Victorian Decorated Trade Bindings
1830–1880

VICTORIAN DECORATED TRADE BINDINGS 1830–1880

A Descriptive Bibliography

EDMUND M. B. KING

THE BRITISH LIBRARY
AND
OAK KNOLL PRESS

First published 2003 by
The British Library
96 Euston Road
St Pancras
London NW1 2DB

Published in North and South America by
Oak Knoll Press
310 Delaware Street
New Castle
DE 19720

British Library Cataloguing in Publication Data
A CIP record is available from The British Library

ISBN 0–7123–4723–2 (BL)

Library of Congress Cataloging-in-Publication Data
King, Edmund M. B.
Victorian decorated trade bindings, 1830–1880: a descriptive bibliography /
Edmund M. B. King.
p. cm.
Includes bibliographical references and indexes.
ISBN 1–58456–095–9
1. Bookbinding, Victorian—Bibliography. 2. Book covers—Great Britain—
Bibliography. 3. Book covers—Great Britain—History—19th century. I. Title.
Z270.G7 K46 2003 016.7416′4′094109034—dc21 2002034649

Designed by Bob Elliott
Typeset by Hope Services (Abingdon) Ltd.
Printed in Great Britain by
St Edmundsbury Press, Bury St Edmunds

For Alec Hyatt and Eve King, and for Alison

Contents

Acknowledgements

Note about photographs: all are made by the British Library, unless otherwise stated.

Many people have helped in a variety of ways to realise this book. I am very grateful to all who have assisted me as the work has developed, and to those who have encouraged me to persevere. I pay particular thanks to those outside the British Library:

Jane E. Brown, who took time to show me her extensive collection of John Leighton cover designs; Tessa Chester, Curator, Bethnal Green Museum of Childhood, for assistance in finding cover designs in the Renier Collection of Children's Books; the Gledhill family, for the loan of *The Works of Shakespeare*, which contains a design by Rogers reproduced well after his death; Dr. Beryl Gray, for drawing my attention to Leighton's design for the paper wrappers of the Blackwood Edition of George Eliot's *Novels*; Antony Griffiths, Keeper, Prints and Drawings, British Museum for permission to consult *the Robin de Beaumont Collection of 1860s Illustrators, Books, Drawings and Proofs*; David Hall, Deputy Librarian, Cambridge University Library for permssion to look for cover designs at the Library; Gregory Jones and Jane E. Brown for sending me their article on the cover designs of William Ralston, and for their permission to quote from it; my mother, Eve King, whose proficiency at proofreading ensured that many keyboarding and grammatical mistakes did not get into print; my brother David Hyatt King, who provided reassurance, advice, and widened my perspective of the artistic influences upon the designers of the period; Mrs. Julie Anne Lambert, Curator, John Johnson Collection, Bodleian Library, for assistance in consulting the John Leighton boxes in the Collection; John Morris, National Library of Scotland, for help in finding cover designs by John Leighton; Philip Oldfield, Thomas Fisher Rare Books Library, University of Toronto, for providing a list of John Leighton cover designs from the Sybille Pantazzi donation; Michael Snodin, Head of Design, Prints, Drawings and Paintings, Victoria and Albert Museum, for permission to see the Albums containing designs of William Harry Rogers; Tom Valentine, who drew my attention to *Gems from the poets . . .*, and for the loan of the book for its cataloguing; Clive Wainright, who gave knowledgeable advice before his untimely death.

I owe two debts to Paul Goldman: firstly, for encouraging me to start on the quest for designs, and secondly, for reading a draft of the text, making many useful suggestions for its improvement. I am also most grateful to Susannah Avery-Quash for enlarging my knowledge of Henry Cole, and showing his influence on John Leighton, and who read the text in draft, providing many useful comments.

In Robin de Beaumont, I have had an understanding mentor, wise companion and co-enthusiast, who has assisted me at many stages in the work; happy hours have been spent seeking out what each of us has wanted. It has been a rare privilege to have access to his private collection, where an inexhaustible flow of books was produced to delight the eye, all in the best condition imaginable. Through his determination and exceptional abilities, one of the finest collections of books of this period has been assembled, and I owe a great debt to him for his patience, stimulation, and humour as I came to learn more about cover designs.

To all the Reader Services staff of the British Library that I have dealt with, both when at the British Museum and in the Library's new building at St. Pancras, I am indebted for many hundreds of books fetched, and for many queries answered, often at short notice.

Acknowledgements

I would like to thank colleagues and friends in the British Library:

Peter Barber, Map Library, British Library, for assistance in naming globes; Tamara Carpenter, for designing the Access database of records so well; Maria Cavedaschi, for carrying out copying of research material; Mirjam Foot, for her time and helpful advice at the outset of the project, and for ensuring that proper thought was given to the use of preferred terms for binding tools and their consistency of application; Kevin Fromings has helped over many years to have books repaired and boxed, with ready understanding; Annie Gilbert, for many fascinating conversations which illuminated relationships between cover design artists and photographers; John Goldfinch, for sorting out some knotty queries relating to British Library shelfmarks; Richard Goulden, for ensuring that some books with signed designs by John Leighton were drawn to my attention; Kathleen Houghton, for help in organising the material for this book; Elizabeth James, for advice on the form of catalogue entries, and for enlightening me regarding some of the bibliographic oddities encountered during the course of the work; David McLachlan for drawing my attention to a signed design on a volume of printed music; Graham Marsh, for assistance with photography for lectures; Deborah Novotny, for lending her thesis on papier mâché covers; Maurice Packer, for many stimulating conversations regarding Victorian cover designs; Laurence Pordes, for much invaluable work in scanning book covers, and for his excellent photographs of John Leighton's tomb, reproduced in the *British Library Journal*; David Way, who has steered and supported the work from its early state; Chris Wootton, for assisting with database enquiries during the course of the work, and arranging the sort order for records within the database, which made possible the printing of entries in the order published.

Finally, I would like to thank my wife Alison, who has lived with the subject of Trade Bindings for many years, provided a useful sense of proportion during the course of the work, and without whose support the project would have been impossible.

St. Albans, Herts.
July 2002

Introduction

The artistic and cultural setting for book designs

The impulses that resulted in book cover designs for edition bindings[1] were many and varied. Technical developments provided the means for artists to attempt wide experimentation with design. The production of starched, filled and dyed cloth from the mid 1820s permitted its embossing or its blocking[2]. In the 1830s, ribbon embossing of cloth imparted patterns to it. This was done by the passing of cloth through heated rollers, which had engraved patterns cut into them.[3] The development of the arming press by the early 1830s permitted the use of pre-cut heated brass blocks for blocking onto cloth, with or without the use of gold.[4] The necessity was obvious of replicating the embossing or the blocking of a design before the cloth and boards were attached to the text block. Once this step was made, mass production of designs blocked onto cloth covers became feasible.

Contrast in design could also be attempted through the use of 'in relievo' work and also with the use of coloured onlays. Patterns could be made by the embossing of the blockwork onto the cloth, leaving portions of it raised. By the 1850s, 'in relievo' work had reached a high level of sophistication, with its extensive employment for bindings both cheap and expensive, applied to both covers and to spines. Onlays and inlays were also extensively used at this time, most usually to fit with design elements such as rectangles, circles, diamonds or ovals. These technical developments coincided with the movement to improve the quality of design applied to the manufacturing arts. Henry Cole provided book cover designs in the 1840s, which assisted the process of applying designs drawn from previous ages to book covers.[5]

It was the exhibition movement of the 1840s, culminating in the Great Exhibition of 1851, which gave great impetus to the development of book cover design for edition bindings. It was possible for an artist such as John Leighton, among many others, to create book designs for the Exhibition itself.[6] The enormous popularity of the Great Exhibition, visited by over six million people, helped create the market for books about it, which publishers eagerly filled. Moreover, the market for books of all subjects grew significantly in the 1850s.[7] Editions of many thousands of copies were made and bound for all kinds of subjects, many with cover designs created *ab initio*. Those engaged in this work did not consider themselves to be cover designers *per se*. Rather, they thought of themselves as artists, executing but one part of the whole. Frequently,

[1] *Edition bindings* is the term for the binding of mass produced books, with texts frequently being reprinted from metal copies made from the original hand-set type.

[2] For a discussion of the development and early use of bookcloth, see Tomlinson, William and Masters, Richard. *Bookcloth, 1823–1980*. Stockport, D. Tomlinson, 1996. pp. 6–9.

[3] *Bookcloth, 1823–1980*, p.116.; see also G. Dodd. *Days at the factories*. London, Charles Knight, 1844. pp. 380–81. A cloth embossing machine is illustrated on p.381.

[4] There is a description of how the blocking work was done by the 1850s in Tomlinson, Charles (Editor). *Cyclopaedia of Useful Arts*. 1854, p. 159, which illustrates the gold-blocking press.

[5] Avery-Quash, Susannah. *Henry Cole and the Society of Arts* ... RSA History Study Group, 1998/99, p. 3.

[6] For example, see Leighton's designs in plate 96 in: Matthew Digby Wyatt. *The industrial arts of the nineteenth century. A series of illustrations of the choicest specimens produced by every nation at the Great Exhibition of works of industry, 1851. Dedicated, by permission, to his Royal Highness the Prince Albert.* London, Day & Sons, lithographers to the Queen, 1851. 2 vols. 158 plates, with descriptions.

[7] Eliot, Simon. *Some patterns and trends in British Publishing 1800–1919*. London: The Bibliographical Society, 1994, pp.30–31 and Appendix B, pp.121–122. *Bent's Monthly Literary Advertiser* listed 64% more titles for the decade 1850–59, over 1840–49. *Publisher's Circular* listed 36% more titles for 1850–59 over the decade 1840–49.

artists who provided the illustrations for the engravings, or the lithographs, of a book also drew designs for engravers to create brass dies for blocking onto the covers.

Where ascertained in publishers' catalogues bound at the end of volumes, a common price listed is between 2s. 6d. and 3s. 6d. The range 2s. 1d. to 3s. 6d. accounts for a fifth (or just less) of books prices for titles listed in trade journals of the period.[8] For this price range, cloth over boards was the preferred covering medium. An elaborate spine design and an upper cover vignette would be made with new dies, and blocked in gold, with the lower cover being blocked in blind only. The borders and the corners would be frequently blocked using fillets and small decorative tools, that were re-used. The virtuosity of the artwork provided ranged from ordinary, derivative work, to the highly original. Books priced at 10s. 6d. or at one guinea commanded artwork of a far more elaborate nature. Several designs by John Leighton (*Shakespeare's Household Words*, *The Bridal Souvenir*), some by John Sliegh, and by William Harry Rogers, Albert Warren and many unsigned designs attest to this.

Some artists were more interested in exploring the use of other materials for bindings. Leather, wood, and papier mâché were all employed in a variety of ways. Owen Jones experimented with compressed wood for *The Preacher*, probably adopting a technique originally created in the 1820s.[9] Henry Noel Humphreys worked with papier mâché designs, which complemented the texts over which he had also exerted a degree of artistic control. Published by Longman from the mid-1840s, they form a distinct, but short-lived, corpus, proving the potential of papier mâché for mass production.[10] Humphreys also experimented with designs in leather, with coloured onlays.[11]

The influence of Gothic Revival on book cover design of this period was obvious. Pugin's great advocacy of this led him into designing book covers amongst the myriad of objects he created in this style.[12] The cover design work of William Harry Rogers and of Henry Noel Humphreys shows strong Gothic influences. However, the designs of all previous ages were considered for a cover design appropriate to the subject matter of a book, if suitable parallels could be simply made. John Leighton had published in 1852–53 *Suggestions in Design. Including original compositions in all styles . . . for the use of artists and art-workmen*. The forty-seven plates provided ample scope for the re-deployment of ornament from previous eras to manufactured goods, including books. The work predates Owen Jones' *Grammar of Ornament* by four years. However, the one hundred and twelve richly chromolithographed plates by Day and Son for the *Grammar* . . . provided the stimulus of colour, and Jones' work became enormously popular.

Brief biographies of leading artists

The artists who were employed in book production were many. For those where identification has been possible, details are given below.

Charles Henry Bennett (1829–1867) was a prolific book illustrator in his short lifetime.[13] His work is frequently brilliant, showing high levels of originality. His illustrations for children's books provided ample scope for his inventiveness. He also could be strongly satirical: his illus-

[8] Eliot, Simon, ibid. Appendix D, pp. 134–135.

[9] *On a method of producing embossed designs on wood. J. Straker.* MS. Transactions of the Society of Arts April 14, 1824; and Minutes of the Committee of Polite Arts, 3 May 1824. I am indebted to Robin de Beaumont for this information.

[10] Leathlean, Howard. *Henry Noel Humphreys and the Getting-Up of Books in the Mid-Nineteenth Century.* **In:** *The Book Collector.* Vol. 38. no.2. Summer 1989. pp. 192–209.

[11] cf *Maxims and Precepts of the Saviour*; entry no. 58.

[12] These are discussed in: Atterbury, Paul and Wainwright, Clive, Editors. *Pugin. A Gothic passion.* New Haven and London: Yale Univeristy Press, [1994], chapter eleven.

[13] Details of Bennett's book illustrations are in: Goldman, Paul. *Victorian Book Illustration: the Pre-Raphaelites, the Idyllic School and the High Victorians.* Aldershot: Scolar, 1996. pp 230–232.

trations for *Character Sketches* are a witty, yet profoundly perceptive satire on Darwin's *Origin of Species*.[14] In several instances, engravers copied his illustrations within the book directly onto brass for cover blocking. Bennett's monogram of joined 'CHB' is distinctive, and on occasion is cut onto book cover blocks. This is so for *The nine lives of a cat*, and *Mr. Wind and Madam Rain*.[15] His monogram on the spine of *Quarles's Emblems* is used to great effect in combination with that of William Harry Rogers.[16]

Walter Crane (1845–1915) has fame as a painter, illustrator, designer, writer and teacher.[17] He was apprenticed to William James Linton in 1859, and in the next three years learnt the technique of draughtmanship on wood blocks. An early example of Crane's work is his drawings for John Wise's *The New Forest*, drawings which were engraved by Linton. In the same year, Crane also provided fourteen plates for Caroline Hadley's *Stories of Old* . . .[18] Both these works were published by Smith Elder, and have cover designs provided by John Leighton. *King Luckieboy's Picture Book* is listed as a cover design to show that Crane's distinctive work was gaining ground with publishers when he was still quite young.[19]

Richard Doyle (1824–1883) was well known as book illustrator. He was the uncle of Arthur Conan Doyle. He joined the staff of *Punch* in 1843, and his design for the magazine was retained for over one hundred years.[20] The only two cover designs included are those derived from his illustrations within the book. These are for *The Scouring of The White Horse*[21] and *The adventures of a watch*.[22] His use of the distortion of line transfers well to the covers of these two books.

Robert Dudley (active 1858–1891) worked in Matthew Digby Wyatt's office. He was Superintendent of the restorations and of the monuments and principal draughtsman, under Wyatt, of the Mediaeval and Renaissance Courts of the Sydenham Crystal Palace, 1854. He designed for Goodall & Son, and accompanied The Great Eastern on its cable laying expedition on the Atlantic Ocean in 1866.[23] The design for The Atlantic Telegraph, displaying the core of the telegraph cable as an onlay on the centre of the upper cover, is likely to be a design of Dudley's.[24] He provided illustrations for a number of books.[25] He designed a set of Christmas cards in 1887, and wrote the story of *King Fo, the Lord of Misrule. A twelfth night story* in 1884.[26] His work shows mainly vignettes, several for elaborate designs, such as *Poet's Wit and Humour*.[27] Like Leighton, he used pictorial effects in his designs, not relying on figurative work alone.

Owen Jones (1809–1874) was more consciously involved with the minutiae of book production for a long period, from the early 1840s to the late 1860s. He experimented with techniques, using a design impressed upon wood for *The Preacher*, published in 1849.[28] The renown of *The Grammar Of Ornament* should not obscure his other achievements in chromolithography also published by Day And Son, such as *Paradise and the Peri*, *One Thousand and One Initial Letters* and *The History of Joseph and his Brethren*.[29] Jones provided cover designs to accompany his

[14] See entry no. 512.
[15] See entry nos: 10 and 13.
[16] See entry no. 579.
[17] Grove Dictionary of Art, vol.8.
[18] See entry nos. 428, 393, 394.
[19] See entry no. 26.
[20] Grove Dictionary of Art, vol. 9. p.209.
[21] See entry no. 30.
[22] See entry no. 31.
[23] Pantazzi, Sybille. *Four designers of English Publishers' Bindings, 1850–1880, and Their Signatures.* **In**: *Papers of the Bibliographical Society of America*. 55. 1961. p. 96.
[24] See entry no. 45.
[25] *A Memorial of the Marriage of Albert Edward Prince of Wales and Princess Alexandra of Denmark*, [1864]; *Manchester Art Treasures Exhibition*, 1858; *The Library Shakespeare*, 1873; *The Twigs*, 1890; *Shakespeare Pictures*, 1896.
[26] *King Fo* . . .BL copy at 12811.h.4(4).
[27] See entry no. 34.
[28] See entry no. 78 and J. Straker's invention of 1824 cited above.
[29] See entry nos. 83, 86, 87.

artwork for the text. His cover design for *Winged Thoughts* is an excellent piece of blocking on leather – elegant, unified and understated.[30]

John Leighton's (1822–1912) originality was only exceeded by his proficiency.[31] Dying on his ninetieth birthday in 1912, his known cover designs span the period 1845–1902. He was possessed of a powerful imagination, which was applied time and again to create designs for vignettes and for spine designs, with deft touches and with humour, often in keeping with a book's subject. Leighton was capable of providing work on a small or on a large scale. His designs for *Blackie's Literary and Commercial Almanack*, made between 1853 and 1872, were for a publication not more than 55 mm wide and 85 mm high.[32] By contrast, Leighton's design for *The Life of Man* is on a book measuring 225 mm wide and 288 mm high.[33] This size permitted a complex and intricate design. Leighton provided humour in a number of vignettes or full cover designs.[34] He also had a strong eye for detailing groups of objects within a small space, especially so for spine designs[35] All of this is ample evidence of his graphic skill, as well as his calligraphic gifts in the designs of novel lettering, albeit at one remove in the production process. Fortunately, drawings of Leighton's survive, which show amply his abilities in original form.[36] Leighton's work for William Mackenzie in the 1870s and 1880s demonstrates his artistic staying power, even though many of the designs were done in a similar manner, within the publisher's formula for the size of the book.[37]

Leighton possessed considerable knowledge of heraldry; coats of arms feature on many of his designs. His most single minded heraldic design is for Hodgkin's *Monograms*.[38] His Scottish ancestry possibly provided impetus to heraldic designs for the covers of Walter Scott's *Marmion* and *Lay of the Last Minstrel*.[39] His link by kinship to the bookbinding firm of Leighton Son & Hodge should not be underestimated in providing experience in how to maximise design elements within the constraints of executing the designs on cloth in this period.[40] Leighton signed his designs equally with his monogram, the crossed 'L' and 'J', or with these initials separately.

William Harry Rogers (1825–1874) was a contemporary of Leighton.[41] The eldest son of William Gibbs Rogers, a renowned wood carver, he began drawing artwork for book covers in his twenties. His illustrations for page borders, head and tail-pieces, are to be found in many books. He is notable for intricate cover design work, often showing elaboration of title letters, or dense foliage. Three of his most elaborate overall designs for covers are those for *Spiritual Conceits* and for Tupper's *Proverbial philosophy*, and, with Charles Henry Bennett, *Quarles' Emblems*. One of his most delightful is the design blocked on Rimmel's *Book of perfumes*, which displays the coat of arms of the parfumiers.

He invariably used his full initials **WHR** as a monogram. He is also distinctive for the way he placed his monogram in his designs, sometimes small or very small, and, at other times, inserting

[30] See entry no. 82.

[31] A more detailed assessment of Leighton's life and his cover designs is to be found in: 1. Edmund M.B. King. *The book cover designs of John Leighton F.S.A.* **In**: The British Library Journal Vol. 24, no.2., Autumn 1998, pp.234–255; 2. Pantazzi, Sybille. *John Leighton, 1822–1912. A versatile Victorian designer: his designs for book covers.* **In** *The Connoisseur*, Vol. 152, April 1963, pp. 262–273.

[32] See entry no. 138.

[33] See entry no. 472.

[34] See *Jack Frost and Betty Snow*, or *Jingles and Jokes for Little Folks*; entry nos. 276 and 456.

[35] For example, *Dew drops for Spring Flowers*, or for *The Plants of the Bible*; entry nos. 257 and 234.

[36] The drawings are in the John Leighton boxes, John Johnson Collection, Bodleian Library, Oxford.

[37] Leighton made designs for several Mackenzie publications originally issued in successive parts, which had paper wrappers. The parts were bound also in cloth, for which Leighton provided a different design. Seven designs are listed.

[38] See entry no. 467.

[39] See entry nos. 208 and 184

[40] Of some 456 Leighton designs catalogued, 51 have bookbinder's tickets of Leighton Son & Hodge.

[41] For a further account of Rogers's cover designs, see Edmund M.B. King *The book cover designs of William Harry Rogers*. **In**: *For the Love of Binding. Studies in Historical Bookbinding Presented to Mirjam Foot.* Edited by David Pearson. London British Library, 2000, pp. 319–329.

it within a design, seemingly inviting the viewer to hunt for it. Unlike Leighton, his imaginative powers did not extend much into the pictorial, as the delineation of human or of animal forms scarcely occurs on his cover designs. His death in 1874 prevented any further development of his draughtsmanship. However, he paid a strong attention to the detail of ornament, a mastery of the forms of its proportions, seeming to delight in providing intricacy and denseness.

Dante Gabriel Rossetti (1828–1882) found fame within the Pre-Raphaelites. His work illustrating books formed only a small part of his artistic endeavour, creating but ten significant illustrations in four books published between 1855 and 1866.[42] The involvement of Rossetti in the designs of a number of books in the 1860s exerted a real influence in favour of simplicity of line for book cover design.[43] Rossetti provided the design for Christina Rossetti's *Goblin Market and other poems*, which was first published in 1862, at a price of five shillings. The second edition was issued in 1865, and as for the 1862 edition, has bright blue ungrained cloth, with the use of broad fillets intersecting horizontally and vertically, continuing across the spine.[44] The blocking of three small circles at the intersections of the fillets focuses the eye at these points, providing a simple symmetry. The identical design was used over thirty years later, on a copy of Christina Rossetti's *Poems*, 1896, bound in green ungrained cloth.[45] This design for *Goblin Market* introduced a simplicity of line out of step with many of the showy, densely ornamented designs of the 1850s and 1860s, and was much copied.

In 1865, Macmillan also issued William Michael Rossetti's translation of Dante's *Inferno*.[46] Dante Gabriel Rossetti provided the design for Burn to bind, which was done by mid-February 1865. D. G. Rossetti made use of fillets and circles on the upper cover, with the symbolism of stars, flames, alphas and omegas.[47] It seems likely that an adaptation of these designs was made by D. G. Rossetti for W. M. Rossetti's *Spectator* essays, re-published by Macmillan in 1867 under the title *Fine art chiefly contemporary*, at a price of ten shillings and sixpence. Burn bound this work in orange ungrained cloth, with a design of a single fillet on the borders of the upper cover, and three pendant-balls, which show the Macmillan monogram.[48] Darley called the work done by Burn in the 1860s: 'The new Macmillan syle of simplicity . . .'[49]

John Sliegh (active 1841–1872) was clearly a gifted artist. He was one of the twenty artists employed on copying exhibits at the Hyde Park Great Exhibition for Digby Wyatt's *The industrial arts of the nineteenth century*. His cover designs show a good sense of proportion of design in relation to the size of the covers. Sliegh used the Gothic style, particularly for *Evangeline* and *Gertrude of Wyoming*, with elaborate use of fanciful letters.[50]

William Robert Tymms (active 1859–1868) was an accomplished artist and engraver. He provided the chromolithographic work for J. B. Waring's *Masterpieces of the Industrial Art & sculpture at the International Exhibition, 1862*;[51] and also for J. O. *Westwood's Facsimiles of the Miniatures & Ornaments of Anglo-Saxon & Irish Manuscripts*, 1868.[52] His cover designs are on two works: *The Indian Fables*[53] and Tennyson's *The May Queen*.[54]

[42] Goldman, Paul. *Victorian Illustration*. London: Scolar Press, 1996. *The Pre-Raphaelites: The Inner Circle*, p. 2.

[43] For a full discussion of Rossetti's cover designs, see: Barber, Giles. *Rossetti, Ricketts, and Some English Publishers' Bindings of the Nineties*. **In**: *The Library*. 5th series. 1970. p. 311–330.

[44] Entry nos. 603, 605.

[45] BL staff copy.

[46] Price: five shillings. Entry no. 604; BL C.116.b.9.

[47] Barber, op. cit., p. 316.

[48] The Macmillan Archive copy is in Box 024.

[49] Darley, Lionel. *Bookbinding then and now*. Faber, 1959. Caption to plate opposite p. 38.

[50] See Entries 610–615.

[51] Entry no. 691.

[52] BL copy at Tab.437.a.2.

[53] Entry no. 622.

[54] Entry no. 621.

Albert Henry Warren (1830–1911) was the eldest son of Henry Warren (1794–1879), President of the Royal Institute of Painters in Water Colour. He was articled to Owen Jones and worked with him on the construction and decoration of the 1851 and 1862 Exhibitions. He assisted Jones with the illustration of *The Grammar of Ornament* and *The Alhambra*.[55] He made the drawings for St. James's Hall, Piccadilly, assisted his father in painting panoramas of the Nile and the Holy Land, and helped his uncle John Martin with the designs for the Thames Embankment. He was Professor of Landscape at Queen's College, London, and gave lessons in illuminating and floral painting to Princess Alice and Princess Helena. His work was exhibited at the Royal Academy and elsewhere in London between 1860–1870. He was a volunteer in the Artists' Corps (20th Middlesex). He received grants from the Royal Bounty Fund in 1893, 1896, and 1900.[56]

Pantazzi refers to Warren using his monogram, with the capital 'A' within the capital 'W', and also to the use of separate initials 'A W'.[57] Independent evidence has not been found for the separately blocked letters 'A W' being designs by Warren, so they are grouped together just before the Warren entries. The twenty one designs listed show Warren's artistic abilities well adapted to the medium of design on covers, with designs from the expensive to the simple.

Matthew Digby Wyatt (1820–1877) is a national figure of the period, often known for his work as an architect. As Secretary to the Executive Committee of the Commissioners of the Great Exhibition, he was also the Superintendent Architect for the Crystal Palace. He collaborated with Brunel on the design for Paddington Station, 1851–54[58] He carried out significant work for the Sydenham re-build of the Crystal Palace, being appointed Superintendent of the Fine Arts Department, collaborating with Owen Jones in the erection of the Fine Arts Courts, and co-writing with J.B. Waring two of the Crystal Palace Official Publications, *The Byzantine Court* and *The Italian Court*. As Surveyor to The India Office, he worked in partnership with George Gilbert Scott on the building of the Foreign Office, 1861–68, designing and building the interior of the India Office.[59] He designed a reconstruction of Addenbrooke's Hospital in 1866, mainly of the facade, which stands today.[60]

His involvement with book production certainly dates from his supervision of the production of *The industrial arts of the nineteenth century* . . .[61] Digby Wyatt also assisted Owen Jones with the production of *The Grammar of Ornament*, and, with William Robert Tymms, produced *The art of illuminating* in 1860. It is perhaps no surprise that Digby Wyatt ventured into book cover design. *The Campaign in the Crimea* was a topical work, for which he produced an elaborate design, featuring the battle names of the campaign on the upper cover, together with corner medallions.[62] The design for *Curry and Rice* reflects the Indian army scene, and perhaps came about through his involvement with the India Office and through his previous work for the lithographic company of Day & Son.[63] For each design, Digby Wyatt's name is clearly to be seen on the covers.

[55] Warren worked with W. R. Tymms on J. B. Waring. *Masterpieces of Industrial Art & Sculpture at the International Exhibition, 1862*. London: Day & Son, 1863.

[56] *Who was Who, 1897–1916*; and Pantazzi, *4D* p. 93.

[57] Pantazzi, *4D* p. 93.

[58] Information from the Macmillan House website.

[59] Information from the Foreign and Commonwealth Office website; www.fco.gov.uk

[60] Information from the Judge Institute of Management Studies website, now occupying the former Addenbrooke's site.

[61] *The industrial arts of the nineteenth century. A series of illustrations of the choicest specimens produced by every nation at the Great Exhibition of works of industry, 1851. Dedicated, by permission, to his Royal Highness the Prince Albert.* London, Day & Sons, lithographers to the Queen, 1851. 2 vols. 158 plates, with descriptions.

[62] The upper cover is reproduced in R. McLean. *Victorian publishers' book-bindings in cloth and leather.* London, Gordon Fraser, 1974, p. 73.

[63] For further details of the history of this block through several editions, see Edmund M.B. King. *Curry and Rice.* **In**: The Book Collector, vol. 45 no. 4, Winter 1996, pp. 568–570.

Summary

Up to the early 1800s, books were usually sold without bindings, often in paper covers. They were then bound to the purchaser's wishes. Improved technical methods made mass production techniques possible, at the same time as a large middle class developed, with the money to purchase more books. The rapid development of the railways in the 1840s and 1850s also meant the national distribution of books for sale on a greater scale than before. To market and sell increasing numbers of books, publishers needed attractive cover and spine designs, using standardised materials, such as cloth or paper, together with new designs, or mixtures of existing ones. Publishers and bookbinders were quick to expand the use of cloth for board coverings, to ensure that the cloth and boards were assembled separately from other steps in the bookbinding production, and to develop the decoration that could be blocked onto the cloth. Mass produced covers reduced the costs previously associated with the working of leather around each individual book. The production of books in the period 1840–1880 permitted 'high' investment either in cover designs with much individual artistic involvement, or at the other end, a 'low' investment, with far less complexity in designs. Many of the designs fully complement either the text alone or the text and its illustrations. In some instances, the cover design unquestionably exceeds the quality of what lies within.

Technical developments in book cover decoration throughout this period created a new artistic medium, and designs were produced in tens of thousands to embellish covers. In this specialised field, the work of the artists on cover designs in this period is an endless source of fascination. There is no doubt that many of the artists knew each other, collaborating as they did on numbers of high quality expensive works, such as those published by Day & Son in the 1850s and 1860s. With hindsight, we can see that Leighton's work dominates the field. There is little evidence to show that he was seen in this light by his contemporaries. Today, one can also see how influential D. G. Rossetti's designs for book covers were, introducing design concepts entirely novel for the time. The particular abilities of Charles Bennett, Walter Crane, Henry Noel Humphreys and Owen Jones were evident in their book illustration work. Owen Jones created innovative and striking book cover designs. Humphreys is well known for his inventive approach to book designs, and his experimentation with papier mâché as a material for book covers. William Harry Rogers developed his own form: often dense and intricate designs where his mastery of line is readily apparent.

The fashion for Gothic revival in the 1840s and 1850s found full expression in book cover designs. Church arches, niches, imitation clasps, chivalric figures in armour, heraldic devices, together with the symbolic foliage of the Bible – all found their way onto book covers. Oriental, Renaissance and Jacobean motifs were also popular. The abiding vein of delight that the British took in fantasy, comedy and satire was also much in evidence, particularly in the work of Leighton and of Bennett, and often exercised for the designs of children's books.

This period was marked by a prolific output and great achievement in popularising design concepts on book covers. There was undoubtedly cover design work to be shared amongst many, with numerous fine designs awaiting attribution. The variety of design was enormous, the virtuosity on some occasions outstanding, and on other book covers the designs were of mediocre standard and repetitive. The desire by publishers to offer book buyers something special resulted in the creation of books with cover designs that could be visually hugely impressive. The best of this great range in quality and of inventiveness deserves much wider recognition.

Preface to the Bibliography

Antecedents and scope

Work was begun on this bibliography in 1994. A number of books and articles have been published detailing book illustrations and book publishing of this period. Others have been published on bookbindings and their designs. Mass production of book covers and of the designs blocked on them began in this period, and publishers' edition bindings provide the bulk of the output with which this work is concerned. It was the artwork blocked on the covers which provided the attraction and the impetus to catalogue them. A further incentive was the knowledge that many of these books were inexpensively produced, have worn over time, with the artwork needing recording before further deterioration takes place.

This work owes a great deal to McLean's *Victorian Book Design, Victorian Publishers' Bookbindings, Victorian publishers' bookbindings in paper*, to Douglas Ball's *Victorian Publishers' Bindings*, together with Ball's *Catalogue of the Appleton Collection*. Ball listed cover designers in Appendix D to *Victorian Publishers' Bindings*, together with examples of their work. However, Ball did not set out to describe the designs on covers in a systematic fashion in *Victorian Publishers' Bindings*, but did so in his work on the Appleton Collection, which has remained unpublished. This work is intended to remedy this. The scope is confined to designs blocked onto books (or printed on paper covers) published in the UK (including Ireland) in the mid-Victorian period. The essential feature of this work is its incompleteness. The number of designs executed on cloth between the mid-1830s and 1880 was vast, with the great majority of designs being unsigned. Lack of time dictated a concentration of effort in finding and cataloguing designs of artists who either signed their work, or who are known through stylistic or other independent evidence to be the cover designer of a book. A guiding rule has been to describe in words the elements of the design, in order that accurate identification can be made, for the researcher or reader to be confident that the copy being examined elsewhere is the same as the one described in this bibliography, or a variant.

Categories of design included and excluded

The term *cover designer* is used inclusively in this bibliography. Often, it is only the upper or lower cover vignette, or a spine design that has the artist's initials. On occasion, both the designs on covers and on the spine have signatures. In other instances, the design is clearly all in one; neverthless, only one signature is blocked, on the cover or on the spine.

As I worked for the British Library, it was logical to find and catalogue the BL copy of a binding and its design wherever possible, using the references within previously published works as the starting point. These works are cited in the list of Books and Articles referred to. Whenever possible, time has been spent in cataloguing in other libraries rich in designs of the period, as it has frequently proved that the BL copy lacks original covers, which have survived elsewhere. All entries have been keyed into a Microsoft Access database, which has the advantage of permitting single or multiple searches for each field into which data is entered (e.g. Publisher, Binder, Printer, Author, Illustrator, Cover Designer, etc., or combinations of these). A disadvantage is the lack of special characters that can be keyed. What appears in this publication is the text

without indications of lettering (gothic or italic) or normally of special characters, such as accents. Occasionally, these can be found, but only where it was deemed particularly necessary to re-enter the text. Systematic cross checking of multiple copies of titles and designs in different libraries has not been attempted.

In addition to signed designs, attention has also been paid to four other categories. Firstly, unsigned designs of the 1830–1880 period have been included on a selective basis. Inclusion has been the result of the beauty of the design, of the closeness of a design to other examples that are signed, or of the design including an object that is striking or unusual. Secondly, small numbers of UK pre-1840 cloth graining and embossing came to my attention during the course of the work. The grains and patterns embossed onto books after 1825 and before 1840 possess a distinctiveness quite their own. It was not possible to work systematically on these; they have been catalogued and included as found. (Regrettably, lack of space has not permitted the inclusion of pre-1840 cloth grains and embossing for US publications.) After 1840, there was a distinct change in what publishers chose to have blocked on the covers, and these earlier designs and embossing were superseded. Thirdly, post-1840 unusual or rare bookcloths are included, even though the cover design elements may be insignificant. Fourthly, a small number of books with pasted-in photographs are included. The cover designs made to accompany these books show how publishers wished to enhance the effects of the still developing technology of photographs in the 1850s and 1860s.

For cloth covers, no particular distinction has been made between the name of an engraver or that of a cover designer, as in practice the difference is not easily seen. All are recorded in the General index as ‘cover designer’. However, for unusual examples where both the cover designer’s and the engraver’s name are given, the term ‘cover engraver’ is used. Where paper covers are used to accompany the issue of publications in parts, and the covers have engravings signed by the illustrator, these are included, even where they may only be a repeat of an illustration within the text.

Exclusions

Cataloguing designs blocked on books published in the United States up to 1880 is very worthwhile. However, work has been left to a later volume, in order to show their merits separately. A separate volume can also be compiled for UK designs 1880–1914, a period of renewed, re-invigorated, and varied designs by many talented artists. Also, designs of books published in Europe have been excluded, as the field is undoubtedly a large one. Hand-tooled designs are also excluded. Bindings in paper covers have been excluded from systematic enquiry. To have included these would have taken too much time, and made this volume unwieldy. Books with paper covers where the artist has made designs executed predominantly on cloth are included, with the aim of showing as complete a range as possible of the artist’s work.

Arrangement of the Bibliography

During the course of the work for this bibliography, it was necessary to adopt methods of working and a list of preferred terms to give consistency of description across entries. The individual entry is the basis upon which this work has developed. Records for the entries have been keyed into a relational database for each bibliographic work possessing a design. In the database, separate records have often been made for different editions, or for annual publications, even if the works possess the same design on the covers. For the purposes of publication, amalgamation of such entries is necessary to save space.

Each entry has been allocated a unique number in a single sequence. Within this, the sequence of the entries is by artist surname, A–Z. Within each artist, the entries are in date of publication order. For multiple publications designed by one artist in one year, the order is by title A–Z (ignoring 'A' and 'The'), then by author, A–Z. Those designs which are unsigned are grouped under the heading **Unsigned UK**, by year, and within a year, by title A–Z, then author A–Z, as with named artists. Exceptions to the general sequence are:

- entries for annuals, which are placed within the year when an artist's design first appears on the covers.
- if two (or more) volumes of the same work are published in different years, the entry for all is made under the first year of publication.

Books with designs blocked by more than one artist are entered at the end of the sequence for the artist, whose signature or initials are on the upper cover design. However, separate editions issued in different years have separate entries.

Parts of the Description

For each entry, the order of fields is: entry number; cover designer; main heading/author; title; place of publication; publisher; date of publication; place of printing; printer; pagination; lists of publisher's titles; size; shelfmark of the holding library; notes about the plates, or the illustrations, or the price of the book etc; notes relating to the binding and the cover design; references to other published works.

The **main heading** generally follows that of the British Library General Catalogue of Printed Books. Epithets are normally omitted, but titles denoting rank have been retained. Pseudonyms are used in preference to real names, where the practice of the day showed this. Appropriate cross-references are made in the General Index. In the case of John Leighton, an exception is made: works issued under his pseudonym of Luke Limner are indexed also. Books without authors are indexed under the title. Books with multiple authors (normally more than three), or compilations do not have the names indexed separately.

Titles are transcribed as printed on title pages. Where they have been printed in small capitals, they have been treated as though they were in lower case. Words have been capitalized if they are printed as such, or if they are proper nouns. Author statements are normally omitted. An exception to this is the quotation of other titles by the same author and these are transcribed, where the author's name has not been established. Editor and translator names are normally stated. Line markers have reluctantly been omitted from the title page descriptions, but are given normally in the notes field for bookbinders' tickets, and for titles and spines blocked or printed. Three dots means the omission of text on the title page, often quotations of poetry. Title words in gothic, italic, or other characters are not noted.

Capitalisation within titles: unless the title page type or the cover or spine blocking indicate otherwise, lower case is used for the title descriptions. Imprints are normally written as printed on title pages. Printers are stated after the imprint, to make the entries more concise; although they are not normally printed on title pages.

Where **illustrators, photographers, engravers, translators and editors** are cited on the title page, or otherwise obviously cited (e.g. initials or a name on book illustrations), index entries have been made for these. Where more than three illustrators are cited on a title page, normally only the first three are indexed. As with main headings, pseudonyms are used in preference to real names, where the practice of the day showed this. Illustrators and engravers are often cited at the head of (or within) lists of illustrations; these have not been indexed.

Publishers are given in each entry as printed. However, for the index, a common name form has been adopted for publishers with variant names. Where multiple publishers are printed on title pages, only the first named is indexed. **Printer names** are as printed. Full stops at the end of the printer statement are added as appropriate, together with a colon between the place of printing and the printer name, to standardise the layout.

Book measurements are given as: width from spine hinge to foredge; height; thickness. Doublures and paper covers bound in are measured separately.

Bookbinders' tickets are a fascinating study in their own right. They were applied at least in their tens of thousands by the binders in this period for edition bindings, and variant forms are many. This work reproduces those found in books where the designs are the prime reason for inclusion. It is regretted that these are not measured, nor a description given of the design. It is hoped that the reproductions of those found , together with a description in each entry and their indexing, will aid others in their more systematic enumeration. Almost invariably, binders' tickets are pasted on the recto of the lower cover, lower left. **Booksellers' tickets** are far less numerous. These receive an index entry, but are not reproduced.

Provenance: where possible, details are transcribed. However, work has not been systematic on researching coats of arms on bookplates, or on transcribing difficult handwriting. The names of dedicatees or of previous owners are not indexed separately.

The **Notes field** of each entry contains the details of the bookbinding and the description of the design blocked. Designs have been described as though the reader does not have an illustration of the design. This entails a degree of detailed description of the design elements, in order that accurate identification and comparison may be made with a copy elsewhere. The need to save space meant the avoidance of indicators for each element described in the notes. The use of terms to describe binding tools (and their combinations) and to describe the huge quantity of designs has largely been done from scratch, as there has been no previous thesaurus of this period to draw upon. It was also necessary to have terms which could be used in as many entries as possible. Descriptive terminology of blocking has been attempted. This arose out of two considerations: firstly, the desire to record accurately, secondly, the fashion in this period for decoration and ornament as applied to book covers resulted in much figurative and representational work not seen on covers in earlier periods. Heraldic descriptions of coats of arms, and other devices has been attempted in the interests of brevity. Errors and omissions of heraldic description are my responsibility, and hopefully there will be indulgence forthcoming from the really knowledgeable in this field.

In the Notes field, the order of description of book covers, spine and design is generally as follows: individual volume details for multi-volume sets; details of the plates, and of the illustrators or engravers; details of the price of the work ; sewing; edges; boards; endpapers, dye colour and grain of the cloth; design blocked on lower cover; design blocked on upper cover; design blocked on the spine. For the covers, description is from the borders inwards to the centre; or, alternatively, from the head to the tail of the design on each cover. For the spine, description is normally from the head down to the tail. Titles blocked on the covers, or on the spine, may vary from those printed on title pages.

Bibliographical References

Titles of works referred to are listed in full at the end in the section: *Books and Articles Referred to, with Abbreviated Titles*. The author and abbreviation of the work being cited are given before the full citation, and the abbreviations are used in main entries.

There is no easy certainty about the description of the cloth dye colour for individual books. Normally it is not a problem to identify a colour. However, owing to dye bleaching or fading, particular difficulty has been experienced with mauve and purple. Cloth grain descriptions are drawn almost entirely from the schemes published by Tanselle and by Gaskell, and occasionally by Sadleir. Ball has provided useful evidence of unusual grains (eg. trefoil leaf trellis).

Occasionally, objects can be difficult to describe accurately. The gold of some designs has faded so severely that identification is not certain. For other cover designs, an original object is varied by artistic licence, to the point where accuracy is again doubtful. Rather than register uncertainty with a question mark, the reader is asked to judge the description, when looking at the entry with a copy of the book in the hand.

With regard to the indexes, the result of combined enquiries is not shown. For example, which publisher a designer worked for, or which printers were used by which publisher. Such enquiries can be done by searching the database, from which this text is derived.

Suggestions for amendments to the text, or for future additions, should be addressed to the author and sent to him c/o The British Library Publishing Office.

BIBLIOGRAPHY

1 B., C.

Bonar, Andrew Alexander. *Palestine for the young.* . . . London: The Religious Tract Society; 56, Paternoster Row, 65, St. Paul's Churchyard, and 164 Piccadilly, [1865]. London: Printed by William Clowes and Sons, Limited, Stamford Street and Charing Cross. [2], 368 p., 1 plate; 1 fold-out map. With twelve pages of publisher's titles bound at the end.

136 × 190 × 36 mm. 3127.bbb.34.

Gilt edges. Bevelled boards. White endpapers and pastedowns. Binder's ticket on lower pastedown: '| Bound by | Westleys | & Co. | London. |' Purple sand-grain cloth. Both covers identically blocked in blind on the borders and on the corners. Three fillets are blocked on the borders, one thick, two thin. The two thin fillets form a central frame, which is oval-shaped. The upper cover central vignette is blocked in gold. It shows a semi-circular decorative design, with straps blocked at the head and at the tail. On the centre, the title: '| Palestine for the young |' is blocked in gold in a semi-circle within decoration; the author: '| A. Bonar |' is also blocked in gold. Signed 'CB' in gold as separate letters at the base of the vignette. The spine is blocked in gold and relief. From the head downwards, the decoration is: two fillets; the title: '| Palestine | for the | young |' blocked in relief within three curved gold lettering-pieces with vertical hatch on their borders; the lettering-pieces are themselves blocked within a decorative panel; this panel has decoration blocked at its head and at its tail; signed 'CB' in gold as separate letters at the base of the decoration underneath the title panel; near the tail of the spine, a rectangular gold lettering-piece is blocked, with decoration above and below in gold; the words: '| A. Bonar |' are blocked in relief within this; two fillets in gold at the base. [It is suggested that the cover designer 'CB' might be Charles Bayman.]

Ball, *VPB* p. 93.

2 B., C.

Beeton's Annual; a Book for the Young. With illustrations printed in colours, and many woodcuts from original designs by eminent artists. [Edited by S. O. Beeton and the Rev. J. G. Wood] London: Frederick Warne & Co., Bedford Street, Covent Garden, 1866. Hertford: Printed by Stephen Austin. [6], 491 p., 19 plates. With two pages of publisher's titles bound at the end.

123 × 190 × 41 mm. P.P.6751.

Another copy of this work is in Cambridge University Library, shelfmark 147.3.49. The ornamental header for page 1, 'Samuel Beeton's Annual' is a wood engraving signed 'WHR' as a monogram [i.e. William Harry Rogers.] The pun on the editor's surname is provided by a picture of a beehive. The decorated tail-piece on p. 491, entitled: '| Even so for ever | Amen |', is also signed 'WHR' as a monogram. [The original drawing for this design is in one of the Rogers albums at the Victoria and Albert Museum.] Text sewn on three sawn-in cords. Brown endpapers and pastedowns. Binder's ticket on lower pastedown: '| Bound by | Bone & Son. | [rule] | 76 Fleet Street, | London. |' Red sand-grain cloth. Both covers are blocked identically in blind and in relief on the borders and on the corners. Three fillets are blocked on the borders, the innermost of which has repeating half-circles blocked in relief within it. A medallion is blocked in blind on each corner. Within each, blocked in relief, are: a rabbit, a pheasant, a cockerel, and a squirrel. A central oval is formed by a single fillet, which has repeating half-circles blocked in relief within it. Small flowers are blocked in relief on the sides of the oval. The oval is filled with a medley of sporting objects, above and below the centre – all blocked in gold. There are: swords, arrows, fishing equipment, a cricket bat and ball, a racquet, a rifle, oars, stumps, a cricket ball, a kite, stirrups. A medallion is blocked on the centre. This is formed by three circular fillets and a hatch gold border, with small decoration blocked in relief within it. The medallion is bisected by two ovals. The ovals each contain a rectangular gold lettering-piece. The words: '| Beeton's | Annual |' are blocked in relief within each gold lettering-piece. The spine is blocked in gold. Two fillets are blocked on the borders: 1. in gold with repeating dots blocked in relief within it 2. diagonal gold hatch. On the upper half, there is an elaborate decoration of curling stems, leaves and flowers, blocked around a circle. The circle is formed by a single fillet, which has much small decoration blocked in gold within it. Within the circle, a semi-circular gold lettering-piece, is blocked, with the word: 'Beeton's' blocked in relief within it. There is also a rectangular gold lettering-piece, with the word: '| Annual |' blocked in relief within it. On the bottom half of the spine, another group of sporting equipment is blocked in gold: a cricket bat, a rifle, oars, fishing rod, a hoop. Signed 'CB' in gold as separate letters underneath this group. At the base of the spine, small decoration, then a fillet, then more small decoration are blocked in gold. The word: '| Illustrated |' is blocked in gold at the tail.

3 B., C.

Bell, Catherine Douglas. *The Huguenot family; or, help in time of need. With illustrations.* [Monogram of F. Warne.] London: Frederick Warne & Co., Bedford Street, Covent Garden, 1866. Ballantyne, Roberts and Company, Printers, Edinburgh. vi, 270 p. With ten pages of publisher's advertisements bound at the end.

115 × 172 × 28 mm. 4414.bbb.11.

The plates are signed 'Dalziel'. Yellow endpapers and pastedowns. Red sand-grain cloth. Both covers are identically blocked in blind on the borders. Two fillets are blocked on the

outer borders, the outer thin, the inner thick. Two groups of three fillets (one thick between two thin) run vertically from head to tail and horizontally from spine to fore-edge. These form squares on the corners, and within each square, leaf decoration is blocked in relief. The fillets also form four rectangular panels: on the head and on the tail, and one on each side. Within each of these panels, a repeating 'trefoil' leaf pattern is blocked in relief. On each inner corner, a single flower, thin stems, and hatched leaves are blocked in blind. The upper cover central vignette is blocked in gold. There are two semi-circular gold lettering-pieces blocked at the head and at the tail of the vignette. These lettering-pieces have vertical gold hatch on their borders. The title: '| Huguenot Family | Help in time of need |' is blocked in relief within each lettering-piece. The word: '| or |' is blocked on the centre of the cover, within a rectangular gold lettering-piece with vertical gold hatch on its borders. Curling stem and hatch gold leaves surround the word '| or |'. A 'fan-shape' is blocked at the head and the tail of the vignette, and on each side. Signed 'CB' in gold as separate letters at the base of the vignette. The spine is blocked in gold and in relief. A single fillet is blocked in at the head and at the tail. A mandorla is blocked in gold on the upper half of the spine. It has fillets and much small decoration blocked in relief on its borders. The words: '| The | Huguenot | Family | or help in time | of need | by | Catherine D. Bell | Illustrated |' are blocked in relief within eight gold lettering-pieces – each has a single fillet blocked in relief on its borders. Small decoration is blocked in gold underneath the mandorla. Near the base, a medallion is blocked in gold, overlaid with a rectangular gold lettering-piece, with a single fillet in gold on its borders. The words: '| Cousin Kate's | Library |' are blocked in relief within this lettering-piece.

4 B., C.

The Trinity of Italy: or, the Pope, the Bourbon, and the Victor; being historical revelations of the past, present, and future of Italy. By an English Civilian. . . . [Monogram of Edward Moxon.] London: Edward Moxon & Co., Dover Street, 1867. London: Swift and Co., King Street, Regent Street, W. xxviii, 334 p., 1 plate.

145 × 230 × 40 mm. 8032.i.9.

Light brown endpapers and pastedowns. Green ungrained cloth. A single fillet is blocked in blind on the borders of the lower cover. On the upper cover, a single fillet is blocked on the borders in gold. The upper cover central vignette is blocked in gold and, possibly, in silver. It shows a cross, with trefoil ends, and 'arrow heads' blocked between the arms of the cross. Around the cross, a pattern of thin leaves is blocked in silver (?), with decoration highlighted in relief. The spine is blocked in gold. A single gold fillet is blocked at the head and at the tail. The title: '| The Trinity | of | Italy |' is blocked in gold, within a decorated circle formed by three gold fillets. Immediately below this, the crowns of Bourbon and of Victor Emmanuel, are blocked inside medallions. The Papal crown is blocked beneath these two. Signed 'CB' in gold as separate letters below the Papal crown. The imprint: '| London: | E. Moxon & Co. |' is blocked in gold at the tail.

5 B., C.

Craik, Georgiana Marion. *Cousin Trix and her welcome tales. Illustrations by F. W. Keyl.* [Griffith and Farran monogram.] London: Griffith and Farran, Successors to Newbery and Harris Corner of St. Paul's Churchyard, 1868. [3], 207 p. With thirty-two pages of publisher's titles bound at the end. Edinburgh: T. Constable, Printer to the Queen, and to the University.

126 × 175 × 22 mm. 12806.ee.19.

Gilt edges. Light yellow endpapers and pastedowns. Red sand-grain cloth. Both covers are blocked identically in black on the borders, on the corners and on the sides, the head and the tail. A border is blocked in black. This consists of two fillets with a curling stem pattern blocked between them. On each side, near the head and the tail, the fillets form straps. A quatrefoil is blocked on each corner. Cartouches are blocked in black on the centre head and on the centre tail. Inside the cartouches, is a fan-shape, with a flower head blocked on the centre. On each cover, an inner square is formed by fillets and small decoration blocked in black. A semi-circle is blocked in black on each side of the square. On the upper cover, the central vignette is blocked in gold. It shows a central rectangle, formed by four gold fillets. The outermost fillet forms straps at the sides. Around the perimeter of the rectangle, small stem and leaf decoration is blocked in gold. Flower heads are blocked on the centre of each side of the rectangle. Small 'acorn-shaped' decoration is blocked on each corner of the rectangle. Inside the rectangle, the title words: '| Cousin Trix | and her | Welcome Tales |' are blocked in gold. Signed 'CB' in gold as separate letters above the flower decoration at the base of the rectangle. The spine is blocked in gold and in relief. Two fillets are blocked in gold at the head, followed underneath by 'dog-tooth' decoration, blocked in gold. The title: '| Cousin Trix |' is blocked in relief within a vertical hatch rectangular gold lettering-piece. Below this, the words: '| & her |' are blocked in gold. The words: '| Welcome Tales |' are blocked in relief within another vertical hatch rectangular gold lettering-piece. Above and below the title, straps and flower decoration are blocked in gold. Signed 'CB' in gold as separate letters near the base of the flower decoration. At the tail of the spine, the words: '| Griffith & Farran |' are blocked in relief within a vertical hatch rectangular hatched gold lettering-piece, which has small decoration blocked in gold just above it.

6 B., C. FIG. 1

Lemon, Mark *Fairy tales. With upwards of fifty illustrations by Richard Doyle and Charles H. Bennett.* London: Bradbury, Evans, & Co., 11 Bouverie Street, 1868. [London]: Bradbury,

Evans, and Co., Printers, Whitefriars. xi,189p., 7 plates. With two pages of publisher's titles bound at the end.
140 × 195 × 25 mm. 12807.f.60.

Several of the plates are signed with Bennett's monogram 'CHB' and Doyle's monogram 'RD'. Some of the plates are engraved by Swain.

Gilt edges. Bevelled boards. Brown endpapers and pastedowns. Blue pebble-grain cloth. The lower cover is blocked in blind. The three fillets blocked on the borders intersect and overlap slightly at the corners. At the point of intersection, a small single flower is blocked. The central vignette is a roundel, and consists of small leaf patterns blocked in relief. The upper cover is blocked in gold and in blind. Three fillets are blocked on the borders, with small three-pointed leaves on each corner, and small decoration on the centres of the sides, the head and the tail. A single fillet is blocked in blind on the inner borders, with small decoration on each corner. The central vignette is blocked in gold. Its borders form a semi-circle at the top. It shows a reproduction of the illustration bound in opposite page 40, which has the caption from the text: '[. . . a beautiful lady sitting on the grass] nursing a little shapeless cub in her lap, while a full grown bear sported around her . . .' Signed 'CB' in gold as separate letters at the base of the vignette. The spine is blocked in gold. The decoration from the head is: small decorative design; a bear's head; the words: '| Fairy | Tales | By | Mark Lemon |', within a fillet-frame; a seated fairy; 'CB' in gold as separate letters on either side of the fairy's legs; small decoration; the words: '| Illustrated | by | R. Doyle | and C. H. Bennett. |' in gold; small decoration; a semi-circle and small decoration at the tail.

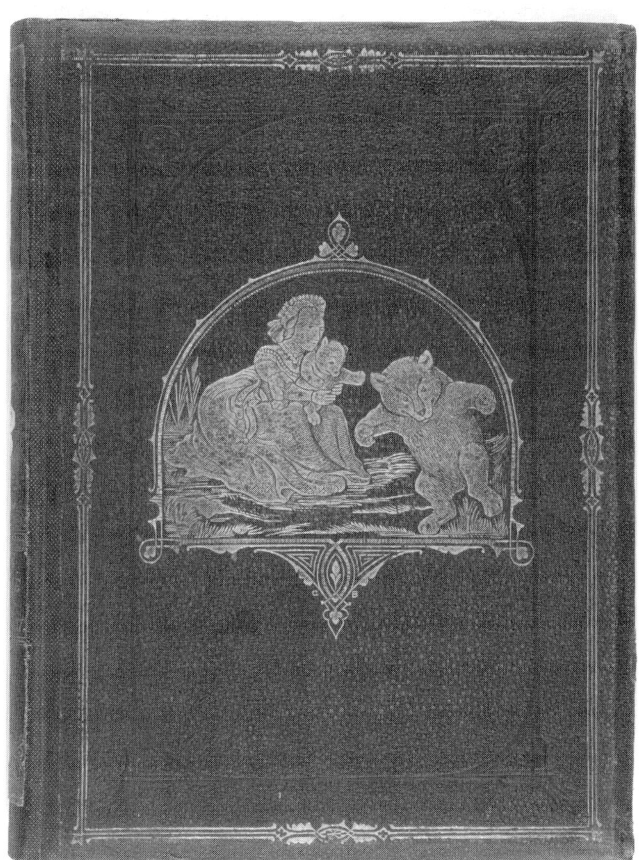

FIG. 1

7 B., C.

Letters everywhere. Stories and rhymes for children. By the author of 'The dove, and other stories of old,' etc. etc. With twenty-eight illustrations by Theophile Schuler. London: Seeley, Jackson, & Halliday, 54 Fleet St, 1869. London: R. Clay, Sons, and Taylor, Printers, Bread Street Hill. viii, 228 p., 26 plates. With four pages of publisher's titles bound at the end.
155 × 208 × 22 mm. 12807.f.74.

Dark green endpapers and pastedowns. Brown sand-grain cloth. Both covers blocked identically on the borders, the upper in black, the lower in blind. A single fillet is blocked on the borders. Inside this, two cartouches are blocked in black on each side. On each corner, another border fillet in black forms a near-square. Within each of these, leaf and flower decoration is blocked with straps. A fillet joins the straps to form the inner rectangle. The upper cover central vignette is blocked in gold and in black. It is square-shaped, being formed by three gold fillets. At the head and the base and on the sides, four circular gold lettering pieces contain the capitals 'A, D, B, C ', blocked in relief. These lettering-pieces are blocked within half circles formed by three gold fillets. The capital letters are linked by three fillets blocked in gold. Small decoration is blocked in black between the gold fillets and between the capitals. The title: '| Letters | Everywhere' is blocked in relief on the centre, within a rectangular gold lettering-piece. Four 'butterfly wing' shapes are blocked in gold on the four corners of the square. Signed 'CB' in gold as separate letters just above the capital letter 'D'. The spine is blocked in gold and relief. From the head downwards, the decoration is: two gold fillets; a pattern of circles and crosses; two gold fillets; the title: '| Letters | Everywhere |' blocked in relief, within a rectangular gold lettering-piece, with fillet and panel decoration blocked above and below the title; signed 'CB' in gold as separate letters within this decoration; near the base, the words: '| Seeley & Co. |' are blocked in relief within a circular gold lettering-piece, which has small decoration blocked above and below it; the blocking at the tail is the same as at the head: two fillets, pattern of circles, two fillets – all in gold.

8 Balfour

Levinge, Godfrey. *The Traveller in the East; being a guide through Greece and the Levant, Syria and Palestine, Egypt and Nubia, with practical information; containing descriptions of the principal cities, antiquities, and interesting localities: excursions through the southern provinces of the Kingdom of Naples, Albania, the Ionian Islands, and the principal islands of the Archipelago; and A Variety of Tours, with Distances. The whole interspersed*

with anecdotes, narrative, historical sketches, and remarks on the present state of each country. [Vol. I only.] London: Printed by the Author, Curzon Street, Mayfair, 1839 [i.e. 1846.]. vi, 331 p.
141 × 230 × 32 mm. 10077.h.11.

The Author states in the Preface that . . . 'the printing of this volume has extended over a period of nearly seven years.' [1839–1846.] The Preface is signed: Chilean, Mullingar, July 1846.

Purple diaper-grain cloth. Both covers identically blocked in blind on the borders and on the corners. Two fillets are blocked on the borders, the outer thick, the inner thin. A curling leaf and stem pattern is blocked on each corner. The same central vignette is blocked on both covers, in blind on the lower, and in gold on the upper. It shows a desert scene, a caravan train, with two camels and two men in the foreground; palm trees and more camels are in the background. The vignette is signed: '| Balfour |' in relief at the base. The spine is missing.

9 Bennett, Charles Henry

Bennett, Charles Henry. *The frog who would a wooing go.* London: G. Routledge & Co., [1858]. [London]: Edmd. Evans, Engraver and Printer, Raquet Court, Fleet Street. [16p.] Eight pages, with illustrations printed on each recto and verso.
167 × 212 × 4 mm. 12807.f.24.

The illustrations are hand coloured. The text is a single gathering sewn with a single cord, stab stitched in three places. Yellow endpapers and pastedowns. Yellow-dyed paper over boards. the lower cover has a list of publisher's titles. The upper cover has a black fillet blocked on its borders. It shows, on the centre, the frog advancing out of pond plants. he has a hat in his left hand, a stick in his right. He has a scarf around his neck, tied in a bow. Above the frog, the title is printed. Below the frog, the author and imprint are printed. The engraving is clearly the work of Bennett. All the illustrations within the text are signed by him. Blue date stamp: '9 JA[nuary 18]58'.

10 Bennett, Charles Henry

Bennett, Charles Henry. *The nine lives of a cat. A tale of wonder.* London: Griffith and Farran. Corner of St. Paul's Churchyard, 1860. [3], 20, [1] p.
140 × 187 × 9 mm. 12806.c.14.

Text sewn on three cords. Red ink speckled edges. Yellow endpapers and pastedowns. Blue bead-grain cloth. Both covers identically blocked in blind on the borders and on the corners. Four fillets are blocked in blind on the borders. The corners have stylised stem and leaf decoration, blocked in relief. The central oval is formed by repeating joined semi-circles, blocked in blind. The upper cover central vignette is blocked in gold. It shows a cat's head. The word: '| The |' is blocked in gold above the cat's head. The words: '| Nine lives of a cat | by | Charles Bennett |' are blocked in gold underneath the cat's head. The whole is intertwined with a cord, blocked in gold. This makes a diamond-shape for the vignette. Signed 'CHB' in gold as a monogram at the base of the vignette. [The monogram measures 2 mm across.] The spine is missing.

11 Bennett, Charles Henry PLATE I

Bennett, Charles Henry. *The book of blockheads. How and why they shot, got; said, had; fought, followed; gave, sold; hunted, governed; mended, built; kissed, played; lived, drank; whipped and watched. How they did, and what they did not.* London: Sampson Low, Son, and Co. 47 Ludgate Hill, 1863. London: R. Clay, Son, and Taylor, Printers, Bread Street Hill. iv, 54 p., 29 plates. With two pages of publisher's advertisements bound at the end.
170 × 235 × 12 mm. 12806.f.34.

Text sewn on two sawn-in cords. Beige endpapers and pastedowns. Green honeycomb-grain. Both covers are blocked in blind on the borders and corners with the same design. Three fillets are blocked on the borders, one thick between two thin. On the corners, large leaves and stems are blocked in blind. On the upper cover, the central vignette is blocked in blind. It shows a replica of the half-title page illustration. It shows Zephania the Zany, a 'Z' on his chest, seated – feet up – on a round wall, and holding hat stands. The title and author words: '| The book of blockheads, | by | Charles Bennett. |' are blocked in gold above and below the centre, in a semi-circle. The spine is unsigned. The cover design is not signed, nor is the half title page. However, many of the other plates are signed by Bennett, and the work is sylistically that of Bennett.

12 Bennett, Charles Henry

Bennett, Charles Henry. *The stories that Little Breeches told, and the pictures which Charles Bennett drew for them.* London: Sampson Low, Son and Co. 47, Ludgate Hill, 1863. London: R. Clay, Son and Taylor, Printers, Bread Street Hill. 55 p., 20 plates.
180 × 242 × 13 mm. 12807.g.51.

The plates are hand coloured. Text sewn on two sawn-in cords. Gilt edges. Beige endpapers and pastedowns. Red bead-grain cloth. Both covers blocked identically in blind on the borders, the corners and on the sides. Three fillets are blocked on the borders, one thick between two thin. On each corner, curling stems, leaves and buds are blocked in blind. The upper cover central vignette is blocked in gold. It shows a jug and loaf, as engraved also on the frontispiece plate, which is signed 'CHB'. Little Breeches is dancing on top of the loaf, and Muncher's body is within the loaf, with his head, arms and legs protruding from the base of the loaf. The vignette design is clearly derived from Bennett's work. The words: 'Little Breeches' are blocked in gold in a semi-circle above the jug and the loaf. The spine is not blocked.

13 Bennett, Charles Henry

Musset, Paul De. *Mr. Wind and Madam Rain. Translated, with permission of the author, by Emily Makepeace. With illustrations*

by Charles Bennett. London: Sampson Low, Son, & Co., 47 Ludgate Hill, 1864. London: Printed by William Clowes and Sons, Stamford Street, and Charing Cross. 112 p.
140 × 190 × 20 mm. 12808.bbb.26.

Gilt edges. Bevelled boards. Purple pebble-grain cloth. Both covers blocked identically in blind on the borders and the corners. Two fillets are blocked on the borders. Plant decoration is blocked on the sides. On the upper cover, a central vignette is blocked in gold. It shows a winged 'Mr Wind' blowing from within clouds upon the title: '| Mr Wind | and Madam Rain |'. The letters are blocked in gold, and they are scattered lopsidedly down the cover by the effects of the wind. Signed 'CHB' in gold as a monogram at the base of the vignette. The spine shows the title: '| Mr. Wind & Madam Rain |' blocked in gold, along the length of the spine.

14 Bennett, Charles Henry PLATE II

Bennett, Charles Henry. *The sorrowful ending of Noodledoo, with the fortunes of fate of her neighbours and friends.* London: Sampson Low, Son, and Marston, 14 Ludgate Hill, 1865. London: Printed by R. Clay, Son and Taylor, Bread Street Hill. 38 p., 16 plates. With two pages of publisher's titles bound at the end.
170 × 233 × 11 mm. 12806.f.35.

The plates are hand-coloured. Gilt edges. Beige endpapers and pastedowns. Red honeycomb-grain cloth. Both covers are blocked in blind with the same design on the borders and the corners. There are three fillets blocked on the borders, one thick between two thin. On the corners, large stem and leaf decoration is blocked in blind. On the upper cover, the central vignette is blocked in gold. The words: '| Noodle | doo | by | Charles Bennett |' are blocked in gold. The animals and birds blocked around these words are copied from the illustrations of the books, which are signed with Bennett's monogram. The cat is a copy of the one at the head of the illustration: 'Said the cat'. The two hatted rooks blocked either side of the word: 'doo' are copied from the illustration 'Corn in the field'. No spine blocking.

15 Bennett, Charles Henry FIG. 2

Bennett, Charles Henry. *The surprising, unheard of and never-to-be-surpassed adventures of Young Munchausen; related and illustrated by C. H.Bennett, in twelve stories.* London: Routledge, Warne and Routledge, Broadway, Ludgate Hill. New York; 129, Grand Street, 1865. London: R. Clay, Son, and Taylor, Printers, Bread Street Hill. [3], 107 p., 12 plates. The plates are engraved by Dalziel.
185 × 255 × 18 mm. 12819.i.57.

Light yellow endpapers and pastedowns. Green pebble grain-cloth. Both covers are blocked identically in blind on the borders, corners, and sides. Four fillets are blocked on the borders, two thin and two wide. The corners and sides are blocked with

FIG. 2

a leaf pattern. On the upper cover, the central vignette is blocked in gold. The words: '| The | adventures | of | Young Munchausen | by Charles Bennett |' are blocked in gold. In between the words, two figures of 'Young Munchausen' are blocked. These figures copy those of the illustration 'Story of the sixth-Wagers', bound between pages 46–47, which is signed with Bennett's monogram. The spine is blocked with the words: '| Young Munchausen. by C. H. Bennett. |', along the spine in gold.

16 Bennett, Charles Henry FIG. 3

Bennett, Charles Henry. *Lightsome, and the Little Golden Lady. With twenty-four illustrations by the author.* London: Griffith and Farran, Successors to Newbery and Harris, Corner of St Paul's Churchyard, 1867. London: R. Clay, Son, and Taylor, Printers, Bread Street Hill. xi, 54 p., 4 plates. With six pages of publisher's titles bound at the end.
170 × 217 × 13 mm. 12806.f.36.

The plates are hand-coloured. The plates and many other engravings in the text are signed with Bennett's monogram. The 'C' and 'B' are joined to the 'H' in the middle.

Text sewn on three sawn-in cords. Gilt edges. Yellow endpapers and pastedowns. Green sand-grain cloth. Both covers blocked identically on the borders and on the corners. The

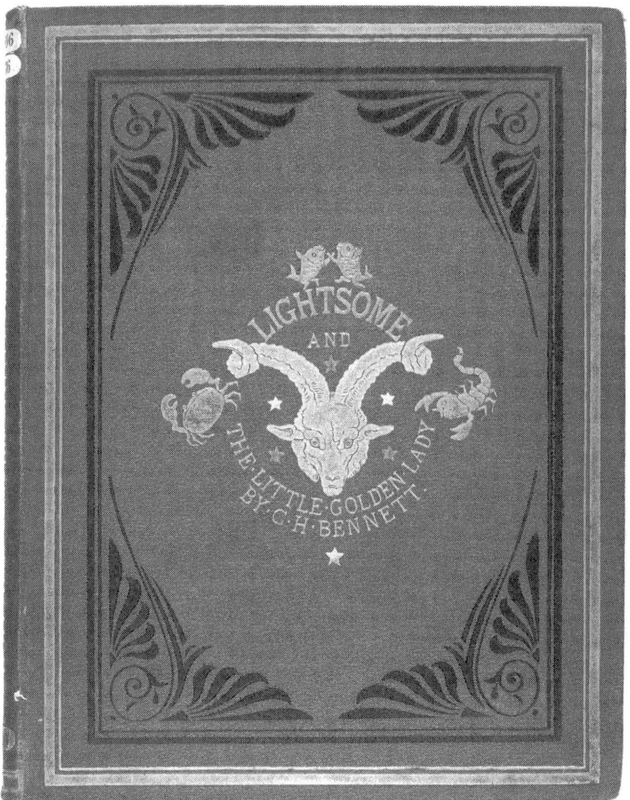

FIG. 3

lower is blocked in blind only; the upper cover is blocked in gold and in black. On the upper cover, four fillets are blocked on the borders, two in gold, two in black. Leaf decoration is blocked on each corner in black. The upper cover has a central vignette blocked in gold. It shows at the top two dancing fishes; on the left – a crab; on the right – a scorpion; on the centre a ram's head. Five hatched stars are blocked in gold around the ram's head. All of these animals are copies of illustrations signed by Bennett in the text. The words: '| Lightsome | and | the Little Golden Lady | by C. H. Bennett. |' are blocked in gold in a circle around the animals. The spine is blocked in gold. Two gold fillets are blocked at the head and at the tail. The title: 'Lightsome and the Golden Lady |' are blocked along the spine. Each word is separated by a hatched gold star.

17 Bibby, H.

Tallis's History and Description of the Crystal Palace, and Exhibition of the World's Industry in 1851; Illustrated by beautiful steel engravings, from original drawings and daguerrotypes, by Beard Mayall, etc., etc. [Royal Coat of Arms.] 6 vols. London and New York: Printed and Published by John Tallis & Co., [1852–1854].
The size of all volumes is:
218 × 280 × 16–20 mm. J/7955.e.11.

The set of three volumes is bound in six Divisions.

Div. I .138p, 25 plates.
Div. 2 [II]. pp.139–268, 23 plates. } Vol. I.
Div. III. 108p, 24 plates.
Div. IV. pp.109–196, 24 plates.
Div. V. pp.197–262, 24 plates. } Vol. II.
Div. V. 30p. (of Vol. III.)
Div. VI. pp.30–110, 23 plates. } Vol. III.
Div. VI. also has the title pages for Vols II. and III., the Contents and list of Illustrations for Vols I–III.

All volumes are sewn on four sawn-in cords, and have: gilt edges, yellow endpapers and pastedowns; blue moiré rib-horizontal-grain cloth. All volumes are blocked identically. The lower covers are blocked in blind only. On the outer borders, two fillets are blocked in blind, the outer thick, the inner thin. On the inner borders, two fillets are blocked in blind, with curling stems, leaves and flowers blocked in blind on the corners. The upper covers are blocked in gold. A single gold fillet is blocked on the borders. The rest of the cover is a large block, showing the facade and transept of the Crystal Palace within a circular frame, formed by branches and leaves. The title: '| The | Crystal Palace [in a semi-circle] |' is blocked in gold above the facade. At the head, at the top left and right are: 1. an angel with trumpet; 2&3. angels holding a laurel wreath above the title, with a dove of peace above this; 4. Britannia seated in clouds. Stars are blocked around these four figures. Near the tail, two groups of well dressed British and foreign men, women, and children are looking at the facade, as though about to enter the building. A royal coat of arms is blocked in gold between the two groups, together with branches acting as supports, which also form a frame for the imprint: '| London Printing and Publishing Company |' blocked in gold. Signed 'HB' in gold as a monogram on the centre tail, and also 'Staples Sc.' in gold underneath the group of people on the right hand side. The spines are blocked identically in gold. Double gold fillets are blocked at the head and at the tail. Double gold fillets divide the spine into six main panels, and four smaller ones. The smaller are blocked in gold with a small ornamental frieze. In the main panels: 1. ornament of leaves, curling stems, flowers, with one flower head on the centre; 2. the title: '| The | Crystal | Palace |' is blocked in gold 3. as for panel 1; 4. the volume number: '| Div. I [2, III–VI] | [rule] | Price 10/6 |' is blocked in gold; panel 5. as for panel 1; 6. at the tail, the imprint: '| London | Printing & Publishing | Company |'.

Morris & Levin, *ABP* no. 229. States the binding design to be by H. Bibby; executed by Thomas Staples.

18 Browne, Hablot Knight PLATE III

Rattlebrain *pseud.*[i.e. William Eassie.]. *Sir Guy de Guy: A Stiring Romaunt. Showing how a Briton drilled for his fatherland; won a heiress; got a pedigree; and caught the rheumatism. Illustrated by Phiz.* [i.e. Hablot K. Browne] London: Routledge, Warne and Routledge, Farringdon Street; New York: 56, Walker Street, 1864. London: Edmund Evans, Engraver and Printer, Raquet Court, Fleet Street. [5], 167 p.
147 × 203 × 20 mm. 11649.bb.19.

Several of the full page illustrations are signed: ' Phiz' and 'E. Evans Sc.'

Gilt edges. Bevelled boards. Binder's ticket on lower pastedown: '| Bound by | Bone & | Son, | 76, Fleet Street, | London. |' Red pebble-grain cloth. The lower cover has three fillets blocked on the borders in blind. On the upper cover, the same three fillets are blocked in gold. The upper cover has a central vignette blocked in gold. The title words: '| Sir Guy de Guy |' are blocked in gold, in rustic lettering, in a semi-circle above the central roundel. Below the central roundel, the words: '| By Rattlebrain | & | Phiz |' are blocked in gold in rustic lettering, in a semi-circle. The central roundel shows Sir Guy pasting a poster of 'Arabella' on a tree in a forest. Sir Guy is watched by an ass, and a moon with a face. The tree, on which the poster is being affixed, also has a face above the poster. All the decoration is picked out with blocking in relief. Unsigned. The attribution of this cover design to Phiz is based on a strong stylistic similarity of the design to the many illustrations of Sir Guy within the body of the text. The spine is blocked in gold and in relief. Two gold fillets are blocked at the head and at the tail. At the head the words: '| Sir | Guy de Guy | Illustrated | by | Phiz |' are all blocked in relief within five gold lettering-pieces which all have single fillets blocked in relief within the borders of each; the words are all surrounded by stem and small leaf decoration blocked in gold.

Muir, *VIB* p. 125. This work not listed.

19 C., M.A.

Martin, William. *The birthday gift, for boys and girls.* London: Darton and Co., 58 Holborn Hill, [1860]. iv, 296 p. 7 plates.
140 × 186 × 31 mm. 12804.c.38.

Text sewn on two tapes. Gilt edges. Yellow endpapers and pastedowns. Red morocco horizontal-grain cloth. Both covers blocked identically, in blind on the lower cover and in gold on the upper. On the upper cover, a single fillet is blocked in gold on the borders. Inside this, an 'oak branch-shaped' fillet is blocked on the borders, which crosses to form single straps at the centre head, the centre tail and on the centre of the sides. Oval panels are formed on each corner by the oak branches. Within each corner panel, scenes are blocked in gold: top left – a sunrise over the sea and two ladies on a cliff; top right – two men, one holding a cricket bat over his right shoulder, the other holding three stumps; bottom right – a 'blind man's buff' game; bottom left – boys are throwing snowballs. Oak leaves and acorns surround these oval corner panels. On the centre, the words: '| The| Birthday | Gift. |' are blocked in gold in 'branch-like' letters. Signed 'MAC' in gold within the strap on the centre tail. The spine is blocked in gold. A single fillet is blocked in gold on the perimeter. From the head downwards, the decoration is: a group of leaves, blocked in gold; the words: '| A | Birthday | Gift |' blocked in gold in 'branch-like' letters; a young lady, who is reaching out to pick pears from a tree; a young girl by the lady holds a basket and is stretching to reach a pear.

In The BL *General Catalogue of Printed Books*: C, M.A. is possibly M.A. Cooke. Author of works of imaginative literature, 1862–1873.

20 C., M.A.

Periodical Publications – *London. Peter Parley's Annual. A Christmas and New Year's present, for Young People. Edited by William Martin, Author of 'Parley's tales about India,' 'The illustrated natural philosopher,' etc.* London: Darton and Co., 58 Holborn Hill, 1860. viii, 296 p., 8 plates. With thirty-two pages of advertisements and one fold-out advertisement bound at the end.
138 × 185 × 40 mm. P.P.6750. [1860.]

The frontispiece plate is signed: 'Collins & Co. 107 Dorset St Fleet St.'

Yellow endpapers and pastedowns. Written on the front pastedown: '| Dec. 21st 1859 | [rule] | To My Dear Son Denis | [rule] | A Reward for | attention to his studies | D H Donnell | [rule] |' Gilt edges. Red bead-grain cloth. Both covers blocked identically in blind on the lower, in gold on the upper. Two gold fillets are blocked on the borders, one thick, one thin. At the head, the title: '| Peter | Parley's | Annual. |' is blocked in relief within two ribbon-shaped gold lettering-pieces. On the head, the tail, the corners, and the sides, vine leaves, grapes and tendrils are blocked. The vine branches form two ovals towards the base, and a circle above, with strapwork between. The circle has a family group, in a snow scene, blocked within it; to the left, is a hunter; to the right is a warrior, with bow and arrow. Within the left oval, at the tail, a man, holding a horse, is hunting a kangaroo; within the right oval at the tail, a postman is delivering a letter to two children and their mother. On the centre tail, '| 1860 |' is blocked, with the signature 'MAC' blocked in gold as separate letters underneath. The spine is blocked in gold. A single gold fillet is blocked around the perimeter. From the head downwards, the decoration is: moon and stars; a balloon and its basket; the basket contains a group of people and flags, with an anchor hanging from it; the title: '| Peter | Parley's | Annual |' blocked in relief within the balloon mantle; below the balloon, a kite is flying with a streamer tail; birds are blocked flying around the balloon and the kite; a church steeple is blocked to the left and right of the tail; between the steeples, a banner-shaped gold lettering-piece is blocked, with the words: '| A | merry Christmas | [&] | Happy New Year |' blocked in relief within it.

21 C., M.A.

Scoresby, Rev. William, *the Younger. The Whaleman's adventures in the Southern Ocean; as gathered by the Rev. Henry T. Cheever, on the homeward cruise of the 'Commodore Preble'. Edited by the Rev. W. Scoresby, D.D., F.R.S. . . . Fifth Edition.* London: Darton & Co., 58, Holborn Hill, 1861. Winchester: Printed by Hugh Barclay, High Street. xiv, 304 p., 8 plates.
107 × 170 × 28 mm. 12805.bbb.16.

The plate opposite p. 36 is signed 'W. H. Prior'.

Text sewn on two tapes. Yellow endpapers and pastedowns. Purple wave vertical-grain cloth. Both covers blocked identically in blind with two fillets on the borders. The upper cover vignette is blocked in gold. It features a flagpole and a large flag, which is blocked as a gold lettering-piece. The words: '| The | Whaleman's | adventures. |' are blocked in relief within the flag. Below this, a scene of a whaling boat on water is blocked. The boat has six men inside it. The man at the rear is steering. The man at the bow is standing with a harpoon held in his raised right hand. He is about to throw the harpoon into a whale just by the boat. The whale has already been speared by one harpoon, and it has its head underwater. One harpoon is in the water. Signed 'MAC' in gold on the left hand base of the vignette. The spine is blocked in gold and in relief. At the head, a beached whaling ship is blocked. It has full sails blocked as gold lettering-pieces, hanging limply. The word: '| The |' is blocked in relief within the topsail; the words: '| Whaleman's | adventures |' are blocked in relief within two pennant-shaped gold lettering-pieces, with scroll ends. Beneath this, an albatross is blocked. At the tail, a lighthouse by the sea is blocked in gold.

22 C., M.A.

De L'Isle, F. Louis Jaquerod. *Wayside warblings and other poems.* . . . London: Thomas Bosworth, 215, Regent Street, 1868. London: Printed by C.W. Stevens, 5, Great Queen-street. xii, 343 p. With two pages of publisher's titles bound at the end.
120 × 195 × 30 mm. 11649.bbb.8.

Gilt edges. Light yellow endpapers and pastedowns. Green pebble-grain cloth. Both covers blocked identically in gold. Four fillets are blocked on the borders. Inside these, a fifth fillet ends small decoration blocked in gold on each corner. The central oval panel is blocked in gold. Leaves and stems are blocked around the perimeter of the oval. The spine is blocked in gold. Two gold fillets are blocked at the head and at the tail. Three panels are formed on the spine by single gold fillets. From the head downwards, the decoration is: panel one – gold leaf and stems and vertical gold hatch, with the title: '| Wayside warblings and other poems. |' blocked in gold; panel two – the same leaf and gold decorations for panel one, then two mandorlas, one larger, together with leaf decoration, and the signature 'MAC' in gold as separate letters at the base of this panel; panel three – decoration as for panel one, but inverted.

23 C., T.

Milner, Mary. *The garden, the grove, and the field: a garland of the months* . . . Bath: Binns and Goodwin. And at their London Depot, Sampson's Low's, 169, Fleet Street. London: Whittaker and Co. Edinburgh: Oliver and Boyd. Dublin: J. M'Glashan, [1852]. [Bath]: Printed by Binns and Goodwin. xxii, 242 p. 2 frontis. plates. With twenty-two pages of publisher's titles bound at the end.
112 × 180 × 25 mm. 7055.d.25.

Text sewn on three sawn-in cords. Yellow endpapers and pastedowns. Blue ripple vertical-grain cloth. Both covers blocked identically in blind and in relief on the borders and on the corners. A single fillet is blocked in blind on the borders. A curling leaf pattern is blocked in relief on each corner. The upper cover is blocked in gold. Curling branches form three circles. Each circle has different leaves , flowers, and reeds growing from it. (E.g. Fuchsias and roses come out of the circle of branches at the top.) The title: '| The | Garden | The | Grove | & | The | Field. |' is blocked in gold in rustic lettering within each circle. Signed 'TC' in gold as a monogram at the base of the vignette. The spine is blocked in gold. A single gold fillet is blocked on the perimeter. A tree grows from near the tail. It has two small plants blocked at its base, and small branches and leaves are blocked further up its trunk. Two branches of the tree form a panel, in which the title: '| The | Garden | The | Grove | The | Field. |' is blocked in gold. A flower, a pot and a plant are blocked at the head. (The plant resembles an Arum, with its spathe around the spadix.) At the tail, the words: '| Bath | Binns and | Goodwin |' are blocked in gold within a rectangle formed by a single gold fillet.

24 C., T.

Marryat, afterwards, Norris, Emilia. *The children's pic-nic and what came of it. With illustrations by Augusta Marryat.* London: Griffith and Farran, Successors to Newbery and Harris, Corner of St. Paul's Churchyard, 1868. Edinburgh: T. Constable, Printer to the Queen, and to the University. [2], 122 p., 4 plates. With thirty-two pages of publisher's titles bound at the end.
125 × 175 × 20 mm. 12806.ee.35.

The plates are hand-coloured.

Gilt edges. Brown endpapers and pastedowns. Binder's ticket on lower pastedown: '| Bound by | Burn. | 37 & 38 | Kirby St. |' Green sand-grain cloth. Both covers blocked identically in blind on the borders and on the corners. Three fillets are blocked on the borders, the outer thick, the middle thin. The innermost fillet forms a 'spade-shape' on each corner, with leaves blocked inside each, and on either side of the spade-shape, all in blind. The upper cover central vignette is blocked in gold. It shows a medallion, formed by: 1. repeated dots in relief; 2. a hatch gold fillet; 3. a gold fillet. Inside, two children are shown, one seated in front of a picnic basket, the other bending over and reaching into it. Above and to the left and right of the medallion, six gold lettering-pieces have the title: '| The children's [semi-circular] | picnic | and | what | came | of it |' blocked in relief inside each. Below the medallion, crossed sticks hold a kettle above a fire. Groups of leaves are blocked to the left, to the right and below the medallion. Signed 'TC' in gold as a monogram at the base of the vignette. The spine is blocked in gold. From the head downwards, the decoration is: small leaf decoration in gold; the title: '| The | Children's | pic nic | and | what | came | of it |' blocked in gold; leaf and stem decoration are blocked in gold underneath the title.

25 C., W.S

Owen, Mrs Octavius Freire. *The Spirit of the Holly*.... London: G. Routledge & Co., Farringdon Street; New York: 18, Beekman Street, 1856. [London]: Cox (Bros) & Wyman, Printers, Great Queen Street.[3], 154 p., 8 plates.
130 × 182 × 15 mm. 12807.d.28.

The plates are signed 'G. L. Johnson'.

Yellow endpapers and pastedowns. Binder's ticket on lower pastedown: '| Leighton | Son & | Hodge. | Shoe Lane | London. |' Blue morocco vertical-grain cloth. Both covers blocked identically in blind on the borders and on the corners. Four fillets are blocked in blind on the borders. A leaf and stem pattern is blocked on each corner in relief. An oval central frame is formed by a pattern of small semi-circles, blocked in blind. The upper cover vignette is blocked in gold. It is diamond-shaped, formed by holly branches blocked on the sides, with holly leaves, stems, berries around the branches. Within the diamond, the words: '| The | spirit | of the | Holly | By | Mrs Owen |' are blocked in gold, some in fanciful 'holly-like' letters. Signed 'WSC' in gold at the base of the vignette. The spine is blocked in gold. From the head downwards, the decoration is: three gold fillets; a holly sprig; the title: '| The | spirit | of the | holly. |' blocked in gold diagonally down the spine; the word '| Owen |' is blocked in gold between gold fillets; holly stems, leaves and berries are blocked in gold; three gold fillets are blocked at the tail.

Ball, *VPB* p. 95. Cites William Stephen Coleman as being one of a number of artists who worked for Edmund Evans, providing woodblocks for yellowbacks pasted onto covers.

26 Crane, Walter

King Luckieboy's Picture Book. Containing King Luckieboy's Party. 'This little pig went to market.' The Old Courtier, Picture Book of Horses. With thirty-two pages of illustrations, printed in colours. London: George Routledge and Sons, The Broadway, Ludgate. New York: 416, Broome Street, [1871]. [London]: [Printed by Edmund Evans and Leighton Bros.] [2, 32 p.] With two pages of publisher's titles bound at the end.
187 × 250 × 13 mm. 12806.h.20.

Each story additionally has its own title page.

Yellow endpapers and pastedowns. Yellow-dyed paper over boards, with quarter sand-grain cloth spine. The lower cover has a printed list of Routledge titles. This work is advertised as part of the series: '| Routledge's coloured pictured books. | Super-royal 8vo, with Illustrations by Walter Crane, Charles H. Bennett, and others; beautifully printed in colours by Edmund Evans and Leighton Brothers. | Price 2s. 6d. each. |' The upper cover has a reproduction in different colours of page 1 of 'King Luckieboy's Party'. This shows a scene in which General Janus comes into a room with his footman Aquarius, to present a choice of fresh colds to King Luckieboy. The engraving is signed with Crane's monogram (as are all the illustrations). Printed at the head: 'Price two shillings & sixpence'; at the tail: '| London: George Routledge & Son |'. A single red fillet is printed on the borders. The words: '| King Luckieboy's | Picture Book |' are printed in red capitals at the head. The spine is unblocked.

27 Crane, Walter

The Blue Beard Picture Book containing Blue Beard, Little Red Riding Hood, Jack and the Bean-Stalk, Baby's Own ABC. With Thirty-two pages of illustrations by Walter Crane. Printed in Colours by Edmund Evans. London: George Routledge and Sons The Broadway, Ludgate; New York, 416 Broome Street, [1875]. [2, 32 p.] The title page verso has a list of publisher's titles.
186 × 248 × 10 mm. 12806.g.23.

Beige endpapers and pastedowns. Blue ungrained cloth. The lower cover is not blocked. The upper cover is fully blocked in gold. On the head and on the tail, a 'candle-flame' border is blocked. Fillets divide the cover into panels. Within the panel at the head, Little Red Riding Hood and the Wolf are blocked. Down the fore-edge, Jack is climbing up the beanstalk, which is growing out of a vase underneath him. The beanstalk grows up and around Red Riding Hood and the Wolf. Near the centre, the figure of Bluebeard holds the key to the small closet in his right hand. He holds two more keys in his left hand. His wife is on her knees in front of him, begging for her life. The doorway of the small closet is behind her. Within the door, the title: '| The | Bluebeard | Picture | Book. |' is blocked in gold. Underneath the doorway, the words: '| 32 | pages of | design | by | Walter | Crane |' are blocked in gold, on either side of the wife. A large version of Crane's rebus is blocked in gold above Bluebeard's head. The spine is blocked in gold only. Candle-flame decoration is blocked at the head and at the base, then a single gold fillet. The head of Bluebeard is blocked near the head. The title: '| The Bluebeard Picture Book |' is blocked in gold along the spine.

28 Cruikshank, George

Ainsworth, William Harrison. *The Tower of London. A Historical Romance. Illustrated by George Cruikshank.* London: George Routledge & Co., Farringdon-Street, 1854. xvi, 439 p., 40 plates.
140 × 225 × 42 mm. 12619.g.31.

Originally issued in thirteen parts. The paper covers for each part are bound in sequence. Each part has the same title page printed, as follows: '| Part 1]–13]. | Price sixpence | Popular Illustrated Weekly | [double rule] | Weekly, in penny numbers; or in monthly parts, Five Numbers, with Wrapper, sixpence. |[double rule] | The | Tower of London. | By | W. Harrison Ainsworth, |[rule] | Illustrated by George Cruikshank. | [Wood engraving.] | London: George Vickers, Holywell Street, | and all booksellers and newsmen in the United Kingdom. |'

The engraving on each upper cover recto shows an execution scene, in front of the Tower of London, with a crowd looking

on. The engraving is signed 'GCK' at its base. All the plates in the text are signed 'George Cruikshank'.

Part 1 is date stamped: '15 DE[CEMBER]53'; Part 13 is date stamped: '3 M[A]Y [18]55'. Publisher's titles are printed on the verso of each upper paper cover, and on the verso of each lower paper cover.

Buchanan-Brown, John, BIGC p. 28 and illustrations, 140–149.

29 D., C.

The casquet of lyric gems with accompaniments for the piano. Glasgow: David Jack; 61, Jamaica St.; London: Houlston and Wright, [1857]. Bell and Bain, Printers, Glasgow. vi, 240 p.
166 × 211 × 22 mm. BL Music Library. C.461.

Gilt edges. Yellow endpapers and pastedowns. Red morocco vertical-grain cloth. Both covers identically blocked, in blind on the lower cover, and in gold and blind on the upper. Two fillets are blocked on the borders, the outer thick, the inner thin. A leaf pattern is blocked on the head, the tail, and the sides, with scrolls on the corners – all in blind. The upper cover central vignette is blocked in gold. The title: '| The | Casquet | of | Lyric | Gems. | With Music. |' is blocked in gold, in fanciful and gothic letters. The capitals 'L' and 'G' are blocked within horizontal hatch gold lettering-pieces. The spine is blocked in gold. A single gold fillet is blocked on the perimeter. From the head downwards, the decoration is: two fillets; straps; the title: '| The | Casquet | of | Lyric | Gems |' blocked in gold, in fanciful and gothic letters; straps; a pennant-shaped gold lettering-piece wraps downwards around a plant stem; the words: '| Songs | Duets | Glees, &c | with | accompaniments |' are blocked in relief within the pennant; the words: 'David Jack' are blocked in relief, within a gold lettering-piece shaped as an open book; two fillets at the tail. On each side of the spine, just below the mid-point, the initials 'D C' are blocked in gold, outside the gold fillet on the perimeter.

30 Doyle, Richard PLATE IV

Hughes, Thomas. *The Scouring of the White Horse; or, the Long Vacation of a London Clerk. By the Author of 'Tom Brown's School Days.' . . . Illustrated by Richard Doyle.* Cambridge: Macmillan and Co. and 23, Henrietta Street, Covent Garden, London, 1859. [London]: R. Clay, Printer, Bread Street Hill. xi, 228 p. With sixteen pages of publisher's titles bound at the end.
141 × 185 × 20 mm. 12632.d.27.

This work is advertised in the publisher's titles at the end: 'With numerous engravings by Richard Doyle, engraved by W. J. Linton. Imperial 16mo. beautifully printed on toned paper, and bound in extra cloth, with gilt leaves, 8s. 6d.'

Gilt edges. [Edges of original pink endpapers and pastedowns underneath the white endpapers and pastedowns.] Blue morocco horizontal-grain cloth. Both covers blocked identically, in blind on the lower and in gold on the upper. A single gold fillet is blocked on the borders. Down each side, tree branches and leaves are blocked; on the left hand side, people are holding onto a pole among the foliage, with men hunting pigs at the bottom. On the right hand side, groups of figures are blocked on the branches. On the head, centre, the title: '| The Scouring of the White Horse |' is blocked, in rustic 'branch-like' letters. The White Horse is blocked underneath this. On the base, centre, a figure sits with a shawl over his head. The spine is blocked in gold. From the head downwards, the decoration is: two fillets; the title: '| The | Scouring | of | the | White | Horse. |' blocked diagonally across and down the spine, with a curling stem rising up through the letters; at the tail: '| Macmillan & Co. |' is blocked; two gold fillets are blocked at the tail.

The design is unsigned. Attributed to Doyle on stylistic grounds, as the cover design is close to the illustrations within the text, and especially that on the double half-title page, which has a busy scene, dense with many figures scouring the figure of the White Horse.

McLean, *VBD* p. 164.

31 Doyle, Richard

Gouraud, Julie *pseud.* [i.e. Louise d'Aulnay.] *The adventures of a watch. Translated from the French. With a title and frontispiece designed by Richard Doyle Esq. Engraved by the Brothers Dalziel.* Dublin: James Duffy, 15, Wellington Quay; London: Paternoster Row, [1864]. [London]: Dalziel Brothers, Camden Press. 83 p., 2 plates.
125 × 173 × 15 mm. 12806.bbb.23.

The frontispiece is signed with the monogram 'RD'. On the lower pastedown is printed: '| New book for Christmas. | Just published, imperial 16mo., richly gilt, price 1s.6d., with Two | Illustrations, designed expressley[sic] for the work, | By Richard Doyle, Esq, | . . . |'

Text sewn on two cords. Gilt edges. White endpapers and pastedowns, which have publisher's titles printed on them. Blue pebble-grain cloth. Both covers are blocked identically in blind on the borders and on the corners. Three fillets are blocked on the borders, the outer two being thick, the innermost thin. Arabesques are blocked on each corner, with a small flower blocked on their centres. The upper cover vignette is blocked in gold. It is an exact reproduction of the engraving on the title page plate, which is stated to be by Doyle. The title: '| The | adventures | of a | watch |' is blocked in gold, in greatly elaborated 'branch-style' letters. These letters have stems and leaves sprouting from their ends. A pocket watch, which has a roman face, is blocked below the title, hanging from the letter 'T'. The spine is not blocked.

32 Dudley, Robert PLATE V

Longfellow, Henry Wadsworth. *The Song of Hiawatha. Illustrated, from designs by George H. Thomas. Engraved on Wood by W. Thomas & H. Harral.* London: W. Kent & Co, (Late D. Bogue), 86, Fleet Street, 1860. London: Savill and Edwards, Printers, Chandos Street, Covent Garden. viii, 224 p.
145 × 218 × 25 mm. RdeB.I.23.

The British Museum de Beaumont copy.

Gilt edges. Bevelled boards. Yellow endpapers and pastedowns. de Beaumont bookplate on upper pastedown. Bookseller's ticket on upper pastedown: '| S & T. Gilbert, | Booksellers, | 4, Copthall Buildings, | Back of the Bank. |' Binder's ticket on lower pastedown: '| Bound | by | Leighton | Son and | Hodge |'. Blue morocco vertical-grain cloth. Both covers identically blocked in gold, in blind and in relief. Blocked on the borders are: 1. a single thin gold fillet; 2. hatch gold fillet; 3. a repeating pattern of semi-circles and dots, blocked in gold; 4. a hatch gold fillet. On the corners and on the sides, ten medallions are blocked – each formed by a hatch gold fillet and four dots. Each medallion has plant decoration blocked in relief within it, surrounded by horizontal gold hatch blocking. Between the medallions, rectangular panels are formed by single gold fillets, with plants blocked in relief within each. The inner rectangle on the covers is formed by: 1. a thin gold fillet; 2. semi-circles and dots blocked in gold. Above and below the central oval, two rectangular panels are formed by hatch gold fillets and a single thin gold fillet; within each rectangle, the title: '| The Song of | Hiawatha |' is blocked in gold. The central oval has three groups of decoration on its borders: 1. a hatch gold fillet, blocked between two thin gold fillets; 2. a repeating plant pattern blocked in gold; 3. a hatch gold fillet, blocked between two thin gold fillets . On the head, the tail and the sides, plant decoration is blocked in relief within gold lettering-pieces. The inner central oval has a white paper onlay. Within it, a vignette is blocked, showing an Indian chief and a squaw standing on the right; another squaw is seated on the ground to the left – all in gold. Signed 'RD' in gold at the base of the vignette. The spine is blocked in gold and in relief. A single hatch gold fillet is blocked on the borders. Panels are blocked down the spine, formed by single gold fillets. From the head downwards, the decoration is: 1. gold dots and semi-circles; 2. a medallion formed by two fillets, the inner of which is hatch, with maize plant decoration blocked in relief, surrounded by horizontal gold hatch; around the medallion, plant decoration is blocked in relief; 3. the title: '| The | Song | of | Hiawatha |' blocked in gold within an oval formed by two gold fillets, the inner of which is of hatch gold; 4. a medallion, with the same formation as no. 2. and plant decoration blocked in relief within, together with horizontal gold hatch; 5. the words: '| Longfellow | [rule] | Illustrated | by | Geo. Thomas |' are blocked in gold, within an oval formed by two fillets, the inner of which is of gold hatch; 6. a medallion – the same as no. 2; 7. the same decoration as no. 1; 8. a rectangle formed by a single fillet; 9. the same as nos. 1 and 7. The spine is not signed.

de Beaumont, *RdeB1* no. 185. Goldman, *VIB*, no.185.

33 Dudley, Robert

Bunyan, John. *The Pilgrim's Progress from this world to that which is to come. A new edition with a memoir, and notes by George Offer. Illustrated with one hundred and ten designs by J. D. Watson, engraved on wood by the Brothers Dalziel.* London: Routledge, Warne, and Routledge, Farringdon Street. New York: 56, Walker Street, 1861. London: Richard Clay, Bread St. Hill. [6], xxii, 408 p.

170 × 228 × 45 mm. RdeB.G.12.

The British Museum de Beaumont copy.

Gilt edges. Bevelled boards. Yellow endpapers and pastedowns. The upper endpaper is missing. Binder's ticket on lower pastedown: '| Bound | by | Leighton | Son and | Hodge |'. Maroon morocco horizontal-grain cloth. Both covers blocked identically in gold, in blind and in relief. On the borders are: 1. three gold fillets, the middle being thicker, with repeating dots blocked in relief within it; 2. a pattern of flowers, blocked in relief; 3. as for 1, which forms the inner rectangle. On each inner corner, circles are formed by two gold fillets. Hatch gold leaves are blocked inside each circle. The central oval is formed by: 1. two gold fillets, the inner of which has repeating dots blocked within it; 2. a repeating pattern of leaves blocked in relief; 3. two gold fillets, the outer of which has repeating dots blocked within in relief. Leaves and flowers are blocked in vertical gold hatch at the head, at the tail and on each side of the central oval. The inner oval is a light purple ungrained cloth onlay; the oval is recessed, with two thin gold fillets blocked on its borders. A pattern of stems, of leaves and of flowers is blocked on the onlay in relief, with the flower petals being of vertical hatch gold and the flower stamens being gold dots. The title: '| The | Pilgrim's | Progress.' is blocked in gold on the centre. Signed 'RD' in relief at the base of the recessed oval. The spine is blocked in gold and in relief. On the borders, three gold fillets are blocked, the middle having repeating dots blocked in relief within it. The spine is divided into eight panels by groups of three fillets blocked horizontally, the middle of which has repeating dots blocked in relief within it. From the head, the decoration in the panels is: 1. bunches of flowers, blocked in relief; 2. the words: '| The | Pilgrim's | Progress | [decorative device] | Bunyan |' are blocked in gold, within an oval formed by two gold fillets; 3. bunches of flowers; 4. stems and flowers, blocked in gold within an oval -all in gold; 5. the word: '| Illustrated |' is blocked in gold; 6. repeating hatch leaves are blocked in gold within a circle formed by two gold fillets; 7. the words: '| Geo. Routledge & Co. |' are blocked in gold; 8. a single fillet is blocked in relief at the tail. Unsigned.

de Beaumont, *RdeB1* no.40. Goldman, *VIB* no.40.

34 Dudley, Robert

Wills, W. Henry. *Poet's wit and humour. Selected by W. H. Wills. Illustrated with one hundred engravings from drawings by Charles H. Bennett and George H. Thomas.* London: Joseph Cundall, 168, New Bond Street, [1861]. London: Petter and Galpin, Belle Sauvage Printing Works, Ludgate Hill. E.C. [7], 284 p.

170 × 232 × 40 mm. RdeB.K.6.

The British Museum de Beaumont copy.

Text sewn on three tapes. Gilt edges. Bevelled boards. Yellow endpapers and pastedowns. Green sand-grain cloth. Both

covers blocked identically, in blind and relief on the lower and in gold and relief on the upper. On the upper cover, a hatch gold fillet is blocked on the borders. Horizontal hatch gold is blocked on the corners, with small plant patterns blocked within each corner in relief. Fillets of vertical hatch gold, with repeating circles blocked in relief within them form: 1. an inner border; 2. a cartouche on each side; 3. an inner central rectangle; 4. a circle at the centre head and at the centre tail; 5. a central diamond. Around the perimeter of the central rectangle, plant and flower patterns are blocked in relief, with flower heads blocked in gold. Arabesques of horizontal hatch gold are blocked on the middle of each cartouche, with small decoration in relief within each arabesque. On each corner of the central rectangle, a scroll-shaped hatch gold lettering-piece is blocked, with a one word of the title blocked within each in relief: '| Poet's | wit | and | humour |'. The central vignette, blocked in gold, shows a winged putto, wearing a jester's hat, holding a lyre on its left. The jester's staff is on the ground in front. Signed 'RD' in gold as separate letters at the base of the central diamond. The spine is blocked in gold. A single hatch gold fillet and a single thin gold fillet are blocked on the perimeter. A single hatch gold fillet, with repeating circles blocked in relief within, forms, from the head downwards: 1. a circle, with flower decoration blocked in gold and relief within; 2. a panel with the title: '| Poet's | wit | and | humour |' blocked in gold within; 3. a cartouche with flower decoration blocked in relief within, surrounding an arabesque blocked in gold; 4. a panel with the words: '| Selected by | Henry. Wills |' blocked in gold; 5. a circle, with decoration as for the circle at the head; 6. at the tail, a rectangle, with a single gold fillet forming another rectangle within.

Ball, *VPB* p. 147. de Beaumont, *RdeB1* no.266. Goldman, *VIB* no. 266. McLean, *VPBB* p. 14. Morris & Levin, *APB* p. 33, no. 44.

35 Dudley, Robert PLATE VI

Favourite English poems of modern times. Unabridged. Illustrated with upwards of two hundred engravings on wood, from drawings by the most eminent artists. London: Sampson Low, Son, and Co., 1862. London: R. Clay, Son, and Taylor, Printers. xii, 372 p.
165 × 230 × 40 mm. C.109.d.1.

The monogram of Joseph Cundall is printed on the title page verso.

Gilt edges. Bevelled boards. Light yellow endpapers and pastedowns. Brown morocco horizontal-grain cloth. Both covers are blocked identically in gold and in blind. Two thin fillets with a hatched fillet between them are blocked in gold on the borders. There is an inner border pattern of small leaves and stems, in gold. At the head, the tail and on the corners and on the sides, small leaf and stem decorations are blocked in relief and in blind. The large central oval has two fillets blocked in gold on the borders. In between these fillets are blocked poets' names in gold, each name inside small panels. In between the panels, small leaf and stem decorations are blocked in relief and in blind. At the head of the central oval, the word: '| Favourite |' is blocked in relief inside a hatched semi-circular cartouche; at the base of the central oval are the words: '| English poems |' blocked in the same way. The central panel is recessed. It has white coarse-grain cloth. The whole is blocked in gold, with fruit and flower decoration blocked in relief (showing the white cloth). The very centre has a blue paper onlay, which is blocked in gold and in relief. The relief shows a winged putto holding a garland of flowers. The spine is blocked in gold and in relief. A fillet is blocked on the perimeter in gold. A hatch gold fillet is blocked on the head and at the tail. Strapwork forming a square, with small leaves and dots, is blocked at the head, and also in the middle in gold. The title: '| Favourite | English | Poems |' is blocked in gold, inside a circle, formed by two gold fillets. Beneath the title, crossing gold hatch fillets form small squares, with leaf and berry decoration blocked in gold around and within them. There is more leaf and stem intertwined decoration blocked in relief and in blind on the lower half of the spine. At the tail, there are two small squares, with dots, above a small rectangle, formed by a single gold fillet, which contains stem decoration. Signed 'RD' in gold as separate letters in the middle of this rectangle. Formerly shelved at 1347.f.15.

Ball, *VPB* p. 148. Cites Cundall as the Editor. McLean, *Cundall* p. 86. McLean, *VPBB* p .91.

36 Dudley, Robert

Willmott, Robert Eldridge Aris. *English sacred poetry of the sixteenth, seventeenth, eighteenth, and nineteenth centuries. Selected and edited by Robert Aris Willmott, Illustrated by Holman Hunt, T. D. Watson, John Gilbert, J. Wolf, etc. Engraved by the Brothers Dalziel.* London: Routledge, Warne & Routledge, Farringdon Street. New York: 56, Walker Street, 1862. London: Printed by R. Clay, Son, and Taylor, Bread Street Hill. xix, 387 p.
170 × 230 × 42 mm. 1347.f.13.

Original upper yellow endpaper bound at the front. Binder's ticket on upper pastedown: '| Bound | by | Leighton | Son and | Hodge |'. Blue morocco horizontal-grain cloth. Both covers identically blocked in gold, in blind and in relief. Two gold fillets are blocked on the borders, with repeating dots blocked in relief between them. On the inner borders, a wide elaborate patterns of thin stems, hatched leaves and clusters of three small berries is blocked in gold. Inside this, another border of two more gold fillets with semi-circular corners, and a border of repeating dots blocked in relief between them. A pattern of stems and five-petalled flowers is blocked in relief within the central rectangle. A large oval, and a recessed oval are blocked on the centre. The borders of the oval have two groups of three gold fillets, the middle of which is 'cord-shaped'. The words: '| English | sacred | poetry | Willmott. |' are blocked in gold between these groups of fillets. Within the recessed oval, a piece of white paper is onlaid, and bordered with a single gold fillet. A lyre and a man in Celtic-type dress are blocked in gold on the onlay. The spine is blocked in gold and in relief. A single thin gold fillet is blocked on the perimeter. Horizontal hatched gold fillets divide the spine into panels. From the head downwards, the decoration is: a thin rectangular panel with

small gold decoration blocked within; a semi-circular panel with curling leaves and stems blocked within; the words: '| English | sacred | poetry | [rule] | Illustrated | [rule] Willmott |' are blocked in gold within a panel formed by: 1. a hatch gold fillet; 2. a single thin gold fillet; 3. repeating dots, blocked in relief; 4. a hatch gold fillet; 5. a thin gold fillet; the lower half of the spine has a panel formed by four gold fillets and dots in relief; this panel is semi-circular at its head; it has a pattern of elaborate curling stems and vertical hatch leaves blocked in gold within; beneath this, a small rectangular panel is blocked with the same gold decoration as for the panel at the head; a rectangular panel formed by a single gold fillet has the word: '| Routledge & Co |' blocked in gold within; at the tail, a small rectangle is formed by a single gold fillet and five small gold circles are blocked within.

The British Museum de Beaumont copy is at RdeB.M.2. It has the text sewn on three tapes. Gilt edges. Bevelled Boards. Binder's ticket of Leighton Son & Hodge. Brown morocco horizontal-grain cloth. Both covers blocked identically in gold, in blind and in relief. The central vignette of this copy is signed 'RD' in gold as separate letters at the lower right.

de Beaumont, *RdeB1* no. 399. Goldman, *Cat1*., no. 107, states that the central ovals for this design are signed 'RD' [i.e. Robert Dudley] on the 1863 edition. Goldman, *VIB* no. 399. Morris & Levin, *APB* p. 102, no. 226.

37 Dudley, Robert

Edgar, John George. *Danes, Saxons, and Normans; or, Stories of our Ancestors.* London: S. O.Beeton, 248 Strand, 1863. London: Savill and Edwards, Printers, Chandos Street, Covent Garden. xxii, 249 p.
142 × 223 × 22 mm. 9504.g.7.

Many of the ornamented capital letters, and the tail-pieces and the half-title illustrations are signed 'RD' or 'R. Dudley'.

Gilt edges. Light yellow endpapers and pastedowns. Red morocco vertical-grain cloth. The borders and corners of both covers are blocked identically in blind. Three fillets are blocked on the borders. A leaf and stem pattern is blocked on the sides and on the 'inner' corners, ending as three leaves blocked on each corner. The upper cover central vignette is blocked in gold. It has a heraldic theme with three shields, with three ribbon-shaped gold lettering-pieces surrounding them, forming a circle. The title: '| Danes | Saxons | and | Normans |' is blocked in relief within the ribbons. The three shields show: or, an eagle; azure, five birds and a moline cross; gules, two lions. A crown is blocked in gold at the top of the vignette, with two flowers and leaves at the base. Signed 'RD' in gold as separate letters beneath the word: 'And' at the centre. The spine is blocked in gold and in relief. A single fillet is blocked in gold on the perimeter. From the head downwards, the decoration is: a shield: or, an eagle; the title: '| Danes | Saxons | & | Normans |' blocked in relief within ribbon-shaped gold lettering-pieces; a shield: azure, five birds and a moline cross; the words: '| by | J. G. Edgar | Illustrated by | Robert Dudley |' are blocked in relief within three ribbon-shaped gold lettering-pieces; a shield: gules, two lions; one flower on each side of this shield; at the tail, the words: '| London | S. O. Beeton |' are blocked in relief within two gold lettering-pieces, which are separated by two fillets blocked in gold.

38 Dudley, Robert

Kingston, William Henry Giles. *Our soldiers: or, anecdotes of the campaigns and gallant deeds of the British Army During the Reign of Her Majesty Queen Victoria.* London: Griffith and Farran, (Successors to Newbery and Harris) Corner of St. Paul's Churchyard, 1863. Billing, Printer and Sterotyper, Guildford, Surrey. ix, 284 p., 1 plate. With thirty six pages of publisher's titles bound at the end.
110 × 177 × 35 mm. 8827.aa.42.

On page three of the publisher's titles: 'With Frontispiece from a Painting in the Queen Victoria Cross Gallery. Fcap 8vo, price 3s. cloth; 3s. 6d. gilt edges.'

Original yellow endpaper bound at the front. Binder's ticket on lower pastedown: '| Hanbury & Co. | Binders | 80, Coleman St. | E.C. |' Red morocco horizontal-grain cloth. Both covers blocked identically in blind and in relief on the borders and on the corners. Three fillets blocked in blind on the borders. A medallion, formed by two fillets blocked in blind, is blocked on each corner, with a quatrefoil blocked inside blocked in relief. One leaf is blocked in blind on each side of each medallion. The central mandorla is formed by two fillets blocked in blind. The upper cover central vignette is blocked in gold. It shows a Victoria Cross, hung from a ribbon with a pennant-shaped gold lettering-piece blocked in gold around the ribbon. The title: '| Our Soldiers |' is blocked in relief within the pennant. A crown is blocked in gold above the pennant. Signed 'RD' in gold as separate letters at the base of the vignette.

Ball, *VPB* p. 148.

39 Dudley, Robert

Lushington, Henrietta. *The happy home; or, the children at the Red House. With illustrations by G. J. Pinwell.* London: Griffith and Farran, Successors to Newbery and Harris, Corner of St. Paul's Churchyard, 1864. London: Printed by R. Clay, Son and Taylor, Bread Street Hill. [1],vii, 229 p., 3 plates.
128 × 174 × 25 mm. 12806.bb.49.

The plates are signed 'GJP' as a monogram. The plate opposite page 118 is signed 'Swain Sc.' The plates are hand-coloured. [Rebound paper conservation in early 1980s. No original endpapers or pastedowns.]

Red pebble-grain cloth. Both covers identically blocked in blind on the borders, on the corners and on the sides. Two fillets are blocked on the borders. Stylised leaf and stem and flower decoration is blocked on each corner in blind. [This is the same decoration as on the borders of BL 12806.b.57. – *Day of a baby boy*.] The upper cover vignette is blocked in gold. It shows a

large central circle, which is formed by a single fillet. On the top of the circle, the words: 'The Happy Home' are blocked in relief within a rectangular gold lettering-piece with 'scroll-shaped' ends. Within the circle, a garden scene is blocked, showing a husband and wife, with their three children. Signed 'RD' in gold as separate letters at the base of the vignette. The spine is blocked in gold. Fillets are blocked in gold at the head. Leaf decoration and a bird are blocked in gold above the title. The title: '| The | Happy | Home |' is blocked in gold, within a panel formed by a single branch-like fillet. Leaf decoration is blocked in gold below the title. At the tail, the words: '| London | [Griffith &] Farran |' are blocked in gold.

—— Another copy. London: Griffith and Farran, Successors to Newbery and Harris, Corner of St. Paul's Churchyard, 1864. London: Printed by R. Clay, Son, and Taylor, Bread Street Hill. vii, 229 p., 4 plates. With thirty-two pages of publisher's titles bound at the end.
127 × 173 × 25 mm. RdeB.D.7.

The British Museum de Beaumont copy.

On page three of the publisher's titles: '. . . Super royal 16mo., price 3s. 6d. cloth 4s. 6d., coloured, gilt edges.' Text sewn on three sawn-in cords. Brown endpaper and pastedowns. Binder's ticket on lower pastedown: '| Hanbury & Co. | Binders | 80 Coleman St. | E.C. |' [printed in red]. Purple pebble-grain cloth. Both covers blocked identically in blind and in relief on the borders, on the corners and on the sides. Two fillets are blocked in blind on the borders. The sides and each corner have stylised plant and stem decoration blocked in blind and in relief. The upper cover circular central vignette is formed by a single fillet, blocked in gold. The title: '| The Happy Home |' is blocked in relief at the head of the vignette, within a gold lettering-piece with scroll-shaped ends. Groups of three clover leaves are blocked in gold above and around the title. Within the vignette, a family scene is blocked in gold. A man to the right is picking leaves from a tree; a woman in a hat is at the centre, holding a pot plant; three children are blocked on the left. Signed 'RD' in gold as separate letters at the base of the vignette. The spine is blocked in gold. Two gold fillets are blocked at the head and at the tail. A branch-like fillet forms a panel, with the title: '| The | Happy | Home |' blocked in gold within it. An owl is blocked in gold within branches blocked above the title panel. Small leaf and plant decoration is blocked in gold below the title panel.

Ball, *VPB* p. 148. de Beaumont, *RdeB1* no. 187. Goldman, *VIB* no. 187.

40 Dudley, Robert

Russell, William Howard, *Sir. A Memorial of the Marriage of H.R.H. Albert Edward Prince of Wales and H.R.H. Alexandra Princess of Denmark. The Various Events and the Bridal Gifts. Illustrated by Robert Dudley.* [All letters are gothic, coloured.] Published by Day and Son. London, Lithographers to the Queen & to HRH The Prince of Wales, 1864. [London]: Bradbury and Evans, Printers Extraordinary to the Queen, Whitefriars. [8],122, xvi p., 41 chromolithographs.
290 × 430 × 35 mm. 1754.d.32.

Gilt edges. Original upper cover used as a doublure. Red pebble-grain cloth. The cover is blocked in gold in blind and in relief. On the borders are: 1. two gold fillets; 2. a fillet blocked in blind, with a repeating pattern of cartouches and two dots blocked in relief within it; 3. two gold fillets; 4. a wide decorative border, composed of two gold fillets, each with repeating dots blocked in relief within, which form straps on the side and on the corners, with groups of flowers, leaves and seeds being blocked on the sides, the head and the tail; 5. two gold fillets; 6. as for no.2; 7. two gold fillets. The central rectangle has a 'background' decoration of leaves, buds, flowers – all blocked in relief. Two shields are blocked at the head and at the tail of the inner rectangle. Blocked within shields at head: three lions of England, lion of Scotland; at the tail, Irish harp, the three lions of England. On the centre, a large block showing the Prince of Wales' feathers, and the motto: '| Ich Dien |' blocked between them in gold. The word: '| Houmont |' is blocked in gold on each side, together with ribbons. A crown is blocked underneath the feathers; a large elaborate ribbon is blocked as a gold lettering-piece underneath the crown. The title: '| The Wedding | at [in gold] | Windsor |' is blocked in relief within the ribbon. Signed 'RD' in gold as separate letters at the base of the centre.

Ball, *VPB* p. 148. Cover illustrated on plate 11.

41 Dudley, Robert

Edgar, John George. *Cressy and Poictiers; or, The Story of the Black Prince's Page. Illustrated with numerous engravings, principally from designs by Robert Dudley and Gustave Doré.* [Device of S. O. Beeton] London: S. O. Beeton, 248, Strand, W.C., 1865. Stephen Austin, Printer, Hertford. xvi, 382 p., 16 plates.
142 × 220 × 32 mm. 12621.h.19.

The monogram device of Stephen Austin is printed on the verso of the title page. The plates are signed 'W. Thomas Sc.'.

Gilt edges. Dark grey endpapers and pastedowns. Binder's ticket on lower pastedown: '| Bound by Bone & Son | [rule] | 76, Fleet Street, | London. |' Black sand-grain cloth. Both covers blocked identically in blind and in relief on the borders and on the corners. Two fillets are blocked in blind on the borders, the outer thick, the inner thin. Three leaves and curling stems form a circle on each corner, with a flower head blocked in relief within each. The central mandorla is formed by three fillets blocked in blind, one thick between two thin. The thick fillet has repeating dots blocked in relief within it. Inside this, small line decoration and straps are blocked in blind on the inner mandorla border. The upper cover vignette is blocked in gold and in relief. It shows a shield, blocked as a gold lettering-piece, argent, surmounted by a crown and the three Prince of Wales feathers, together with three six-pointed hatch gold stars. A ribbon-shaped gold lettering-piece runs between the feathers. The motto: '| Ich Dien |' and 'Houmont' are blocked

twice in relief within the ribbon. The central shield is supported by two gryphons, each gripping the end of a ribbon in its jaws. Their tails wind round the shafts of a sword blocked to the left and to the right of the shield. The title: '| Cressy and | Poictiers |' is blocked in relief in gothic letters within the central shield. The words, '| By J. G. Edgar | Illustrated | S. O Beeton |' are blocked in relief within the ribbons held by the gryphons, which wind around the swords, to come in front of the lower portion of the central shield. Signed 'RD' in gold as separate letters at the base of the vignette, above a vertical hatch gold fleur-de-lis. The spine is blocked in gold and in relief. From the head to the tail, a dense pattern of pointed leaves of flowers and thin stems is blocked in gold. In the middle, a banner gold lettering-piece with tassels hangs from the stems, with the title: '| Cressy | and Poictiers |' blocked in relief in gothic letters within the banner. On the lower half of the spine, a circle is formed by double gold fillets. Between the fillets, the words: '| By | J.G. Edgar | Illustrated |' are blocked in gold; on the centre of the circle, a shield and the Prince of Wales feathers are blocked in gold. Near the tail, a seated figure of a man in fourteenth century dress is blocked in gold. At the tail, the imprint: '| London | S. O. Beeton |' is blocked in relief within a rectangular gold lettering-piece, which has a single gold fillet blocked above and below it, each fillet with zig-zag decoration blocked in relief within it.

Ball, *VPB* p. 148.

42 Dudley, Robert

Edgar, John George. *Historical anecdotes of animals.* [Monogram of S. O. Beeton, in a beehive, within an oval frame.] London: S. O.Beeton, 248 Strand, W.C., [1865]. [London]: Savill and Edwards, Printers, Chandos Street, Covent Garden. vi, 90 p., 4 plates.
133 × 149 × 14 mm. 7207.a.24.

The plates are signed: 'J. W. Wood' and W. Thomas Sc.'

Gilt edges. Original yellow endpaper bound at the front. Both original cloth covers bound at the end. Red pebble-grain cloth. Both covers blocked identically in blind on the borders and on the corners. Two fillets are blocked on the borders, the outer thick, the inner thin. On each corner, a small leaf and stem pattern is blocked in relief. The upper cover central vignette is blocked in gold. It shows a wooden rectangular frame, with the wooden poles nailed together and overlapping. A bear clings to the wooden upright on the left; a monkey clings to the upright on the right. A lion is blocked on the centre of the upper crossbar. Palm plants and lilies rise up on either side of the lion. The lower crossbar has a semi-circular piece of wood nailed onto its middle. A greyhound is blocked within this semi-circle. Signed 'RD' in gold as separate letters underneath the greyhound. On the centre within the wooden frame, a gold lettering-piece is blocked. It has the title: '| Historical | anecdotes | of animals |' blocked in relief within.

43 Dudley, Robert

Lushington, Henrietta. *Hacco, the Dwarf, or the Tower on the Mountain; and other tales. With illustrations by G. J. Pinwell.* London: Griffith and Farran, (Successors to Newbery & Harris), Corner of St. Paul's Churchyard, 1865. Printed by R. & R. Clark, Edinburgh. [2], 238 p., 4 plates. With thirty-two pages of publisher's titles bound at the end.
130 × 175 × 35 mm. 12804.bbb.30.

The plates are signed 'GJP' and Swain'. On page 3 of the publisher's titles at the end: '. . . Super royal 16mo., price 3s. 6d. cloth, 4s. 6d. coloured, gilt edges.'

Binder's ticket on lower pastedown: '| Bound by | Bone & Son. | [rule] | 76, Fleet Street, | London. |' Blue sand-grain cloth. Both covers blocked identically in blind on the borders and on the corners. Three fillets are blocked on the borders. A leaf and stem pattern is blocked on each corner. The lower cover central vignette is blocked in blind and in relief. It is lozenge-shaped, and shows patterned decoration blocked in blind and in relief. The upper cover central vignette is blocked in gold, with a circular central vignette, formed by a single gold fillet. Just above the vignette, the title: '| Hacco | the Dwarf | &c. |' is blocked in gold in stylised letters. Ten stars are blocked at the head of the circle. The centre shows Hacco and a ram. Hacco is seated on a branch, with the ram standing beside him. These are set in a rural mountain landscape with plants and the sun rising behind. Signed 'RD' in gold as a monogram at the base of the vignette. The spine is blocked in gold in blind and in relief. At the head and at the tail are: 1. a blind fillet; 2. a blind fillet, with dots and a diamond blocked in relief within it; 3. two blind fillets. Below the head, three panels are formed by dense plant | woodland decoration, blocked in gold. In panel one an owl is blocked in gold. Panel two has the title: '| Hacco | the Dwarf | and other | tales. |' blocked in gold. Panel three has two rabbits blocked in gold.

The British Museum de Beaumont copy is at shelfmark RdeB.D.6. It has hand-coloured plates, gilt edges, green sand-grain cloth, also bound by Bone & Son.

de Beaumont, *RdeB1* no. 186. Goldman, *VIB* no. 186.

44 Dudley, Robert

Lushington, Henrietta. *Almeira's Castle; or, my early life in India and in England . . . With Twelve Illustrations.* London: Griffith and Farran, Successors to Newbery and Harris, Corner of St. Paul's Churchyard, 1866. London: Gilbert and Rivington, Printers, St. John's Square. [8], 312 p., 4 plates. With thirty-two pages of publisher's titles bound at the end.
127 × 175 × 30 mm. 12804.ccc.9.

Some of the plates are signed: 'Pearson sc.'

Edges speckled with red ink. Light yellow endpapers and pastedowns. Green sand-grain cloth. The lower cover is blocked in blind only. Three fillets are blocked on the borders. A pattern of leaves, curling stems and berries is blocked in blind on each corner. The upper cover is blocked in gold, in blind and

in relief. Three fillets are blocked in blind on the borders. Arabesques are blocked in blind and in relief on the centre head and on the centre tail. The upper cover central vignette is blocked in gold and in relief. It is square-shaped, with a 'peacock's feathers' pattern blocked in hatched gold on each corner. The central circle is a gold lettering-piece with flowers and leaves blocked in relief within it. The words: '| Almeira's Castle |' are blocked on the centre in relief within a rectangle formed by a single fillet, also blocked in relief. The spine is blocked in gold, in blind, and in relief. From the head downwards, the decoration is: four fillets in blind, with a pattern in the middle; a gold lettering-piece, broken up to form patterns – hatch, arrows, zig-zag – by blocking in blind; the title: '| Almeira's Castle |' blocked in relief within a rectangular gold lettering piece; a flower pattern blocked in relief; more small patterns; a pattern of 'hanging objects', blocked in gold; signed 'RD' in relief within a decorative motif; four fillets in blind are blocked at the tail, the same as for the head.

45 Dudley, Robert

Russell, William Howard, *Sir. The Atlantic Telegraph. Illustrated by Robert Dudley. Dedicated by Special Permission to His Royal Highness Albert Edward Prince of Wales.* London: Day & Son Limited 6 Gate Street, [1866]. [London]: Bradbury, Evans, and Co., Printers, Whitefriars. v, 117 p., 26 plates.
204 × 287 × 23 mm. 8756.f.28.

The plates are executed by a number of artists from 'Drawing[s] by R. Dudley'; all are signed 'London. Day & Son, Limited. Lith.' The engravers are: R.Dudley (the title-page); F. Jones; R. M. Bryson; G. McCulloch, T. Picken; E. Walker. The lithographs, with the exception of the title page, are all tinted.

Original upper cover used as a doublure. Doublure size: 195 × 285 mm. Green sand-grain cloth. Two intertwined fillets are blocked in blind on the borders. There is a wide border, shaped as a picture frame, with shells blocked in gold within it, and Atlantic Telegraph cabling interlaced through it. There are four medallions blocked on the cover: the two upper ones show the UK and US flags; the two lower show (to the left) Britannia with the shields of the UK and the US, and (to the right) a globe with latitude and longitude markings. A medallion is blocked on the centre. Eagles' wings are blocked above it, with a royal coat of arms between the wings. Below the medallion, an eagle is blocked. The medallion has two borders: a fillet, and a 'wave' pattern in hatch gold. At the very centre, an onlay (possibly of paper) shows a cross section of the Atlantic Telegraph cable. This consists of seven central copper conduction wires, protected by iron wires embedded in layers of gutta percha, hemp and tar. Unsigned.

Ball, *VPB* p. 148. Lists this design as 'probably by Dudley'. McLean, *VBD* pp. 127 & 139. Reproduces the title page, the upper cover and spine; says the onlay at the centre, which shows the Atlantic cable, is chromolithographed. Oldfield, *BC* no. 86.

46 Dudley, Robert

Dickens, Charles. *Household words. Christmas stories. 1851–1858. Conducted by Charles Dickens. Consisting of What Christmas is as we grow older. A round of stories by the Christmas fire. Another round of stories by the Christmas fire. The Seven poor travellers. The Holly-Tree Inn. The Wreck of 'The Golden Mary'. The perils of certain English prisoners. A house to let.* London: Ward, Lock, and Tyler, Warwick House, Paternoster Row, [1874]. [London]: Printed by W. Clowes and Sons, Stamford Street and Charing Cross. [Stories paginated separately.] With three pages of publisher's titles bound at the front and ten pages bound at the end; also two pages of advertisements at the end.
143 × 230 × 30 mm. 12452.m.22.

Each story paginated separately. 1851 – 36 p.; 1853 – 36 p.; 1854 – 36 p.; 1855 – 36 p.; 1856 – 36 p.; 1857 – 36 p. 1858 – 36 p.] The printer's name appears as the colophon for the years 1854 and 1858.

Red ink on edges. Bevelled boards. Original yellow endpaper bound at the front. The lower cover is blocked in blind only. A single fillet is blocked on the borders, with three more forming an inner rectangle. The upper cover is blocked in gold and in black. Two fillets are blocked in black on the borders. Inside this, another border, of dots and lines, is blocked in black. The central rectangle is formed of double fillets in gold to show an arch rounded at the head. At the centre of the head, the words: '| Household words |' are blocked in black; to the left of the centre, the word: 'Conducted' is blocked in black. Two crossed red paper onlays are 'hung' diagonally across the arch. One has a border of three gold fillets, and inside the words: '| Charles Dickens. |' are blocked in gold. The other onlay is blocked as a gold lettering-piece, with three fillets on the borders, and the words: '| The Christmas Stories |' blocked in relief within. Underneath this, six medallions are hanging from a Christmas tree, which is blocked in black. Each medallion is a gold lettering-piece, with a gold fillet on its perimeter, and the story titles blocked within in relief. The titles are: '| A | round | of | stories |'; '| A | house | to | let |'; '| The | Holly | Tree | Inn |'; '| Seven | poor | travellers |'; '| Island | of | silver-store |'; '| The | wreck | of the | Golden Mary |'. The columns of the arch have leaf and stem decoration blocked in black. The trailing ends of the red onlays are blocked in gold and in black. Signed 'RD' in black as separate letters on the centre tail of the upper cover. The spine is blocked in gold and in black. Two fillets are blocked on the perimeter in gold. From the head downwards, the decoration is: an arch; crossed gold lettering-pieces, with the title: '| Christmas | Stories |' blocked in relief within them; a heron blocked in black; at the tail, the words: '| London | Ward Lock & Tyler |' are blocked in gold within a rectangle formed by a single gold fillet.

47 E.

Hibberd, Shirley. *The book of the aquariums; or practical instructions on the formation, stocking and management in all seasons, of collections of marine and river animals and plants. A new edition,*

revised and enlarged. London: Groombridge and Sons, 5, Paternoster Row, 1860. vii, 128 p., 1 plate. With eight pages of publisher's titles bound at the end.
110 × 172 × 30 mm. 1256.b.23.

The title page is composite for two works by Hibberd: 1. The fresh-water aquarium; 2. The marine aquarium.

[Conserved and rebound in the early 1990s.] Binder's ticket on lower pastedown: '| Bound by | Westleys | & Co. | London. |' Purple horizontal morocco-grain cloth. Both covers are blocked identically in blind and in relief on the borders and on the corners. Two fillets are blocked in blind on the borders. A 'water plant' pattern is blocked on each corner in relief, with leaves and stem decoration extending on the sides. The upper cover central vignette is blocked in gold. It shows six rectangular gold lettering-pieces, each with a single fillet blocked in relief on its borders. The words: '| The | book | of the | aquarium | by | Shirley Hibberd |' are blocked in relief within the six gold lettering-pieces. Small decoration is blocked in gold around and between the lettering-pieces. Signed 'E' in relief within a small 'drop' blocked at the base of the vignette. The spine is blocked in gold. Three fillets are blocked in gold at the head and at the base. The title: '| The | book | of the | aquarium |' is blocked in relief within four gold lettering-pieces. Small decoration is blocked in gold around and between the lettering-pieces.

48 E., R.

Bell, Catherine Douglas. *Ella and Marian; or, rest and unrest . . . With illustrations.* London: Frederick Warne & Co., Bedford Street, Covent Garden, 1866. Ballantyne, Roberts, & Co., Printers, Edinburgh. [8], 402 p., 6 plates. With six pages of publisher's titles bound at the end.
116 × 174 × 40 mm. 12807.e.14.

The plates are signed 'Dalziel'. Bevelled boards. Light yellow endpapers and pastedowns. Binder's ticket on lower pastedown: '| Bound by | Westley's | & Co. | London. |' Red pebble-grain cloth. Both covers identically blocked in blind on the borders and on the corners. Two fillets are blocked on the borders. A single leaf is blocked on each corner. The upper cover vignette is blocked in gold. It shows three gold rectangular gold lettering-pieces, each with single gold fillet borders. The words: '| Ella and Marian[in a semi-circle] | or rest and unrest. | C. D. Bell [in a semi-circle] |' are blocked in relief within each of the lettering-pieces. There is border decoration to each lettering-piece. There is also circular and fan-shaped decoration between each lettering-piece. A small device with eight leaves around a diamond is blocked at the head in gold. A small device with seven leaves around a diamond is blocked at the tail in gold. Signed 'RE' in gold as separate letters at the base of the vignette. The spine is blocked in gold and in relief. Two gold fillets are blocked at the head and at the tail. A mandorla is blocked on the middle of the spine. It has decorated inner borders of hatch, dots, etc., and horizontal gold hatch on its middle. Overlaying the mandorla are seven rectangular gold lettering-pieces, each with a single fillet blocked in relief on its borders. The words: '| Ella | and Marian [in a semi-circle] | or | rest and unrest | by | Catherine D. Bell [in a semi-circle] |' are blocked in relief within each of the seven lettering-pieces. A small hatch leaf decorative device is blocked below the mandorla. Signed 'RE' in gold as separate letters at the base of this device. Near the tail, a hatch circle gold lettering-piece is overlaid with a rectangular gold lettering-piece. The words: '| Cousin Kate's | Library |' are blocked in relief within the rectangular gold lettering-piece.

49 E., R.

Mateaux, Clara L. *Home chat with our young folks on People and Things they See or Hear About . . .* London: Cassell, Petter, and Galpin; and 596, Broadway, New York, [1870]. Cassell, Petter and Galpin, Belle Sauvage Works, London, E.C. 260 p., 2 plates. With sixteen pages of publisher's titles bound at the end.
170 × 225 × 40 mm. 12806.f.44.

The plate printed opposite page 82, entitled 'The last of poor Bruin' is signed 'A Houghton' . The plate printed opposite page 185 is entitled 'A flying visit' and is signed 'Morten'. On page ten of the publisher's titles at the end, this work is listed as: 'F cap 4to . . . 5s.'

[No original endpapers or pastedowns.] Green sand-grain cloth. The lower cover is blocked in blind only. A repeating pattern of buds, leaves, half circles, and hatch triangles is blocked in blind on the borders, with a single fillet blocked just inside this. The central rectangle is formed by two fillets. An oval is blocked on each corner of this, together with a leaf shape inside each of the ovals. A trefoil is blocked on each centre side. The upper cover is blocked in gold, in black and in red. Fillets in black are blocked horizontally across the cover, dividing it into three panels. The panel at the head has the title: '| Home chat | with our young folks. |' blocked in red inside. The middle panel has a dining room 'family' scene, blocked in gold. It shows a mother seated at a round table. Her left arm is around the shoulders of a girl looking at an open book in her lap. A boy and another girl at the table are looking at the mother. To their left, a boy is seated on a small bench, looking at the mother. In the panel at the tail, the words: '| With | 200, pictures. |' are blocked in red. On the bottom left of the cover, a medallion is blocked. It is formed by: 1 a black fillet; 2. a single circle of repeating dots; 3. a single gold fillet. Within it, a posy of roses is blocked in gold. Signed: 'RE' in gold at the base of the medallion. The spine is blocked in gold, in black and in red. From the head downwards, the decoration is: a red fillet; a row of red triangles; a black fillet; small decoration blocked in red and in black; the title: '| Home | Chat | with our | Young Folks |' blocked in gold; lattice work is blocked in red and in black, around a medallion formed by a single gold fillet; within, a girl reading a book is blocked; the words: '| Cassell Petter | & Galpin |' are blocked in red; a black fillet is blocked at the tail.

50 E., T.

Copsley Annuals. *Copsley Annuals preserved in proverbs.* [By Emily Steele Elliott] London: Seeley, Jackson, and Halliday, 54 Fleet Street, 1867. London: Strangeways and Walden, Printers, Castle St. Leicester Sq. v, 341 p. With two pages of publisher's titles bound at the end.
125 × 187 × 32 mm. 12805.f.43.

Bevelled boards. Dark green endpapers and pastedowns. Brown sand-grain cloth. Both covers identically blocked in blind and in relief on the borders, on the corners, and on the sides. Three fillets are blocked on the borders: 1. a thick fillet; 2. a thin fillet; 3. a fillet with repeating dots blocked in relief inside it. A stem, leaf, bud and flower pattern is blocked in blind on the corners and on the sides. A fillet, blocked in blind, forms the central oval. There is a border of repeating dots blocked in relief just inside the fillet. The upper cover central vignette is blocked in gold. It shows a central circle, which has decoration of leaves, of stems, and of buds blocked around its perimeter. The centre has a gold lettering-piece blocked as a ring, with the title: '| Copsley Annuals | preserved in proverbs |' blocked in relief inside the ring. On the centre, an ink pot and quill pens are blocked in gold. The inkpot rests on a sheaf of papers, which are blocked as a gold lettering-piece. The title: '| Copsley | Annuals |' is blocked in relief within the sheaf of papers. Signed 'TE' in gold as separate letters near the base of the vignette. The spine is blocked in gold and in relief. At the head, a gold fillet and a hatched gold border are blocked. The title: '| Copsley | Annuals, | preserved in proverbs |' is blocked in relief within two rectangular gold lettering-pieces, each with a single fillet blocked on its borders, and with leaf and stem decoration surrounding them. Underneath this, a group of leaves and acorns is blocked. Signed 'E' amongst the leaves. A gold fillet and a gold vertical hatch are blocked at the tail.

51 H., C.

Longfellow, Henry Wadsworth. *Evangeline: A Tale of Acadie. Illustrated with forty-five engravings on wood, from designs by Jane E. Benham, Birket Foster and John Gilbert.* London: David Bogue, 86, Fleet Street, 1850. London: Henry Vizetelly, Printer and Engraver, Gough Square, Fleet Street. vii, 102 p. With two pages of publisher's titles bound at the end.
133 × 207 × 23 mm. 11688.g.22.

Gilt edges. Bevelled boards. Yellow glazed paper over boards. Light brown rib horizontal-grain cloth on spine. Light blue endpapers and pastedowns. Written on the upper pastedown: '| Mr. A. Pierpont | 1850. | Stella | from Katherine Isobel | Tuesday | Cheltenham | S Eustasius – |' The same design is printed on both covers. The pattern over the corners and the sides is of curling thin stems and leaves, printed in green. The title '| Evangeline | A Tale of Acadie |' is in gothic letters above and below the central roundel. On the lower cover, the central roundel shows an engraving of an angel. On the upper cover, the central roundel shows an engraving of two adults. Signed CH (or HC) as a monogram near the centre tail. The spine has the words: '| Evangeline | Illustrated | [rule] | Longfellow | [rule |' blocked in gold.

52 Halswelle, Keeley

Cummins, Maria Susanna. *The Lamplighter.* London: T. Nelson and Sons. London and Edinburgh, [1854]. Edinburgh: Printed by T. Nelson and Sons. 543 p., 8 plates. With sixteen pages of publisher's titles bound at the end.
120 × 190 × 35 mm. 12706.d.18.

The title page is engraved and signed 'Keeley Haswell [i.e. Halswelle]del; F. Borders Sc'. The plates are signed 'Keeley Haswell'.

Beige endpapers and pastedowns. Blue wave horizontal-grain cloth. Both covers blocked identically in blind on the borders. Two fillets are blocked on the borders, with a decorated pattern on the border inside. The lower cover has a central vignette of a Maltese cross, plus a wreath, blocked in blind. The upper cover has a central vignette blocked in gold. It shows a crown above a roundel, which is formed by three fillets blocked in gold. St George is slaying the dragon at the base of the vignette. The title: '| Lamp | lighter | [rule]' is blocked in gold on the centre. The spine is blocked in gold. A single fillet is blocked on the perimeter. A single gold fillet is blocked at the head and at the tail. The words: '| The | Lamplighter | Illustrated |' are blocked in relief within a gold lettering-piece shaped as a pennant. Beneath this, a winged angel holds a crown of laurel leaves above a girl reading and pointing to an open book. Signed 'K.H.' in gold as separate letters underneath the book. At the tail, the imprint: '| T. Nelson & Sons | London & Edinburgh |' is blocked in gold within a rectangle formed by a single gold fillet.

53 Humphreys, Henry Noel

Ephemerides. *The home and Illuminated diary Calendar for 1845.* London: Longman and Co., [1845]. Unpaginated. [53 p.] With two pages of publisher's titles bound at the end.
195 × 275 × 20 mm. C.30.l.3.

The paper covers are over a mull cloth base. Printed at the end of the 'Description of the Illuminated Calendar': 'The present is an attempt to render mechanism an auxiliary of art, as far as it is now practicable, and to point the way to greater and higher efforts. The flower borders are printed entirely by the lithographic press of Mr. Owen Jones, and it is believed are excellent specimens of that delicate process. The figure subjects are coloured by hand.'

Gilt edges. White paper over cloth over boards. The lower cover is blocked with a blue fillet on the borders, and a single strap on each corner. On the centre, fillets blocked in gold form a strap pattern, with the shape of a lozenge. The upper cover is blocked in gold, and painted in colours. A fillet is blocked in gold on the borders, with straps blocked on each corner. There is a border pattern, blocked in gold, of a 'continuous contorted line' shape. Elaborate fillets and straps are blocked in gold on

the centre head, on the centre tail, and on the sides, which together form the central frame. There are blue and red colours between the fillets and the straps. Each inner corner has a coloured tree depicting the four seasons. On the centre, the title: '| The | Illuminated | Calendar | [rule] | 1845' is blocked in gold, in gothic lettering. On this copy, the spine is of modern leather, with modern lettering.

Ball, *App.* 44b. Copy bound in paper. Ball, *VPB* p. 149. States Humphreys: 'may be assumed to have designed the cover for this work.' McLean, *VBD* p. 88 & plate IV. States: 'design presumably by Humphreys'.

54 Humphreys, Henry Noel

Ephemerides. *The illuminated calendar for m.dccc.xlvi.* London: Longman and Co., 1846. Unpaginated. [59 p.]
187 × 277 × 17 mm. C.30.l.4.

The historical introduction is signed: 'HNH'. No more produced after 1846. The lithography is suggested to be in nine colours. (Each leaf is hinged on a paper guard.)

Gilt edges. Yellow endpapers and pastedowns. White morocco leather. Both covers are blocked identically, which is in blind only on the lower cover. The upper cover is blocked in gold, with portions painted in red and blue. [It looks as though the colours were painted on the upper cover first; then the gold laid on, and the whole blocked.] Decoration resembling clasps are blocked on each corner. The decoration in these clasps is of rings, with blue arms, both within a gold lettering-piece. Fillets blocked in gold and in relief are blocked on the inner borders, with straps on the head, the tail, and the sides. Between these two groups of fillets, a fillet is blocked in relief, and painted in red. The inner corners are painted in blue, having patterns of curling stems and flowers blocked in gold inside. The central lozenge is elongated, with 'wavy' fillets blocked in gold and on its perimeter. The centre of the lozenge is painted in red, with the words. '| The | illuminated | calendar | for | mdcccxlvi |' blocked in gold within the red. The spine is not blocked.

Ball, *VPB* 149. (The 1845 issue.) McLean, *VBD* p. 88.

55 Humphreys, Henry Noel

Humphreys, Henry Noel. *The coins of England.* London: William Smith, 113, Fleet Street, 1846. iv, xii, 136 p., 23 plates.
130 × 200 × 20 mm. C.30.g.4.

The title page is a chromolithograph. Signed: 'On stone by F. Bauer. H. Woods & Co. lith.'. The coins on the plates are lithographed variously in gold, silver and copper. This work is described in the publisher's titles at the end of the 'Record of the Black Prince' as: 'In a rich ornamental binding of novel design . . . 18s.'

Gilt edges. Light blue endpapers and pastedowns. The turn-ins and the board edges are lined in gold. Red paper over boards, with a 'leaf' and horizontal rib pattern. Both covers blocked identically. On the head, the tail and the fore-edge, a raised pattern of strapwork, stems and leaves is blocked in gold. On the upper and lower parts of each cover, decoration in the shape of clasps is blocked, with the centre of each clasp being blocked in gold on the spine. On the spine the title: '| English coins |' is raised and blocked in gold, in gothic lettering.

Ball, *VPB* p. 149. McLean, *VPBP* p. 34 '. . .a simulation in paper of gold clasps on red velvet'.

56 Humphreys, Henry Noel PLATE VII

Humphreys, Henry Noel. *Parables of Our Lord.* London: Longman & Co., 1847. Unpaginated [30 leaves].
120 × 168 × 20 mm. C.30.g.5.

The borders to the text are chromolithographs. The colophon of this work reads: 'In designing ornaments to the sacred parables contained in this volume, the illuminator has sought to render them in each instance appropriate. The work of illumination was commenced the first day of May in the year of Our Lord MDCCCXLV and terminated on the tenth day of Febry MDCCCXLVI. HNH.' The description of this work in the publisher's titles at the end of: 1. the 'Record of the Black Prince': 'In rich binding, in high relief, imitative of carved ebony, 21s.' 2. the 'Book of Ruth': In an imitative carved ebony binding, price 21s.'

Gilt edges. Marbled endpapers and pastedowns. The turn-ins are blocked in gold. Black 'papier mache'. The design is the same for both covers. Four vertical and two horizontal columns divide each cover into nine panels. Leaves are shown on the corners, and studs are shown where the columns cross each other, and at the column ends. Animal heads are shown in the corner panels, and there are leaves in the panels at centre head and the centre tail. Trees are on the central panel, to the left and to the right. On the centre panel is a sower inside a wreath, with ribbons above and below ending in straps. Within the ribbons, the words: '| Scripture | Parables |' are in relief. The spine is light leather (possibly bleached), blocked in black with fillets forming three rectangular panels. The title is blocked along the spine, with the words: 'Of Our' in the tail panel; 'The Parables' in the middle panel; 'Lord' in the panel at the head – all words blocked in relief.

Ball, *App.* 47d. Ball, *VPB* p. 149. de Beaumont, *PB* p. 17–21. Leathlean, *HNH* p. 196. McLean, *VBD* pp. 99–100. McLean, *VPBP* p. 51.

57 Humphreys, Henry Noel PLATE VIII

Gospels, Selections, English. *The miracles of Our Lord.* London: Longman & Co., 1848. 31, iv p.
118 × 172 × 20 mm. C.30.b.3.

The borders to the text are chromolithographs: alternately pink, blue and silver; then black, grey and gold. The 'descriptive index of the miracles' at the end is signed: 'HNH'. The list of publisher's titles bound at the end of the *Record of the Black Prince* states this work is: 'In a carved binding of appropriate design, 21s.'

Gilt edges. Bevelled boards. Marbled endpapers and pastedowns. The turn-ins are blocked in gold. Black 'papier mache', with black [paper] backing. The design is the same for both covers. There are beads on the borders, and, inside this, a border of leaves and straps between two fillets. There are two fish at the centre head, and one bird on each corner, and two gryphons at centre tail. Within the central rectangle, six ovals depict miracles of Christ. The title: '| The | Miracles | of | Our | Lord |' is placed between the ovals. There is also strapwork between the ovals. The spine is leather. Dots are blocked in relief on the perimeter. The title: '| The | Miracles of Our Lord |' is blocked in relief along the spine, with straps blocked in relief at the head and at the tail.

Ball, *App*. 48e. Ball, *VPB* p. 149. de Beaumont, *PB* p. 17. Leathlean, *HNH* p. 196. McLean, *VBD* p. 104. McLean, *VPBP* p. 53.

58 Humphreys, Henry Noel PLATE IX

Humphreys, Henry Noel. *Maxims and Precepts of the Saviour.* [London]: [1848]. [1], 31 p. With one page of other titles by Humphreys bound at the end.

127 × 178 × 20 mm. C.30.b.41.

The colophon states: 'The illuminator began his work Septr. A.D. 1847 and finished April 6 1848'. The borders are chomolithographs. They are of flowers or of birds, with text at the head, within a panel formed by interweaving lines. At the base, a scroll contains the scientific and popular names of the birds or flowers. Printed at the base of the descriptive index: 'The binding is designed from a peculiar style of ornament, supposed to be the 'Opus Anglicum,' so much prized on the continent in the 10th and the 11th centuries. The model which has furnished the present design is a border in a MS. copy of the Gospels executed for King Cnut (Canute). The principal school for the execution of this peculiar style of ornament appears to have been established at Winchester.' In the publisher's titles at the end of BL C.30.g.7 – The Book of Ruth, this title stated to be: 'In a new and richly gilt leather binding, in the Grolier taste, price 21s.'

Gilt edges, gauffered. Bevelled boards. The turn-ins are blocked in gold. Paper covers over leather. Much of the design is in relief, with the colours likely to be applied by hand. Both covers identically blocked, with colours of black, red, blue, green, gold and grey. A single fillet is blocked in gold on the borders. Squares and circles are blocked on each corner, in gold, with coloured pairs of leaves at each corner of each square. Fillets on the sides, the head and the tail join together the corner squares. On the centre of each side, circles are blocked in gold, with leaves coloured in red and green. Small decorated circles are blocked in gold on the centre head and centre tail, within rectangles each formed by a single gold fillet. The central rectangle has an onlay of grey paper. The title: '| Maxims | & | Precepts | of the | Saviour |' is blocked in gold and in relief, with the smaller letters interspersed between large capital letters. The spine is blocked in gold. A single fillet is blocked on the perimeter. The title: '| Maxims & Precepts of the Saviour |' is blocked in gold along the spine. Small decoration is blocked in gold on the head and on the tail.

Ball, *App*. 48f. Leathlean, *HNH* p. 193. McLean, *VBD* p. 104. The border chromolithographs '. . .in up to about twelve colours'.

59 Humphreys, Henry Noel

Humphreys, Henry Noel. *The art of illumination and Missal Painting. A guide to Modern Illuminators. Illustrated by a series of specimens, from richly illuminated MSS. of various periods, accompanied by a Set of Outlines, to be coloured by the Student according to the theories developed in the Work.* London: H. G. Bohn, York Street, Covent Garden, 1849. [London]: Charles Whittingham, Chiswick. [1], 64 p., 24 plates.

137 × 172 × 22 mm. 1401.b.15.

The description in the publisher's titles at the end of the *Record of the Black Prince* states that this work is: 'In an ornamental cover, 21s.'

Original upper and lower covers used as doublures. White leather. The upper and lower covers have: 1. a fillet blocked in gold on the borders; 2. inside this, is an onlay border of blue paper, blocked in gold; the blocking on the blue paper shows leaves, long stems and small flowers blocked in relief; 3. inside this, another small border fillet is blocked in gold. On the lower cover, another inner border is blocked in gold. A fillet then forms the inner rectangle. On the upper cover, a fillet in black forms the inner rectangle. The border of the inner rectangle has a paper onlay, with six divisions. Each division has a scroll, with writing in it. The division at the top left has gold stems against a red background; the words: '| Giulio Clovio |' are on the scroll. The division at the top right has grey leaves, stems and flowers against a blue background; the words: '| Girolamo Libri |' are on the scroll. The division centre right has white stems, leaves and flowers against a red background. The division bottom right has the same decoration as for the top left. The division bottom left has the same decoration as for the top right. The division centre left has light green flowers against a dark green background. [The text on the scrolls of the last four divisions of this copy are not readable. On the copy reproduced in Morris & Levin, they are: Ion Sifrewas | Isr vn Meghenem | Lucas von Leyden | Iean Fouquet.] The rectangle on the centre of the upper cover is a paper onlay, with a border of a single fillet blocked in black. It shows lilies against a crimson background. The words: '| The art of |' are in blue inside a scroll; the word: '| Illumination |' is in red inside a scroll.

Ball, *App*. 49d. Copy in white leather. Ball, *VPB* p. 149. States that the decoration is 'chromolitho onlay on gold-blocked white leather.' Leathlean, *HNH* p. 203. McLean, *VBD* Plate XV. Shows the upper cover. Morris & Levin, *APB* p. 29, no. 32.

60 Humphreys, Henry Noel PLATE X

Humphreys, Henry Noel. *A Record of the Black Prince. Being a selection of such passages in his life as have been most quaintly and strikingly narrated by chroniclers of the period, embellished with*

highly wrought miniatures and borderings selected from various illuminated MSS, referring to events connected with English history. London: Longman, Brown, Green, and Longmans, 1849. London: Vizetelley Brothers and Co. Printers and Engravers, Peterborough Court, Fleet Street. [6], xcv, ii p. With one page of publishers titles bound at the end.
137 × 195 × 27 mm. C.30.g.1.

The design is described by Humphreys in paragraph 8 of the 'descriptive index' at the end: '8. The carved cover is taken from one of the compartments of the Prince's tomb at Canterbury, slightly altered for its present purpose by the addition of the label to receive the title, and the extra enrichment of the mouldings; in which, however, the decorative feeling of the period has been carefully preserved.' In the publisher's titles at the end of BL C.30.g.7. – *The Book of Ruth*, this work is stated to be: 'In a carved and pierced binding, price 21s.'

Gilt edges. The turn-ins are blocked in gold. Black pierced 'papier mache', with a red paper background. The design is identical for both covers. Two decorated raised borders are separated by a border of bosses. The central rectangle is filled with symmetrical medieval decorative motifs – there are small pointed arches on each corner, together with bosses, and leaves. Semi-circles are on the centre head, the centre tail, and the sides. The coat of arms of the Black Prince is on the centre. The title words are within a ribbon, which is above and on each side of the coat of arms. Above: '| A Record of |'; to the sides: '| Black Prince | Houmont Ich dien |'. The spine is of leather. The title: '| A Record of the Black Prince |' is blocked in relief along the spine. Above and below these words, repeating pattern of two lines and three small leaves is blocked.

Ball, *App.* 49f. Ball, *VPB* p. 149. de Beaumont, *PB* p. 18, 21. Leathlean, *HNH* p. 202. McLean, *VBD* pp. 104–106, 113. '. . . one thousand copies were printed.' McLean, *VPBP* p. 54. Morris & Levin, *APB* p. 75, no. 160.

61 Humphreys, Henry Noel PLATE XI

Humphreys, Henry Noel. *The Book of Ruth, from the Holy Scriptures. Enriched with Coloured Borders, selected from Illuminated MSS. in the British Museum, Bibliotheque Nationale, Paris, Soane Museum, and other libraries. The Illuminations arranged and executed under the direction of H. Noel Humphreys.* London: Longman, Brown, Green, and Longmans, 1850. [London]: Vizetelley & Company, Printers, 135 Fleet St. [1], 31 p. With two pages of other titles by Humphreys bound at the end.
120 × 167 × 15 mm. C.30.g.7.

The title page is printed in gold. Each opening is alternately printed in gold and grey, and in several colours. The text has chromolithographed borders. In the list of works at the end is the description: 'In a highly embossed leather binding, price 21s. (Just ready.)'

Gilt edges. Bevelled boards, with gauffered edges. The turn-ins are blocked in gold. Marbled endpapers and pastedowns. Red leather over the boards. Both covers identically embossed with the same design. The blocking is in blind and in relief. On the borders, two fillets are blocked in blind, with a border of joined single flowers and leaves between the fillets. There is a pattern of flowers and cornstalks blocked inside the central rectangle. Poppies are blocked on the top left hand and bottom right hand corners of the inner rectangle. Cornstalks are blocked on the centre sides. Flower stems form a central frame, with straps at its head and its tail. Inside the frame, the title: '| The | Book | of | Ruth |' is blocked in relief, in gothic lettering. The spine is blocked in blind. A cornstalk is blocked at the head and at the tail. The title: '| The Book of Ruth |' is blocked in relief along the spine.

Ball, *VPB* p. 146. Lists this work under 'Relievo Bindings'. Leathlean, *HNH* p. 193. McLean, *VBD* p. 108. Morris & Levin, *APB* p. 69, no. 143.

62 Humphreys, Henry Noel PLATE XII

Shakespeare, William. *Sentiments and similes. A classified selection of similes, definitions, descriptions, and other remarkable passages in the plays and poems of Shakespeare.* London: Longman, Brown, Green and Longmans, 1851. London: Vizetelley and Company, Printers and Engravers, Peterborough Court, Fleet Street. [4], 100 p.
155 × 204 × 25 mm. C.30.g.6.

The borders and capital decoration on each page are printed in gold. Silk head and tailbands. Black leather on borders and on spine. The edges are gauffered, and the turn-ins are blocked in gold. Yellow endpapers and pastedowns. Both covers have the same design executed in black 'papier mache', with gold rib diagonal-grain backing paper. The design shows a renaissance frame with studs on the borders, and interlocking straps within. The ribbon at the head contains the words: '| Sentiments & similes |'; at the base, another ribbon contains the words: '| of William Shakespeare |'. The recessed central oval has a wreath and flower border, with a mask above and below. The oval contains, on the upper cover, a bust of Shakespeare in terracotta; on the lower cover, the central oval contains the monogram 'WS' in terracotta. The spine is blocked in blind and in relief. Dots are blocked in relief on the perimeter. The title: '| Sentiments &c of Shakespeare |' is blocked in relief along the spine.

Ball, *App.* 51d. Ball, *VPB* pp. 149–150. Leathlean, *HNH* pp. 193, 195, 198. McLean, *VBD* pp. 108, 110, 210. Morris & Levin, *APB* p. 75, no. 161. Oldfield, *BC* no. 44. Exhibited the second edition of 1857.

63 Humphreys, Henry Noel

The Book of Exotic Birds. A Series of Richly Coloured Plates Accompanied by Descriptions. London: Paul Jerrard, 111 Fleet Street, [1852]. Unpaginated. [22 p.] With three leaves of publisher's titles bound at the end, printed on the recto only.
185 × 275 × 20 mm. C.27.m.8.

All text is printed in gold. The letters on the title page are fanciful, with extravagant use of tendrils at the ends. The colour lithographs of the birds are printed separately and pasted onto

the verso of leaves, within a gold printed border. The leaves are sewn on three sawn-in cords. In the publisher's titles at the end of BL C.27.m.9. 'Flower painting in twelve lessons', this work is advertised as: 'Preparing for Publication, Exotic Birds. Price 21s. In one handsome volume, Imperial 8vo. Richly bound, suitable for Birth-day or Marriage Presents, with Ornamental Decoration Page, and 10 Plates.'

Gilt edges. Yellow endpapers and pastedowns are printed in gold, with a rococo design of stems and flowers. Beige fine net-grain cloth. The lower cover is blocked in gold only. A single fillet is blocked in gold on the borders. The central vignette shows a spray of summer flowers, tied together by a ribbon. The upper cover has a single fillet blocked in gold on the borders. Within this, a single coloured lithograph on a sheet of paper has been pasted onto the board. It has elaborate tendrils and a branch border pattern, and shows flowers at the end of long stems, with the title: 'The book of exotic birds' attached to the stems. The letters are shaped like small stems. The lithograph has been lacquered and this has cracked. The words: 'London. Paul Jerrard 111 Fleet St.' are printed in black near the base.

Another copy is at BL 7286.dd.8. [22 p.] It has the same design as for C.27.m.8. Endpapers and pastedowns are in good condition. White net-grain cloth and upper cover decoration, both in poor condition. Original gutta percha binding has now given way, with leaves loose.

Gaskell, *NIB* p. 242, fig. 90. Leathlean, *HNH* pp. 204–208. Leathlean, *Jerrard* p. 185.

64 Humphreys, Henry Noel

Jerrard, Paul. *Flower painting. In twelve Progressive Lessons.* London: Paul Jerrard. 111 Fleet Street, [1852]. Unpaginated. [30 p.] With three pages of publisher's titles bound at the end, printed in gold on rectos.
185 × 277 × 13 mm. C.27.m.9.

The title page has extravagant title lettering in gold, with numerous tendrils at the ends of letters. The text portions of the work have a lithograph on each recto, and gold printed text on each verso. Several of the lithographs in colour have the words: 'Paul Jerrard. Lithr. 111 Fleet St London' printed at the base, on the left hand side. Publisher's titles are printed on the recto of the last two leaves. The publisher's titles at the end of 'Flowers from Stratford on Avon' lists this work: 'In a handsome volume imperial 8vo, price 1l 1s; or extra bound in Patent Binding for Special Presents, price 1l 11s 6d, richly decorated.'

Gilt edges. Yellow endpapers and pastedowns, with the same rococo pattern as for BL C.27.m.10. [Shakespeare. Flowers from Stratford on Avon.] and BL C.27.m.8. [The book of exotic birds.] Green morocco horizontal-grain cloth. The lower cover has two fillets blocked on the border in blind, with single straps on each corner. The central vignette is blocked in gold, and is the same as for BL C.27.m.8. The upper cover is blocked in gold only. There is a border of rose branches, rose stems and flowers, which forms a frame. On the centre, the title: '| Flower painting | in | Twelve Lessons. |' is blocked in gold in rustic lettering. The spine is not blocked. This is the copyright copy, date stamped: 15 M[A]Y [18]52.

Leathlean, *HNH* pp. 204–208. Leathlean, *Jerrard* pp. 182, 187. Plate 3 illustrates the title page.

65 Humphreys, Henry Noel PLATE XIV

Shakespeare, William. *Flowers from Stratford on Avon. A selection from the flowers mentioned in the plays and poems [of] Shakespeare. Highly coloured from the original drawings by Paul Jerrard.* London: Paul Jerrard, 111 Fleet Street, [1852]. Unpaginated. [15 folios.] With two folios of publisher's titles for other books in this series by Jerrard, bound at the end.
195 × 283 × 20 mm. C.27.m.10.

The text is printed in gold. All the plates have: 'Paul Jerrard, litho. 111 Fleet Street' printed at the base. In the publisher's titles at the end, this work is advertised as: 'In Patented Binding, imperial 8vo, price 1l 11s 6d.' Jerrard's patent application is dated 1 November 1852, no. 604: 'Ornamenting japanned and papier-mâché surfaces, as also the surfaces of varnished and polished woods.' This provisional specification was made void by the Commissioners of Patents: '. . . by reason of notice to proceed not having been given within the time prescribed by the Act.' The blue date stamp is: '30 DE[CEMBER 18]52'.

Gutta percha binding. Gilt edges. The boards are made up to resemble the thickness of wood, and are smooth bevelled. Yellow endpapers and pastedowns printed in gold, featuring an elaborate rococo pattern. Paper (yellow dyed in appearance) has been drawn over the boards, which has then been lacquered. The lower cover is not blocked. The upper cover is blocked in gold with an ornate rococo design of intermingled flowers and ornament. On the centre, the title: '| Flowers | from | Stratford | on | Avon |' is blocked in rustic lettering. At the base of the design, on the right hand side, the words: '| Paul Jerrard | Patentee |' are blocked in gold. The spine is of leather, unblocked.

Leathlean, *HNH* pp. 204–208. 'This is one of a series of gift books issued under Jerrard's name, which has a substantial artistic input from Humphreys, as evidenced by the Journal of Humphreys' son, also named Humphreys, Henry Noel.' Leathlean, *Jerrard* pp. 177–178; 185–186; 192.

66 Humphreys, Henry Noel PLATE XIII

Humphreys, Henry Noel. *The origin and progress of the art of writing: A connected Narrative of the development of the art, its primeval phases in Egypt, China, Mexico, etc.; its middle state in the Cuneatic systems of Nineveh and Persepolis, to its introduction to Europe through the medium of the Hebrew, Phoenician, and Greek systems, and its subsequent progress to the present day. Illustrated by a number of specimens of the writing of all ages, and a series of facsimiles from autograph letters from the fifteenth to the nineteenth century.* London: Ingram, Cooke, and Co., 1853.

London: Printed by Robson, Levey and Franklyn, Great New Street and Fetter Lane. viii, 176 p., 8 plates.
180 × 265 × 40 mm. C.30.l.12.

All colour plates are signed: 'H. N. Humphreys. Lith. Day & Son Lith.rs to The Queen.' All the black and white plates are signed: 'Printed by Paul Jerrard, 111, Fleet St.'

Marbled endpapers and pastedowns. Gilt edges. Green head and tail bands. Black 'papier mache', with red backing paper. The design is the same on both covers. There is a leaf and flower border, with three fillets inside. The centre is occupied by a large foliage stem which surrounds the title. It originates as the horizontal bar for the capital 'T' of 'The'; it then encircles the title: '| The | history | of writing |'. The curling end of the stem forms the bar of the lower case 't' of the word 'writing'. The letters of the title words have tendrils. Red [paper] backing is placed underneath the 'papier mache'. The turn-ins appear to be of dark blue paper, printed with a flower pattern in gold. The spine is of black leather, blocked in gold. At the head and at the tail, two fillets and tendrils are blocked in gold. The title: '| history of writing |' is blocked in gold along the spine.

Ball, *App*. 55e. de Beaumont, *PB*, p. 17. Leathlean, *HNH* pp. 197–198. McLean, *VBD* p. 212. Reproduces the 1853 edition; the same as the BL copy. McLean, *VPBB* p. 47. Shows the 1853 edition in a cloth binding, with blue ripple-grain (or wave diagonal-grain) cloth. McLean, *VPBP* p. 58.

67 Humphreys, Henry Noel

PLATE XV

Mackay, Charles. *The Salamandrine. With Illustrations, drawn by John Gilbert; engraved by the Brothers Dalziel.* London: Ingram, Cooke, and Co., 1853. London: Printed by Robson, Levey and Franklyn, Great New Street and Fetter Lane. xii, 140 p.
RdeB.J.1.

The British Museum de Beaumont copy.

Gilt edges. Bevelled boards. Yellow endpapers and pastedowns. The bookplate of Edward Dalziel is pasted on the upper pastedown. A letter of John Gilbert of 18 October 1864 is tipped onto the upper endpaper. Written on the upper endpaper: '| J. Dalziel |'. Blue morocco horizontal-grain cloth. Both covers blocked identically; in blind only on the lower cover. Two fillets are blocked in blind on the borders – the outer thick the inner thin. The title: '| The | Salamandrine |' is blocked in gold in elaborate branch-like letters on the centre of the upper cover. Curling stems weave between the letters, and flowers and leaves surround the title. The capital 'S' is bisected by a branch ending in thin roots at the head and at the tail. A vertical branch is also blocked near the fore-edge. The spine is blocked in gold. The words: '| The | Salamandrine | by | Cha Mackay | Illustrated | by | Gilbert |' are blocked in gold in elaborate letters, within and between four 'spade-shapes', which are formed by single gold fillets. Small leaf and berries decoration is blocked in gold at the head, on the middle and on the tail.

de Beaumont, *RdeB1* no. 194. Goldman, *VIB* no. 194.

68 Humphreys, Henry Noel

Humphreys, Henry Noel. *The coinage of the British Empire: an outline of the progress of the coinage in Great Britain and her dependencies, from the earliest period to the present time. Illustrated by fac-similies of the coins of each period, worked in gold silver and copper.* London: Nathaniel Cooke, Milford House, Strand, 1854. 160 p., 24 plates.
172 × 245 × 28 mm. C.30.k.1.

Gilt edges. Yellow endpapers and pastedowns. Binder's ticket on lower pastedown: '| Leighton | Son & | Hodge, | Shoe Lane | London. |' Brown morocco horizontal-grain cloth. Both covers blocked identically in blind. On each cover, decorative fillets are blocked in blind on the borders, with straps blocked in relief on the corners, the head, the tail, and the sides. Rose flowers and leaves are blocked in relief on the inner corners. The title in the central oval: '| The coinage of the British Empire |' is blocked in relief in gothic capital letters. The upper cover has a central vignette, consisting of seven coins. Four are blocked in black and three in gold. The coin designs are blocked in relief. The spine is blocked in gold and in black. The title: '| Coinage of the British Empire |' is blocked in gold along the spine. Between the words 'the' and 'British', a coin is blocked in black. Three fillets, decorated and with strapwork, border the title words. A single coin is blocked in gold at the head and at the tail.

The 1861 edition is at BL 7755.df.6. London and Glasgow: Richard and Griffin and Company, Publishers to the University of Glasgow, 1861. 207 p., 24 plates. Printed by Bell and Bain, St. Enoch Square.

Ball, *App*. 54d. Cites copy in 'papier mache' covers. Ball, *VPB* p. 150. Leathlean, *HNH* pp. 197, 199. McLean, *VBD* pp. 210, 213. Page 213 illustrates the work in 'papier mache' covers. McLean, *VPBP* p. 59. Illustrates the work in 'papier mache' covers.

69 Humphreys, Henry Noel

Humphreys, Henry Noel. *Ocean Gardens: The History of the Marine Aquarium, and the best methods now adapted for its establishment and preservation.* London: Sampson Low, Son, and Co., 57 Ludgate Hill, 1857. London: Thomas Harrild, Printer, Salisbury Square, Fleet Street; and Silver Street, Falcon Square. viii, 112 p., 12 plates.
133 × 187 × 15 mm. 1257.d.8.

The plates are hand-coloured. Gilt edges. Binder's ticket on lower pastedown: '| Bound by | Bone & Son, | [rule] | 76, Fleet Street, | London. |' Blue ripple vertical-grain cloth. Both covers blocked identically in blind on the borders and on the corners. A single fillet is blocked in blind on the borders. Inside this, a border of repeating three-pointed leaves is blocked alternating in blind and in relief, within triangles blocked in blind. A fillet blocked in blind forms the inner triangle. A conch shell and seaweed are blocked in blind on each inner corner. The upper cover central vignette is blocked in gold. It shows a circle, composed by joined curved fillets. Within the circle, the title: '| Ocean Gardens | [rule] |

Glimpses Beneath the | Waters | [rule] |' is blocked in gold in gothic letters. Seaweed above and below the title is blocked in gold. The spine is blocked in gold. The title: '| Ocean | Gardens |' is blocked in gold, with seaweed blocked above and below it, also in gold. Unsigned.

Ball, *VPB* p. 150.

70 Humphreys, Henry Noel

Humphreys, Henry Noel. *River Gardens; being An Account of the Best Methods of cultivating fresh-water plants in aquaria, in such a manner as to afford suitable abodes to ornamental fish, and many interesting kinds of aquatic animals.* London: Sampson Low, Son, and Co. 47 Ludgate Hill, 1857. London: Thomas Harrild, Printer, Salisbury Square, Fleet Street. viii, 108 p., 8 plates. With four pages of publisher's titles bound at the end.
135 × 187 × 19 mm. 1257.d.9.

Gilt edges. Yellow endpapers and pastedowns. Binder's ticket on the lower pastedown: 'Bound by | Bone & Son, | [rule] | 76, Fleet Street, | London. |' Blue wave diagonal-grain cloth. Both covers blocked identically in blind and in relief on the borders and on the corners. Two thick fillets are blocked in blind on the borders. Between these, stems of bulrushes rise from the base to form leaves and the rush, blocked in relief on each upper corner. On the lower inner corners of each cover, ivy leaves and stems are blocked in blind. The lower cover central vignette is blocked in blind and it consists of thin stems, intertwined, which form an oval. The upper cover central vignette is blocked in gold, in a semi-circle, above an aquarium scene of lilies, water plants and fish. The spine is blocked in gold and in relief. On the upper half of it, an aquarium tank is blocked in gold, as a lettering-piece. The title: '| River | Gardens |' is blocked in relief within this tank. Bulrushes and a frog are blocked above the tank; fish are blocked below it – all in gold. Unsigned.

Ball, *VPB* p. 150.

71 Humphreys, Henry Noel

Longfellow, Henry Wadsworth. *Kavanagh: a tale. Illustrated with original designs by Birket Foster, engraved by H. N. Woods.* London: W. Kent and Co. (Late D. Bogue), 86, Fleet Street, 1858. London: Henry Vizetelly, Printer and Engraver, Gough Square, Fleet Street. 136 p. With four pages of publisher's titles bound at the end.
140 × 220 × 20 mm. 1347.h.9.

Gilt edges. Bevelled boards. Yellow endpapers and pastedowns. Binder's ticket on lower pastedown: '| Bound by | Leighton | Son & | Hodge, | Shoe Lane | London. |' Dark red morocco horizontal-grain cloth. Both covers blocked identically in blind and in relief on the borders, the corners, and the sides. Two fillets are blocked on the borders, with strapwork blocked in relief on the corners. Inside the fillets, rose branches, rose flowers and leaves are blocked in relief on the sides and on the corners. On the upper cover, the centre is blocked in gold. It shows a bouquet of stems, leaves and flowers. (This is derived from an illustration by Humphreys on page 7). The title: '| Kavanagh |' is blocked in rustic lettering, with the letters running down the length of the bouquet. The spine has the words: '| Longfellow's Kavanagh |' blocked in gold in rustic letters along its length, within a cartouche. The cartouche is formed by a single 'branch-like' gold fillet, which forms straps at the head and at the tail.

Ball, *VPB* p. 150.

72 Humphreys, Henry Noel PLATE XVI

Humphreys, Henry Noel. *The Penitential Psalms.* London: Printed and Published by Day & Son Limited, Gate St. W.C., [1861]. [32 p.]
125 × 176 × 18 mm. C.44.c.4.

The BL General Catalogue of Printed Books states the illuminated initials and borders are by Humphreys. These are chromolithographed.

Gilt edges. Bevelled boards. Yellow endpapers and pastedowns. Brown morocco horizontal-grain cloth. Both covers blocked identically in gold and in blind and in relief. A single fillet is blocked in gold on the borders. Inside, two fillets are blocked, one in blind, and one in gold, with points blocked in blind on the corners. There is a wide border, blocked in gold, showing groups of flowers and leaves, resembling dahlias and strawberries; all are surrounded by small circles. The centrepiece is rectangular, with a point at the head and at the tail, and semi-circles blocked on its corners. There are two fillets blocked on the borders, one in gold, and one in blind. The centre-piece is a gold lettering-piece with the title: '| The | Penitential | Psalms |', surrounded by small curling stems, both blocked in relief. The spine is blocked in gold. A single gold fillet is blocked on the perimeter. The title: '| The Penitential Psalms |' is blocked in gold along the spine, with small decorative pieces at the head and at the tail.

Another copy is at BL 3089.d.46. The same design is blocked on the covers and on the spine. This copy has a gutta percha binding, now given way.

Ball, *App.* 61a. Cites copy in brown sand-grain cloth. Ball, *VPB* p. 150. The design 'attributable to Humphreys'. McLean, *VBD* p. 110.

73 Humphreys, Henry Noel

Manning, Samuel. *The Months illustrated by pen and pencil. The designs by Noel Humphreys, John Gilbert, Barnes, Wimperis, North, Lee, Sulman, and other eminent Artists: Engraved by Butterworth and Heath.* London: The Religious Tract Society, 56 Paternoster Row; 65 St. Pauls Churchyard; and 164 Piccadilly, [1864]. London: R. Clay, Son, and Taylor, Printers, Bread Street Hill. xvi, 224 p.
155 × 222 × 23 mm. 11601.h.1.

Gilt edges. Bevelled boards. Light yellow endpapers and pastedowns. Green pebble-grain cloth. Both covers blocked in

gold and in blind. Two gold fillets are blocked on the borders. Inside, a border of single branches is blocked, which cross at the corners. Sprays of flowers are attached to the branches on each side. At the head, a garland of flowers is blocked. At the tail, a winter scene is blocked, with a hawthorn-like plant blocked on the centre. The central rectangle has three fillets on its borders, one blocked in blind between two in gold. On the centre, the title: '| The Months | Illustrated | by | Pen & Pencil |' is blocked in gold, in gothic letters. The capital letters 'T', 'M' and 'I' are enlarged, with small decoration blocked in relief inside each letter. Many tendrils are attached to the title letters. The spine is blocked in gold. A single fillet is blocked in gold on the perimeter. From the head downwards, the decoration is: two diamond panels, surrounded by 'branch-like' fillets, which cross and form single straps; gold lettering-pieces shaped as ribbons; the title: '| The | Months | Illustrated | by | Pen & Pencil |' blocked in relief within these ribbons; two more diamond panels; small decoration is blocked at the base. All the diamonds are gold lettering-pieces, with decoration of the seasons blocked in relief within each panel. The decorations in each panel are, from the head: winter; spring; summer; autumn.
The detail of the clustered flowers on branches, and the tendrils attached to the gothic letters – both are characteristic of Humphrey's work in his engravings and lithographs.

The 1876 edition is at BL 11652.bb.18. Gilt edges. White endpapers and pastedowns. Binder's ticket on lower pastedown: 'Bound by Westley's & Co. London'. Green rib diagonal-grain cloth. Both covers blocked identically, in blind on the lower, and in gold and in black on the upper. The same design is used for the title lettering as for the 1864 edition, within a smaller rectangle, with a fillet in black around its perimeter. The spine has the title blocked in relief within ribbon-shaped gold lettering-pieces.

Ball, *VPB* p. 150. 'Attributed by a bookseller's catalogue to Humphreys.'

74 Humphreys, Henry Noel and Leighton, John

Jerrard, Paul. *The Humming Bird Keepsake Book of Bird Beauty. The Birds Painted among Nests and Flowers by Paul Jerrard, The Poems by FWN Bayley Esq.* London: Paul Jerrard, 111 Fleet Street, [1852]. Unpaginated [28 p.].
270 × 375 × 10 mm. C.194.c.2.

White net vertical-grain cloth. Light yellow endpapers and pastedowns, ribbed diagonally, are printed in gold with a repeating floral pattern. The lower cover is blocked in gold and in blind. Two fillets are blocked in blind on the borders, the outer thick, the inner thin. The inner rectangle is formed by two fillets, with repeating rectangles, themselves crossed within, and with diamonds, blocked between the fillets – all in blind. Flowers, leaves and stems are blocked on the inner corners, on the sides, the head and the tail. On the centre, the vignette is blocked in gold. It shows a stag's head and antlers surrounded by groups of oak leaves and acorns. Signed 'JL' in gold as separate letters at the base of the vignette. The upper cover has a glazed white paper onlay, printed in gold and chromolithographed. The onlay is bordered by a single gold fillet on the cloth. The title: '| The hummingbird keepsake | A book of bird beauty. |' is printed in gold at the head. A lattice pattern, with interlocking branches, and with flowers and stems with long tendrils, is printed in gold down each side of the onlay. On the centre tail: '| London: | Paul | Jerrard, 111 Fleet Street. |' is printed in gold in gothic letters. On the centre, the chromolithograph shows two humming birds stated to be: '| White eared humming bird ; Black breasted humming bird |' printed in black. Signed: '| Paul Jerrard litho | 111 Fleet St. |' in black.

Ball, *VPB* p. 68. Leathlean, *HNH* p. 207.

75 Jones, Owen

Calabrella, E. C. de, *Baroness. The prism of imagination . . .* London: Longman, Brown, Green and Longmans, 1844. Unpaginated. [70 leaves.]
145 × 215 × 30 mm. 1457.h.9.

Printed on leaf 3, recto: '| The | Illustrations to the Tales | by Henry Warren: | [decorated rule] | The | Borders and Ornamental Titles | by | Owen Jones, Archt. |'. Leaf 5 has a good specimen of Warren's monogram, 'AHW'.

Gilt edges. White endpapers and pastedowns. Light brown morocco. The lower cover is blocked in blind and in relief. Two fillets are blocked in blind on the outer border. Two more fillets are blocked in blind on the inner border, with straps blocked in relief on the corners, on the centre head, and on the tail. The latter two groups of straps join on to the diamond-shaped centre, which is formed of multiple straps, blocked in relief. The upper cover is blocked in gold and in blind. Three fillets are blocked in gold on the borders. Inside these, a fourth fillet, blocked in gold, has straps on the corners, the centre head and the centre tail. A profusion of curling stems and small leaf decoration is blocked in gold around the central rectangular panel. This is formed by two fillets, the inner of which forms straps on the corners, on the centre head and the centre tail, and on the sides. Curling thick leaf decoration is blocked on the corners of the inner rectangle. Straps are linked by double fillets to form a diamond-shape on the centre. Inside the diamond, the title: '| The | Prism | of | Imagination | 1844. |' is blocked in gold in gothic letters. The spine is blocked in gold. A single fillet is blocked on the perimeter. From the head downwards, the decoration is: two gold fillets; the title: '| The | Prism | of | Imagination |' blocked in gold in gothic letters; the date: '| 1844 |' is blocked on the centre of the spine in gold; curling stem and small leaf decoration rises from the base to form 'panels' for the date and the title; a gold fillet is blocked near the tail; the words: '| Longman & Co. |' are blocked in gold; at the tail, three gold fillets are blocked, one thick between two thin.

Ball, *VPB* p. 151. McLean, *VBD* p. 68.

76 Jones, Owen

Gray, Thomas. *Gray's Elegy.* London: Longman and Co.; New York: Wiley and Putnam, 1846. Unpaginated. [36 p.]
175 × 255 × 25 mm. C.30.l.6.

There are two border fillets on each page: one in red, one in black. The central panels containing the text and ornamental capitals are in gold, red and blue. The panels are surrounded by plant decoration in gold, in red, blue and black. Printed on the title page verso: '| Illuminated | by | Owen Jones |' The last leaf has the monogram 'ONJ' [i.e. Owen Jones.]

Text sewn on three sawn-in cords. Gilt edges. Bevelled boards. The edges and turn-ins are blocked in gold. White endpapers and pastedowns. Brown calf over boards. The bevels are blocked with hatch in blind and in relief hatch. The inside border has a pattern of large holly leaves and berries, blocked in deep relief. The 'background' to these is rib horizontal-grain. On the lower cover, the central panel is formed by two 'fillets', which interlock on the corners and on the sides, with diamond straps at the head and at the tail. Inside, a pattern of trefoils and stems is blocked in relief. At the centre the signature 'ONJ' is blocked in relief as a monogram. The 'background' is bead-grain effect. On the upper cover, the same two fillets form the central panel. Inside, the title: '| Gray's | Elegy' is blocked in relief in gothic letters, surrounded by leaves and stems in relief. The background is also bead-grain. The spine is blocked in blind and in relief. From the head to the tail, a pattern of trefoils is blocked. The trefoils are attached to a branch which runs down the centre of the spine.

McLean, *VPBB* pp. 11 & 15. Morris & Levin, *APB* p. 70, no. 144. Oldfield, *BC* no. 45.

77 Jones, Owen

Hunt, Leigh. *A jar of honey from Mount Hybla, Illustrated by Richard Doyle.* London: Smith, Elder & Co, 65 Cornhill, 1848. London: Vizetelly, Brothers, and Co. Printers and Engravers, Peterborough Court, Fleet Street. viii, xxiii, 200 p.
140 × 208 × 22 mm. 11805.d.31.

The original paper cover size is 135 × 202 mm. At the base of the List of Illustrations: 'The cover designed by Owen Jones.'

Original upper endpaper is bound at the front. It shows a repeating pattern of tendrils, thin leaves and bud heads, blocked in gold on white glazed paper. The original upper and lower paper covers are bound in. Each is of yellow glazed paper. The border shows twin branches which interlock to form a frame, with straps on the sides, the head and the tail. Gold is printed between the branches. Leaves (possibly passion flower) are printed in green, and cling on to the frame. On the centre of each cover, a blue jar is printed with passion flower leaves in gold. On the upper cover, the title: '| A | Jar of Honey |' is printed in gold above the jar; the words: '| from | Hybla |' are printed in gold below it. The jar is surrounded by an oval, formed by single green branches, crossing at the tail, with leaves in green and buds and flowers in gold. On the lower cover, the jar on the centre is supported by a plinth of multiple straps, extending upwards from the centre base. Above the jar, there are extended straps, with a pattern of green (passion flower) leaves.

Ball, *VPB* p. 152. McLean, *VBD* p. 132; plate XV. Morris & Levin, *APB* p. 66, no. 132.

78 Jones, Owen PLATE XVII

Jones, Owen. *The Preacher.* [London]: Longman & Co., 1849. Unpaginated. [17 leaves.]
200 × 295 × 40 mm. C.43.d.10.

Printed on the last leaf: '| Illuminated by Owen Jones. |'. The borders of each leaf are ornamented in the gothic style.

Gutta percha binding. Gilt edges. The original decorated endpapers are bound in. They show a curling stem and large leaf decorated pattern, printed in blue and in red. Wooden boards, either carved or pressed. The edges and turn-ins are gauffered. On the lower cover, a leaf is shown on each corner, on the centre of the sides, and on the centre head and the centre tail. The border has words in it. An arch is formed at the head by leaves. Within the central panel, a symmetrical pattern is shown of two curling stems and leaves, with a single leaf above. The upper cover has the same border and words within the border. The same two curling stems and leaves are shown at the base. Above this, the title: '| The | Preacher |' is shown in high relief, with the capitals 'T' and 'P' ornamented. The effect of the whole is extravagantly exaggerated. The spine is of leather, ribbed vertically. There are letters blocked along the spine, but the spine is too worn to decipher them. Formerly shelved at: [1. C44.i. [2. C.30.m.5.

Ball, *VPB* p. 153. McLean, *VBD* pp. 95; 210. McLean, *VPBB* p. 31. Morris & Levin, *APB* p. 78, no. 166.

79 Jones, Owen

Jones, Owen. *The Song of Songs.* [London]: Longman & Co., 1849. [London]: [Day & Son]. Unpaginated [32 p.]
142 × 210 × 15 mm. 1346.h.24.

On the title page verso: '| Illuminated | by | Owen Jones |'. Each leaf has chromolithograph borders. Gutta percha binding, in pieces. Gilt edges. Bevelled boards. The leather turn-ins are blocked in gold with a repeating pattern of zig-zag fillets and stylised leaf decoration between each zig-zag. Light yellow endpapers and pastedowns, decorated in gold and in blue with a repeating pattern of curling leaves and stems. The first (blank) flyleaf has stamped on its tail: '| Bound by Remnant Edmonds & Remnants. |' in black letters. Both covers blocked identically on the borders and on the corners in blind and in relief. On the borders, there is a zig-zag repeating pattern, with leaf and a single berry blocked between each zig-zag. Inside this, two fillets are blocked on the borders, with beads in relief between them. The fillets and the beads form circular straps on the sides, the head, and the tail. A large leaf pattern is blocked in relief on each corner. Two groups of double fillets, and of beads between them, form the central mandorla. On the lower

cover, the monogram of Day and Son is blocked in relief, surrounded by thick leaves, and smaller clover leaves and stems. On the upper cover, the central mandorla has the title: '| The | Song of | Songs |' blocked in relief in gothic letters. The spine is blocked in relief, showing four 'spade-shapes' blocked in relief from head to tail, with elongated 'fleurs-de-lis' blocked in relief inside each. No gold blocking on the spine.

Ball, *VPB* p. 153. McLean, *VBD* pp. 92–94. McLean, *VPBB* p. 33. Morris & Levin, *APB* p. 69, no. 142.

80 Jones, Owen

PLATE XVIII

Liturgies. *Holy Matrimony.* [London]: Longman & Co., [1849]. Unpaginated [24 leaves]
90 × 132 × 15 mm. C.30.a.8.

The half title page has: '| The form of | Solmenization | of | Matrimony |'. The title page verso has: '| Illuminated by Owen Jones |'. Each leaf is printed on the recto and the verso only, with ornamental borders in gold, red and blue.

Gilt edges. Bevelled boards. Beige calf. The turn-ins are blocked in gold with repeating semi-circles, and with a 'leaf and bud' pattern. Both covers blocked identically, apart from the centres. The borders are blocked in gold, with oval-shaped linked straps blocked in relief. An inner rectangle is formed by two fillets blocked in gold, with two crossing leaves blocked in gold on each inner corner. On the centre of the lower cover, a lozenge-shaped series of straps is blocked in relief, with blocking in gold surrounding them, and highlighting them. On the centre of the upper cover, a single plant stem is blocked in gold from the base upwards. The stem bisects the title words: '| Ho | ly Matri | mony', which are blocked in gold in gothic letters. Above the title, the plant has two open flowers, and two nearly open flowers, plus three buds – all blocked in gold. The spine is blocked in gold and in relief. Two fillets are blocked in gold at the head and at the tail. The rest of the spine is blocked with straps in relief, with gold blocking in between.

Ball, *VPB* p. 153. McLean, *VBD* p. 94.

81 Jones, Owen

Bacon, Mary Ann. *Fruits from the Garden and Field.* [London]: Longman & Co., 1850. Unpaginated. [16 leaves.]
182 × 265 × 15 mm. 1347.l.18.

Originally a gutta percha binding. Gilt edges. Bevelled boards. Gauffered turn-ins. Buff endpapers and pastedowns, impressed with diaper pattern and printed in gold with a pattern of corn stalks, vine leaves and grapes. Printed on the blank endpaper at the front: '| Bound by Remnant Edmonds & Remnants. |' Brown calf. On the lower cover, a stem pattern is blocked in blind on the bevels. A fillet is blocked in blind on the borders. Inside this, a 'double-branch' border is blocked, with berries, buds and leaves attached to, or hanging from, the branches. A group of corn stalks is blocked on the centre tail, rising upwards to show five stems, with ears of corn of the stalks. Fruit, berries, and ears of corn are blocked in relief. On the upper cover, there is the same border decoration in blind. However, there is different plant decoration on the branches. It consists of curling stems at the head, and corn stalks on each side; On the centre, the title: '| Fruits | from the | Garden and | Field |' is blocked in gothic letters, with a 'branch-like' shape to each letter. The capitals 'F' of 'Fruits' and of 'Field' are greatly elaborated, almost to the point of the grotesque. The spine is missing. [Formerly shelved at C.30.l.10.]

Ball, *VPB* p. 153. McLean, *VBD* pp. 93–94. McLean, *VPBB* pp. 10–11.

82 Jones, Owen

Bacon, Mary Ann. *Winged thoughts.* [London]: Longman & Co., 1851. Unpaginated. [28 leaves.]
185 × 265 × 17 mm. C.30.l.11.

Printed in gold on leaf 5: '| Poetry by M A Bacon. | Drawn on stone by E.L. Bateman. | Owen Jones direxit. |'

Gilt edges. Bevelled boards. Cream endpapers and pastedowns, decorated in gold with bronze and swirling wings. Printed on upper endpaper verso, at the tail: '| Bound by Remnant Edmonds & Remnants. |' Turn-ins decorated in gold with the same 'dog-tooth' pattern as for BL 1347.l.18. The bevels are blocked with the same curling stem and leaf decoration as for BL1347.l.18. The lower cover has two fillets blocked on its borders. An arch is formed by massed feathers blocked up the sides, to meet at the centre head. From the base, more massed feathers form a 'peacock's fan tail' on the centre – all the decoration uses the contrast between blind and relief to harmonious effect. On the upper cover, the same two fillets are blocked on the borders, and the same arch is formed at the centre head by massed feathers. On the tail, more massed feathers are blocked in blind and in relief. A feathered wing is blocked on the left and on the right of the upper cover. On the centre, the title: '| Winged | thoughts |' is blocked in gothic, with the capitals 'W' and 'F' being in 'bird-like' ornamental style. On the spine, feathers are blocked from the head to the tail in blind and in relief.

Ball, *VPB* p. 153.

83 Jones, Owen

FIG. 4

Moore, Thomas. *Paradise and the Peri.* [London]: Day & Son, [1860]. [2], 52 p.
245 × 335 × 20 mm. C.43.g.5.

Printed on the title page verso: '| Illuminators Owen Jones and Henry Warren. | On stone by Albert Warren | Day & Son Chros Lith: |'. In the list of titles bound at the end of BL 12304.h.1., this work is described as: '. . . Small folio, 54 splendidly illuminated pages, elegantly bound, bevelled boards, 2l. 2s., or calf embossed extra elegant, price 2l. 12s. 6d.'

Gilt edges. Yellow endpapers and pastedowns. Brown calf. The turn-ins are blocked in gold with a repeating leaf, curling

FIG. 4

stem and bud pattern. Both covers are blocked identically in blind and in relief. A single fillet is blocked on the borders, and inside this, there is a border of circles and leaves, blocked in relief. The decoration on the covers, apart from on the centre, shows an elaborate pattern of large leaves, blocked in relief. There is a 'background' decoration of horizontal ribs and small berries. The large leaves form the central frame, which is approximately square-shaped. Inside this, a dense pattern of small leaves is blocked in relief. The title: '| Paradise | and the | Peri |' is blocked in relief on the centre of the upper cover. On the centre of the lower cover, the monogram of Day & Son is blocked in relief. The spine is blocked in blind and in relief. Two fillets are blocked in blind on the perimeter. Between these, repeating dots are blocked in relief. Curling leaf decoration is blocked in relief at the head and at the tail. The title: '| Paradise and the Peri |' is blocked in relief along the spine.

Ball, *VPB* p. 154. McLean, *VBD* p. 11. Cites a copy with the binder's ticket of Leighton, Son & Hodge. McLean, *VPBB* p. 102. Illustrates the design on cloth.

84 Jones, Owen

PLATE XX

Taylor, Tom. *Birket Foster's Pictures of English landscape. (Engraved by the Brothers Dalziel) With Pictures in words by Tom Taylor.* London: Routledge, Warne, and Routledge. New York: 56, Walker Street, 1863. [London]: Dalziel Brothers, Engravers & Printers, Camden Press. Unpaginated. (6, 30p.] 30 plates. With one page of publisher's advertisement bound at the end.

202 × 262 × 40 mm. RdeB.J.23.

The British Museum de Beaumont copy.

Each page of text and plate is printed on the recto only. Bookplate of de Beaumont on upper pastedown. Written by R. de Beaumont on half-title page verso: 'The binding design is by Owen Jones. See advert at rear of: *The Golden Harp*. 1864' [which reads] '. . . superb binding, designed by Owen Jones – One Guinea.'

Gilt edges. Bevelled boards. Yellow endpapers and pastedowns. Green pebble-grain cloth. Both covers blocked identically in gold. Blocked on the borders in gold are: 1. 'dog-tooth' decoration; 2. a gold fillet, blocked between two thin gold fillets; 3. a gold fillet, with repeating rectangles blocked in relief within it, blocked between two thin gold fillets. These last three fillets are blocked horizontally and vertically to form a rectangle; an elaborate swirling pattern of acanthus-like leaves is outlined in relief by gold blocking on the inner corners, and around the large central oval panel. The borders of the central oval have the same group of three fillets (no. 3 above) blocked on its borders. Between them, the words: '| Birket Foster Tom Taylor |' are blocked in gold. On the centre, the title, '| Pictures | of | English | Landscape |' is blocked in gold, surrounded by tree stem and leaf decoration blocked in gold. The spine is blocked in gold. From the head downwards, the decoration is: a thin gold fillet; a thick gold fillet; a group of three gold fillets – two thin, with the middle having repeating rectangles blocked in relief within it; leaf decoration blocked in gold; a group of fillets, blocked as above; leaf decoration; a group of three gold fillets, as above; the words: '| Birket Foster |' are blocked in gold; a group of three fillets, as above; the words: '| Pictures | of | English | Landscape |' are blocked in gold, surrounded by tree stem and leaf decoration blocked in gold; a group of three fillets, as above; the words: '| Routledge &Co |' are blocked in gold; a group of three fillets, as above; at the tail, a thick gold fillet and a thin gold fillet are blocked.

de Beaumont, *RdeB1* no. 259. Goldman, *VIB* no. 259.

85 Jones, Owen

Tennyson, Alfred. *A welcome. To Her Royal Highness the Princess of Wales From the Poet Laureate. Owen Jones illuminator.* [London]: Day & Son Lithographers to the Queen, 1863. Unpaginated.

215 × 297 × 15 mm. C.43.d.2.

The recto of each leaf is a chromolithograph. The embellished text and the ornamental borders are printed in various colours.

Gilt edges. Bevelled boards. Glazed white endpapers and pastedowns, which are embossed with rib diagonal-grain, also moiré. Red pebble-grain cloth. Both covers blocked identically in gold and in relief. A single gold fillet is blocked in gold on the head, the tail and the fore-edge. A pattern of straps is blocked in

gold on the sides, the head and the tail, with leaf decoration blocked on each corner. Above and below the centre is a white paper rectangular onlay. Each onlay has double fillets blocked in gold on its borders. The words: '| A welcome | to Alexandra |' are blocked in gold on each onlay. The centre of each cover has a square white paper onlay, blocked in gold with an elaborate strapwork pattern, which is shown in relief by the blocking in gold. Gold 'fillets' are blocked on the borders of the square and straps (ending in points) are blocked on each corner. The spine has the title: '| A Welcome to Alexandra |' blocked in gold along its length, tail to head.

Ball, *VPB* p. 154. McLean, *VBD* pp. 129–132. 'It was sold at 21s. in an exotic cloth binding of red, gold and white, the Danish colours.' McLean, *VPBB* p. 72.

86 Jones, Owen

Jones, Owen. *One thousand and one Initial Letters Designed and Illuminated by Owen Jones*. London: Day & Son, Lithographers to the Queen, 1864. [London]: Day & Son. Unpaginated. [28 leaves.]

320 × 422 × 15 mm. 1757.b.28.

The recto of each leaf is chromolithographed with the multiple forms of each alphabetical letter, in gold, in red, in blue, and in black. At the base of each leaf: 'London. Chromolithographed & Published April 1st 1864, by Day & Son, Lithrs to the Queen & to H.R.H. The Prince of Wales.'

The original upper cover is used as a doublure. Original upper cover size: 278 × 400 mm. Deep maroon coarse pebble-grain cloth. Two fillets are blocked in blind on the borders. The centre of the cover is occupied by a block, stylistically similar to the design of the title page. The title words: '| 1,001 | Initial | Letters |' are blocked in gold on the centre. The words '1,001' and 'letters' are in floriated gothic letters, with an elaborate filigree of leaf foliage surrounding them to form rectangles. The capital 'I' of 'Initial' runs down the left hand side of the centre. It is highly decorated with stems and leaves. The cover design is an extension of the many designs for the initials printed within.

Ball, *VPB* p. 154.

87 Jones, Owen

PLATE XIX

Bible. Selections. Genesis. English. *The history of Joseph and his brethren. Genesis Chaprs XXXVII. XXXVIII. XL.* London: Published by Day & Son, Lithographers to the Queen & H.R.H. The Prince of Wales, [1865]. Unpaginated. [52 p.]

220 × 290 × 19 mm. C.43.d.16.

The verso of each leaf is printed with a quotation from Genesis in black and in red, against a gold background. The recto of each leaf shows an illustration accompanying the quotation from Genesis. The chromolithographic ornamental borders are all of Egyptian designs and are identical for each opening. The last leaf has: '| Illustrators | Owen Jones. Henry Warren. | On stone A. Warren. |'

The text is sewn on five slightly sawn-in cords. Gilt edges. Bevelled boards. Red pebble-grain cloth. Both covers are blocked identically in gold. A thin fillet is blocked on the borders. A beige paper onlay forms a rectangle within. The middle portion of the onlay is stained green. The whole onlay has been blocked in gold with three patterns. The outer pattern shows repeating rectangles; the inner pattern shows two fillets, pointed at intervals, which form repeating cartouches; the pattern in the middle is blocked on the green, and shows a repeating 'three layered' zig-zag pattern, with stylised plants blocked between each zig-zag. Within the inner rectangle, wings and a sun in the Egyptian style are blocked in gold on the centre head. Eleven five-point stars, a quarter moon and a sun are blocked below. The title: '| Joseph | and | his Brethen |' is blocked in gold in Egyptian letters. The spine is blocked in gold. On the head and the base, the same decoration is blocked, of fillets, cartouches, plant decoration and rectangles. The title: '| Joseph and his Brethen |' is blocked in gold along the spine, in Egyptian letters. The title is blocked within a rectangle formed by a single gold fillet, with Chinese angles blocked at the head and at the tail.

Ball, *VPB* p. 154.

88 Jones, Owen

Shakespeare, William. *Scenes from the Winter's Tale.* London: Day and Son Limited, [1866]. Unpaginated. [48 p.]

230 × 285 × 17 mm. J/11765.h.17.

Apart from the title page and the colophon, the recto of each leaf contains a chromolithograph. The verso of each leaf has text from the Winter's Tale printed in red and in black against a gold background. The colophon has the text: '| Illuminators | Owen Jones | and Henry Warren. | On stone | A. Warren |' The ornamental borders of each leaf are also chromolithographs.

Red ink edges. Original upper and lower covers used as doublures; cover size: 216 × 272 mm. Coarse brown pebble-grain cloth. Both covers are blocked identically in gold. Two thin fillets are blocked in gold on the outer borders. Three patterned borders are blocked in gold on rectangular paper onlays, coloured in red and in blue. Each rectangular onlay is separated by a gold fillet. The outer and inner onlays are red, and have a repeating pattern of flower heads and four dots blocked in gold. The blue onlay between these shows a stylised leaf and stem pattern blocked in gold. The inner rectangle formed by these three onlays has spade-shaped and leaf decoration blocked in gold on each corner. From the centre tail upwards, a plant is blocked in gold. The thin stems of the plant end in leaves. The title: '| Scenes | from the | Winter's | Tale |' is blocked in gold amongst and between the plant's stems.

Ball, *VPB* p. 154. McLean, *VPBB* p. 72.

89 K., W.

Leonora. *Donald Cameron; or, trust winneth troth. A tale.* London: Darton & Co., 42, Paternoster Row, E.C., 1866. Westminster: Printed by Faithfull & Co., Victoria Press, 1a Princes Street, Storey's Gate; and 83a, Farringdon Street. [2], 142 p., 1 plate.
105 × 167 × 17 mm. 12804.bbb.27.

The plate is signed with the monogram 'NP'.

Gilt edges. Yellow endpapers and pastedowns. Purple bead-grain cloth. Both covers blocked identically in blind on the borders, and on the corners. Two fillets are blocked on the borders. Single leaf decoration is blocked in blind on each corner. The upper cover vignette is blocked in gold. It shows a tracery of stem and hatched leaf decoration blocked in gold. This decoration surrounds three gold lettering-pieces, the top being semi-circular, the two underneath being rectangular. The title: '| Donald Cameron | or | Trust winneth troth |' is blocked in relief within the three gold lettering-pieces. Signed 'WK' in gold as separate letters at the base of the vignette. The spine is blocked in gold. Fillets and vertical hatch are blocked in gold at the head and at the tail. The title: '| Donald Cameron |' is blocked in gold along the spine, within a cartouche formed by two gold fillets, one of which is hatch. The capitals 'D' and 'C' are blocked in relief within rectangular gold lettering-pieces, which have single gold fillets blocked on their borders.

The artist or engraver of the upper cover vignette is possibly W. Kelsall.

90 Leighton, John

Knapp, Andrew and Baldwin, William. *The Newgate calendar; comprising interesting memoirs of the most notorious characters who have been convicted of outrages on the Laws of England since the commencement of the Eighteenth Century; with occasional anecdotes and observations, speeches, confessions, and last exclamations of sufferers.* 4 vols. London: J. Robins and Co. Ivy Lane, Paternoster Row, 1824–1828. Printed by J. Robins and Co. Ivy-Lane, London.

1379.h.12–14.

Vol. I. 1824. iv, 516 p., 3 plates. 142 × 226 × 32 mm.
Vol.II. 1825. [2], 502 p., 3 plates. 140 × 226 × 33 mm.
Vol. III. 1828. [2], 502 p., 9 plates. } 140 × 226 × 63 mm.
Vol. IV. [1828.] 406 p., 7 plates. }

The set of Henry Spencer Ashbee, whose bookplate is on each upper pastedown. There is no title page for Vol. IV. Volumes III and IV are bound together.

Mauve dot and line vertical-grain cloth. All the covers of this three volume set are blocked identically. Two fillets are blocked on the borders. An inner rectangle is formed with the blocking of a further two fillets, which have strapwork on the corners, the sides, and on the head and the tail. On the inner borders, a pattern of small strapwork, flowers and circles is blocked in blind and in relief. On each upper cover, the same central vignette is blocked in gold. It shows a wooden treasure chest, with its lid open. The chest has studded corners. Around the outside of the chest, a snake is coiled. It has the key to the lock of the chest on its tail. At the 'head' of the snake is a hand, holding a quill over an open book, propped up against the front of the box and the lid of the chest. There is a rolled-up scroll showing on the left hand side of the chest. On it, 'JL' is blocked in relief as a monogram. All the decorative features of the chest are picked out in relief. Only the spine of Vol. II survives on this set. The spine is blocked in gold. It has curling leaves and stems blocked from the head to half way down the spine. Within circles formed by this, the title: '| The | Newgate | Calendar |' is blocked near the head; below this, the words: '| Memoirs | of the | most | notorious | characters |'; then below: '| by | Knapp | and | Baldwin. | II. |' Underneath this, the figure of a gaoler is blocked, an axe on his right shoulder, his left hand holding a flag. At the tail the words: '| London. | Robins [&Co]. |' are blocked in gold.

There is another copy of this work in the London Metropolitan Archives, in the Burns Collection. It has four volumes also bound in three. The spines are all identical in this set and the same as Vol II of the BL copy. This set has the same cloth, grain, dye colour and blocking as the British Library set. It seems likely that the work was bound some thirty years or more after original publication, as dot and line grain did not come into use until the 1860s.

Ball, *VPB* p. 132. Gaskell, *NIB* p. 242, no. 58. Tanselle, *BDP* p. 96, no. 110.

91 Leighton, John

Cowper, William. *The diverting history of John Gilpin: showing how he went further than he intended, and came safe home again. With ten illustrations by a young artist.* [i.e. John Leighton.] London: Joseph Cundall, 12, Old Bond Street, 1845. [London] Chiswick: Printed by C. Whittingham. 24 p., 10 plates.
290 × 230 × 10 mm. L.49/575.

The plates are lithographs.

All the signatures on the plates are signed with Leighton's monogram, with the 'J' crossing below the 'L'.

Plate I. Frontispiece. Signed 'JL', at the base of the plinth.

Plate II. Interior of room. Signed 'JL', on the parcel.

Plate III. Street scene in London. Signed 'JL', on the doorstep.

Plate IV. Street scene in London. Signed 'JL', on the door column.

Plate V. Interior of inn. Signed 'JL', on the wooden box.

Plate VI. Horse in the road outside inn. Signed 'JL', on the base of the wall column.

Plate VII. Horse in pond. Signed 'JL', on the vase.

Plate VIII. Horse galloping. Signed 'JL', as part of the first floor window glazing.

Plate IX. Horse in street. Signed 'JL', at base of the gate column.

Plate X. Galloping horse. Signed 'JL', at the base of the toll gatepost.

All of the signatures are without serifs. Rebacked. Red pebble-grain cloth. The cloth has been ribbon embossed with a repeating frond pattern. Both covers are blocked identically in blind. Two fillets, the outer thick, the inner thin, are blocked in blind on the borders. Strapwork is blocked in blind on the corners. On the upper cover, the title: '| The | diverting history | of | John Gilpin |' is blocked in gold, in rustic letters. Unsigned.

McLean, *Cundall* p. 58. States that the illustrations are said to be the first Leighton published. Pantazzi, *JL* p. 273.

92 Leighton, John

Limner, Luke *pseud.* [i.e. John Leighton.] *Ancient story of the Old dame and Her Pig. A legend of obstinacy. Shewing how it cost the Old Lady a world of trouble, & the pig his tail. Illustrated by Luke Limner.* London: David Bogue Fleet St, 1847. London: Printed at the Lithographic Press of C. Blair [&] Leighton, Percy Street. [14 plates.]
147 × 145 × 8 mm. 12805.c.1.

The plates are stab-stitched.

Both covers of paper pasted onto thin boards. Lithographed in brown and blue ink. The upper cover shows the title [as above] printed on the farmhouse gate, and the old dame & her pig who are in a rural farmyard setting. The lower cover has a series title: '| Pictures | poems & | legendary lore | for the | homes of England. | Collected & illustrated | by | Luke Limner Esq. | No. 1 | The ancient legend | of the | Old Woman and her pig. | London | Published | by | David | Bogue | 86 Fleet St. |'. The background is a Renaissance bolt and panel design, with the initials 'J' and 'L' to the left and the right, printed in blue.

Pantazzi, *JL* p. 273.

93 Leighton, John

Limner, Luke *pseud.* [i.e. John Leighton.] *Contrasts & conceits for contemplation.* London: Ackermann & Co, Strand, [1847]. [20 plates]
16 × 26 × 0 mm. Johnson d.4233.

Copy in the Bodleian Library. Pencil note on flyleaf: 'Author's proof copy'.

A man [Leighton?] is seated at a desk, looking forwards. Black and white engravings. The plates feature contrasts: 'tragedy-comedy'; 'wedding clothes-funeral clothes'; 'within-without'; 'lucky-unlucky'; 'before and after the railway'. The unpublished memoir of Leighton, also in the John Johnson Collection, suggests that the cover features a self-portrait of Leighton.

King, *JL* p. 235. Pantazzi, *JL* p. 273.

94 Leighton, John

Limner, Luke *pseud.* [i.e. John Leighton.] *The London cries & Public Edifices from sketches on the spot.* London: Grant & Griffith Successors to Newbery and Harris, corner of St Paul's Churchyard, 1847. [London]: Printed at the Litho Press of Leighton & Taylor, 19 Lamb's Conduit Street. 24 p., 24 plates.
140 × 145 × 15 mm. 1303.a.28.

There are twenty four plates, apart from the frontispiece. Each shows a famous London building or place, together with the figure of a crier, with a quote of their cry. Most of the plates are signed 'JL', many as a monogram. All the monograms of Leighton are small, and often they are cunningly placed, as in plate 3. They are:

1. The Tower of London. 'Pots and kettles to mend: bellows to mend'. Signed 'LJ' as a monogram on the box on the tinker's back.
2. The East India House. 'Rhubarb'. Signed 'LJ' as a monogram on the pavement.
3. The Bank of England. 'Matches'. Signed 'LJ' as a monogram on a poster affixed to railings.
4. The Royal Exchange. 'Oranges, sweet St. Michael oranges'. Signed 'LJ' as a monogram on a canvas cover.
5. The Mansion House. 'Bring a cage for your fine singing bird'. Signed 'LJ' as a monogram on barrel of a wagon.
6. The Old College of Physicians. 'Old chairs to mend'. Signed 'LJ' as a monogram on the pavement.
7. Smithfield. 'Cat's meat dogs meat'. Signed 'LJ' as a monogram on top of column.
8. St. John's Gate Clerkenwell. 'Dust O !!!'. Signed 'LJ' as a monogram on the pavement.
9. Temple Bar. 'But a lace of the poor blind'. Signed 'LJ' as a monogram on the rear of the horse.
10. Somerset House. 'Umbrellas to mend, my old ones to sell'. Signed 'LJ' as a monogram on a wooden fence, as a poster.
11. Covent Garden Market. 'Cherry ripe: round and sound 4d a pound'. Signed 'J L' as separate letters on the blanket on the horse.
12. Covent Garden Theatre. 'The costardmonger. Heath stones, and Flanders brick'. Unsigned ?
13. Trafalgar Square. 'Images, buy images'. Signed 'LJ' as a monogram on the base of a pillar.
14. Charing Cross. 'Baked potatoes all hot'. Signed 'LJ' as a monogram on the pavement.
15. White Hall. 'Bow pots'. Signed 'LJ' as a monogram on rear of the cart.
16. Burlington House Gateway. 'Wild duck rabbit or fowl. Strawberries'. Unsigned ?
17. Saint George's Hanover Sq. 'New mackerel'. Signed 'LJ' as a monogram on the mackerel basket.
18. St James Palace. 'Old cloths buy a box, a band box'. Signed 'LJ' as a monogram on the pavement.
19. Westminster Abbey. 'Milk below'. Signed 'LJ' as a monogram on the milk churn.
20. Lambeth Palace. 'Water cresses'. Signed 'LJ' as a monogram on the bucket.
21. New Hall Lincoln's Inn. 'Knives & scissors to grind. Buy a mat, a rope or a parlour mat'. Signed 'J' and 'L' at top LH and RH corners.

22. Foundling Hospital. 'Sweep'. Unsigned?
23. North Western Railway. 'Muffins, crumpets'. Signed ' L' on trunk.
24. Coliseum. 'Buy a broom'. Signed 'LJ' as a monogram on the scrap of paper on the ground.

The original covers are paper, lithographed. There is a red endpaper bound at the front. On the upper cover a Renaissance bolt and panel design is printed with emblems and figures at the head, and an artist's studio with objects at the tail. The title: '| The | Cries | of | London | & | Public | Edifices | from | sketches | on the | spot |' is printed on the centre. The words 'public edifices' sketches', 'LL' [Luke Limner], are printed in blue. The words 'London' and 'on the spot' are printed in red. On the lower cover, the same Renaissance bolt and panel design is printed. Within it is printed in the following colours: '| Published by [in blue] | Grant & Griffith [in red] | Successors to [in blue] | Newbery & Harris [in red] | at [in blue] | the [in blue] | Bible & Sun [in red] |'. The monogram of Grant & Griffith shows crossed capital 'G' letters, one 'G' [in black] ,'&' [in red], and the other 'G' [in blue]. Underneath, are the words '| Holy Bible |' [in red], on a spine of a Bible. On the line underneath this, is '| estabd a [in blue] century [in red] |'. On the next lines below, are : '| The corner of' [in red] | Saint [in blue] | Pauls [in red] | Church yard [in blue] |'. The letters 'LL' [i.e. Luke Limner] are printed in red.

The Library of Congress copy is at shelfmark DA688.L37 Rare books. It has white endpapers and pastedowns. Printed paper over boards. The same design is lithographed on both covers. There are three fillets blocked on the borders. Flowers and leaves on the corners. At the head 'In twenty six illustrations' is printed in a scroll. [the 26 plates being 24, the text, and two for the covers.] At the centre, a shield of the City of London is printed, with the title overprinted. A lamp-post is on either side of the shield, each with a shield of its own. The word 'Westminster' is printed in the shield on the left; 'Southwarke' in the shield on the right. A street scene is printed at the base.

King, *JL* p. 235. Pantazzi, *JL* p. 273.

95 Leighton, John

Limner, Luke *pseud.* [i.e. John Leighton.] *London out of town. Or the adventures of the Browns at the sea side.* [London]: Published by David Bogue 86 Fleet Street, [1848]. London: Printed at the Lithographic Pr[ess] Leighton [& Taylor?], 19 Lamb's Conduit Street. 14 plates.

143 × 110 × 10 mm. 12352.a.3.

The cover states: '154 illustrations. Price one shilling.'

Both covers of paper pasted onto thin boards. Both covers have an identical bolt and panel Renaissance design. The upper cover features medallions of events in 'watering places'. The lower cover shows the front wall and gate of 'Victoria Villa' with members of a family attempting to gain entrance to it. The initials 'JL' and the monogram 'DB'[David Bogue] are printed in blue on the lower cover. The lithographs are not signed.

Pantazzi, *JL* p. 273.

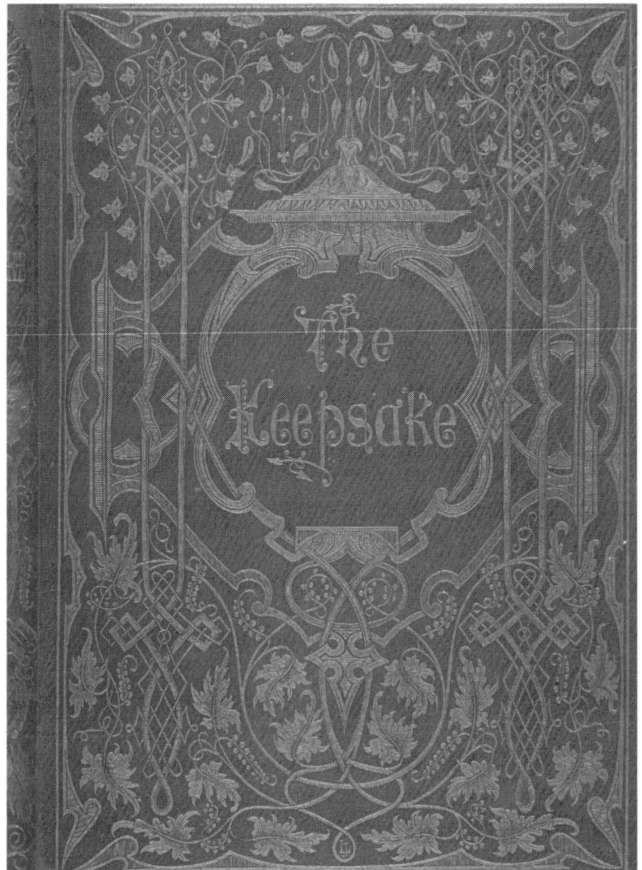

FIG. 5

96 Leighton, John FIG. 5

Periodical Publications – *London. The Keepsake.* London: David Bogue, 86, Fleet Street, 1828–1857. [London]: George Barclay, Castle St., Leicester Square.

P.P. 6670.

Published annually from 1828. The last volume in the British Library set is 1857. The years 1836, 1837, 1840, 1843, 1844, and 1845 are bound in red moiré grain cloth, with lettering in gold on the spines. The year 1838 has pink pebble grain cloth, blocked in blind, with a large central roundel showing a classical scene – a man playing a lyre. The year 1842 is bound in red morocco leather, with central lozenges blocked in gold on both covers. The year 1847 is of red morocco-grain cloth, with an elaborate neo-classical design blocked in gold. The design is signed 'E. Smith. Binder. Ivy Lane' in relief at the base of both covers. The year 1848 is of brown morocco vertical-grain cloth, blocked in gold, with a rectangular design, and neo-classical centre pieces. [Dry, op. Cit., p.30 and note 184, suggests that the 1848 volume had a cover design by Vivant Beauce.] The volume of 1830 has the binder's ticket for 'F. Westley. Binder. Friar Street, Near Doctor's Commons.' The 1848 volume has the ticket: '| Bound by | Josiah | Westley | London. |' The cover design by John Leighton is blocked on the covers for years 1849–1857. The volumes for these years have gilt edges. The volumes had originally yellow endpapers and pastedowns. The

same blocking is repeated throughout these years. Red morocco horizontal-grain cloth. An identical design is blocked in gold on the upper and in blind on the lower covers. The design is an intricate tracery with grapes and vine leaves, intermingled with strapwork. The title: '| The | Keepsake |', in fanciful lettering, is centrally blocked in gold on each upper cover. It is surmounted by a 'vase bowl' lid, oriental style. All copies are signed 'JL' in gold as a monogram, on the centre tail of each upper cover. The upper cover for 1850 shows evidence of the design being executed in two blocks, as the two halves do not join. The spine for 1854 is the only original spine fully intact; however the design is the same for these years. It is blocked in gold, and repeats the vine leaves, grapes, tracery and strapwork patterns of the covers. The title: '| The | Keepsake | 18[49–57]. |' is blocked in gold within a panel formed by columns, a decorated base (with a lyre), and a lantern above.

The titles in this series with covers designed by Leighton are:

The Keepsake 1849. Edited by The Countess of Blessington. With beautifully finished engravings, from drawings by the first artists, engraved under the superintendence of Mr. Charles Heath. London: David Bogue, 86 Fleet Street; New York, Appleton & Co.; H. Mandeville, Paris, 1849. London: Printed by George Barclay, Castle Street, Leicester Square. [7], 275 p., 12 plates. 175 × 245 × 30 mm. Binder's ticket on lower pastedown: '| Bound by | Westleys & Co. | [rule] | London. |'

The Keepsake 1850. Edited by The Countess of Blessington. With beautifully finished engravings, from drawings by the first artists, engraved under the superintendence of Mr. Frederick A. Heath. London: David Bogue, 86 Fleet Street, New York, Appleton & Co.; H. Mandeville, Paris, 1850. London: Printed by G. Barclay, Castle St., Leicester Sq. ix, 271 p., 12 plates. 170 × 245 × 30 mm.

The Keepsake 1851. Edited by Miss Power. With beautifully finished engravings, from drawings by the first artists, engraved under the superintendence of Mr. Frederick A. Heath. London: David Bogue, 86 Fleet Street, New York, Appleton & Co.; H. Mandeville, Paris. 1851. London: Printed by G. Barclay, Castle St., Leicester Sq. viii, 272 p., 12 plates. 175 × 245 × 30 mm.

The Keepsake 1852. Edited by Miss Power. With beautifully finished engravings, from drawings by the first artists, engraved under the superintendence of Mr. Frederick A. Heath. London: David Bogue, 86 Fleet Street: Bangs, Brothers & Co, New York; H. Mandeville, Paris, 1852. London: Printed by G. Barclay, Castle St. Leicester Sq. viii, 272 p., 12 plates. 170 × 245 × 30 mm.

The Keepsake 1853. Edited by Miss Power. With beautifully finished engravings, from drawings by the first artists, engraved under the superintendence of Mr. Frederick A. Heath. London: David Bogue, 86 Fleet Street; Bangs, Brothers & Co., New York; H. Mandeville, Paris, 1853. London: Printed by G. Barclay, Castle St., Leicester Sq. viii, 272 p., 12 plates. 175 × 245 × 30 mm. Binder's ticket on lower pastedown: '| Leighton, | Son & | Hodge, | Shoe Lane, | London. |'

The Keepsake 1854. Edited by Miss Power. With beautifully finished engravings, from drawings by the first artists, engraved under the superintendence of Mr. Frederick A. Heath. London: David Bogue, 86 Fleet Street; Bangs, Brothers & Co., New York; H. Mandeville, Paris, 1854. London: Printed by G. Barclay, Castle St., Leicester Sq. viii, 272 p., 12 plates. 170 × 245 × 30 mm. Binder's ticket on lower pastedown: '| Leighton, | Son & | Hodge, | Shoe Lane, | London. |'.

The Keepsake 1855. Edited by Miss Power. With beautifully finished engravings, from drawings by the first artists, engraved under the superintendence of Mr. Frederick A. Heath. London: David Bogue, 86 Fleet Street; Bangs, Brothers & Co., New York; H. Mandeville, 15 Rue Dauphin, Paris, 1854. London: Printed by G. Barclay, Castle Street Leicester Square. viii, 272 p., 12 plates. 170 × 245 × 30 mm. Original cover size: 170 × 245 mm. Binder's ticket on lower pastedown: '| Leighton, | Son & | Hodge, | Shoe Lane, | London. |'. Conserved and rebound in 1995 by Cedric Chivers. The lower cover is with the rebound book, and is identical to all the others.

The Keepsake 1856. Edited by Miss Power. With beautifully finished engravings, from drawings by the first artists, engraved under the superintendence of Mr. Frederick A. Heath. London: David Bogue, 86 Fleet Street; Bangs, Brothers & Co., New York; H. Mandeville, 15 Rue Dauphine, Paris, 1856. London: Printed by G. Barclay, Castle St. Leicester Sq. viii, 272 p., 12 plates. 170 × 245 × 30 mm. Binder's ticket on lower pastedown: '| Leighton, | Son & | Hodge, | Shoe Lane, | London. |'.

The Keepsake 1857. Edited by Miss Power. With beautifully finished engravings, from drawings by the first artists, engraved under the superintendence of Mr. Frederick A. Heath. London: David Bogue, 86 Fleet Street; Bangs, Brothers & Co., New York; H. Mandeville, 15 Rue Dauphine, Paris, 1857. London: Printed by G. Barclay, Castle St. Leicester Sq. viii, 272 p., 12 plates. 170 × 245 × 30 mm.

Ball, *VPB* ref.3, p. 179. Dry, *JL* no. 8. King, *JL* p. 237. McLean, *VPBB* p. 44. Morris & Levin, *APB* p. 31 no. 38. Shows the upper cover and spine for 1851.

97 Leighton, John

Best, M. C. *The works of creation illustrated.* London: Darton & Co., Holborn Hill; Bath: Binns and Goodwin, 1849. Bath: Printed by Binns & Goodwin. xiii, 256 p., 6 plates. With four pages of publisher's titles bound at the end.
140 × 180 × 25 mm. 1256.b.8.

Gilt edges. Yellow endpapers and pastedowns. Binder's ticket on lower pastedown: '| Bound by | Josiah Westley | [rule] | London. |'. Red fine vertical-rib grain cloth. Both covers are blocked identically in blind. There are five fillets blocked on the borders, and tropical plant leaves blocked on the corners. The stems of the leaves all join in a continuous series of branches, which are linked together to form an oval. The upper cover has a central vignette, blocked in gold and in relief. Around the perimeter, two fillets are blocked, forming a diamond shape. Where the

fillets link, strapwork is formed. To the left of the vignette is blocked the sun; to the right is blocked the moon. In the centre is blocked a globe. A gold lettering-piece, resembling a pennant, is blocked above, across and below the globe. Above the globe, the words: '| The | works of |' are blocked in relief within the pennant above the centre. The word '| Creation |' is blocked in relief on the portion of the lettering piece running across the globe. The word '| Illustrated |' is blocked in relief within the pennant below the globe. Stars are blocked in gold around all the above. Signed 'JL' in gold as a monogram, at the base of the vignette. The spine is blocked in gold. A single gold fillet is blocked on the perimeter. Branches are blocked in gold down each side of the spine. There are leaves and flowers in an arch above the title: '| Works | of | creation | illustrated |', blocked in gold. A lion, a snake curled in branches, and a whale spouting water, are all blocked below the title. Signed 'JL' in gold as a monogram at the tail.

Dry, *JL* no. 5.

98 Leighton, John

Limner, Luke *pseud.* [i.e. John Leighton.] *Comic art-manufactures. Collected by Luke Limner Esq.* London: David Bogue, 86 Fleet St, [1848]. London: Printed at the Lithographic Press of Leighton & Taylor, 19 Lamb's Conduit Street. 8 plates.
230 × 145 × 7 mm. 012331.de.79(1).

The cover states, top left and top right: 'Sixty four designs. Price one shilling.'

The upper cover is of orange paper, printed in black. Underneath the plaques containing the title: '| Comic. | Art-Manufactures. |', there is a quote by Felix Summerly [i.e. Henry Cole]: '| The aim of this collection is to decorate objects | of every day life, and to associate poetical invention | with every thing. To decorate each article with appro- | priate details relating to its use, and to obtain | these examples as directly as possible from nature. |' Underneath the title, an artist is seated in a chair in front of an easel, looking pensively at a drawing (on the easel) of: 'The 'cold' | Grecian nosed | gruill mug |'. The Grecian is holding a handkerchief to his dripping nose. At the base of the drawing is Leighton's monogram 'LJ', with the 'J' below the 'L', and crossing it. Two bottles are labelled 'Rum' and 'Shrub', and in their necks, are the stems of plants that rise up to form plant medallion borders, which contain parodies of animals and nature. At the left and right hand tail of the page is the text: '| Botanical and zoological border, from a screen, after a great (made o'evil) artist. (Devilish clever) |'. The art manufactures drawn within amply parody Summerly's words quoted above.

It is suggested (in the life of Leighton by Straker(?) in the John Johnson Collection), that the artist seated in the chair is a self-portrait of Leighton. On page 5 of the 'Rejected Contributions . . .', there is an engraving of the Grecian nosed mug, entitled: ' "The Cold" A Grecian nosed mug for slops Being a portrait of the noted Dr. Slop. Rejected because the design could not be considered happy.'

King, *JL* p. 234. Pantazzi, *JL* p. 273. '. . .first printed by Leighton Brothers, then by Vincent Brooks, and by David Bogue . . .'

99 Leighton, John PLATE XXI

Limner, Luke *pseud.* [i.e. John Leighton.] *Our Tom Cat & his nine lives.* London: Ackermann & Co., Strand, [1849]. London: Leighton & Taylor, 19 Lamb's Conduit Street. 16 p.
145 × 110 × 7 mm. 012807.de.69.

At the base of the upper cover is printed: 'Plain 1/-; coloured 2/6'. The illustrations are hand coloured.

Rebacked 1995. Blue endpapers and pastedowns. The covers are paper pasted over boards. The upper cover is printed in red and black. A Tom Cat is seated in the centre, hatted, with a feather held in his left paw against his lips. The Tom is surrounded by books. The letters of the words '| Our Tom |' above his head are printed to resemble books on a shelf. The word '| cat |' is printed on a large book with fore-edge clasps and metal tips on the fore-edge corners. Four other cats climb and play amongst leaves and plants around the centre piece. The lower cover is printed in red and in black, showing titles of other works by Luke Limner.

Pantazzi, *JL* p. 273. Gives a date of 1848 for the work.

100 Leighton, John FIGS. 6–9

The Court Album: Fourteen Portraits of the female aristocracy. Engraved by the best artists, from drawings by John Hayter. London: David Bogue, 86, Fleet Street, 1850. London: Savill and Edwards, Printers, Chandos Street, Covent Garden. Unpaginated [33 p., 15 plates.] [All original cloth covers used as doublures.]
220 × 295 × 20 mm.
Doublure size: 210 × 285. 10815.f.3.[1850–1857]

Light green morocco horizontal-grain cloth. Upper and lower original covers used as doublures. Both covers fully blocked in gold, with an identical design. There are three thin fillets blocked in gold on the outer border. There are 'lily-shape' flowers blocked in gold on the corners. There is another fillet blocked in gold, which forms the inner rectangle, and it has small repeating dots, blocked in relief within. The branches, leaves and seeds of a horse chestnut tree wind around the inner rectangle, forming an oval-shaped centre. Within the centre, is blocked a diamond-shaped lettering piece. The title: '| The | Court | Album |' is blocked within, together with a crown and a rose, all in relief. Signed 'JL' in gold as monogram at the base of the design.

—— London: David Bogue, 86, Fleet Street, 1851. Unpaginated [30 p; 14 plates]
220 × 295 × 20 mm. Doublure size: 210 × 285 mm.

The design blocked on both covers is identical to that for 1850. Light green morocco horizontal-grain cloth. Upper and lower

FIG. 6 [1850–1852]

FIG. 8 [1855]

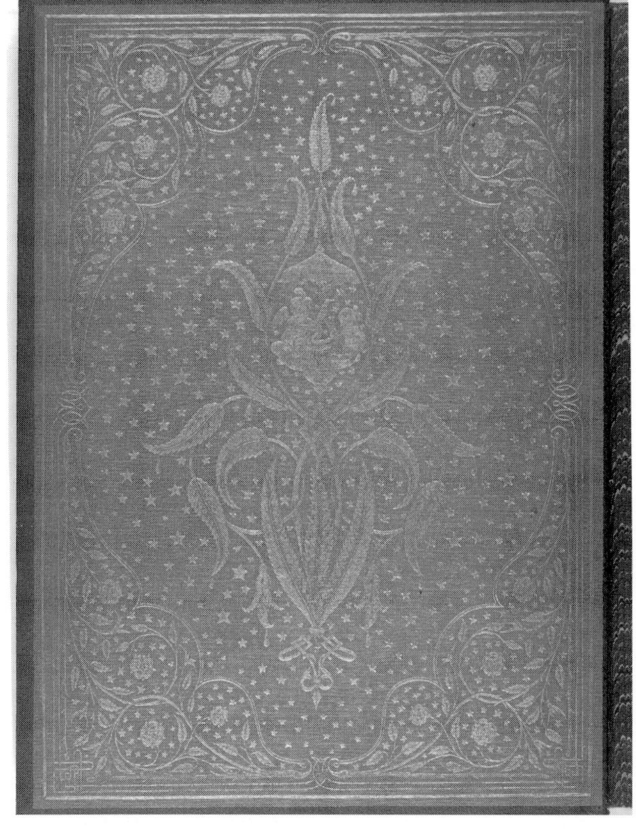

FIG. 7 [1853–1854]

FIG. 9 [1857]

original covers used as doublures. Both covers fully blocked in gold, with an identical design. There are three thin fillets blocked in gold on the outer border. There are 'lily-shape' flowers blocked in gold on the corners. There is another fillet blocked in gold, which forms the inner rectangle, and it has small repeating dots, blocked in relief within. The branches, leaves and seeds of a horse chestnut tree wind around the inner rectangle, forming an oval-shaped centre. Within the centre, is blocked a diamond-shaped lettering piece. The title: '| The | Court | Album |' is blocked within, together with a crown and a rose, all in relief. Signed 'JL' in gold as monogram at the base of the design.

—— London: David Bogue, 86, Fleet Street, 1852. London: Savill and Edwards, Printers, Chandos Street, Covent Garden. Unpaginated. [54 p; 12 plates]
220 × 295 × 20 mm. Doublure size: 210 × 290 mm.

The design blocked on both covers is identical to that for 1850 and 1851. Light green morocco horizontal-grain cloth. Upper and lower original covers used as doublures. Both covers fully blocked in gold, with an identical design. There are three thin fillets blocked in gold on the outer border. There are 'lily-shape' flowers blocked in gold on the corners. There is another fillet blocked in gold, which forms the inner rectangle, and it has small repeating dots, blocked in relief within. The branches, leaves and seeds of a horse chestnut tree wind around the inner rectangle, forming an oval-shaped centre. Within the centre a diamond-shaped lettering piece is blocked. The title: '| The | Court | Album |' is blocked within, together with a crown and a rose, all in relief. Signed 'JL' in gold as monogram at the base of the design.

—— London: David Bogue, 86, Fleet Street, 1853. London: Savill and Edwards, Printers, Chandos Street, Covent Garden. Unpaginated. [59 p; 12 plates.]
220 × 295 × 20 mm. Doublure size: 210 × 290 mm.

Light green morocco horizontal-grain cloth. Original upper and lower covers used as doublures. Both covers fully blocked in gold and in blind, with an identical design. There is a single fillet blocked in gold on the borders. Two more thin fillets are blocked inside this, forming strapwork on the corners and onion shapes on the centre sides. Rose branches are blocked along the sides, with rose stems, leaves and flowers blocked on the corners. The veins of the leaves, and petals of the flowers are highlighted by blocking in relief. Surrounding the centre-piece are multiple stars, in gold, resembling an open sky. The base of the centre-piece shows a triplet of leaves, and their veins, blocked in blind. At the sides are two flowers, with water drops below them. Above, more leaves surround two figures. An angel putto is playing a stringed instrument to a fashionably dressed lady, who is reclining on cushions shaped like mushrooms. The lady's hair is tied in two buns at the back of her head, and her right hand holds a fan. Above the two figures is a cupola, hanging from leaves and stems. The cupola has a lamp suspended from it. Signed 'JL' in gold as a monogram twice: once underneath the triplet of leaves at the base of the centre-piece; once on the centre of the tail of the cover.

—— London: David Bogue, 86, Fleet Street, 1854. London: Thomas Harrild, Printer, Silver Street, Falcon Square. Unpaginated. [25 p; 11 plates.]
220 × 295 × 20 mm. Doublure size: 210 × 285 mm.

Original upper and lower covers used as doublures. The cloth and the design is identical to 1853. The exception is that the monogram 'JL' is absent from the centre of the tail of the covers.

—— London: David Bogue, 86, Fleet Street, 1855. London: Thomas Harrild, Printer, Silver Street, Falcon Square. Unpaginated. [28 p., 11 plates.]
220 × 295 × 20 mm. Doublure size: 210 × 280 mm.

Light green ripple vertical-grain cloth. Original upper and lower covers used as doublures. Both covers blocked identically. The borders and corners are blocked as for 1853 and 1854. The centre-piece for 1855 is a new design, showing a recessed central diamond. Around the border of the diamond, a pattern of repeating three headed flowers and Maltese crosses is blocked in gold. Fuchsia-like flowers are blocked at the head and the tail of the diamond, with onion-shaped flowers at the sides – all in gold. On the borders inside the recess, a pattern of fuchsia stems, leaves and flowers is blocked in blind and relief, the inner portions of which forms an arabesque. At the centre, a single rose with a crown of stars are blocked in gold. Signed 'JL' in gold as a monogram at the centre of the tail of the upper cover.

—— London: David Bogue, 86, Fleet Street, 1856. London: Thomas Harrild, Printer, Silver Street, Falcon Square. Unpaginated. [27 p., 11 plates.].
220 × 295 × 15 mm. Doublure size: 225 × 280 mm.

Red sheepskin leather. Blocked in gold and in blind, with an identical design on both covers. The borders and corners have repeating small massed tool patterns, with a tracery of geometric lines – all blocked between fillets which form rectangles on the covers. The centre-piece is blocked in blind, as a diamond shape, with a quatrefoil at the centre. The whole effect is of an imitation of an earlier C16 design. Unsigned; design probably not by Leighton.

—— London: David Bogue, 86, Fleet Street, 1857. London: Thomas Harrild, Printer, 11, Salisbury Square, Fleet Street, and Silver Street, Falcon Square. [27 p; 11 plates]
220 × 295 × 15 mm. Doublure size: 210 × 280 mm.

Original upper and lower covers used as doublures. Green rib vertical-grain cloth. Blocked in gold, with an identical design on both covers. There are three fillets blocked in gold on the borders. Between the second and third fillets, a repeating pattern of diamonds and ovals is blocked in gold. The inner border side decoration imitates a renaissance design, with joined small pillars, and scroll-like patterns at the sides. Two ovals are

blocked on the centre, linked with strapwork, which at the head and the tail end in leaves and flowers. Signed 'JL' in gold as a monogram on both covers at the base of the centre-piece.

Dry, *JL* no. 14. King, *JL* p. 237.

101 Leighton, John

Bryant, William Cullen. *Poems. Collected and Arranged by the Author. With an introductory essay, on the genius & writings of the author, by George Gilfillan.* Liverpool: John Walker, Hanover Street; London: David Bogue; Hamilton, Adams and Co.; Johnstone and Hunter; H. Washburne; Edinburgh: Oliver and Boyd; Johnstone and Hunter; Dublin: J. M'Glashan, 1850. Liverpool: D. Marples, Printer, Liverpool xvi, 275 p.
120 × 171 × 22 mm. 11687.b.33.

Yellow endpapers and pastedowns. Binder's ticket on lower pastedown: '| Bound by | Josiah Westley, | adjoining 'The Times' Office | London. |' Blue ripple horizontal-grain cloth. The same design is blocked in blind on both covers. Two fillets are blocked on the borders. There are curling stems and leaves blocked in relief on the corners. On each cover, a central vignette is blocked. Each consists of four linked heart-shapes, with pointed ends. The spine is blocked in gold. There is a single fillet blocked on the perimeter. A single lily plant is blocked on the spine, with its roots at the base. There are three stems up the spine, with leaves blocked at intervals. There are four flowers at the head above the title words: '| Bryant's | Poems. |' blocked in gold, within a shield-shape, formed by a single gold fillet. Signed 'JL' in gold as a monogram at the tail.

Dry, *JL* no. 11.

102 Leighton, John

Emerson, Ralph Waldo. *Poems. Second Edition.* London: George Routledge & Co., Soho Square, 1850. vii, 200 p.
122 × 195 × 18 mm. 11689.a.44.

Gilt edges. Yellow endpapers and pastedowns. Binder's ticket on lower pastedown: '| Bound by | Josiah Westley, | adjoining 'the Times' Office | London. |'. Green fine vertical rib-grain cloth. Both covers blocked identically in blind on the borders. A single fillet is blocked on the borders; then a wide repeating pattern of curling stems and leaves blocked in blind. Straps are blocked on the corners. Three fillets in blind form the inner rectangle. The upper cover has a central vignette blocked in gold, showing a lyre and branches and leaves intertwined. Signed 'JL' in gold as a monogram at base of the vignette. The spine is blocked in gold. A pattern of curling stems and leaves form 'S' shapes down the spine. In an oval formed by these stems, the words: '| Emerson's | Poems |' are blocked in gold. The upper cover vignette block is repeated on both covers of B.L. 11649.c.4, Sophia Milligen, Original poems . . ., 1856; and also on the lower cover of B.L. 1347.g.25, A book of modern ballads . . .[1866].

King, *JL* p. 239.

103 Leighton, John

Limner, Luke *pseud.* [i.e. John Leighton.] *Christmas comes but once a year. Showing what Mr. Brown did, thought, and intended to do, during that festive season. Now first edited from the original MSS. (MESS). With Notes and Ilustrations.* London: William Tegg and Co., 85, Queen Street, Cheapside, 1850. [3], 101 p., 16 plates. With eighteen pages of publisher's titles bound at the end.
140 × 150 × 15 mm. c.194.a.74.

Many of the plates are signed with Leighton's monogram. Some of the text vignettes are also signed 'JL' as a monogram. The colophon has: '| The Cuts, | inserted in the text, are | engraved by the Brothers DALZIEL; | the Plates (from zinc) printed | by LEIGHTONS & TAYLOR; | and the Letter-press by | BENTLEY & FLEY, | BANGOR HOUSE, | SHOE LANE. |'

Test sewn on three sawn-in cords. Light blue endpapers and pastedowns. (The lower endpaper is missing.) Brown rib vertical-grain cloth. Both covers blocked identically in blind on the lower, and in gold and in blind on the upper. Two fillets are blocked in blind on the borders. On the corners, and the sides around the centre, a pattern of holly branches, leaves and berries is blocked in blind. The central vignette is blocked in gold on the upper cover. It shows a cross at the head. The title: '| Christmas | comes | but | once a year |' is blocked in gold in rustic and fantastic letters. The first 'S' of 'Christmas' is wrapped around the stem of the cross, as is the 'm' of 'Comes'. From the horizontal bar of the 'A', a strap and buckle support a shield, (argent) with two five-pointed stars blocked within it at the centre, plus small stars around it – all in gold. The message: '| Good tidings | of | great | joy | to all | people. |' is blocked in relief within ribbon-shaped gold lettering-pieces blocked on each side of the shield. Signed 'JL' in blind as separate letters at the centre tail of each cover. The spine is blocked in gold. From the head downwards, the decoration is: two gold fillets; holly branch, stem and berries in gold; the title: '| Christ | [rule] | mas | comes | but | once | a year |' blocked in gold; holly berries, leaves and stems; a panel hangs from a strap around the holly branch; within the panel: '| Luke | Limner |' is blocked in relief within two scroll-shaped gold lettering-pieces blocked at right angles to each other; the date '| 1850 |' is blocked in gold within a circle formed by stems in gold; more holly leaves, stems, and berries; two gold fillets blocked at the tail.

Dry, *JL* no. 17. Pantazzi, *JL* p. 273.

104 Leighton, John FIG. 10

Marryat, Frederick. *The floral telegraph: or affection's signals.* London: Saunders and Otley, Conduit-Street, [1850]. xv, 324 p., 6 plates.
110 × 154 × 26 mm. 12614.ccc.18.

Gilt edges. Light endpapers and pastedowns. Green ripple horizontal-grain cloth. Both covers are blocked identically in blind on the borders and on the corners. Two fillets are blocked on the

FIG. 10

borders, one thin, one thick. Flowers shaped like fleurs-de-lis are blocked in blind on each corner, ending in scrollwork. On the upper cover, a central vignette is blocked in gold. This shows rose branches, leaves and flowers, all intertwined. At the very centre, the rose branches form a 'heart-shape', with two birds perched on top. Signed 'JL' in gold as a monogram at the base of the vignette. The spine is blocked in gold. Two branches curl upwards from the tail to the head. One has fuchsia leaves and flowers; the other has small daisy-like flowers. The branches and stems interlock, and form an oval frame near the head. In this frame, the words: '| Floral telegraph |' are blocked in gold in rustic lettering. Signed 'JL' in gold as a monogram at the tail of the spine.

Dry, *JL* no. 62.

105 Leighton, John

Michell, Nicholas. *Ruins of many lands. A descriptive poem. Second edition, enlarged.* London: William Tegg and Co., Pancras-Lane, Cheapside, 1850. London: John K. Chapman & Company, Printers, 5, Shoe-Lane and Peterborough-Court, Fleet-Street. viii, 9–394 p. With two pages of publisher's titles bound at the end.

130 × 195 × 25 mm. 1490.b.9.

Yellow endpapers and pastedowns. Binder's ticket on lower pastedown: '| Bound by | Josiah Westley | London. |' Brown fine rib vertical-grain cloth. Both covers identically blocked in blind, with fillets on the borders and a grapevine pattern on the corners. The upper cover has vignette blocked in gold, featuring two columns blocked in gold. The words 'Thebes' and 'Athens' are blocked in relief at the base of the columns. Medallions containing figures representing Nineveh and Rome are blocked to the left and right, with the words: 'Nineveh' and 'Rome' blocked in gold underneath. Branches and leaves form a lyre at top of the columns. The words 'Ruins of' are blocked in gold above a hatch gold pyramid. The word: '| Many |' is blocked in gold within the pyramid. The word: '| Lands |' is blocked in relief within the gold base of the pyramid. Underneath this, the curling stems and small leaves that surround the columns and the pyramid then form into a circular snake holding its own tail. An hour glass is blocked in gold within the circle formed by the snake. Signed 'JL' as a monogram in gold, at the base of vignette. The spine is blocked in gold and in blind and in relief. Two fillets are blocked in blind at the head and four fillets are in blind at the tail. The blockwork in blind and in relief forms four panels down the spine, with a single fillet in blind enclosing each panel. Leaves , a diamond and a quatrefoil are blocked in relief within each panel. Between the first and second panel, the words: '| Michell's | Ruins of | Many | Lands. |' are blocked in gold. Between the third and fourth panels, the words: '| Second | edition. |' are blocked in gold.

King, *JL* p. 240. Pantazzi, *JL* p. 263. Copy illustrated bound in 'Green fine ribbed silky cloth. Bound by Josiah Westley'.

106 Leighton, John

Andersen, Hans Christian. *Pictures of Sweden.* London: Richard Bentley, New Burlington Street, 1851. London: Printed by Schulze and Co., 13, Poland Street. iv, 324 p.

128 × 205 × 30 mm. 10280.c.19.

Light yellow endpapers and pastedowns. Binder's ticket on the lower pastedown: '| Bound by | Josiah Westley, | adjoining 'The Times' Office | London. |' Olive green fine rib vertical-grain cloth. Both covers are blocked identically in blind and in relief. Three fillets are blocked on the borders, with an inner decorative surround, of leaves and branches blocked in relief. This copy has no spine. The covers are not signed.

Ball, *App.* 51e. States that the spine has Leighton's monogram.

107 Leighton, John

Limner, Luke *pseud.* [i.e. John Leighton.] *The rejected contributions to the Great Exhibition of all nations. Collected by Luke Limner, Esq. With the classes in which they will not be found. If the public maintain that many of the articles are not rejected, but still occupy distinguished positions, the collector distinctly states it is no fault of his – they ought to have been.* London: Ackermann & Co, Strand, [1851]. London: Printed by Leighton Bros. 8 plates.

230 × 145 × 5 mm. 012331.de.79(2).

The cover states: 'Seventy odd illustrations. Price one shilling. An edition upon large paper. India proofs, 2/6.' The upper cover is of plain paper, printed in black. The title and sub-title are printed within a lithograph of the facade of the central bar-

rel-vaulted transept of the Hyde Park Crystal Palace. To either side of the transept is an angel, left, blowing a horn saying 'Puff', and, on the right, a winged Mercury with the word 'Speed' printed alongside. The figures of 'Paxton' and 'O[wen] Jones' stand on either side of the transept, at roof level. Each holds a book: Paxton's is 'Chatsworth'. Jones holds 'Alhambra'. The sub-title is in the shape of a flag, draped in front of the building. Below it, is a crowd of people, many comically depicted, who are swarming in and out of the Crystal Palace.

King, *JL* p. 235. Pantazzi, *JL* p. 273.

108 Leighton, John

May, Emily Juliana. *Louis' school days: a story for boys.* Bath: Binns and Goodwin; London: Whittaker and Co.; Hall, Virtue, and Co; Simpkin, Marshall, and Co.; and Hamilton, Adams, and Co.; Edinburgh: Oliver and Boyd; Dublin: John Robertson and Co., Grafton Street, 1851. Bath: Printed by Binns and Goodwin. vii, 340 p. With sixteen pages of publisher's titles bound at the end.

110 × 176 × 28 mm. 12805.c.51.

Pink endpapers and pastedowns, printed with a pattern of holly-like leaves and flowers. Mauve morocco vertical-grain cloth. Both covers have the same border and corner blocking in blind. There is a single fillet blocked on the borders, with small 'rococo' decorative patterns blocked on the corners. On the upper cover, the central vignette is blocked in gold and in relief. At the head, '| Louis' | school | days |' are blocked in gold in rustic lettering. Between the words: 'school' and 'days', a hand holds a ribbon, which is attached to a medal below. This is blocked as a gold lettering-piece. Within the medal, the words: '| Ashfield House | To | Louis | Mortimer | for | good | conduct. | Dr Wilkinson. |' are blocked in relief. Underneath, and to either side of the medal, is blocked a scroll-shaped gold lettering-piece, with the motto: 'Bear ye one anothers burdens and so fulfil the law of Christ' blocked in relief inside. The title letters, the medal and the scroll are all surrounded by small stems and leaves, all blocked in gold. Signed 'JL' in gold as a monogram at the base of the vignette. The spine is blocked in gold. The design is of linking branches, ending in leaves, which form three circular and oval patterns, within which further decoration is blocked. At the head, a bell and small birds are blocked. Underneath this, the words: '| Louis' | school | days |' are blocked in gold in rustic letters. Beneath, a small rectangular gold lettering-piece is blocked , with the word: '| Study |' blocked in relief inside. Underneath this, an open book is blocked with a cross above it. At the tail: '| Bath Binns & Goodwin | London Hall & Co. |' are blocked in gold.

Dry, *JL* no. 27.

109 Leighton, John

The Birth-day gift: a Christmas and New Year's present. By Agnes Strickland, Alan Cunningham, W. C Taylor, L.L.D. W. H. Harrison, Leitch Ritchie, G. P. R. James, Alfred Tennyson, J. A. St. John, T. Crofton Croker, T. K. Hervey, Thomas Miller, Mrs. Abdy, Sarah Stickney, Emma Roberts. With Beautifully Finished Engravings. London: George Routledge and Co. Farringdon Street, [1852]. North Shields: Printed by Philipson and Hare. vii, 316 p., 10 plates.

104 × 168 × 22 mm. 12354.b.16.

Text sewn on two sawn-in cords. Gilt edges. Yellow endpapers and pastedowns. Binder's ticket on lower pastedown: '| Leighton | Son & | Hodge, | Shoe Lane | London. |' Blue wave diagonal-grain cloth. Both covers blocked identically in blind on the borders and on the corners. Two fillets are blocked on the borders, the outer thick, the inner thin. Sprigs of ivy leaves and berries are blocked in blind on each corner. The upper cover central vignette is blocked in gold. It shows a plant growing from a bulb, and roots. The plant has unfurling leaves and four flower heads. The figure of a lady emerges out of the leaves. Her arms are held aloft, her hair flows out behind her. In her right hand is a jug, with drops of water below it. Water droplets are also below the lady's left hand. A quarter moon and a five-point star are blocked in gold above the lady. Signed 'JL' in gold as separate letters at the base of the vignette. The spine is blocked in gold. It shows a basket containing rose flowers, which hangs from ribbons at the head. Rose leaves, flowers and petals are tipped out of the basket, and 'fall down' the spine. The title: '| The | Birth-Day | Gift |' is blocked in gold underneath the rose basket. The rose leaves, and petals are being caught by a young girl, blocked near the base, who is kneeling on a cushion, and holds her apron to catch them. Strapwork is blocked in gold underneath the girl.

Dry, *JL* no. 31.

110 Leighton, John

The winter's wreath; a literary album and Christmas and New Year's present; with beautifully finished engravings. London: George Routledge & Co., Farringdon Street, [1852]. Brampton: Robert Latimer, Printer, Front Street. viii, 316 p., 9 plates.

105 × 166 × 21 mm. 12354.b.34.

Gilt edges. Yellow endpapers and pastedowns. Binder's ticket on lower pastedown: '| Leighton | Son & | Hodge, | Shoe Lane | London. |' Red morocco vertical-grain cloth. The same design is blocked in blind on the borders and corners of both covers. Two fillets are blocked on the borders. Ivy leaves, stems, and berries are blocked on the corners. The central vignette is blocked in gold on the upper cover. It shows a maiden arising out of a lily plant, which has its roots showing at the base, The maiden is watering the flowers, a jug in her right hand. A moon and a star are blocked above the maiden's head. Signed 'JL' in gold as separate letters at the base of the vignette. The spine is blocked in gold. A basket, blocked at the head, has been tipped over, with roses tumbling down the spine from it. '| The

Winter's | Wreath | ' blocked in gold in fanciful letters, near the head.

Dry, *JL* no. 59.

111 Leighton, John

FIG. 11

Buckley, Theodore Alois William. *The great cities of the ancient world, in their Glory and their Desolation. With illustrations.* London: G. Routledge & Co., 2, Farringdon Street, 1852. London: Printed by Stewart and Murray, Old Bailey. viii, 380 p., 8 plates. With eight pages of publisher's advertisements bound at the end.

110 × 180 × 30 mm. 1309.b.32.

In the publisher's titles at the end: . . . 'Fols. 8vo., cloth, emblematically gilt, plain edges, 3s. 6d.'

Rebound in 1995. Binder's ticket on lower pastedown: '| Leighton | Son & | Hodge, | Shoe Lane | London. |'. Red morocco vertical-grain cloth. Both covers blocked identically in blind on the borders. Four fillets are blocked on the borders: 1. a single fillet; 2. three more fillets which interlock at the centre sides, the centre head and the centre tail, and also on the corners. The upper cover has a central vignette blocked in gold, featuring a globe surmounted by a castellated crown. The title word: '| Ancient |' is blocked in gold above the globe. The words: '| Cities of |' are blocked in relief inside the globe. The words: '| The world |' are blocked in gold beneath the globe. The spine is blocked in gold. Fillets delineate panels on the spine. In panel one, a crown is blocked in gold. In panel two, the words: '| Ancient | cities | of | the world |' are blocked in gold. In panel three, a heron is perched on an ancient column, at the edge of water. Signed 'JL' in gold as separate letters at base of spine. [The 1878 edition is at 1295.b.26., and is not signed.]

FIG. 11

—— Another copy. London: G. Routledge & Co., 2, Farringdon Street, 1852. London: Printed by Stewart & Murray, Old Bailey. viii, 380 p., 8 plates.

105 × 167 × 30 mm. 010005.e.69.

The plates are hand coloured. In the publisher's titles on the endpapers of Macfarlane's 'Life of Marlborough', BL shelfmark 1452.b.47., this work is offered in the following binding styles:

> . . . 'cloth, emblematically gilt, 380 pages, 4s.
> The same edition, cloth, gilt edges, 4s. 6d.
> The same edition, with plates coloured 5s. 6d.
> The same edition, morocco extra, different patterns, 9s.'

Gilt edges. Yellow endpapers and pastedowns. Written on the upper pastedown: '| Presented to | Master Thomas Weston, | of Hackney, Middlesex, | by his cousin | Henry Whalley | Of Middleton, Lancashire, | this 15th. May 1856. |' Binder's ticket on lower pastedown: '| Leighton | Son & | Hodge, | Shoe Lane | London. |'. Blue ripple horizontal-grain cloth. Both covers are blocked identically in blind. Two fillets are blocked on the borders, the outer thick, the inner thin. There is a leaf and flower pattern blocked on the borders and on the corners. The upper cover has a central vignette blocked in gold, featuring a globe surmounted by a castellated crown. The title word: '| Ancient |' is blocked in gold above the globe. The words: '| Cities of |' are blocked in relief inside the globe. The words: '| The world |' are blocked in gold beneath the globe. The spine is blocked in gold. Fillets delineate panels on the spine. In panel one, a crown is blocked in gold. In panel two, the words: '| Ancient | cities | of | the world |' are blocked in gold. In panel three, a heron is perched on an ancient column, at the edge of water. Signed 'JL' in gold as separate letters as base of spine.

Dry, *JL* no. 33

112 Leighton, John

Flygare, afterwards Carlen, Emilie. *Ivar: or the Skuts-Boy. Translated from the Swedish, By Professor A.L. Krause.* London: Office of the National Illustrated Library, 227, Strand, 1852. London: Savill and Edwards, Printers, Chandos Street, Covent Garden. xi, 318 p. With one page of publisher's titles bound at the end.

127 × 196 × 21 mm. 12580.d.13.

The frontispiece is engraved by Edmund Evans.

Yellow endpapers and pastedowns. Binder's ticket on lower pastedown: ' | Leighton | Son & | Hodge, | Shoe Lane | London. | ' Pink rib vertical-grain cloth. Both covers blocked identically on the borders, on the corners and on the sides, in

blind on the lower cover, and in silver on the upper. Three fillets are blocked on the borders, with half-circles blocked on the corners, the centre of the sides, and on the head and the tail. Straps are blocked also on the corners. Inside the border blocking, a symmetrical design shows the curling stems, leaves and flowers of fuchsias. The fuchsia flower heads have five stamens, which are greatly lengthened. This is typical of Leighton of this period. (See BL P.P.6965, The book of home beauty. Putnam, 1852.) The stems of the fuchsias form a central 'hour-glass' frame. On the upper cover, the words: 'Ivar | or the | Skjuts = Boy | [rule] | A tale | by | Emile Carlen | ' are blocked in silver. The spine is blocked in silver. From the head downwards, the decoration is: three vine leaves; a fillet in silver; the title: 'Ivar | or the | Skjuts – Boy | [rule] | Emile Carlen | ' blocked in silver; a fillet in silver; vine leaves and branches of grapes grow up around a pole from the base; signed 'JL' in silver as separate letters in a small circle at the tail.

113 Leighton, John

Kennedy, Jane. *Light hearts and happy days: or, tales of wisdom for children and youth.* Bath: Binns and Goodwin. London: Whittaker and Co.; Edinburgh: Oliver and Boyd; Dublin: J. McGlashan, [1852]. Bath: Printed by Binns and Goodwin. [Three stories paginated separately.] With six pages of publisher's titles bound at the end.
108 × 140 × 20 mm. 12805.c.48.

Three stories in one volume. Mrs Shenstone's birthday – 70 p., 1 plate. Arthur Seymour – 80 p., 1 plate. The sister's retaliation – 91 p., 1 plate. All plates: 'Printed in colours by Binns and Goodwin, Bath'.

Edges speckled with red ink. Yellow endpapers and pastedowns. Binder's ticket on lower pastedown: '| Leighton | Son & | Hodge, | Shoe Lane | London. | ' Red cord vertical-grain cloth. The same design is blocked in blind on the borders and on the corners of both covers. There is a tracery of small thin stems and leaves blocked in relief on the corners and on the sides, with straps blocked in blind on the inner border. On the upper cover, within the central frame, a vignette is blocked in gold. This shows a volcano in eruption and a young man thrown off a horse. The title words: '| Light hearts | & | happy days | ' are blocked above and below the man and the horse, in rustic lettering. Signed 'JL' in gold as a monogram at the base of the vignette. The spine design is the same as BL 12805.e.36., 'The Westons'. [There is no lettering discernible at the base of the spine of 12805.c.48.] The title: Light | hearts | and | happy | days | ' is blocked on the spine in gold, within a square formed by a single gold fillet.

Dry, *JL* no. 41. Tanselle, *BDP* p. 99, no. 306.

114 Leighton, John

PLATE XXIII

Kirkland, Caroline Matilda. *The book of home beauty. With twelve portraits of American ladies, from drawings by Charles Martin Esq., engraved on steel by eminent artists.* New York: G.P. Putnam, 155, Broadway, 1852. [New York]: John F. Trow, Printer, 49 Ann-street. 6, 145 p., 13 plates.
246 × 315 × 30 mm. P.P.6965.

Gilt edges. Bevelled boards. The endpapers and pastedowns are decorated with red shells, against a gold background. Black pebble-grain leather. The turn-ins are blocked in gold with a repeating pattern of stems, buds and leaves. Both covers are blocked identically in gold. On the borders, six fillets are blocked. In the middle of these fillets, a repeating leaf and stem pattern is blocked. There are two fillets blocked on the inner border with small strapwork on the corners. The design of the central rectangle is based upon interlacing arched stems, leaves and fuchsias. The central arch formed by the stems and the leaves is stylistically close to plate 34 [XXXIV] in 'Suggestions in Design', 1853, entitled 'Fanciful superficial pattern'. Six 'portrait frames' hang from the branches, in three pairs. The stems come out from an artist's palette blocked near the base. There are ten fuchsias in the design, whose five-stamened flowers are a feature. The words: '| The | Book | of | Home | Beauty | ' are blocked in gothic letters on the centre. Above the title, a shield is blocked, which contains United States stars and stripes. Signed 'JL' in gold as separate letters at the base of the palette. The spine is divided into six panels by bands. Each panel has the same decoration of a centre-piece and four spiral-shapes blocked in gold in small tools, within a panel formed by two fillets. The title: '| The | Book | of | Home | Beauty | ' is blocked on the second panel.

Dry, *JL* no. 43.

115 Leighton, John

Lynch, Henry, *Mrs. The mountain pastor.* London: Published for the Author by Darton & Co., Holborn Hill, 1852. London: E. Varty, Printer, 27 & 15, Camomile Street, Bishopsgate. xiii, 214 p. With one page of publisher's titles bound at the end.
110 × 175 × 20 mm. 4415.d.45.

Yellow endpapers and pastedowns. Binder's ticket on lower pastedown: '| Bound | by | Charles H. Clarke. | [2]5 Bouverie St. Fleet St. | London | '. Dark green morocco horizontal-grain cloth. Both covers are blocked in blind with an identical design. There are two fillets blocked on the borders, and scroll patterns blocked on the corners. The upper cover has a central vignette blocked in gold. The title: '| The Mountain | Pastor | ' is blocked in gold, in rustic letters, above and below the central decoration. The centre shows a pastor, seated on a branch, surrounded by curling branches and tendrils, and ivy-shaped leaves. Signed 'JL' in gold as a monogram at the base of the vignette. The spine is blocked in gold. A single gold fillet is blocked on the perimeter. From the head downwards, the decoration is: a branch and leaves; the title: '| The | Mountain | Pastor | ' in gold in rustic letters; a candle, blocked in gold, is divided into seven panels, with quatrefoils blocked in relief in each panel; the candle is surrounded by leaves, tendrils and branches. Signed 'JL' at the tail in gold as a monogram.

Dry, *JL* no. 45.

116 Leighton, John

Macfarlane, Charles. *A life of Marlborough. In four books.* London: G. Routledge & Co., Farringdon Street, 1852. London: Stewart and Murray, Old Bailey. viii, 326 p., 2 plates. The plates are signed 'Geo. Mesom'. With two pages of publisher's titles bound at the end.

110 × 177 × 27 mm. 1452.b.47.

Yellow endpapers and pastedowns, with publisher's titles printed on them. Blue morocco horizontal-grain cloth. Both covers are blocked in blind with the same design on the borders and corners. There are two fillets blocked on the borders; with curling stem and leaf decorations blocked in the corners. (This is the same blocking as on 'Guizot's moral tales'.) The central vignette on the upper cover is blocked in blind. The words: '| Macfarlane's | Marlborough |' are blocked at the head and at the tail. The words: '| Life of the Duke of |' are blocked on either side of the shield showing the royal coat of arms. The word '| Blenheim |' is blocked in blind above the shield. The spine is blocked in gold and in relief. A sword runs from tail to the head. Around the blade of the sword is a ribbon-pennant, blocked as a gold lettering-piece. Within the pennant, the words: '| Macfarlane's | Life | of | Marlborough |' are blocked in relief. Signed 'JL' in gold as separate letters at the base of the sword handle.

Dry, *JL* no. 46.

117 Leighton, John

Meulan, afterwards, Guizot, Elisabeth Charlotte Pauline de. *Moral tales. Translated from the French, by Mrs. L. Burke. With illustrations by O. R. Campbell.* London: George Routledge and Co., Farringdon Street, 1852. [London]: Cox (Brothers) and Wyman, Printers, Great Queen Street. v, 426 p, 8 plates.

110 × 176 × 35 mm. 12510.c.32.

The plates are engraved by Dalziel. One of 'Routledge's Illustrated standard juveniles'.

Yellow endpapers and pastedowns, with publisher's titles printed on them. Blue wave diagonal-grain. Both covers have borders and corners blocked identically in blind. Two fillets are blocked on the borders, and curling stems and leaves on the corners. The upper cover has a central vignette blocked in gold and in relief. It shows an oval writing tablet, blocked as a hatched gold lettering-piece. Within it, '| Guizot's | moral | tales |' are blocked in relief. Beneath this, a hand, clasping a quill, is holding the handle of the writing tablet. Stems and small leaves are blocked in gold around the centre. The veins of the leaves are picked out in relief. Signed 'JL' in gold as separate letters at the base of the vignette. The spine is blocked in gold. There is a single gold fillet blocked around the perimeter. The words: '| Guizot's | moral | tales |' are blocked at the head within a rectangle formed by a single fillet. The remainder of the spine is blocked with curling leaves, stems, flower heads, all coming out of a vase shape at the base. Signed 'JL' in gold as a monogram near the tail.

Dry, *JL* no. 40.

118 Leighton, John

Nieritz, Carl Gustav. *The little drummer; or, filial affection: a story of the Russian campaign. Translated from the German of Gustav Nieritz, by H. W. Dulcken. With four illustrations, drawn by Gilbert, engraved by Dalziels.* London: Addey and Co., 21, Old Bond Street, 1852. London: Thompson and Davidson, Printers, 19, Great St. Helens. viii, 132 p., 4 plates. With twenty pages of publisher's titles bound at the end.

113 × 177 × 14 mm. 12551.c.10.

Printed on page eight of the publisher's titles: ' Foolscap 8vo., 2s. 6d. cloth gilt.'

Light yellow endpapers and pastedowns. Red morocco diagonal-grain cloth. Both covers are blocked identically in blind. Two fillets are blocked on the borders, the inner with small squares blocked on the corners. The design on the centre is of interlocking stems and trefoils, with a 'spade-shape' being formed by the design. The design on the covers is unsigned. The spine is blocked in gold. There is a single fillet blocked at the head; then a bird; then the title words: '| The | little | drummer |', in rustic letters. From the tail upwards, a tree is blocked, its roots showing at the base. The leaves of the tree are thin, pointed. At the top of the tree is a bird's nest with three chicks. The mother above the nest is about to land. Signed 'JL' in gold as separate letters in the roots of the tree near the tail. The Routledge edition of 1856 is on blue morocco horizontal-grain cloth, Unsigned. BL shelfmark: 12805.c.36.

Dry, *JL* no. 48.

119 Leighton, John

Periodical Publications – *London. Peter Parley's annual. A Christmas and New Year's Present for Young People.* [Edited by W. Martin.] London: Darton and Co., 58 Holborn Hill, and all Booksellers, 1852. London: Printed by J.O. Clarke, 121, Fleet Street, and Raquet Court. vii, 384 p., 5 plates. With four pages of advertisements bound at the end.

124 × 155 × 34 mm. P.P.6750 [1852.]

The half title is a coloured plate and signed: 'T. H. Nicholson del. Printed in colours by W. B. Collins. W. G. Mason Sc.'

Gilt edges. Red morocco vertical-grain cloth. Both covers blocked identically in blind on the borders, the corners and on the sides. Three fillets are blocked on the borders, one thick between two thin. Holly branches, stems, leaves and berries are blocked on the lower corners and the tail. Single branches, leaves and berries rise up each side, forming an arch on the top corners and on the head. Signed 'JL' in blind as a monogram on the centre of the tail. The upper cover has a central vignette blocked in gold. It shows a boy in an armchair reading a book. A hat and a coat are blocked on the right of the armchair. At the base of the armchair: on the left, a stick and a book entitled; '| Geography |'; on the right, two books are blocked, entitled: '| Astronomy | Poetry |' – the three titles are blocked in relief on the spines of the books, which are blocked as gold lettering-pieces. A tracery of curling stems and small leaves surrounds

the chair. The title: '| Peter | Parley's | Annual |' is blocked in gold in rustic lettering above and on each side of the centre. Signed 'JL' in gold as a monogram at the base of the vignette. [Original spine missing.]

Dry, *JL* no. 50.

120 Leighton, John

Redding, Cyrus. *Every man his own butler. Second edition.* London: William Tegg & Co., 85, Queen Street, Cheapside, 1852. London: Bradbury and Evans, Printers, Whitefriars. xx, 143 p. With thirty-two pages of publisher's titles bound at the end.

105 × 164 × 21 mm. 1037.b.49.

Yellow endpapers and pastedowns. Green rib vertical-grain cloth. The same design is blocked in blind on the borders and corners of both covers. There are two fillets blocked on the borders. Inside this, there is a repeating stem pattern, with a single flower blocked on each corner. Within this, another fillet is blocked on the inner border, with a single strap on each corner. The upper cover has a central vignette blocked in gold. This shows an oval frame composed of vine stems, vine leaves and bunches of grapes. Vine tendrils hold a wine cup on each side of the central oval, and a wine bottle is blocked at the base of the oval. In the middle is a butler, wine glass in his right hand, a candle in his left hand. The title words: '| Every man | his own | butler. |' are blocked in gold in 'rustic style' lettering, above, below and each side of the butler. Signed 'JL' in gold as a monogram at the base of the vignette. The spine is blocked in gold and in relief. It is divided into five panels by groups of two fillets, with repeating dots blocked in relief between them. A single fillet is blocked in blind at the head and at the tail.

The 1839 Whitaker edition is at BL 1037.b.30. Red rib vertical-grain cloth. Upper cover gold vignette. Unsigned.

Dry, *JL* no. 51.

121 Leighton, John

Sharpe, Richard Scrafton. *The Westons or, scenes in a village consisting of Cottage Prose and Cottage Poetry. Second edition.* London: Parry and Co., 32 and 33 Leadenhall Street, [1852]. London: Savill and Edwards, Printers, Chandos Street, Covent Garden. xii, 179 p., 4 plates.

105 × 137 × 16 mm. 12805.e.36.

The plates are engraved by Leighton Bros. This work advertised in the rear of 'All the best', BL 12805.c.55. as 'square 16mo., 3s. cloth, gilt edges'.

Gilt edges. Light yellow endpapers and pastedowns. Brown ripple horizontal-grain cloth. Both covers are blocked in blind with the same design on the borders, corners and the sides. There are two fillets blocked on the borders. The stems of a rush-like plant curl out and upwards from the centre tail, with leaves and flowers blocked towards the top. The whole forms a frame. On the upper cover, a central vignette is blocked in gold within this frame. It shows a boy reading, seated on an upturned bucket. A hoop is propped up on the small tree behind him, and his feathered hat is hanging on a branch above him. The stems and small leaves of the tree curl around him. Signed 'JL' in gold as a monogram at the base of the vignette. The spine is blocked in gold. It shows a shrub, growing from a pot blocked at the base. On the pot, the words: '| Parry | & | Co. |' are blocked in relief. The stem, leaves, and flowers of the shrub are blocked all the way up the spine to the head, with the title: '| The | Westons |' blocked in gold near the head. Signed 'JL' in gold as a monogram at the tail. Apart from the title, the blocking is the same as for BL 12805.c.56. 'Edith Templeton'; and BL 12805.c.55. 'All the best'.

Dry, *JL* no. 49c.

122 Leighton, John

Stebbing, Henry. *The Christian graces in olden time. A series of female portraits. With Poetical Illustrations.* London: David Bogue, Fleet Street, 1852. London: Printed by G. Barclay, Castle St., Leicester Sq. 36 p., 16 plates.

190 × 280 × 20 mm. 11647.g.11.

Gilt edges. Bevelled boards. Yellow endpapers and pastedowns. Binder's ticket on lower pastedown: '| Leighton | Son & | Hodge | Shoe Lane | London. | Est. 1767. |' Green ripple vertical-grain cloth. Both covers blocked identically in gold and in relief. Lattice-work is blocked in gold on the borders. On the corners and on the sides, a tracery of thin stems, leaves and flowers is blocked in gold. The stems and small leaves curl around larger flower heads. There is a recessed oval central panel. Around its perimeter, a repeating pattern of crowns and pointed leaves is blocked in gold. Within the recessed panel, a wide border is blocked, with the small leaf and flowers pattern blocked in relief. Inside this, more small decoration is blocked in relief. On the centre of the panel, a small rose is blocked in gold, with a circle of stars above it. Signed 'JL' in gold as a monogram on the centre of the base of the upper cover. The spine is fully blocked in gold. The decoration is of intertwining long thin plant stems, with flower heads and small leaves blocked from head to tail. The title words: '| The | Christian | graces | in olden | time |' is blocked in gold within a panel 'hanging' from stems near the head. [The original gutta percha binding is in pieces.]

Dry, *JL* no. 54.

123 Leighton, John

Sunshine, *Sir* Shadowy *pseud. New stories suggested by Old Rhymes. With illustrations. A book for young people . . . By Sir Shadowy Sunshine, Knight of the Order of Light and Shade.* London: Darton and Co., Holborn Hill, 1852. London: Stevens and Co., Printers, Bell Yard, Temple Bar. 188 p. With four pages of publisher's titles bound at the end.

122 × 162 × 27 mm. 12805.e.37.

Yellow endpapers and pastedowns. Binder's ticket on the lower pastedown: '| Bound by | Bone & Son, | 76, Fleet Street, |

London. | ' Blue wave diagonal-grain cloth. Both covers blocked identically in blind on the borders, corners and sides. Two fillets are blocked on the borders. A decorative pattern of stems, three-leafed plants and berries is blocked in blind on the sides and on each corner. On the upper cover, a central vignette is blocked in gold. The title: ' | New | stories suggested | by old rhymes | ' is blocked in rustic lettering above and below the central decoration, which shows a boy, a feather in his hat, and a dog seated on a branch, with leaves and fruit blocked in gold around them. Signed 'JL' in gold as a monogram at the base of the vignette. The spine is blocked in gold. From the head downwards, the decoration is: a curling branch supports three books, whose titles on the spines are: ' | Tales | Pictures | Rhymes | ' blocked in relief; the title: ' | New | stories | suggested | by | old rhymes | ' blocked in gold in rustic lettering; a girl is blocked with her back to the viewer, standing on a foot cushion, with her outstretched right hand holding a branch which curls around her; signed 'JL' in gold as separate letters underneath the foot cushion.

Dry, *JL* no. 55. Tanselle, *BDP* no. 106ae.

124 Leighton, John

Tayler, Charles Benjamin. *Thankfulness: a narrative. Comprising passages from the diary of the Rev. Allan Temple. Third edition.* London: Sampson Low, 169 , Fleet Street, 1852. [London]: Printed by Mary S. Rickerby, Sherbourn Lane, King William Street, City. vii, 200 p. With eleven pages of publisher's titles bound at the end.
112 × 180 × 15 mm. 4416.g.31.

On page 10 of the publisher's titles: 'Third edition. Fcap., cloth 2s. 6d. * . . . Volumes marked thus * are in 'Low's Series.'

Yellow endpapers and pastedowns. Bookseller's ticket on the upper pastedown: 'Seton Bookseller Edinburgh'. Binder's ticket on lower pastedown: ' | Bound by | Bone & Son, | 76, Fleet Street, | London. | ' Maroon wave diagonal-grain cloth. Both covers are blocked identically in blind. There are two fillets blocked on the borders in blind. On the corner of each cover at the base, sprays of ivy leaves & stems are blocked in blind. Up the sides and on the upper corners, stems, leaves and flowers are blocked in blind. This decoration forms an 'onion-topped' central frame, in which a vignette is blocked in blind and in relief. It shows a bookcase with a pediment and an urn on top of the pediment. On each of three book shelves are blocked in relief the words: ' | Low's | family | series | '. Signed 'JL' in blind as a monogram near the tail. The spine is blocked in gold. Two gold fillets are blocked at the head and at the tail. The words: ' | Thankfulness | by the | Rev. C.B Tayler | ' are blocked in gold near the head. A lily plant is blocked up the spine from the tail to underneath the title. Small stars are blocked around the stems, leaves and flowers of the lily. At its base, inside a 'bulb-root' shape, the monogram of Sampson Low & Son – 'SLS' – is blocked in gold. Signed 'JL' in gold as separate letters at the base of the bulb. Underneath this, a rectangle formed by two gold fillets contains the words: ' | Sampson Low | and Son | ', blocked in gold. Two gold fillets are blocked underneath the rectangle.

Dry, *JL* no. 56.

125 Leighton, John

Toulmin, afterwards Crosland, Camilla. *Lays and legends, illustrative of English life. With illustrations by several distinguished artists.* London: George Routledge and Co., Farringdon Street, 1852. London: Spottiswoodes and Shaw, New-street-Square. viii, 194 p.
207 × 252 × 20 mm. 12354.k.3.

The colophon reads: ' | London: Printed by A. Spottiswoode, New-Street-Square. | ' The bookplate of Richard James Spiers, Oxford is on the upper pastedown.

Gilt edges. Light yellow endpapers and pastedowns. Blue ripple vertical-grain cloth. The same design is blocked in blind on the borders and on the corners of both covers. Two fillets are blocked on the borders, the outer thick, the inner thin. There are large leaf patterns blocked on each corner. The same central vignette is blocked on both covers, in blind on the lower, and in gold on the upper. It shows a double oval, on its side, with lines and small circles picked out in relief within the two principal fillets that form the ovals. On the left and the right of the oval, strapwork is blocked. At the top and bottom of the ovals, there is an elaborate pattern of plant stems, leaves and flowers, which also form straps at the ends – all blocked in gold. Signed 'JL' in gold as a monogram at the base of the vignette. The words: ' | English Life | Illustrated | ' are blocked in gold on the centre, within the oval. The spine is blocked in gold. A vase is blocked at the head. Beneath this, an oval Renaissance frame is blocked, and the words: ' | Lays | and | legends | ' are blocked within in gold. Underneath this, two more frames are blocked, then a third, with the words: ' | Camilla | Toulmin | ' in gold inside. At the tail, another frame and small decoration within it are blocked in gold.

Dry, *JL* no. 58.

126 Leighton, John

Upcher, Frances. *All for the best: or, Minnie's motto.* London: Parry and Co., Leadenhall Street, [1852]. London: Savill and Edwards, Printers, Chandos Street, Covent Garden. 185 p., 4 plates. With two pages of publisher's titles bound at the end.
106 × 137 × 15 mm. 12805.c.55.

The plates are engraved by Leighton Bros.

Gilt edges. Yellow endpapers and pastedowns. Binder's ticket on the lower pastedown: ' | Leighton | Son & | Hodge, | Shoe Lane | London. | ' Green wave diagonal-grain cloth. Both covers are blocked in blind with the same design on the borders, corners and the sides. There are two fillets blocked on the borders. The stems of a rush-like plant curl out and upwards from the base, with leaves and flowers blocked towards the top. The whole forms a frame. On the upper cover, a central

vignette is blocked in gold within this frame. It shows a boy reading, seated on a bucket. A hoop is propped up on the small tree behind him, and his feathered hat is hanging on a branch above him. The stems and small leaves of the tree curl around him. Signed 'JL' in gold as a monogram at the base of the vignette. The spine is blocked in gold. It shows a shrub, growing from a pot blocked at the tail. On the pot, the words: '| Parry | & | Co. |' are blocked in relief. The stem, leaves, and flowers of the shrub are blocked all the way up the spine to the head, with the title: '| All for | the | best |' blocked in gold near the head. Signed 'JL' in gold as a monogram at the tail. Advertised in the rear of 'Edith Templeton', BL 12805.c.56., as 'square 16mo., 3s. With four beautiful coloured illustrations and handsomely bound in cloth, gilt edges'. Apart from the spine title, this is the same blockwork as BL 12805.c.56., Edith Templeton, and BL 12805.e.36., The Westons.

Dry, *JL* no. 49b.

127 Leighton, John

Upcher, Frances. *Edith Templeton: or, a little girl's duty. Third edition.* London: Parry and Co., Leadenhall Street, [1852]. London: Savill and Edwards, Printers, Chandos Street, Covent Garden. iv, 186 p., 4 plates. With two pages of publisher's titles bound at the end.

105 × 137 × 16 mm. 12805.c.56.

The colour plates are engraved by Leighton Bros.

Gilt edges. Light yellow endpapers and pastedowns. Binder's ticket on lower pastedown: '| Leighton | Son & | Hodge, | Shoe Lane | London. |' Blue wave diagonal-grain cloth. Both covers are blocked in blind with the same design on the borders, corners and the sides. There are two fillets blocked on the borders. The stems of a rush-like plant curl out and upwards from the base, with leaves and flowers blocked towards the top. The whole forms a frame. On the upper cover, a central vignette is blocked in gold within this frame. It shows a boy reading, seated on a bucket. A hoop is propped up on the small tree behind him, and his feathered hat is hanging on a branch above him. The stems and small leaves of the tree curl around him. Signed 'JL' in gold as a monogram at the base of the vignette. The spine is blocked in gold. It shows a shrub, growing from a pot blocked at the tail. On the pot, the words: '| Parry | & | Co. |' are blocked in relief. The stem, leaves, and flowers of the shrub are blocked all the way up the spine to the head, with the title: '| Edith | Templeton |' blocked in gold near the head. Signed 'JL' in gold as a monogram at the tail. Advertised in the rear of this volume, as 'Square 16mo., 3s. With Four new and beautiful Coloured illustrations, and Handsomely bound in cloth, gilt edges'. Part of the 'Frances Upcher's Juvenile Works'. Apart from the title, this has the same blockwork as BL 12805.c.55. 'All for the Bset', and BL 12805.e.36. 'The Westons'.

Dry, *JL* no. 49a.

128 Leighton, John

Braggadocio: A Tale for boys and girls. With Illustrations. London: George Routledge and Co. Farringdon Street, 1853. London: Printed by Levey, Robson, and Franklyn, Great New Street, Fetter Lane. [1], 190 p., 4 plates.

98 × 158 × 14 mm. 12806.c.4.

The plates are signed with the monogram 'JD' and 'Dalziel'. Beige endpapers and pastedowns. Dark brown net-grain cloth. Both covers identically blocked in blind on the borders and on the corners. Two fillets are blocked on the borders. A cartouche is blocked at the head and at the tail. A pattern of leaves and stems is blocked around each cartouche on the head, the tail, and corners and on the sides. [This is the same design as for BL 12805.f.38. – Uncle Frank's home stories.] The upper cover vignette is blocked in gold. '| Braggadocio |' is blocked in gold on the centre. Above and below this, small groups of stems, leaves and flowers are blocked in gold. Signed 'JL' in gold as separate letters at the base of the vignette. The spine is blocked in gold. From the head downwards, the decoration is: two fillets, zig-zag and dots in gold; a gold fillet; the title: '| Braggodocio |' blocked in gold (the letters are very close together on the thin spine); a gold fillet; stem and bud decoration; zig-zag and dots and two fillets – all in gold. Blue date stamp: 18 FE[BRUARY 18]53.

Another copy of this edition is at BL 12806.d.9. Same title page. The same illustrations are bound in a different order throughout the text. Date stamped: 9 NO[VEMBER 18]55. Red ink speckled edges. Yellow endpapers and pastedowns. Red wave diagonal-grain cloth. Unsigned design.

129 Leighton, John

Laura Temple. A tale for the young . . . London: George Routledge and Co. Farringdon Street, 1853. London: M'Corquodale and Co., Printers, London, Works – Newton. 231 p.

104 × 167 × 25 mm. 12806.c.38.

Yellow endpapers and pastedowns. Binder's ticket on lower pastedown: '| Leighton | Son & | Hodge, | Shoe Lane | London. |' Blue wave diagonal-grain cloth. Both covers are blocked identically in blind on the borders and on the corners. Two fillets are blocked on the borders, one thick, one thin. A spray of leaves and flowers is blocked on each corner. The upper cover has a central vignette blocked in gold. It shows a 'double bowl' shape, defined by a fillet in gold with repeating dots within it blocked in relief. Around the 'bowls', ivy leaves, stems and berries are blocked in gold. Within the 'bowl', the title words: '| Laura | Temple |' are blocked in gold in rustic lettering. Signed 'JL' in gold as separate letters near the base of the vignette. The spine is blocked in gold. Ivy leaves, stems and berries are blocked in gold from the tail to the head. The stems form an oval frame near the head. Inside this, the words: '| Laura | Temple |' are blocked in gold.

Dry, *JL* no. 100.

130 Leighton, John

Poets of England and America; being Selections from the Best Authors of both Countries, designed as a companion to all lovers of poetry. With an introductory essay . . . London: Whittaker & Co., Ave Maria Lane. Liverpool: Edward Howell, Church Street, 1853. D. Marples, Printer, Liverpool. xxxiv, 472 p.
120 × 168 × 34 mm. 11602.c.14.

The title page has a red fillet and a black small plant decoration on its borders.

Yellow endpapers and pastedowns. Binder's ticket on the lower pastedown: '| Leighton | Son & | Hodge, | Shoe Lane | London. |' Blue morocco vertical-grain cloth. Both covers are blocked identically in blind on the borders and the corners. Two fillets are blocked on the borders. On each corner, small 'leaf-like' decoration is blocked. On the upper cover, the central vignette is blocked in gold. The centre has a circle, formed by a single gold fillet. There are four spade shapes formed by an interlocking cord blocked in gold at the head, the tail and each side. Each spade-shape contains a flower and leaves blocked in gold. Small flowers are blocked in gold between the spades. The central circle is formed by the cord and, within this, with a small gold fillet. In it, the title: '| Poets | of | England | and | America. |' is blocked in gold. Signed 'JL' in gold as separate letters at the base of the vignette. The spine is blocked in gold. A single gold fillet is blocked around the perimeter. The decoration is placed within an interlocking 'branch-shaped' fillet, which runs from head to tail. At the head, the fillet forms an oval, with leaves blocked around it. Inside, a single fuchsia flower is blocked in gold. Beneath this, the fillet forms a rectangular panel which contains the title: '| Poets | of | England | and America. |'. Two more fuchsia leaves, stems and flowers are blocked beneath the title. The fillet then forms a mandorla in the middle of the spine. This has a lyre blocked inside. Two more fuchsia leaves, stems and flowers are blocked underneath the mandorla. Small fleurs-de-lis are blocked in a rectangular frame formed by a single fillet at the tail. Signed 'JL' in gold as a monogram at the base of the mandorla.

The upper cover vignette is the same design as BL shelfmarks: 12304.b.10.; 12631.f.21.; 12807.a.55.; 12807.a.58.; 12804.b.36.

Dry, *JL* no. 94. Leighton, *SID, 1880* Plate 75, no. 1.

131 Leighton, John

Tales and sketches . . . With Twenty-Seven Illustrations. London: Addey & Co., 21, Old Bond Street, 1853. Unpaginated [B4–G4, G16.] With eight pages of publisher's titles bound at the end.
138 × 195 × 8 mm. 12806.e.17.

Both original paper covers are bound at the end. Yellow paper, printed in brown. The upper cover shows a single fillet on the border. The design shows strapwork on the corners and on the sides. On the corners and sides, rose leaves, rose stems and flowers are printed. Straps printed inside this form a central 'oval' panel. Printed inside this panel are the words: '| Books | for young readers. | Tales and sketches. | [rule] | Addey & Co. | 21. Old Bond Street | London. |'. Signed in the strap work at the base: 'Luke Limner del. H. Leighton Sc.[i.e. Henry Leighton]'. The lower cover has lists of the publisher's titles and states: 'Books for young readers. No. IV. price one shilling each'.

Dry, *JL* no. 67d.

132 Leighton, John

Archer, Richard *pseud.* [i.e. Bowman, James F.] *The island home: or, the adventures of six young Crusoes* . . . London: George Routledge and Co., Farringdon Street, 1853. London: M'Corquodale and Co., Printers, London-Works, Newton. 383 p., 4 plates.
103 × 173 × 30 mm. 12806.c.8.

The plates engraved by Dalziel. Yellow endpapers and pastedowns. Binder's ticket on lower pastedown: '| Leighton | Son & | Hodge, | Shoe Lane | London. |' Green wave diagonal-grain cloth. Both covers are blocked identically in blind on the borders and on the corners. A single fillet is blocked on the borders. On each corner, a spray of ivy leaves and berries is blocked. On the upper cover, the central vignette is blocked in gold. It shows an angel flying above a boat on water. The title: '| The | Island | Home |' is blocked in gold in fanciful letters around the angel. Small stars are blocked around the angel. Underneath the boat, the quote: '| Water, water everywhere | But not a drop to drink. |' is blocked in gold. Signed 'JL' in gold as separate letters at the base of the vignette. The spine is blocked in gold. A single gold fillet is blocked around the perimeter. The title: '| The | Island | Home |' is blocked in gold inside a panel formed by a single fillet. A palm tree is blocked from the tail to the title panel. Signed 'JL' in gold as separate letters at the base of the palm tree. The word: '| Illustrated |' is blocked in gold within a rectangle formed by two gold fillets blocked underneath the base of the palm tree. Small decoration is blocked in gold at the tail.

Dry, *JL* no. 65. Tanselle, *BDP* no. 106ae.

133 Leighton, John

Bowman, Anne. *Travels of Rolando; or, a tour around the world. Second series, containing a journey through Mesopotamia, Persia, Siberia, Kamschatka, China, and Thibet. With illustrations by William Harvey.* London: George Routledge and Co., Farringdon Street, 1853. [London]: Printed by Cox (Bros.) and Wyman, Great Queen Street. xv, 400 p., 8 plates.
110 × 174 × 30 mm. 12806.c.30.

Blue ripple horizontal-grain cloth. Both covers blocked identically in blind on the borders and on the corners. Two fillets are blocked on the borders, one thick, one thin. Sprays of ivy leaves and berries are blocked on each corner. The upper cover has a central vignette blocked in gold. It shows a Chinese pagoda roof,

adorned with bells. There are two decorated ball-lanterns on either side. Lattice work is blocked below the centre. Within the central panel, the words: '| The | travels | of | Rolando. | 2nd series. |' are blocked in gold in Chinese style lettering. Signed 'JL' in gold as separate letters at the base of the vignette. The spine is blocked in gold. A single gold fillet is blocked around the perimeter. An arch is blocked at the head. Underneath, the words: '| The | travels | of | Rolando | [rule] | Second series. |' are blocked in gold, in rustic lettering. From the tail upwards, a palm tree is blocked, with a weather vane at its top. Signed 'JL' in gold as a monogram in the roots of the tree. Below the roots at the tail, a rectangular panel is formed by a single gold fillet, with small decoration blocked in gold inside it.

The Renier Collection copy is in blue wave diagonal-grain cloth.

Dry, *JL* no. 68.

134 Leighton, John

Buckley, Theodore Alois. *The dawnings of genius exemplified and exhibited in the early lives of distinguished men.* London: G. Routledge & Co., Farringdon Street, 1853. London: Reed and Parton, Printers, Paternoster Row. viii, 408 p.,8 plates.
106 × 175 × 32 mm. 10604.c.15.

Yellow endpapers and pastedowns. Blue morocco horizontal-grain cloth. Binder's ticket on lower pastedown: '| Leighton | Son & | Hodge, | Shoe Lane | London. |' Both covers blocked identically in blind. A single fillet is blocked in blind on the borders; leaf and stem decoration on the corners. On the upper cover, a central vignette is blocked in gold. It shows a flame, with rays, blocked at the top. A wreath of leaves and small berries surrounds the title words: '| The dawnings | of | genius. |' The stems of the wreath are knotted at the base with a ribbon. Signed 'JL' in gold as a monogram at the base. The spine is blocked in gold and in relief. A single fillet is blocked in gold around the perimeter. At the head, a sun is blocked in gold, with the head of a child inside it. The title: '| The | dawnings | of | genius. |' is blocked in gold under this. The remainder of the spine is occupied by a single plant, a single flower at its head, with curling stems and leaves emanating from its main stem. A gold lettering piece in the shape of a pennant curls around the stem to the tail. In it are blocked in relief the words: '| Newton | Mozart | Chatterton |'. Signed 'JL' in gold as separate letters on either side of the base of the plant. At the tail, small decoration is blocked in gold inside a rectangle formed by a single fillet.

Dry, *JL* no. 70.

135 Leighton, John

Campbell, Pamela, *Lady. The story of an apple. Illustrated by John Gilbert.* London: George Routledge and Co. Farringdon Street, 1853. London: R.Clay, Printer, Bread Street Hill. [1], 152 p., 4 plates. With eight pages of publisher's titles bound at the front and thirty-six pages bound at the end.
108 × 175 × 16 mm. 12806.c.36.

The plates are engraved by Dalziel.

Yellow endpapers and pastedowns. Binder's ticket on lower pastedown: '| Leighton | Son & | Hodge, | Shoe Lane | London. |' Blue ripple vertical-grain cloth. The same design is blocked in blind on the borders and on the corners of both covers. Two fillets are blocked on the borders, one thick, one thin. Sprays of ivy leaves, stems and berries are blocked on each corner. The upper cover has a central vignette blocked in gold. It shows an apple tree in leaf, with fruit. Its roots at the base end in tendrils. A pennant-shaped gold lettering-piece winds around the tree. The title: '| The | story | of | an | apple. |' is blocked in relief within five rectangular gold lettering-pieces that are part of the pennant. Signed 'JL' in gold as a monogram at the base of the vignette. The spine is blocked in gold. At the head and at the tail, small decoration above and below a single fillet, blocked in gold. The title: '| The | story | of | an | apple |' is blocked in gold, in rustic lettering. Below this, an apple hangs from a cord. A thick ribbon gold lettering-piece around the cord contains the words: '| This apple was given | by Esther Regina Jones – I've 1800 to keep' blocked in relief; the apple has a face blocked within it in relief. Signed 'JL' in gold as separate letters in decoration near the tail.

Dry, *JL* no. 98.

136 Leighton, John

Draper, Bourne Hall. *The Bible story book. First and Second Series . . . Thirteenth edition.* London: Ward & Co., Paternoster Row, [1853]. London: Reed & Pardon, Printers, Paternoster Row. viii, 259 p., 15 plates. The frontispiece and half-title page plates are signed: 'W. Dickes'.
95 × 150 × 22 mm. 3127.b.15.

Some of the plates are signed: 'E. Whymper Sc.' Yellow endpapers and pastedowns. Binder's ticket on lower pastedown: '| Leighton | Son & | Hodge, | Shoe Lane | London. |' Green wave diagonal-grain cloth. Both covers blocked identically in blind on the borders. Fillets on the borders and inside form rectangular panels at the centre head, the centre tail, and two on each side. Celtic knot strapwork is blocked in relief inside these panels. On each corner, the fillets form a square, with leaves blocked in relief inside. The upper cover central vignette is blocked in gold. An ivy branch and its leaves form a panel. The title: '| Bible | story | book |' is blocked in gold inside this panel. The spine is blocked in gold. A plant, in a pot at the tail, rises all the way up the spine, showing flowers, buds and thin stems. The title: '| Bible | story | book |' is blocked near the head in gold within a square formed by a single gold fillet. Signed 'JL' in gold as a monogram at the tail, underneath the pot. [The monogram is small, 1 mm. across.]

137 Leighton, John

Elwes, Alfred. *The Richmonds' tour through Europe. Holland Norway; Sweden Denmark; Iceland Belgium. With seventeen illustrations.* London: Addey & Co., 21, Old Bond Street, 1853.

Unpaginated [1, B4–L4.] With eight pages of publisher's titles bound at the end.
137 × 194 × 10 mm. 12806.e.14.

Both original paper covers are bound at the end. Yellow paper, printed in brown. The upper cover shows a single fillet on the border. The design shows strapwork on the corners and on the sides. On the corners and sides, rose leaves, rose stems and flowers are printed. Fillets printed inside this form a central 'oval' panel. Printed inside this panel are the words: '| Books for young readers. | [rule] | The Richmonds' | tour through Europe. | Addey & Co. | 21. Old Bond Street | London. |'. Signed in the strap work at the base: 'Luke Limner del. H. Leighton Sc. [i.e. Henry Leighton]'. The lower cover has lists of publisher's titles and states: 'Books for young readers. No. II. price one shilling each'.

Dry, *JL* no. 67b.

138 Leighton, John

Ephemerides. *Blackie's Literary and Commercial Almanac [sic].* Glasgow, Edinburgh, London, and New York.: Blackie & Son, [1853–1872]. Glasgow: W. G. Blackie & Co, Printers, Villafield.
P.P.2468.cc. [1853–72]

All the paper covers spell 'Almanack' with a 'k'. The years 1853–57, 1858–61 and 1862–69 are bound in three volumes.

1853. Ninth publication. 55 × 82 × 7 mm. 72 p. Gilt edges. No lower cover. The upper white paper cover is printed in red, green and black. Four roundels on the corners – Spring, Summer, Autumn, Winter. A tree, reflecting each season, is printed in each roundel. The frame in the centre contains the title words: '| Blackie's | Literary | & Commercial | Almanack | 1853. |' The words 'Literary' and 'Almanack' are printed in red. Signed 'Luke Limner Del' in black at the centre tail of the cover.

1854. Tenth publication. 55 × 82 × 5 mm. 96 p. Gilt edges. Paper covers. Black printed on bright green-dyed paper. The upper and lower cover have a single fillet on their borders. The lower cover shows a scroll and quill; the verses of the poem: '| The Almanack to its friends |'; printed at the tail are: a military standard (with two snakes and wings at its top), an anchor and rope. The upper cover has a design of leaves on stems emerging from a vase at the base, together with the titles, as for 1853. On each leaf, a month of the year is printed. The ampersand '&' of 'literary & commercial' is printed on a sunflower in the middle. Thin strapwork printed at the base. Signed 'JL del' in black at the tail.

1855. Eleventh publication. 55 × 82 × 5 mm. 96 p. Gilt edges. Paper covers. Printed in black on pink-dyed paper. The lower cover features a mandorla with oriental decoration printed inside. The upper cover has a single fillet on the borders. The title: '| Blackie's | Literary | & Commercial | Almanack |' is printed above and below the central medallion. The medallion shows a sunflower head, with the months printed in the petals, and '1855' printed at the very centre. Signed 'JM Culloch del et lith' at the tail.

1856. Twelfth publication 55 × 82 × 5 mm. 96 p. Gilt edges. Paper covers. Printed in black on pink-dyed paper. A single fillet is printed on the borders of both covers. The lower cover shows plant decoration, with a monogram date printed inside an 'onion' shape'. The upper cover shows Father Time shaking the years off a tree. [Designer's name obscured by a label.] 'Maclure & Macdonald lith.' is printed on the right hand tail.

1857. Thirteenth publication. 55 × 82 × 5 mm. Gilt edges. Printed in black on pink-dyed paper. Two fillets are printed on the borders of both covers. The lower cover shows a dove and an olive branch between the words: '| Peace & plenty | to | 1857 |'. The upper cover shows an elderly angel, seated, an open book on his lap. The page on the left has the word: '1857'; the page on the right has the word: '1858', each date with the words: 'Past Present Future' printed above it. The design is not signed, but stylistically that of Leighton , particularly in the use of the snake, its tail in its mouth, around the centre.

1858. Fourteenth publication. 55 × 80 × 5 mm. 96 p. Printed in black on blue-dyed paper covers. Two fillets are printed on the borders of both covers. On the upper cover, the title: '| Blackie's | Literary | and Commercial | Almanack. |' is printed above and below the central medallion. The medallion shows Father Time on the sea shore, about to launch a small, toy-like, sailing boat – marked '[18]58' – onto the water. The sailing boat for 1857 is in the distance, and the boat for 1859 is on the sand beside him. '| God prosper '58 |' is printed on the edge of the medallion. Signed '| Luke Limner del |' at the base of the medallion, and '| Maclure and Macdonald lith. Glasgow, Liverpool, Manchester, & London |' at the tail.

1859. Fifteenth publication. 55 × 82 × 5 mm. 96 p. Printed in black on pink-dyed paper covers. Two fillets are printed on the borders of both covers. The title: '| Blackie's | Literary | and Commercial | Almanack. |' is printed above a central frame. This shows Father Time watching the sun rising across a lake, as '| The New Year | rises | 1859 |'. Signed at the tail: '| Luke Limner del ; Maclure and Macdonald lith. |' The lower cover has the same design as the upper; however, the words: '| The old year sinks | to rest | 1858 |' are printed with a setting sun. A lighthouse has also been inserted at the right hand side of the scene.

1860. Sixteenth publication. 55 × 80 × 5 mm. 96 p. Green dyed paper covers. Both covers have two fillets on the borders, the inner of which has straps on the corners. '| Blackie's | Literary & Commercial | Almanack |' is printed a the head. '| 1860 |' is printed at the tail, in a cartouche. On the centre, Father Time is looking at a potted shrub, which has books on its branches. Father time says: '| What! A booke | bouquet at Christ-mas? – Yes it is a hardy | little Annual that always appears | at this time. |' Signed at the tail: 'Luke Limner del. Maclure & Macdonald lith.' The lower cover has the same design as the upper, with the exception of the centre. This shows a winged

putto, a trumpet in its right hand, with '| 1860 |' on a flag attached to the trumpet. Under the putto's left arm is a copy of '| Blackie's | Almanack |'; underneath the putto is the quote: '| Prosperity to the new decade |', with '| 1860 |' underneath, printed within a cartouche.

1861. Seventeenth publication. 55 × 80 × 5 mm. 96 p. Orange dyed paper covers. The upper cover has the title: '| Blackie's | Literary & Commercial | Almanack | 1861 |' printed at the head. Below, an old man in a dressing gown is seated in a wicker chair at a desk. He holds spectacles in his left hand. Above him, an inscription reads: '| Old time rubs his spectacles | and consults his | little oracle | for 1861. |' On the desk, an open book is perched, with the words: '| Wit | & | wis | dom | 18 | 61 |' printed on the opening. A cat, with a scowling face, a globe lamp on the desk (with facial features), and an hour-glass adorn the design. Signed at the tail: '| Luke Limner del. Maclure & Macdonald lith. |' The lower cover shows a balloon in the clouds above the world. The word: '| L'anniversaire |' is printed on the balloon, with '1860' printed on the basket.

1862. Eighteenth publication. 55 × 80 × 5 mm. 96 p. Orange dyed paper covers. Two fillets are printed on the borders of both covers. The upper cover has quotations printed on the borders. At the head: '| Time is the herald of truth. |'; on the fore-edge: '| Literature is the hoarding of our ancestors. Not to be spent. |'; on the tail: '| Time and tide wait for no man |'. The centre shows a winged man with a telescope. The title: '| Blackie's | Literary & Commercial | Almanack | For the year 1862 |' is printed beside and below the man. The lower cover has a border, with four medallions containing sea motifs. On the centre is a ship with the words: '| 1862 | for the Great Exhibition |' printed on its sail. Two oarsmen hold oars; a man in the ship's crow's nest, with a feather in his hat, holds a flag with the letter 'B' printed in it.

1863. Nineteenth publication. 55 × 80 × 5 mm. Orange dyed paper covers. Both covers have two fillets printed on the borders. Within this, a diamond design is formed by a single fillet, which has single straps at the head, the tail, the centre sides. The title: '| AD | 1863. | Blackie's | Literary & Commercial | Almanack |' is printed inside the diamond, together with the monogram of Blackie, and the motto: 'Lucem libris disseminamus'. Signed 'JL' as a monogram beneath the motto. On the four inner corners are men representing the seasons, in various poses, consulting books or papers. The words accompanying these men are: 'Spring. Plant & Prune. | Summer. Work & Build. | Autumn. Trade & Store. | Winter. Tranquil Repose. |' The lower cover has the same design, with the exception of the centre. This is a mandorla, with a fruit tree printed within. Hung on the fruit tree is a ribbon, with two mottoes printed within it: '| A | good book | is a true | friend. | A | wise | author | a public | benefactor |'.

1864. Twentieth publication. 55 × 80 × 5 mm. 96 p. 'Being Leap Year'. Green dyed paper covers. The design for both covers is identical to 1863.

1865. Twenty-first publication. 55 × 80 × 5 mm. 96 p. Mauve dyed paper covers. The design for both covers is identical to 1863, and 1864.

1866. Twenty-second publication. 55 × 85 × 5 mm. 96 p. Red ink edges. Blue dyed paper covers. The design for both covers is identical to 1863–1865.

1867. Twenty-third publication. 55 × 85 × 5 mm. 96 p. Gilt edges. Orange dyed paper covers. The design for both covers is identical to 1863–1866.

1868. Twenty-fourth publication. 55 × 85 × 5 mm. 96 p. 'Being Leap Year'. Red ink edges. Green dyed paper covers. The design for both covers is identical to 1863–1867.

1869. Twenty-fifth publication. 55 × 80 × 5 mm. 96 p. Red ink edges. Pink dyed paper covers. The design for both covers is identical to 1863–1868.

1870. Twenty-sixth publication. 59 × 85 × 5 mm. 96 p. Gilt edges. Orange dyed paper covers. The design for both covers is identical to 1863–1869. [This year is as issued, not bound into a volume.]

1871. Twenty-seventh publication. 57 × 85 × 5 mm. 96 p. Mauve dyed paper covers. The design for both covers is identical to 1863–1870. [This year is as issued, not bound into a volume.]

1872. Twenty-eighth publication. 57 × 85 × 5 mm. 96 p. 'Being Bissextile or Leap Year'. Gilt edges. Blue dyed paper covers, with design printed in brown. The design for both covers is identical to 1863–1871. [This year is as issued, not bound into a volume.]

Dry, *JL* no. 65. King, *JL* p. 247.

139 Leighton, John

Gazewell, Berenice. *Every-day astronomy: or, practical lessons on the celestial sphere. Second edition.* Bath: Binns and Goodwin. London: Whittaker and Co. Hamilton and Co. Simpkin and Co. Low, Son and Co. Edinburgh: Oliver and Boyd; Dublin: J. McGlashan, [1853]. Bath: Printed by Binns and Goodwin. xviii, 184 p., 9 plates.
110 × 174 × 15 mm. 8560.aa.43.

Yellow endpapers and pastedowns. Binder's ticket on lower pastedown: '| Bound by | Bone & Son, | [rule] | 76 Fleet Street, | London. |' Blue wave diagonal-grain cloth. Both covers blocked identically in blind on the borders and on the corners. Two fillets are blocked on the borders, one thick, one thin. Leaf decoration is blocked on each corner. The lower cover has a central vignette blocked in blind. It shows an eight pointed star design, with a leaf pattern blocked in relief within. On the upper cover, a central vignette is blocked in gold and relief. It shows a circle with twelve panels; each panel incorporates one sign of the zodiac, blocked in gold. On the centre, the title words: '| Every |' and '| astronomy |' are blocked in a semicircle above and below a sun-shaped gold lettering-piece. Each letter of these two words is blocked in relief within a five pointed star gold lettering-piece. Within this, at the very centre, the

word: 'day' is blocked in relief within the sun. Signed JL' in gold as separate letters at the base of the zodiac panels. The spine is blocked in gold. A moon and small stars are blocked at the head above the title. The title: '| Every | day | astronomy |' is blocked in gold. Beneath this, a plant and small stars are blocked in gold.

Dry, *JL* no. 80.

140 Leighton, John

Gilbert, J. A. *The change; or, the passage from death unto life. A Memoir of Lieut.-Col. Holcomb, C.B., late of the Royal Artillery. New edition.* Bath: Binns and Goodwin. London: Hamilton; Simpkin; Whittaker. Edinburgh: Oliver and Boyd. Dublin: J M'Glashan, [1853]. Bath: Printed by Binns and Goodwin. xv, 200p., 1 plate. With twenty pages of publisher's titles bound at the end.

112 × 177 × 18 mm. 4903.aaa.23.

Text sewn on two sawn-in cords. Yellow endpapers and pastedowns. Binder's ticket on lower pastedown: '| Leighton | Son & | Hodge, | Shoe Lane | London. |' Blue morocco horizontal-grain cloth. Both covers blocked identically in blind on the borders and on the corners. A single fillet is blocked in blind on the borders. Curling stem and leaves, plus a single flower, are blocked in blind on each corner. The upper cover vignette is blocked in gold. It shows a winged angel, 'floating' in the sky. She carries a staff, which has a cross at its top. A ribbon-shaped pennant, formed by a single fillet, streams downwards behind the angel. The title: '| The change | or | the passage from | death unto | life. |' is blocked in gold within the pennant. Signed 'JL' in relief as separate letters at the base of the angel's dress. The spine is blocked in gold. A single gold fillet is blocked on the perimeter. From the head downwards, the decoration is: a crown in gold; the title: '| The | change | a memoir | of | Lieut. Coll. | Holcombe. |'; fillets in gold; a chain in gold forms a circle, and the word: '| Bondage |' is blocked in gold within; a single fillet forms a rectangle, topped by a pair of wings, and the word: '| Freedom |' is blocked in gold within; a pair of laurel leaves encircle the word: '| Victory |' blocked in gold; two stars and a cross are blocked above and below this word; signed 'JL' in gold as a monogram; a gold fillet; the words: '| Bath. | Binns & Goodwin. |' are blocked in gold within a rectangle formed by a single fillet.

141 Leighton, John

H., J. *The seven wonders of the world, and their associations. With illustrations by William Harvey.* London: George Routledge & Co., Farringdon Street, 1853. [London]: Printed by Cox (Brothers) and Wyman, Great Queen Street, Lincoln's-Inn Fields. xv, 303 p., 8 plates.

105 × 174 × 25 mm. 10002.a.16.

The plates are engraved by Dalziel. Text sewn on two sawn-in cords. Yellow endpapers and pastedowns. Binder's ticket on lower pastedown: '| Leighton | Son & | Hodge, | Shoe Lane | London. |' Orange ripple vertical-grain cloth. Both covers blocked identically in blind on the borders and on the corners. Two fillets are blocked on the borders, one thick, one thin. Ivy leaves, stems and berries are blocked in blind on each corner. The upper cover has a central vignette blocked in gold. It is a gold lettering-piece shaped as a pyramid, with the words: '| The | seven | wonders | of | the world. |' blocked in hatch relief inside. There is a small landscape beneath the title words, picked out in relief. Stems, leaves and flower pods are blocked in gold around the pyramid. A winged hour glass is blocked in gold at the head of the vignette. Signed 'JL' in gold as a monogram at the base of the vignette. The spine is blocked in gold. A single gold fillet is blocked around the perimeter. Two fillets are blocked in gold at the head. At the head, seven stars are blocked in a semi-circle above the words: '| The | seven | wonders | of the | world |'. Underneath this, a circle is blocked. Beneath this, a winged figure on a plinth is blocked – all in gold. Beneath the plinth, small repeating flower decoration is blocked in gold, between pairs of gold fillets.

Dry, *JL* no. 96.

142 Leighton, John

Jamieson, Robert. *Cyclopaedia of religious biography: a series of memoirs of the most eminent religious characters of modern times, intended for family reading.* London: Published by John Joseph Griffin and Co. 53 Baker-Street, Portman Square; and Richard Griffin and Co. Glasgow, 1853. Glasgow: Printed by Bell and Bain. iv, 412 p. With eight pages of publisher's titles bound at the end.

130 × 197 × 30 mm. 4903.d.52.

Bolts uncut. Yellow endpapers and pastedowns. Brown morocco vertical-grain cloth. Both covers are blocked identically. The lower cover is blocked in blind only; the upper cover in blind on borders, and on corners, with a central vignette in gold. There are two fillets on the borders, one thick, one thin. On each corner in blind is a group of passion flower leaves, stems, tendrils and buds. The leaves have six lobes. The vignette at the centre is shaped as a ring, with passion flowers, stems, buds and tendrils all blocked in gold on the circle. At the head and at the tail, and the sides, there are small rings, each containing a flower. Within the main ring, the title: '| Cyclopaedia | of | modern | religious | biography. |' is blocked in gold. Signed 'JL' in gold as separate letters at the base of the vignette. The spine is blocked in gold. There is a single gold fillet blocked around the perimeter, with another fillet blocked inside, forming an arch at the head. From the head downwards, the decoration is: web tracery; a pointed arch, a star, and an eagle blocked in gold; the title: '| Cyclopaedia | of | modern | religious | biography |'; ivy leaves, stems and berries are blocked in gold; a gold fillet; a lily plant, with a small 'vase-like' frame around it; small decoration is blocked in gold between two gold fillets; the words: '| Griffin and Co. |' are blocked at the tail in gold.

Dry, *JL* no. 83. Leighton, *SID, 1852*. plate XXXVI, no. XII. Shows a group of passion flowers.

143 Leighton, John

Limner, Luke *pseud.* [i.e. John Leighton]. *Suggestions in Design. Including original compositions in all styles, with descriptive notes, for the use of artists and art-workmen: containing nearly six hundred hints for workers in metal, wood, ivory, glass and leather; the potter, weaver, printer in colours, engraver, decorator, &c. &c. &c.* London: David Bogue, Fleet Street, 1853. London: Printed by G. Barclay, Castle St. Leicester Sq. 26 p. 47 plates.
220 × 286 × 21 mm. 1269.g.8.

At the base of plate XLII: '| Printed from zinc plates, | at the Press of Leighton Bros. | No. 4, Red Lion Sq, London, | 1853. |'

Issued in parts with paper covers [1852–1853]. Paper cover size: 210 × 280 mm. The cover to issue no. 1 is light green, and bound at the front. The price of Issue no. 1 was one shilling. Both the cover and page 26 feature the medal Luke Limner was awarded at the Great Exhibition, 'For a variety of designs. Fine Art Jury 1851'. The colophon on page twenty-six reads: 'The whole of the designs have been printed from zinc plates, from drawings on that material by the artist.' Each of the 47 plates has a Leighton signature; some are in Leighton's monogram. Each of the signatures has the letters 'JL' presented in accordance with the style of the designs of the period shown on each plate. For example, on plate XLVI, Egyptian, or on plate VII, Jacobean, the letters are highly stylised.' Cover to be preserved' has been written in pencil at the top of the paper cover of Issue 1.

Dry, *JL* no. 84. King, *JL* pp. 235–236.

144 Leighton, John

FIG. 12

Longfellow, Henry Wadsworth. *Hyperion: a romance . . . Illustrated with nearly one hundred engravings on wood, from drawings by Birket Foster.* London: David Bogue, 86 Fleet Street, 1853. London: Henry Vizetelly, Printer & Engraver, Gough Square, Fleet Street. xiii, 304 p. With eighteen pages of publisher's titles bound at the end.
135 × 210 × 35 mm. 1570/1285.

In the publisher's titles at the end, this work is advertised as: '21s. cloth; 30s. morocco antique.'

Text sewn on three tapes. Bevelled boards. Gilt edges. Yellow endpapers and pastedowns. Blue ripple horizontal-grain cloth. Both covers blocked identically in gold, in blind and in relief. Two gold fillets are blocked on the borders. On each corner a triangle is formed by four gold fillets. Long leaves and lily-like flowers are blocked in gold within each triangle. The recessed central diamond reaches from head to tail. A single fillet is blocked in blind on its borders, with a wide fillet blocked inside this. The latter has a patterns of semi-circular stems and buds blocked in relief within it. The central vignette is blocked in gold. It shows eight lily-like flowers and four buds, surrounding a heart-shape. Signed 'JL' in gold as separate letters at the base of the vignette. The spine is fully blocked in gold. A single fillet is blocked on the perimeter. From the head downwards, the decoration is: lily-like flowers and buds are blocked in gold

FIG. 12

within and around two 'balloon-shaped' panels at the head; a heart-shaped gold lettering-piece; the words: '| Longfellow's | Hyperion | [rule] | Illustrated |' are blocked in gold within a panel formed by a single gold fillet; an elaborate symmetrical pattern of lily-like flowers, leaves and buds between, within and around fillets; signed 'JL' in gold as separate letters; two gold fillets; four lily-like leaves and two buds in gold; two gold fillets are blocked at the tail.

Dry, *JL* no. 85. King, *JL* p. 241. McLean, *VPBB* p. 113 Illustrates the AW Bennett edition of 1865 which also has a cover design by Leighton. Pantazzi, *JL* p. 266.

145 Leighton, John

Marryat, Frederick. *The children of the New Forest. A new edition, in one volume, with illustrations by John Gilbert.* London: George Routledge & Co., Farringdon Street, 1853. [London]: Cox (Brothers) and Wyman, Printers, Great Queen Street. [2], 428 p., 8 plates.
105 × 165 × 35 mm. 12806.c.34.

Gilt edges. Yellow endpapers and pastedowns. Binder's ticket on lower pastedown: '| Leighton | Son & | Hodge, | Shoe Lane | London. |' Blue ripple horizontal-grain cloth. Both covers blocked identically in blind on the borders and on the corners. Two fillets are blocked on the borders, one thick, one thin. Oak leaves, stems, and acorns are blocked on each corner. On the upper cover, the central vignette is blocked in gold. It shows four sprigs of oak leaves blocked around a stag's head and antlers. Three acorns are blocked at the head of the vignette. Signed 'JL' in gold as separate letters at the base of the vignette. On the spine, The words: '| The | children | of | the | New Forest | by | Capt. Marryat |' are blocked at the head, in rustic lettering. Below this, an oak branch rises from the base, showing oak leaves and acorns, all blocked in gold.

Dry, JL no. 88.

146 Leighton, John

Marryat, Frederick. *The little savage. A new edition, in one volume. With illustrations by John Gilbert.* London: George Routledge & Co., Farringdon Street, 1853. [London]: Cox (Bros) and Wyman, Printers, Great Queen Street. [2], 412 p., 7 plates.

107 × 175 × 37 mm. 12805.d.61.

The plates are engraved by Dalziel.

Yellow endpapers and pastedowns. Binder's ticket on lower pastedown: '| Leighton | Son & | Hodge, | Shoe Lane | London. |' Blue wave diagonal-grain cloth. Both covers blocked identically in blind on the borders and on the corners. Two fillets are blocked on the borders, one thick, one thin. A group of flowers, leaves, stems, and buds are blocked on each corner. The upper cover has a central vignette blocked in gold. A circle is formed by a rope-like fillet, with strapwork at the base. Eight scallop shells are blocked around the circle. Fronds of seaweed are blocked at the head and at the tail of the vignette. Eight mussels are joined by a ribbon to form an inner circle. Inside this, the title: '| The | little | savage |' is blocked in gold in 'rope-like' letters. Signed 'JL' in gold as separate letters within the strapwork. The spine is blocked in gold. At the head is blocked a seabird, with a fish in its beak. Below this, the words: '| The | little | savage | by | Capt. | Marryat |' are blocked in gold, in 'rope-like' letters. Beneath this, a sea plant and flowers are blocked, with a coiled rope at the base of the plant. Signed 'JL' in gold as separate letters at the tail, within the coil of rope.

Dry, *JL* no. 89.

147 Leighton, John

Marsh, Anne. *Helen's fault; a tale for the young.* London: George Routledge and Co., Farringdon Street, 1853. [London]: Cox (Brothers) and Wyman, Printers, Great Queen Street. [1], 190 p., 4 plates.

97 × 158 × 15 mm. 12805.e.24.

The plates are signed 'C.H.W.' and 'W.C.M.' [i.e. C. H. Weigall and W. C. Mason.]

White endpapers and pastedowns. Orange net-grain cloth. Both covers blocked identically in blind on the borders and on the corners, the head and the tail. The blocking has been done after casing-in. Two fillets in blind are blocked on the borders, the outer thin, the inner thick. A pattern of curling stems and leaves is blocked in blind on the corners, the head, the tail, and the sides. These patterns surround cartouches blocked on the head and the tail. The upper cover vignette is blocked in gold. It has two gold fillets blocked on its perimeter. It is diamond-shaped, with small plant decoration blocked in side at the top and at the bottom. The title: '| Helen's | Fault. |' is blocked in gold in fanciful letters on the centre. Signed 'JL' in gold as separate letters, within a small diamond blocked at the base of the vignette. [This is a small, but clear, signature of 1mm across.] The spine is blocked in gold. The title: '| Helen's | Fault |' is blocked in gold near the head. Small fillets and decoration are blocked above and below the title. Blue date stamped: '18 FE[BRUARY 18]53'.

Another copy is at BL 12806.d.19. Yellow endpapers and pastedowns. Blue morocco vertical-grain cloth. Blocking in blind on the borders and on the corners. The upper cover vignette is blocked in gold, with the title on the centre, within circular decoration of straps and rings. Unsigned.

Dry, *JL* no. 82.

148 Leighton, John

Moses, Henry. *An Englishman's life in India: or, Travel and Adventure in the East*... London: Binns & Goodwin, 44, Fleet Street, and 19, Cheap Street, Bath. Edinburgh: Oliver and Boyd. Dublin: J. M'Glashan, 1853. Bath: Printed by Binns and Goodwin. xx, 342 p. 1 plate. With eighteen pages of publisher's titles bound at the end.

108 × 172 × 25 mm. 10056.a.12.

Yellow endpapers and pastedowns. Red wave diagonal-grain cloth. Both covers blocked identically in blind on the borders and on the corners. A single fillet is blocked on the borders. On the corners, flower and leaf decoration is blocked in relief. The upper cover has a central vignette blocked in gold. The shape is a 'bowl', formed by interlocking 'S's. The 'S' shapes contain dotted gold fillets. Four-petal flowers, leaves and stems are blocked inside circles formed by the 'S' shapes. On the centre, the title: '| An | Englishman's | life | in | India. |' is blocked in gold. Signed 'JL' in gold as separate letters at the base of the vignette. The spine is blocked in gold. A single gold fillet is blocked around the perimeter, forming straps at the head. From the head downwards the decoration is: the crown of a palm tree; the title: '| An | Englishman's | life | in | India. |' blocked in gold; a climbing plant grows up a pole from the tail; near the tail: '| Binns | and Goodwin. |' are blocked in gold; the roots of the plant form a triangle near the tail, with a gold fillet below this.

Dry, JL no. 92.

149 Leighton, John

Mulock, afterwards, Craik, Dinah Maria. *A Hero. Philip's book. . . . With illustrations by James Godwin.* London: Addey & Co., 21, Old Bond Street, 1853. London: Thompson and Davidson, Printers, 19, Great St. Helens. viii, 150 p., 4 plates. With sixteen pages of publisher's titles bound at the end.
113 × 178 × 14 mm. 12805.e.25.

Yellow endpapers and pastedowns. Blue wave diagonal-grain cloth. Both covers blocked identically in blind. Two fillets are blocked on the borders, the inner having a single strap on each corner. The design inside the fillets shows a flowing pattern of stems, clover leaves and flowers. The design forms an onion-shape, on the lower half of each cover. The spine is blocked in gold. A single fillet is blocked in gold on the perimeter. From the head downwards, the decoration is: the title: '| A | Hero |' blocked in gold; from beneath the title to the tail, a tree is blocked in gold; a spider's web is blocked near the base and a spider hangs from it by a thread; a squirrel is blocked on the lower branches of the tree; small insects and a butterfly are blocked on each side of the tree; a bird's nest is blocked at the top of the tree; the nest has three chicks inside, and a parent bird above is about to land on the nest – all in gold; signed 'JL' in gold as separate letters in a circle made by the roots of the tree.

150 Leighton, John

Myrtle, Harriet, Mrs. *pseud.* [i.e. Lydia Falconer Miller.] *Amusing tales . . . With ten illustrations.* London: Addey & Co., 21, Old Bond Street, 1853. Unpaginated. [7 p., D4, B4–C4; E4–L4], 1 plate.
136 × 195 × 10 mm. 12806.e.15.

Both original paper covers are bound at the end. Yellow paper, printed in brown. The upper cover shows a single fillet on the border. The design shows strapwork on the corners and on the sides. On the corners and sides, rose leaves, rose stems and flowers are printed. Straps printed inside this form a central 'oval' panel. Printed inside this panel are the words: '| Books | for | young readers. | [rule] | Amusing tales | by Mrs Myrtle. | [rule] | Addey & Co. | 21. Old Bond Street | London. |'. Signed in the strap work at the base: 'Luke Limner del. H. Leighton Sc. [i.e. Henry Leighton]'. The lower cover has lists of publisher's titles and states: 'Books for young readers. No. I. price one shilling each'.

Dry, *JL* no. 67a.

151 Leighton, John

Scott, *Sir* Walter *Bart. The Lady of the Lake. With all his introductions, various readings, and the Editor's notes. Illustrated by numerous engravings on wood from drawings by Birket Foster and John Gilbert.* Edinburgh: Adam and Charles Black, North Bridge, 1853. Edinburgh: Printed by R. & R. Clark. 375 p., 2 plates.
134 × 205 × 41 mm. 11641.d.70.

The frontispiece and half title page plates are signed: 'J. M. W. Turner, R. A. W. Miller.' The text engravings are by J. W. Whymper and Edmund Evans.

This design attributed to John Leighton, as there are similarities to 'The Lay of the Last Minstrel', particularly for the spine design. BL 11642.e.27, published by Black in 1854.

Gilt edges. Bevelled boards. Binder's ticket on lower pastedown: '| Bound by | John Gray | [rule] | Edinburgh |'. Brown morocco horizontal-grain cloth. Both covers identically blocked in gold and in blind. A single fillet is blocked in gold on the borders. Inside this, a wide border is blocked, with medieval decoration. A shield is blocked in gold on each corner. Coats of arms – top left and bottom right: argent, crescent, and two five-point stars, vert; top right and bottom left: argent, 'pierced gold circle', three diamonds in bend. On the centre at the head, a hound is blocked; on the centre at the tail, a stag is blocked. Each is blocked within an oval formed by two gold fillets. On each side at the centre, figures are blocked in niches with decorated gothic arches. The figure on the left is headed '| Roderic Dhu |'; the figure on the right is headed '| Fitz James |' – each of these titles is blocked in gold within ribbons above the niches. The ribbons are blocked with quatrefoils formed by two gold fillets. Below each figure, the titles: left – '| Malcolm | Graeme |' and right – '| Ellen | Douglas |' are blocked below the niches in ribbons within quatrefoils. The central rectangle has rounded corners, and is recessed. A single gold fillet is blocked on its borders, above the recess. Within the recess, two fillets are blocked in blind on its borders. On the centre, the title words: '| The | Lady | of the | Lake |' are blocked in gold, in gothic letters. The spine is blocked in gold. A single fillet is blocked on the perimeter. From the head downwards, the decoration is: the title: '| The | Lady | of | the | Lake |' blocked in gold, within a decorated panel; the words: '| Authors | Edition | Illustrated |' are blocked in gold, within a hatched gold lettering-piece shaped as a ribbon – all within a quatrefoil; gothic decoration; within a gothic arch, a lady stands in a boat on water, holding a pole; the words: '| A & C Black Edinburgh |' are blocked in gold, in gothic letters between two gold fillets; Unsigned. [Compiler's copy is bound in blue wave diagonal-grain cloth, also bound by Gray.]

Dry, *JL* no. 460. Cites copy of 1863.

152 Leighton, John

Smith, Albert. *The story of Mont Blanc.* London: David Bogue, Fleet Street, 1853. xii, 219 p., 1 plate. With eight pages of publisher's titles bound at the end.
126 × 204 × 25 mm. 10195.b.17.

Yellow endpapers and pastedowns. Binder's ticket on lower pastedown: '| Leighton | Son & | Hodge, | Shoe Lane | London. |' Orange ripple horizontal-grain cloth. Both covers blocked identically in blind. A single fillet is blocked on the borders. Strapwork is blocked on the inner corners, with fillets on the inner sides. Leaf and stem decoration is blocked, rising from the base. A mandorla is blocked in blind just above the

centre. It contains a 'fleur-de-lis' shape, blocked in relief. Signed 'JL' as a monogram in relief near the base of each cover. The spine is blocked in gold. At the head, the outline of an alpine hut is formed by a single gold fillet. In it, a goat's head is blocked. Beneath are the words: '| The | story | of | Mont Blanc | by | Albert | Smith. |'. Underneath this, a hat, a cloak, and climbing boots are hung on a stand – all in gold. Signed 'JL' in gold as a monogram at the tail.

Dry, *JL* no. 97.

153 Leighton, John

Stowe, Harriet Elizabeth Beecher. *Uncle Tom's cabin. Adapted for young persons. By Mrs. Crowe. With eight illustrations.* London: George Routledge and Co., Farringdon Street, 1853. [3], 404 p., 8 plates. With eight pages of publisher's titles bound at the front, and thirty-two pages of publisher's titles bound at the end.
105 × 167 × 40 mm. 12705.c.36.

The original upper cover is used as a doublure. Doublure size: 95 × 152 mm. Red morocco horizontal-grain cloth. Blocked in blind on the corners. On each corner, a spray of ivy leaves and berries is blocked in blind. The central vignette is blocked in gold. It shows oak leaves and stems curling upwards from the centre to form a semi-circle. On the left hand side of the semi-circle within a flower, the torso of a black boy is blocked in gold. He wears a turban, with a feather in it. On the right hand side, a girl holding a lily is blocked in gold. The title: '| Uncle Tom's | cabin; | adapted | for | juvenile | readers. |' is blocked in gold, rustic-style, above and within the semi-circle formed by the oak leaves and stems. Signed 'JL' in gold as separate letters at the base of the vignette.

Dry, *JL* no. 76.

154 Leighton, John

W., C. J. *Etchings from nature.* Bath: Simms & Son, 1853. Bath: Simms & Son, Printers. x, 228 p.
110 × 177 × 20 mm. 11646.g.12.

Yellow endpapers. Green fine rib vertical-grain cloth. The upper and lower covers are blocked identically in blind. Two fillets are blocked in blind on the borders. The third inner border fillet in blind forms straps on the lower corners. Branch and leaf decoration is blocked in blind on each upper corner. A group of three leaves is blocked in blind on the lower centre of each cover. Signed JL' in blind as separate letters, at the base of the leaves. The spine is blocked in gold. From the head downwards, the decoration is: a broad gold fillet is blocked with a single arch underneath; the title: '| Etchings | from | nature. |' blocked in gold; a pattern of lily-like leaves and flowers is blocked in gold from the middle of the spine to near the tail; signed 'JL' in gold in separate letters just above the broad gold fillet blocked at the tail.

Dry, *JL* no. 101.

155 Leighton, John

Woodworth, Francis C. *Uncle Frank's home stories. With illustrations.* London: George Routledge and Co. Farringdon Street, 1853. London: Printed by Levey, Robson, and Franklyn, Great New Street, Fetter Lane. iv, 188 p., 4 plates.
97 × 157 × 15 mm. 12805.f.38.

Two of the four plates are signed with the monogram 'JRH' and with the initials 'A.J.M.'

Yellow endpapers and pastedowns. Orange ripple vertical-grain cloth. Both covers identically blocked in blind on the borders and on the corners. Two fillets are blocked on the borders. A cartouche is blocked in blind at the head and at the tail. A pattern of leaves and stems is blocked around each cartouche on the head, the tail, and corners and on the sides. [This is the same design as for BL 12806.c.4. – Braggadocio.] The upper cover vignette is blocked in gold. A single fillet forms a circle, with straps blocked at the head, the tail, and on each side. The title: '| Uncle | Frank's | Home | Stories |' is blocked in gold within the circle. Signed 'JL' in relief as separate letters within a small gold lettering-piece suspended from the strapwork at the tail of the circle. [This is one of the smallest JL signatures seen. The gold lettering-piece that contains the signature is one millimetre wide, and both letters are blocked inside it.] The spine is blocked in gold. The title: '| Uncle | Frank's | Home | Stories |' is blocked in gold, with small decorative pieces blocked in gold above and below the title. Unsigned. Blue date stamp: 18 FE[BRUARY 18]53.

156 Leighton, John

The doll and her friends; or, Memoirs of the Lady Seraphina. By the author of 'Dog and cat, or puss and the captain;' [i.e. Maitland, Julia Charlotte.] *'Letters from Madras,' etc., etc. Second edition. With four illustrations by Hablot K. Browne.* London: Grant & Griffith (Successors to Newbery and Harris,) Corner of St Paul's Churchyard, 1854. London: Printed by Levey, Robson, and Franklyn, Great New Street and Fetter Lane. [3], 91 p., 4 plates. With sixteen pages of publisher's titles bound at the end.
125 × 175 × 10 mm. 1568/9155.

On page 7 of the publisher's titles at the end: '. . . 2nd Edition, small 4to., cloth 2s.6d. plain; 3s.6d. coloured, gilt edges.'

Yellow endpapers and pastedowns. Written on the upper endpaper: '| Jessie Grantham | from her Uncle John. | Decr. 1856 |' Blue ripple horizontal-grain cloth. Both covers are blocked identically in blind on the borders the corners and the sides. A single fillet is blocked on the border. Curling stems are blocked in blind on the corners and on the sides. On the centre of the lower cover, a lozenge is blocked. On the upper cover, the central vignette is blocked in gold. It shows a doll's house standing on a table. Two dolls are at the windows, and another, seated, leans against the house. There are books, a tea set on a tray, and a vase with flowers around the doll's house. The title: '| The | doll | and | her friends | or | memoirs of |' is blocked in relief on the wall of the house. The words: '| the Lady Seraphina |' are blocked in relief on one of the books propped

against the house. The spine is fully blocked in gold. The title: '| The Doll | & | Her | Friends |' is blocked in gold at the head, and down to the middle. Underneath the title a doll is blocked, wrapped to look like a mummy. Signed 'JL' in gold as a monogram at the tail.

157 Leighton, John

FIG. 13

Oriental fairy Tales, or fancy's wanderings in the East. With thirty-two illustrations, by William Harvey, engraved by the Brothers Dalziel. London: George Routledge & Co. 2 Farringdon Street, 1854. London: Printed by Richard Clay, Bread Street Hill. [3], 338 p., 8 plates
115 × 182 × 25 mm. 12430.f.11.

White endpapers and pastedowns. Blue morocco horizontal-grain cloth. Both covers are blocked identically in blind and in relief on the borders, corners and sides . There are three fillets blocked in blind on the borders, the middle having repeating dots in relief. Onion shapes are blocked on the corners. There is an oval frame on the inner portion of the cover, with lace work of stems blocked in relief. On the upper cover, a central vignette is blocked in gold. There is a gold fillet blocked around its perimeter, which forms strapwork on the upper corners, with very small dots blocked in relief within the fillet. The inner decoration is onion-shaped, showing stems and leaves. At the very centre, the title: '| Oriental | fairy | Tales |' is blocked in gold. Signed 'JL' in gold as separate letters at the base of the vignette. The spine is blocked in gold. The decoration from the head is: small stars; the title: '| Oriental | Fairy | Tales |' is blocked within an arabesque; a single star is blocked at the top of a lance – the star has the word 'FAIRY' blocked in its angles. Signed 'JL' in gold as a monogram at the tail.

Dry, *JL* no. 143.

FIG. 13

158 Leighton, John

Round games for all parties: a collection of the greatest variety of family amusements for fireside or pic-nic; consisting of Games of Action; Games simply taxing the attention; Games of Memory; Catch Games, depending upon the Assistance of an Accomplice or Secret knowledge for the purpose of Mystification; Games requiring the Exercise of Fancy, Intelligence, and Imagination; Directions for the Crying of Forfeits, &c. &c. For the Use of Old and Young; and adapted to the understandings of children from the ages of seven to seventy. London: David Bogue, 86 Fleet Street, 1854. [London]: Savill and Edwards, Printers, 4, Chandos Street, Covent Garden. x, 164 p., 12 plates. With two pages of publisher's titles bound at the end.
123 × 160 × 19 mm. 7915.a.9.

Text sewn on two tapes. Gilt edges. Yellow endpapers and pastedowns. Bookseller's label on the front pastedown, lower left hand corner: '| Jarrold & Sons | Booksellers &c. | Norwich. |' Blue ripple horizontal-grain cloth. Both covers blocked identically in blind on the borders and on the corners. Two fillets are blocked on the borders, the outer thick, the inner thin. On each corner, leaves and stems are blocked in blind. The upper cover has a central vignette blocked in gold. It shows a hand (with a ruff), holding a trencher upright. Around its edge, within dividers, the title: '| Round games for all parties |', blocked in relief. The trencher is surrounded by holly leaves, berries and stems, blocked in gold. The words: '| Spin the trencher!!! |' are blocked in gold at the base of the vignette. The spine is blocked in gold. A single gold fillet is blocked around the perimeter. Small decoration blocked at the head. The title: '| Round games |' is blocked in gold down the spine. Signed 'JL' in gold as joined italic letters at the tail.

Dry, *JL* no. 150.

159 Leighton, John

Adams, Charlotte. *Boys at home. The second edition, Illustrated by John Gilbert.* London: George Routledge and Co. Farringdon Street, 1854. [London]: Printed by Cox (Bros.) and Wyman, Great Queen Street. 414 p., 8 plates.
107 × 172 × 43 mm. 12806.d.5.

The plates engraved by Dalziel.

Yellow pastedowns. Blue morocco vertical-grain cloth. The same design is blocked in blind on the borders and on the corners of both covers. Two fillets are blocked on the borders, one thick, one thin. Passion flower leaves, flowers and stems are blocked on each corner. (This is the same design as on BL 10604.b.5.) On the centre of the upper cover, a roundel in the form of a garter is blocked in blind. The words: 'In the exercise of the social virtues lies man's greatest happiness' are blocked in relief within the garter strap. The title: 'Boys at home' is blocked in blind on the centre. Signed 'JL' in blind as separate letters at the base of the roundel. The spine is blocked in gold. A single fillet is blocked in gold around the perimeter. The spine is divided into three main square panels, each of which is formed by a single gold fillet. There are four smaller rectangular panels at the

head, the tail and between the square panels. Square panel one has the title: '| Boys | at | home |' blocked in gold. Square panel two has an upraised hand, with leaf decoration, blocked in gold. Square panel three has a heart and leaf decoration, blocked in gold. The small panels have ovals blocked within them. Small leaf decoration is blocked in gold around the ovals. Signed 'JL' in gold as separate letters at the tail.

160 Leighton, John

Ainsworth, William Harrison. *The Flitch of Bacon: or, the Custom of Dunmow. A tale of English home . . . With illustrations by John Gilbert.* London: Geo. Routledge & Co., Farringdon Street. New York, 18, Beekman Street, 1854. [London]: Savill, & Edwards, Printers, 4, Chandos-street, Covent-garden. xii, 376 p., 8 plates.
108 × 174 × 35 mm. 12619.b.21.

The plates engraved by Dalziel.

Original yellow endpaper bound at the front. Red morocco horizontal-grain cloth. Both covers are blocked identically in blind and relief. Two fillets are blocked on the borders, one thick, one thin. Stem patterns are blocked in relief on each corner. The central vignette is blocked on both covers. It shows a spit, with a pig on it. The words: '| Flitch |' and '| Bacon |' are blocked on either side of the pig, in rustic lettering; the word '| The |' is blocked in relief within the pig's body. Below the pig are two heart shapes, formed by a ribbon. A girl's head is blocked within each heart. Each girl wears a hat. Signed 'JL' in blind as separate letters at the base of the vignette. The spine is blocked in gold. Two gold fillets are blocked on the perimeter. From the head down, the decoration in gold is: an inn-sign; inside it, the words: '| Painted in gold | Ye Flitch behold | Of Fam'd Dunmow Ye boast | By Nettle | Jonas Bed. | Then here should call | Fond couples all | and pledge it in a toast |'; a pig's carcass is blocked in the middle of the inn-sign; the supporting column for the sign has a pennant-shaped gold lettering-piece, with the words: '| The | Flitch | of | Bacon | by Ainsworth |' blocked in relief within a pennant which wraps itself around the column. Lower half of spine is missing.

Dry, *JL* no. 106.

161 Leighton, John

Bechstein, Ludwig. *The old story-teller. Popular German Tales collected by Ludwig Bechstein. One hundred illustrations by Richter.* London: Addey and Co., 21 Old Bond Street, 1854. London: Printed by Levey, Robson, and Franklyn, Great New Street and Fetter Lane. 287 p., 8 plates
123 × 190 × 25 mm. 12430.f.12.

Text sewn on three sawn-in cords. Gilt edges. Yellow endpapers and pastedowns. Blue ripple horizontal-grain cloth. The blocking appears to have been done after the covers were attached to the text block. Both covers are blocked identically in blind only. Two fillets are blocked on the borders of the covers. The central vignette, blocked in blind, shows curling leaves and stems, forming a 'heart' shape. Signed 'JL' in relief as separate letters at the base of the vignette. The spine is blocked in gold. A single gold fillet is blocked on the perimeter. From the head downwards, the decoration is : a roundel, formed by a single gold fillet, showing a man carrying faggots; the words: '| The old | story teller | [rule] | Bechstein |' are blocked in gold; a shoe, with a boy in it, holding a whip; the words: '| 100 | illustrations |'; a gnome holding a stick; at the tail: '| Addey & Co. |' is blocked in gold.

Dry, *JL* no. 109.

162 Leighton, John

Besset, Jane M. *The Black Princess. A True Story for Young Persons.* London: G. Routledge & Co., Farringdon Street, 1854. London: Reed and Pardon, Printers, Paternoster Row. viii, 168 p., 4 plates. With thirty-one pages of publisher's titles bound at the end.
110 × 174 × 16 mm. 12805.f.8.

The plates engraved by Dalziel and have John Gilbert's monogram.

Yellow endpapers and pastedowns. Dark maroon morocco horizontal-grain cloth. Both covers blocked identically in blind on the borders and on the corners. Two fillets are blocked on the borders, one thick, one thin. Flower heads, leaves and stems are blocked on each corner. On the upper cover, the central vignette is blocked in gold. It shows the figure of the Black Princess standing on a flower head. She holds a leaf canopy over her head. On either side of her, symmetrical flower leaf and stem decoration is blocked in gold. The title words: '| The | Black |' are blocked in gold above the Princess; the word: '| Princess |' is blocked below her, within a rectangular scroll-shaped frame. Signed 'JL' in gold as a monogram at the base of the vignette. The spine is blocked in gold. A single gold fillet is blocked on the perimeter. The words: '| The | Black | Princess |' are blocked in gold at the head. From the tail up to beneath the title, a chain is blocked. This has plant leaves and stems curling around the links of the chain. A single flower is blocked above a chain ring at the top. There is small decoration at the tail, with a single fillet underneath, all in gold.

Dry, *JL* no. 111.

163 Leighton, John

Bray, Anna Eliza. *A peep at the pixies; or, legends of the west. With illustrations by Hablot K. Browne. (Phiz.)* London: Grant and Griffith, (Successors to Newbery and Harris,) Corner of St. Paul's Churchyard, 1854. London: Printed by Wertheimer, and Co. Finsbury Circus. [6], 162 p., 6 plates. With eight pages of publisher's titles bound at the end.
130 × 178 × 15 mm. 12430.c.9.

Original yellow endpaper bound at the front. Blue wave diagonal-grain cloth. Both covers are blocked in blind with the same design on the borders and on the corners. Two fillets are

blocked on the borders. Leaves and stems are blocked on the corners, in relief. The upper cover has a central vignette, blocked in gold. It shows a pixie, with its legs crossed, seated on the stem of a flowering plant, surrounded by leaves and flowers. Above this, the title: '| A | peep | at the pixies. |' is blocked in gold in rustic letters. Below, the words: '| By Mrs | Bray. |' are blocked in gold in rustic lettering. Signed 'JL' in gold as separate letters at the base of the vignette. The spine is blocked in gold. At the head a crescent moon is blocked, surrounded by small stars. The words: '| A | peep | at | the | pixies | by | Mrs Bray |' are blocked in gold in rustic lettering. A pixie, with a tail, is blocked in gold underneath the title words.

Dry, *JL* no. 114.

164 Leighton, John

Cockayne, M. S. *History and adventure; or, Stories of Remarkable Men of All Nations.* London: Binns & Goodwin, 44, Fleet Street; and 19, Cheap Street, Bath, 1854. London: W. Clowes and Sons, Stamford Street. [3],344 p., 8 plates. With twenty pages of publisher's titles bound at the end.

110 × 177 × 29 mm. 10604.b.5.

The frontispiece engraved by Bonner.

Text sewn on two sawn-in cords. Yellow endpapers and pastedowns. Blue morocco horizontal-grain cloth. Both covers have the same design blocked in blind on the borders and on the corners. Two fillets are blocked on the borders, one thick, one thin. A passion flower leaf, flowers and stems are blocked on each corner. (This is the same design as on BL 12806.d.5.) The upper cover has a central vignette blocked in gold. It shows a circular wreath formed by branch stems, three-pointed leaves and berries. A five-pointed star is blocked at the top. A scroll-shaped gold lettering-piece is blocked at the bottom. A trumpet is inserted through the hollow of the scroll. The words: 'History; Biography' are blocked in relief on the scroll. The title: '| History | & | adventure | of | Remarkable Men | of | All Nations |' is blocked in gold within the circular wreath. Signed 'JL' in gold as separate letters at the base of the vignette. The spine is fully blocked in gold. A single fillet is blocked in gold on the perimeter. There are four square panels, each formed by single gold fillets. From the head: panel one has a circle blocked, with small decoration blocked on its corners; blocked within the circle are a crown and the words: 'Henry IV.'. Panel two has the words: '| History | & | adventure. |' blocked in gold. Panel three has a circle with small decoration on the corners; the words: '| Luther [-spine of a book-] Cranmer. |' are blocked in gold within the circle. Panel four has a circle with small decoration blocked on the corners. Within the circle, the words: '| Wellington | [-sword-] | Washington. |' are blocked in gold. Above and below panel four are rectangular panels with small circle and flower decoration inside. Signed 'JL' in gold as separate letters within the circle of the lower of these two panels. The words: '| Binns & | Goodwin |' are blocked in gold within a rectangle formed by a single gold fillet at the tail.

Dry, *JL* no. 116.

165 Leighton, John

Cummins, Maria Susanna. *The Lamplighter . . . Eighth Thousand. Illustrated by John Gilbert.* London: G. Routledge & Co., Farringdon Street, 1854. London: Savill and Edwards, Printers, Chandos Street. [1],396 p. 6 plates.

118 × 190 × 37 mm. 12706.d.16.

The plates are engraved by Dalziel.

Yellow endpapers and pastedowns. Blue wave diagonal-grain cloth. Both covers blocked identically in blind on the borders. Three fillets are blocked on the borders; between two of them, a border of curving stems and berries is blocked in groups of three. The upper cover has a central vignette blocked in gold. It shows a winged angel, who holds a lamp aloft in her left hand. In front of the angel, a child with crossed arms is blocked. Both figures are walking on the rungs of a ladder. A snake is curled around the ladder. The word: '| The |' is blocked above the angel; the word: '| Lamp-lighter |' is blocked on either side of the figures. Signed 'JL' in gold as separate letters, within the curled tail of the snake at the base of the vignette. The spine is fully blocked in gold. A single fillet is blocked around the perimeter. From the base to the head, a lamp-post is blocked. Ivy stems and leaves curl around the lamp-post, with stars dotted around these. The lamp and its rays blocked at the head, with icicles hanging on the ladder rest beneath. The words: '| The | Lamplighter |' are blocked in relief within a gold lettering-piece shaped as a pennant, which curls around the lamp-post. Signed 'JL' in gold as separate letters at the base of the lamp-post. The word: '| Illustrated |' is blocked in gold at the tail.

Dry, *JL* no. 133.

166 Leighton, John

Cundall, Joseph. *The photographic primer for the use of beginners in the collodion process. Illustrated with a Facsimile of a Photographic Picture of Birds, showing the Difference of tone produced by various colours.* London: Photographic Institution, 168 New Bond Street, 1854. London: Printed by G. Barclay, Castle St. Leicester Sq. 32 p., 1 plate. With eight pages of advertisements bound at the end.

105 × 175 × 15 mm. 787.d.22.

Two pages of the advertisements advertise the products and the work done by the Photographic Institution.

Yellow endpapers and pastedowns. Original paper covers are bound at front and rear of rebound book. Original paper cover size: 100 × 165 mm. The paper covers are yellow, printed in red. The same design is printed on both covers. There are three fillets blocked on the borders. Sunflowers are printed in the corners at the head. Between is the head of a goddess-like figure. The title: '| The | Photographic | Primer. |' is printed within a panel which is semi-circular at the head. The words have tracery around them. At the sides and at the base, leaves and 'vein-like' branches are printed. Signed 'H Leighton Sc' as a monogram at the centre of the base. Just above this is the

monogram of John Leighton, printed in faint outline. The 'J' does not cross the 'L', it joins onto the end of the 'L'.

McLean, Cundall p. 33 'Bound in yellow paper with an elaborate design printed in red from a wood cut by John Leighton.' Dry, *JL* no. 118.

167 Leighton, John

Elwes, Alfred. *Ocean and her rulers; A Narrative of the Nations who have from the earliest ages held dominion over the sea, comprising a brief history of navigation from the remotest periods up to the present time.* London: Grant and Griffith, Successors to Newbery and Harris, Corner of St Paul's Churchyard, 1854. London: Printed by J. Wertheimer and Co., Finsbury Circus. xvi, 422 p., 1 plate. With twenty-four pages of publisher's titles bound at the end.

110 × 177 × 35 mm. 1424.c.5

Yellow endpapers and pastedowns. Binder's ticket on lower pastedown: '| Bound by | Bone & Son. | [rule] | 76 Fleet Street, | London. |' Blue morocco vertical-grain cloth. The same design is blocked in blind on both covers. Three fillets are blocked on the borders. The middle of these has repeating dots within it, in relief. On each corner, 'bulb'- shaped ornaments are blocked in relief. A central oval panel is formed of lattice work and leaves. The spine is blocked in gold. A fillet is blocked in gold on the perimeter. A single fillet is blocked in gold at the head and the tail. From the head downwards, the decoration blocked in gold is: an arch; a crown with ships' sails and sterns atop it; the title words: '| Ocean | and her | rulers |', blocked in 'rope' lettering; a mast, with a Union Jack at the head; a lion seated on a plinth at the base of the mast. Within the plinth, two lines of text are blocked in relief: [first line] '| The flag that's braved a thousand years. |' [second line obscured by a label]. Seaweed is blocked in gold underneath the plinth. Signed 'JL' in gold as separate letters within a circle at the centre of the seaweed.

Dry, *JL* no. 120.

168 Leighton, John

Fern, Fanny *pseud.* [i.e. Sarah Payson Willis, afterwards Eldredge, afterwards Parton.] *Little ferns for Fanny's little friends. With Illustrations by Birket Foster, engraved by E. Evans.* London: Nathaniel Cooke, Milford House, Strand, 1854. London: Savill, and Edwards, Printers, Chandos Street, Covent Garden. vi, 186 p., 8 plates.

125 × 172 × 15 mm. 12354.b.23.

Edges speckled with red ink. Yellow endpapers and pastedowns. Green wave diagonal-grain cloth. Both covers blocked identically in blind on the borders, on the corners and on the sides. There is a single fillet blocked on the borders, and a leaf and stem pattern blocked on the corners, which forms a central panel. A lozenge is blocked on the centre of the lower cover. It has a star-shaped centre, with a circle blocked within the star. The upper cover centre has a vignette blocked in gold. It shows a right hand, with its little finger crooked. The hand holds a quill pen. Instead of a feather, the end of the quill pen has a fern leaf. The fern leaf bisects the title: '| Little | Ferns | for Fanny's | Little Friends |' blocked in gold in fanciful italic letters with leaves and stems running out from the ends of the letters. The quill pen is writing on an open book, which is blocked in gold. Signed 'JL' in gold as a monogram underneath the book. The spine is blocked in gold. A single gold fillet is blocked on the perimeter. From the head downwards, the decoration is: an arch at the head, formed by two gold fillets; curling stems and straps; the words: '| Little | Ferns | for | Little | Friends | By the | Author | of Fern | Leaves |' blocked in gold; a birds' nest; a beetle is blocked at the tail.

169 Leighton, John

Fullom, Stephen Watson. *The great highway: A Story of the World's Struggles. With Illustrations on Steel by John Leech . . . Third Edition.* London: George Routledge & Co. Farringdon Street; New York: 18, Beekman Street, 1854. [London]: Printed by Cox (Bros.) and Wyman, Great Queen Street. vii, 428 p., 4 plates. With four pages of publisher's titles bound at the end.

120 × 190 × 33 mm. 12620.b.32.

Yellow endpapers and pastedowns. Blue morocco vertical-grain cloth. The same design is blocked in blind on the borders and on the corners of both covers. Two fillets are blocked on the borders, one thick, one thin. Honeysuckle is blocked in relief on the corners. The upper has a central vignette blocked in gold. It shows an open book, blocked as a gold lettering-piece. On its left hand page, the words: '| Mormon | and Mammon |' are blocked in relief. On the right hand page, the word: '| 185[4] |' is blocked in relief. A snake runs through the book as a bookmark. Its tail is coiled around thorny branches which surround the book. Above the book, the title: '| The | great highway. |' is blocked in gold in rustic lettering. A hand and wrist are blocked in gold between 'great' and 'highway'. There is a snake curled around the hand and wrist. Signed 'JL' in gold as a monogram at the base of the vignette. The spine is fully blocked in gold. A single gold fillet is blocked around the perimeter. A brick arch is blocked at the head. A signpost is blocked from the base to the head. At the head, two of the signpost direction boards are blocked in hatch gold; they point four ways. The words: 'Hope; hate; despair; [love?]' are blocked in relief on each board. Below these, a gold lettering piece shaped as a pennant winds around the signpost. Within the pennant, the words: '| The | great | highway | by S. W. | Fullom |' are blocked in relief. Plants and leaves are blocked around the post at its base. The words: '| Routledge & Co. | London |' are blocked in gold in a rectangle formed by a single fillet at the tail.

Dry, *JL* no. 124.

170 Leighton, John

FIG. 14

Gay, John. *The fables. Illustrated. With an original memoir, introduction, and annotations, by Octavius Freire Owen, M.A.*

F.S.A. . . . With one hundred and twenty six drawings by William Harvey, engraved by the Brothers Dalziel. London: George Routledge & Co. Farringdon Street, 1854. London: Printed by Richard Clay, Bread Street Hill. xv, 271 p.
110 × 175 × 25 mm. 12305.c.33.

Yellow endpapers and pastedowns. Blue morocco horizontal-grain cloth. Both covers blocked identical in blind on the borders and on the corners. The lower cover is blocked in blind, with two fillets on the borders, the outer thick, the inner thin. Scrollwork is blocked in blind on the corners. The upper cover central vignette is blocked in gold. It shows a monkey, wearing a wig and a ruff, a long waistcoat and knee breeches, buckled shoes, and a sword. The monkey is seated on a curling branch, which has leaves and flowers sprouting from it to surround the monkey. The monkey's three-cornered hat is on a branch above its head. The monkey is holding an open book, blocked as a gold lettering-piece, on whose covers are blocked '| Gay's Fables |', in relief. At the base of the branch a plaque is formed by a single gold fillet. The words: '| The monkey | who had seen | the world. |' Signed 'JL' in gold as separate letters, underneath the plaque. The spine is blocked in gold. A single gold fillet is blocked on the perimeter. From the head downwards, the decoration is: a gold fillet; the title: '| Gay's | Fables |' blocked in gold, in rustic letters, surrounded by buds and stems; two owls and a sparrow are seated on branches, with the words: '| The | two | owls & the | sparrow |' blocked in gold beneath; more leaves and a plant stem in gold; a triangle formed by a single fillet, with small decoration blocked in gold within it; at the tail, the words: '| Harvey's | Illustrations |' are blocked in gold within a rectangle formed by a single gold fillet.

Dry, *JL* no. 127.

FIG. 14

171 Leighton, John

Jamieson, Robert. *Scripture readings; or, the Bible familiarly explained to the young. The Patriarchs. Edited by the Rev. Robert Jamieson, D.D.* London and Glasgow: Published by Richard Griffin and Company, 1854. Glasgow: W. G. Blackie & Co, Printers, Villafield. xii, 340 p., 10 plates.
110 × 180 × 27 mm. 3128.d.28.

Bolts uncut. Yellow endpapers and pastedowns. Olive-green wave diagonal-grain cloth. Both covers blocked identically in blind on the borders and on the corners. Two fillets are blocked on the borders, the outer thick, the inner thin. An inner border, blocked in blind, shows repeating ovals, formed by two fillets, blocked in blind, with leaves blocked in relief between ovals. An inner rectangle is formed by a single fillet. The central vignette is blocked and in relief on the lower cover and in gold and in relief on the upper. It shows a winged angel with a single five-point star above its head. The angel holds an open book, blocked as a gold lettering-piece, with the words: '| Jesus said | [rule] | Suffer little | children to come unto | me & forbid | them not: | for of such | is the king | -dom of God | St. Luke | XVIII.16. |' blocked in relief within the opening of the book. The spine is blocked in gold. A single honeysuckle-like plant is blocked from the tail to the head, with three flowers at the head, The title: '| Scripture | readings. | Or | the Bible | Familiarly | explained | for young people |' is blocked in relief within two ribbon-shaped gold lettering-pieces, running downwards around the plant stem. Signed 'JL' in gold as separate letters at the base of the plant. A fillet is blocked near the tail. The word: '| Patriarchs |' is blocked in gold at the tail, between two gold fillets.

172 Leighton, John

Keddie, William. *Cyclopaedia of literary and scientific anecdote; illustrative of the characters, habits, and conversation of men of letters and science. Edited by William Keddie.* London and Glasgow: Published by William Griffin and Company, 1854. Glasgow: W. G. Blackie & Co, Printers, Villafield. Xvi, 368 p. With eight pages of publisher's titles bound at the end.
127 × 195 × 35 mm. 12315.f.23.

No original endpapers and pastedowns. Brown ungrained cloth. (The cloth is very lightly vertically-ribbed.) Both covers blocked identically in blind on the borders and on the corners. Two fillets are blocked on the borders, one thick, one thin. Passion flower plant leaves, stems and buds are blocked in blind on each corner. The same central vignette is blocked on both covers, in blind on the lower, in gold on the upper. It shows a

lamp heating a glass water container. The end of the container drips water onto the pages of an open book. The pages on the right hand side of the book are curled; on the left hand side the text reads: '| Retort | Repartee | & | Words | of Wisdom |' blocked in relief. The title: '| Cyclopaedia | of |' is blocked in gold above the book; the words: '| Literary & scientific | anecdote |' are blocked in gold below the open book. Signed 'JL' in gold as separate letters at the base of the vignette. The spine is blocked in gold. A single gold fillet is blocked around the perimeter. From the head downwards, the decoration is: a laurel wreath; a light with rays; then the title: '| Cyclopaedia | of | literary | & | scientific | anecdote. |' blocked in gold; a torch with scientific instruments and ribbons blocked across it; then lily leaves and stems. Two fillets are blocked in gold at the tail.

Dry, *JL* no. 129.

173 Leighton, John

Krummacher, Frederic Adolphus. *The Parables. With forty Illustrations Drawn by J. R. Clayton; Engraved by the Brothers Dalziel.* London: Nathaniel Cooke, Milford House, Strand, 1854. London: Printed by Levey, Robson, and Franklyn, Great New Street and Fetter Lane. viii, 280 p.
130 × 175 × 25 mm. RdeB.C.24.

The British Museum de Beaumont copy.

Gilt edges. Blue endpapers and pastedowns. Circular bookplate of Edward Dalziel pasted on upper pastedown. Letter from Clayton to Edward Dalziel of the 25 Nov. 1901 is tipped onto the upper endpaper. Blue rib horizontal-grain cloth, also moiré. Both covers blocked identically in blind. Two fillets are blocked in blind on the borders. A pattern of branches, leaves and flowers rises from the tail to the head, blocked in blind. It forms the central frame. The upper cover central vignette is blocked in gold. It shows a man and a boy standing in front of a rose bush. The spine is blocked in gold. From the head downwards, the decoration is: a fillet and small straps in gold; the words: '| The | Parables | of Krummacher | [rule] | Illustrated. |' blocked in gold; an ivy branch is blocked from near the tail to underneath the title, with leaves and berries – all in gold; signed 'JL' in gold as separate letters at the base of the branch; small leaf and berry decoration is blocked in gold between two fillets; the words: '| London. | N. Cooke. |' are blocked in gold; a gold fillet is blocked at the tail.

de Beaumont, *RdeB1* no. 155. Goldman, *VIB* no. 155.

174 Leighton, John PLATE XXII

Longfellow, Henry Wadsworth. *The golden legend. Illustrated with fifty engravings on wood, from designs by Birket Foster and Jane E. Hay.* London: David Bogue, 86 Fleet Street, 1854. London: Henry Vizetelly, Printer & Engraver, Gough Square, Fleet Street. viii, 224 p.
136 × 210 × 28 mm. C.109.b.3.

The plates are signed with the illustrators' names and are also signed 'H. Vizetelly Sc.'.

Text sewn on three tapes. Bevelled boards. Gilt edges. Yellow endpapers and pastedowns. Blue ripple horizontal-grain cloth. Both covers are fully blocked in gold, with an identical design. Two thin fillets are blocked on the borders. There is an 'ivy leaf' pattern, with sprays of buds blocked on the corners and on the sides. Each cover has a recessed centre panel. Around the perimeter of this, two fillets are blocked in gold. The centre panel is 'oriental' shaped at top and bottom. A fillet blocked in blind on the perimeter of the recess. Within this fillet, decoration is blocked in relief. The centre-piece is blocked in gold, showing a nearly formed mandorla, blocked as a gold lettering-piece. The mandorla has small decoration blocked in relief inside, and it is surrounded by lily-like leaves and stems. Signed 'JL' in gold as a monogram at the base of the centre-piece. The spine is blocked in gold. A single gold fillet is blocked on the perimeter. From the head downwards, the decoration is: three 'ivy-like' leaves and groups of buds; the words: '| The | Golden | Legend. | [rule] | Longfellow. |' blocked in gold; a cross botonny in gold; another symmetrical group of ivy-like leaves and berries; a gold fillet; a plant decorative pattern; a gold fillet at the tail. Formerly shelved at 1347.h.14.

Dry, *JL* no. 136. King, *JL* p. 241.

175 Leighton, John

Maitland, Julia Charlotte. *Cat and dog; or, memoirs of Puss and the Captain. A Story founded on Fact. With illustrations by Harrison Weir. Second edition.* London: Grant and Griffith , (Successors to Newbery and Harris,) Corner of St. Paul's Churchyard, 1854. London: Printed by Levey, Robson, and Franklyn, Great New Street, Fetter Lane. 99 p., 3 plates. With eight pages of publisher's titles bound at the end.
130 × 176 × 12 mm. 12837.ff.11.

On page two of the publisher's titles, this work is listed as: 'Price 2s. 6d. cloth, plain; 3s. 6d. coloured gilt edges.'

Blue morocco vertical-grain cloth. Both covers have the same blocking in blind on the borders, on the corners and on the sides. There are two fillets blocked on the borders, one thick, one thin. Leaf and flower decoration is blocked in blind and in relief on the corners, with leaves and stems blocked on the sides, the head and the tail. The upper cover has a central vignette blocked in gold. It shows a dog sleeping in its kennel, with its head and its tail protruding from the kennel entrance. The title: '| Cat & dog | or | Puss and the Captain. |' is blocked in gold, in rustic letters above and below the kennel. The word '| or |' is blocked in relief within the kennel. Signed 'JL' in gold at the bottom right-hand corner of the kennel. The spine is blocked in gold. A cat's head is blocked at the head, with a ribbon hanging from its neck. Below this, the title: '| Cat | & | Dog | A | story |' is blocked in gold. A chain leads down the spine to the tail.

—— Another copy. London: Grant & Griffith, (Successors to Newbery and Harris,) Corner of St. Paul's Churchyard, 1854.

London: Printed by Levey, Robson, and Franklyn, Great New Street and Fetter Lane. 99 p., 4 plates. With eight pages of publisher's titles bound at the end.
125 × 172 × 12 mm. 12806.b.59.

On page 1 of the publisher's titles at the end: 'Price 2s. 6d. cloth, plain; 3s. 6d. coloured, gilt edges.'

Edges speckled with red ink. Light yellow endpapers and pastedowns. Red rib horizontal-grain cloth, lightly moiré. Both covers have the same blocking in blind on the borders, on the corners and on the sides. There are two fillets blocked on the borders, the outer thick, the inner thin. Leaf and flower decoration is blocked on the corners, with leaves and stems blocked on the sides, the head and the tail. The upper cover has a central vignette blocked in gold. It shows a dog sleeping in its kennel, with its head and its tail protruding from the kennel entrance. The title: '| Cat & dog | Puss and the Captain. |' is blocked in gold, in rustic letters above and below the kennel. Signed 'JL' in gold as a monogram on the bottom right hand corner of the kennel. Spine missing.

Dry, *JL* no. 71. The 1853 edition.

176 Leighton, John

Mayhew, Henry. *The story of the peasant-boy philosopher: or, 'A child gathering pebbles on the sea shore.' (Founded on the early life of Ferguson, the shepherd-boy astronomer, and intended to show how a poor lad became acquainted with the principles of natural science.)* . . . London: David Bogue, 86, Fleet Street, 1854. London: Savill and Edwards, Printers, Chandos Street. xvi, 484 p., 8 plates. With twenty-four pages of publisher's titles bound at the end.
114 × 175 × 45 mm. 12806.e.28.

The first page of 'David Bogue's . . .Annual Catalogue' at the end reproduces the frontispiece illustration of Leighton's 'Suggestions in design', and is signed 'Luke Limner del.'

Text sewn on three sawn-in cords. Yellow endpapers and pastedowns. Binder's ticket on lower pastedown: '| Leighton | Son & | Hodge | Shoe Lane | London. |' Red morocco horizontal-grain cloth. Both covers blocked identically in blind and in relief. A single fillet is blocked in blind on the borders. An inner border is blocked in blind of rectangular panels, which are formed by two fillets. Celtic strapwork is blocked in relief within each panel. A square is blocked in blind on each corner, with a four-leaf Celtic motif blocked in relief within each square. From head to tail of each cover, an arabesque is blocked in blind and in relief, with an 'onion-shape' on the centre, which has decorative work within blocked in relief. Signed 'JL' in blind as a monogram at the base of the arabesque. The spine is blocked in gold. Two fillets are blocked on the perimeter. From the head downwards, the decoration is: a hatched gold half-moon, with stars in gold; the words: '| The | story | of the | peasant boy | philosopher | [rule] | Henry Mayhew. |' blocked in gold, within a cup-shaped panel, which is formed by a single thin branch, with leaves on its top; a sextant in gold; an orrery in gold; a measuring scale, a winch, and a sundial – all blocked in gold; the monogram 'JM'; at the tail, flower and stems and strapwork are blocked in gold.

177 Leighton, John

Meadows, Amy. *Happy days of childhood. Illustrated with Twenty-four Pictures by Harrison Weir, and a Frontispiece by Birket Foster.* London: Joseph Cundall, 168 New Bond Street, 1854. London: Printed by G. Barclay, Castle St, Leicester Sq. [51 p.], 25 plates.
170 × 215 × 14 mm. 12805.h.33.

Yellow endpapers and pastedowns. Brown ripple horizontal-grain cloth. The blocking appears to have been done after casing in. Both covers blocked identically in blind on the borders, the corners, and on the sides. Two fillets are blocked in the borders, one thin, one thick. From the tail to the top of each cover, on the left and right, a plant is blocked, showing its roots, bulb. stem, leaves, buds and flower. A dragon fly is blocked in blind on the centre head. Signed 'JL' in blind as separate letters at the centre base, within strapwork. The upper cover has a central vignette blocked in gold. It shows a girl dancing, holding a hoop; sprigs of flowers and leaves are in the girl's hands. A spray of flowers is blocked above the girl. The title: '| Happy days of | child hood |' is blocked in gold above and below the girl, in rustic lettering. Signed 'JL' in gold as a monogram at the base of the vignette. The plates are monochrome.

The Sampson Low copy at BL shelfmark 12807.d.5. has the same plates, which are hand coloured. Each plate is back to back with the letterpress. Paper covers over boards. The upper cover shows a boy on a ladder looking into a dovecote. The lower cover has a list of publisher's titles.

Dry, *JL* no. 139. Leighton, *SID, 1880* plate 80, no. 1. 'Grass-form plant'. McLean, *Cundall* p. 79.

178 Leighton, John

Meulan, afterwards, Guizot, Elisabeth Charlotte Pauline de. *Popular tales. Translated from the French by Mrs. L. Burke. With illustrations.* London: George Routledge & Co., Farringdon Street, 1854. London: Reed and Parton, Printers, Paternoster-Row. [7],357 p., plates. With two pages of publisher's titles bound at the end.
110 × 175 × 27 mm. 12512.c.23.

Yellow endpapers and pastedowns. Binder's ticket on lower pastedown: '| Bound by | Bone & Son, | [rule] | 76, Fleet Street, | London. |' Red wave diagonal-grain cloth. Both covers identically blocked in blind on the borders and on the corners. Three fillets are blocked on the borders. Leaf and stem decoration is blocked on each corner. The lower cover has a central vignette blocked in blind. It shows a torque-shape. The upper cover has a central vignette blocked in gold. It shows fuchsia flowers and buds, with stems forming a circle. The words: '| Guizot's | Popular | Tales |' are blocked in gold within the circle, in fanciful letters. At the base, a hand – with a

ruff at the wrist – holds a stylus. Signed 'JL' in gold as separate letters at the base of the vignette. The spine is blocked in gold. The decoration from the head downwards is: a panel, formed by a single gold fillet, with the words: '| Guizot's | Popular | Tales |' blocked in gold; a bird cage, its door open; a lady on a stool, holding the bird; a cat immediately underneath the stool – all three are within a cord surround, which ends in tassels; a tasselled plinth is blocked at the tail. Signed 'JL' in gold as separate letters at the tail.

Dry, *JL* no. 128. Leighton, *SID, 1852*. Plate XXXV, no. II. Shows fuchsia flowers and buds.

179 Leighton, John

Moore, Thomas *the Poet. Irish melodies.* London: Longman, Brown, Green and Longmans, 1854. xxviii, 139 p. With four pages of publisher's advertisements bound at the end.
70 × 109 × 13 mm. 11647.a.21.

Gilt edges. Yellow endpapers and pastedowns. Binder's ticket on lower pastedown: '| Leighton | Son & | Hodge, | Shoe Lane | London. |'. Blue ripple horizontal-grain cloth. Both covers have two fillets blocked in blind on the borders, the outer thin, the inner thick. The upper cover has a vignette blocked in gold, showing a tracery of clover leaves and stems surrounding an Irish harp. The title: '| Irish | Melodies. |' is blocked in gold. Signed 'JL', as a monogram in gold, at base of vignette. The spine is blocked in gold. The words: '| Irish | Melodies | by | Thomas | Moore. |' are blocked in gold between two gold fillets. Clover leaves and stems are blocked in gold above and below the lettering.

Dry, *JL* no. 140.

180 Leighton, John

FIG. 15

Moore, Thomas *the Poet. Lallah Rookh, an Oriental Romance.* London: Longman, Brown, Green, and Longmans, 1854. xvi, 231 p., 1 plate
70 × 110 × 15 mm. 11647.a.19.

Gilt edges. Yellow endpapers and pastedowns. Binder's ticket on lower pastedown: '| Leighton | Son & | Hodge, | Shoe Lane | London. |'. Green ripple horizontal-grain cloth. Both covers blocked in blind with two fillets blocked on the borders. The upper cover has a vignette blocked in gold, of an arabesque shape, showing flowers, leaves and stems. Signed 'JL', as a monogram in gold, at the base of the vignette. The letters 'JL' are blocked in reverse. The spine is blocked in gold. From the head downwards, the decoration is: leaves blocked in gold within an oval panel formed by several fillets; the title: '| Lalla | Rookh | by | Thomas | Moore. |' blocked in gold, within a panel formed by two gold fillets; a mandorla is formed by three gold fillets and gold dots on its perimeter, and has leaf decoration blocked within it in gold; a small mandorla is formed by two gold fillets and gold dots, with leaf decoration blocked in gold within it.

Dry, *JL* no. 141.

FIG. 15

181 Leighton, John

Osler, Edward. *The life of Viscount Exmouth. A New and Revised Edition.* London: Geo. Routledge & Co., Farringdon Street, and 18, Beekman Street, New York, 1854. London: Printed by Stewart and Murray, Old Bailey. xv, 235 p. With four pages of publisher's titles bound at the end.
110 × 175 × 25 mm. 10816.a.35.

Original upper yellow endpaper bound at the front. Blue ripple horizontal-grain cloth. The borders and corners of both covers are identically blocked in blind. Two fillets are blocked on the borders and a plant pattern on the corners. On the lower cover, the central vignette is blocked in blind, and displays a leaf, stem and bud pattern. On the upper cover, the central vignette is blocked in gold. A lion rampant, dexter, and a sailor, sinister, support the central medallion. Within the medallion, a lion, courant, gules, crossed laurel leaves; three masted sailing ship and castle. A coronet surmounts the medallion, with a crest of a ship and a castle. The sailor holds shackles in his left hand, and a cross in his right. The lion's feet and the sailor's feet rest on a gold lettering piece, with patterns blocked in relief; the word '| Algiers |' is blocked in relief in the middle. The title: '| The | life of | Admiral Viscount | Exmouth. |' is blocked in gold above and below the medallion. Signed 'JL' in gold as a mono-

ruff at the wrist – holds a stylus. Signed 'JL' in gold as separate letters at the base of the vignette. The spine is blocked in gold. The decoration from the head downwards is: a panel, formed by a single gold fillet, with the words: '| Guizot's | Popular | Tales |' blocked in gold; a bird cage, its door open; a lady on a stool, holding the bird; a cat immediately underneath the stool – all three are within a cord surround, which ends in tassels; a tasselled plinth is blocked at the tail. Signed 'JL' in gold as separate letters at the tail.

Dry, *JL* no. 128. Leighton, *SID, 1852*. Plate XXXV, no. II. Shows fuchsia flowers and buds.

179 Leighton, John

Moore, Thomas *the Poet. Irish melodies.* London: Longman, Brown, Green and Longmans, 1854. xxviii, 139 p. With four pages of publisher's advertisements bound at the end.
70 × 109 × 13 mm. 11647.a.21.

Gilt edges. Yellow endpapers and pastedowns. Binder's ticket on lower pastedown: '| Leighton | Son & | Hodge, | Shoe Lane | London. |'. Blue ripple horizontal-grain cloth. Both covers have two fillets blocked in blind on the borders, the outer thin, the inner thick. The upper cover has a vignette blocked in gold, showing a tracery of clover leaves and stems surrounding an Irish harp. The title: '| Irish | Melodies. |' is blocked in gold. Signed 'JL', as a monogram in gold, at base of vignette. The spine is blocked in gold. The words: '| Irish | Melodies | by | Thomas | Moore. |' are blocked in gold between two gold fillets. Clover leaves and stems are blocked in gold above and below the lettering.

Dry, *JL* no. 140.

180 Leighton, John FIG. 15

Moore, Thomas *the Poet. Lallah Rookh, an Oriental Romance.* London: Longman, Brown, Green, and Longmans, 1854. xvi, 231 p., 1 plate
70 × 110 × 15 mm. 11647.a.19.

Gilt edges. Yellow endpapers and pastedowns. Binder's ticket on lower pastedown: '| Leighton | Son & | Hodge, | Shoe Lane | London. |'. Green ripple horizontal-grain cloth. Both covers blocked in blind with two fillets blocked on the borders. The upper cover has a vignette blocked in gold, of an arabesque shape, showing flowers, leaves and stems. Signed 'JL', as a monogram in gold, at the base of the vignette. The letters 'JL' are blocked in reverse. The spine is blocked in gold. From the head downwards, the decoration is: leaves blocked in gold within an oval panel formed by several fillets; the title: '| Lalla | Rookh | by | Thomas | Moore. |' blocked in gold, within a panel formed by two gold fillets; a mandorla is formed by three gold fillets and gold dots on its perimeter, and has leaf decoration blocked within it in gold; a small mandorla is formed by two gold fillets and gold dots, with leaf decoration blocked in gold within it.

Dry, *JL* no. 141.

FIG. 15

181 Leighton, John

Osler, Edward. *The life of Viscount Exmouth. A New and Revised Edition.* London: Geo. Routledge & Co., Farringdon Street, and 18, Beekman Street, New York, 1854. London: Printed by Stewart and Murray, Old Bailey. xv, 235 p. With four pages of publisher's titles bound at the end.
110 × 175 × 25 mm. 10816.a.35.

Original upper yellow endpaper bound at the front. Blue ripple horizontal-grain cloth. The borders and corners of both covers are identically blocked in blind. Two fillets are blocked on the borders and a plant pattern on the corners. On the lower cover, the central vignette is blocked in blind, and displays a leaf, stem and bud pattern. On the upper cover, the central vignette is blocked in gold. A lion rampant, dexter, and a sailor, sinister, support the central medallion. Within the medallion, a lion, courant, gules, crossed laurel leaves; three masted sailing ship and castle. A coronet surmounts the medallion, with a crest of a ship and a castle. The sailor holds shackles in his left hand, and a cross in his right. The lion's feet and the sailor's feet rest on a gold lettering piece, with patterns blocked in relief; the word '| Algiers |' is blocked in relief in the middle. The title: '| The | life of | Admiral Viscount | Exmouth. |' is blocked in gold above and below the medallion. Signed 'JL' in gold as a mono-

London: Printed by Levey, Robson, and Franklyn, Great New Street and Fetter Lane. 99 p., 4 plates. With eight pages of publisher's titles bound at the end.
125 × 172 × 12 mm. 12806.b.59.

On page 1 of the publisher's titles at the end: 'Price 2s. 6d. cloth, plain; 3s. 6d. coloured, gilt edges.'

Edges speckled with red ink. Light yellow endpapers and pastedowns. Red rib horizontal-grain cloth, lightly moiré. Both covers have the same blocking in blind on the borders, on the corners and on the sides. There are two fillets blocked on the borders, the outer thick, the inner thin. Leaf and flower decoration is blocked on the corners, with leaves and stems blocked on the sides, the head and the tail. The upper cover has a central vignette blocked in gold. It shows a dog sleeping in its kennel, with its head and its tail protruding from the kennel entrance. The title: '| Cat & dog | Puss and the Captain. |' is blocked in gold, in rustic letters above and below the kennel. Signed 'JL' in gold as a monogram on the bottom right hand corner of the kennel. Spine missing.

Dry, *JL* no. 71. The 1853 edition.

176 Leighton, John

Mayhew, Henry. *The story of the peasant-boy philosopher: or, 'A child gathering pebbles on the sea shore.' (Founded on the early life of Ferguson, the shepherd-boy astronomer, and intended to show how a poor lad became acquainted with the principles of natural science.)* . . . London: David Bogue, 86, Fleet Street, 1854. London: Savill and Edwards, Printers, Chandos Street. xvi, 484 p., 8 plates. With twenty-four pages of publisher's titles bound at the end.
114 × 175 × 45 mm. 12806.e.28.

The first page of 'David Bogue's . . .Annual Catalogue' at the end reproduces the frontispiece illustration of Leighton's 'Suggestions in design', and is signed 'Luke Limner del.'

Text sewn on three sawn-in cords. Yellow endpapers and pastedowns. Binder's ticket on lower pastedown: '| Leighton | Son & | Hodge | Shoe Lane | London. |' Red morocco horizontal-grain cloth. Both covers blocked identically in blind and in relief. A single fillet is blocked in blind on the borders. An inner border is blocked in blind of rectangular panels, which are formed by two fillets. Celtic strapwork is blocked in relief within each panel. A square is blocked in blind on each corner, with a four-leaf Celtic motif blocked in relief within each square. From head to tail of each cover, an arabesque is blocked in blind and in relief, with an 'onion-shape' on the centre, which has decorative work within blocked in relief. Signed 'JL' in blind as a monogram at the base of the arabesque. The spine is blocked in gold. Two fillets are blocked on the perimeter. From the head downwards, the decoration is: a hatched gold half-moon, with stars in gold; the words: '| The | story | of the | peasant boy | philosopher | [rule] | Henry Mayhew. |' blocked in gold, within a cup-shaped panel, which is formed by a single thin branch, with leaves on its top; a sextant in gold; an orrery in gold; a measuring scale, a winch, and a sundial – all blocked in gold; the monogram 'JM'; at the tail, flower and stems and strapwork are blocked in gold.

177 Leighton, John

Meadows, Amy. *Happy days of childhood. Illustrated with Twenty-four Pictures by Harrison Weir, and a Frontispiece by Birket Foster.* London: Joseph Cundall, 168 New Bond Street, 1854. London: Printed by G. Barclay, Castle St, Leicester Sq. [51 p.], 25 plates.
170 × 215 × 14 mm. 12805.h.33.

Yellow endpapers and pastedowns. Brown ripple horizontal-grain cloth. The blocking appears to have been done after casing in. Both covers blocked identically in blind on the borders, the corners, and on the sides. Two fillets are blocked in the borders, one thin, one thick. From the tail to the top of each cover, on the left and right, a plant is blocked, showing its roots, bulb. stem, leaves, buds and flower. A dragon fly is blocked in blind on the centre head. Signed 'JL' in blind as separate letters at the centre base, within strapwork. The upper cover has a central vignette blocked in gold. It shows a girl dancing, holding a hoop; sprigs of flowers and leaves are in the girl's hands. A spray of flowers is blocked above the girl. The title: '| Happy days of | child hood |' is blocked in gold above and below the girl, in rustic lettering. Signed 'JL' in gold as a monogram at the base of the vignette. The plates are monochrome.

The Sampson Low copy at BL shelfmark 12807.d.5. has the same plates, which are hand coloured. Each plate is back to back with the letterpress. Paper covers over boards. The upper cover shows a boy on a ladder looking into a dovecote. The lower cover has a list of publisher's titles.

Dry, *JL* no. 139. Leighton, *SID, 1880* plate 80, no. 1. 'Grass-form plant'. McLean, *Cundall* p. 79.

178 Leighton, John

Meulan, afterwards, Guizot, Elisabeth Charlotte Pauline de. *Popular tales. Translated from the French by Mrs. L. Burke. With illustrations.* London: George Routledge & Co., Farringdon Street, 1854. London: Reed and Parton, Printers, Paternoster-Row. [7],357 p., plates. With two pages of publisher's titles bound at the end.
110 × 175 × 27 mm. 12512.c.23.

Yellow endpapers and pastedowns. Binder's ticket on lower pastedown: '| Bound by | Bone & Son, | [rule] | 76, Fleet Street, | London. |' Red wave diagonal-grain cloth. Both covers identically blocked in blind on the borders and on the corners. Three fillets are blocked on the borders. Leaf and stem decoration is blocked on each corner. The lower cover has a central vignette blocked in blind. It shows a torque-shape. The upper cover has a central vignette blocked in gold. It shows fuchsia flowers and buds, with stems forming a circle. The words: '| Guizot's | Popular | Tales |' are blocked in gold within the circle, in fanciful letters. At the base, a hand – with a

or Read & think | ' are blocked in gold above and on each side of the easel in fanciful lettering. Signed 'JL' in gold as separate letters at the base of the vignette. The spine is blocked in gold. A single fillet is blocked around the perimeter. Two fillets are blocked in gold at the head and the tail. The spine is divided into five panels: panels 1,3,5 are blocked with thin rectangles with leaf decoration, blocked in gold; panel 2 has the title words: '| John Railton | or | read | & | think' blocked in gold; panel 4 has a lily plant and leaves blocked in gold and relief, with a crossed feather and a paper knife blocked in gold in the middle of the panel.

Dry, *JL* no. 148.

184 Leighton, John

PLATE XXIV

Scott, *Sir* Walter *Bart. The Lay of the Last Minstrel. With all his introductions, and the editor's notes. Illustrated by one hundred engravings on wood from drawings by Birket Foster and John Gilbert.* Edinburgh: Adam and Charles Black, North Bridge, Booksellers and Publishers to the Queen, 1854. Edinburgh: R. & R. Clark. 354 p.

137 × 210 × 37 mm. 11642.e.27.

Bevelled boards. Gilt edges. Yellow endpapers and pastedowns. Red morocco horizontal grain cloth. Both covers blocked identically in gold. A single gold fillet is blocked on the borders. A banner pole, spear tipped at each end, is blocked at the top of the cover, and supports drapery. Within the drapery, top left, a lion rampant is blocked; top right, a cross is blocked. Within niches on each side of the central recessed medieval arch panel, figures are blocked – to the left: a knight in armour, plus shield and axe; to the right: an archer, with bow, arrow and sword. Each is supported on a plinth and is surrounded by tracery. On the tail, left and right, a coat of arms, argent, is blocked within circles formed by three fillets. The arms are: three cranes; two crescents and mallet within bend. Four coats of arms are blocked on the centre tail, within mediaeval decorated arches and columns. From the left the coats of arms, argent, are: 1. three stars in chief, crown and vase; 2. double headed eagle displayed, augmentation saltire; 3. lion rampant; 4. six crosses crosslet fitchy, shield (containing an 'S', possibly denoting Scott), and molet in bend. With the recessed central panel, a gothic window with intersecting tracery is blocked. The title: '| Lay | of | The Last | Minstrel | ' is blocked in gothic letters between the window mullions. The spine is blocked in gold. A single gold fillet is blocked on the perimeter. From the head downwards, the decoration is: decorated gothic window at the head; the title: '| Lay | of | The Last | Minstrel | ' blocked in gold in gothic letters within the window; an arabesque panel formed by two gold fillets, and is surrounded by small decoration; within the arabesque, the words: '| Authors | Edition | Illustrated | ' are blocked in gold within a pennant curling downwards; double pointed thin gothic arches; within these, near the tail, a man is blocked, dressed in knee breeches, stockings and wearing a tartan cloak, holding a harp on his left knee; a gold fillet; at the tail, '| A & C Black Edinburgh | ' is blocked in gold within a rectangle formed by a single gold fillet. [Spine missing from BL copy; description from Compiler's copy.]

Dry, *JL* no. 150A. Pantazzi, *JL* p. 266. Attributes this binding to John Leighton.

185 Leighton, John

Sheppard, Elizabeth Sara. *The day of a baby-boy. A Tale for a Little Child. By E. Berger. The illustrations from drawings by John Absolon . . .* London: Grant & Griffith, (Successors to Newbery and Harris,) corner of St Paul's Churchyard, 1854. London: Printed by Levey, Robson, and Franklyn, Great New Street and Fetter Lane. 90 p., 4 plates. With eight pages of publisher's titles bound at the end.

126 × 172 × 11 mm. 12806.b.57.

Printed on page one of the publisher's titles: 'Price 2s. 6d. cloth, plain; 3s. 6d. coloured [plates], gilt edges'.

Edges speckled with red ink. Light yellow endpapers and pastedowns. Red wave diagonal-grain cloth. Both covers identically blocked in blind. Two fillets are blocked on the borders. Curling stem, stylised leaf, and flower decoration are blocked on each corner and on the side, the flower stamen decoration being blocked in relief. [This is the same decoration in blind on the borders as on BL 12806.bb.49. – Lushington. The happy home.] The upper cover central vignette is blocked in gold. It shows a small tree growing behind a stone wall. The sun and its rays are rising behind the tree. An adult bird is about to land to feed a single chick in a nest at the top of the tree. The title words: '| The | day | of a | baby boy. | ' are blocked in gold in rustic letters, above and on either side of the tree. A wall and its coping stones are blocked in within a hatched gold lettering-piece. Signed 'JL' in gold as separate letters within the wall, on the centre. The spine is blocked in gold. The lower half is missing. A bird is blocked at the head. The title words: '| The | day | of | a | baby | boy. | ' are blocked in gold. Below this leaves on a stem are blocked in gold.

Dry, *JL* no. 110.

186 Leighton, John

Spencer, Edmund. *Turkey, Russia, The Black Sea, and Circassia. Third Thousand. With coloured illustrations, numerous engravings, and a map.* London: George Routledge & Co. Farringdon Street, 1854. London: R. Clay, Printer, Bread Street Hill. xi, 404 p., 4 plates, 1 fold-out map.

120 × 190 × 33 mm. 10027.d.29.

The fold-out map is entitled: 'The | Turkish | Empire, | comprising the Caucasian Isthmus, | with the adjoining Countries, forming a complete map | of the present seat of war in the East. | Revised by the Author from the latest | Russian & Turkish Authorities. | Engraved by Becker & Co.'s patent process on steel, 11 Stationer's Court, City. | '

Yellow endpapers and pastedowns. Red morocco vertical-grain cloth. Both covers blocked identically in blind on the bor-

gram at the base of the vignette. The spine is blocked in gold. A single gold fillet is blocked on the perimeter. From the head downwards, the decoration is: two gold fillets; a crown in gold; the title: '| The | life | of | Admiral | Viscount | Exmouth |' is blocked in gold; a spear, inverted, and a flagpole are blocked in gold; the Union Jack flies from the top of the flagpole; the Union Jack has a long pennant, which winds around the spear and the flagpole; the word '| Algiers |' is blocked in relief within the pennant.

Dry, *JL* no. 144.

182 Leighton, John FIG. 16

Proctor, George. *History of the Crusades: their rise, progress, and results. With illustrations by Gilbert, Sargent, etc.* London and Glasgow: Richard Grffin and Company, Publishers to the University of Glasgow, 1854. Edinburgh: Printed at the University Press. xvi, 208 p., 12 plates. With eight pages of publisher's titles bound at the end.

130 × 200 × 25 mm. 4570.c.17.

The plates engraved by Dalziel, Gorway.

Yellow endpapers and pastedowns. Blue rib vertical-grain cloth. Binder's ticket on lower pastedown: '| Bound by | Adam Gowans, | Glasgow. |' The same design is blocked on both covers, in blind on the lower and in gold on the upper. The borders and corners are blocked in blind on both covers. Two fillets are blocked on the borders, and curling leaves on the corners. The central vignette features a sword which passes from top to bottom of the vignette. The handle of the sword is crossed by a pennant-shaped gold lettering-piece, inside which the words: '| To chace [sic] | these pagans | in those holy fields. |' are blocked in relief. The centre of the vignette is a gold lettering-piece shaped as a shield, argent; it covers the shaft of the sword. In the shield, the words: '| History | of the | Crusades |', and a Maltese cross, are blocked in relief. To the left and right and below the shield are pennant-shaped gold lettering-pieces, with the following words blocked in relief within each: '| Over whose acres | walk'd those blessed | feet, | which | eighteen hundred | years ago, | were nail'd | For our | advantage | on the | bitter + [cross] | . Shakspear [sic]. |' At the point of the sword is a tuft of grass. Beneath it, a small diamond-shaped gold lettering-piece is blocked, with the signature 'JL' blocked inside in relief as separate letters. The spine is blocked in gold. Three gold fillets are blocked at the head. From the head downwards, the decoration is: a cross is blocked, with hatching; four smaller crosses are blocked in the corners of the larger one; the title: '| History | of | the Crusades |' blocked in gold, in gothic letters;. underneath the word 'of', a moon is blocked, with hatch; beneath the title a palm tree is blocked, with a shield in the middle of its trunk; the shield, argent, cross gules, with the lamb of God in the centre; roots are blocked at the base of the tree and underneath this is a Maltese cross, then small decorative device; a gold fillet; the words : '| Griffin & Co. |' are blocked in gold between single gold fillets; three gold fillets blocked at the tail.

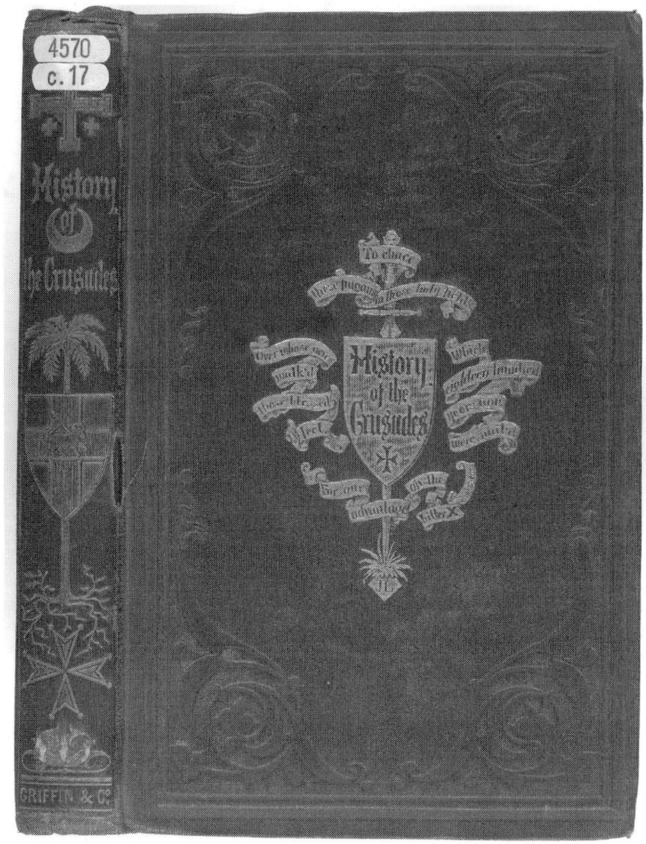

FIG. 16

183 Leighton, John

Robson, William. *John Railton; or, read and think. . . . With illustrations.* London: George Routledge & Co., Farringdon Street, 1854. [London]: Printed by Cox (Bros.) and Wyman, Great Queen Street. viii, 373 p., 7 plates. With two pages of publisher's titles bound at the end.

110 × 177 × 27 mm. 12619.d.11.

The plates are signed: 'Dalziel.'

Bolts uncut. Yellow endpapers and pastedowns. Red morocco vertical-grain cloth. Both covers blocked identically in blind on the borders and the corners. Two fillets are blocked on the borders. Strapwork and fillets blocked on the corners and on the sides. The upper cover has a central vignette blocked in gold. It shows an artist's easel. A wreath hangs from its top, on the left. An open book, blocked as a gold lettering-piece, rests on a bar in the middle of the easel. The words: '| Books | teach us to | refine our | pleasures | when young | & to recall | them with | satisfaction | when old. |' are blocked in relief within the open pages of the book. At the base of the easel on the right, a palette and an artist's wrist-stick are propped, together with a scroll-shaped gold lettering-piece, with the word '| Music |' blocked in relief within it. At the base on the left, a lyre and a portfolio are propped, the portfolio has the word '| Sketches |' blocked in relief on its cover. The title words: '| John Railton |

ders, with an ivy berry and stem pattern between two fillets. A third inner fillet is also blocked in blind, with a small flower head blocked on each corner. The upper cover vignette is blocked in gold. On the centre, a shield is blocked, azure. Within the shield, double-headed crowned eagles are blocked, with each claw holding 1. a ball and sceptre; 2. a staff. An inner shield, gules, shows St. George slaying the Dragon. A crown surmounts the shield. A medallion is blocked above the crown. The words: '| Turkey Russia |' are blocked to the left and to the right of the shield. The words: '| Black Sea | & | Circassia. |' are blocked in gold below the shield. Signed 'JL' in gold as separate letters at the base of the vignette, within a final backwards loop of the '&'. Spine missing.

Dry, *JL* no. 152.

187 Leighton, John

White, Gilbert, *of Selborne. The natural history of Selborne. With additional notes, by the Rev. J. G. Wood., M.A. Illustrated with engravings on wood.* London: G. Routledge & Co. Farringdon Street, 1854. [London]: Richard Clay, Printer, Bread Street Hill. viii, 428 p. With four pages of publisher's titles bound at the end.

118 × 187 × 30 mm. 7005.c.28.

Yellow endpapers and pastedowns. Binder's ticket on lower pastedown: 'Bound by | Burn, | Hatton Garden |'. Red morocco vertical-grain cloth. Both covers blocked in blind on borders. There are three fillets blocked on the outer and inner borders of both covers, with a leaf and branch pattern between the fillets. The upper cover has a vignette blocked in gold, featuring a bird cage, a wooden stool – with a coat and hat draped over it – in front of a desk, which has a lectern on it, with an inkstand, a quill on top of the lectern. A cat seated on the desk looks out at us, or possibly at the dog seated under the desk. Signed 'JL' in gold as separate letters at the base. The spine is blocked in gold. A single gold fillet is blocked on the perimeter. From the head downwards, the decoration is: a gold fillet; a spider's web and leaves and a flower; the title: '| White's | Natural | History | of | Selborne |' is blocked in gold in rustic letters, with gold tendrils at the ends of several letters; a bird holding a quill is perched on an ink-pot, surrounded by leaves, branches; [the copy reproduced by McLean shows 'JL' blocked in gold as separate letters near the tail; this is obscured by the label on the BL copy]; a gold fillet; a decorative pattern; two gold fillets are blocked at the tail.

The S.P.C.K. edition of 1860 has 338 p. is at BL shelfmark 7005.c.29. Binder's ticket on lower pastedown: 'Trickett & Son Binders.' Brown morocco-grain cloth. Blind blocked on both covers. Spine fully blocked in gold. Unsigned.

McLean, *VPBB* p. 62.

188 Leighton, John

Wood, John George. *Sketches and anecdotes of animal life. With illustrations by Harrison Weir.* London: G. Routledge and Co., Farringdon Street. New York: 18, Beekman Street, 1854. London: Printed by Woodfall and Kinder, Angel Court, Skinner Street. [3], 428 p., 8 plates.

110 × 170 × 42 mm. 7205.a.44.

The plates are engraved by Dalziel.

Original yellow endpaper bound at the front. Red morocco horizontal-grain cloth. Both covers blocked identically in blind and in relief. Three fillets are blocked on the borders. Stars are blocked in relief on the inner corners. Each cover has a central vignette, blocked in blind. It shows a bird cage, then the title words: '| Anecdotes | of | animal life |', in rustic lettering; then a stool, a robe, a book, a stick and a cat. Signed 'JL' in blind as a monogram at the base of the vignette. The spine is blocked in gold. The decoration from the head down is: a cat curled up in its own long tail; the words: '| Anecdotes | of | animal | life | JAG. Wood |', in gold in rustic lettering; small leaves and berries. [The spine is damaged – the lower third is missing.]

Dry, *JL* no. 156. Oldfield, *BC* no. 66.

189 Leighton, John

'Suffer little children to come unto me.' A series of scripture lessons for the young. [London]: T. Nelson and Sons, London; Edinburgh; and New York, 1855. Edinburgh: Printed by T. Nelson and Sons. 128 p., 3 plates.

105 × 170 × 15 mm. 3128.c.18.

Edges speckled with red ink. Yellow endpapers and pastedowns. Blue wave diagonal-grain cloth. Both covers are blocked identically in blind on the borders, and on the corners. Two fillets are blocked on the borders, with two more inside this, which end in frets blocked on each corner; small flowers are blocked on the corners. The upper cover central vignette is blocked in gold. The title: '| Suffer little children |' is blocked in gold in a semi-circle above the central picture. The words: '| To come unto me |' are blocked in gold underneath the central picture. The title is blocked in rustic lettering. The central picture consists of a white cloth onlay, blocked in gold, showing Jesus and two children. Signed 'JL' in gold as a monogram at the base of the vignette. The spine is blocked in gold. A single gold fillet is blocked on the perimeter. From the head downwards, the decoration is: a fleur-de-lis, blocked in hatch gold, within circles blocked on either side of an arch formed by two gold fillets; the title: '| Suffer | little | children | to come | unto me |' blocked in gold; the words: '| See that | ye refuse | not him | that | speaketh |' are blocked in gold within a shield formed by three gold fillets; two gold fillets; a fleur-de-lis, blocked in hatch gold, within a circle – both within an oval; a gold fillet is blocked at the tail.

190 Leighton, John

Adams, Charlotte. *Matilda Lonsdale; or the eldest sister. Illustrated by Birket Foster.* London: G. Routledge & Co. Farringdon Street; New York: 18, Beekman Street, 1855. London: Printed by Cox (Bros.) and Wyman, Great Queen

Street. viii, 347 p., 5 plates. With four pages of publisher's titles bound at the end.
110 × 175 × 35 mm. 12631.b.18.

Yellow endpapers and pastedowns. Binder's ticket on the lower pastedown: '| Leighton Son & | Hodge, | Shoe Lane | London. |' Red morocco horizontal-grain cloth. Both covers are blocked identically in blind on the borders and the corners. Three fillets are blocked on the borders. Flowers and leaves are blocked on the corners. On the upper cover, the central vignette is blocked in gold. It shows a bird's nest, with chicks, and two birds in flight. The nest, birds, branches and leaves surround the title: '| Matilda Lonsdale |'. The letters are blocked 'in double', with the capital 'M' of 'Matilda' being blocked inside a square gold lettering-piece, which also has small decoration blocked in relief within it. Signed 'JL' in gold as a monogram at the right-hand base of the vignette. [A small monogram – only 1 mm across.] The spine is blocked in gold. There is a single fillet blocked in gold on the perimeter. The title: '| Matilda Lonsdale |' is blocked in gold. Down the rest of the spine is a single lily with leaves and flowers blocked in gold. The imprint: '| London | Routledge & Co |' is blocked in gold at the tail, inside a rectangle formed by a single gold fillet.

Dry, *JL* no. 157.

191 Leighton, John

Aikman, James. *One hundred animals; or, book of natural history.* London; Edinburgh and New York: T. Nelson and Sons, 1855. Edinburgh: Printed by T. Nelson and Sons. xii, 372 p., 29 plates.
97 × 153 × 30 mm. 7205.a.5.

Yellow endpapers and pastedowns. Blue wave diagonal-grain cloth. Both covers blocked identically in blind only on the borders and on the corners. Two fillets blocked on the borders, one thick, one thin. Leaf and stem decoration is blocked on each corner. The spine is blocked in gold. A single gold fillet is blocked around the perimeter. Two gold fillets are blocked at the head. The words: '| One | hundred | animals | by | James | Aikman | Esq. |' are blocked in gold in rustic lettering within a panel bordered by a single gold fillet. Below this, two monkeys play in a cage; a seated bear is in another cage. Signed 'JL' in relief, within the base of the bear's cage, blocked in gold. Small decoration and two fillets are blocked in gold at the tail.

Dry, *JL* no. 158.

192 Leighton, John FIG. 17

Ainsworth, William Harrison. *The miser's daughter: A Tale . . . With illustrations by George Cruikshank. . . .* London: G. Routledge & Co., Farringdon Street. New York: 18, Beekman Street, 1855. London: Savill, and Edwards, Printers, Chandos Street, Covent Garden. xi, 302 p., 19 plates. With six pages of publisher's titles bound at the end.
142 × 225 × 31 mm. 12603.f.21.

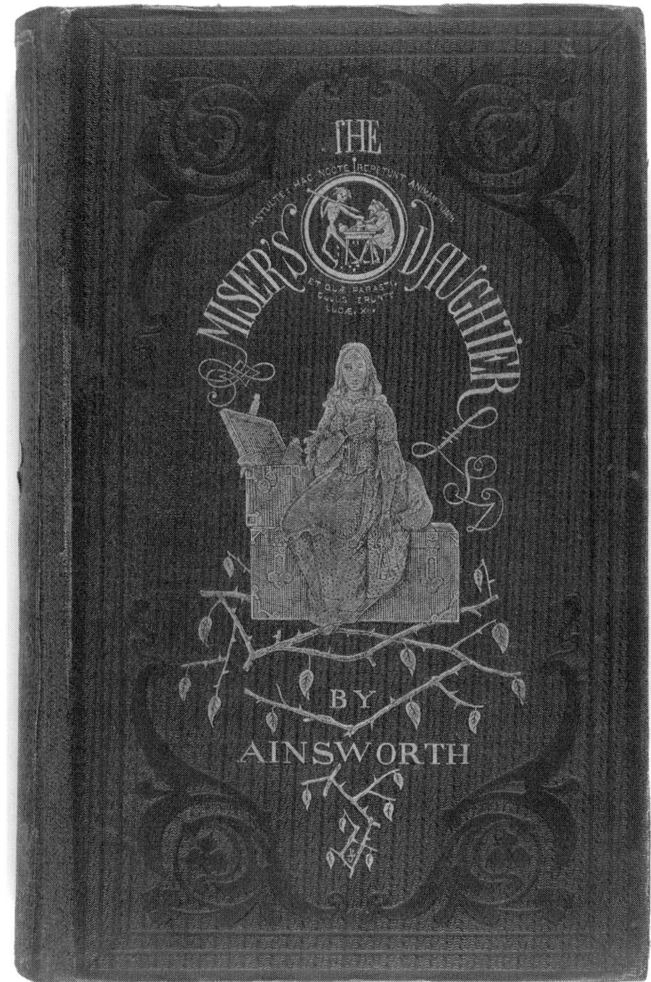

FIG. 17

Yellow endpapers and pastedowns. Blue ripple horizontal-grain cloth. Both covers identically blocked in blind on the borders and on the corners. Three fillets are blocked on the borders, the outer thick, the two inner thin. A leaf and flower pattern is blocked in blind on each corner. The upper cover central panel is blocked in gold. At the head, the title: 'The miser's daughter' is blocked in gold, with a medallion blocked between 'Miser ' and 'daughter' . The medallion shows death pointing a spear at an apothecary, who is seated at a table. The words: ' "Stulte hac nocte repetunt animam tuam | et quae parasti cuus erunt" Lucae. XII. |' is blocked in gold above and below the medallion. The capital 'M' of 'Miser' ends in strapwork. The letter 'R' of 'daughter' ends in the letters '£SD'. At the centre, the daughter (Hilda) is seated on a chest, her left hand holding keys, her right hand holding a packet of papers. Another smaller chest, with its lid open is blocked to her right. Thorn branches are blocked beneath it. The words: '| by | Ainsworth |' are blocked in gold between the thorn branches. Signed 'JL' in gold as a monogram at the base of the branches. The spine is blocked in gold. A single gold fillet is blocked on the perimeter. From the head downwards, the decoration is: a gold fillet; the words: '| The | Miser's | daughter | [rule] |

W. Harrison | Ainsworth. | '; a pole is blocked in gold from the tail upwards – a spade and a vase are blocked at the base of the pole; hung on top of it is a hat; around the middle of the pole, a group of objects is secured by ropes: a lantern, a scroll (the scroll has 'Plot James 3 D' blocked in relief on it), a purse, a vase, a sword, and a bunch of keys; at the tail: '| Geo Cruikshank | Illustrations | ' is blocked in gold within a rectangle formed by a single gold fillet.

Dry, *JL* no. 160.

193 Leighton, John FIG. 18

Ainsworth, William Harrison. *Old Saint Paul's: A Tale of the Plague and the Fire. With illustrations by John Franklin, and H. K.Browne.* London: G. Routledge and Co., Farringdon Street. New York: 18, Beekman Street, 1855. [7],426 p., 22 plates.
137 × 216 × 38 mm. 12619.g.32.

Two plates are signed 'Phiz'.

Original yellow endpaper bound at the front. Original upper cover used as a doublure. Doublure size: 130 × 209 mm. Red morocco horizontal-grain cloth. Two fillets are blocked in blind on the borders. Leaf and stem decoration is blocked in blind on each corner. The central block in gold shows the figure of a man astride a crucifix, both on the top of St. Paul's roof. The man has a brazier on his head. Above and below the brazier, the words: '| Ainsworth's | Old Saint Paul's. | ' are blocked in gold. Near the base, a flaming torch and arrow, crossed, are blocked in gold. Signed 'JL' in gold as a monogram at the base.

Dry, *JL* no. 161.

FIG. 18

194 Leighton, John

Ayton, Emily. *Words by the way-side; or, the children and the flowers. With illustrations by H. Anelay.* London: Grant and Griffith, Successors to Newbery and Harris, corner of St Paul's Churchyard, 1855. London: Printed by J. Wertheimer and Co., Circus Place, Finsbury Circus. [1], ii, 159 p., 4 plates. With eight pages of publisher's titles bound at the end.
128 × 177 × 16 mm. 12806.d.6.

The plates engraved by Edmund Evans. On page one of the publisher's titles: 'Small 4to; price 3s. 6d. cloth; 4s. 6d. coloured gilt edges.'

Yellow endpapers and pastedowns. Blue morocco horizontal-grain cloth. Both covers identically blocked in blind on the borders and on the corners. A single fillet is blocked on the borders. A circle and leaves are blocked on each corner. The upper cover has a central vignette blocked in gold. It shows a girl dancing. Her head has a garland of flowers. She carries other flowers in the folds of her dress, held in each hand. The title: '| Words | by the wayside; | or the children & the flowers | ' is blocked in rustic lettering in a circle above and below the girl. Signed 'JL' in gold as separate letters at the base of the vignette. The spine is blocked in gold. At the head, the title: '| Words | by the | way- | side; | or | the | children | & the | flowers | ' is blocked in gold. Small flowers and leaf decoration are blocked in gold above and below the title.

Dry, *JL* no. 162.

195 Leighton, John

Bowman, Anne. *Esperanza; or, the home of the wanderers.* London: G. Routledge & Co., Farringdon Street; New York: 18, Beekman Street, 1855. [London]: Printed by Cox (Bros.) and Wyman, Great Queen Street. ix, 435 p., 8 plates.
110 × 175 × 35 mm. 12806.d.8.

The plates engraved by Dalziel.

Yellow endpapers and pastedowns. Blue ripple vertical-grain cloth. Both covers identically blocked in blind on the borders, the corners and the sides. Three fillets blocked on the borders. Leaf and stem decoration blocked on each corner and the sides. The lower cover has a central vignette blocked in blind. It shows a series of circles at the centre, with strapwork around them. The upper cover has a central vignette blocked in gold. It shows two of the wanderers walking in a jungle. They hold a pole on

their shoulders. The pole is hung with game and fish. The wanderer on the right holds a rifle over his shoulder with his right hand; on the end of a rifle hangs a baby crocodile. The wanderer on the left holds a spear in his left hand. There is a palm tree blocked to the left of the vignette. The title: '| Esperanza; | or the home | of the | wanderers |' is blocked in gold above the two men, with 'Esperanza' being blocked in rustic lettering. Signed 'JL' in gold as a monogram at the left hand base of the vignette. The spine is blocked in gold. A single gold fillet is blocked on the perimeter. From the head downwards, the decoration is: a fillet blocked at the head; the title: '| Esperanza | or | the home | of the | wanderer |' blocked in gold; a bamboo frame house, with tropical creepers: a bird sits on top of the house; a man is seated inside the house; near the tail, the word: '| Illustrated |' is blocked in gold, within a rectangular fillet-frame formed by a single fillet. Signed 'JL' in gold as separate letters below this. [The signature is only 1mm wide.] Two fillets blocked in gold at the tail.

Dry, *JL* no. 164.

196 Leighton, John

Crosland, Camilla. *Hildred: the daughter. Illustrated by John Gilbert*. London: G. Routledge & Co., Farringdon Street. New York: 18, Beekman Street, 1855. London: Savill & Edwards, Printers, 4, Chandos-street, Covent Garden. 338 p. With ten pages of publisher's titles bound at the end.
110 × 175 × 30 mm. 12619.c.37.

Yellow endpapers and pastedowns. Binder's ticket on lower pastedown: '| Leighton | Son & | Hodge, | Shoe Lane | London. |' Red morocco horizontal-grain cloth. Both covers have borders and corner pieces blocked in blind. There are fillets blocked on the borders and passion flower leaves and buds blocked on the corners. The upper cover vignette is blocked in gold, featuring the title: '| Hildred | The daughter. |' blocked in gold above and below rose branches and flowers, and documents – all blocked in gold. One document has 'Dowry £20,000' blocked in relief on it; another has 'To be read last', also in relief. Signed 'JL' in gold as a monogram, at the base of vignette. The spine is blocked in gold. A single gold fillet is blocked on the perimeter. From the head downwards, the decoration is: two gold fillets; the words: '| Hildred: | The | daughter | by | Mrs | Newton | Crosland. |' blocked in gold; two gold fillets; lily-like leaves and stems surround three bishop's (or curate's) neck vestments, which are blocked down the spine. The words: '| Faith | Hope | Charity. |' are blocked in relief within these; a gold fillet; the words: '| London | Routledge & Co |' are blocked in gold; two gold fillets are blocked at the tail.

Dry, *JL* no. 167. McLean, *VPBB* p. 15.

197 Leighton, John

PLATE XXV

Donaldson, John, *Professor of Botany. The Geological Staircase, Containing The Steps of Rocks and Floors of Alluvium*. London: James Cornish, 297 High Holborn; 37, Lord Street, Liverpool; and 18, Grafton Street, Dublin, [1855]. ix, 526 p., 2 fold-out charts.
106 × 175 × 40 mm. 7107.a.21.

The half title page is dated 1855, and is lithographed 'T. Torne lith Hatton Garden.' The specimens pasted within the text are chromolithographs.

Yellow endpapers and pastedowns. Binder's ticket on lower pastedown: '| Leighton | Son & | Hodge, | Shoe Lane | London. |' Both covers identically blocked in blind on the borders and on the corners. Two fillets are blocked on the borders. Passion leaves, stems and flowers are blocked on each corner. The upper cover has a central vignette blocked in gold. The title: '| The | Geological | Staircase |' is blocked in gold above an open book, blocked as a gold lettering-piece. A geologist's hammer, a rock and a fossil lie upon the open book. The book is supported by palm leaves. Signed 'JL' in gold as a monogram at the base of the vignette. Spine missing.

Dry, *JL* no. 168.

198 Leighton, John

Doran, John. *Habits and men, with Remnants of Record touching the makers of both . . . Third edition*. London: Richard Bentley, New Burlington Street, Publisher in Ordinary to Her Majesty, 1855. London]: Printed by John Edward Taylor, Little Queen Street, Lincoln's Inn Fields. vi, 417 p. With two pages of publisher's titles bound at the end.
126 × 205 × 30 mm. 1609 / 5956.

Yellow endpapers and pastedowns. Binder's ticket on lower pastedown: '| Bound by | Edmonds & Remnants, | London. |' Orange moiré rib horizontal-grain cloth. Both covers blocked identically in blind. Four fillets are blocked on the borders. The innermost of these has straps blocked in relief on the sides, the head and at the tail. Three flowers and leaves are blocked on each corner. A lozenge-shaped central vignette is blocked in blind and in relief on the centre of each cover. The spine is blocked in gold. Two gold fillets are blocked at the head and at the tail, one thick, one thin. At the head, the words: '| Habits | and | men | [rule] | Doran. |' are blocked in gold. Up the spine from the tail runs an ivy branch, with berries and leaves. Signed 'JL' in gold as a monogram at the base of the ivy branch. The imprint: '| London. | Bentley |' is blocked at the tail, above the two fillets.

The upper cover of the 1854 edition at BL 7742.b.25. has the same central lozenge-shaped vignette blocked in blind. The decoration on the corners is different, showing bunches of grapes on the corners.

Dry, *JL* no. 119. The 1854 edition.

199 Leighton, John

Forbes, James David. *The tour of Mont Blanc, and of Monte Rosa being a personal narrative, abridged from the Author's 'Travels in the Alps of Savoy,' etc*. . . Edinburgh: Adam and Charles Black,

1855. Edinburgh: Printed by R. and R. Clark. xl, 320 p., 2 fold-out maps. With twenty-four pages of publisher's titles bound at the end. A page of publisher's titles is tipped in at the front.
110 × 177 × 28 mm. 10195.a.27.

The fold-out map bound at the front is entitled: 'The Pennine chain of Alps', printed in black and white. The fold-out map bound at the end is entitled: 'Map of the Mer de Glace of Chamouni and of the adjoining district from an actual survey in 1842–4–6 and 1850 by Professor James D.Forbes.' Drawn by Dr Augustus Peterman. Lith. by C. Hellforth Gotha. Edinburgh, published by A&C Black, 1855. The map is tinted in blue.

Sixteen of the twenty-four pages of publisher's titles at the end are: '| Catalogue | of the | various | editions | of | Sir Walter Scott's | writings | & | life. |' The title page of this catalogue has a design by John Leighton. It shows a medieval arch at the top, with decorated niches to the left and right. In the niche on the left is a knight in armour holding a lance; in the niche on the right is a saint holding a staff. At the base is a mixture of objects: a harp, a shield, an ornamented book, spears, an axe, swords, with a seated dog. The monogram of Walter Scott is within a shield with a pair of antlers at its top. Signed 'JL' at the left hand base as a monogram; signed 'H. [i.e. Henry] Leighton S.' at the right hand base.

Text sewn on two tapes. Light yellow endpapers and pastedowns. Brown morocco horizontal-grain cloth. Both covers blocked identically. Two fillets are blocked on the borders in blind, one thick, one thin. The same central vignette is blocked on both covers, in blind on the lower and in gold on the upper. It shows a mountain goat on a ledge, against a backdrop of high mountains. Above this, the title: '| Tour | of | Mont Blanc |' is blocked in gold in 'icicle-like' lettering. Signed 'JL' in gold as a monogram at the base of the vignette. Spine missing.

Dry, *JL* no. 171. Oldfield, *BC* no. 67.

200 Leighton, John

Gerstaecker, Friedrich Wilhelm Christian. *Frank Wildman's Adventures on Land & Water. Translated and Revised by Lascelles Wraxall. With tinted illustrations by Harrison Weir.* London: Geo. Routledge & Co. Farringdon Street. New York, 18, Beekman Street, 1855. [London]: Printed by Cox (Bros.) and Wyman, Great Queen Street. viii, 296 p., 8 plates. The plates engraved by Edmund Evans.
117 × 187 × 27 mm. 12807.e.47.

Yellow endpapers and pastedowns. Red morocco vertical-grain cloth. Both covers blocked identically in blind on the borders, the corners and the sides. A single fillet is blocked on the borders. Trefoil leaf decoration is blocked on each corner and on the sides. The upper cover has a central vignette blocked in gold. A circle is formed by a rope, knotted at the sides. Above and below the circle, the title: '| Frank | Wildman's | Adventures |' is blocked in rustic lettering. Inside the circle, a scene is blocked of a young man clinging to wreckage in a stormy sea. He is waving a cloth in his left hand, to attract attention. This is a reproduction of the illustration opposite p. 91. Signed 'JL' in gold as a monogram at the base of the vignette. The spine is blocked in gold. A single gold fillet is blocked around the perimeter. From the head downwards, the decoration is: two gold fillets; the words: '| Frank | Wildman's | Adventures | Gerstaecker |', blocked in gold, in rustic lettering; then a crescent-shaped room, above a small tree, which is blocked from the tail up; a bag of gold is blocked at the base of the tree; a man is digging with a spade at the base of the tree, together with a bag of gold; a gold fillet; the words: '| London | Routledge & Co. |' are blocked in gold within a rectangle formed by a single gold fillet; two gold fillets blocked at the tail.

Dry, *JL* no. 173.

201 Leighton, John

Gerstaecker, Friedrich Wilhelm Christian. *Wild sports in The Far West. Translated from the German. With tinted illustrations, by Harrison Weir. Fourth thousand.* London: Geo. Routledge & Co., Farringdon Street. New York, 18, Beekman Street, 1855. [London]: Savill Edwards, Printers, 4, Chandos-street, Covent-garden. vi, 314 p., 8 plates. With thirty-two pages of publisher's titles bound at the end.
120 × 191 × 30 mm. 7920.aaa.7.

The plates are engraved by Edmund Evans. On page eighteen of the publishers titles, this work is listed as: ' In 1 vol. Price 5s. cloth lettered.'

Yellow endpapers and pastedowns. Bookseller's name embossed on upper pastedown: '| W.H. Smith & Son | 138 | Strand | London |'. Bookplate & coat of arms of Joseph Teale on upper pastedown. Binder's ticket on lower pastedown: '| Leighton | Son & | Hodge, | Shoe Lane | London. |' Blue morocco vertical-grain cloth. Both covers identically blocked in blind on the borders and on the corners. Two fillets are blocked on the borders, the outer thick, the inner thin. A leaf and stem pattern is blocked on each corner. The upper cover has a central vignette blocked in gold. It shows the heads of three wild animals, with a rectangular gold lettering piece blocked underneath. The words: '| Wild sports |' are blocked in relief within the rectangle; beneath it, the words : '| in the | Far West. | By | Gerstaecker. |' are blocked in gold in rustic lettering. A branch and leaves, with its stems ending in circle, is blocked in gold across the vignette. Signed 'JL' in gold as separate letters at the base of the vignette. The spine is blocked in gold. A single gold fillet is blocked on the perimeter. From the head downwards, the decoration is: two gold fillets shaped as branches; the words: '| Wild sports | in the | Far West. | by | Gerstaecker. |' blocked in gold in rustic lettering; a man clinging onto a branch above water, with his hat falling towards the water; in the water, a crocodile's head and water plants are blocked; at the tail: '| Routledge & Co | London |' is blocked in gold within a rectangle formed by a single 'branch-like' gold fillet.

Dry, *JL* no. 172.

202 Leighton, John

Goldsmith, Oliver. *The deserted village. Illustrated by the Etching Club.* London: Published for Joseph Cundall by Sampson Low and Son, 47 Ludgate Hill, 1855. 46 p. With two pages of publisher's titles bound at the end.
140 × 205 × 20 mm. 11640.ee.51.

Bevelled boards. Gilt edges. Yellow endpapers and pastedowns. Binder's ticket on lower pastedown: '| Leighton | Son & | Hodge, | Shoe Lane | London. |' Green morocco horizontal-grain cloth. Both covers are blocked identically in blind on the borders. Two fillets are blocked in blind on the borders. Inside these, a wide border pattern of leaves and flowers is blocked in relief. On the upper cover, within the central rectangle, a vignette is blocked in gold. The words: '| The | Deserted | Village | Illustrated | by the | Etching Club |' are blocked in gold in elaborate 'branch-like' lettering, with roots from the bottom of letters. Two etching tools are blocked near the base of the vignette. Signed 'JL' in gold as a monogram, at the base of the vignette. On the spine, the title: '| Goldsmith | Deserted | Village is blocked in gold near the head. The 1859 edition is at BL RB23.a.5278. It has a cover design by Albert Warren.

Dry, *JL* no. 174. McLean, *Cundall* p. 79. McLean, *VPPB* p. 78.

203 Leighton, John

FIG. 19

Grimm, Jacob Ludwig Carl. *Home stories, collected by the Brothers Grimm. Newly translated by Matilda Louisa Davis. Illustrated by George Thompson.* London: G. Routledge & Co. Farringdon Street; New York: 18, Beekman Street, 1855. London: Printed by Cox (Bros.) and Wyman, Great Queen Street. viii, 376 p., 8 plates.
105 × 172 × 30 mm. 12430.c.11.

FIG. 19

The plates are engraved by Dalziel.

White endpapers and pastedowns. Blue morocco horizontal-grain cloth. Both covers have the borders and corners blocked identically in blind. There are three fillets blocked on the borders, with circles blocked in blind and stars blocked in relief on the corners. The upper cover has a square-shaped central vignette, blocked in gold. The words: '| Grimm's | Home Stories. |' are blocked in gold in fanciful letters. The capitals 'G' and 'S' are embellished. The 'G' has fire grate bars across it, and has a kettle on top of the grate, with bellows below. A poker, fire tongs, and a small shovel stand on the top of the capital 'S'. The fire tongs have a face within the ball at their head. A cat and two fairy figures are blocked in and around the capital 'S'. Signed 'JL' in gold as separate letters at the base of the vignette. The spine is blocked in gold. From the head downwards, the decoration is: three fillets blocked at the head; the words: '| Grimms | Home | Stories |' blocked in fanciful letters; a quill runs down the spine, held in position by child-fairies; the tip of the quill is writing on a scroll, held open by two more fairy figures; signed 'JL' in gold as separate letters, within the tail of a fairy; the word: '| Illustrated |' is blocked in gold within gold fillets; a gold fillet is blocked at the tail.

Dry, *JL* no. 176.

204 Leighton, John

Huntley, afterwards Sigourney, Lydia Howard. *Mary Rice: And Other Tales.* London; Edinburgh and New York.: T.Nelson and Sons, 1855. 237 p., 6 plates. With six pages of publisher's titles bound at the end.
94 × 147 × 18 mm. 12806.d.18.

Yellow endpapers and pastedowns. Blue wave diagonal-grain cloth. Both covers blocked identically in blind on the borders, on the corners and on the sides. Two fillets are blocked in relief on the borders. Stems and flowers are blocked on the borders, head and tail. An extended single stem is blocked in blind on each side. The upper cover has a central vignette blocked in gold. It shows a roundel, formed on its perimeter by two fillets, with repeating dots blocked in gold between. Inside, a dog guards a sleeping girl, her head on a pillow. The words: '| Sleeping infant |' are blocked in gold at the base of the roundel. Signed 'JL' in gold as a monogram under the girl's pillow. [This is the usual Leighton monogram, but it is small, only one millimetre across.] Above and below the roundel, the words: '| Tales | and | Pencilings | by Mrs. Sigourney. |' are blocked in gold in fanciful lettering. The spine is blocked in gold. A single fillet is blocked on the perimeter of the upper half. From the head downwards, the decoration is: an arch formed by small leaves and branches; the title: '| Mary Rice | and other | Tales | and | Pencilings | in | prose & verse | by | Mrs Sigourney |'; two palm trees, which cross at their heads; between the trees, a young woman is blocked, with an urn on her head; the word '| Orpamel |' is blocked in gold, within a rectangle frame formed by a single gold fillet; at the tail, small decoration is blocked in gold.

Dry, *JL* no. 189.

205 Leighton, John

Napoleon I, *Emperor of the French. A life of Napoleon Bonaparte. In four books. With five illustrations.* London: George Routledge and Co. London: Farringdon Street. New York: 18 Beekman Street, 1855. London: Printed by Woodfall and Kinder, Angel Court, Skinner Street. vii, 387 p., 5 plates. With four pages of publisher's titles bound at the end.
110 × 175 × 28 mm. 10659.a.31.

The plates are signed: 'Henry Linton'; 'H.L. Sc.'; 'E. Morin'.

Yellow endpapers and pastedowns. Red morocco horizontal-grain cloth. Both covers identically blocked in blind on the borders and on the corners. Four fillets are blocked on the borders. Curling leaf and stem decoration is blocked on each corner. On the lower cover, the central vignette is blocked in blind. It shows an octagon and fillets with curling ends. Pointed leaves are blocked between the fillets. The upper cover has a central vignette blocked in gold. It shows a laurel wreath, two ribbons and a shield. The arms are: argent, an eagle displayed, wings inverted; crest: Pope's mitre. The shield is crossed diagonally by two staffs. One staff has a hand at the head, the other staff has a seated figure, holding a chasuble and a staff. Signed 'JL' in gold as a monogram near the base of the vignette, just above a medal. The spine is blocked in gold. [The upper half is missing.] The decoration is: a capital 'N'; a bee within a circle; a wreath with '| 1821 |' blocked within it. '| St. Helena |' is blocked in gold below the wreath. Signed 'JL' in gold as separate letters underneath.

Dry, *JL* no. 180.

206 Leighton, John

Palmer, Francis Paul. *Old tales for the young. As newly told. Illustrated by Alfred Crowquill.* London: G. Routledge & Co., Farringdon Street. New York: 18, Beekman Street, 1855. London: Savill and Edwards, Printers, Chandos Street. viii, 407 p., 7 plates.
107 × 175 × 30 mm. 12410.c.6.

Yellow endpapers and pastedowns. Binder's ticket on lower pastedown: '| Leighton | Son & | Hodge, | Shoe Lane | London. |' Blue morocco horizontal-grain cloth. Both covers blocked identically in blind on the borders and on the corners. Three fillets are blocked on the borders, and a (passion) flower pattern on each corner. The upper cover has a central vignette blocked in gold. It shows at the centre a diamond-shaped square, formed by two gold fillets, with two children lying inside. Atop the diamond is a genie's lamp. Underneath the diamond, a key and an oriental sabre are blocked. To the left of the diamond, a cat is seated, its left paw on its forehead. To the right is a mouse clothed in ermine, holding a staff on its shoulder. The title: '| Old | tales | for the | Young. |' is blocked above and below the vignette in gold. Signed 'JL' in gold as a monogram at the base of the vignette. The spine is blocked in gold. From the head downwards, the decoration is: a winged wizard floating above, and pointing down, at the title: '| Old | Tales | for the | Young. |', all blocked in gold; the words: 'Old tales' are in fanciful letters; beneath this is blocked the figure of Jack, about to strike at the head of the giant with a pickaxe; signed 'JL' in gold as separate letters; crouched 'stick-like' figures, repeating in gold, are blocked between gold fillets; a gold fillet is blocked at the tail.

Dry, *JL* no. 185.

207 Leighton, John

Robson, William. *The great sieges of history. Illustrated by John Gilbert.* London: G. Routledge & Co., Farringdon Street; New York: 18, Beekman Street, 1855. [London]: Cox (Bros) & Wyman, Printers, Great Queen Street. xii, 627 p., 8 plates.
120 × 190 × 45 mm. 9005.b.27.

The plates are engraved by Dalziel.

Original upper cover bound at the front. Original cover size: 112 × 182 mm. Stepped wave horizontal-grain cloth. The cloth is dyed red. Three fillets are blocked in blind on the borders, with a repeating 'stem and berries' pattern blocked in blind between these two fillets. The upper cover vignette is blocked in gold. It shows a star above a crown which is held aloft by two soldiers. The crown has the word: 'Sebastopol' blocked in relief within it. The soldier on the left is in oriental uniform, and holds a musket in his right hand, and the crown in his left. The soldier on the right is in Scottish uniform (kilt and socks), plus a sabre. He holds a musket upright in his left hand, and the crown with his right hand. Between the two soldiers, the title: '| The | great | sieges | of | history |' is blocked in gold. On the ground underneath, a triangular pile of cannon balls is blocked in gold. Signed 'JL' in relief as separate letters within one of the cannon balls at the base of the pile. The book is date stamped in blue: 9 NO[VEMBER 18]55.

Ball, *VPB* p. 137. Illustrates this grain type.

208 Leighton, John

Scott, *Sir* Walter, *Bart. Marmion. A tale of Flodden Field. With all his introductions, and the Editor's notes.Illustrated by eighty engravings on wood from drawings by Birket Foster and John Gilbert.* Edinburgh: Adam and Charles Black, North Bridge, Booksellers and Publishers to the Queen, 1855. Edinburgh: Printed by R. & R. Clark. 408 p. With frontispiece and engraved half title page bound at the front as part of the main sequence.
136 × 202 × 38 mm. Compiler's copy.

Text sewn on three tapes. Bevelled boards. Gilt edges. Bookplate of Robin de Beaumont on upper pastedown. Binder's ticket on lower pastedown: '| Leighton | Son & | Hodge, | Shoe Lane | London. |' Yellow endpapers and pastedowns. Blue morocco vertical-grain cloth. Both covers identically blocked in gold in blind and in relief. Five gold fillets are blocked on the borders, the innermost being dotted. On each side, from tail to head, a [mediaeval knight's] lance is blocked in gold. On the left, thistle heads and leaves are blocked around the

lance from the tail to the middle. The thistle heads are drooping, indicating Scottish defeat. At the head of the 'Scottish' lance, a pennant-shaped gold lettering-piece is blocked, tied to the top by a cord with tassel ends. A shield is blocked within the pennant, showing the lion rampant of Scotland, or. The lance on the right has roses and leaves blocked around it in gold. At the head of the 'English' lance, a pennant-shaped gold lettering-piece is blocked, tied to the top by a cord with tassel ends. The shield blocked within the pennant shows the three lions of England, gules. All are surrounded by numerous stars and dots blocked in gold. The title: '| Marmion | A Tale of Flodden Field |' is blocked in gothic letters in relief within two rectangular gold lettering-pieces with scroll-shaped ends, which are blocked above and below the recessed central oval. The oval has three gold fillets blocked on its outer border. On its inner border, in the recess, a wide fillet is blocked in blind, with a zig-zag flower and dot pattern blocked in relief inside. A mandorla is blocked on the centre. It has a gold fillet on its borders. A shield is blocked on the centre, showing an eagle, wings displayed, azure. The shield is surmounted by a helm, closed, with animate crest and panache (the feathers) tumbling down on either side of the helm. Below the shield, within a pennant-shaped gold lettering-piece, the words: '| Who checks at me | To death is dight. |' are blocked in relief in gothic letters. Signed 'JL' in gold as a monogram at the base of the mandorla.

The spine is blocked in gold and in relief. A thin gold fillet is blocked on the perimeter. A second thin gold fillet is blocked on the perimeter of all but the tail, and this fillet forms an arch at the head. From the head downwards, the decoration is: triangles formed by three fillets are blocked above the arch in gold, with a cross blocked within each triangle; a sword in gold is blocked from the head to near the tail, with its hilt near the head; one rose and one thistle and their leaves are blocked around the hilt in gold; a shield is superimposed over the sword blade; the shield is formed by a single gold fillet and repeating gold dots blocked inside the gold fillet; a cross is blocked within the shield, with the words: '| Marmion | by | Sir Walter | Scott. |' blocked in gold in gothic letters within; a pennant-shaped gold lettering-piece is blocked in gold around the sword blade underneath the shield; the words: '| Author's | Edition | Illustrated. |' are blocked within the pennant in relief; roses and thistle flowers and leaves surround the sword blade; stars and dots blocked in gold surround all the above decoration; signed 'JL' in gold as a monogram at the tip of the sword; the words: '| Edinburgh: | A & C. [sic] Black |' are blocked in gold within a rectangle formed by three gold fillets; at the tail, a rectangle formed by a single fillet is blocked in gold. The BL copy is at 11642.e.28. It is blue date stamped: 20 NO[VEMBER 18]54'. No original covers.

An original drawing by Leighton of the spine and upper cover of this design is owned by the compiler (previously owned by Robin de Beaumont and Sir Robert Leighton, of Leighton-Straker Bookbinders). It is signed 'Luke Limner'. It is identical to the above description, with one exception: the 'd' of the word 'Field' is missing from the lower lettering-piece of the upper cover.

Dry, *JL* no. 188. Pantazzi, *JL* p. 270. Illustrates copy in crimson cloth, bound by Leighton Son & Hodge.

209 Leighton, John

Warren, Eliza and Pullan, Mrs. *Treasures in needlework; comprising Instructions in Knitting, Netting, Crochet, Point Lace, Tatting, Braiding and Embroidery: illustrated with useful and ornamental designs, patterns, etc.* London: Ward and Lock, 158, Fleet Street, [1855]. London: Printed by Adams and Gee, Middle Street, Cloth Fair, Smithfield. xvi, 448 p.
125 × 194 × 30 mm. 1044.g.27.

Binder's ticket on lower pastedown: '| Leighton | Son & | Hodge | Shoe Lane | London. |'. Blue morocco vertical-grain cloth. Both covers blocked identically in blind. Two fillets blocked on the borders. A Moorish design blocked in blind, of three pointed stems and leaves surrounds the centre. On the centre, the words: '| Treasures | in | Needlework | by Mrs Warren | Mrs Pullan |' are blocked in blind in fanciful letters. The spine is blocked in gold. A single gold fillet is blocked in gold around the perimeter. From the head downwards, the decoration is: two hands and knitting needles; the title: '| Treasures | in Needle work |', blocked in gold in fanciful letters; then an urn, suspended by decorated cords; small decoration in gold at the tail; signed 'JL' in gold as separate letters within the decoration. (Each letter is less than 1 mm wide.)

Dry, *JL* no. 193.

210 Leighton, John

Wittich, William. *Curiosities of physical geography. New Edition.* London and Glasgow: Richard Griffin and Company, 1855. London: William Clowes and Sons, Stamford Street. 412 p.
107 × 163 × 30 mm. 10002.a.23.

Yellow endpapers and pastedowns. Green morocco horizontal-grain cloth. Both covers blocked identically in blind. A single fillet is blocked on the borders. Rose flowers and leaves are blocked on each corner, on the middle of the sides and on the centre. The spine is blocked in gold. A single gold fillet is blocked around its perimeter. From the head downwards, the decoration is: a sun in clouds; a bird; the title words: '| Curiosities | of physical | geography | Wittich. |' , in rustic lettering; a volcano by the sea is in eruption, with lava raining down. Signed 'JL' in gold as separate letters at the base of the waters. The words: '| Griffin & Co. |' are blocked at the tail within a rectangular frame formed by a single gold fillet.

211 Leighton, John

Wolf, Johann Wilhelm. *Fairy tales, collected in the Odenwald. Edited, with a preface, by Kenneth R.H.Mackenzie. Illustrated by W. Harvey.* London: George Routledge & Co., Farringdon Street. New York: 18 Beekman-Street, 1855. London: Printed

by Stewart and Murray, Old Bailey. xii, 337 p, 8 plates. With two pages of publisher's titles bound at the end.
110 × 175 × 27 mm. 12430.c.20.

The engravings are by Dalziel.

An original yellow endpaper is bound in at the front. Blue wave diagonal-grain cloth. Both covers are blocked in blind with the same design on the borders and on the corners. Two fillets are blocked on the borders. Thin curling stems and flowerheads are blocked on the corners. On the upper cover, the central vignette is blocked in gold. At the centre of the vignette, the words: '| Wolff's [sic] | Fairy tales | & | stories |' are blocked in gold. These are surrounded, in a circle, by twelve fairy figures, dancing and holding hands. Signed 'JL' in gold as separate letters at the base of the vignette. The spine is blocked in gold. A single gold fillet is blocked on the perimeter. From the head downwards, the decoration is: two gold fillets; an adult female fairy figure, standing on a quarter moon, is blocked in gold; the words: '| Wolf's | Fairy | Tales & | Stories. |' blocked in gold; a 'butterfly-winged' fairy crouches on the head of a toadstool; two more fairies are reading books underneath the toadstool; signed 'JL' in gold as separate letters at the base of the toadstool; the word: '| Illustrated |' is blocked in gold inside a rectangle formed by two fillets; a gold fillet is blocked at the tail.

Dry, *JL* no. 194.

212 Leighton, John

Wood, John George. *The illustrated natural history. With four hundred and eighty original designs, by William Harvey. New Edition, corrected and considerably enlarged.* London: George Routledge & Co. Farringdon Street. New York: 18, Beekman Street, 1855. London: R. Clay, Printer, Bread Street Hill. xx, 444 p., 2 plates. The two plates at the front form the frontispiece and the half title page.
120 × 188 × 35 mm. 1568 | 4304.

The two plates are signed: 'Dalziel Sc.'

Yellow endpapers and pastedowns. Blue ripple horizontal-grain cloth. Both covers are blocked identically in blind on the borders and on the corners. Two fillets are blocked on the borders, one thick, one thin, with leaf decoration on the corners and on the sides. The upper cover has a central vignette blocked in gold. The words: '| Wood's | Illustrated | natural | history. |' are blocked in gold in rustic lettering on the centre. Around the outside of the vignette, clockwise, are: the bust of a man; a snake; an eagle; a whale; an octopus; a crab; a crocodile; a lion. Small leaves and branches curl between these animals – all blocked in gold. Signed 'JL' in gold as a monogram at the base of the vignette. The spine is blocked in gold. A single gold fillet is blocked around the perimeter. From the head downwards, the decoration is: two fillets; the words: '| Wood's | Illustrated | Natural | History. |' blocked in gold in rustic lettering; a small tree, beside a pond or river; at the side of the water and in it are: a water vole, a beaver, a pike, a fish, an eel, a frog; a snake curls up the lower half of the tree trunk; two gold fillets; the words: '| Illustrated by | William Harvey. |' are blocked in gold; two gold fillets; a thick gold fillet is blocked at the tail.

Dry, *JL* no. 195.

213 Leighton, John FIG. 20

Theakston's Guide to Scarborough; comprising a brief sketch of the antiquities, natural productions, and romantic scenery, of the town and neighbourhood. Sixth edition. Illustrated with numerous Engavings on Steel and Wood. Scarborough: Published by S. W. Theakston, Gazette Office, 31, St. Nicholas-Street, 1856. viii, 198, 5 p., 5 plates, 1 fold-out map. With fifteen pages of advertisements bound at the end.
108 × 173 × 17 mm. 1607/5776.

The monogram of S. W. Theakston is printed on the title page. The plates are drawn by H. B. Carter.

Yellow endpapers and pastedowns. The pastedowns and endpapers have printed advertisements relating to Scarborough. Brown morocco vertical-grain cloth. Both covers identically blocked in blind on the borders and on the corners. Two fillets blocked on the borders, one thick, one thin. A spray of ivy leaves and berries is blocked on each corner. The upper cover has a central vignette blocked in gold. It shows a medieval gate, with three arches, castellation, and two small castellated turrets at the top. The title words: '| Theakston's | Scarborough |' are blocked in relief within the front of the gate. The word: '| Guide |' is blocked in gold below the gate. Signed 'JL' in gold as a monogram at the base of the gate. The spine is blocked in gold. At the head, the words: '| Theakson's

FIG. 20

Scarboro [sic] | guide. |' are blocked in gold, between two fillets. From the tail upwards, a lily-like plant is blocked in gold, with buds and a flower.

Dry, *JL* no. 153. The fifth edition of 1854.

214 Leighton, John

Adams, Charlotte. *Edgar Clifton; or, Right and Wrong. A story of school life. Third Edition, Revised and Corrected. With new illustrations.* London: G. Routledge & Co. Farringdon Street; New York: 18, Beekman Street, 1856. [London]: Cox (Bros) & Wyman, Printers, Great Queen Street. [1], 400 p., 8 plates.
110 × 177 × 32 mm. RB.23.a.15912.

The plates are signed 'BF' [i.e. Birket Foster] and 'Dalziel'.

Light yellow endpapers and pastedowns. Red bead-grain cloth. Both covers blocked identically in blind and in relief on the borders and on the corners. Two fillets are blocked in blind on the borders; leaf and stem decoration is blocked in relief on each corner. The upper cover vignette is blocked in gold. It shows a hand, at the top, holding the scales of justice. Each scale is weighed down with plaques, blocked as gold lettering-pieces. The one on the left weighs more, and the words: '| Candour | and | truth |' are blocked in relief within it. On the right hand plaque, the words: '| Prejudice | and | pride |' are blocked in relief. The words: '| Edgar Clifton |' are blocked within a ribbon-shaped gold lettering-piece above the scales; the word: '| or |' is blocked in relief within a gold lettering-piece, shaped as a weight; the words: '| right | and | wrong |' are blocked in relief within scroll-shaped gold lettering-pieces. Small stems and buds are interspersed within the design. Signed 'JL' in relief as a monogram, at the base of the vignette. The spine is blocked in gold. An arrow is blocked in gold from the tail to the head, the point at the tail. The words: '| Edgar | Clifton | or | right | & | wrong |' are blocked in relief within six ribbon-shaped gold lettering-pieces, which wrap themselves around the tree. Flowers are blocked in gold around the point of the arrow near the tail. Signed 'JL' in gold as separate letters at the tail.

215 Leighton, John

Bishop, Frederick. *The Wife's Own Book of Cookery, containing upwards of fifteen hundred original receipts, prepared with great care, and a proper attention to economy, and embodying all the latest improvements in the culinary art; accompanied by important remarks and counsel on the arrangement and well-ordering of the kitchen, combined with useful hints on domestic economy. The whole based on many years' constant practice and experience; and addressed to Private Families as well as the Highest Circles. Illustrated with 250 descriptive engravings.* London: Ward and Lock, 158, Fleet Street, and all Booksellers, [1856]. J. T. Norris, Printer, 128, Aldersgate Street, London. xvi, 398 p., 1 plate. With two pages of publisher's titles bound at the end.
125 × 194 × 37 mm. 1406.f.8.

Original cover size: 125 × 187 mm. Original covers bound in at the front and at the end. Original cover size: 120 × 185 mm. Dark green morocco vertical-grain cloth. Both covers blocked identically in blind and in relief on the borders, the corners and the sides. A single fillet is blocked on the borders. The corners, the head, the tail and the sides are blocked in blind with an elaborate stem and leaf pattern, showing in relief. A central panel is formed by the blocking in blind. The upper cover has a central vignette blocked in gold. It shows a lady (wearing an apron, with a servant's hat and ribbons) holding a serving-dish with a domed cover. The title: '| The wife's | own book | of | cookery |' is blocked in gold in rustic lettering above, below and to each side of the lady. Some of the letters have sprigs of leaves sprouting from their ends. The letters of the word: 'own' are pierced by a fork; the letters of the word: 'book' are pierced by a knife. Signed 'JL' in gold as a monogram at the base of the vignette.

Dry, *JL* no. 197.

216 Leighton, John FIG. 21

Crowquill, Alfred *pseud.* [i.e. Alfred Henry Forrester.] *Tales of magic and meaning. Written and illustrated by Alfred Crowquill.* London: Grant & Griffith, Successors to Newbery and Harris, Corner of St Paul's Churchyard, 1856. London: Wertheimer and Co., Printers, Circus Place, Finsbury Circus. xi, 175 p., 4 plates. With sixteen pages of publisher's titles bound at the end.
125 × 175 × 20 mm. 12807.c.22.

In page one of the publisher's titles at the end, this title is advertised as: 'Small 4to.; price 3s. 6d. cloth; 4s. 6d. coloured, gilt edges.'

Text sewn on two sawn-in cords. Yellow endpapers and pastedowns. Binder's ticket on lower pastedown: '| Bound by |

FIG. 21

Burn, | 37 & 38 | Kirby St. |' Green morocco horizontal-grain cloth. Both covers blocked identically in blind on the borders and on the corners. Two fillets blocked on the borders. Leaves and flower buds are blocked on each corner. The upper cover has a central diamond-shaped vignette blocked in gold. It shows a set of dancing fairies and grotesques, holding hands. Within this group, the words: '| Tales | of | magic & meaning |' are blocked in gold above and below a quarter moon. The words '| By | Alfred | Crowquill |' are blocked below the group. Signed 'JL' in gold as separate letters at the base of the vignette. The spine is missing.

Dry, *JL* no. 201.

217 Leighton, John

De Vere, Florence. *Eugenie; or, the Spanish bride. (The Author reserves the right of translating or acting this tragedy and comedy.)* London: Ward and Lock, 158, Fleet Street, 1856. London: Printed by Petter and Galpin, La Belle Sauvage Yard, Ludgate Hill. 302 p.

122 × 1187 × 22 mm. 11781.e.8.

Yellow endpapers and pastedowns. Blue morocco horizontal-grain cloth. Both covers are blocked in blind with the same design on the borders and on the corners. There are four fillets blocked on the borders. There are flower-head patterns blocked in blind on the sides, on the corners, and on the head and the tail. The upper cover has a central vignette, blocked in gold. It shows a pattern of thin stems and flowers around a central shield. The shield is formed by: 1. a thin gold fillet; 2. a thicker gold fillet with a 'diamond and dot' pattern blocked in gold and in relief; 3. an inner border of gold dots. The title: '| Eugenie | or the | Spanish | bride |' is blocked in gold, within the shield. Signed 'JL' in gold as a monogram at the base of the vignette. The spine is blocked in gold. Four gold fillets are blocked at the head. The spine is divided into three panels, each formed by double gold fillets, and three small dots on the corners of each panel. Panel one has flowers blocked in gold. Panel two contains the title: '| Eugenie | or the | Spanish | bride |', blocked in gold. Panel three (the largest) shows an elaborate 'oriental' flower pattern. Signed 'JL' in gold as separate letters at the base of the third panel, inside an inverted heart. Four fillets are blocked in gold. The publisher's name '| Ward Lock |' is blocked at the base in gold. Two gold fillets are blocked at the tail.

218 Leighton, John

Dulcken, Henry William. *The Book of German Songs: from The Sixteenth to the Nineteenth century. Translated and edited by H. W. Dulcken.* London: Ward and Lock, 158, Fleet Street, 1856. London: Printed by Petter and Galpin, Playhouse Yard, adjoining 'The Times' office. 324 p., 6 plates.

122 × 190 × 30 mm. 11525.c.15.

Some of the plates are signed: 'Dalziel'

Original upper and lower covers used as doublures. Doublure size: 115 × 185 mm. Red morocco vertical-grain cloth. Both covers are identically blocked in blind on borders and corners, with a branch and leaf pattern blocked in relief. The upper cover has a central vignette blocked in gold, showing a youth, in a military uniform, seated on a branch, feather in a hat, holding a tankard in left hand and a sword in right hand. The title; '| The | Book of | German Songs. |' is blocked in gold, in rustic letters. Signed 'JL' in gold as a monogram at base of vignette.

219 Leighton, John

Edgeworth, Maria. *Moral tales for young people. With Eight illustrations.* London: G. Routledge & Co. Farringdon Street; New York: 18, Beekman Street, 1856. [London]: Printed by Cox (Bros.) and Wyman, Great Queen-Street. vii, 414 p., 8 plates. With two pages of publisher's titles bound at the end.

105 × 173 × 33 mm. 12807.d.26.

The plates are engraved by Dalziel.

Yellow endpapers and pastedowns. Red ripple horizontal-grain cloth. Both covers blocked identically in blind on the borders and on the corners. Two fillets are blocked on the borders, the outer thick, the inner thin. Curling stems and fuchsia-like leaves are blocked on each corner. The upper cover has a central vignette blocked in gold. From the top downwards, the decoration is: a five pointed star; the word: '| Edgeworth's |' in gold in rustic lettering; a wreath, containing the words: '| To | point | a moral | & | adorn | a | tale |', blocked in gold; two children are seated on a wooden trellis; the one to the left has a fan in its right hand, the left hand resting on a book; the child on the right holds a ball, a sword and a scales in its left hand; beneath these figures, the words: '| Moral tales |' are blocked in gold within a rectangular frame formed by 'branch-like' fillets. Signed 'JL' in gold as separate letters at the base of the vignette. The spine is blocked in gold. A single gold fillet is blocked around the perimeter. From the head downwards, the decoration is: an arch, formed by lilies; the words: '| Edgeworth's | Moral | tales |' blocked in gold; an urn, with two winged female figures as handles; lily flowers and buds; a rectangle, formed by a single gold fillet, is blocked at the tail.

Dry, *JL* no. 203.

220 Leighton, John

Edgeworth, Maria. *Popular tales. With illustrations.* London: G. Routledge & Co. Farringdon Street; New York: 18, Beekman Street, 1856. [London]: Cox (Bros) & Wyman, Printers, Great Queen Street. vii, 413 p., 7 plates. With two pages of publisher's titles bound at the end.

106 × 174 × 36 mm. 12807.d.27.

The plates are engraved by Dalziel.

Yellow endpapers and pastedowns. Red ripple horizontal-grain cloth. The covers are identically blocked as for BL 12807.d.26. – Edgeworth, Moral tales. The exception is the

word 'Popular' substituted for 'Moral' within the upper cover vignette. The spine is missing from this copy.

Dry, *JL* no. 204.

221 Leighton, John

Hibberd, Shirley. *Rustic adornments for homes of taste, and recreations for town folk, in the study and imitation of nature . . .* London: Groombridge and Sons, 5, Paternoster Row, 1856. Driffield: B. Fawcett, Engraver and Printer, Driffield. vi, 353 p., 7 plates.
130 × 190 × 25 mm. 7004.a.26.

The plates are signed variously: 'G. Voyez del.' and 'B. Fawcett'.

Original upper and lower covers used as doublures; the cloth is cropped at head and tail. Doublure size 120 × 180 mm. Red morocco vertical grain cloth. Both covers are blocked identically in gold. The title: '| Rustic | adornments |' is blocked in gold in rustic letters, with elaborate tendrils and leaves attached. The letters are also interwoven with leaves and branches, in fanciful 'gothic rustic' style. A fish bowl in the centre contains a rock garden and a fish, from the centre of which arises a fountain, which sprouts upwards to bisect the 's' and 't' of: 'Rustic.' Signed 'JL' in gold as separate letters near the tail.

King, *JL* p. 241. McLean, *VPBB* p. 62.

222 Leighton, John

Jerrold, Douglas William. *Mrs Caudle's curtain lectures.* London: Bradbury and Evans, 11 Bouverie Street, 1856. London: Bradbury and Evans, Printers, Whitefriars. viii, 97 p. With two pages of publisher's titles bound at rear.
117 × 180 × 12 mm. 12354.c.41.

The paper cover measures: 110 × 172 mm. The blue paper upper cover, printed in black, is bound at the front of the volume. 'Price one shilling' is printed at the centre head. A border of branches and brambles is printed at the head. Lilies are printed at tail, around the monogram of Bradbury and Evans. The words: '| Mrs. Caudle's | Curtain | Lectures | By | Douglas Jerrold |' is printed within panels on the upper half of the cover. Signed 'JL' as separate letters at the tail of the cover.

223 Leighton, John — PLATE XXVI

Jewsbury, Geraldine Endsor. *Angelo; or, the pine forest in the Alps. With illustrations by John Absolon.* London: Grant & Griffith, (Successors to Newbery and Harris,) corner of St Paul's Churchyard, 1856. London: Printed by Wertheimer and Co, Circus Place, Finsbury Circus. 96 p., 4 plates. With sixteen pages of publisher's titles bound at the end.
130 × 175 × 15 mm. 12807.c.24.

Red morocco horizontal-grain cloth. Both covers are blocked in blind on the borders and the corners. Two fillets are blocked on the border in blind, the outer thick, the inner thin. On the corners, branch and leaf patterns are blocked . The upper cover has a vignette blocked in gold, depicting a child [Angelo?], leading two goats. The title: '| Angelo: | or the | pine forest | in the | Alps |' is blocked in gold, in rustic letters. Signed 'JL' in gold in separate letters at the base of vignette. The spine is missing. The list of titles issued by Griffith and Farran, bound at the end of 'Nursery nonsense or rhymes without reason', 1864, (BL shelfmark 12806.bb.13.) has the following description of this publication: 'Small 4to; price 2s. 6d. cloth. 3s. 6d. coloured, gilt edges.' In the list of publisher's titles at the end of 'Our Eastern Empire', BL 9056.b.14., 'Angelo . . .' is stated to be 'price 2s. 6d. cloth; 3s. 6d. coloured, gilt edges'.

King, *JL* p. 237. McLean, *VPBB* p. 65.

224 Leighton, John

Kirby, Mary and Kirby, Elizabeth. *The talking bird; or, the little girl who knew what was going to happen. With illustrations by Hablot K. Browne. (Phiz.)* London: Grant and Griffith, (Successors to Newbery and Harris,) Corner of St. Paul's Churchyard, 1856. London: Printed by Wertheimer and Co., Circus Place, Finsbury Circus. 96 p., 4 plates. With sixteen pages of publisher's titles bound at the end.
127 × 173 × 13 mm. 12807.c.38.

In page one of the publisher's titles, this work is cited as: 'Small 4vo; price 2s. 6d. cloth; 3s. 6d. coloured, gilt edges.'

Edges speckled with red ink. Yellow endpapers and pastedowns. Green morocco horizontal-grain cloth. The blocking appears to be done after casing in. Both covers blocked identically in blind on the borders and on the corners. Two fillets blocked on the borders. A spray of leaves is blocked in blind on each corner. The upper cover has a central vignette blocked in gold. It shows Rose (the little girl) and the Tiny Old Woman, a near reproduction of the Frontispiece illustration by Browne. A bird cage, with its door open, lies at Rose's feet. Above the two figures , the title: '| The | talking bird; |' is blocked in gold in rustic lettering. Groups of holly leaves and berries come out of these letters. Underneath the two figures, the sub-title: '| or | the little girl who knew | what was going to happen. |' is blocked in gold. Signed 'JL' in relief, within a leaf-shaped gold lettering-piece blocked at the base of the vignette. The spine has the words: '| The talking bird |' blocked in gold along the spine. Beneath the word 'The', a bird on a branch is blocked in gold.

Dry, *JL* no. 207.

225 Leighton, John — PLATE XXVII

Limner, Luke *pseud.* [i.e. John Leighton.] *The Royal picture alphabet.* London: Ward and Lock, 158, Fleet Street, 1856. London: Printed by Petter and Galpin, Playhouse Yard, adjoining The 'Times' office. [31 p.]
140 × 186 × 5 mm. 12985.e.46.

The BL copy has printed paper covers pasted on boards. The upper and lower covers are printed identically in red and in black. Two red fillets are printed on the borders. At the head, centred, is a royal coat of arms, with, as supporters, a seated lion and unicorn. Two roses, a thistle, and a shamrock are printed in red on the top corners. Below the coat of arms the words: '| The Royal |' are printed in black, within a red plaque, with scroll ends. A young woman, wearing a bonnet, stands on a plinth on the left, and a young man, wearing a cap and holding a spindle, stands on the plinth on the right. Three more people are standing within a central arch. The central figure is a man, dressed in an elaborate red bow tie, and with a large red feather in his lopsided hat. He holds open a book, which rests upon a plinth. The book contains the remainder of the title: '| Picture alphabet [printed in red] | ; | of humour [printed in black] | ; | and droll [printed in red] | ; | moral tales or words & [printed in black] | ; | their meanings [printed in red] | ; | illustrated [printed in black] |'. The monogram 'JL' is printed at the bottom left hand side both covers, with 'H. Leighton Sc.' printed on the bottom right hand side. '| Price one shilling |' is printed at the tail in black. The imprint is printed in red at the base of the plinth. Henry Leighton engraved the lithographs in this work. Not all the lithographs are signed. The following are:

Frontispiece: 'H. Leighton Sc.'
Title page: Ditto
Letter 'A': Ditto
Letter 'B': 'HLs'. The monogram 'HL'; the 'L' is joined to the right hand side of the 'H'.
Letter 'J': 'H. Leighton S.'
Letter 'S' 'HL Sc'. The monogram 'HL'; the 'L' is joined to the right hand side of the 'H'.
Letter 'X: 'HL', as separate letters.
Letter 'Z': 'H. Leighton Sc.'

The Bodleian Library copy (loose in sections) is in the John Johnson Collection, John Leighton boxes, no. 4.

King, *JL* p. 235; title page reproduced on p. 236.

226 Leighton, John

Longfellow, Henry Wadsworth. *Poetical works. Evangeline. – Voices of the night. The seaside and the fireside. – The golden legend. Miscellaneous poems. Illustrated with upwards of one hundred and sixty engravings on wood, from designs by Jane E. Benham, Birket Foster, etc.* London: David Bogue, 86, Fleet Street, 1856. London: Henry Vizetelly, Printer and Engraver, Gough Square, Fleet Street. xii, 422 p. With two pages of publisher's titles bound at the end.

131 × 215 × 40 mm. 11686.g.27.

Rebound in 1978. Doublure size: 130 × 205 mm. Gilt edges. The original upper cover used as a doublure at the front. Blue ripple horizontal-grain cloth. A single gold fillet is blocked on the borders. Between two more gold border fillets, a repeating pattern of gold hatch ovals is blocked in gold. Each of the ovals is bordered by two gold fillets. Each oval has small leaf decoration blocked within it in relief. Triangles are blocked on the corners, each formed by two gold fillets, with plant decoration blocked in gold. On the inside of the central diamond-shaped recess a border of two gold fillets is blocked, with a border of leaves and stems blocked in relief. The centre piece is diamond-shaped, with lily-like flowers and acorn-like seeds blocked in gold. The four heart-shapes blocked in gold at the centre have their decoration within blocked in relief. Unsigned. Except for the centre piece, the design is the same as for Longfellow's Hyperion (BL copy at 1570/1285), Bogue, 1853.

227 Leighton, John

Longfellow, Henry Wadsworth. *Poetical works. Evangeline. – Voices of the night. The seaside and the fireside. – The golden legend. Miscellaneous poems. Illustrated with upwards of one hundred and sixty engravings on wood, from designs by Jane E. Benham, Birket Foster, etc.* London: David Bogue, 86, Fleet Street, 1856. London: Henry Vizetelly, Printer and Engraver, Gough Square, Fleet Street. xvi, 422 p., 1 plate. With two pages of publisher's titles bound at the end.

140 × 213 × 40 mm. RdeB.I.21.

The British Museum de Beaumont copy.

Text sewn on three tapes. Gilt edges. Bevelled boards. Yellow endpapers and pastedowns. Bookseller's ticket on upper pastedown, upper left: '| Noble | Boston. |' Inscription on frontispiece plate recto: '| Mary Ann Maidens | from her Affet husband. |' Blue ripple horizontal-grain cloth. Both covers blocked identically in gold and in blind. Five fillets are blocked in gold on the borders. Between the second and the third, a border of repeating ovals is blocked in gold, each oval being formed by two gold fillets. Within each oval, hatch and small leaves are blocked in gold. Triangular panels of leaves are blocked in gold on each inner corner. A recessed diamond-shaped panel is blocked on the centre of each cover. Two fillets are blocked in gold on the borders of the diamond, with a leaf and stem border, blocked in relief within the recess. The centre is occupied by a symmetrical design with four 'heart shapes' linked. Fillets join these heart shapes together. The cover design is not signed. The spine is blocked in gold and in relief. Two thin fillets are blocked in gold on the perimeter. From the head downwards, the decoration is: a gold fillet; the words: '| Longfellow's | poetical | works. | [rule] | Illustrated. |' blocked in gold; small stem and tendril decoration, blocked in gold; a fir tree and a lyre, which is attached by a ribbon to the trunk of the tree – all blocked within a panel formed by a single gold fillet; small straps are blocked in gold on the left and the right centre of each side of the spine; 'heart shaped' decoration with leaves and flowers, blocked in gold; signed 'JL' in gold as separate letters, within a small panel near the tail; a gold fillet; at the tail, the words: '| London: | David Bogue. |' are blocked in gold, within a rectangle formed by a single fillet.

Dry, *JL* no. 210. de Beaumont, *RdeB1* no.180. Goldman, *VIB* no.180. Pantazzi, *JL* p. 271.

228 Leighton, John

PLATE XXVIII

Mary-Lafon, Jean Bernard. *Jaufrey the Knight and the Fair Brunissende. A tale of the times of King Arthur. Translated from the French version of Mary Lafon by Alfred Elwes. Illustrated with Twenty Engravings by G. Doré.* London: Addey and Co. Henrietta Street, Covent Garden, 1856. London: Printed by Robson, Levey and Franklyn, Great New Street and Fetter Lane. 158 p., 20 plates. With two pages of publisher's titles bound at the end.
170 × 260 × 32 mm. 11498.g.50.

Gilt edges. Grey endpapers and pastedowns. The same design is blocked in blind on the borders and on the corners. Two fillets are blocked on the borders, the outer thick, the inner thin. A single flower head is blocked on each corner, surrounded by leaves and stems. The upper cover has a central vignette blocked in gold. It shows a knight in full armour on horseback. He carries a lance in his right hand; a pennant attached to the head of the lance shows the arms, gules, of three hearts. The reins of the horse are in the knight's left hand. Long feathers flow from the knight's helmet. The horse is fully caparisoned. There are feathers on the horse's forehead; the drapes on its body end in ribbons. There are ribbons tied on its tail. The knight's shield is fastened to the horse's rear flank. The arms are: or, three hearts, gules. Below the knight and horse, a heart is blocked in hatched gold. Signed 'JL' in gold as separate letters at the base of this heart. The spine is blocked in gold. A single gold fillet is blocked around the perimeter. From the head downwards, the decoration is: a raven on a branch holds the tip of a lance in its beak; the title: '| Jaufrey | the Knight | & | the Fair | Brunissende |' blocked in gold in gothic lettering; from the tail upwards, a lance is blocked; it has a frog at its base, a snake curled around its length, and an owl perched on the snake's body near the top of the lance; signed 'JL' in gold as separate letters at the base of the lance; at the tail: 'London Addey & Co.' are blocked in gold, within a rectangle formed by a single gold fillet.

Dry, *JL* no. 208.

229 Leighton, John

Milligen, Sophia. *Original poems with Translations from Scandinavian and other Poets.* London: Hurst and Blackett 13 Great Marlborough Street, 1856. vi, 338 p. With three pages of notes to translations & errata bound at the end.
108 × 175 × 27 mm. 11649.c.4.

Light green endpapers and pastedowns. Binder's ticket on lower pastedown: '| Leighton | Son & | Hodge. | Shoe Lane | London. |'. Brown morocco horizontal-grain cloth. Both covers are blocked identically in blind. A single fillet is blocked on the borders. Inside this, another fillet is blocked with a single leaf on each inner corner. The central vignettes on both covers are blocked in blind with the same design, which is of a lyre surrounded by stems and leaves. At the base of each vignette, the monogram 'JL' is blocked in blind. These vignettes are identical to those used on the covers of BL.11689.a.44., Ralph Waldo Emerson, Poems, 1850; and also on the lower cover of BL.1347.g.25., A book of favourite ballads, [1866]. The spine is blocked in gold and blind and relief. Two fillets are blocked in blind on the head and on the tail. On the upper half of the spine, a gold lettering-piece is shaped as an oval. Leaves and stems are blocked in gold above and below this. The words: '| Poems | Original | and | Translated | by | Sophia | Milligen |' are blocked in relief within the oval. Thin curling stems and dots are blocked in relief around the title. Near the tail, the words: '| Hurst & | Blackett. |' are blocked in gold.

King, *JL* p. 239.

230 Leighton, John

Periodical Publications – *London. Peter Parley's Annual. A Christmas and New Year's Present for Young people.* London: Darton and Co., 58, Holborn Hill, 1856. London: Printed by Aird and Tunstall, 18, Exeter Street, Strand. v, 296 p., 9 plates.
137 × 185 × 35 mm. P.P.6750. [1856]

The half title page is a chromolithograph signed: 'George C. Leighton.'

Gilt edges. Yellow endpapers and pastedowns. Red morocco vertical-grain cloth. Both covers blocked identically, in blind on the lower, in gold and in relief on the upper. Two fillets are blocked on the borders. On the bottom right hand corner, ivy is blocked, plus a racquet; on the top right hand corner, horse chestnut leaves; on the left hand top corner, a cord tassel hangs from a stem; on the left hand bottom corner, leaves, stems, berries, and two sticks. Pages of books (as gold lettering-pieces) are blocked around the centre at the head, the tail and the sides. One of the pages at the head displays a girl skipping; one of the pages at the tail displays a ship; on the left hand side, one of the pages displays a ship in sail; on the right hand side, one of the pages displays a giraffe. All of these features are blocked in relief. Branches form a circle on the centre. Within it, the title: '| Peter | Parley's | Annual. | 1856. |' is blocked in gold in rustic lettering. Signed 'JL' in gold as separate letters on the centre tail. The spine is blocked in gold, now faded. A single fillet is blocked around the perimeter. From the head downwards, the decoration is: leaves, tendrils and a plant; the title: '| Peter | Parley's | annual. |'; a man, his top hat held aloft in his right hand, and a girl underneath a small tree; ground decoration; a fillet; '1856' blocked in gold within a cartouche; a fillet is blocked at the tail.

Dry, *JL* no. 212. Leighton, *SID, 1880* plate 77, nos. 9 & 12. Examples of ivy and horse chestnut.

231 Leighton, John

Saunders, Frederick. *Salad for the social.* London: Richard Bentley, 8, New Burlington Street, Publisher in Ordinary to Her Majesty, 1856. London: Bradbury and Evans, Printers, Whitefriars. viii, 358 p. With two pages of publisher's titles bound at the end.
123 × 203 × 27 mm. 12315.e.19.

Text sewn on two sawn-in cords. Yellow endpapers and pastedowns. Green morocco horizontal-grain cloth. Both covers identically blocked in blind and relief. Two fillets blocked in blind on the borders, the outer thick, the inner thin. On each corner, straps and squares are blocked in blind. At the head, the tail and on the sides (two on each side), a 'shamrock' plant is blocked, showing its roots, its stem and leaves – all blocked in relief. These are within pointed panels. The effect of the pattern is to resemble a medieval clasp binding. The spine is blocked in gold and in blind. From the head downwards, the decoration is: a vase with thin handles; two stems come out of the head of the vase, and curl around it, crossing at its base, and ending in shamrock leaves; the title: '| Salad | for the | social |' blocked in gold in rustic lettering, blocked within a frame formed by two thin gold fillets; a bowl with food and two utensils; shamrock leaves and stems; a 'spade' shape, blocked in blind, with a shamrock blocked inside in relief; signed 'JL' in blind as a monogram; two fillets in blind; the words: '| London | Bentley |' are blocked in gold; two fillets blocked at the tail.

The US edition of 1856 is at BL 12355.f.28. 401p. The imprint is: New York: De Witt & Davenport, 160 & 162 Nassau Street; London: Richard Bentley, 1856. Printed on the title page verso: 'W.H. Tinson, Stereotyper. George Russell, Printer. G.W. Alexander, Binder.' The text is embellished with engravings at Chapter headings and endings. Many of these and the frontispiece plate are signed 'Avery Sc.' The title page has an engraving signed '[H?]ORRETT'. It shows a man eating out of a large dish, with a fork and a spoon. This engraving is reproduced on the upper central vignette, which is not signed. The book has brown endpapers and pastedowns. Blue morocco vertical-grain cloth. Four fillets are blocked on the borders in blind on both covers. The spine is blocked in gold. [The upper cover vignette has the title words: 'Salad for the social', blocked in gold, with letters ending in tendrils – very reminiscent of Feely's work.]

Dry, *JL* no. 216.

232 Leighton, John

Stickney, afterwards Ellis, Sarah. *The Mother's Mistake. . . . With illustrations by Anelay.* London: Houlston and Stoneman, 65, Paternoster Row, [1856]. London: Printed by Adams and Gee, Middle Street, West Smithfield. viii, 207 p.

125 × 190 × 17 mm. 12631.f.21.

Gilt edges. Yellow endpapers and pastedowns. Binder's ticket on lower pastedown: '| Leighton | Son & | Hodge, | Shoe Lane | London. |' Blue morocco horizontal-grain cloth. Both covers identically blocked in blind on the borders and on the corners. Two fillets are blocked on the borders, the outer thin, the inner thick. Curling stem, leaf and flower patterns are blocked on each corner. The upper cover has a central vignette blocked in gold. The central roundel is formed by a single gold fillet. Around its perimeter, a repeating flower border of roses is blocked in gold. At the head, the tail and on each side, individual flowers are blocked within 'card-spade' shapes. Within the roundel, the words: '| The | Mother's | Mistake | by | Mrs. Ellis. |' are blocked in gold. [This vignette design is also used on BL 12304.b.10. , W.R. Evans A century of fables. Hardwicke, 1860. This copy is also bound by Leighton Son & Hodge. This design is also repeated on BL 12807.a.55., and BL 12807.a.58.] Signed 'JL' in gold as separate letters at the base of the vignette. The spine is blocked in gold. At the head and at the tail, small decoration is blocked between groups of three fillets. Rose branches, leaves and flowers are blocked above and below the title words: '| The | mother's | mistake | by | Mrs. Ellis. |'

Dry, *JL* no. 205.

233 Leighton, John

Weymouth as a watering place; with a description of the town and neighbourhood, the Breakwater and its construction, the Portland Quarries, the Chesil Beach, etc., etc. For the use of intending and actual visitors. Illustrated. London: Simpkin and Marshall. Weymouth: D. Archer,[1857]. Weymouth: Printed by D. Archer, Weymouth. 138 p., 6 plates. With eighteen pages of advertisements bound at the end.

122 × 190 × 13 mm. 10368.b.35.

Light yellow endpapers and pastedowns. Binder's ticket on lower pastedown: '| Leighton | Son & | Hodge, | Shoe Lane | London. |' Red moiré fine rib vertical-grain cloth. Both covers identically blocked in blind on the borders and on the corners. Two fillets are blocked on the borders. Onion-shaped stems are blocked in relief on each corner. The lower cover has a central vignette blocked in blind. It is diamond-shaped, with a circle at the centre. Around the central circle, the decoration of stems and leaves is blocked in relief. The upper cover has a central vignette blocked in gold. A rope forms a circle, with straps at the base. Seven shells and fronds of seaweed are blocked around the perimeter of the circle. The title: '| Weymouth | as a | Watering | Place. |' is blocked in gold within the circle. Signed 'JL' in gold as separate letters within the rope work at the base of the vignette. [Spine missing.]

Dry, *JL* no. 264.

234 Leighton, John FIG. 22

Balfour, John Hutton. *The plants of the Bible. Trees and shrubs . . .* London: T. Nelson and Sons, Paternoster Row; Edinburgh; and New York, 1857. iv, 2, 54 p., 12 colour plates.

165 × 245 × 20 mm. 03128.k.12.

Gilt edges. Bevelled boards. Yellow endpapers and pastedowns. Blue diagonal wave-grain cloth. Both covers are blocked in blind with an identical design. Four fillets are blocked in blind on the borders. On the inner rectangle, stem decoration is blocked in relief at the head and the tail, with more stem decoration blocked in relief on the middle, forming a central oval. On the upper cover, a central vignette is blocked in gold. Five fern fronds cross upwards, and emerge behind a ribbon-shaped gold lettering-piece which contains the title: '| Plants | of |

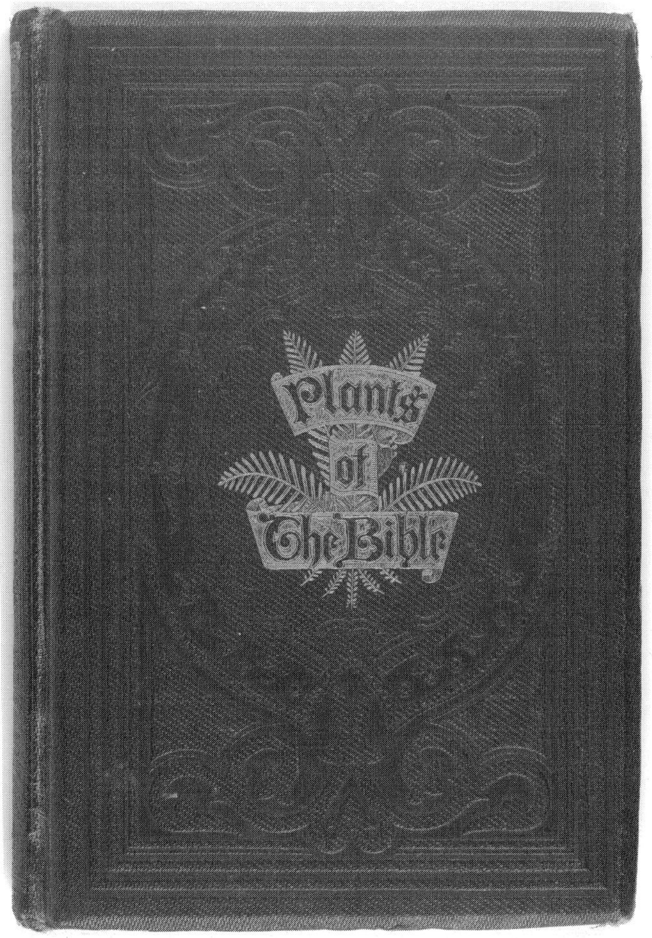

FIG. 22

The Bible |' blocked in relief. Signed 'JL' in gold as separate letters at the base of the vignette. The spine is fully blocked in gold and relief. A single gold fillet and gold dots are blocked on the perimeter. The spine is divided into six panels by horizontal and vertical gold fillets. Running the length of the centre of the spine is a coconut tree. The leaves are at the top, the nuts underneath. In panel one, stars are blocked in gold; in panel two, the title: '| Plants | of The | Bible |' is blocked in relief within a gold lettering-piece; in panel three, a medallion is blocked in gold, with the words '| by Professor Balfour |' blocked in relief inside; in panel four, the words: '| Trees | and | shrubs |' are blocked in gold within a rectangle formed by a single gold fillet; in panel five, the roots of the tree contain the Bible quotation: '| Behold | the | fig-trees | & | all | the | trees |' [Luke xxi., 29; this quotation is also on the title page.]; the words: '| T.Nelson | & | Sons. |' are blocked in relief within a rectangular gold lettering-piece, with a single gold fillet blocked on its borders.

Ball, *App.* 57i. King, *JL* p. 239. Dry, *JL* no. 223.

235 Leighton, John

Bell, Caroline. *Pictures from the Pyrenees; or Agnes and Kate's travels.* [Engraving of 'Cradle of Henri Quatre at Pau'.] *With numerous illustrations.* London: Griffith and Farran, Late Grant & Griffith, Successors to Newbery and Harris, Corner of St. Paul's Churchyard, 1857. London: Printed by J. Wertheimer and Co., Circus Place, Finsbury Circus. iv, 202 p., 8 plates. With sixteen pages of publisher's titles bound at the end.
128 × 177 × 26 mm. 10173.b.42.

Details of this work printed on page 1 of the list of publisher's titles: 'Small 4to.; price 3s. 6d. cloth; 4s. 6d., coloured, gilt edges.'

[Resewn and re-cased. No original endpapers or pastedowns.] Blue ripple vertical-grain cloth. Both covers identically blocked in blind on the borders and on the corners. A single fillet is blocked on the borders. A leaf and stem pattern is blocked on the corners in blind, and down the sides. On the lower cover, the centre-piece is lozenge-shaped, and consists of strapwork. The upper cover central vignette is blocked in gold. The title: '| Pictures from the Pyrenees |' is blocked in gold, in rustic letters, in a semi-circle at the top. Stems and leaves are attached to the letters. Below the title, on the left, a woman holds a basket of goods on her head , with her left hand. Her right hand holds a small bucket. A tree stump is blocked on the centre. To the right, a hatted man is seated on another, lower, tree stump. Below these figures, the words: '| Agnes' & Kate's | Travels. |' are blocked in gold. Signed 'JL' in gold as separate letters at the base of the vignette. The spine is blocked in gold. Near the head: the title: '| Pictures | from | the | Pyrenees |' is blocked in gold in rustic letters. Small groups of stems and of leaves are blocked in gold above and below the title.

Dry, *JL* no. 224.

236 Leighton, John

Bowman, Anne. *The castaways; or, the Adventures of a Family in the Wilds of Africa . . . Illustrated by Harrison Weir.* London: G. Routledge & Co. Farringdon Street; New York: 18, Beekman Street, 1857. [London]: Printed by Cox (Bros.) and Wyman, Great Queen Street. [3], 444 p., 8 plates.
110 × 176 × 35 mm. 12807.c.48.

Original yellow endpaper bound at the front. Blue ripple vertical-grain cloth. Both covers identically blocked in blind on the borders and on the corners. Two fillets are blocked on the borders. Sprays of stems, small leaves and buds blocked on each corner. The lower cover has a central vignette blocked in blind. It shows an oval, with a floral border, and a diamond-shaped centre-piece consisting of stems and flower buds. The upper cover has a central vignette blocked in gold. On the centre is a large lion, with a hunter underneath, with oxen and a wagon to the left of the lion. Above the lion are the words: '| The castaways |'; below the lion are the words: '| or, the | adventures of a family | in the | wilds | of | Africa |', all blocked in gold, in rustic lettering. Small stems, leaves, tendrils are at the end of some of the title letters. The spine is blocked in gold. A single gold fillet is blocked on the perimeter of the spine. From the head downwards, the decoration is: a single fillet; then: '| The | castaways | or | adventures | in Africa | [rule] | Bowman. |';

all the words except 'Bowman' are in rustic lettering; a jungle scene, with a man about to spear a snake, which is coiled at the base. Signed 'JL' in gold as separate letters to the left and to the right underneath the snake; the word : '| Illustrated |' is blocked in gold within a rectangle formed by a single gold fillet.

Dry, *JL* no. 226.

237 Leighton, John

Buckland, Francis Trevelyan. *Curiosities of natural history.* London: Richard Bentley, New Burlington Street, 1857. London: Printed by W. Clowes and Sons, Stamford Street. xvi, 319 p., 3 plates
110 × 175 × 27 mm. 7205.a.19.

[Rebound 1995. No original spine.] Original brown endpaper bound at the front. Binder's ticket on lower pastedown: '| Bound by | Edmonds & Remnants. | [rule] | London |'. Green morocco vertical-grain cloth. On both covers, two fillets are blocked in blind on the borders. On the upper cover, the central vignette is blocked in gold. It shows clockwise around the central roundel, a lion, a snake, an eagle, and ichthyosaurus. All these figures are surrounded by stems, small leaves and berries. The central roundel is a gold lettering-piece, with the words: '| Buckland's | Curiosities | of | natural | history |' blocked in relief within. Signed 'JL' in gold as separate letters underneath the eagle at the base of the vignette.

The second edition of 1858 is at BL 7205.a.20. xvi, 319 p. Printed by Clowes. 110 × 176 × 25 mm. Brown endpapers and pastedowns. Purple (? now faded) wave diagonal-grain cloth. Both covers are blocked identically in blind. The upper cover central medallion, with the author and title in relief within, is the same as for the 1857 edition. However, there is no outer decorative work, signed by Leighton. The spine is in gold.

238 Leighton, John

Bunyan, John. *The Pilgrim's progress from this world to that which is to come. Delivered under the Similitude of a Dream. With twenty illustrations, drawn by George Thomas, and engraved by W. L. Thomas.* London: James Nisbet and Co., 21, Berners Street, 1857. Edinburgh: Printed by Ballantyne and Company, Paul's Work. xii, 223 p., 20 plates.
186 × 252 × 27 mm. 4417.i.36.

The plates are hand-coloured. Gilt edges. Bevelled boards. Yellow endpapers and pastedowns. Binder's ticket on lower pastedown: '| Bound by | Westleys & Co. | London |'. Brown rib diagonal-grain cloth. Both covers identically blocked in black on the borders and on the corners. Three fillets blocked on the borders, one thin between two thick. Patterns of curling stems, leaves and flowers are blocked on each corner in black. The corner decoration forms a large quatrefoil central frame, with pointed ends. The upper cover has a central vignette blocked in gold, showing a five-pointed crown with stars blocked on each point. Rays are blocked around the crown. The spine is fully blocked in gold. Two gold fillets are blocked on the perimeter. From the head downwards, the decoration is: a seven pointed crown, with five point stars on each crown tip; the title: '| The | Pilgrim's | Progress | by | Iohn [sic] | Bunyan |' blocked in relief within six gold lettering-pieces, five of which are rectangular, the sixth being circular – all have gold fillets blocked on their borders, and dots blocked inside them blocked in relief; from the tail upwards, a wooden staff is blocked, with a knight's helmet on its top, and a shield, or, cross, gules; a sword is blocked underneath – vine leaves and stars surround all these; signed 'JL' in gold as separate letters at the base. All of the above is within an extended cartouche, with two thin fillets and dots down its sides. At the tail, the word: '| Illustrated |' is blocked in relief within a rectangular gold lettering-piece, with a single gold fillet on its borders.

Dry, *JL* no. 227.

239 Leighton, John PLATE XXIX

Burrows, E. *Our Eastern Empire: or, stories from the history of British India. With Illustrations.* London: Griffith & Farran, (late Grant & Griffith), The corner of St. Paul's Churchyard, 1857. London: Savill and Edwards, Printers, Chandos Street, Covent Garden. xii, 236 p., 4 plates. With eight pages of publisher's titles bound at the end.
125 × 160 × 25 mm. 9056.b.14.

Edges speckled with red ink. Yellow endpapers and pastedowns. Green wave diagonal-grain cloth. Both covers are blocked identically in blind on the borders and on the corners. There is a single fillet blocked on the borders. There are leaf and stem patterns blocked on the corners. The central vignette on the upper cover is blocked in gold. At the sides and the base of the vignette are circles, with 'lily-like' flowers blocked in the circles. The arabesque of the centre shows a coat of arms which contains two lions rampant, standing on a pennant, blocked as a gold lettering-piece, with the motto: 'Auspicio regis et senatus angliae', blocked in relief within. The lions support a shield, argent, cross, gules. Above the shield is a small lion holding a crown. The two lions each hold a flagpole. At the tops of the flagpoles fly the flags of St. George. The title: '| Our | Eastern | Empire |' is blocked in relief in three gold lettering-pieces above the centre. Signed 'JL' in gold as separate letters at the base of the vignette. The spine is blocked in gold. A crown is blocked at the head. Above and below the title panel, a pattern of leaves and flowers is blocked in gold. In the panel, the title: '| Our Eastern | Empire. |' is blocked in gold.

Dry, *JL* no. 234.

240 Leighton, John

Crowquill, Alfred *pseud.* [i.e. Alfred Henry Forrester.] *Fairy tales, comprising Patty and her pitcher, The Selfish Man, Tiny and her Vanity, Peter and his Goose, The Giant and the Dwarf, The Giant Hands. Written and illustrated by Alfred Crowquill.* London: Geo. Routledge & Co., Farringdon Street. New York:

– 18, Beekman Street, 1857. Each story paginated separately with 31 pages.
132 × 180 × 20 mm. 12431.c.23.

White endpapers and pastedowns. Red ripple-horizontal grain cloth. Both covers blocked identically in blind on the borders and on the corners. A single fillet is blocked on the borders. Stems, small leaves and flowers are blocked on each corner. The upper cover has a central vignette blocked in gold. It is diamond-shaped, and is formed of vine leaves and small figures, representing the six stories. Clockwise, the figures are: a small winged girl-fairy; a goose with human legs; a boy standing on the palm of a hand; a giant's head, with a small boy standing alongside; a pitcher, with human arms and legs; The Selfish Man. The title: '| Fairy | tales |' is blocked at the centre, in rustic lettering; the words: '| By | Alfred | Crowquill |' are blocked below the centre, all in gold. Signed 'JL' in gold as a monogram at the base of the vignette. Spine missing.

Dry, *JL* no. 231.

241 Leighton, John

Dalton, William. *The wolf-boy of China; or Incidents and Adventures in the life of Lyn-Payo.* Bath: Binns and Goodwin. Sold by all booksellers, 1857. [London]: Printed by W. Clowes and Sons, Stamford Street, and Charing Cross. vii, 383 p., 4 plates. With four pages of publisher's titles bound at the end.
112 × 177 × 30 mm. 12631.d.11.

The publisher's information at the end states for this work: 'Small 8vo., with several engravings, cloth, price 5s.'

Yellow endpapers and pastedowns. Orange morocco horizontal-grain cloth. The borders and corners of both covers are blocked identically in blind. Two fillets are blocked on the borders, with intertwined leaf work on the corners. On the lower cover, the central lozenge is blocked in blind. On the upper cover, the central vignette is blocked in gold and in relief. It shows two elongated dragons curled around a ball in the centre. The ball has a fillet border, with small decoration picked out in relief. At the very centre, a ball is blocked as a gold lettering-piece, with the words: '| The | wolf-boy | of | China |' blocked in relief. Signed 'JL' in gold as separate letters between the tips of the dragons' tails. The spine is blocked in gold. There is a single fillet blocked around the perimeter. There is lattice-work blocked in gold above and below the title: '| The | wolf-boy | of | China |'. In the middle, stars surround a circle with a pointed top. The circle is a gold lettering-piece, with a dragon picked out in fine relief. Below this, birds perch on branches, amid flowers and leaves. Signed 'JL' in gold as a monogram near the tail, immediately above the word: '| Illustrated |', blocked in gold at the tail in rectangle formed by single gold fillet.

Dry, *JL* no. 232.

242 Leighton, John PLATE XXX

Ewles, Alfred. *The adventures of a cat and a fine cat too! With eight illustrations by Harrison Weir.* London: Addey and Co., Henrietta Street, Covent Garden, 1857. [London]: Printed by John Edward Taylor, Little Queen Street, Lincoln's Inn Fields. 64 p., 8 plates.
165 × 212 × 12 mm. 12807.dd.33.

Gilt edges. Yellow endpapers and pastedowns. Blue morocco horizontal-grain cloth. Both covers blocked identically in blind on the borders and on the corners. Two fillets are blocked on the outer borders, one thick, one thin. Two fillets form an inner frame with plants, stems, and flowers blocked on each corner. The upper cover has a central vignette blocked in gold. On the centre is the head of a cat, holding a quill in its mouth. Above and below the centre, the title: '| The | adventures | of a | Cat |' is blocked in gold, in fanciful lettering. The 'A' and 'S' of 'Adventures' have stems attached, which end in leaves, small buds, and tendrils. Signed 'JL' in gold as a monogram at the base of the vignette. The spine title: '| The adventures of a cat |' is blocked in gold along the spine.

Dry, *JL* no. 236.

243 Leighton, John

Gay, John. *The fables. With an original memoir, introduction, and annotations by Octavius Freire Owen, M.A. F.S.A. . . . Second edition. With one hundred and twenty six drawings by William Harvey, engraved by the Brothers Dalziel.* London: George Routledge & Co. Farringdon Street, 18, Beekman Street, New York, 1857. London: Richard Clay, Printer, Bread Street Hill. xv, 271 p.
125 × 185 × 25 mm. 1162.f.41.

Yellow endpapers and pastedowns. On the upper pastedown is the bookplate of: '| H(?) B. Money Coutts, | Ancote, Weybridge. |' On the upper endpaper is blind stamped: '| W. T. Clark. | Bookseller and newsagent. | Upper | Sydenham | & | Crystal Palace. |' Blue bead-grain cloth. Both the covers are blocked identically in blind on the borders, on the corners and on the sides. Three fillets are blocked in blind on the borders. Groups of four leaves are blocked on each side; groups of six leaves are blocked on the centre head and on the centre tail. The upper cover central vignette is blocked in gold. It shows a monkey, wearing a wig and a ruff, a long waistcoat and knee breeches, buckled shoes, and a sword. The monkey is seated on a curling branch, which has leaves and flowers sprouting from it to surround the monkey. The monkey's three-cornered hat is on a branch above its head. The monkey is holding an open book, blocked as a gold lettering-piece, on whose covers are blocked '| Gay's Fables |', in relief. At the base of the branch a plaque is formed by a single gold fillet. The words: '| The monkey | who had seen | the world. |' Signed 'JL' in gold as separate letters, underneath the plaque. The spine is blocked in gold. The upper half is missing. The lower half has three medallions: 1. shows a lion; 2. shows a fox with a hat; 3. shows a leopard's head. Signed 'JL' in gold as separate letters at the tail.

Pantazzi, *JL* p. 272. Shows the same spine as the 1857 BL edition.

244 Leighton, John

Gerstaecker, Friedrich Willhelm Christian. *The Little Whaler; or, The Adventures of Charles Hollberg. Illustrated by Harrison Weir.* London: G. Routledge & Co., Farringdon Street. New York: 18, Beekman Street, 1857. London: Savill and Edwards, Printers, Chandos Street. viii, 343 p., 8 plates.
107 × 175 × 28 mm. 12807.c.37.

The plates are engraved by Dalziel.

Yellow endpapers and pastedowns. Blue ripple horizontal-grain cloth. Both covers blocked identically in blind on the borders and on the corners. Two fillets are blocked on the borders. Curling stems, trefoils, leaves and flowers are blocked on each corner. The upper cover has a central vignette blocked in gold. It shows a whaling ship on the right, and an iceberg on the left. On the centre, a rowing boat from the whaler has been tossed into the air by a whale, its harpoon all adrift. The whale's tail fin shows in the water. Two figures are clinging onto the boat, one is in mid-air. Three more figures are in the water. The title: '| The | Little | Whaler |' is blocked in gold above and below the centre, in 'harpoon-rope' lettering. The spine is blocked in gold. A single gold fillet is blocked around the perimeter. From the head downwards, the decoration is: a harpoon rope forming an arch at the head; this provides a frame for a circular lamp, on a plinth supported by a stem and a base; the words: '| The | Little | Whaler. | Gerstaecker. |' blocked in gold below this; on either side of the title, and down each side of the spine, a harpoon is blocked, with rope attached; between, small stars and a whale spout, with a whale blocked near the base; a gold fillet; the word: '| Illustrated |'; a 'rope-like' gold fillet; signed 'JL' in gold as separate letters; a gold fillet.

Dry, *JL* no. 238.

245 Leighton, John

PLATE XXXI

Hibberd, Shirley. *Rustic adornments for homes of taste, and recreations for town folk, in the study and imitation of nature. Second edition.* London: Groombridge and Sons, 5, Paternoster Row, 1857. Driffield: B. Fawcett, Engraver and Printer, Driffield. xv, 508 p., 7 plates. With four pages of publisher's titles bound at the end.
140 × 190 × 40 mm. 1608 / 3947.

Gilt edges. Moiré grey and white pattern on endpapers and pastedowns. Binder's ticket on lower pastedown: '| Bound by | Westley's | & Co. | London. |' Green morocco horizontal-grain cloth. Both covers are blocked identically in gold. Four fillets are blocked in gold on the borders. On both covers, the same rustic ornamental title letters are blocked above and below the centre as for the 1856 edition. The central vignette features a landscape of trees, a statue on a plinth, an urn and a fountain. Signed 'JL' in gold in separate letters at the tail. The spine is fully blocked in gold. A trellis-like gold fillet is blocked on the perimeter. This has plant stems, tendrils and leaves curling around it. From the head downwards, the decoration is: leaves blocked in gold; a bird cage; the title: '| Rustic | adornments |' in gold in rustic letters; a glass container with house plants inside; an ornamental fish tank has water ferns blocked inside; the words: '| By | Shirley | Hibberd |' are blocked in gold within a pennant-shaped flag, formed by a single fillet, which wraps itself around the single pole supporting the fish tank; a single gold fillet; at the tail, the words: '| Groombridge & Sons |' are blocked within a rectangle formed by a single gold fillet. [New edition of 1870 at BL 7004.bb.24. not signed.]

King, *JL* p. 241. McLean, *VPBB* pp. 63 & 104.

246 Leighton, John

Hood, Thomas. *Pen and pencil pictures.* London: Hurst and Blackett, Publishers, Successors to Henry Colborn, 13, Great Marlborough Street, 1857. [London]: Printed by Schulze and Co., 13, Poland Street. viii, 337 p. With sixteen pages of publisher's titles bound at the end.
122 × 200 × 30 mm. 12355.d.14.

Text sewn on three sawn-in cords. Yellow endpapers and pastedowns. Binder's ticket on lower pastedown: '| Leighton | Son & | Hodge, | Shoe Lane | London. |'. Blue morocco horizontal-grain cloth. Both covers blocked identically in blind. A wide decorative frame is blocked on the borders, showing flowers, stems and leaf patterns blocked inside elongated cartouches. On the centre of each cover, a vignette is blocked , in the shape of a flower bud, with leaves above and below it. Signed 'JL' in blind as a monogram at the base of the vignette. The spine is blocked in gold. Curling stems end in straps above and below the title panel, which has the words: '| Hood's | Pen | and | pencil | pictures. |' Below the title, a bouquet of flowers is blocked down the spine. The words: '| Hurst & | Blackett |' are blocked in gold near the tail. Two fillets blocked at the tail.

The second edition of this work, also of 1857, is at BL shelfmark 12355.d.15. vi,376p.. With twenty-four pages of publisher's titles bound at the end. Also bound by Leighton Son & Hodge. Yellow endpapers and pastedowns. Red wave vertical-grain cloth. Two fillets blocked in blind on the borders of both covers. The title and publisher blocked in gold on the spine.

Dry, *JL* no. 240.

247 Leighton, John

Kingston, William Henry Giles. *Salt water: or, the sea life and adventures of Neil D'Arcy, the Midshipman. Illustrated by H. Anelay.* London: Griffith and Farran, late Grant and Griffith, Successors to Newbery & Harris, Corner of St. Paul's Churchyard, 1857. London: Savill and Edwards, Printers, Chandos Street. viii, 407 p., 8 plates. With twenty-four pages of publisher's titles bound at the end.
110 × 180 × 34 mm. 12807.c.52.

Page one of the catalogue of publisher's titles at the end has: 'Fcap. 8vo., price 5s. cloth; 5s. 6d. gilt edges.'

Light yellow endpapers and pastedowns. Red morocco horizontal-grain cloth. Both covers blocked identically in blind. A single fillet is blocked in blind on the borders. Two more fillets

form an inner rectangle, with diamonds and three pointed leaves blocked on each inner corner. The spine is blocked in gold. A single gold fillet is blocked on the perimeter. An anchor rope is blocked on the inner perimeter, from the anchor near the tail, up to form an arch at the head. From the head downwards, the decoration is: seaweed by the arch at the head; a seagull; the title: '| Salt-water | or the | sea life | & | adventures | of Niel [sic] D'Arcy. |'; flying fish; a squid, a dolphin, and a lobster in the sea around an anchor; signed 'JL' in gold as separate letters to the left and the right of the lobster; the word: '| Illustrated |' is blocked in gold within a rectangle formed by a single gold fillet; a gold fillet is blocked at the tail.

Dry, *JL* no. 242.

248 Leighton, John FIG. 23

Kirby (afterwards Gregg), Mary and Kirby, Elizabeth. *Julia Maitland; or, pride goes before a fall. With Illustrations by John Absolon.* London: Griffith and Farran, Late Grant and Griffith, Successors to Newbery and Harris, Corner of St. Paul's Churchyard, 1857. London: H.W. Hutchings, Printer, 63, Snow Hill. 98 p., 4 plates. With sixteen pages of publisher's titles bound at the end.

127 × 177 × 12 mm. 12807.b.52.

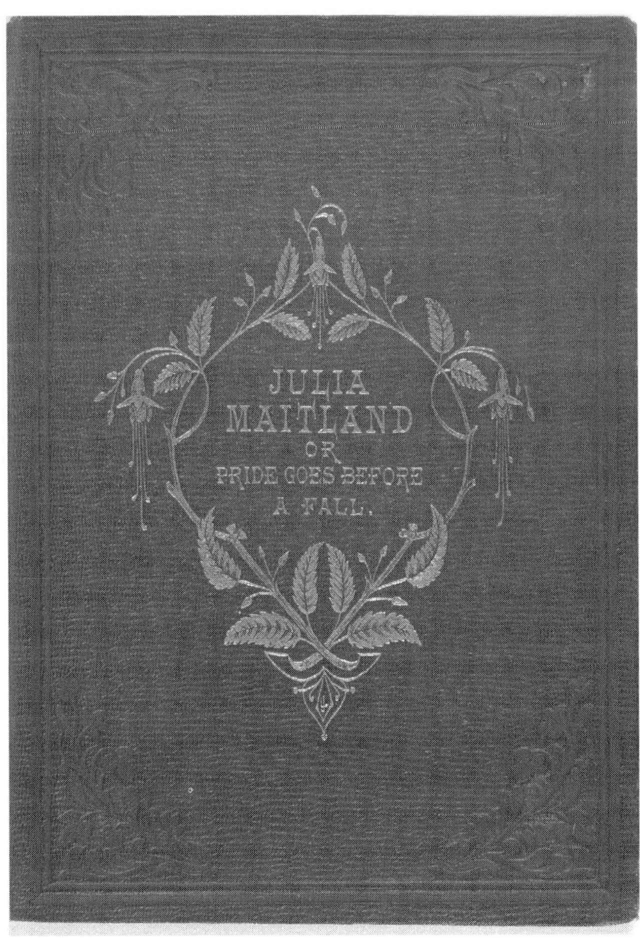

FIG. 23

Yellow endpapers and pastedowns. Red morocco horizontal-grain cloth. Blind blocked as for BL 12807.c.24, Geraldine E. Jewsbury, Angelo. . . ., 1856. The upper cover has a vignette blocked in gold. The title, centred: '| Julia | Maitland | or | pride goes before | a fall. |' is blocked in gold and surrounded by the branches, leaves, buds of a fuchsia and three open fuchsia flowers, which have long stamens. Signed 'JL' in gold as a monogram, at the base of vignette. The title: '| Julia Maitland |' is blocked in gold along the spine. The list of titles issued by Griffith and Farran, bound at the end of 'Nursery nonsense or rhymes without reason ', 1864, (BL shelfmark 12806.bb.13.) has the following description of this publication: 'Price 2s. 6d. cloth; 3s. 6d. coloured gilt edges.' In the list of publisher's titles at the end of 'Our Eastern Empire', BL 9056.b.14., this work is stated to be 'price 2s. 6d. cloth; 3s. 6d. coloured, gilt edges'.

Dry, *JL* no. 243. King, *JL* p. 237. McLean, *VBPP* p. 7.

249 Leighton, John

May, Emily Juliana. *Saxelford; a story for the young* . . . London: G. Routledge & Co., Farringdon Street; New York: 18, Beekman Street, 1857. [London]: Printed by Cox (Bros.) and Wyman, Great Queen-Street. [1], 375 p., plates. With four pages of publisher's titles bound at the end.

109 × 176 × 33 mm. 12807.bb.35.

The plates are signed by Dalziel.

Yellow endpapers and pastedowns. Binder's ticket on lower pastedown: '| Bound by Bone & Son, | 76, Fleet Street, | London. |' Blue ripple horizontal-grain cloth. Both covers identically blocked in blind on the borders and on the corners. A single fillet is blocked on the borders. A spray of rose-like leaves, stems, and flowers is blocked in blind on each corner. The lower cover has an oval shaped central vignette. The upper cover has a central vignette blocked in gold. It shows an angel, her left hand on the shoulder of a boy holding a book; her right hand rests on a circle formed out of a passion flower stem. Inside this circle, the words: '| Take | heed | to the thing | that is | right. |' are blocked in gold. Passion flowers, leaves, curling stems, tendrils and flowers are blocked to the left and to the right of the vignette. The title: '| Saxelford |' is blocked in gold above these two figures; the words: '| By the author of | Louis' | school | days. |' are blocked below the figures – all in gold. Signed 'JL' in gold, as a monogram at the base of the vignette. The spine is blocked in gold and in relief. A single gold fillet is blocked on the perimeter. A vine is blocked in gold from tail to head, with leaves, bunches of grapes and tendrils. Near the head, the words: '| Saxelford | by | E J May |' are blocked in gold, within a circle formed by two fillets. A ribbon-pennant gold lettering-piece runs downwards around the main stem of the vine. The words: '| Jesus said | I am the true vine | & | ye are the branches | without me ye can | do nothing |' are blocked in relief within the ribbon-pennant. Underneath the roots of the vine, leaf decoration is blocked in gold between double gold fillets. A gold fillet is blocked at the tail.

Dry, *JL* no. 247. Leighton, SID, 1880 Plate 79, item 10. Example of passion flowers.

250 Leighton, John

PLATE XXXII

Northcote, James. *Fables, original and selected. Illustrated by two hundred and seventy-five engravings on wood.* London: G. Routledge & Co. Farringdon Street; New York: 18, Beekman Street, 1857. London: Printed by Richard Clay, Bread Street Hill. xii, 244 p.
120 × 185 × 29 mm. 12304.d.26.

Untrimmed edges. Yellow endpapers and pastedowns. Blue ripple horizontal-grain cloth. Both covers are blocked identically in blind on the borders, on the corners and on the sides. Four fillets are blocked in blind on the borders. A fifth inner fillet joins leaf decoration blocked on the sides, the head and the tail: there are two groups of three leaves on each side, and one of five leaves on the centre head and on the centre tail. A single leaf is blocked on each corner. The upper cover central vignette is blocked in gold, showing a lion's head on a pillar, a copy of Aesop (Fables) resting against it. A boy, seated, is painting a picture. Another picture, entitled: 'Dog and crane', is blocked between the boy and the lion. To the left and the right, tendrils end in an eagle's head and a peacock's head. A semi-circle of stems and leaves surrounds the whole. Signed 'JL' in gold in separate letters at the base of the vignette. The spine is blocked in gold. A single gold fillet is blocked on the perimeter. From the head downwards, the decoration is: an arch; an open book, blocked as a gold lettering-piece; the title: '| The | parrot | & | singing | birds |' blocked in relief on the pages; the open book is held in the claw of a parrot, perched on a branch; the words: '| Northcote's | Fables. | [rule] | Illustrated |' are blocked in gold in rustic letters; two monkeys are blocked on branches, the lower of which holds a book, which is blocked as a gold lettering-piece; this has the words: '| The | Mon- | key |' blocked in relief on the cover; the lower monkey also has a waist-belt, a ring and a chain hanging from the ring – all amidst curling stems and leaves, all blocked in gold; signed 'JL' in gold as separate letters near the tail, within a small heart-shaped panel formed by a single fillet; a single gold fillet; a rectangular panel formed by a single gold fillet; a single gold fillet is blocked at the tail.

Dry, *JL* no. 250. King, *JL* p. 238. Pantazzi, *JL* p. 264. Illustrates copy in crimson fine ripple-grain cloth.

251 Leighton, John

Pardoe, Julia S. H. *Abroad and at Home: tales here and there.* London: Lambert & Co, 1857. London: R. Clay, Printer, Bread Street Hill. viii, 293 p. With two pages of publisher's titles bound at the end.
105 × 168 × 22 mm. 12603.c.27.

In the publisher's titles, page 2, this work is listed as: '| Tales at Home and Abroad. By Miss Pardoe. | 2s. Cloth 2s. 6d. |'

Edges speckled with red ink. White endpapers and pastedowns. Publisher's titles printed on endpapers and pastedowns. Blue morocco horizontal-grain cloth. Both covers identically blocked in blind on the borders and on the corners. Two fillets are blocked on the borders. Curling stems and leaves are blocked on each corner. The upper cover central vignette is blocked in gold. This is diamond-shaped. Around the centre, flowers and long stamens are blocked in gold, with some leaves blocked in relief. A shield is blocked on the centre, with a patterned border. The words: '| Pardoe's | Tales |' are blocked in gold within the shield on the centre. A five point star is blocked at the top of the vignette. Signed 'JL' in gold as a monogram at the base of the vignette. The spine is blocked in gold. A single gold fillet is blocked on the perimeter. Three panels are formed by single gold fillets. From the head downwards, the decoration is: panel one – two leaves and Greek fret; panel two has the words: '| Pardoe's | Tales |' blocked in gold; panel three has three leaves, four flower buds and angular spirals at top and bottom; a rectangle formed by a single gold fillet is blocked at the tail.

Dry, *JL* no. 251.

252 Leighton, John

Pardoe, Julia S.H. *The Thousand and One Days; a companion to the 'Arabian Nights.' With an introduction by Miss Pardoe.* London: William Lay, King William Street, Strand, 1857. Gilbert and Rivington, Printers, St. John's Square, London. x, 358 p., 6 plates. With eight pages of publisher's titles bound at the end.
110 × 175 × 36 mm. 12806.d.38.

Some of the plates are signed 'Jules Collignon', and 'E. Guillaumot'. Brown endpapers and pastedowns. Green morocco horizontal-grain cloth. Both covers blocked identically in blind and in relief on the borders, the corners and on the sides. A single fillet is blocked on the borders in blind. A pattern of curling stems and leaves (of the passion-flower plant) is blocked in relief on each corner. The upper cover vignette is blocked in gold. It shows arabesques, which form a diamond-shape. Within the arabesques, stems, leaves are blocked in gold, with some clover leaf decoration blocked in relief. On the centre, the title: '| A | thousand | and one | days. | Or | Arabian tales |' is blocked in gold. Signed 'JL' in gold as separate letters at the base of the vignette. The spine is blocked in gold. A double fillet is blocked in gold on the perimeter. From the head downwards, the decoration is: a gold fillet and a 'dotted' fillet; a panel formed by fillets, with an ogee arch blocked at the top of the panel and dotted straps below in gold; within the panel, the title: '| Thousand | & | one | days | or | Arabian | tales. |' blocked in gold; a stylised lily plant and arabesques; a gold fillet; a rectangle formed by a single fillet in gold; a gold fillet; a dotted gold fillet.

Dry, *JL* no. 251.

253 Leighton, John

Paul, Adrien. *Adventures of Willis the Pilot. A Sequel to the Swiss Family Robinson. With twenty-four illustrations.* London: Charles H. Clarke, 23A, Paternoster Row, [1857]. London: Jas.

Wade, Printer, 26, Bridge Street, Strand. 342 p., 24 plates, With one page of publisher's titles bound at the front and at the end.
106 × 175 × 34 mm. 12842.ee.11.

Light yellow endpapers and pastedowns. Brown morocco horizontal-grain cloth. Both covers blocked identically in blind on the borders: two fillets are blocked on the borders, the outer thin, the inner thick. The lower cover has a central vignette blocked in blind. It shows a diamond-shape, made by a wide border of stems and leaves, which are blocked in relief. A circle is formed on the centre by a single fillet blocked in relief. The upper cover has a central vignette blocked in gold. From the head downwards, the decoration is: a monkey, holding a wine glass and bottle; the title: '| Willis the Pilot. |' is blocked in gold in rustic lettering; Willis stands in front of a ship's steering wheel in storm dress; a coiling rope and a tuna fish, with seaweed underneath; Signed 'JL' in gold as separate letters within the seaweed. The spine is blocked in gold. A single gold fillet is blocked around the perimeter. From the head downwards, the decoration is: a fillet; the title: '| Willis | the | Pilot. |' blocked in gold in rustic lettering, within a panel formed by a single rope-shaped fillet; a man on a ladder propped against a tree is coiling up rope; a man with an axe is kneeling at the base of the tree; at the base, the word: '| Illustrated |' is blocked in gold within a rectangle formed by a single gold fillet.

Dry, *JL* no. 221.

254 Leighton, John

Peregrine, Uncle. *Uncle Peregrine; or, annals and incidents of romantic adventure.* London: James Nisbet and Co. 21 Berners Street, 1857. Edinburgh: Printed by Ballantyne and Company, Paul's Work. viii, 316 p., 6 plates.
116 × 176 × 26 mm. 12807.c.43.

The plates are signed 'H. Weir' and 'Pearson Sc.'

Yellow endpapers and pastedowns. Binder's ticket on lower pastedown: '| Bound by | Westleys | & Co. | London. |' Blue morocco vertical-grain cloth. Both covers blocked identically in blind on the borders and on the corners. Two fillets are blocked on the borders, the outer thick, the inner thin. Leaf and stem decoration is blocked in blind on each corner. The upper cover has a central vignette blocked in gold. It shows an elephant, with a rider and two hunters in the basket on the elephant's back. The hunters are shooting at game with rifles. The spine is blocked in gold. A single gold fillet is blocked on the perimeter. From the head downwards, the decoration is: a bird in flight; the title: '| Uncle | Peregrine |' blocked in gold in rustic lettering; a panther leaping out of a tree at a hunter, whose spear is raised to meet its charge; a snake in plants is blocked near the base; signed 'JL' in gold as a monogram underneath the snake; at the tail, the word: '| Illustrated |' is blocked in gold within a rectangle formed by a single gold fillet.

Dry, *JL* no. 262.

255 Leighton, John

Periodical Publications – *London. Peter Parley's Annual. A Christmas and New Year's Present for young people.* London: Darton and Co., 58 Holborn Hill, 1857. D. M. Aird, Printer, 18, Exeter-Street, Strand, London. vi, 280 p., 8 plates. With thirty-four pages of advertisements bound at the end.
136 × 185 × 30 mm. P.P.6750. [1857]

Gilt edges. Yellow endpapers and pastedowns. The covers have been blocked after casing in. Red morocco vertical-grain cloth. Both covers blocked identically in blind on the lower, in gold on the upper. The block has the same design on the borders, the corners, the sides, and the head as the 1856 annual. The changes made to the 1856 design are: a hanging game bird blocked at the tail; a vulture-like bird blocked near the centre; the title: '| Peter | Parley's | Annual |' is blocked in gold in a circular fashion, with '| 1857 |' being blocked in gold to the left of the hanging bird; a sun and its rays are blocked to the left of the vulture. Signed 'JL' in gold as separate letters at the centre of the tail of the upper cover. The spine is blocked in gold, now faded. A single fillet is blocked around the perimeter. From the head downwards, the decoration is: a fillet; palm tree leaves; the title: '| Peter | Parley's | Annual |' blocked in relief within a roundel gold lettering-piece; the figure of a man holding a rifle; a palm tree, with a lion at its base; a fillet; '| 1857 |' in gold with small decoration; a fillet at the tail.

Dry, *JL* no. 252.

256 Leighton, John FIG. 24

Pierce, Charles. *The household manager: being a practical treatise upon the various duties in large or small establishments, from the Drawing-Room to the Kitchen.* London: Geo. Routledge & Co., Farringdon Street; New York: 18, Beekman Street, 1857. London: Savill and Edwards, Printers, Chandos Street, Covent Garden. viii, 376 p.
110 × 180 × 25 mm. 7953.b.34.

Yellow endpaper and pastedowns. (The front endpaper is missing.) Blue ripple horizontal-grain cloth. Both covers blocked identically in blind on the borders and on the corners. Two fillets are blocked on the borders, with a leaf and stem pattern blocked on the corners. On the lower cover, the centre-piece is formed of stems and small leaves curling into six circles. The upper cover central vignette is blocked in gold and shows a bunch of keys on a ring. The title: '| The | Household | Manager |' is blocked in gold inside the ring. There are key tags, blocked in relief, each indicating the door to which the key gives access (e.g. steward's room, wine, medicine, etc.). The spine is blocked in gold. A single gold fillet is blocked on the perimeter. From the head downwards, the decoration is: a bell in a servant's pantry, the title: '| The | Household | Manager |' blocked in gold; a spike for household accounts; two books, one entitled 'memoranda'. Signed 'JL' in gold as separate letters near the tail; a gold fillet; the imprint: '| London: Routledge & Co |' is blocked in gold within a rec-

FIG. 24

tangle formed by a single gold fillet; a gold fillet is blocked at the tail.

Dry, *JL* no. 253. King, *JL* p. 238.

257 Leighton, John

Prentice, Emily. *Dew-drops for spring flowers.* London: Ward and Co., 27, Paternoster Row, 1857. [London]: John Childs & Son, Printers. iv, 90 p.
105 × 170 × 8 mm. 11649.b.30.

Gilt edges. Yellow endpapers and pastedowns. Blue diagonal wave-grain cloth. Both covers are blocked in blind with an identical design. Two fillets are blocked on the borders in blind, the outer thick, the inner thin. Flower, leaf and stem patterns are blocked in blind on the corners. A decorated centre-piece is blocked in blind on the lower cover, resembling a lyre. On the upper cover, a central vignette is blocked in gold. The title: '| Dew | drops | for | spring flowers |' is blocked in rustic branch style, with roots shooting from some of the letters. Above and below the title are spring flowers, with their leaves, bulbs and roots all showing. Signed 'JL' in gold as a monogram blocked in the bulb of the flower at the base of the vignette. The spine is blocked in gold. At the head and at the tail, stem and leaf decoration is blocked in gold, with two fillets. The title: '| Dew drops | for | spring flowers |' is blocked in gold in the same style as for the upper cover. The letters curl down the spine. There is a spring flower blocked above and below the letters, plus the bulb and its roots.

[This is one of the smallest Leighton monograms, being 1 mm square.]

Dry, *JL* no. 254. King, *JL* p. 239.

258 Leighton, John PLATE XXXIII

Scott, *Sir* Walter, *Bart. The Lord of the Isles. With all his introductions, and the editor's notes. Illustrated by numerous engravings on wood from drawings by Birket Foster and John Gilbert.* Edinburgh: Adam & Charles Black, North Bridge, Booksellers and publishers to the Queen, 1857. Edinburgh: R. & R. Clark, Edinburgh. 367 p., 2 plates.
140 × 213 × 40 mm. C.109.bb.3.

Bevelled boards. Gilt edges. Yellow endpapers and pastedowns. Binder's ticket on lower pastedown: '| Leighton | Son & | Hodge, | London. |'. [De luxe cloth issue.] Red morocco vertical-grain cloth. Both covers are blocked identically in gold, in blue and in blind and in relief. The blocking on the borders is: 1. a gold fillet and small decoration blocked in relief within it; 2. a border of alternating fleurs-de-lis and clover leaves; 3. a fillet blocked in blind, with hexagons and buds blocked in relief within it; 4. a single gold fillet. The pattern in the central rectangle is a large 'flower-petal' one, with the bands raised, blocked in gold. The areas between the petals are recessed and blocked with small patterns in relief, and coloured blue. The words: '| The | Lord of the | Isles | By Sir | Walter | Scott | Bart. |' are blocked in relief within gold lettering-pieces shaped as pennants. The central medallion has a fillet blocked in gold on its perimeter with small circles blocked inside it in blind. In the middle is a gold lettering-piece which shows a shield, or, and a lion rampant, blocked in relief within it. To the left and to the right of the shield are lizards, blocked in gold.

The spine is fully blocked in gold. The spine has a gold fillet blocked on the perimeter. Inside this, there is an inner border of a fillet with alternating fleurs-de-lis and clover leaves attached to it. From the head downwards, the decoration is: a knight's lance blocked from the tail to the head; the title: '| The Lord | of the Isles |' blocked in relief within three pennant-shaped gold lettering-pieces; a shield is formed by three gold fillets; a lion rampant, or; the words: '| Sir | Wal | ter | Scott | Bart. | Authors | Illustrated | Edition |' are blocked in relief within seven pennant-shaped gold lettering-pieces; a gold fillet; the imprint: '| Edinburgh. | A &C Black |' is blocked in gold at the tail within a rectangle formed by a gold fillet on three sides.

The Compiler's copy, formerly in the Private Collection of Robin de Beaumont, is a de luxe cloth issue; it has bright green morocco-horizontal grain cloth, with red coloured central

roundel, and the recessed floral pattern painted in blue. Text sewn on three tapes.

McLean, *VPBB* p. 35 States '. . . unsigned but almost certainly by John Leighton.' Morris & Levin, *APB* p. 50, nos. 89–91. The same design is blocked on cloth of three copies with: 1. Green pebble-grain; 2. on magenta bead-grain; 3. On blue morocco-grain cloth.

259 Leighton, John FIG. 25

Scott, *Sir* Walter, *Bart. The poetical works. Including his great metrical romances, copyright lyrical pieces, miscellaneous poems and ballads. With a memoir of the author. Illustrated by many engravings on steel and wood.* Edinburgh: Adam and Charles Black, North Bridge, 1857. 747 p., 7 plates.
120 × 195 × 45 mm. 11611.c.25.

Text sewn on three tapes. Gilt edges. Cream endpapers and pastedowns. Binder's ticket on lower pastedown: '| Bound by | John Gray | [rule] | Edinburgh |'. Blue trefoil leaf trellis-grain cloth. Both covers are blocked identically, with the same design. There are fillets blocked in blind on borders, the outer thick, the inner thin; thistle leaves and flowers are blocked in relief on the sides and on the corners. The central vignette is blocked in gold and consists of a ten point star, with thistle leaves and flowers blocked in gold between the star points. Every second star point contains one letter of 'SCOTT', blocked in relief, within a shield, or. There is a central medallion, with two gold fillets blocked on its borders. It is a gold lettering-piece, showing a lion, rampant, blocked in relief, or. Signed 'JL', in relief as separate letters, within the point of the star at the base. The spine is blocked in gold. A single gold fillet is blocked on the perimeter. From the head downwards, the decoration is: a gold fillet; leaf and stem decoration on either side on an arch formed by three fillets – all blocked in gold; within the arch, the words: '| Scott's | Poetical | Works [in fanciful gothic letters] | [rule] | Author's edition | with life | & | numerous illustrations |' blocked in gold – all within a panel formed by a single gold fillet, arched at the head; a shield, argent, saltire, gules; a medallion is blocked in gold on each side of the shield; a mandorla is formed by six borders: 1. a thin gold fillet; 2–4. a pattern of repeating dots, between two thin gold fillets; 5–6. a slightly thicker gold fillet, and a thin gold fillet.; a man in Celtic dress is blocked within the mandorla; his right arm is raised, and his left hand holds a harp upright on the ground in front of him; a shield, a sword and sword strap are on the ground beneath him; signed 'JL' in gold as separate letters underneath the shield; a medallion is blocked in gold on each side of the base of the mandorla; a gold fillet; the imprint: '| A & C Black |' is blocked in gold, within a rectangle formed by a single fillet; two gold fillets are blocked at the tail.

Ball, *App.* no. 571. The same text; different covers and designer. Ball, *VPB* pp. 94, 99. Dry, *JL* no. 256.

FIG. 25

260 Leighton, John FIG. 26

Tennyson, Alfred. *The miller's daughter. Illustrated by A. L. Bond, by permission of the author.* London: Published by W. Kent & Co., late David Bogue, Fleet Street and Paternoster Row, 1857. Unpaginated. [19 plates.]
195 × 252 × 25 mm. 1347.l.21

Text printed on recto only of each plate.

Bevelled boards. Gilt edges. Original yellow endpaper bound at the front. Binder's ticket on lower pastedown: '| Leighton | Son & | Hodge, | Shoe Lane | London. |'. Blue morocco horizontal grain cloth. Both covers are blocked with an identical

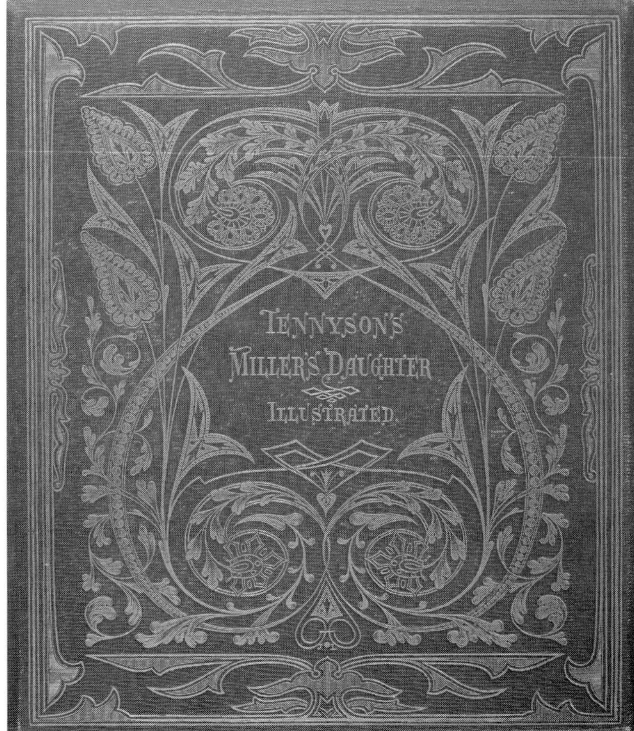

FIG. 26

Gilt edges. Bevelled boards. Yellow endpapers and pastedowns. Binder's ticket on lower pastedown: '| Leighton | Son & | Hodge. | Shoe Lane. | London. |' Bright green morocco vertical-grain cloth. Both covers and spine blocked identically in gold and in relief. There is a sea shell and rope pattern on the borders. Three gold fillets are blocked on the borders inside this, which form straps at the head, at the tail and on each centre side. Each corner-piece is formed by five gold fillets, the middle of which is dotted. Within each corner-piece, a dolphin, surrounded by seaweed, is blocked, all in gold. The recessed central oval has three gold fillets blocked on its upper borders, and a fillet in blind blocked on its recessed border, which has a 'rope' pattern blocked in relief within it. On the inner perimeter of the oval, two more fillets are blocked, and, within these, a ship's anchor chain and stars – all in gold. The centre shows a ship's sail, blocked as a gold lettering-piece. Within it, the words: '| The | Shipwreck | by | William | Falconer |' are blocked in relief. Above the sail, within a pennant-shaped gold lettering-piece blocked in gold, the words: '| WF Born at Edin: 1732 | Lost at sea. 1769 |' are blocked in relief. Below the sail, within other pennant-shaped gold lettering-pieces, the words: '| Life & this | I struggled | alone | to save |' are blocked in relief. A gold medallion is hanging from the sail spar. Within the medallion, the silhouette of a lady, with ribbon and bonnet is blocked in relief. Signed 'JL' in relief as separate letters on the shoulder of the lady.

The spine is blocked in gold and in relief. Two fillets are blocked in gold on the perimeter. From the head downwards, the decoration is: a rectangular panel, formed by a single gold fillet, with small decoration blocked within; a lyre, surrounded by stars; the words: '| The | Shipwreck | A | poem | by | William | Falconer | Illustrated |' blocked in relief within seven rectangular gold lettering-pieces – the eighth contains the word '| A |' within a heart-shaped gold lettering-piece; an anchor and a curling rope, which surrounds six pennant-shaped gold lettering-pieces; these contains the words: '| Yet | Hope with | flattering | voice | betrayed | them on |' are blocked in relief; ribbons blocked in gold surround the anchor; a scallop shell is blocked below the anchor; signed 'JL' in gold as separate letters underneath the shell; a gold fillet; the words: '| A & C Black |' are blocked in relief within a rectangular gold lettering-piece, with a single gold fillet blocked on its borders; a gold fillet; a thick gold fillet and two gold fillets are blocked at the tail.

McLean, *VBD* p. 219. Morris & Levin, *APB* p. 33, no. 42. Oldfield, *BC* no. 53. Pantazzi, *JL* pp. 266–67. Reproduces a copy bound in blue morocco cloth by Leighton Son & Hodge.

282 Leighton, John

Forrest, George *pseud.* [i.e. John George Wood.] *The Playground; or, the boy's book of games.* London: G. Routledge & Co. 2, Farringdon Street. New York: 18 Beekman Street, 1858. London: R. Clay, Printer, Bread Street Hill. x, 267 p., 1 plate.

105 × 170 × 20 mm. 7906.b.19

Light yellow endpapers and pastedowns. Written on the upper endpaper: '| J.B. White | As a souvenir of | my pleasant visit | to Brighton. | Jany. 1860. | . . . |' Bookseller's ticket on upper pastedown: '[H?] & C. Treacher, late King & Co. | Booksellers | Publishers, | 7 Stationers, | [4?] North St. & 44 East St. | Brighton. |' Blue bead-grain cloth. Both covers blocked identically in blind and in relief. Two fillets are blocked on the borders, the outer thick, the inner thin. A single leaf is blocked on each corner, the veins outlined in relief. A third fillet is blocked on the borders, with a single strap on each corner, and two leaves on each side attached to the strap. A single leaf is blocked on each corner. A group of three leaves is blocked in blind and in relief on the centre head and on the centre tail. The spine is blocked in gold and in relief. A single fillet is blocked in gold on the perimeter. From the head downwards, the decoration is: a kite with tail streamers, a ball, a shuttlecock; the title: '| The | Play | Ground |' blocked in relief within a gold lettering-piece with a single fillet blocked on its borders; the words: '| A | boy's book | of | games. |' are blocked in gold; the words 'a' and 'of' are blocked within circles formed by a single fillet; the words 'boy's book' and 'games' are blocked in gold within rectangles formed by a single gold fillet; an archery board is blocked in gold, supported by stilts; an arrow shaft and arrow head, together with a holder full of arrows – are hung in front of the archery board; between the stilts, a group of objects is blocked – a cricket bat, a pair of cricket stumps, a cricket ball, a racquet, a stick with strands on its end; a fillet in gold; the word: '| Illustrated |' is blocked in gold within a rectangle formed by a single gold fillet; a gold fillet; signed 'JL' in gold as separate letters, at the tail.

Another copy in Cambridge University Library at CUL.140.4.308.

283 Leighton, John

Goldsmith, Oliver. *The poetical works of Oliver Goldsmith, Tobias Smollett, Samuel Johnson, and William Shenstone. With biographical notices and notes. Illustrated by John Gilbert.* London: G. Routledge & Co., Farringdon Street; New York: 18, Beekman Street, 1858. London: Savill, and Edwards, Printers, Chandos Street. xvi, 84 p.; xv, 33 p.; xvi, 88 p.; xxxi, 196 p., 8 plates. With twelve pages of publisher's titles bound at the end.

105 × 170 × 22 mm. 11603.e.19

Routledge's British poets. Engravings executed by Dalziel.

Gilt edges. Yellow endpapers and pastedowns. Binder's ticket on lower pastedown: '| Bound by | Bone & Son. | [rule] | 76 Fleet Street, London.'. Red bead-grain cloth. Blocked identically as 11603.e.14. Cowper, William. The poetical works.

Dry, *JL* no. 281.

284 Leighton, John FIG. 35

Hall, Anna Maria. *The adventures and experiences of Biddy Dorking. To which is added the story of the Yellow Frog. Edited by*

FIG. 35

Mrs S.C. Hall. With illustrations by Harrison Weir. London: Griffith and Farran, late Grant & Griffith, Successors to Newbery & Harris, Corner of St. Paul's Churchyard, 1858. London: Savill and Edwards, Printers, Chandos Street, Covent Garden. [2], 94 p., 4 plates. With sixteen pages of publisher's titles bound at the end.
125 × 176 × 12 mm. 12808.a.34.

On page 2 of the publisher's titles at the end, this work is listed as: '2s.6d. cloth; 3s.6d. coloured, gilt edges.' The plates are coloured.

Text sewn on two tapes. Gilt edges. Yellow endpapers and pastedowns. Blue morocco horizontal-grain cloth. Both covers identically blocked in blind on the borders and on the corners. Two fillets blocked on the borders. Flower, leaf and seed head decoration on each lower corner, with joined stems and leaves on the lower centre; stems rise up each side, ending in more flowers, leaves and seed heads on each upper corner. (This is the same design as for BL 12807.b.53. Jack Frost and Betty Snow) The upper cover has a central vignette blocked in gold. It shows a hen standing on corn stalks, with the heads and leaves of the stalks around the hen. The words: '| Biddy Dorking |' are blocked in gold, in a semi-circle, above the hen, in rustic lettering with tendrils. An egg is blocked above these words. Signed 'JL' in gold as separate letters at the base of the vignette. The spine is blocked in gold. From the head downwards, the decoration is: an egg, with a chick with its head out of the shell; the title words: '| Biddy | Dorking | & the | Fat Frog. |' blocked in gold; a frog in gold, with reeds.

Dry, *JL* no. 283.

285 Leighton, John FIG. 36

Hey, Wilhelm. *Picture fables. Drawn by Otto Speckter, engraved by the Brothers Dalziel. With rhymes translated from the German of F. Hey by Henry W. Dulcken.* London: G. Routledge and Co. Farringdon Street. New York: 18 Beekman Street, 1858. London: Printed by Richard Clay, Bread Street Hill. ix, 101 p.
136 × 203 × 17 mm. 12305.d.13.

Gilt edges. Bevelled boards. Pink endpapers and pastedowns. Binder's ticket on lower pastedown: '| Bound by | Westleys | & Co. | London. |'. Blue morocco horizontal-grain cloth. Both covers blocked identically in blind and in relief on the borders and on the corners. Two fillets are blocked on the borders, the outer thick, the inner thin. Curling rose stems and flowers are blocked in blind on each corner, with the centre of each rose

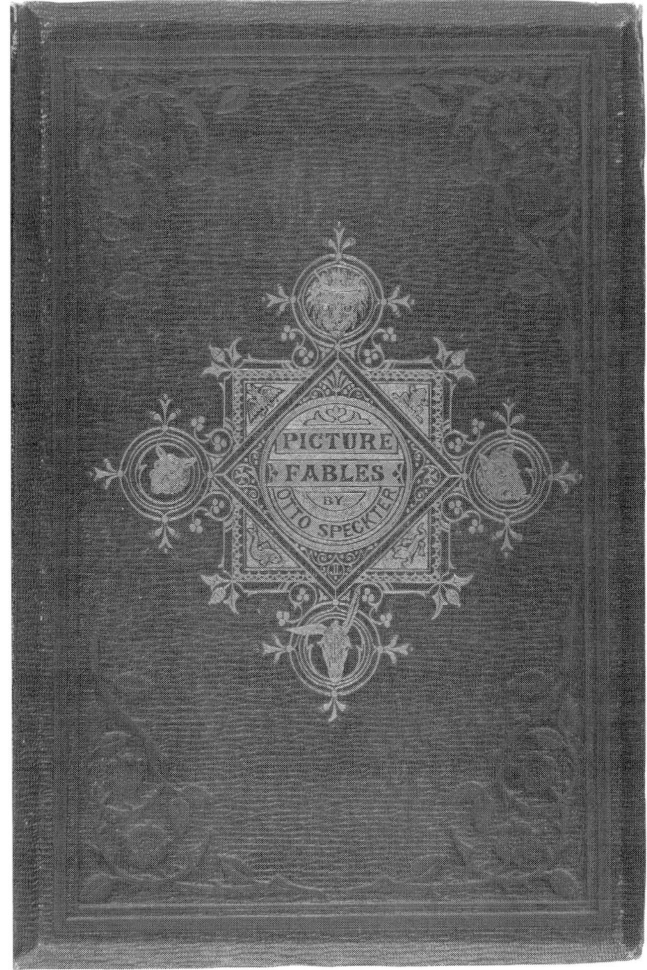

FIG. 36

flower being blocked in relief. A central vignette blocked in gold shows a diamond enclosing a medallion gold lettering-piece. The title: '| Picture | fables | By | Otto Speckter [in a semicircle] |' is blocked in relief within the medallion. A medallion, each formed by four gold fillets, is blocked on each corner of the diamond.. Within each, a sheep, an ass, a lion – crowned and a wolf, are blocked in gold. A square with decorated borders surrounds the diamond; a bat, a frog, a lizard and fish are blocked within each corner of the square. Signed 'JL' in gold as separate letters at the base of diamond. The spine is blocked in gold and in relief. From the head downwards, the decoration is: the words: '| Picture | Fables | by | Otto | Speckter |' blocked in gold; a gold rectangle with decoration blocked in relief within it; an arabesque; an elongated arabesque in gold, with an owl within its lower centre; signed 'JL' in relief as separate letters within a 'teardrop' underneath the arabesque; the words: '| Routledge | [& Co] |' are blocked in relief within a rectangular gold lettering-piece, with a single gold fillet blocked on its borders; a gold fillet is blocked at the tail.

286 Leighton, John FIG. 37

James, George Payne Rainsford. *Memoirs of great commanders. A new edition. With illustrations by Phiz.* London: G. Routledge & Co. Farringdon Street; New York: 18, Beekman Street, 1858. Printed by Cox and Wyman, Great Queen-Street, London. iv, 459 p., 8 plates.
115 × 185 × 35 mm. 10603.c.8.

The plates are signed: 'Edward H. Corbould' and 'Dalziel'. Text sewn on three sawn-in cords. Light endpapers and pastedowns. Blue morocco horizontal-grain cloth. Both covers blocked identically in blind on the borders and on the corners. Two fillets blocked on the borders, the outer thin, the inner thick. Lattice work is blocked in blind on each corner. The upper cover has a central vignette blocked in gold. It shows a medallion gold lettering-piece, with linked branches forming triangles around its perimeter. Within the medallion, the title: '| The | great | commanders | of | Europe. |' is blocked in relief. Underneath, two crossed marshal's batons with ribbons are blocked in relief. A small tie for the batons holds a model of St. George, on a horse, sword in hand, about to slay the dragon. Signed 'JL' in gold as separate letters underneath the dragon's tail. The spine is blocked in gold. Two gold fillets are blocked on the perimeter. From the head downwards, the decoration is: a knight's helmet with two plumed feathers; the words: '| The | great | commanders | of | Europe. | [rule] | G.P.R. James. |' blocked in gold; a sword, blocked from the tail upwards, has a laurel wreath and castellated crown across it. Stars surround the sword. All of the above is blocked within a cartouche, formed by two gold fillets, with a border of gold dots. Signed 'JL' in gold as separate letters underneath the hilt of the sword. At the tail, the word: '| Illustrated.' is blocked in gold, within a rectangle formed by two gold fillets.

[A well proportioned spine design, still in good condition.]

Dry, *JL* no. 286.

FIG. 37

287 Leighton, John

Kemp, Edward. *How to lay out a garden: intended as a General Guide in choosing, forming, or improving an estate, (From a Quarter of an Acre to a Hundred Acres in extent,) with reference to both design and execution . . . Second edition: greatly enlarged, and illustrated with numerous plans, sections, and sketches of gardens and garden objects.* London: Bradbury & Evans, 11, Bouverie Street, 1858. London: Bradbury and Evans, Printers, Whitefriars. xxxii, 403 p.
125 × 190 × 30 mm. 7055.c.30.

Text sewn on three sawn-in cords. Gilt edges. Light yellow endpapers and pastedowns. Green bead-grain cloth. Both covers blocked identically in blind on the borders and on the corners. Two fillets are blocked in blind on the borders; then a border of fillets, which delineate straps blocked in relief. Between the straps, cartouches are blocked in relief. A flower head and leaf outline is blocked in relief on each corner. The upper cover has a central vignette blocked in gold. It shows a central gold lettering-piece medallion. This has the words: '| How | to | lay

out | a | garden |' blocked in relief within five gold lettering-pieces, formed by single fillets blocked in relief. The words are surrounded by small trefoils and stems, blocked in relief. The medallion has four ovals blocked at the head, the tail, and on each side. Each contains a plant representing: 'Summer' – a rose; 'Autumn' – apples; 'Winter' – a leafless bush; 'Spring' – a bush sprouting leaves. Groups of seasonal flowers are blocked between the ovals. Signed 'JL' in gold as separate letters underneath the word 'Winter', at the base of the vignette. The spine is blocked in gold. From the head downwards, the decoration is: tendrils forming a panel; the words: '| How | to | lay out | a | garden | [rule] | E. Kemp. |' blocked in gold within the panel; a fountain, showing an angel on a ball, sprouting water through a trumpet held in its right hand; dolphins support the fountain basin [the dolphins are very much a Leighton decoration-piece]; a line of leaves blocked in gold at the rim of the fountain pond; signed 'JL' in relief as separate letters within one of these leaves [a tiny signature; only 1 mm wide]; the words: '| London | Bradbury & Evans |' are blocked within a rectangle formed by two gold fillets; three gold fillets blocked at the tail.

Dry, *JL* no. 288.

288 Leighton, John

Kingston, William Henry Giles. *Fred Markham in Russia; or, the boy travellers in the land of the Czar. With Illustrations by R. T. Landells.* London: Griffith & Farran, late Grant & Griffith, Successors to Newbery & Harris, Corner of St. Paul's Churchyard, 1858. London: Savill and Edwards, Printers, Chandos Street, Covent Garden. xii, 372 p. 8 plates. With twenty-four pages of publisher's titles bound at the end. The verso of the half-title page also has publisher's titles.

110 × 175 × 35 mm. 12807.bb.34.

Yellow endpapers and pastedowns. Blue morocco horizontal-grain cloth. Both covers blocked identically in blind and in relief. Two fillets blocked on the borders. Leaf motifs are blocked in relief on the corners, the head and the tail. The spine is blocked in gold. A single gold fillet is blocked on the perimeter. Inside this, another gold fillet and gold dots are blocked on the inner perimeter. From the head downwards, the decoration is: an arch; a Russian crown and ribbons; the words: '| Fred | Markham | in | Russia | Kingston. |' blocked in gold within four rectangles formed by single gold fillets, with the word 'in', being blocked within a circle formed by a single gold fillet; a Russian double-headed eagle is blocked in relief within a gold lettering-piece; St. George slaying a dragon; signed 'JL' in gold as separate letters within a 'spade-shape' formed by a single gold fillet; a gold fillet; the word: '| Illustrated |' is blocked in gold within a rectangle formed by a single gold fillet, with gold dots blocked within; two gold fillets blocked at the tail.

Dry, *JL* no. 289.

289 Leighton, John

Kirkland, Caroline Matilda. *Garden walks with the poets.* London: T. Nelson & Sons, Paternoster Row; Edinburgh and New York, 1858. 192 p., 6 plates.

95 × 152 × 22 mm. 11601.e.10.

Text sewn on three sawn-in cords. Gilt edges. Yellow endpapers and pastedowns. Wave diagonal-grain cloth. Both covers blocked identically in blind with four fillets on the borders. The upper cover has a central vignette blocked in gold. It shows a garden urn with twisted 'branch-like' handles. The urn is filled with leaves and flowers. Above the urn, the title words: '| Garden walks | with the |' are blocked; below the urn, the word: '| poets |' is blocked. The words: 'Garden walks' and 'poets' are blocked in gold in rustic lettering. The letters of the word 'poets' also have only their upper half blocked in gold. Signed 'JL' in relief as separate letters on the plinth of the urn. The spine is blocked in gold. A single gold fillet is blocked around the perimeter. Honeysuckle and ivy rise as stems up the sides, with their leaves and flowers blocked at the head. Below this, the title: '| Garden | walks | with the | poets. |' is blocked in rustic lettering; then a rose bush, with a lyre supported in its middle. A rectangle, formed by a single gold fillet, is blocked at the tail, with a single 'branch-like' gold fillet blocked within the rectangle.

Dry, *JL* no. 280.

290 Leighton, John

Knowles, James Sheridan. *The dramatic works. A New Edition in One Volume.* London: G. Routledge & Co. Farringdon Street; New York: 18, Beekman Street, 1858. London: Cox (Bros) and Wyman, Printers, Great Queen Street. Two vols in one. Vol. 1. vi, 448 p. Vol. 2. 457 p. With two pages of publisher's titles bound at the end.

125 × 190 × 55 mm. 1568/2770.

Untrimmed edges. Yellow endpapers and pastedowns. Blue bead-grain cloth. Both covers are blocked identically in blind with four fillets on the borders. The inner border is of a wide fillet blocked in blind, with a repeating leaf and stem pattern blocked in relief within it. The spine is blocked in gold. A single gold fillet is blocked on the perimeter. Groups of three fillets (one thick between two thin) divide the spine into panels. Within the panel at the head, the words: '| The | dramatic | works | of | James Sheridan Knowles |' are blocked in gold; underneath this, within a long rectangle formed by the three fillets, a long pole is blocked, with a pineapple-like plant at its head, surrounded by vine leaves and tendrils, with two face masks hanging at the middle on either side; signed 'JL' in gold as separate letters at the base of the pole; at the tail, the words: '| London: G. Routledge & Co. |' are blocked in gold within a rectangle formed by a single gold fillet, which is surrounded by the three fillets.

291 Leighton, John

May, Emily Juliana. *Bertram Noel. A Story for Youth . . .* London: E. Marlborough & Co., Ave Maria Lane. Bath: Binns and Goodwin, [1858]. vi, 409 p., 5 plates. With four pages of publisher's titles bound at the end.
110 × 178 × 35 mm. 12808.a.52.

Four of the plates are signed 'J H Nicholson' and 'C. W. Sheeres'. On page two of the publisher's titles: 'Price 5s.'

Text sewn on three sawn-in cords. Bolts uncut. Yellow endpapers and pastedowns. Brown morocco horizontal-grain cloth. Both covers blocked identically in blind on the borders and on the corners. Two fillets are blocked on the borders. the outer thick, the inner thin. On each corner, leaves and curling stems form a circle, with small leaves blocked inside in relief. The upper cover central vignette is blocked in gold. At the head, a ribbon-shaped gold lettering-piece is blocked in gold, with the words: '| He that | ruleth his spirit | is more mighty than he that taketh a city |' blocked in relief inside. A medallion, formed by two fillets blocked in gold, shows a boy inside with his arms crossed holding a book. The words: '| Bertram Noel | a | Story for Youth | by | E. J. May. |' are blocked in relief within five gold lettering-pieces, of which three are rectangles, and two are circular, each with a single gold fillet blocked on its borders. Signed 'JL' in gold as separate letters at the base of the vignette. The spine is blocked in gold. From the head downwards, the decoration is: small plants; the title: '| Bertram | Noel. |' blocked in gold within a panel formed by a fillet blocked on each side, and small decoration above and below; an urn on a plinth, blocked in gold, has a bouquet of leaves and flowers, some of which hang downwards; a fillet; the words: '| London | Marlborough & Co |' are blocked in gold within a rectangle formed by two gold fillets; two gold fillets are blocked at the tail.

Dry, *JL* no. 292.

292 Leighton, John

Milton, John. *The poetical works. A new edition, carefully revised, from the text of Thomas Newton, D. D. With illustrations by William Harvey.* London: G. Routledge & Co., Farringdon Street. New York: 18, Beekman Street, 1858. London: Savill and Edwards, Printers, Chandos Street, Covent Garden. viii,570 p., 7 plates.
110 × 170 × 30 mm. 11603.e.17.

Routledge's British poets. Engravings executed by Dalziel.

Gilt edges. Yellow endpapers and pastedowns. Blue thick pebble-grain cloth. Blocked identically as BL 11603.e.14. Cowper, William. *The poetical works.*

293 Leighton, John

FIG. 38

Munchausen, Baron. *The surprising travel and adventures of Baron Munchausen in Russia, the Caspian Sea, and through the centre of Mount Etna into the South Sea, etc., etc. Humbly Dedicated to Mr Bruce, the Abyssinian Traveller, &c.* Edinburgh: Adam and Charles Black, 1858. Printed by R. and R. Clark Edinburgh. xvi, 159 p.
100 × 153 × 14 mm. 12804.b.42.

FIG. 38

Text sewn on two tapes. Gilt edges. Light brown endpapers and pastedowns. Blue morocco vertical-grain cloth. Both covers blocked identically, in blind only on the lower, in gold and in blind on the upper. Two fillets are blocked in blind on the borders, the outer thick, the inner thin. The central vignette is blocked in gold on the upper cover. It shows the words: '| Baron | Munchausen |' blocked in gold, in gothic letters. The capitals 'B' and 'M' are blocked in relief within gold lettering-pieces. The 'M' has facial features, with the nose, eyes on either side and a mouth being on each side and below the middle serif. To the left of the capital 'B' is a quarter moon, shaped as a face, smoking a pipe. The title letters are surrounded by tendrils and trefoils. The trefoils have faces. Signed 'JL' in gold as separate letters at the left hand base of the vignette. The spine is blocked in gold. Two gold fillets are blocked at the head and the tail; the words: '| Baron Munchausen. |' are blocked in gold along the spine; a gold fillet; the words: '| Illustrated | edition |' in gold are blocked near the tail.

Dry, *JL* no. 302.

294 Leighton, John

Myrtle, Harriet, Mrs. *pseud.* [i.e. Lydia Falconer Miller.] *The Ocean Child; or, showers and sunshine. A Tale of Girlhood. Second edition.* London: G. Routledge & Co. Farringdon Street; New York: 18, Beekman Street, 1858. Cox and Wyman, Printers, 74–75, Great Queen-Street, London. vii, 308 p., 8 plates. With four pages of publisher's titles bound a the end.
105 × 167 × 27 mm. 12806.c.35.

The plates are signed 'B. Foster' and 'Dalziel' The design has been blocked after casing in. Yellow endpapers and pastedowns. Blue morocco horizontal-grain cloth. Both covers blocked identically in blind on the borders and on the corners, with the leaf and stem decoration blocked in relief. An inner border of

leaves and stems, blocked in relief, forms a central oval. The upper cover has a central vignette blocked in gold. It shows a girl, wearing a hat, seated side saddle on a pony, looking out at the ocean. Above and below the girl, the title: '| The | Ocean | Child |' is blocked in gold, in rustic lettering. A shell and seaweed are blocked below the word: 'Child'. Signed 'JL' in gold as a monogram in the seaweed below the shell. The spine is blocked in gold. Two gold fillets are blocked around the perimeter. From the head downwards, the decoration is: an arch and stars; the title: '| The | Ocean | Child |' blocked in fanciful letters; a hand holding a lamp, which is lit, emitting rays; a girl seated among plants; signed 'JL' in gold as separate letters to the left and to the right underneath the girl; the word '| Illustrated |' is blocked in gold at the tail within a rectangle formed by a single gold fillet.

The Addey & Co. edition of 1857 is at BL 12631.a.24. It has green morocco horizontal-grain cloth. Blocked in blind only on both covers. Unsigned.

Dry, *JL* no. 294.

295 Leighton, John

Robson, William. *The great sieges of history. With the addition of Delhi and Lucknow by Captain Thomas Spankie, Bengal Retired List. The fifth Thousand.* London: G. Routledge & Co. Farringdon Street; New York: 18, Beekman Street, 1858. Cox and Wyman, Printers, Great Queen Street, London. xii, 681 p., 8 plates. With four pages of publisher's titles bound at the end.
117 × 189 × 50 mm. 9005.b.26.

The plates are signed: 'JG' [i.e. John Gilbert] and 'Dalziel'. Text sewn on two sawn-in cords. Light yellow endpapers and pastedowns. Blue bead-grain cloth. Both covers are blocked identically in blind on the borders. Two fillets are blocked on the borders. Between them, a repeating pattern of curling stem and three berries is blocked, with six berries blocked in relief on each corner. The upper cover vignette is blocked in gold. It shows a star and also a crown which is held aloft by two soldiers. The crown has the word: 'Sebastopol' blocked in relief within it. The soldier on the left is in oriental uniform, and holds a musket in his right hand, and the crown in his left. The soldier on the right is in Scottish uniform (kilt and socks), plus a sabre. He holds a musket upright in his left hand, and the crown with his right hand. Between the two soldiers, the title: '| The | great | sieges | of | history |' is blocked in gold. On the ground underneath, a triangular pile of cannon balls is blocked in gold. Signed 'JL' in relief as separate letters within one of the cannon balls at the base of the pile. [This is the same upper cover vignette as for the 1855 edition at BL 9005.b.27.] The spine is blocked in gold. A single fillet is blocked in gold on the perimeter. From the head downwards, the decoration is: a group of military equipment for conducting a siege, which includes a rocket; the words: '| The | great | sieges | of | history. | [rule] | Robson. |' blocked in gold; a group of objects, blocked in gold – a musket, a bayonet, a spade, a pickaxe, a saw, an axe, a smaller pickaxe – all tied together in the middle with a rope; the words: '| London | Routledge & Co |' are blocked in gold at the base within a rectangle formed by a single gold fillet. [This is likely to be the spine blocked on earlier edition(s), as its width of 35mm is clearly less than the spine width of this edition of 50 mm.] Blue date stamp: '22 M[A]Y [18]58'.

296 Leighton, John

Southey, Robert. *Minor poems, ballads and Joan of Arc. With Illustrations by John Gilbert.* London: G. Routledge & Co., Farringdon Street. New York: 18, Beekman Street, 1858. London: Savill and Edwards, Printers, Chandos Street. xxiv, 469, 8 plates. With two pages of publisher's titles bound at the end.
105 × 170 × 40 mm. 11603.e.20.

Routledge's British poets. Engravings executed by Dalziel. In the publisher's titles at the end, the series is advertised as: 'In Fcap. 8vo, elegantly printed in new type, cloth, gilt edges, 5s. each; . . .'

Gilt edges. Yellow endpapers and pastedowns. Red bead-grain cloth. Blocked identically as BL 11603.e.14. Cowper, William. *The poetical works.*

297 Leighton, John PLATE XXXIV

Stanesby, Samuel. *The Bridal Souvenir. Illuminated by Samuel Stanesby.* London: Griffith and Farran, Corner of St. Paul's Churchyard, 1858. London: Ashbee & Dangerfield, 22 Bedford St., Covent Garden. [38 p.]
175 × 223 × 16 mm. 1347.h.24.

The borders and capital letters of each page are chromolithographed. In the Preface: 'The flowers introduced into the illuminated borders are selected in accordance with their signification in the language of flowers.' [A list of the flowers and of their characteristics follows.]

Bevelled boards. Gilt edges. Light yellow endpapers and pastedowns. White coarse pebble-grain cloth. Binder's ticket on front pastedown: '| Bound by | Bone & Son, | 76 Fleet Street, | London. |' Both covers fully blocked in gold and in blind, with an identical design. Nine borders are blocked on each cover: 1. a gold fillet; 2. dog-tooth decoration; 3 & 4. single gold fillets; 5. a repeating pattern of cartouches, each with small decoration blocked within; 6. a repeating 'heart-shape and semi-circle' pattern; 7. a gold fillet; 8. repeating small dots; 9. a gold fillet. Rose leaves and flowers are blocked on the corners of the inner borders. Turquoise paper onlays form a thin oval-shaped arabesque, which are gold stamped in gold, showing a leaf and flower pattern in relief. Four border fillets are blocked on the outside of the arabesque. Rose medallions and crossing hearts shapes formed by five fillets surround the title. The title: '| The | Bridal | Souvenir |' is blocked in relief within a quatrefoil gold lettering-piece, which is within a circle. Signed 'JL' in relief as separate letters at base of title. On the spine, the title: '| The Bridal Souvenir |' is blocked in letters with 'double' relief, within a gold lettering-piece blocked along the spine.

Gilt edges. Bevelled boards. Yellow endpapers and pastedowns. Binder's ticket on lower pastedown: '| Leighton | Son & | Hodge. | Shoe Lane. | London. |' Bright green morocco vertical-grain cloth. Both covers and spine blocked identically in gold and in relief. There is a sea shell and rope pattern on the borders. Three gold fillets are blocked on the borders inside this, which form straps at the head, at the tail and on each centre side. Each corner-piece is formed by five gold fillets, the middle of which is dotted. Within each corner-piece, a dolphin, surrounded by seaweed, is blocked, all in gold. The recessed central oval has three gold fillets blocked on its upper borders, and a fillet in blind blocked on its recessed border, which has a 'rope' pattern blocked in relief within it. On the inner perimeter of the oval, two more fillets are blocked, and, within these, a ship's anchor chain and stars – all in gold. The centre shows a ship's sail, blocked as a gold lettering-piece. Within it, the words: '| The | Shipwreck | by | William | Falconer |' are blocked in relief. Above the sail, within a pennant-shaped gold lettering-piece blocked in gold, the words: '| WF Born at Edin: 1732 | Lost at sea. 1769 |' are blocked in relief. Below the sail, within other pennant-shaped gold lettering-pieces, the words: '| Life & this | I struggled | alone | to save |' are blocked in relief. A gold medallion is hanging from the sail spar. Within the medallion, the silhouette of a lady, with ribbon and bonnet is blocked in relief. Signed 'JL' in relief as separate letters on the shoulder of the lady.

The spine is blocked in gold and in relief. Two fillets are blocked in gold on the perimeter. From the head downwards, the decoration is: a rectangular panel, formed by a single gold fillet, with small decoration blocked within; a lyre, surrounded by stars; the words: '| The | Shipwreck | A | poem | by | William | Falconer | Illustrated |' blocked in relief within seven rectangular gold lettering-pieces – the eighth contains the word '| A |' within a heart-shaped gold lettering-piece; an anchor and a curling rope, which surrounds six pennant-shaped gold lettering-pieces; these contains the words: '| Yet | Hope with | flattering | voice | betrayed | them on |' are blocked in relief; ribbons blocked in gold surround the anchor; a scallop shell is blocked below the anchor; signed 'JL' in gold as separate letters underneath the shell; a gold fillet; the words: '| A & C Black |' are blocked in relief within a rectangular gold lettering-piece, with a single gold fillet blocked on its borders; a gold fillet; a thick gold fillet and two gold fillets are blocked at the tail.

McLean, *VBD* p. 219. Morris & Levin, *APB* p. 33, no. 42. Oldfield, *BC* no. 53. Pantazzi, *JL* pp. 266–67. Reproduces a copy bound in blue morocco cloth by Leighton Son & Hodge.

282 Leighton, John

Forrest, George *pseud.* [i.e. John George Wood.] *The Playground; or, the boy's book of games.* London: G. Routledge & Co. 2, Farringdon Street. New York: 18 Beekman Street, 1858. London: R. Clay, Printer, Bread Street Hill. x, 267 p., 1 plate.
105 × 170 × 20 mm. 7906.b.19

Light yellow endpapers and pastedowns. Written on the upper endpaper: '| J.B. White | As a souvenir of | my pleasant visit | to Brighton. | Jany. 1860. | . . . |' Bookseller's ticket on upper pastedown: '[H?] & C. Treacher, late King & Co. | Booksellers | Publishers, | 7 Stationers, | [4?] North St. & 44 East St. | Brighton. |' Blue bead-grain cloth. Both covers blocked identically in blind and in relief. Two fillets are blocked on the borders, the outer thick, the inner thin. A single leaf is blocked on each corner, the veins outlined in relief. A third fillet is blocked on the borders, with a single strap on each corner, and two leaves on each side attached to the strap. A single leaf is blocked on each corner. A group of three leaves is blocked in blind and in relief on the centre head and on the centre tail. The spine is blocked in gold and in relief. A single fillet is blocked in gold on the perimeter. From the head downwards, the decoration is: a kite with tail streamers, a ball, a shuttlecock; the title: '| The | Play | Ground |' blocked in relief within a gold lettering-piece with a single fillet blocked on its borders; the words: '| A | boy's book | of | games. |' are blocked in gold; the words 'a' and 'of' are blocked within circles formed by a single fillet; the words 'boy's book' and 'games' are blocked in gold within rectangles formed by a single gold fillet; an archery board is blocked in gold, supported by stilts; an arrow shaft and arrow head, together with a holder full of arrows – are hung in front of the archery board; between the stilts, a group of objects is blocked – a cricket bat, a pair of cricket stumps, a cricket ball, a racquet, a stick with strands on its end; a fillet in gold; the word: '| Illustrated |' is blocked in gold within a rectangle formed by a single gold fillet; a gold fillet; signed 'JL' in gold as separate letters, at the tail.

Another copy in Cambridge University Library at CUL.140.4.308.

283 Leighton, John

Goldsmith, Oliver. *The poetical works of Oliver Goldsmith, Tobias Smollett, Samuel Johnson, and William Shenstone. With biographical notices and notes. Illustrated by John Gilbert.* London: G. Routledge & Co., Farringdon Street; New York: 18, Beekman Street, 1858. London: Savill, and Edwards, Printers, Chandos Street. xvi, 84 p.; xv, 33 p.; xvi, 88 p.; xxxi, 196 p., 8 plates. With twelve pages of publisher's titles bound at the end.
105 × 170 × 22 mm. 11603.e.19

Routledge's British poets. Engravings executed by Dalziel.

Gilt edges. Yellow endpapers and pastedowns. Binder's ticket on lower pastedown: '| Bound by | Bone & Son. | [rule] | 76 Fleet Street, London.'. Red bead-grain cloth. Blocked identically as 11603.e.14. Cowper, William. The poetical works.

Dry, *JL* no. 281.

284 Leighton, John FIG. 35

Hall, Anna Maria. *The adventures and experiences of Biddy Dorking. To which is added the story of the Yellow Frog. Edited by*

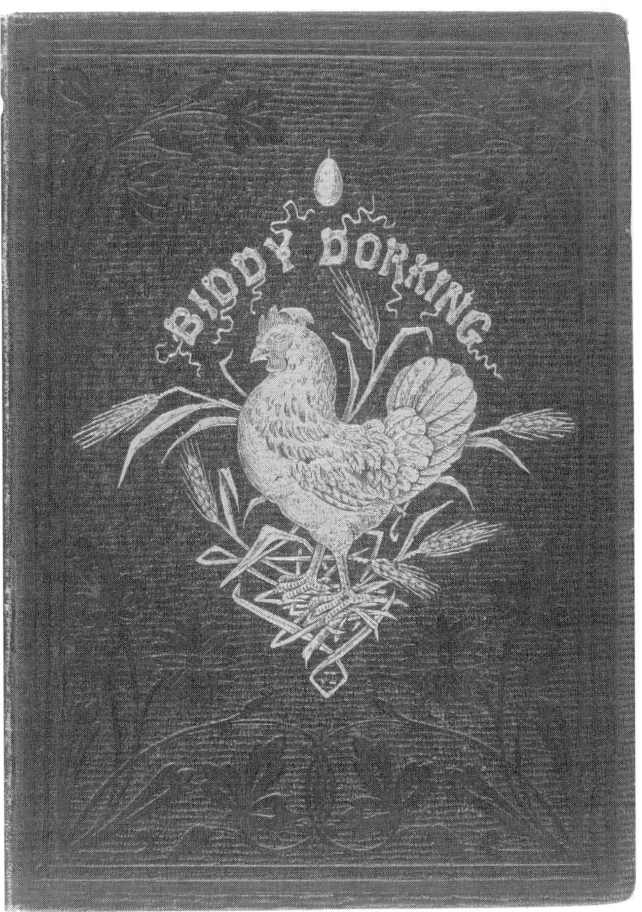

FIG. 35

Mrs S.C. Hall. With illustrations by Harrison Weir. London: Griffith and Farran, late Grant & Griffith, Successors to Newbery & Harris, Corner of St. Paul's Churchyard, 1858. London: Savill and Edwards, Printers, Chandos Street, Covent Garden. [2], 94 p., 4 plates. With sixteen pages of publisher's titles bound at the end.
125 × 176 × 12 mm. 12808.a.34.

On page 2 of the publisher's titles at the end, this work is listed as: '2s.6d. cloth; 3s.6d. coloured, gilt edges.' The plates are coloured.

Text sewn on two tapes. Gilt edges. Yellow endpapers and pastedowns. Blue morocco horizontal-grain cloth. Both covers identically blocked in blind on the borders and on the corners. Two fillets blocked on the borders. Flower, leaf and seed head decoration on each lower corner, with joined stems and leaves on the lower centre; stems rise up each side, ending in more flowers, leaves and seed heads on each upper corner. (This is the same design as for BL 12807.b.53. Jack Frost and Betty Snow) The upper cover has a central vignette blocked in gold. It shows a hen standing on corn stalks, with the heads and leaves of the stalks around the hen. The words: '| Biddy Dorking |' are blocked in gold, in a semi-circle, above the hen, in rustic lettering with tendrils. An egg is blocked above these words. Signed 'JL' in gold as separate letters at the base of the vignette. The spine is blocked in gold. From the head downwards, the decoration is: an egg, with a chick with its head out of the shell; the title words: '| Biddy | Dorking | & the | Fat Frog. |' blocked in gold; a frog in gold, with reeds.

Dry, *JL* no. 283.

285 Leighton, John FIG. 36

Hey, Wilhelm. *Picture fables. Drawn by Otto Speckter, engraved by the Brothers Dalziel. With rhymes translated from the German of F. Hey by Henry W. Dulcken.* London: G. Routledge and Co. Farringdon Street. New York: 18 Beekman Street, 1858. London: Printed by Richard Clay, Bread Street Hill. ix, 101 p.
136 × 203 × 17 mm. 12305.d.13.

Gilt edges. Bevelled boards. Pink endpapers and pastedowns. Binder's ticket on lower pastedown: '| Bound by | Westleys | & Co. | London. |'. Blue morocco horizontal-grain cloth. Both covers blocked identically in blind and in relief on the borders and on the corners. Two fillets are blocked on the borders, the outer thick, the inner thin. Curling rose stems and flowers are blocked in blind on each corner, with the centre of each rose

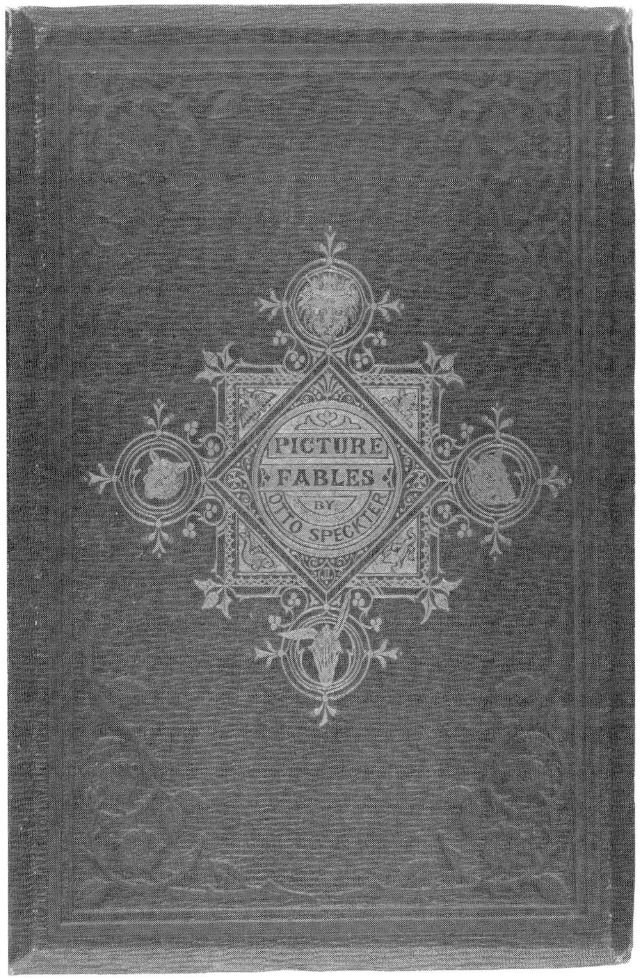

FIG. 36

flower being blocked in relief. A central vignette blocked in gold shows a diamond enclosing a medallion gold lettering-piece. The title : '| Picture | fables | By | Otto Speckter [in a semi-circle] |' is blocked in relief within the medallion. A medallion, each formed by four gold fillets, is blocked on each corner of the diamond.. Within each, a sheep, an ass, a lion – crowned and a wolf, are blocked in gold. A square with decorated borders surrounds the diamond; a bat, a frog, a lizard and fish are blocked within each corner of the square. Signed 'JL' in gold as separate letters at the base of diamond. The spine is blocked in gold and in relief. From the head downwards, the decoration is: the words: '| Picture | Fables | by | Otto | Speckter |' blocked in gold; a gold rectangle with decoration blocked in relief within it; an arabesque; an elongated arabesque in gold, with an owl within its lower centre; signed 'JL' in relief as separate letters within a 'teardrop' underneath the arabesque; the words: '| Routledge | [& Co] |' are blocked in relief within a rectangular gold lettering-piece, with a single gold fillet blocked on its borders; a gold fillet is blocked at the tail.

286 Leighton, John FIG. 37

James, George Payne Rainsford. *Memoirs of great commanders. A new edition. With illustrations by Phiz.* London: G. Routledge & Co. Farringdon Street; New York: 18, Beekman Street, 1858. Printed by Cox and Wyman, Great Queen-Street, London. iv, 459 p., 8 plates.
115 × 185 × 35 mm. 10603.c.8.

The plates are signed: 'Edward H. Corbould' and 'Dalziel'. Text sewn on three sawn-in cords. Light endpapers and pastedowns. Blue morocco horizontal-grain cloth. Both covers blocked identically in blind on the borders and on the corners. Two fillets blocked on the borders, the outer thin, the inner thick. Lattice work is blocked in blind on each corner. The upper cover has a central vignette blocked in gold. It shows a medallion gold lettering-piece, with linked branches forming triangles around its perimeter. Within the medallion, the title: '| The | great | commanders | of | Europe. |' is blocked in relief. Underneath, two crossed marshal's batons with ribbons are blocked in relief. A small tie for the batons holds a model of St. George, on a horse, sword in hand, about to slay the dragon. Signed 'JL' in gold as separate letters underneath the dragon's tail. The spine is blocked in gold. Two gold fillets are blocked on the perimeter. From the head downwards, the decoration is: a knight's helmet with two plumed feathers; the words: '| The | great | commanders | of | Europe. | [rule] | G.P.R. James. |' blocked in gold; a sword, blocked from the tail upwards, has a laurel wreath and castellated crown across it. Stars surround the sword. All of the above is blocked within a cartouche, formed by two gold fillets, with a border of gold dots. Signed 'JL' in gold as separate letters underneath the hilt of the sword. At the tail, the word: '| Illustrated.' is blocked in gold, within a rectangle formed by two gold fillets.

[A well proportioned spine design, still in good condition.]

Dry, *JL* no. 286.

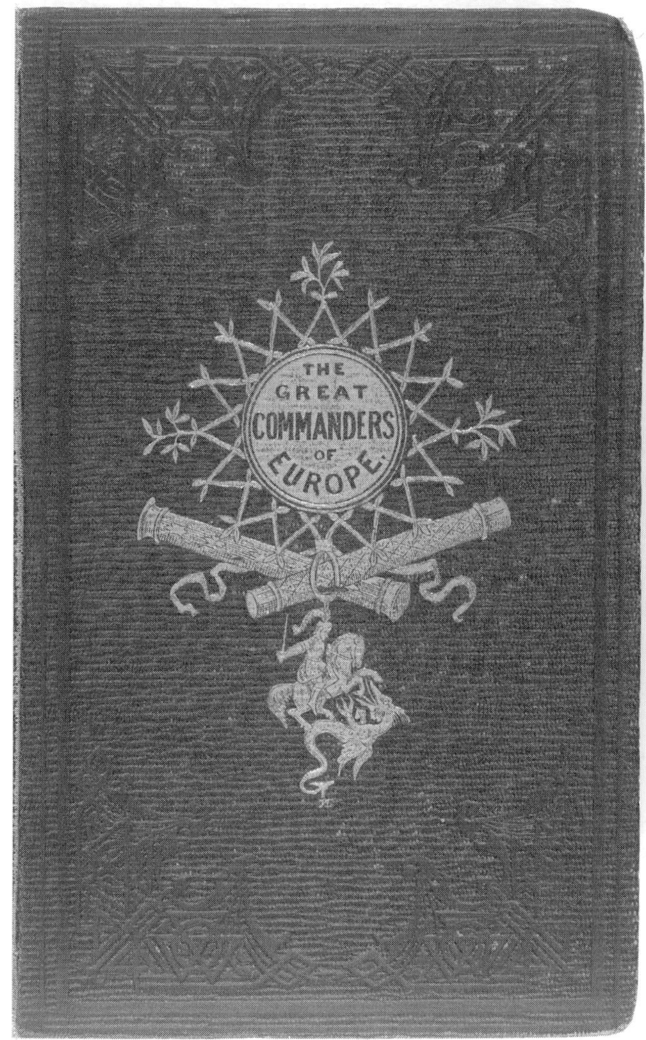

FIG. 37

287 Leighton, John

Kemp, Edward. *How to lay out a garden: intended as a General Guide in choosing, forming, or improving an estate, (From a Quarter of an Acre to a Hundred Acres in extent,) with reference to both design and execution . . . Second edition: greatly enlarged, and illustrated with numerous plans, sections, and sketches of gardens and garden objects.* London: Bradbury & Evans, 11, Bouverie Street, 1858. London: Bradbury and Evans, Printers, Whitefriars. xxxii, 403 p.
125 × 190 × 30 mm. 7055.c.30.

Text sewn on three sawn-in cords. Gilt edges. Light yellow endpapers and pastedowns. Green bead-grain cloth. Both covers blocked identically in blind on the borders and on the corners. Two fillets are blocked in blind on the borders; then a border of fillets, which delineate straps blocked in relief. Between the straps, cartouches are blocked in relief. A flower head and leaf outline is blocked in relief on each corner. The upper cover has a central vignette blocked in gold. It shows a central gold lettering-piece medallion. This has the words: '| How | to | lay

out | a | garden |' blocked in relief within five gold lettering-pieces, formed by single fillets blocked in relief. The words are surrounded by small trefoils and stems, blocked in relief. The medallion has four ovals blocked at the head, the tail, and on each side. Each contains a plant representing: 'Summer' – a rose; 'Autumn' – apples; 'Winter' – a leafless bush; 'Spring' – a bush sprouting leaves. Groups of seasonal flowers are blocked between the ovals. Signed 'JL' in gold as separate letters underneath the word 'Winter', at the base of the vignette. The spine is blocked in gold. From the head downwards, the decoration is: tendrils forming a panel; the words: '| How | to | lay out | a | garden | [rule] | E. Kemp. |' blocked in gold within the panel; a fountain, showing an angel on a ball, sprouting water through a trumpet held in its right hand; dolphins support the fountain basin [the dolphins are very much a Leighton decoration-piece]; a line of leaves blocked in gold at the rim of the fountain pond; signed 'JL' in relief as separate letters within one of these leaves [a tiny signature; only 1 mm wide]; the words: '| London | Bradbury & Evans |' are blocked within a rectangle formed by two gold fillets; three gold fillets blocked at the tail.

Dry, *JL* no. 288.

288 Leighton, John

Kingston, William Henry Giles. *Fred Markham in Russia; or, the boy travellers in the land of the Czar. With Illustrations by R. T. Landells.* London: Griffith & Farran, late Grant & Griffith, Successors to Newbery & Harris, Corner of St. Paul's Churchyard, 1858. London: Savill and Edwards, Printers, Chandos Street, Covent Garden. xii, 372 p. 8 plates. With twenty-four pages of publisher's titles bound at the end. The verso of the half-title page also has publisher's titles.

110 × 175 × 35 mm. 12807.bb.34.

Yellow endpapers and pastedowns. Blue morocco horizontal-grain cloth. Both covers blocked identically in blind and in relief. Two fillets blocked on the borders. Leaf motifs are blocked in relief on the corners, the head and the tail. The spine is blocked in gold. A single gold fillet is blocked on the perimeter. Inside this, another gold fillet and gold dots are blocked on the inner perimeter. From the head downwards, the decoration is: an arch; a Russian crown and ribbons; the words: '| Fred | Markham | in | Russia | Kingston. |' blocked in gold within four rectangles formed by single gold fillets, with the word 'in', being blocked within a circle formed by a single gold fillet; a Russian double-headed eagle is blocked in relief within a gold lettering-piece; St. George slaying a dragon; signed 'JL' in gold as separate letters within a 'spade-shape' formed by a single gold fillet; a gold fillet; the word: '| Illustrated |' is blocked in gold within a rectangle formed by a single gold fillet, with gold dots blocked within; two gold fillets blocked at the tail.

Dry, *JL* no. 289.

289 Leighton, John

Kirkland, Caroline Matilda. *Garden walks with the poets.* London: T. Nelson & Sons, Paternoster Row; Edinburgh and New York, 1858. 192 p., 6 plates.

95 × 152 × 22 mm. 11601.e.10.

Text sewn on three sawn-in cords. Gilt edges. Yellow endpapers and pastedowns. Wave diagonal-grain cloth. Both covers blocked identically in blind with four fillets on the borders. The upper cover has a central vignette blocked in gold. It shows a garden urn with twisted 'branch-like' handles. The urn is filled with leaves and flowers. Above the urn, the title words: '| Garden walks | with the |' are blocked; below the urn, the word: '| poets |' is blocked. The words: 'Garden walks' and 'poets' are blocked in gold in rustic lettering. The letters of the word 'poets' also have only their upper half blocked in gold. Signed 'JL' in relief as separate letters on the plinth of the urn. The spine is blocked in gold. A single gold fillet is blocked around the perimeter. Honeysuckle and ivy rise as stems up the sides, with their leaves and flowers blocked at the head. Below this, the title: '| Garden | walks | with the | poets. |' is blocked in rustic lettering; then a rose bush, with a lyre supported in its middle. A rectangle, formed by a single gold fillet, is blocked at the tail, with a single 'branch-like' gold fillet blocked within the rectangle.

Dry, *JL* no. 280.

290 Leighton, John

Knowles, James Sheridan. *The dramatic works. A New Edition in One Volume.* London: G. Routledge & Co. Farringdon Street; New York: 18, Beekman Street, 1858. London: Cox (Bros) and Wyman, Printers, Great Queen Street. Two vols in one. Vol. 1. vi, 448 p. Vol. 2. 457 p. With two pages of publisher's titles bound at the end.

125 × 190 × 55 mm. 1568/2770.

Untrimmed edges. Yellow endpapers and pastedowns. Blue bead-grain cloth. Both covers are blocked identically in blind with four fillets on the borders. The inner border is of a wide fillet blocked in blind, with a repeating leaf and stem pattern blocked in relief within it. The spine is blocked in gold. A single gold fillet is blocked on the perimeter. Groups of three fillets (one thick between two thin) divide the spine into panels. Within the panel at the head, the words: '| The | dramatic | works | of | James Sheridan Knowles |' are blocked in gold; underneath this, within a long rectangle formed by the three fillets, a long pole is blocked, with a pineapple-like plant at its head, surrounded by vine leaves and tendrils, with two face masks hanging at the middle on either side; signed 'JL' in gold as separate letters at the base of the pole; at the tail, the words: '| London: G. Routledge & Co. |' are blocked in gold within a rectangle formed by a single gold fillet, which is surrounded by the three fillets.

291 Leighton, John

May, Emily Juliana. *Bertram Noel. A Story for Youth . . .* London: E. Marlborough & Co., Ave Maria Lane. Bath: Binns and Goodwin, [1858]. vi, 409 p., 5 plates. With four pages of publisher's titles bound at the end.
110 × 178 × 35 mm. 12808.a.52.

Four of the plates are signed 'J H Nicholson' and 'C. W. Sheeres'. On page two of the publisher's titles: 'Price 5s.'

Text sewn on three sawn-in cords. Bolts uncut. Yellow endpapers and pastedowns. Brown morocco horizontal-grain cloth. Both covers blocked identically in blind on the borders and on the corners. Two fillets are blocked on the borders. the outer thick, the inner thin. On each corner, leaves and curling stems form a circle, with small leaves blocked inside in relief. The upper cover central vignette is blocked in gold. At the head, a ribbon-shaped gold lettering-piece is blocked in gold, with the words: '| He that | ruleth his spirit | is more mighty than he that taketh a city |' blocked in relief inside. A medallion, formed by two fillets blocked in gold, shows a boy inside with his arms crossed holding a book. The words: '| Bertram Noel | a | Story for Youth | by | E. J. May. |' are blocked in relief within five gold lettering-pieces, of which three are rectangles, and two are circular, each with a single gold fillet blocked on its borders. Signed 'JL' in gold as separate letters at the base of the vignette. The spine is blocked in gold. From the head downwards, the decoration is: small plants; the title: '| Bertram | Noel. |' blocked in gold within a panel formed by a fillet blocked on each side, and small decoration above and below; an urn on a plinth, blocked in gold, has a bouquet of leaves and flowers, some of which hang downwards; a fillet; the words: '| London | Marlborough & Co |' are blocked in gold within a rectangle formed by two gold fillets; two gold fillets are blocked at the tail.

Dry, *JL* no. 292.

292 Leighton, John

Milton, John. *The poetical works. A new edition, carefully revised, from the text of Thomas Newton, D. D. With illustrations by William Harvey.* London: G. Routledge & Co., Farringdon Street. New York: 18, Beekman Street, 1858. London: Savill and Edwards, Printers, Chandos Street, Covent Garden. viii,570 p., 7 plates.
110 × 170 × 30 mm. 11603.e.17.

Routledge's British poets. Engravings executed by Dalziel.

Gilt edges. Yellow endpapers and pastedowns. Blue thick pebble-grain cloth. Blocked identically as BL 11603.e.14. Cowper, William. *The poetical works.*

293 Leighton, John FIG. 38

Munchausen, Baron. *The surprising travel and adventures of Baron Munchausen in Russia, the Caspian Sea, and through the centre of Mount Etna into the South Sea, etc., etc. Humbly Dedicated to Mr Bruce, the Abyssinian Traveller, &c.* Edinburgh: Adam and Charles Black, 1858. Printed by R. and R. Clark Edinburgh. xvi, 159 p.
100 × 153 × 14 mm. 12804.b.42.

FIG. 38

Text sewn on two tapes. Gilt edges. Light brown endpapers and pastedowns. Blue morocco vertical-grain cloth. Both covers blocked identically, in blind only on the lower, in gold and in blind on the upper. Two fillets are blocked in blind on the borders, the outer thick, the inner thin. The central vignette is blocked in gold on the upper cover. It shows the words: '| Baron | Munchausen |' blocked in gold, in gothic letters. The capitals 'B' and 'M' are blocked in relief within gold lettering-pieces. The 'M' has facial features, with the nose, eyes on either side and a mouth being on each side and below the middle serif. To the left of the capital 'B' is a quarter moon, shaped as a face, smoking a pipe. The title letters are surrounded by tendrils and trefoils. The trefoils have faces. Signed 'JL' in gold as separate letters at the left hand base of the vignette. The spine is blocked in gold. Two gold fillets are blocked at the head and the tail; the words: '| Baron Munchausen. |' are blocked in gold along the spine; a gold fillet; the words: '| Illustrated | edition |' in gold are blocked near the tail.

Dry, *JL* no. 302.

294 Leighton, John

Myrtle, Harriet, Mrs. *pseud.* [i.e. Lydia Falconer Miller.] *The Ocean Child; or, showers and sunshine. A Tale of Girlhood. Second edition.* London: G. Routledge & Co. Farringdon Street; New York: 18, Beekman Street, 1858. Cox and Wyman, Printers, 74–75, Great Queen-Street, London. vii, 308 p., 8 plates. With four pages of publisher's titles bound a the end.
105 × 167 × 27 mm. 12806.c.35.

The plates are signed 'B. Foster' and 'Dalziel' The design has been blocked after casing in. Yellow endpapers and pastedowns. Blue morocco horizontal-grain cloth. Both covers blocked identically in blind on the borders and on the corners, with the leaf and stem decoration blocked in relief. An inner border of

leaves and stems, blocked in relief, forms a central oval. The upper cover has a central vignette blocked in gold. It shows a girl, wearing a hat, seated side saddle on a pony, looking out at the ocean. Above and below the girl, the title: '| The | Ocean | Child |' is blocked in gold, in rustic lettering. A shell and seaweed are blocked below the word: 'Child'. Signed 'JL' in gold as a monogram in the seaweed below the shell. The spine is blocked in gold. Two gold fillets are blocked around the perimeter. From the head downwards, the decoration is: an arch and stars; the title: '| The | Ocean | Child |' blocked in fanciful letters; a hand holding a lamp, which is lit, emitting rays; a girl seated among plants; signed 'JL' in gold as separate letters to the left and to the right underneath the girl; the word '| Illustrated |' is blocked in gold at the tail within a rectangle formed by a single gold fillet.

The Addey & Co. edition of 1857 is at BL 12631.a.24. It has green morocco horizontal-grain cloth. Blocked in blind only on both covers. Unsigned.

Dry, *JL* no. 294.

295 Leighton, John

Robson, William. *The great sieges of history. With the addition of Delhi and Lucknow by Captain Thomas Spankie, Bengal Retired List. The fifth Thousand.* London: G. Routledge & Co. Farringdon Street; New York: 18, Beekman Street, 1858. Cox and Wyman, Printers, Great Queen Street, London. xii, 681 p., 8 plates. With four pages of publisher's titles bound at the end.
117 × 189 × 50 mm. 9005.b.26.

The plates are signed: 'JG' [i.e. John Gilbert] and 'Dalziel'. Text sewn on two sawn-in cords. Light yellow endpapers and pastedowns. Blue bead-grain cloth. Both covers are blocked identically in blind on the borders. Two fillets are blocked on the borders. Between them, a repeating pattern of curling stem and three berries is blocked, with six berries blocked in relief on each corner. The upper cover vignette is blocked in gold. It shows a star and also a crown which is held aloft by two soldiers. The crown has the word: 'Sebastopol' blocked in relief within it. The soldier on the left is in oriental uniform, and holds a musket in his right hand, and the crown in his left. The soldier on the right is in Scottish uniform (kilt and socks), plus a sabre. He holds a musket upright in his left hand, and the crown with his right hand. Between the two soldiers, the title: '| The | great | sieges | of | history |' is blocked in gold. On the ground underneath, a triangular pile of cannon balls is blocked in gold. Signed 'JL' in relief as separate letters within one of the cannon balls at the base of the pile. [This is the same upper cover vignette as for the 1855 edition at BL 9005.b.27.] The spine is blocked in gold. A single fillet is blocked in gold on the perimeter. From the head downwards, the decoration is: a group of military equipment for conducting a siege, which includes a rocket; the words: '| The | great | sieges | of | history. | [rule] | Robson. |' blocked in gold; a group of objects, blocked in gold – a musket, a bayonet, a spade, a pickaxe, a saw, an axe, a smaller pickaxe – all tied together in the middle with a rope; the words: '| London | Routledge & Co |' are blocked in gold at the base within a rectangle formed by a single gold fillet. [This is likely to be the spine blocked on earlier edition(s), as its width of 35mm is clearly less than the spine width of this edition of 50 mm.] Blue date stamp: '22 M[A]Y [18]58'.

296 Leighton, John

Southey, Robert. *Minor poems, ballads and Joan of Arc. With Illustrations by John Gilbert.* London: G. Routledge & Co., Farringdon Street. New York: 18, Beekman Street, 1858. London: Savill and Edwards, Printers, Chandos Street. xxiv, 469, 8 plates. With two pages of publisher's titles bound at the end.
105 × 170 × 40 mm. 11603.e.20.

Routledge's British poets. Engravings executed by Dalziel. In the publisher's titles at the end, the series is advertised as: 'In Fcap. 8vo, elegantly printed in new type, cloth, gilt edges, 5s. each; . . .'

Gilt edges. Yellow endpapers and pastedowns. Red bead-grain cloth. Blocked identically as BL 11603.e.14. Cowper, William. *The poetical works.*

297 Leighton, John

PLATE XXXIV

Stanesby, Samuel. *The Bridal Souvenir. Illuminated by Samuel Stanesby.* London: Griffith and Farran, Corner of St. Paul's Churchyard, 1858. London: Ashbee & Dangerfield, 22 Bedford St., Covent Garden. [38 p.]
175 × 223 × 16 mm. 1347.h.24.

The borders and capital letters of each page are chromolithographed. In the Preface: 'The flowers introduced into the illuminated borders are selected in accordance with their signification in the language of flowers.' [A list of the flowers and of their characteristics follows.]

Bevelled boards. Gilt edges. Light yellow endpapers and pastedowns. White coarse pebble-grain cloth. Binder's ticket on front pastedown: '| Bound by | Bone & Son, | 76 Fleet Street, | London. |' Both covers fully blocked in gold and in blind, with an identical design. Nine borders are blocked on each cover: 1. a gold fillet; 2. dog-tooth decoration; 3 & 4. single gold fillets; 5. a repeating pattern of cartouches, each with small decoration blocked within; 6. a repeating 'heart-shape and semi-circle' pattern; 7. a gold fillet; 8. repeating small dots; 9. a gold fillet. Rose leaves and flowers are blocked on the corners of the inner borders. Turquoise paper onlays form a thin oval-shaped arabesque, which are gold stamped in gold, showing a leaf and flower pattern in relief. Four border fillets are blocked on the outside of the arabesque. Rose medallions and crossing hearts shapes formed by five fillets surround the title. The title: '| The | Bridal | Souvenir |' is blocked in relief within a quatrefoil gold lettering-piece, which is within a circle. Signed 'JL' in relief as separate letters at base of title. On the spine, the title: '| The Bridal Souvenir |' is blocked in letters with 'double' relief, within a gold lettering-piece blocked along the spine.

Small decoration in gold is blocked at the head and at the tail. The list of titles issued by Griffith and Farran, bound at the end of 'Nursery nonsense or rhymes without reason ', 1864, (BL shelfmark 12806.bb.13.) has the following description of this publication: 'Elegantly bound in white and gold, price 21s.'. The list of titles at the rear of BL 12807.f.70. 'Old nurse's book of rhymes, jingles and ditties' has the description: 'Elegantly bound in a new white morocco cloth, with richly gilt sides. Quarto, price One Guinea.' [Formerly shelfmarked at B.L. C.30.f.6.]

Dry, *JL* no. 357. King, *JL* p. 238. McLean, *VPBB* p. 70. Oldfield, *BC* no. 52. Pantazzi, *JL* pp. 266, 270.

298 Leighton, John

Walpole, Horace. *The Castle of Otranto. A Gothic Story . . .* Edinburgh: Adam & Charles Black, 1858. Neill and Co., Printers, Edinburgh. xvi, 181 p.
106 × 166 × 18 mm. 12614.a.11.

Gilt edges. Brown endpapers and pastedowns. Brown bead grain-cloth. Both covers blocked identically in blind with two fillets blocked on the borders, the outer thick, the inner thin. Both covers have the same central vignette, blocked in blind and in relief on the lower, in gold and in relief on the upper. It shows a knight's helmet, with a bird and four plumed feathers on the crest. The helmet rests on a gold lettering-piece, shaped as cushion resting on top of a plinth. The plinth has the title: '| Castle of Otranto |' blocked in relief within it. Signed 'JL' in relief as separate letters to the left and to the right above the cushion. The spine is blocked in gold. From the head downwards, the decoration is: a gold fillet; a sword with a handle; a gold lettering-piece shaped as a shield suspended by straps on the hilt of the sword; the shield has dots on its border, blocked in relief; the words: '| The | Castle | of | Otranto | by | Horace | Walpole. |' blocked in relief within the shield; tendrils are blocked in gold underneath the shield; the words: '| A. & C. Black | Edinburgh | are blocked in gold near the tail; a gold fillet at the tail.

Dry, *JL* no. 303.

299 Leighton, John

Wood, John George. *My feathered friends. With illustrations by Harrison Weir.* London: G. Routledge & Co., Farringdon Street. New York: 18, Beekman Street, 1858. Printed by Woodfall and Kinder, Angel Court, Skinner Street, London. xii, 396 p., 8 plates.
105 × 170 × 30 mm. 7006.a.28.

Text sewn on three sawn-in cords. Blue wave diagonal-grain cloth. Both covers blocked identically in blind on the borders and on the corners. Two fillets are blocked on the borders, the outer thick, the inner thin. Circles and leaves are blocked in relief on each corner. The upper cover has a central vignette blocked in gold. It shows a bird standing on the spine of a book, shaped as a gold lettering-piece, which is lying on its fore-edge. The bird is surrounded by ivy stems and leaves (the leaf veins being picked out in relief). The title: '| My | feathered friends |' is blocked in gold in rustic letters above and on each side of the bird. The words: '| By | J.G. Wood | M.A. F.L.S. |' are blocked in relief within the upper cover of the book. Signed 'JL' in gold as separate letters at the base of the vignette. The spine is blocked in gold. A single fillet is blocked in gold on the perimeter. From the head downwards, the decoration is: a gold fillet; curling stems and buds; the words: '| My | feathered | friends. | [rule] | J.G. Wood. |' blocked in gold near the head; feathers are blocked on top of a medallion, which is mounted on a claw base; a bird's head and the motto: 'My talking friend' are blocked in gold, within a medallion; small decoration; a gold fillet; the words: '| London | Routledge & Co. |' are blocked in gold within a rectangle formed by a single fillet; a gold fillet at the tail.

Dry, *JL* no. 304.

300 Leighton, John

Wordsworth, William. *The poetical works. A new edition, carefully edited. With a life.* London: G. Routledge & Co. Farringdon Street; New York: 18, Beekman Street, 1858. London: Cox and Wyman, Printers, Great Queen Street, Lincoln's inn Fields. xxiii, 496 p., 8 plates.
105 × 170 × 30 mm. 11603.e.23.

Routledge's British poets. Engravings by Dalziel.

Gilt edges. Yellow endpapers and pastedowns. Binder's ticket on lower pastedown: '| Bound by | Bone & Son. | [rule] | 76 Fleet Street, | London. |'. Blue bead-grain cloth. Blocked identically as 11603.e.14. Cowper, William. *The poetical works.*

301 Leighton, John

The nursery library of Pictures and Stories for little folk. London: Darton and Co., Holborn Hill, [1859].
172 × 216 × 12 mm. 12807.g.53.

The work has a composite title page and a frontispiece plate for four stories paginated separately. These are: *Holiday scenes.* 16 p., 8 plates. *My new story book.* 16 p., 8 plates. *Shadows.* 16 p., 8 plates. *Home and its joys.* 16 p., 8 plates. All the plates are hand coloured.

The text is stab stitched on six cords. Original yellow endpapers. Pink dyed paper over boards, printed in red and blue. Both covers printed identically. Two fillets in blue are printed on the borders. Inside this a border of blue is printed, with small stems and leaves inside, printed in red. Bunches of leaves are printed on the upper inner corners. On the centre the title: '| The | Nursery | Library |' is printed. Below these, a lady, a boy and a girl are seated on a bench. The boy and the girl have an open book on their laps. Above the lady is a kite, with its 'face' looking down on this group, and its tail streamers rising above. There is a hoop to the right of the bench. Ivy leaves and stems are underneath the bench. Signed, bottom left: 'Luke Limner del'; and bottom right: 'H. Leighton'. At the tail, within the

blue border: '| Darton & Co. Holborn Hill. London. |' is printed in red. The spine is of brown morocco vertical-grain cloth, and is not blocked.

Dry, *JL* no. 323.

302 Leighton, John

Atkinson, John Christopher. *Walks, talks, travels and exploits of two schoolboys; A Book for Boys.* London: Routledge, Warne & Routledge, Farringdon Street. New York: 56, Walker Street, 1859. London: Savill and Edwards, Printers, Chandos-Street, Covent Garden. xi, 433 p., 6 plates. With thirty-four pages of publisher's titles bound at the end.

111 × 177 × 40 mm. 12804.g.21.

The plates are signed 'H. Weir' and 'Dalziel'.

Text sewn on three sawn-in cords. Yellow endpapers and pastedowns. Binder's ticket on lower pastedown: '| Bound by | Edmonds & Remnants. | [rule] | London |'. Blue bead-grain cloth. Both covers blocked identically in blind on the borders and on the corners. Two fillets are blocked on the borders, the outer thick, the inner thin. Groups of three leaves are blocked in blind on each corner. The upper cover has a central vignette blocked in gold. It shows two schoolboys, wearing caps, standing on a plinth. Their left hands are clasped together, with their right hands holding aloft a bird's nest. Between the boys, an open book is blocked as a gold lettering-piece. It has the words: '| Walks | Talks | Travels & | Exploits |' blocked in relief within the opening. The words: 'of' and 'Two School Boys' are blocked in relief within rectangular gold lettering-pieces with a single fillet on the borders. Small leaf and stem decoration is blocked on each side of the boys and below the title. A necklace is blocked at the base. Signed 'JL' in gold as separate letters beneath the necklace. The spine is blocked in gold. A single fillet is blocked on the perimeter. From the head downwards, the decoration is: leaves and birds on either side of a bell; the words: '| Walks, | Talks. | Travels & Exploits | of | Two School Boys | A | book for boys | [rule] | Atkinson. |' blocked in gold within a frame formed by a single fillet; a group of bulrushes, oak leaves, ferns, and a school class slate are blocked above a water scene, which has a frog, a nesting bird, fish, a water rat, and an eel – all blocked in gold; signed 'JL' in gold as separate letters to the left and the right of the base of the water; a fillet; the word: '| Illustrated |' is blocked in gold within a rectangular gold lettering piece, which has a fillet border; a gold fillet blocked at the tail.

Dry, *JL* no. 307.

303 Leighton, John

Bowman, Anne. *The kangaroo hunters; or, adventures in the bush.* . . . London: G. Routledge & Co. Farringdon Street; New York: 18, Beekman Street, 1859. Cox and Wyman, Printers, Great Queen Street, London. iv, 444 p., 7 plates.

107 × 175 × 48 mm. 12808.a.45.

Some of the plates are signed: 'H. Weir'; and all are signed 'Dalziel'.

Original yellow endpaper bound at the front. Red bead-grain cloth. Both covers blocked identically in blind on the borders, on the corners and on the sides. Two fillets are blocked on the borders. Inside these, plant decoration is blocked in relief in the form of small groups of 'stylised' leaves, with three on each side and one group on each corner, and one on the centre head and the centre tail. All these are joined by a single fillet, blocked in blind. The upper cover central vignette is blocked in gold. It shows an aborigine, half-crouching on his left knee, with a spear held horizontally in his right hand, resting on his right shoulder. His left hand reaches out to the dog by his side. A group of plants is blocked behind the aborigine. The title: '| The | kangaroo | hunters. |' is blocked above and below the aborigine, in gold in rustic letters with tendrils. Signed 'JL' in gold as separate letters at the base of the vignette. [Spine missing]

304 Leighton, John

Brough, John Cargill. *The fairy tales of science. A book for youth. With sixteen illustrations by Charles H. Bennett.* London: Griffith and Farran, Successors to Newbery & Harris, Corner of St. Paul's Churchyard, 1859. London: Savill and Edwards, Printers, Chandos Street, Covent Garden. xi, 338 p., 12 plates. With twenty-four pages of publisher's titles bound at the end.

110 × 178 × 32 mm. 8704.b.20.

The plates are signed: 'CHB' as a monogram; some of the plates are also signed 'Swain Sc.'

Original endpapers bound in. Red wave diagonal grain cloth. Both covers are blocked identically in blind on the borders and on the corners. Two fillets are blocked on the borders. On the corners leaves and stems are blocked in blind. On the upper cover, the central vignette is blocked in gold. It features four roundels, each formed by two gold fillets, one blocked on each side of a square. Inside each roundel is decoration. In the roundel at the top is a putto's head and wings, blowing air. On the right is a hand holding a torch. At the base is a mallet, a pickaxe, and a sack. Signed 'JL' in gold as separate letters at the base of this roundel. On the left is a hand pouring a pitcher of water. On the corners of the square, blocked in capitals inside small gold lettering pieces in relief are the words: 'earth; air; fire; water'. The central roundel has dog-tooth and fillets blocked on the border. It contains the title. The word: '| The |' is blocked in relief inside a small gold lettering piece shaped as a star. The words: '| fairy tales |' are blocked in gold within lines , which are blocked between two firework rockets. The words: '| of science |' are blocked in gold. All are surrounded by small stars blocked in gold. The spine is blocked in gold. Within a panel formed by a single fillet, the title: '| The | fairy tales | of | science. |' is blocked in gold. An oil lamp with a handle is lit. The lamp rests on a plinth blocked in gold, which is blocked underneath the title panel.

Dry, *JL* no. 309.

305 Leighton, John

Burrows, Mrs E. *The triumphs of steam; or, Stories from the Lives of Watt, Arkwright, and Stephenson. With illustrations by John Gilbert.* London: Griffith and Farran, Late Grant and Griffith, Successors to Newbery and Harris, Corner of St. Paul's Churchyard, 1859. London: Gilbert and Rivington, Printers, St. John's Square. viii, 263 p., 4 plates. With thirty-two pages of publisher's titles bound at the end.
124 × 160 × 25 mm. 10804.a.32.

In page 3 of the list of publisher's titles at the end: ' Royal 16mo., price 3s. 6d., cloth; 4s. 6d. coloured, gilt edges.' The plates are hand coloured and engraved by Dalziel.

Gilt edges. Original upper cover used as a doublure. Blue morocco horizontal-grain cloth. The borders and the corners are blocked in blind. Three fillets blocked on the borders. Stems and trefoils are blocked on the corners. The stems form an arch at the centre head, crossing to make straps. Quatrefoils are blocked along the inner tail. The central vignette is blocked in gold. It shows a model of an early steam engine, with six wheels, the decoration for the detail of the engine being blocked in relief. The word: '| Stephenson |' is blocked in relief within a plaque mounted on the side of the engine. The words: '| The | Triumphs |' are blocked above the engine; the words: '| of | steam |' are blocked below it – all in gold. Signed 'JL' in gold as separate letters at the base of the vignette.

Dry, *JL* no. 330

306 Leighton, John

Dalton, William. *The War Tiger; or, adventures and wonderful fortunes of the young sea chief and his lad Chow: a tale of the conquest of China. With illustrations by H. S. Melville.* London: Griffith and Farran, late Grant and Griffith, Successors to Newbery and Harris, Corner of St. Paul's Church Yard, 1859. London: Gilbert and Rivington, Printers, St. John's Square. xi, 371 p., 8 plates. With twenty-four pages of publisher's titles bound at the end.
110 × 177 × 32 mm. 12808.a.49.

In the list of publisher's titles at the end of BL 10804.a.32. 'The triumphs of steam' is the description of this work: '. . .price 5s. cloth; 5s. 6d. cloth, gilt edges.'

Text sewn on three sawn-in cords. Yellow endpapers and pastedowns. Blue morocco vertical-grain cloth. Both covers identically blocked in blind and in relief. There are three fillets blocked on the borders: 1. a single fillet; 2. repeating cartouches and diamonds are blocked in relief, within a fillet blocked in blind; 3. a fillet with small circles within. A leaf, flower, and stem pattern blocked in relief on each corner forms a central oval. The spine is blocked in gold. Two fillets are blocked in gold on the perimeter. From the tail upwards, the decoration is: two fillets; the word: '| Illustrated |' blocked in relief, in Chinese lettering, within a rectangular gold lettering-piece; a fillet; signed 'JL' in gold as separate letters; a Chinese soldier stands to attention, his rifle on the ground, held in his right hand. A standard rises above the soldier: it has a dragon on its top; then a gold lettering-piece shaped as a medallion, with the words: '| The | War | Tiger |' blocked in relief within it; below the medallion, a gold lettering-piece shaped as a flag is attached to the pole, and has the sub title: 'or adven | tures | of the | young | Sea | Chief | &c. |' blocked in relief within the flag.

Dry, *JL* no. 311.

307 Leighton, John

Defoe, Daniel. *The Life and Adventures of Robinson Crusoe. With a memoir of the author, and essay on his writings. Illustrated by [J. J.] Grandville.* London: Routledge, Warne, & Routledge, Farringdon Street. New York: 56, Walker Street, 1859. 599 p.
130 × 200 × 35 mm. C.188.a.26.

Light yellow endpapers and pastedowns. Binder's ticket on lower pastedown: '| Bound | by | Leighton | Son and | Hodge |'. Red bead-grain cloth. Both covers identically blocked in blind on the borders and on the corners. Three fillets are blocked on the borders. Between the second and the third fillets, a pattern of repeating diamonds is blocked in relief. A plant decoration pattern is blocked in blind on the corners and down the sides. The upper cover vignette is blocked in gold. It shows a palm leaf umbrella, with a bird on its top. The umbrella is supported by wooden poles, tied together with a rope around the central pole. The rope also holds together a group of objects around the pole: a sword, an axe, a musket, a saw. The rope forms a medallion to the left and to the right of the pole. The heads of Man Friday, and of Crusoe are blocked in gold within each medallion. Two pairs of palm leaves are blocked below the medallions. A ribbon-shaped gold lettering-piece is blocked amongst these leaves. The words: '| Juan Fernandez |' are blocked in relief within the ribbon. Signed 'JL' in gold as a monogram at the base of the vignette. The spine is blocked in gold. A rope-like gold fillet is blocked on the perimeter. From the head downwards, the decoration is: the title: '| Life | & | adventures | of | Robinson | Crusoe | [straps] | Illustrated |' blocked in gold in fanciful letters; from the tail upwards, a wooden pole is blocked to beneath the title; a wooden notice board gold lettering-piece is nailed to the top of the pole; within the board, the words: '| I came on | shore here | on the 30th of | September 1659 |' are blocked in relief within it; crossed palm leaves are blocked in gold below this; seagulls and turtles are blocked at the base of the pole, by water. Unsigned spine.

308 Leighton, John FIG. 39

Defoe, Daniel. *The life and surprising adventures of Robinson Crusoe. Illustrated by C. A.Doyle.* Edinburgh: Adam and Charles Black, 1859. Printed by R & R Clark, Edinburgh. viii, 338 p., 4 plates. With six pages of publisher's titles bound at the end.
145 × 190 × 30 mm. 12613.c.28.

Gilt edges. Light brown endpapers and pastedowns. Brown pebble-grain cloth. The upper and lower covers are blocked identically in blind with two fillets on the borders, the outer

FIG. 39

thick, the inner thin. Both covers have the same central vignette, blocked in blind on the lower cover, and in gold on the upper. At the head of the vignette, a parrot is blocked atop a 'roof' of palm leaves. The head of Crusoe is blocked in gold, with dog to left and cat to right, with a ram's head below – all in medallions. The title: '| Robinson | Crusoe |' is blocked in gold, in rustic lettering, above and below the medallion of Crusoe, within rectangles formed by single branch-like fillets. Signed 'JL', in gold as separate letters, at base of vignette. The spine is fully blocked in gold. A single fillet is blocked on the perimeter. A palm tree is blocked from the tail to the head, with leaves and branches near the head. From the head downwards, the decoration is: the title: '| Robinson | Crusoe |' blocked in relief within two rectangular gold lettering-pieces, with a single gold fillet on their borders; beneath this, a gold medallion is blocked, showing the head of '| Man Friday |' blocked in relief; a group of objects is blocked in gold 'behind' the medallion' – an oar, two sabres, a musket, an axe, a spade, a spear and a rope; single thin gold fillet; the words: '| A & C Black |' are blocked in relief within a rectangular gold lettering-piece with a single gold fillet blocked on its borders; at the tail, a gold fillet is blocked.

Dry, *JL* no. 312. King, *JL* p. 240.

309 Leighton, John FIG. 40

Grimalkin, Tabitha *pseud. Tales from Catland, written for little kittens. By an Old Tabby. Fourth edition. With four illustrations by Harrison Weir.* London: Griffith and Farran, late Grant and Griffith, Successors to Newbery & Harris, Corner of St. Paul's Churchyard, 1859. [London]: John Edward Taylor, Printer, Little Queen Street, Lincoln's Inn Fields. 94 p., 4 plates. With thirty-two pages of publisher's titles bound at the end.
125 × 175 × 12 mm. RB.23.a.12925.

The dedication reads: 'To the kittens of England, the following pages are very affectionately dedicated by their sincere friend and well-wisher Tabitha Grimalkin.' On the publisher's titles, page 17: 'Third edition. Small 4to., 2s. 6d. plain; 3s. 6d. coloured gilt edges.' The list of titles issued by Griffith and Farran, bound at the end of 'Nursery nonsense or rhymes without reason', 1864, (BL 12806.bb.13.) has: 'Fourth edition. Small 4to, 2s. 6d. plain; 3s. 6d. coloured, gilt edges.'

Yellow endpapers and pastedowns. Binder's ticket on lower pastedown: '| Bound by | Burn. | 37 & 38 | Kirby Street. |' Red bead-grain cloth. Both covers are blocked identically in blind on the borders and on the corners. Two fillets are blocked on the borders, one thick, one thin. Leaf, stem and flower decoration are blocked on each corner, with stems blocked on the sides. On the upper cover, a central vignette is blocked in gold. It shows, at the centre, an Old Tabby, seated in an armchair, its legs on a footstool. The Tabby wears a dressing gown, its left paw holding spectacles; its right paw holding a quill just above the open page of a book, which is suspended on foliage in front of the tabby. Its open pages form a gold lettering-piece, with the words: '| Tab | by's | tales |' blocked within in relief. There is small mouse blocked on the left on a stem, holding a quill pen and an inkpot. The title words:

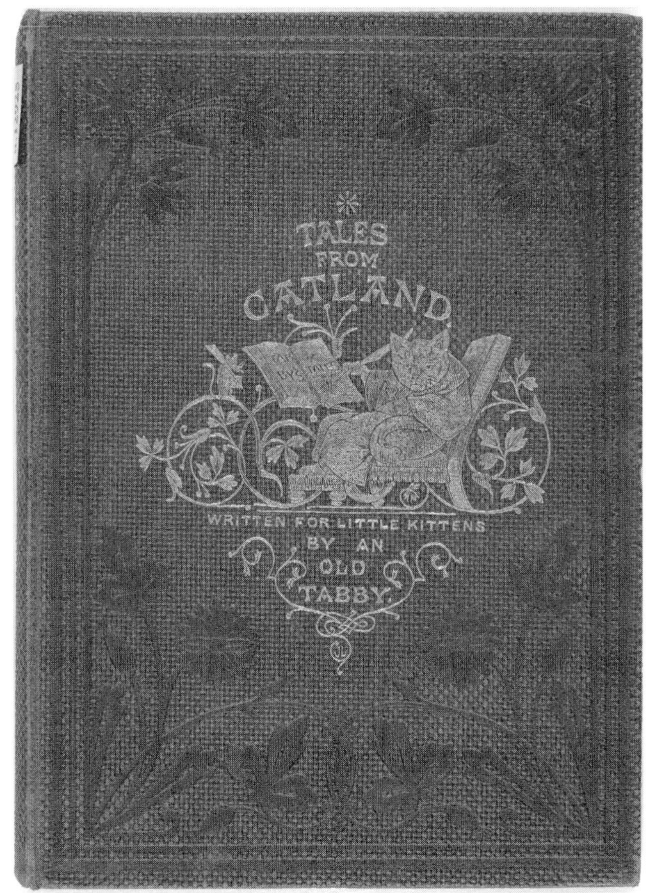

FIG. 40

'| Tales | from | Catland. |' are blocked in gold above the Tabby. Below him, the words: '| Written for little kittens | by an | Old | Tabby. |' are blocked in gold. Signed 'JL' in gold as separate letters, at the base of the vignette. On the spine, the title words: '| Tales from | Cat | land |' are blocked in gold in rustic letters. Tendrils and stems emerge from the letters. A mouse is blocked at the base of the tendrils, sitting on a stem.

310 Leighton, John

Hall, Anna Maria and Hall, Samuel Carter. *The book of the Thames, from Its Rise to its Fall....* London: Arthur Hall, Virtue and Co., 25, Paternoster Row, 1859. London: Printed by James S. Virtue, City Road. xii, 516 p.
158 × 227 × 43 mm. 10350.d.32.

Original covers used as doublures. Doublure size: 153 × 225 mm. Green morocco vertical-grain cloth. Both covers identically blocked in gold and in relief. Five borders are blocked on each cover: 1. a thin fillet, with repeating small diamonds and spikes; 2. a border of crossed, decorated semi-circles; 3. a rope-shaped gold fillet; 4. a gold fillet with a small pattern of alternating diamonds and circles, blocked in relief; 5. a fillet, with small dots blocked at intervals. On the inner border, an alternating pattern of three leaves and three dots is blocked. A dolphin is blocked on each inner corner, within a triangle formed by a gold fillet and small repeating dots. On the centre is a large mandorla, with three smaller ones blocked inside. A crown is at the head of the large mandorla; a shell is blocked at its tail. The three smaller mandorlas are blocked in a row on the centre. There are gold fillet borders for each of these three mandorlas. Within the central mandorla of the three, a man is blocked with fish in his beard. The mandorla on the left has crossed snakes on a staff, blocked underneath a winged helmet. There are also two shields: 1. azure, a ring and cross, crossed with triangular staff; 2. the arms of the Corporation of London. The mandorla on the right has a bishop's mitre and a staff and two shields: 1. argent, a bull, gules, on waves, azure; 2. the arms of the Oxford University Press. At the head and the tail of the three small mandorlas, panels are blocked, containing groups of leaves blocked in vertical hatch gold. Above and below the three mandorlas, the title: '| The | Book | of | the | Thames |' is blocked in relief within rectangular and circular gold lettering-pieces, each of which has a single gold fillet blocked on its borders. Signed 'JL' in relief as separate letters within the shell at the base of the larger outer mandorla.

Dry, *JL* no. 314. Morris & Levin, *APB* p. 35, no. 48.

311 Leighton, John

Howitt, William. *A country book: for the Field, the Forest and the Fireside. Third edition, With Illustrations from Designs by Birket Foster.* London: G. Routledge & Co. Farringdon Street; New York: 18, Beekman Street, 1859. London: Cox and Wyman, Printers, Great Queen-Street. viii, 392 p., 8 plates.
110 × 180 × 30 mm. 12354.b.42.

The engravings are signed 'Dalziel Sc.'.

Text sewn on three sawn-in cords. Light yellow endpapers and pastedowns. Binder's ticket on lower pastedown: '| Bound by | Edmonds and Remnants | [rule] | London |'. Blue bead-grain cloth. The borders and corners of both covers are blocked identically in blind. There are two fillets blocked in blind on the borders, and there are plant and leaf patterns blocked in blind on the corners. The upper has a central vignette, blocked in gold. There is a small bird blocked at the top. Beneath this, is a fox, astride a weather vane. Below this, the title: '| Howitt's | Country | Book |' is blocked in relief, within three rectangular gold lettering-pieces. The lettering-pieces each have a small dot border, blocked in relief, and outside this, a single fillet is blocked in gold on the borders. Crossing underneath the gold lettering-pieces are a scythe, a rake, a fish net holding a fish, a rifle. A water flask hangs from the pole of the fish net. At the base of the vignette hangs a drum, a drumstick and a small wind instrument (a shawm?). Signed 'JL' in gold as a monogram at the base of the vignette. The spine is blocked in gold. A single fillet is blocked in gold on the perimeter. From the head downwards , the decoration is: at the head, an arch is formed by two fillets, and a bird is blocked near the top of the arch; the title word '| A |' blocked in relief in a spade-shaped gold lettering-piece; the words: '| Country | book |' blocked in relief, within two rectangular gold lettering-pieces, with border fillets the same as for the upper vignette; the word '| by |' blocked in gold; the words: '| William | Howitt |' blocked in gold within two rectangular lettering-pieces, each formed by a thin gold fillet; ivy leaves and plants and bushes are blocked near the base; a rabbit is blocked within the plants; signed 'JL' in gold as separate letters to the left and to the right of the spine underneath the rabbit; at the tail, the word '| Illustrated |' is blocked in relief in a rectangular gold lettering-piece, which has a single gold fillet blocked on its borders.

312 Leighton, John

Mary, *Sister. Sister Mary's Annual: a series of delightful tales and stories, written expressly for the amusement and instruction of youth.* Dublin: Published by James Duffy, 7, Wellington-Quay, 1859. J. M. O'Toole, 13 Hawkins'-Street, Dublin. [Ten stories separately paginated.] With two pages of publisher's titles bound at the end.
107 × 141 × 25 mm. 12804.b.36.

The title page and frontispiece are plates. The frontispiece is signed: 'Geo Measom Sc.'

Gilt edges. Yellow endpapers and pastedowns. Red bead-grain cloth. Both covers blocked identically in blind on the borders, on the corners, and on the sides. A pattern of stems and leaves is blocked in relief on the borders, on the corners, and on the sides. The pattern forms a rectangular central frame. The upper cover vignette is blocked in gold. A medallion, formed by a single fillet, is blocked on the centre. Within it, the title: '| Sister | Mary's | annual |' is blocked in gold. Around it, four 'card-spade' shapes are blocked. Inside each, leaves and a single

flower are blocked in gold. A border of roses links the 'card-spade' shapes. [This is the same blocking as on BL 12304.b.10.; 12631.f.21.; 12807.a.55.; 12807.a.58.] The spine is blocked in gold. The title: '| Sister | Mary's | annual |' is blocked in gold within a panel formed by a single fillet. Passion flower leaves and tendrils are blocked down the spine in gold; two gold fillets are blocked at the tail. [Lower half of spine missing.]

313 Leighton, John

Miller, Thomas, *Miscellaneous writer. English country life. Consisting of descriptions of rural habits, country scenery, and the seasons. With nearly three hundred illustrations, by Birket Foster, John Gilbert, William Harvey, etc.* London: Routledge, Warne and Routledge, Farringdon Street. New York: 18, Beekman Street, 1859. London: R.Clay, Printer, Bread Street Hill. xvi, 479 p.
120 × 182 × 33 mm. 12355.c.31.

Gilt edges. Original yellow endpaper bound at the front. Blue bead-grain cloth. The borders and corners of both covers are blocked identically in blind. There are two fillets blocked in blind on the borders, with leaf and stem patterns blocked in relief on the corners. The upper cover has a central vignette blocked in gold. It shows four putti representing the seasons: Spring, Summer, Autumn, and Winter. The putti are blocked at the head, the tail and at the sides of the vignette. Linking the four putti is a tracery of branches, leaves and flowers, which forms a central frame. In the frame the words: '| English | Country | Life | by | Thomas | Miller. |' are blocked in gold. The capital 'C' of 'country' is blocked in the shape of a sickle. The capital 'L' of 'Life' is blocked in the shape of a horse whip. The head of the horsewhip rises to cross the bar of the 'L' of the word 'English' blocked on the line above. Signed 'JL' in gold as separate letters at the base of the vignette. The tracery of branches and small birds blocked at the base of the vignette is similar to 'Sunshine in the country', and to 'Gems from the poets'. The spine is fully blocked in gold. A single gold fillet is blocked on the perimeter, which forms an arch at the head. At the tail of the spine a trellis is blocked, with leaves and flowers growing through it. Rising up from this is a pole, with ivy leaves and stems twined around it. Towards the head, the pole supports three rectangular gold lettering-pieces in which the title words '| English | Country | Life |' are blocked in relief.

Dry, *JL* no. 320.

314 Leighton, John

Munchausen, *Baron. The travels and surprising adventures of Baron Munchausen. [Engraving of the tombstone of Baron Munchausen; inscribed: 'Here | lies | Baron | Mun | chausen | '] Illustrated by Alfred Crowquill.* London: Trubner & Co. 60, Paternoster Row, 1859. London: R. Clay, Printer, Bread Street Hill. xii, 194 p., 8 plates.
125 × 190 × 30 mm. 12808.c.22.

The plates are coloured. Gilt edges. Bevelled boards. [No original endpapers or pastedowns.] Binder's ticket on lower pastedown: '| Bound | by Westleys | & Co. | London. |' Brown bead-grain cloth. Both covers blocked identically in gold and in blind and in relief. Three fillets are blocked in gold on the borders. A pattern of lily-like leaves, flowers, stems and tendrils is blocked in blind on each corner, on the head and on the tail, and on the sides. On the sides, the pattern ends in straps. Two fillets form the central frame. Inside, a border of small leaves is blocked in relief. The centre-piece is blocked in gold. It shows a similar pattern of lily-like leaves, etc. The spine is blocked in gold. From the head downwards, the decoration is: lily and tendril decoration blocked in gold; two gold fillets; the title: '| The | travels | of | Baron | Munchausen |' blocked in gold, within a rectangular panel formed by a single fillet; two gold fillets; lily flowers, leaves, stems, are blocked in gold, forming an extended 'figure of eight' pattern down the spine; signed 'JL' in gold as separate letters at the base of this decoration; two gold fillets; a row of small flower decoration is blocked in gold; at the tail, a single gold fillet.

315 Leighton, John

Puzzewell, Peter, *Esq. pseud. Home amusements; a choice collection of riddles, charades, rebuses, conundrums, parlour games, forfeits, etc. New edition, Revised and Enlarged.* London: Griffith and Farran, Successors to Newbery and Harris, Corner of St. Paul's Churchyard, 1859. London: Savill and Edwards, Printers, Chandos Street, Covent Garden. 224 p., 1 plate. With thirty-two pages of publisher's titles bound at the end.
110 × 140 × 22 mm. 12804.b.45.

Yellow endpapers and pastedowns. Binder's ticket on lower pastedown: '| Bound by | Bone & Son | [rule] | 76, Fleet Street, | London. |' Green morocco horizontal-grain cloth. The borders and the corners of both covers are blocked identically in blind. Two fillets are blocked on the borders. A leaf and stem pattern is blocked in relief on each corner. The lower cover central vignette shows a medallion and a diamond, both blocked in blind. The upper cover central vignette is blocked in gold. The central medallion is formed by two gold fillets. The title: '| Riddles games | Home | Amusements | charades |' is blocked in gold. The words: 'Home' and 'Amusements' are blocked within rectangles formed by single gold fillets. On the left and the right, satyr-like figures are blocked in gold. The figure to the left is winged, with a jester's hat and a trumpet; the figure to the right is winged, with hair flowing upwards, holding a triangle in its right hand, and the beater of the triangle in its left hand. Leaves are blocked below each figure in gold. At the head of the medallion, two oil lamps are blocked, each held symmetrically on brackets, the whole suspended by two strings. At the base of the vignette, an animal-headed satyr is blocked in gold, holding a bell in each upraised arm. Signed 'JL' in relief as separate letters at the base of the vignette, within a small leaf decoration, blocked in gold. The spine is blocked in gold. The title: '| Home | amusements. | Riddles. | Charades. | Games.

&c. | ' is blocked in gold; above and below the title, the decoration is blocked in gold.

316 Leighton, John

Ramble, Reuben *pseud. The child's treasury of Knowledge and Amusement; or, Reuben Ramble's picture lessons.* London: Darton and Co., Holborn Hill, [1859]. London: W. Stevens, Printer, 37, Bell Yard, Temple Bar. [16p., 9 plates; 16 p., 8 plates; 32 p.; 32 p.]
167 × 215 × 15 mm. 12807.f.50.

The plates are hand-coloured. [Modern yellow endpapers and pastedowns.] Pink printed paper over boards. The same design is printed on both covers. Red and blue rules are printed on the borders. There is a floral inner border, with red flowers printed on black. The central rectangle shows a lady standing behind two children seated on a bench. The children are looking at an open book. Above this group, the title: '| The | child's treasury | ' is printed in rustic letters. Around the group are ivy leaves and stems and flowers. Signed at the left hand corner: 'Luke Limner del.'. At the base of the right hand corner is: 'H.Leighton [the 'n' is printed in reverse] S'. Printed in red at the base of the floral border is 'Darton & Co., Holborn Hill. London.' The spine is printed in red, with rustic lettering along its length.

317 Leighton, John

Shakespeare, William. *Shakespeare's Household Words. A Selection from the wise saws of the Immortal Bard. Illuminated by Saml Stanesby.* London: Griffith & Farran, Corner of St. Paul's Churchyard, [1859]. London: Printed in colors [sic] by Ashbee and Dangerfield. [2], 28 p.
105 × 145 × 17 mm. 11765.a.31.

All pages have chromolithographed borders.

The frontispiece displays a photographic print of Shakespeare in a central oval. The bard's nose is pointing to the right. The list of titles issued by Griffith and Farran, bound at the end of 'Nursery nonsense or rhymes without reason', 1864, (BL shelfmark 12806.bb.13.) has the following description of this publication: 'With a photographic portrait taken from the monument at Stratford-on-Avon. Price 9s. cloth elegant; 14s. morocco antique.'

Gilt edges. Green endpapers and pastedowns. Brown morocco horizontal-grain cloth. Both covers are blocked identically. A single fillet is blocked in blind on the borders. Inside this is a border of repeating leaves and plant heads, blocked in gold. Within this, a border, of a navy blue paper onlay, is blocked in gold between two fillets, and shows a small pattern in blue relief. The central rectangle has white paper onlays in each corner. These are blocked in gold, showing ivy leaves and stems. The central panel is a blue paper onlay, shaped as an arabesque. The panel has two fillets around the perimeter, blocked in gold, with gold dots between. A lance is blocked in gold, from the base to the top of the arabesque and around it curls a pennant-shaped gold lettering-piece. The title words: '| Shakespeare's | Household | Words | ' are blocked in relief within the pennant. Signed 'JL' in relief as separate letters at the base of the pennant. Stars, blocked in gold, surround the pennant. The spine is blocked in gold. A single gold fillet is blocked on the perimeter. The title: '| Shakespeare's Household Words | ' is blocked along the spine in relief inside rectangular gold lettering-pieces. The imprint: '| Griffith | and | Farran | ' is blocked in relief within a rectangular gold lettering-piece, with a gold fillet blocked above and below it. At the tail, a small rectangular gold lettering-piece is blocked, with leaf decoration blocked in relief inside. Date stamped in blue: '7 DE[CEMBER 18] 59'.

Dry, *JL* no. 326. McLean, *VBD* p. 134. Oldfield, *BC* no. 54.

318 Leighton, John

Thornbury, George Walter. *Life in Spain: past and present. . . . In two volumes. With eight tinted illustrations.* London: Smith, Elder & Co., 65, Cornhill, 1859. London: Printed by Smith, Elder and Co., Little Green Arbour Court, Old Bailey, E.C.
127 × 205 × 30 mm. 10160.b.13.

Vol. I. vii, 318 p., 5 plates. Some of the plates are signed: 'E. Evans Sc'.

Vol. II. [2], 307 p., 5 plates. Some of the plates are signed: 'E. Evans Sc'. With twenty-four plates of publisher's titles bound at the end.

Original yellow upper endpapers bound at the front of each volume. Both volumes have brown morocco-grain cloth. On volume I, the cloth is applied vertical-grain; on volume II, the cloth is applied horizontal-grain. Both covers blocked identically in gold and in blind and in relief. On the borders of all the covers, three fillets are blocked in blind – one thick fillet between two thin ones. The upper cover central vignette is blocked in gold. It shows a diamond-shape, with a curved fillet and a dotted fillet blocked on its borders, and horizontal gold hatch stylised leaves blocked around the centre. A crown is blocked at the head in gold. The title words: '| Life | in | Spain | ' are blocked in relief within two rectangular and one circular gold lettering-pieces, all with single fillets blocked on their borders. On the centre, the coat of arms is blocked in gold. (Possibly a Spanish royal coat of arms.) To the left and the right of the coat of arms, an Ionic column is blocked in gold. The word 'Plus' is blocked in relief within a gold lettering-piece on the left column; the word: 'Ultra' is blocked in relief within a gold lettering-piece on the right column. Signed 'JL' in relief as separate letters within small horizontal hatch gold decoration at the base of the vignette. The spines of both volumes are blocked in gold, with an identical design. A panel is formed by two fillets, which have elaborate straps and hatched gold decoration blocked above and below it. The words: '| Life | in | Spain | by | W. Thornbury. | ' are blocked in gold inside the panel. The word: 'Vol' is blocked in relief within a heart-shaped gold lettering-piece; 'I [II]' is blocked in gold within a panel formed by a single fillet in the middle of decoration in the lower

half of the spine. The words: '| London | Smith Elder & Co |' are blocked in gold at the tail.

Dry, *JL* no. 327.

319 Leighton, John

Every boy's stories. A choice collection of standard tales, rhymes, and allegories. London: James Hogg and Sons, [1860]. 569 p., 10 plates. With six pages of publisher's titles bound at the end.
115 × 175 × 37 mm. 12804.c.23.

The plates are signed: 'F. Borders Sc.' Text sewn on two tapes. Yellow endpapers and pastedowns. Brown bead-grain cloth. The upper cover is blocked in gold and in blind. Two fillets are blocked on the borders in blind, the outer thick, the inner thin. The central vignette is blocked in gold. It shows a boy, wearing wings, carrying board advertisements on his shoulders, also holding two quills on his right shoulder. The front board is a gold lettering-piece, with the title: '| Every boy's | stories | A | choice collection | of | standard tales | rhymes | & allegories |' blocked in relief on the board. Signed 'JL' in gold as separate letters at the base of the vignette. [No spine, no lower cover.]

320 Leighton, John

Italian lyrics and other poems. London: Sanders, Otley, and Co., Conduit Street, 1860. London: F. Schoberl, Printer, 37, Dean Street, Soho, W. [7], 126 p. With seven pages of publisher's titles bound at the end.
107 × 173 × 13 mm. 11648.b.16.

The monogram of Saunders, Otley & Co. is printed on the title page, within a medallion and shield, with the motto: 'Sans Changer'.

Text sewn on two sawn-in cords. Light blue endpapers and pastedowns. Binder's ticket on lower pastedown: '| Bound by | Burn. | 37 & 38 | Kirby St. |' White bead-grain cloth. Both covers blocked identically in blind on the borders and on the corners. Two fillets are blocked on the borders, the outer thick, the inner thin. Stems and three leaves are blocked in blind and in relief on each corner. The upper cover central vignette is blocked in gold. It shows a trefoil frame formed by gold fillets, with small leaf and arabesques on its perimeter. On the centre, the title: '| Italian | lyrics |' is blocked in gold. Signed 'JL' in gold as separate letters at the base of the vignette. The spine is blocked in gold. From the head downwards, the decoration is: small decoration; the title: '| Italian | lyrics | and | other | poems' blocked in gold; small leaves are blocked in relief within two oriental-shaped gold lettering-pieces; near the tail, the date: '| 1860. |' is blocked in gold within a rectangle formed by a single gold fillet; three fillets blocked at the tail in gold.

Dry, *JL* no. 355.

FIG. 41

321 Leighton, John FIG. 41

Social etiquette. The art of cookery and hints on carving. Fourth thousand. London: Houlston and Wright, 65, Paternoster Row, 1860. 248 p.
113 × 177 × 20 mm. 7953.aa.46.

Cream endpapers and pastedowns. Brown rib diagonal-grain cloth. Both covers are blocked identically in blind, with an identical design. A single fillet is blocked in blind on the borders of both covers. Inside these, a strapwork, leaf and branch design is blocked on the head, the tail, and the sides. The upper cover central vignette is blocked in gold on the upper cover, featuring a gold lettering-piece blocked as an open book, with the title: '| Cookery, | carving | & | etiquette | of the | table |' blocked in relief within the book. The spine is blocked in gold. From the head downwards, the decoration is: the title: '| Cookery. | Carving, | & | Etiquette | of the | table. |' blocked in gold; a bunch of keys on a ring is blocked amidst ivy leaves and branches, all in gold; signed 'JL' in gold as a monogram near the tail, within the roots of an ivy plant; the publisher: '| Houlston | & Sons |' is blocked in gold; a single gold fillet is blocked at the tail.

322 Leighton, John

Aikin, John and Aikin, afterwards Barbauld, Anna Letitia. *Evenings at home: or, the juvenile budget opened. Consisting of a*

variety of miscellaneous pieces for the instruction and amusement of youth. Illustrated with one hundred engravings by the Brothers Dalziel. New edition, carefully revised. London: Ward and Lock, 158, Fleet Street, 1860. Dalziel Brothers, Camden Press, London. viii, 455 p., 1 plate.
114 × 182 × 36 mm. 12807.d.16.

Text sewn on two sawn-in cords. Edges speckled with red ink. Beige endpapers and pastedowns. Binder's ticket on lower pastedown: '| Bound by | Burn. | 37 & 38 | Kirby St. |' Red bead-grain cloth. Both covers blocked identically in blind and in relief on the borders and on the corners. Two fillets are blocked in blind on the borders. A leaf and stem pattern is blocked in relief on each corner. The upper cover vignette is blocked in gold. It shows four medallions, containing, clockwise: a bird in flight; an oak sprig; a cat's head; an apple tree sprig. On the centre, the words: '| Evenings at home | by | Dr. Aikin & | Mrs Barbauld. |' are blocked in relief within four gold lettering-pieces. Signed 'JL' in gold as separate letters at the base of the vignette. The spine is blocked in gold. Three fillets are blocked on the sides. From the head downwards, the decoration is: an arch; a quarter moon and stars; the title: '| Evenings | at | home | .' blocked in relief, within gold lettering-pieces; the words: '| 100 illustrations |' are blocked in gold; a pendulum clock is blocked in gold, surmounted by a winged ball; three fillets; the words: '| London | Ward & Lock |' are blocked in gold near the tail; gold fillet on the tail.

Dry, *JL* no. 332.

323 Leighton, John

Atkinson, John Christopher. *Playhours and half-holidays: or, further experiences of Two Schoolboys. Illustrated by Coleman.* London: Routledge, Warne & Routledge, Farringdon Street; New York: 56, Walker Street, 1860. London: Savill and Edwards, Printers, Chandos-Street, Covent Garden. 445 p., 5 plates. With six pages of publisher's titles bound at the end.
111 × 177 × 35 mm. 12807.bb.22.

The plates are signed W.S. Coleman and 'Dalziel'. Original yellow endpaper bound at the front. Binder's ticket on lower pastedown: '| Bound | by Hanbury & Co. | Binders, | 80, Coleman St. | E.C. |' Red bead-grain cloth. Both covers blocked identically in blind on the borders and on the corners. Two fillets blocked on the borders, the outer thick, the inner thin. Panels are blocked on the corners, showing curling stems blocked in relief. The upper cover vignette is blocked in gold. At the head, a fish is hanging from some netting. The title: '| Play Hours | and | half holidays | A book | for | boys. |' is blocked above and below the centre. On the centre a fishing boat is blocked. It is moored on the water, with a boy and a lady, holding fishing rods, blocked at each end of it. In the middle of the boat, another man is holding a freshly caught fish, with a rod slung over his left shoulder. The title words: 'Half Holidays' are blocked in relief within the base of the boat, which is blocked in gold. Signed 'JL' in gold as separate letters at the base of the vignette. The spine is blocked in gold. A single gold fillet is blocked on the perimeter. From the head downwards, the decoration is: a gold fillet; branches and leaves form an arch; the words: '| Play | hours | and half | holidays | A book for boys | [rule] | Atkinson |' blocked in gold; a heron is blocked beside a pond, in shallow water; a gold fillet; the word '| Illustrated |' is blocked in gold within a rectangle formed by a single gold fillet; a gold fillet is blocked at the tail.

Dry, *JL* no. 334.

324 Leighton, John FIG. 42

Atkinson, Thomas Witlam. *Travels in the regions of the Upper and Lower Amoor and the Russian acquisitions on the confines of India and China. With adventures among the mountain Kirghis; and the Manjours, Manyyargs, Toungouz, Touzmetz, Goldi and Gelyeks: the Huntung and Pastoral tribes. With a map and numerous illustrations.* London: Hurst and Blackett, Publishers, Successors to Henry Colborn, 13 Great Marlborough Street, 1860. London: Printed by Spottiswoode and Co. New-Street Square. xiii, 553 p., 1 plate, 1 fold-out map.
160 × 250 × 45 mm. 010058.ff.2.

FIG. 42

The frontispiece is a chromolithograph, entitled: '| A view on the Amoor . . . |' It is signed: '| T.W. Atkinson delt T. Picken lith. Day & Son Lithrs to the Queen. |' The fold-out map bound at the end is entitled: '| Central Asia, from the | Caspian Sea to the Pacific Ocean, | including the Regions between | Cashmere and Pekin, on the South, | and | Siberia, on the North; | to accompany the Travels of T.W. Atkinson Esq. |' The map is signed : '| John Arrowsmith. |'

The original upper cover used as doublure. Doublure size: 146 × 240 mm. Mauve morocco horizontal-grain cloth. The two fillets on the borders are blocked in blind. Oriental patterns are blocked on the corners in relief. The central vignette is blocked in gold. The title: '| The | Upper and Lower | Amoor. |' is blocked in relief within three gold lettering-pieces, with surrounding decoration of stems and leaves in gold. The centre shows a sleigh pulled by three horses. The wicker basket of the sleigh contains a man holding its sides, his cape flowing out behind him; his fur hat has fallen off. Signed 'JL' in gold as separate letters at the base of the vignette.

Dry, *JL* no. 335.

325 Leighton, John

Bede, Cuthbert *pseud.* [i.e. Edward Bradley.] *The adventures of Mr Verdant Green, an Oxford Freshman. With numerous illustrations designed and drawn on wood by the author. The one hundredth thousand.* London: James Blackwood & Co., Lovell's Court, Paternoster Row, [1860]. London: Robert K Burt, Printer, Wine Office Court, Fleet Street. vi, 118 p. + 112 p.

XL.823.8BRA

The University of Durham Library copy.

Mauve sand-grain cloth. Both covers blocked identically in blind on the borders. Fillets blocked on the borders. The upper cover has a central vignette blocked in gold. It shows a bust [of Mr Verdant Green?], being crowned with a teacher's hat by a gentleman on either side, each of which holds a shield. The bust rests on two books. The gentleman on the left stands on a crook; the one on the right stands on a mace. The title is blocked in gold, in rustic letters. The words: 'The one hundredth thousand' are blocked in gold at the top of the vignette. Signed 'JL' in gold as a monogram at the base of the vignette.

326 Leighton, John

Broderip, Frances Freeling. *Funny fables for little folks. With Illustrations by her Brother, Thomas Hood.* London: Griffith and Farran, Successors to Newbery & Harris, Corner of St. Paul's Churchyard, 1860. London: Savill and Edwards, Printers, Chandos Street, Covent Garden. [5], 98 p., 4 plates. With thirty-two pages of publisher's titles bound at the end.

127 × 175 × 15 mm. 12807.bb.12.

Edges speckled with red ink. Yellow endpapers and pastedowns. Binder's ticket on lower pastedown: '| Bound by | Burn. | 37 & 38 | Kirby St. |' Red bead-grain cloth. Both covers blocked identically in blind on the borders and on the corners. Two fillets are blocked on the borders. A third fillet is blocked on each side, rising to make leaves grouped on the left and right upper corners. On the left and right lower corners, a leaf, flower and bud are blocked in a group. The upper cover has a central vignette blocked in gold. It shows the heads of animals inside circles. The heads are (clockwise from top): a pig; a dog; a kettle; a cat. In between these, within smaller circles, are: a bird; a foxglove; a daisy; a crab. The central medallion is blocked in gold. It has a cross on the centre, and the title: '| Funny Fables for little folks |' is blocked in relief within the medallion's border, which is blocked between two fillets. Signed 'JL' in gold as separate letters at the base of the vignette. The spine is blocked in gold. From the head downwards, the decoration is: a moth; the title: '| Funny | fables | for | little | folks |' blocked in gold; a plant.

Dry, *JL* no. 338.

327 Leighton, John FIG. 43

Browne, Frances. *Our Uncle the traveller's stories.* London: W. Kent & Co. (Late D. Bogue), 86, Fleet Street, and Paternoster Row, 1860. Winchester: Printed by Hugh Barclay, High Street. [1], 138 p., 6 plates.

129 × 180 × 26 mm. 12806.c.31.

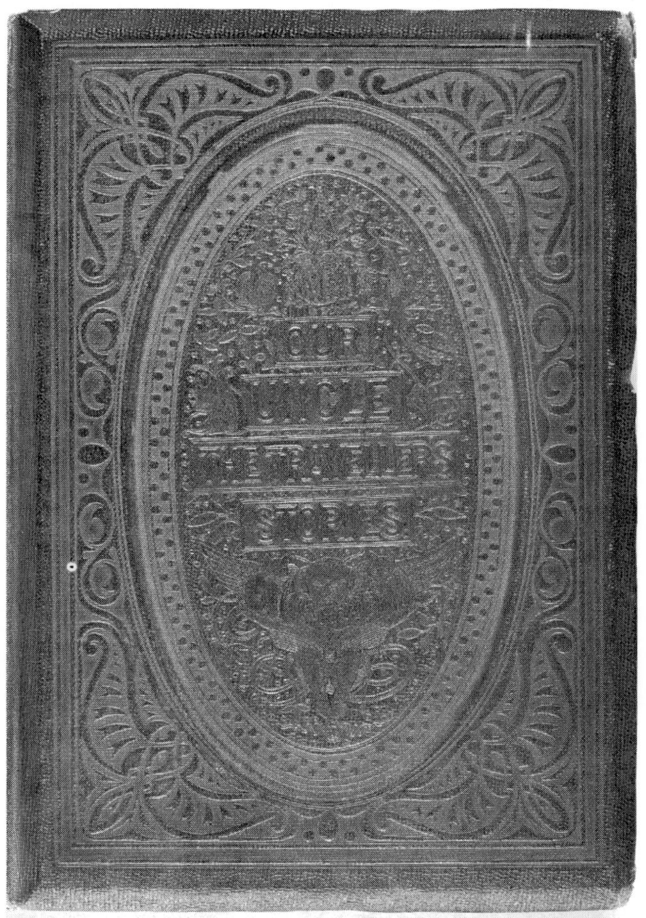

FIG. 43

The plates are signed 'H W' [i.e. Harrison Weir] and 'W Dickes'.

Red ink speckled edges. Bevelled boards. Light yellow endpapers and pastedowns. Binder's ticket on lower pastedown: '| Bound | by | Leighton | Son and | Hodge. |' Red morocco vertical-grain cloth. Both covers identically blocked in blind on the borders, on the corners, and on the sides. Two fillets are blocked on the borders, the outer thin, the inner thick. A leaf pattern is blocked on the corners and on the sides – all in relief, and the pattern forms a central oval. Two thin fillets are blocked in blind on the borders of this oval. On the upper cover, the central vignette is recessed. It has five fillets blocked on its borders: 1&2. two fillets blocked in blind; 3. one fillet blocked in blind, with repeating dots blocked in relief inside it; 4. a fillet blocked in blind 5. one fillet blocked in gold. On the centre, four rectangular gold lettering-pieces are blocked with single gold fillets on their borders. Within each lettering-piece, the title: '| Our | Uncle | The traveller's | stories. |' is blocked in relief. Above the title words are: a hanging vase, containing flowers; two birds; a squirrel and a mouse. Below the title, a winged satyr figure is seated, with his knees up, reading an open book; he wears a ruff around his neck; his hands are joined by the thumbs and index fingers, forming a diamond; his tail curls around his legs; a cat is blocked on either side of him, perched on each of his wings. All the above figures are surrounded by curling stems and small leaves, in hatch gold. The spine is blocked in gold. A single fillet is blocked in gold on the perimeter. From the head downwards, the decoration is: an arch; a gold lettering-piece, with the title: '| Our | Uncle | The | traveller's | stories. |' blocked in relief inside; a bird cage; two small birds; small decoration; a rectangle formed by two gold fillets; two gold fillets blocked at the tail.

Dry, *JL* no. 340

328 Leighton, John FIG. 44

Bruce, James. *Bruce's travels and adventures in Abyssinia. Edited by J. Morison Clingan, M.A.* [Illustrated by C. A. Doyle.] Edinburgh: Adam and Charles Black, North Bridge, 1860. Printed by R. and R. Clark Edinburgh. xxviii, 350 p., 4 plates. With six pages of publisher's titles bound at the end.
135 × 180 × 30 mm. 10095.aaa.36.

Gilt edges. Brown endpapers and pastedowns. Brown morocco vertical-grain cloth. On both covers, three fillets are blocked in blind. The central vignette is blocked in blind on the lower cover, in gold on the upper cover. The words: '| Bruce's | travels |' are blocked in gold at the head and at the tail of the vignette. The centre of each letter is picked out in relief. In the middle, a pyramid, two palm trees, and a pharaoh-like figure are blocked in gold and in relief. At the base of the pyramid, the words: '| To the source of the Nile. |' are blocked in relief within a rectangular gold lettering-piece. Signed 'JL' in gold as separate letters underneath a small Egyptian fan at the base of the vignette. The spine is blocked in gold. There is a single fillet blocked in gold on the perimeter. There are four fillets

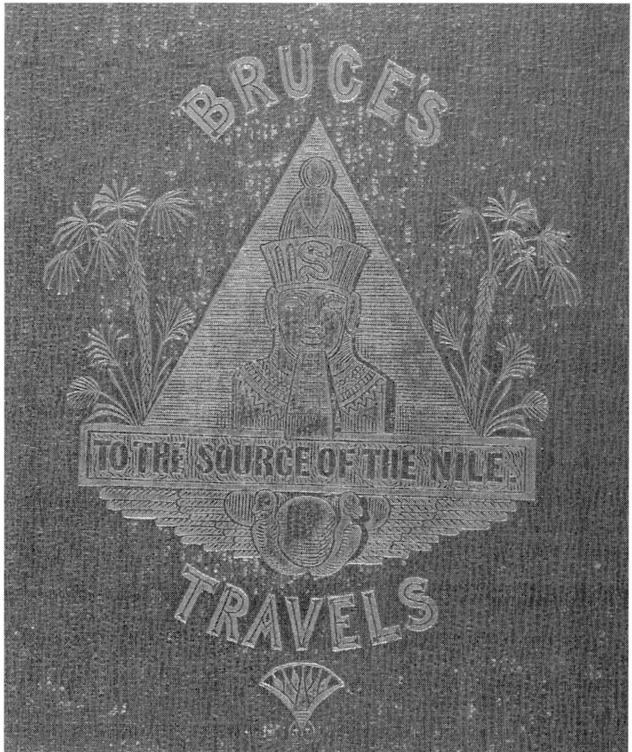

FIG. 44

blocked in gold at the head and at the tail. From the head downwards, the decoration is: a rhinoceros head, within an arch formed by two gold fillets; the words: '| Bruce's | Travels | in | Abyssinia |' blocked in gold; a Cleopatra's needle, blocked as a gold lettering-piece, with pelicans and Egyptian fans around it; within the needle, blocked in relief: '| Alex | andria | Nile | Condar | Bahelazrek | Abyssinia | Nubia'; a dolphin shape is blocked in relief; on the base of the needle, the words: '| James Bruce 1768 |' blocked in relief; at the tail, the words: '| Illustrated by | C.A. Doyle |' blocked in gold, within a rectangle formed by a single gold fillet. [Charles Altamont Doyle was the father of Conan Doyle.]

Dry, *JL* no. 341. Muir, *VIB* p. 22.

329 Leighton, John

Burrows, E., Mrs. *Tuppy; or, the autobiography of a donkey. With four illustrations by Harrison Weir.* London: Griffith and Farran. (Successors to Newbery & Harris), Corner of St. Paul's Churchyard, 1860. iv, 100 p., 4 plates. With thirty-two pages of publisher's titles bound at the end.
126 × 175 × 14 mm. 12808.a.43.

The plates are signed 'H. Weir' and 'Greenaway Sc.'.

Text sewn on two sawn-in cords. Edges speckled with red ink. Yellow endpapers and pastedowns. Binder's ticket on lower pastedown: '| Bound by | Burn, | 37 & 38 | Kirby St. |'. Blue wave diagonal-grain cloth. Both covers blocked identically in blind on the border and on the corners. Two fillets are blocked on the borders. Groups of plants and flowers are blocked on the

lower corners, with rising single stems up each side, with groups of the same leaves and plants on the upper corners. The upper cover vignette is blocked in gold. It shows Tuppy's head, a feather in his mane. Tuppy is looking at an open book, which is blocked as a hatched gold lettering-piece. Thistles are blocked to his left and his right. The title word: '| Tuppy |' is blocked in gold in rustic letters above him. On the lower cover of the book, the words: '| or the | autobiography | of a |' are blocked in relief. The word: '| Donkey |' is blocked in gold in rustic letters, within a rectangle formed by a single 'wood-shaped' fillet. Signed 'JL' in gold as separate letters at the base of the vignette. The spine is blocked in gold. The title: '| Tuppy | or | the | autobiography | of | a | Donkey. |' is blocked in gold.

Dry, *JL* no. 368.

330 Leighton, John

Cats, Jacob and Fairlie, Robert. *Moral emblems with aphorisms, adages, and proverbs, of all ages and nations, . . . With illustrations freely rendered, from designs found in their works, by John Leighton, F.S.A. The whole translated and edited, with additions, by Richard Pigot.* [Renaissance bolt and strap design contains a masted ship in full sail, and '| L & Co. | 1726 |'. Within the bolt, the motto: '| A good book is a true friend | a wise author a public benefactor. |' Signed 'JL' at the base of the panel.] London: Longman, Green, Longman, and Roberts, 1860. London: Richard Clay, Bread St. Hill. xvi, 240 p.
190 × 265 × 35 mm. 1347.i.14.

Each page of text has four proverbs (or adages) printed between one single border fillet and an inner border of two fillets. The illustrations are within the format of: 1. an elaborate bolt and panel Renaissance design; all are on versos, ending with a text; all are signed 'JL' and many of these are engraved by Henry Leighton; 2. the head-piece for each passage of text is a large circle, with brackets at each quarter; all are signed 'JL' at the base. [John Leighton drew the designs.] The contents page lists all the engravers. Where 'Leighton' is cited in this list, it is most likely Henry Leighton.

The illustrations on pp. 129, 177, 205, 229 are signed 'H. Leighton Sc.', as is the frontispiece showing a portrait of Jacob Cats.

Original upper and lower covers used as doublures. Doublure size: 175 × 252 mm Red morocco horizontal-grain cloth. Both covers blocked identically in gold and black. There is a single black fillet blocked on the borders between two gold fillets. On the inner borders, this same combination of fillets forms straps on the corners and on the sides. The strapwork is blocked in black, with parallel rules blocked in gold on either side. Leaves and stems are blocked in gold at the head, the tail and the sides, and on the corners. The fillets form a central rectangle, whose corners are blocked in black, with Latin phrases in relief. The phrases are: 'Animi pabullum', in the top left and the bottom right hand corners. The words 'Animi medicina' are blocked in the top right and bottom left corners. The central mandorla is formed by two gold fillets. In the mandorla, the capitals 'M' and 'E' are blocked in gold. The letters '[M]oral' and '[E]mblems' are blocked in relief, in rectangular gold lettering-pieces, with single gold fillets blocked on their borders. Curling stem and hatch leaf decoration surround the title. A cross and an anchor and a sword are blocked in gold underneath the title. Signed 'JL', in gold as separate letters, at the base of mandorla. The spine is fully blocked in gold and black, featuring a mandorla containing the title and the strapwork blocked in gold and in black. Signed 'JL' in gold at the tail.

de Beaumont, *RdeB1* no. 161. Dry, *JL* no. 342. Goldman, *VIB* no. 161.

331 Leighton, John

Davidson, James Bridge. *The Conway in the Stereoscope. Illustrated by Roger Fenton, Esq., M.A. Vice President of the Photographic Society. With Notes, Descriptive and Historical, . . .* London: Lovell, Reeve, 5, Henrietta Street, Covent Garden, 1860. London: John Edward Taylor, Printer, Little Queen Street, Lincoln's Inn Fields. xi, 187 p., 20 plates of Stereographs. With sixteen pages of publisher's titles bound at the end.
125 × 200 × 35 mm. 10369.d.7.

On page fifteen of the publisher's titles: 'Twenty Stereoscopic Pictures; price 31s. 6d., extra bound, gilt edges.'

Gilt edges, Bevelled boards. Red endpapers and pastedowns. Binder's ticket on lower pastedown: '| Bound by | Westley's | & Co. | London. |' Red bead-grain cloth. Both covers blocked identically on the borders and on the corners. Five gold fillets are blocked on the outer and inner borders. Triangles are formed by two gold fillets blocked on each corner, with leaf and stem decoration blocked in gold within each. On the lower cover, a quatrefoil is blocked on the centre, with the monogram of Lovell Reeve surrounded by horizontal gold hatch within it. On the upper cover, the centre has: the Prince of Wales three feathers blocked above a shield, azure; within the shield, leaves and four gold lettering-pieces are blocked; the title: '| The | Conway | in the | Stereoscope |' is blocked within the lettering-pieces, each of which has a single gold fillet blocked on its borders. Leaves surround the shield. The words: '| Ich dien |' are blocked in relief within a scroll, blocked in gold at the base of the shield. Signed 'JL' in relief as separate letters within the centre of the scroll. The spine is blocked in gold. From the head downwards, the decoration is: a gold fillet, with small gold repeating decoration blocked underneath – this is repeated at the tail; the title: '| The | Conway | in the | Stereoscope |' blocked in gold within an arabesque formed by two gold fillets; a posy of flowers is blocked below the title; near the tail: '| Lovell Reeve |' is blocked in gold.

332 Leighton, John

Day, Thomas. *The history of Sandford and Merton. Illustrated with one hundred engravings by The Brothers Dalziel. New edition, carefully revised.* London: Ward and Lock, 158, Fleet

Street, 1860. Dalziel Brothers, Camden Press, London. xii, 388 p., 2 plates.
117 × 182 × 35 mm. 12807.e.21.

Original upper yellow endpaper bound at the front. Original upper cover bound at the front. Size: 105 × 175 mm. Red bead-grain cloth. Two fillets are blocked in blind on the borders. Leaf decoration is blocked on each corner in relief. The upper cover central vignette is blocked in gold. It shows two young men shaking hands. The man on the left is dressed in simple country clothes.; the man on the right is dressed fashionably in town clothes, with breeches and knee ruffs, and he holds a tricorne hat in his left hand. Fencing is blocked behind the men. To the left, the fencing is rustic, wooden; to the right, the fencing is town inspired, showing metal railings and spikes. The title word: '| Sandford |' is blocked in gold in rustic lettering above the two boys, with tendrils ending in berries attached to the letters. The tendrils also curl round the top of the fencing. The letter: '| & |' is held in the left hand of the boy on the left; the word: '| Merton |' is blocked in relief within a rectangular gold lettering-piece, with a single fillet blocked in gold on its borders. Signed 'JL' in gold as separate letters at the base of the vignette.

Dry, *JL* no. 345.

333 Leighton, John

Dulcken, Henry William. *Pearls from the poets. Specimens of the works of celebrated writers. Selected, with biographical notes, by H. W. Dulcken. With a Preface by the Rev. Thomas Dale . . .* London: Ward and Lock, 158 Fleet Street, [1860]. London: Petter and Galpin, Belle Sauvage Printing Works, Ludgate Hill, E.C. 188 p.
168 × 225 × 25 mm. C.109.d.3.

The title page has the Ward Lock monogram, within a garter with the motto: 'Go well and doubt not'.

Gilt edges. Bevelled boards. Grey endpapers and pastedowns. Binder's ticket on lower pastedown: '| Bound by | Burn. | 37 & 38 | Kirby St. |' Brown wave diagonal-grain cloth. Both covers blocked identically: in blind and black on the lower; and in gold, black and relief on the upper. On the upper cover, the border blocking, from the outside inwards, is: 1. a repeating pattern in gold of leaves and seed heads (resembling dandelions); 2. two fillets blocked in gold; 3. a fillet blocked in black, with small dots inside blocked in relief; 4. two fillets blocked in gold. The inner rectangle has groups of horizontal hatch clover leaves and stems blocked in gold, above small decoration in each corner, and on the centre head and centre tail. The design of the centre is formed into six diamonds by fillets: four small diamonds, a half diamond and the large diamond on the centre. Groups of horizontal hatch clover leaves surround the small diamonds. Inside each small diamond, there is quartering, showing three smaller hatch diamonds and a gold lettering-piece blocked in gold. The central diamond has three fillets on its border: two are blocked in gold, and one in black, with dots inside blocked in relief. The centre has three rectangular gold lettering-pieces, each with a single gold fillet on its borders, with the title: '| Pearls | from the | poets |' blocked inside each lettering-piece in relief. Small plant decoration of horizontal hatch gold is blocked above, between and below the three rectangular gold lettering-pieces. Signed 'JL' in relief as separate letters within a small gold lettering-piece at the base of the large diamond. The spine is blocked in gold. A single fillet is blocked in gold on the perimeter. From the head downwards, the decoration is: small plant decoration; a rectangle formed by three gold fillets with three small diamonds blocked inside, and leaves of horizontal hatch gold below; the title: '| Pearls | from | the | poets. |' blocked in gold; a group of two diamonds, with groups of three clover leaves blocked in hatched gold above and below these diamonds; a rectangle formed by three fillets, with three small diamonds blocked inside; the words: '| London. | Ward & Lock |' blocked in gold; a small rectangle, formed by three fillets, with three small diamonds blocked inside; plant decoration; a gold fillet at the tail. Formerly shelved at BL 1347.f.8.

Dry, *JL* no. 346.

334 Leighton, John

E., A.L.O. *pseud.* [i.e. Tucker, Charlotte M.] *Pride and his prisoners . . .* London: T. Nelson & Sons, Paternoster Row; Edinburgh and New York, 1860. 275 p. With eleven pages of publisher's titles bound at the end.
118 × 180 × 30 mm. 12632.cc.12.

Yellow endpapers and pastedowns. Purple bead-grain cloth. Both covers blocked identically in blind on the borders and on the corners. Five fillets are blocked in blind on the borders. Groups of three horse chestnut leaves and stems are blocked in relief on each corner. A quatrefoil central frame is formed by the blind blocking, which is pointed at the head and at the tail. The upper cover has a central vignette blocked in gold. It shows a stone arch, with a diamond-shaped centre stone at its apex. Within the arch is the base of a portcullis. The title word: '| Pride |' has its letters blocked in gold between the bars of the portcullis. The title words: '| and his | prisoners |' are blocked in gold below this. Ivy creeps up the columns of the arch. The figures of an old woman and a knight are blocked at the base of each column. Signed 'L' in relief on a stone-shaped gold lettering-piece by a fence. A snake is blocked in grass at the base of the vignette. The gold vignette has clearly been blocked after the blocking in blind, as the gold overlaps the blind on the centre sides, left and the right. The spine is blocked in gold. A single gold fillet is blocked on the perimeter. From the head downwards, the decoration is: three gold fillets; small decoration, forming an arch; the words: '| Pride | and his | Prisoners | by A.L.O.E |' blocked in gold; a gold fillet; an arch; the word: 'ALOE' blocked in gold as a monogram within a shield; an inverted arch; small decoration; three gold fillets at the tail.

Dry, *JL* no. 347.

FIG. 45

335 Leighton, John FIG. 45

Evans W. R. *A century of Fables. In verse. For the most part paraphrased or imitated from various languages.* London: Robert Hardwicke, 192, Piccadilly, 1860. London: Cox and Wyman, Printers, Great Queen Street, Lincoln's inn Fields, W.C. xvi, 144 p.
107 × 172 × 10 mm. 12304.b.10.

Cream endpapers and pastedowns. Binder's ticket on lower pastedown: '| Bound | by | Leighton | Son and | Hodge. |'. Dark red bead-grain cloth. Both covers are blocked identically in blind. Four fillets are blocked on the borders; the inner three form a strapwork pattern on the borders and the corners of both covers. There is a central vignette blocked in gold on the upper cover. It features four 'card spade' shapes at the top, bottom and at the sides, in which flowers and leaves are blocked. Between the spades is a tracery of small pairs of leaves and single flowers. The title: '| A century | of | fables. |' is blocked in the central circle in gold. Signed 'JL' in gold as separate letters at the base. The spine is blocked in gold. The words: '| Evans | Fables |' are blocked in gold near the head. A fillet and two passion flower leaves and a tendril are blocked in gold underneath the title.

This Leighton upper cover vignette is repeated on BL 12631.f.21., BL 12807.a.55., and BL 12807.a.58.

336 Leighton, John

George, Uncle. *Stories about ships and shipwrecks, for The Amusement and Instruction of Youth.* New York: John Reynolds and Company, 197, Broadway, 1860. [London]: City Press, Long Lane: W. H. Collingridge. 138 p., 15 plates. With two pages of publisher's titles bound at the end.
105 × 146 × 12 mm. 12807.a.58.

Text sewn on two tapes. Red ink speckled edges. Yellow endpapers and pastedowns. Blue morocco vertical-grain cloth. Both covers blocked identically in blind on the borders and on the corners. Two fillets are blocked on the borders, the outer thick, the inner thin. Leaf patterns are blocked on each corner. The upper cover has a central vignette blocked in gold. It shows a roundel. Around the roundel, a repeating flower border is blocked in gold. At the head, the tail and on each side, individual flowers are blocked within 'card-spade' shapes. Within the roundel, the title: ' Uncle George's | Stories | about | ships &c |' is blocked in gold. Signed 'JL' in gold as separate letters at the base of the vignette. No blocking on the spine. This is the same block as on BL 12304.b.10, and BL, 12631.f.21., and BL 12807.a.55.

Dry, *JL* no. 351.

337 Leighton, John

Hallock, Mary Angelina. *The sweet story of old.* London: The Religious Tract Society; 56, Paternoster Row, and 164, Piccadilly; and sold by the Booksellers, 1860. [London]: Reed and Pardon, Printers, Paternoster Row. [4], 164 p., 3 plates. With eight pages of publisher's titles bound at the end.
124 × 160 × 17 mm. 4805.b.45.

The plates are signed: 'London: J. M. Kronheim & Co.' Gilt edges. Light yellow endpapers and pastedowns. Binder's ticket on lower pastedown: '| Bound by | Lewis & Sons, | [rule] | Gough Square | [rule] | Fleet St. London. |' Both covers blocked identically in blind on the borders, the corners and the sides. Three fillets are blocked on the borders, the outer thick, the inner two thin. A curling leaf and stem pattern is blocked on each corner and on the sides. The inner fillet border has repeating dots blocked in relief inside it, and forms the oval central frame. The upper cover central vignette is blocked in gold. The title words are blocked in gold around the centre: '| The | sweet story | of old |'. On the centre, a shepherd, a lamb and a flower in the ground are blocked in gold. Below this, the words: '| Feed my lambs |' are blocked in gold. The spine is blocked in gold. A single fillet is blocked in gold on the perimeter. From the head downwards, the decoration is: two gold fillets; clover leaf decoration; the title: '| The | sweet story | of | old. |' blocked in gold; an upright book, blocked as a gold lettering-piece, has its spine facing outwards, with the words: '| New | Testament |' blocked in relief within the second panel of the spine; signed 'JL' in gold as separate letters at the base of the book; a fillet; a rectangle formed by a single fillet is blocked near the base; a gold fillet at the tail.

Dry, *JL* no. 411.

338 Leighton, John

Hewlett, Henry Gay. *The heroes of Europe: a Biographical Outline of European History from A.D. 700 to A.D.1700. . . .* London: Bickers and Bush, 1 Leicester Square, 1860. London: Strangeways & Walden (late G. Barclay), Printers, 28 Castle St. Leicester Square. vii, 448 p., 17 plates.
110 × 176 × 53 mm. 10603.aa.12.

Brown morocco horizontal-grain cloth. Both covers identically blocked in blind on the borders and on the corners. A single fillet is blocked on the borders. An inner border of cartouches, and of sprigs (which are blocked in relief) are blocked between two fillets. On each corner, a group of leaves and buds is blocked in blind. The upper cover has a central vignette blocked in gold. It shows Saint George, armoured, on his charger. He holds a staff and a banner, which displays the three lions of England. His shield, also displaying the three lions of England, is by his right leg. The spine is blocked in gold and in relief. A single gold fillet is blocked on the perimeter. From the head downwards, the decoration is: a fillet in gold; an arch, with a fillet descending downwards on each side of the spine; a pope's hat and two crowns; the title: '| The | heroes | of | Europe |' blocked in gold within a panel formed by single fillets, shaped as cords; single tassels hang from the ends of the cords on either side of the panel; the shaft of a lance has the following objects suspended from it – two keys, a medallion blocked in hatched gold, showing Europa on the back of a bull; the word: '| Europa |' is blocked in relief underneath; beneath and behind the medallion – two swords, a double-headed axe, and an arrow are blocked in gold; the base of the lance has small stem decoration blocked on its left and its right, with the signature 'JL' in gold as separate letters also to the left and the right of the lance base; two gold fillets; the word: 'Illustrated' is blocked in gold within a cartouche formed by a single gold fillet, and both these are within a rectangle formed by a single fillet, in gold.
Dry, *JL* no. 354.

339 Leighton, John

Kingston, William Henry Giles. *Digby Heathcote: or, the early days of a country gentleman's son and heir. Illustrated by Harrison Weir.* London: Routledge, Warne, and Routledge, Farringdon Street. New York: 56, Walker Street, 1860. London: Savill and Edwards, Printers, Chandos Street, Covent Garden. vi, 429 p., 8 plates. With ten pages of publisher's titles bound at the end.
110 × 176 × 35 mm. 12807.bb.33.

The engravings are by Dalziel.

Yellow endpapers and pastedowns. Binder's ticket on lower pastedown: '| Bound by | Bone & Son, | 76 Fleet Street, | London. |' Blue bead-grain cloth. Both covers blocked in blind with the same design on the borders and on the corners. There are three fillets on the borders. Leaf decoration is blocked in relief on the corners, with stems and buds blocked within an egg-shaped oval at the centre of each corner. An oval is formed by the corner blocking. The upper cover central vignette is blocked in gold and in relief. At the centre of the vignette is a medallion. It has two fillets in gold around it, one thin, one thick. The thick fillet has repeating dots blocked within it in relief. Within the medallion, the words: '| Digby |' and '| Heathcote |' are blocked in relief within two rectangular gold lettering-pieces. Below these, the words: '| A book for boys |' are blocked in gold. Underneath these, '| W. H. Kingston |' is blocked in relief with a decorated gold lettering-piece. Above the medallion, Digby Heathcote's school slate is blocked, with the words: '| DH | his slate |' blocked in relief within the wooden border of the slate. On the slate, a picture of a teacher is drawn, with the words: '| Mrs Carter |' blocked in gold above it. On the left and the right of the medallion, oak leaves, stems and acorns are blocked, which form a diamond pattern around the vignette. Below the medallion, an open book is blocked as a gold lettering-piece, with page edges picked out in relief. On the open page on the left, the words: '| Kate | Heathcote | her copy | book |' is blocked in relief. The open page on the right has a dog, a house, and '| Blaxholme | Hall |' blocked in relief. Signed 'JL' in gold as separate letters inside a ring at the base. The spine is fully blocked in gold. There is a single fillet blocked around the perimeter. Oak leaves are blocked in gold on the corners of the frame at the head. Underneath, the title: '| Digby | Heathcote | A | Book for boys | [rule] | W. H. Kingston |' is blocked in gold. Beneath this, a boy sits on an oak branch, surrounded by oak leaves. Signed 'JL' in gold as separate letters at the base of the oak branch. At the tail, the word: '| Illustrated |' is blocked in gold between two pairs of gold fillets.
Dry, *JL* no. 357.

340 Leighton, John

Lawford, Louisa. *Every girl's book. A Compendium of entertaining amusements, for Recreation in Home Circles.* London: Routledge, Warne & Routledge, Farringdon Street; New York: 56, Walker Street, 1860. Cox and Wyman, Printers, Great Queen Street, London. viii, 392 p., 1 plate.
110 × 176 × 32 mm. 12804.c.36.

The plate is signed 'HKB' [i.e. Hablot K. Browne.] and 'Dalziel'.

Yellow endpapers and pastedowns. Blue bead-grain cloth. Both covers blocked identically in blind on the borders and on the corners. Two fillets are blocked on the borders. Stylised leaf decoration is blocked in relief on each corner. A fillet blocked in blind on the inner borders forms a central frame. The upper cover central vignette is blocked in gold. It shows a seated lady, with a sewing frame, which has a bird depicted within it. The sewing frame is upright on the lady's lap. A sewing basket is on a stand to her right, and a hanging basket is blocked above to her right. Seven medallions are blocked in vertical hatch gold around the lady. Each medallion has a single fillet on its border, then a fillet with repeating dots blocked in relief inside it. Within each medallion, words are blocked in relief within rectangular gold lettering-pieces. The words, clockwise, are: 1. 'Engines'; 2. '| Acting | Proverbs |'; 3. 'Forfeits'; 4.

'| Ladies | work'; 5. 'Conundrum'; 6. '| Rondes | & music |'; 7. 'Games'. At the head of the vignette, the words: '| Every girl's |' are blocked in relief within a rectangular gold lettering-piece with a single fillet blocked on its borders. Underneath the lady's dress, the title word: '| Book. |' is blocked in relief within a rectangular gold lettering-piece with a single fillet blocked on its borders. Branches, stems, horizontal hatch leaves and tendrils – all blocked in gold – weave from the base of the vignette round the medallions to the top. A bird sits on a stem at the top. The spine is blocked in gold. Two fillets are blocked in gold on the perimeter. From the head downwards, the decoration is: crossing branches; the words: '| Every | girl's | book. | [rule] | Lawford. |' blocked in gold; a vase and a spray of flowers, resting within an oval branch-shaped frame; hatched leaves are blocked around the vase; beneath the vase, a dinner plate warming pan; a gold fillet; at the tail, a rectangular gold lettering-piece, with a single fillet blocked on its borders, has small decoration blocked in relief inside.

Dry, *JL* no. 360.

341 Leighton, John

Lee, Holme *pseud.* [i.e. Miss Harriet Parr.] *Legends from fairy land: narrating the history of Prince Glee and Princess Trill. The cruel persecutions and condign punishment of Aunt Spite, The adventures of the Great Tuflongbo, and The story of the Blackcap in the Giant's well. With eight illustrations by H. Sanderson.* London: Smith, Elder and Co., 65, Cornhill, 1860. London: Printed by Smith, Elder, and Co., Little Green Arbour Court, Old Bailey, E.C. vii, 239 p., 8 plates. With sixteen pages of publisher's titles bound at the end.
113 × 185 × 28 mm. 12804.d.26.

Some of the plates are signed with the monogram 'HS' and 'E. Evans Sc.'

Text sewn on three sawn-in cords. Light yellow endpapers and pastedowns. Purple morocco horizontal-grain cloth. Both covers blocked identically in blind on the borders and on the corners. Two fillets are blocked on the borders, the outer thick, the inner thin. Rose stems, leaves and flowers are blocked on the corners. The upper cover central vignette is blocked in gold. It shows a winged fairy, its right hand holding onto a half moon, which is blocked in horizontal hatch gold. The fairy holds a wand in its left hand, with a star at the head. Three more stars are blocked in gold on the sides and on the tail; all the stars have 'faces' within them, blocked in relief. The words: '| Legends | from |' are blocked in gold above the fairy; the words: '| Fairy Land |' are blocked on each side of the fairy – all in gold. '| By Holme Lee |' are blocked in hatch gold within the quarter moon. Signed 'JL' in gold as separate letters at the base of the vignette. The spine is blocked in gold. A single gold fillet is blocked on the perimeter. From the head downwards, the decoration is: '| Legends | from | fairy | land | by | Holme | Lee |' blocked in gold; a seated boy-figure, holding string, which is also blocked around the inner perimeter of the spine; signed 'JL' in gold as separate letters by the boy's feet to the left and right of the spine; two gold fillets; the words '| Smith Elder & Co |' are blocked in gold, near the tail; two gold fillets at the tail.

Dry, *JL* no. 361.

342 Leighton, John

Leslie, *Sir* John. *Discovery and adventure in the Polar seas and regions. With a narrative of the recent expeditions in search of Sir John Franklin, including the voyage of the 'Fox', and the discovery of the fate of the Franklin expedition. By R. M. Ballantyne.* London: T. Nelson and Sons, Paternoster Row; Edinburgh; and New York, 1860. 652 p., 11 plates.
115 × 180 × 47 mm. 10460.a.35.

Original yellow endpaper bound at the front. Red bead-grain cloth. Both covers identically blocked in blind and in relief on the borders and on the corners. Two fillets are blocked in blind on the borders. Curling stem and leaf decoration is blocked in relief on each corner. The upper cover vignette is blocked in gold. It shows a jagged semi-circle of ice, blocked above a three-masted ship in pack ice. The title: '| The | Polar seas | and | regions. |' is blocked above, between and below the ice and the ship. Signed 'JL' in relief as separate letters on the left hand side of the pack ice. The spine is blocked in gold. Two fillets are blocked on the perimeter, the inner of which is 'rope' shaped. From the head downwards, the decoration is: a bear's head; the title: '| The | Polar seas | & | regions. |' blocked in gold in 'ice-like' letters; a portrait of Sir John Franklin, and his autograph underneath; the words: '| With | a continuation | by | R. M Ballantyne |' blocked in gold in a semi-circle around the head of a walrus; a gold fillet; at the tail, the word: '| Illustrated |' is blocked in gold, within a rectangle formed by a single gold fillet.

Dry, *JL* no. 362.

343 Leighton, John

Miller, Thomas. *Sports and pastimes of Merry England.* London: Darton & Co., Holborn Hill, [1860]. [London]: Printed by W. H. Cox, 5, Great Queen Street, Lincoln's Inn Fields. [2], 184 p., 2 plates.
126 × 189 × 18 mm. CUL.60.7.106.

Cambridge University Library copy.

Gilt edges. Yellow endpapers pastedowns. Binder's ticket on lower pastedown: '| Leighton | Son & | Hodge, | Shoe Lane | London. |' Red fine rib vertical-grain cloth, lightly moiré. The borders and corners of both covers are identically blocked in blind. Two fillets are blocked on the borders in blind, the outer thin, the inner thick. A pattern of curling leaves and stems are blocked on each corner in blind. The lower cover centre-piece is lozenge-shaped, consisting of small straps and leaves blocked in relief. The upper cover central vignette is blocked in gold. it shows a maypole blocked from bottom to the top of the vignette. At the top, a cockerel is blocked, together with a banner-shaped gold lettering-piece, with the words: 'Sports & pastimes' blocked in relief within the banner. Below this, a hoop

hangs on strings, with flower and streamers attached to it. The words: 'of Merry England' are blocked in gold in gothic letters below the hoop. Underneath the title, an archer and a jester stand on either side of the maypole, with their upper arms resting against the maypole. The archer holds a bow in his right hand; the jester holds a stick and a balloon in his left hand. Both figures are surrounded by leaves and curling stems. Signed 'JL' in gold as separate letters within a leaf at the base of the vignette. The spine is blocked in gold. A single fillet is blocked in gold on the perimeter. A stake is blocked from the tail to the head of the spine. From the head downwards, the decoration is: a boar's head, impaled on the point of the stake, amidst small leaves; a fillet in gold; the words: 'Sports | & | Pastimes [gothic letters] | of | Merry | England | by Thomas | Miller |' blocked in gold; the stake, surrounded by curling stems and leaves; a group of objects is tied onto the stake: a sword, a dagger, an axe and a hunting horn; leaves and stems are blocked at the base of the stake; signed 'JL' in gold, to the left and right of the base of the stake; a gold fillet; a rectangle formed by a single fillet; a gold fillet at the tail.

The BL copy is at 7906.d.20. Gilt edges. Prize bookplate of Chipping Hill School on the upper endpaper. Red morocco vertical-grain cloth. Both covers blocked identically in blind on the borders and on the corners. Two fillets are blocked on the borders, the outer thick, the inner thin. Curling stem and leaf decoration is blocked on each corner. The upper cover central vignette is blocked in gold. Joined fuchsias (with long stamens) and leaves and plants grow upwards from the base to form a diamond-shaped panel. The title: '| Sports & pastimes | of | merry | England. |' is blocked in gold within the panel. Unsigned. The spine is blocked in gold. Three gold fillets are blocked at the head and at the tail, the middle fillet being of vertical gold hatch. The words: '| Sports | and | pastimes | of | merry | England | Miller |' are blocked in gold near the head; two gold fillets, together with stem and leaf decoration are blocked in gold down the spine to near the tail. Unsigned.

344 Leighton, John

PLATE XXXV

Moffat, A. S., Mrs. *The Ore-Seeker: a tale of the Harz. With twenty-six illustrations by L.C.H.* Cambridge: Macmillan and Co. and 23, Henrietta Street, Covent Garden, London, 1860. London: Printed by Richard Clay, Bread Street Hill. [11], 195 p.
167 × 215 × 27 mm. 12553.i.19.

The plates are signed with the monogram of 'LCH', and 'Pearson Sc.'

Text sewn on three tapes. Gilt edges. Bevelled boards. Light brown endpapers and pastedowns. Binder's ticket on lower pastedown: '| Bound by | Burn. | 37 & 38 | Kirby St. |' Blue wave diagonal-grain cloth. Both covers blocked with the same design, in blind and black on the lower cover, and in gold and black on the upper. There are seven borders: 1. A single gold fillet; 2. a border of leaves, repeating, blocked in horizontal hatch; 3. a thin gold fillet; 4. hatched gold and circles, repeating, blocked between two gold fillets; 5. & 6. thin gold fillets; 7. a fillet blocked in black. On the outer corners, crossed leaves are blocked. On the inner corners, patterns of curling leaves are blocked in vertical hatch and Chinese gooseberries are blocked in gold. On the upper cover, the centre piece has a fillet blocked in black , and then three thin gold fillets blocked on its borders. It shows a lamp and its rays, at the top. The title: '| The | Ore | Seeker |' is blocked in gold, with capitals 'O' and 'S' blocked in relief within rectangular horizontal hatch gold lettering-pieces, with single fillets blocked on the borders. A spade and a pickaxe are blocked in gold at the base of the centre piece. Signed 'JL' in relief as separate letters within the spade. The spine is blocked in gold. A single gold fillet is blocked on the perimeter. From the head downwards, the decoration is: a gold fillet; a semi-circle and a point, within small decoration; the title: '| The | Ore | Seeker |' blocked in relief within three rectangular gold lettering-pieces with single gold fillets on the borders of each; a mandorla with horizontal gold hatch and leaves blocked inside; a semi-circle and a point, within small decoration; the word; '| Macmillan |' is blocked in gold within a rectangle formed by a single fillet; two gold fillets blocked at the tail.

Macmillan's bibliographical catalogue, pp.67 and 633, gives the price as '15s'. The Edition Book in the Macmillan Archive, folio 420, states that 1,000 copies of this work were printed by Clay in October 1860, price 15s.

The same blocking is on a copy bound in red morocco, in the R. de Beaumont Private Collection.

Dry, *JL* no. 363. Oldfield, *BC* no. 55.

345 Leighton, John

Norman, Frank. *Echoes from dreamland.* London: Ward & Lock, 158 Fleet Street, 1860. London: Petter and Galpin, Belle Sauvage Printing Works, Ludgate Hill. E.C. [2], 197 p.
110 × 170 × 20 mm. 11647.c.5.

Text sewn on two tapes. Gilt edges. Beige endpapers and pastedowns. Binder's ticket on lower pastedown: '| Bound by | Burn | 37 & 38 | Kirby St. |'. Red morocco horizontal-grain cloth. The lower cover is blocked in blind, with two fillets blocked on the borders and flower tracery on the corners. The central vignette shows a lozenge, with leaf decoration blocked within in relief. The upper cover is blocked in gold, with two fillets on the borders and flower tracery blocked on the corners. The ornate central vignette is blocked in gold, showing an arabesque with leaf and stem decoration. The title: '| Echoes | from | dreamland |' is blocked in gold on the centre. Signed 'JL' in gold as separate letters at base of vignette. The spine is blocked in gold. From the head downwards, the decoration is: three gold fillets; the words: '| Echoes | from | dream | land | [rule] | F. Norman |' blocked in gold; a lily-like plant is blocked in gold from near the tail up to beneath the title; three gold fillets are blocked at the tail.

Dry, *JL* no. 364.

346 Leighton, John

Piercy, Mary Jane. *Popular tales; or, deeds of genius . . .* [Renaissance frame around a panel, showing an engraving of a family scene of a mother and four children.] Dublin: James Duffy, 7, Wellington-Quay, 1860. Printed by J. M. O'Toole, 6 & 7, Great Brunswick-street, Dublin. [2], 249 p., 1 plate.
110 × 140 × 20 mm. 12807.a.55.

Gilt edges. Yellow endpapers and pastedowns. Blue bead-grain cloth. Both covers blocked identically in blind on the borders. The border decoration shows curling leaves and stem patterns blocked in relief on the sides, and on the corners, with cartouches on the centre head, the centre tail, and the centre sides. The upper cover vignette is blocked in gold. It shows a roundel. Around the roundel, a repeating flower border is blocked in gold. At the head, the tail and on each side, individual flowers are blocked within 'card-spade' shapes. [This is the same block as on BL 12304.b.10, and BL, 12631.f.21., and BL 12807.a.58.] Within the roundel, the title: '| Popular | tales. or | deeds | of | genius |' is blocked in gold. Signed 'JL' in gold as separate letters at the base of the vignette. The spine is blocked in gold. From the head downwards, the decoration is: a fillet; the title: '| Popular | tales | or | deeds | of | genius |' blocked in gold within a frame formed by a single fillet; two gold fillets; a stem running down the spine, with ten passion flower leaves and tendrils attached to it – all blocked in gold; a fillet in gold at the tail.

Dry, *JL* no. 365.

347 Leighton, John PLATE XXXVI

Planché, Matilda Anne. *A selection of the tales; by the author of 'A trap to catch a sunbeam', etc., etc.* [i.e. Miss M. A. Planché, afterwards Mrs Mackarness.] *With illustrations by John Absolon and Henry Anelay. Engraved by Butterworth and Heath.* London: Lockwood & Co., Stationers' Hall Court, E.C., 1860. London: J. E. Adlard, Printer, Bartholomew Close. [7], 371 p., 5 plates. With four pages of publisher's titles bound at the end.
110 × 180 × 30 mm. 12808.k.8.

This compilation later known as the First Series.

Brown endpapers and pastedowns. Brown morocco horizontal-grain cloth. The border decoration is blocked in blind identically on both covers. Three fillets are blocked on the borders, the inner two of which form straps on each corner, on the centre sides, and on the centre tail. The central vignette is blocked in gold on the upper cover. It features two flying figures, either side of rays spreading from a window. The title words are blocked within the rays; the word 'SUN' is blocked in relief, within the spreading rays blocked in gold. The words: '| Beam | Stories |' are blocked in gold. Underneath, an angel holds up a gold lettering piece, in which the words: '| By the author of | A | Trap to catch a sunbeam. |', are blocked in relief. Signed 'JL' in gold in separate letters at the base of the angel's necklace. The spine is blocked in gold. Two gold fillets are blocked on the perimeter, the inner of which forms an arch at the head. Small decoration is blocked in gold at the sides of the arch. From the head downwards, the decoration is: a sun (showing a face), and clouds; the words: '| Sunbeam | stories. | By the | Author | of A | Trap | to catch | a sunbeam |' blocked in gold; from near the tail to beneath the title, a sword hilt and blade is blocked in gold; at the top of the sword, a pair of scales is blocked; around the middle of the blade, a wheel is blocked; within the wheel and below it, a conch shell, with sea objects in its mouth, is blocked in gold; stars surround the sword and these objects; a gold fillet; a rectangular panel is formed by two gold fillets, blocked at the tail.

—— *Second series.* 1863. 333 p. With two pages of publisher's titles bound at the front and sixteen pages bound at the end. 110 × 177 × 30 mm. Bolts uncut. Yellow endpapers and pastedowns. Mauve pebble-grained cloth. The same cover and spine design is blocked as for the 1860 edition, with the addition of two gold stars within the rectangular panel blocked at the tail of the spine. The First Series advertised on page 5 of the publisher's catalogue for the Second Series: '. . . price 5s. cloth elegant or 5s 6d. gilt edges.'

—— *Third series. With illustrations by James Godwin, etc.* 1869. 344 p. With two pages of publisher's titles bound at the front and sixteen pages bound at the end. 110 × 175 × 30 mm. Bolts mostly uncut. Light yellow endpapers and pastedowns. Blue rib horizontal-grain cloth, also moiré. The same cover and spine design is blocked as for the 1860 and 1863 editions, with the addition of three gold stars within the rectangular panel blocked at the tail of the spine. On page 9 of the publisher's catalogue at the end: 'First series . . . Fcap. 3s. 6d. cloth elegant, or 4s gilt edges.' 'Second series . . . Fcap. 3s. 6d. cloth elegant, or 4s gilt edges.'

—— *Fourth series. With illustrations.* 1870. 340 p. With two pages of publisher's titles bound at the front and sixteen pages bound at the end. 108 × 178 × 33 mm. Bolts uncut. Light yellow endpapers and pastedowns. Blue sand-grain cloth. The same cover and spine design is blocked as for the 1860 and 1863 and 1869 editions, with the addition of four gold stars within the rectangular panel blocked at the tail of the spine. On page 9 of the publisher's catalogue at the end, all the three previous series advertised as: ' Fcap. 3s. 6d. cloth, elegant.'

King, *JL* p. 239.

348 Leighton, John

Shakespeare, William. *Shakespeare's Household Words. A Selection from the wise saws of the Immortal bard. Illuminated by Saml Stanesby.* London: Griffith & Farran, Corner of St. Paul's Churchyard, [1860]. London: Printed in colors [sic] by Ashbee and Dangerfield. [2], 28 p. All the pages have chromolithograph borders.
105 × 145 × 15 mm. 11765.a.32.

The title page is a different chromolithograph from the 1859 edition. The frontispiece displays a photographic print of Shakespeare in a central oval. The bard's nose is pointing to the

left. The list of titles issued by Griffith and Farran, bound at the end of 'Nursery nonsense or rhymes without reason', 1864, (BL shelfmark 12806.bb.13.) has the following description of this publication: 'With a photographic portrait taken from the monument at Stratford-on-Avon. Price 9s. cloth elegant; 14s. morocco antique.'

Gilt edges. Dark green endpapers and pastedowns. Binder's ticket on lower pastedown: '| Bound by | Bone & | Son, | [rule] | 76 Fleet Street. | London. |' Red morocco horizontal-grain cloth. Both covers are blocked identically. A single fillet is blocked in blind on the borders. Inside this is a border of repeating leaves and plant heads, blocked in gold. Within this, a border, of a navy blue paper onlay, is blocked in gold between two fillets, and shows a small pattern in blue relief. The central rectangle has white paper onlays in each corner. These are blocked in gold, showing ivy leaves and stems. The central panel is a blue paper onlay, shaped as an arabesque. The panel has two fillets around the perimeter, blocked in gold, with gold dots between. A lance is blocked in gold, from the base to the top of the arabesque and around it curls a pennant-shaped gold lettering-piece. The title words: '| Shakespeare's | Household | Words |' are blocked in relief within the pennant. Signed 'JL' in relief as separate letters at the base of the pennant. Stars, blocked in gold, surround the pennant. The spine is blocked in gold. A single gold fillet is blocked on the perimeter. The title: '| Shakespeare's Household Words |' is blocked along the spine in relief inside rectangular gold lettering-pieces. The imprint: '| Griffith | and | Farran |' is blocked in relief within a rectangular gold lettering-piece, with a gold fillet blocked above and below it. At the tail, a small rectangular gold lettering-piece is blocked, with leaf decoration blocked in relief inside.

Date stamped in blue: '5 DE[CEMBER 18] 60'.

Dry, *JL* no. 326. The 1859 issue. McLean, *VBD* p. 134.

349 Leighton, John

Smyth, Gillespie. *Fit to be a duchess: with other Stories of Courage & Principle. Illustrated by E. H. Corbould & J. Absolon.* London: James Hogg & Sons, [1860]. Dalziel Brothers, Camden Press, London. [viii], 321 p., 8 plates. With six pages of publisher's titles bound at the end.

122 × 190 × 30 mm. 12632.cc.26.

The plates are engraved by Dalziel.

Text sewn on three sawn-in cords. Gilt edges. Yellow endpapers and pastedowns. Red bead-grain cloth. Both covers blocked identically in blind with two fillets on the borders, the outer thick, the inner thin. The upper cover vignette is blocked in gold. It shows a shield, argent, gold lettering-piece, containing the title: '| Stories | of | courage | & | principle |' blocked in relief within the shield. Above the shield, the helm, and the crest of a hand holding a candle are blocked in gold. Below the shield, the motto: '| Virtus | Praestantior | Auro |' are blocked in relief within a ribbon-shaped gold lettering-piece. Signed 'JL' in gold as separate letters at the base of the vignette. The spine is blocked in gold and in relief. A single fillet is blocked in gold on the perimeter. From the head downwards, the decoration is: a gold fillets; leaf decoration and a quatrefoil medal; the words: '| Fit to be [letters blocked in a semi-circle] | a | duchess | with | other stories of | courage | and principle | by | Mrs Gillespie [letters blocked in a semi-circle] | Smyth |' blocked in relief within gold lettering-pieces, which in turn are within a decorated gold lettering-piece; a quatrefoil medallion, with descending leaves; a gold fillet; near the tail, the words: '| Illustrated by | Corbould & | Absolon. |' are blocked in relief, within a rectangular gold lettering-piece; at the tail, a gold fillet.

Dry, *JL* no. 409.

350 Leighton, John PLATE XXXVII

Stanesby, Samuel. *The Birthday Souvenir. Illuminated by Samuel Stanesby.* London: Griffith & Farran, Corner of St. Paul's Churchyard, [1860]. [London]: Ashbee & Dangerfield. [3], 28 p.

138 × 187 × 18 mm. C.30.b.39.

The borders of every page are chromolithographs. On title-page verso: '| Illuminated by | Saml. Stanesby. | Printed in colors | by Ashbee & Dangerfield. |'

Gilt edges. Bevelled boards. Yellow endpapers and pastedowns. Binder's ticket on lower pastedown: '| Bound by Bone & Son, | [rule] | 76, Fleet Street, | London. |' Green morocco horizontal-grain cloth. Both covers identically blocked in gold and in relief. There are eight borders: 1. – 'dog-tooth' fillet; 2. a single gold fillet; 3. diamonds and dots, in gold; 4. a single gold fillet; 5. a single gold fillet; 6. a single gold fillet, with dots blocked inside in relief; 7. & 8. a single gold fillet. The central design has more borders of fillets linked to the centre. On the centre is a red paper onlay, showing two quatrefoils, densely blocked in gold, with leaf and stem patterns, some in vertical hatch gold. On the centre, the title: '| The | Birth-day | Souvenir |' is blocked in gold. Leaf and stem patterns blocked in gold surround the centre. The spine is blocked in gold. Along the upper portion of the spine a scroll-shaped gold lettering-piece is blocked, with the words: '| The | Birth | Day | Souvenir |' blocked in relief within the scroll. Small gold hatch leaves, stems and berries, blocked in gold, interlock with the scroll. Small decoration is blocked in gold at the base. Signed 'JL' in gold as separate letters near the tail.

Dry, *JL* no. 336.

351 Leighton, John

Steyene. *Steyne's grief; or, losing, seeking and finding. By the creator of 'Bow Garretts,' 'Frank's Madonna,' 'The Lathams,' 'Ben Cheery,' 'Only a trifle,' 'Harriette Gwynne,' 'Bitter bell,' 'Cloud witness,' 'Ferndell,' &c., &c.* London: William Tweedie, 337 Strand, 1860. London: Richard Barratt, Printer, Mark Lane. viii, 404 p.

107 × 168 × 32 mm. 12632.aa.27.

Yellow endpapers and pastedowns. Blue morocco horizontal-grain cloth. Both covers blocked identically in blind. Three fillets are blocked on the borders. Inside these, three more fillets are blocked, intersecting at the corners, and with a single leaf on each inner corner. A central panel is formed by a single fillet blocked in blind, semi-circular at the head and at the tail, with a single leaf blocked on each corner. The spine is blocked in gold. From the head downwards, the decoration is: two gold fillets; a decorative panel; the title: '| Steyne's | grief. |' blocked in gold between single fillets; two decorative panels forming an 'hour-glass' shape; signed 'JL' in relief as separate letters near the tail; a gold fillet is blocked at the tail.

Dry, *JL* no. 367.

352 Leighton, John

Webb, afterwards, Webb-Peploe, Annie. *Helen Mordaunt: or, The Standard of Life.* London: Routledge, Warne and Routledge, Farringdon Street. New York: 56, Walker Street, 1860. London: Savill and Edwards, Printers, Chandos Street, Covent Garden. viii, 381 p., 4 plates. With two pages of publisher's titles bound at the end.

112 × 175 × 36 mm. 12631.a.36.

The plates are signed 'Dalziel'; three of the plates are signed with John Gilbert's monogram.

Text sewn on three sawn-in cords. Beige endpapers and pastedowns. Red bead-grain cloth. Binder's ticket on lower pastedown: '| Bound by | Burn | 37 & 38 | Kirby St. |' Both covers blocked identically in blind only. Three fillets are blocked on the borders, the innermost crossing to form small straps on the corners. The inner border decoration has trefoils and curling stems on each corner, with columns on the sides, and ovals on the centre head and the centre tail. The spine is blocked in gold. A single gold fillet is blocked on the perimeter. From the head downwards, the decoration is: lily leaves and buds; the words: '| Helen | Mordaunt | [rule] | Webb |' blocked in gold; three flowers rise out of a 'bulb' shape; lily buds; signed 'JL' in gold as separate letters underneath two crossed lily leaves; a fillet in gold; a rectangle formed by a single fillet is blocked in gold at the tail.

Dry, *JL* no. 369.

353 Leighton, John

The illustrated girl's own treasury specially designed for The Entertainment of Girls and the development of the best faculties of the female mind; embracing Bible biography of eminent women; rudiments of ornamental needlework with designs for presents; tales of purpose and poems of refinement; chamber birds and bird-keeping; music, history of fans, veils and purses; phenomena of the months, and wild flowers; in-door exercises and out-door recreations; by the editor of the 'Illustrated Boy's Own Treasury.' London: Ward and Lock, 158, Fleet Street, 1861. London: Printed by H. Tuck, 16 & 17, New Street, Cloth Fair.xvi, 480 p., 2 plates.

125 × 188 × 37 mm. 12806.cc.23.

The plates are signed: 'E. Evans Sc.'

Edges speckled with red ink. Light yellow endpapers and pastedowns. Purple bead-grain cloth. Both covers blocked identically in blind on the borders, on the corners and on the sides. Two fillets are blocked in blind on the borders. On each corner, leaves and crossed double stems are blocked in relief, within a triangular panel formed by a single fillet. The upper cover central vignette is blocked in gold and in relief. At the top, a bust of a lady, with her hair in a net, is blocked in gold within a garter circle. Rose stems and leaves form four circles. In the centre of each of these are: 1. A ball of wool, pierced by knitting needles; 2. a pin cushion and scissors; 3. a small bird; 4. a squirrel. A single rose flower is blocked in gold to the left and to the right of the vignette. On the centre, a sewing frame is blocked in gold. It has a piece of cloth stretched out on it, blocked as a gold lettering-piece. The title: '| The | illustrated | girl's own | treasury. |' is blocked in relief within the cloth. Beneath this, a basket is blocked in gold. It contains: balls of wool; two knitting needles; a cloth, and a knitted pattern. Signed 'JL' in gold as a monogram at the base of the vignette. The spine is blocked in gold. From the head downwards, the decoration is: an open book, blocked as a gold-lettering-piece, within a circular panel, which is formed by a single 'branch-like' fillet; tendrils are blocked around this; the title: '| The | illustrated | girl's own | treasury. |' blocked in gold within a panel formed by a single 'branch-like' fillet; a bird in a cage on a stand; the cage has tasselled cords blocked on either side; the cage is blocked within a panel formed by a single fillet; two fish swim in a goldfish bowl on a stand; a spade and another small implement are blocked within a panel formed by a single 'branch-like' fillet; small flower plant decoration blocked in gold; at the tail, the words: '| London | Ward & Lock. |' are blocked in gold within a rectangular panel formed by a 'branch-like' fillet.

Dry, *JL* no. 395.

354 Leighton, John

Sunshine in the country. A book of rural poetry. Embellished with photographs from nature. London: Richard Griffin & Company, 10, Stationer's Hall Court, 1861. London: Printed by Richard Clay, Bread Street Hill. 8, 152 pp.

165 × 230 × 30 mm. 1347.f.9.

Twenty photographs accompany the text. The first paragraph of a slip tipped onto the front endpaper reads: 'N.B. The London Stereoscopic Company of 54 Cheapside, London and 594 Broadway, New York, have purchased the choice collection of Negatives of the late Mr. Grundy, prints from which illustrate the present volume. They have also secured about 200 additional negatives by the same eminent artist, all of which are adapted for the Stereoscope.' On page 8: 'The accompanying Photographs were taken by the late Mr. Grundy, of Sutton Coldfield, near Birmingham.'

Yellow endpapers and pastedowns. Purple morocco horizontal grain cloth. Both covers are blocked identically on the borders in blind and relief. There is a zigzag border, with scroll

work blocked in relief on the four corners of the inner panel. On the upper cover, the central vignette is blocked in gold. Two birds are nesting at the top. There is a nest with eggs blocked on the left of the vignette; newly hatched birds are blocked on the right. A pair of birds are perched on a branch at the bottom. The title: '| Sunshine | in the | Country |' is blocked in gold in the central circle, formed by branches. The capitals 'S' and 'C' are blocked in gold within rectangular hatch gold lettering-pieces, with two gold fillets on their borders. All the motifs are surrounded by flowers, leaves, curling branches, to form a tracery effect. Signed 'JL' in gold as separate letters underneath the birds on the branch. This design around the central roundel is repeated on *Gems from the poets*, which is in a private collection. The spine is blocked in gold. Two gold fillets are blocked on the perimeter. Three gold fillets are blocked on the borders of various decorative devices on the spine. All the decorative devices have hatch gold around them inside the three fillets. From the head downwards, these are: curling stems and leaves; the title: '| Sunshine | in the | country |' blocked in relief within three rectangular gold lettering-pieces; a medallion with a 'sunflower' at its centre; a 'spade' shape, with lily-like leaves blocked within; flowers and leaves; signed 'JL' in gold as separate letters underneath the lily-like leaves; a gold fillet; the words: '| R. Griffin | and Compy |' are blocked in relief within a rectangular gold lettering-piece, with a single gold fillet blocked on its borders; two gold fillets are blocked at the tail.

Dry, *JL* no. 410.

355 Leighton, John

The twins, and their stepmother. A Tale, dedicated to the children of the present day. With illustrations. London: Routledge, Warne & Routledge, Farringdon Street. New York: 56, Walker Street, 1861. Cox and Wyman, Printers, Great Queen Street, London. viii, 288 p., 3 plates.
110 × 175 × 30 mm. 12805.bb.43.

Text sewn on two sawn-in cords. Beige endpapers and pastedowns. Purple bead-grain cloth. Both covers identically blocked in blind. Two fillets are blocked on the borders. Inside this, a wide border of triangular leaf patterns is alternately blocked in blind and in relief. A fillet is blocked in blind on the inner border. A tracery of small leaves and curling stems is blocked around the central oval, which itself has fillets and branches on its borders. These intersect to form straps at the head, the tail and the sides. The spine is blocked in gold. A single gold fillet is blocked on the perimeter. From the head downwards, the decoration is: lily leaves and buds blocked in gold, within a rectangular panel formed by two fillets; a gold fillet; the title: '| The | twins | and | their | stepmother |' blocked in gold; a gold fillet; the leaves and buds of a plant, with its bulb at the base – all blocked within a long rectangular frame, formed by two gold fillets; signed 'JL' in gold as separate letters at the base of the plant; two gold fillets; two gold fillets blocked at the tail.

Dry, *JL* no. 413.

356 Leighton, John

Walks abroad and evenings at home . . . With numerous illustrations. London: Houlston and Wright 65, Paternoster Row, 1861. London: Printed by J. and W. Rider, Bartholemew Close. viii, 328 p., 1 plate.
130 × 187 × 25 mm. 12804.d.37.

Some of the illustrations are signed 'E. Jewitt' and Geo. Measom Sc.'

Text sewn on three sawn-in cords. Gilt edges. Beige endpapers and pastedowns. Binder's ticket on lower pastedown: '| Bound by | Burn | 37 & 38 | Kirby St. |' Green wave horizontal-grain cloth. Both covers blocked identically in blind on the borders and on the corners. Two fillets are blocked on the borders, the outer thick, the inner thin. Stem and three-leaf decoration are blocked in relief on each corner. The upper cover central vignette is blocked in gold. It shows a young female figure seated on a fuchsia branch, her head adorned with a tiara and two feathers. She is surrounded by fuchsia stems, leaves, and a flower on each side. The flowers have long stamens characteristic of Leighton's work. The title: '| Walks abroad |' is blocked in a semi-circle above the figure; the words: '| and | evenings | at | home. |' are blocked below the figure – all in gold. Signed 'JL' in gold as separate letters at the base of the vignette. The spine is blocked in gold. From the head downwards, the decoration is: leaf decoration; the title: '| Walks | abroad | and | evenings | at | home. |' blocked in gold, within a panel formed by a single plant tendril; a winged youth, wearing a cap and a gown, is seated on a branch reading a book; a lamp bowl (with a single tassel), suspended from a branch, is blocked above the youth – together with leaves and stars; below the youth, leaves and stars and berries are blocked – all in gold; signed 'JL' in gold as separate letters to the left and the right of the spine near the tail; the words: '| Houlston | & | Wright | are blocked in gold within a rectangle formed by two gold fillets, the outer of which surrounds the rectangle on three sides only (not the top).

Dry, *JL* no. 414.

357 Leighton, John

Adams, William Henry Davenport. *Neptune's heroes: or, the Sea-Kings of England. From Sir John Hawkins to Sir John Franklin . . . With illustrations by W. S. Morgan and John Gilbert.* London: Griffith and Farran, (Successors to Newbery and Harris) Corner of St. Paul's Churchyard, 1861. viii, 440 p., 6 plates. With thirty-two pages of publisher's titles bound at the end.
110 × 177 × 38 mm. 10817.a.46.

The plates are signed 'W. Thomas'.

Yellow endpapers and pastedowns. Blue morocco vertical-grain cloth. Both covers identically blocked in blind. Three fillets are blocked on the borders. The middle fillet has a repeating pattern of 'cartouches and diamonds' blocked in relief within it. Each inner corner has a group of leaves, flowers, and berries,

blocked in relief. These extend to the head, the tail and to the sides. An oval central frame is formed by this decoration. The spine is blocked in gold. A fillet, blocked as a 'sail rope', winds from the head to the tail on the perimeter, forming a panel on the upper and the lower half of the spine. From the head downwards, the decoration is: a crown, with ship's sails and coats of arms on its spikes – all in gold; the title: '| Neptune's | Heroes | or the | sea kings | of England. |' blocked in gold; Neptune's pole and tripod, are blocked from the tail upwards to underneath the word 'England'; a 'bubble' panel, formed by a single gold fillet, has a silhouette of Nelson blocked in gold within, with the words: 'Nelson nat. 1758 obit. 1805' blocked in gold around the silhouette; a rope fillet of curling knots, in gold; signed 'JL' in gold as separate letters on each side of the base of the pole; the word: '| Illustrated |' is blocked in gold at the tail.

Dry, *JL* no. 375.

358 Leighton, John

Balfour, Clara Lucas. *Uphill work* . . . London: Houlston and Wright 65, Paternoster Row, 1861. [London]: J. & W. Rider, Printers 14, Bartholemew Close, E.C. viii, 320 p., 6 plates.
105 × 168 × 30 mm. 12805.bb.6.

The plates are signed: 'CW' and 'H. Dudley Sc.'

Text sewn on two sawn-in cords. Gilt edges. Beige endpapers and pastedowns. Binder's ticket on lower pastedown: '| Bound by | Burn. | 37 & 38 | Kirby St. |' Both covers blocked identically in blind on the borders and on the corners. Two fillets are blocked in blind on the borders, the outer thick, the inner thin. A single shell is blocked on each corner. The upper cover vignette is blocked in gold. It shows a man climbing a cliff path. He holds a hat and a walking stick in his right hand; a soft hat held on his forehead by his left hand. He wears a backpack. On either side of the man are the words: '| Uphill | Work |'; the capitals 'U' and 'W' are blocked in relief within horizontal hatch gold rectangular lettering-pieces. Signed 'JL' in gold as separate letters at the base of the vignette. The spine is blocked in gold. A single gold fillet is blocked on the perimeter. From the head downwards, the decoration is: three fillets; a panel of small gold dots, around a 'vase' shape; the title: '| Uphill | Work |' blocked in relief within two rectangular gold lettering-pieces; the words: '| Mrs. | C. L. Balfour |' blocked in gold; then a palm leaf within a wreath, and the motto: '| Palmam qui meruit ferat |' is blocked in relief within a ribbon-shaped gold lettering-piece; near the base, '| Houlston | and Wright |' blocked in gold within a rectangle formed by a single gold fillet; two gold fillets blocked at the tail.

The Renier Collection has two copies of this work. The same design is blocked on both. One has blue bead-grain cloth; binder's ticket of Burn. The other has purple bead-grain cloth.

359 Leighton, John

Black, Adam, Publisher and Black, Charles, *Publisher. Black's picturesque guide to the English Lakes including an essay on the geology of the district by John Phillips . . . With twelve Outline Views by Mr. Flintoft, and Numerous Illustrations. Eleventh edition.* Edinburgh: Adam and Charles Black, 6 North Bridge, 1861. Edinburgh: Printed by R. & R. Clark. xxxii, 283 p., 2 fold-out maps; 5 maps; 7 plates. With thirty-two pages of publisher's titles bound at the end.
110 × 170 × 25 mm. 10358.c.8.

The fold-out map of the Lake District bound at page 1 was drawn and engraved by W. Hughes, 6 Brook Street, Holborn, London.

Edges speckled with red ink. Light yellow endpapers and pastedowns. On the front endpaper and pastedown is printed an Index Map. On the lower endpaper and pastedown are printed advertisements for A&C Black publications. Dark green bead-grain cloth. The design blocked is the same as for the 1858 edition, at BL. 10358.d.14. Two gold fillets are blocked at the tail of the spine.

360 Leighton, John FIG. 46

Bowman, Anne. *The bear-hunters of the rocky mountains. Illustrated by Zwecker.* London: Routledge, Warne, &

FIG. 46

Routledge, Farringdon Street. New York: 56, Walker Street, 1861. Cox & Wyman, Printers, Great Queen Street, London. 446 p., 4 plates.
115 × 175 × 45 mm. 12807.bb.11.

Rebound in the 1980s. The paper is laminated. Red bead-grain cloth. Binder's ticket on lower pastedown: '| Bound by | Burn 37 & 38 | Kirby St. |' Two fillets are blocked in blind on the borders, the outer thin, the inner thick. Groups of five flowers are blocked in blind on the sides, on the centre head and on the centre tail, with a single flower blocked in blind on each corner. The upper cover has a central vignette in gold, featuring a bear with its arms around a fir tree, licking the [insects on the] bark. At the base of the tree are placed a rifle with a broken barrel, a shoe, a stick. Signed 'JL' in gold as separate letters at the base of the vignette. The spine is blocked in gold. A single gold fillet is blocked on the perimeter. From the head downwards, the decoration is: an arch at the head, and the head of an Indian; crossed arrows and hatchets blocked in gold below the Indian; the words: '| The | bear | hunters | of the | Rocky | Mountains. | [rule] | Bowman |' blocked in gold; fish and game are hanging from a line; a group of objects are gathered together, consisting of: muskets, a dead bird, small branches of foliage; a semi-circular fillet forms an arch at the tail, with dots blocked within it – all in gold.

Dry, *JL* no. 383. King, *JL* p. 238.

361 Leighton, John FIG. 47

Cook, Eliza. *Poems. Selected and Edited by the Author. Illustrated by John Gilbert, J. Wolf, H. Weir, J. D. Watson, etc., etc. Engraved by the Brothers Dalziel.* London: Routledge, Warne, & Routledge, Farringdon Street; and 56, Walker Street, New York, 1861. London: Printed by Richard Clay, Bread Street Hill. viii, 408 p.
165 × 230 × 40 mm. 1347.i.16.

Gilt edges. Bevelled boards. Yellow endpapers and pastedowns. Binder's ticket on lower pastedown: '| Bound by | Edmonds & Remnants, | [rule] | London |.' Blue morocco horizontal-grain cloth. Both covers identically blocked in gold and in relief. Three gold fillets are blocked on the borders. Inside this are: 1. a border of three fillets, with repeating dots blocked in gold, between the first and second fillets; 2. a border fillet blocked in blind on the sides and on the tail; 3. a border of five fillets, with repeating dots blocked in gold between the second and the third fillets. Straps are formed on each corner by these multiple fillets and dots. A raised pattern of hatch ivy leaves and stems surrounds the centre. The centre circle is formed by multiple gold fillets, with more elaborate straps blocked above and below it on the centre head and on the centre tail. The centre circle has fillets blocked in gold on its borders, and inside, there are three hatch gold lettering-pieces containing lily-like flowers. Also within the circle, a trefoil is formed by three fillets blocked in gold, the middle of which has repeating dots blocked in relief. The words '| Poems | by | Eliza Cook |' are blocked in relief within three gold lettering-pieces with single gold fillets blocked on their borders. Hatch gold decoration surrounds these lettering-pieces. Signed 'JL' in gold as separate letters underneath the title.

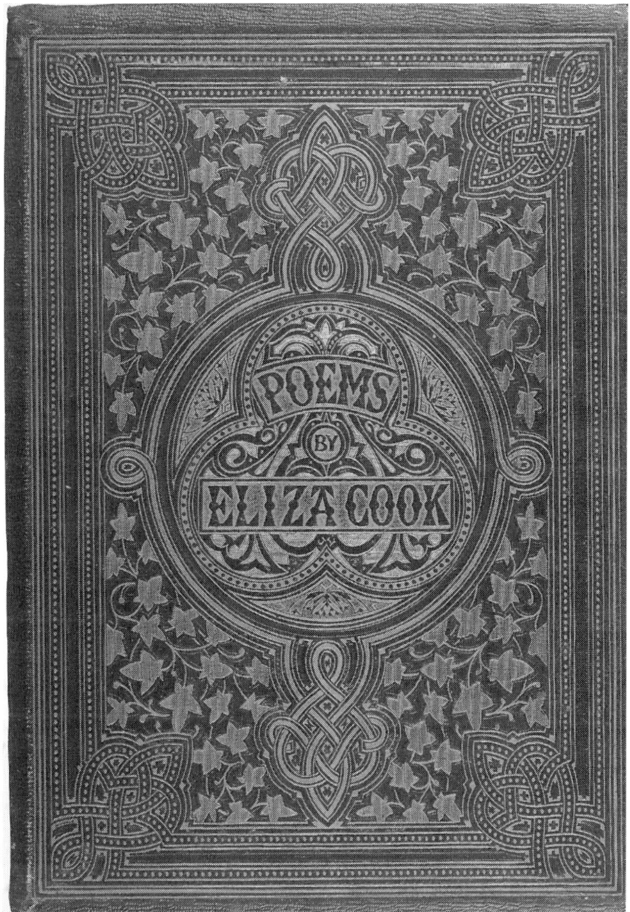

FIG. 47

The spine is blocked in gold. Two gold fillets are blocked on the perimeter. Three groups of elaborate straps are blocked in gold on the head, the middle and near the tail. Each is formed by two gold fillets with repeating gold dots blocked between them. the words '| Poems | by | Eliza | Cook |' are blocked in relief within four rectangular gold lettering-pieces – all being blocked within hatch horizontal gold panel. The word: '| Illustrated |' is blocked in relief within a rectangular gold lettering-piece, which has a single fillet blocked in relief on its borders – both blocked within gold hatch decoration. Signed 'JL' in gold as separate letters near the tail. At the tail, the words: '| Routledge & Co. |' are blocked in relief within a rectangular gold lettering-piece, which has a single fillet blocked in relief on its borders – both blocked within a rectangle formed by a single gold fillet.

The Henry Spencer Ashbee copy of this work is at BL 1347.f.23. Full red morocco, with French style wide border decoration blocked in gold on both covers. Raised bands and panels with tracery decoration in gold on the spine.

Dry, *JL* no. 384. King, *JL* p. 238. McLean, *VPBB* p. 85. Oldfield, *BC* no. 56. Pantazzi, *JL* p. 268.

362 Leighton, John

Cowper, William. *The poet. The poetical works. Edited by the Rev. Robert Aris Willmott, Incumbent of Bear Wood. New Edition, illustrated by Birket Foster.* London: Routledge, Warne and Routledge, Farringdon Street; New York: 56, Walker Street, 1861. London: Savill, and Edwards, Printers, Chandos Street, Covent Garden. lxviii, 631 p., 8 plates.
105 × 170 × 45 mm. 11603.e.24a.

Routledge's British poets. Engravings by Dalziel.

Gilt edges. Yellow endpapers and pastedowns. Binder's ticket on lower pastedown: '| Bound by | Bone & Son. | 76 Fleet Street, | London. |'. Blue bead-grain cloth. Blocked identically as 11603.e.14., Cowper, William. The poetical works. A less incisive impression than the 1858 editions of Routledge's British poets. The width of the block on the spine shows that the block was intended for the earlier, and smaller size, editions. There is a gap between the sides of the block and the spine hinge.

363 Leighton, John FIG. 48

Crowquill, Alfred *pseud.* [i.e. Alfred Henry Forrester.] *Fairy footsteps; or Lessons from Legends. With One Hundred Illustrations designed by Alfred Crowquill.* London: Henry Lea, 22 Warwick Lane, Paternoster Row, 1861. London: Printed by J. E. Adlard, Bartholomew Close. [3], 188 p.,8 plates.
140 × 190 × 22 mm. 12807.d.23.

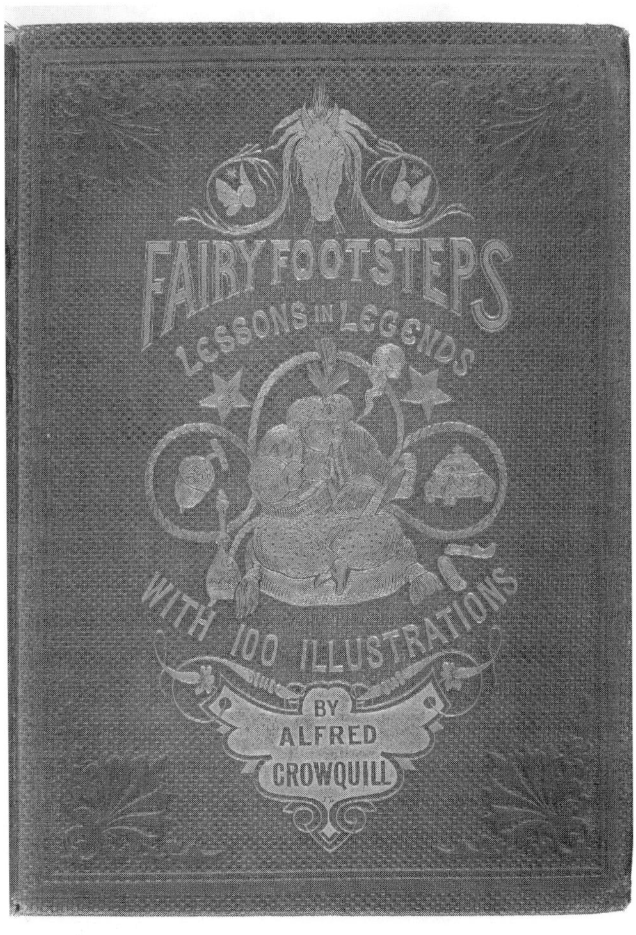

FIG. 48

Gilt edges. Beige endpapers and pastedowns. Binder's ticket on lower pastedown: '| Bound by | Burn. | 37 & 38 | Kirby St. |' Purple bead-grain cloth. Both covers blocked identically in blind and in relief on borders and corners. There are fillets on the borders and shells blocked in blind and in relief on the corners. The upper cover is fully blocked in gold. At the top is blocked a horse's head. The mane hairs of the horse curl outwards to form two circles, which are both blocked with a butterfly and a star. The title: | Fairy Footsteps | Lessons in [sic] Legends |' is blocked in gold, above the central figure of a turbaned oriental; the man is seated on a cushion with tassels, with his legs crossed, reading a book. The hookah is to his right, the pipe curls around and above him before its end reaches his mouth. The decorative elements of the man are all picked out by blocking in relief. Underneath the man, the words: '| With 100 illustrations |' are blocked in gold. At the tail, the words: '| By | Alfred | Crowquill |' are blocked in relief within a gold lettering-piece. Signed 'JL' in relief as separate letters at the base of the design. The spine is fully blocked in gold. The title and author words: '| Fairy | Footsteps | By | Alfred | Crowquill |' are blocked in relief within 'dome-shaped' gold lettering-pieces. Beneath, blocked in gold, is the figure of a fairy, holding a staff, with a star above her. The words: '| 100 illustrations |' are blocked in gold at the tail, within a rectangle formed by a single gold fillet. Just above this, 'JL' is signed in gold as separate letters.

Dry, *JL* no. 385. Pantazzi, *JL* p. 264. Reproduces a copy in dark violet close bead-grain cloth, bound by Burn.

364 Leighton, John

Dalton, William. *Lost in Ceylon: the story of A Boy and Girl's Adventures in the woods and the wilds of the Lion King of Kandy. With Illustrations by Harrison Weir.* London: Griffith and Farran, (Successors to Newbery and Harris), Corner of St. Paul's Churchyard, 1861. London: Savill and Edwards, Printers, Chandos Street, Covent Garden. viii, 408 p., 5 plates. With thirty-two pages of publisher's titles bound at the end.
110 × 178 × 40 mm. 12807.bb.13.

Text sewn on three sawn-in cords. Yellow endpapers and pastedowns. Brown morocco vertical-grain cloth. Both covers blocked identically in blind. A 'dog-tooth' fillet is blocked on the outer border. Three fillets, blocked inside this, cross with three vertical fillets blocked on each side to form panels at the head, the tail and on the sides, with squares on the corners. 'Flower heads' are blocked within each square. The inner rectangle has a thin fillet blocked on its borders. There is small curling stem, leaf and bud decoration on the inside of this fillet, with straps at the head and at the tail. The spine is blocked in gold. A single fillet is blocked on the perimeter. From the head downwards, the decoration is: small decoration blocked in gold at the head; the words: '| Lost | in | Ceylon | by | William |

Dalton | ' in gold; a map of Ceylon Island, with many of the town names blocked in gold on its perimeter; small horizontal hatch leaf decoration; (probably signed 'JL' underneath the spine label, beneath the map); the word: '| Illustrated |' is blocked in gold within a rectangle formed by a single gold fillet; two gold fillets blocked in gold at the tail.

Dry, *JL* no. 386.

365 Leighton, John

E., A.L.O. *pseud.* [i.e.Tucker, Charlotte M.] *Parliament in the play-room* . . . London: T. Nelson and Sons, Paternoster Row; Edinburgh and New York, 1861. 168 p., 1 plate. With thirty-two pages of publisher's titles bound at the end.
108 × 171 × 24 mm. 12804.c.28.

Text sewn on three sawn-in cords. Yellow endpapers and pastedowns. Both covers identically blocked in blind on the borders, the corners and on the sides. Two fillets are blocked on the borders, one thick, one thin. Three horse chestnut leaves are blocked in relief on each corner. (This is the same design on the borders and on the corners as for BL 12632.cc.12., E., A.L.O. Pride and his prisoners . . .) Straps are blocked in relief on the middle of the sides. The blocking in blind on the borders and on the corners forms a central quatrefoil-shape, pointed at the head and at the tail. The upper cover has central vignette blocked in gold. This shows a girl standing on a woolsack, a mace held in her right hand, a scroll in her left. The woolsack is a gold lettering-piece, and has the word: 'Wool' blocked in relief inside with the double 'o' being conjoined. Above the girl, the word: 'Parliament' is blocked in gold. The 'P' and 'T' have extended serifs at the base. The 'A' has three flower heads – the rose of England, the thistle of Scotland, and the trefoil of Ireland – all emerging from the cross-bar of the 'A'. The words: 'in the play room' are blocked in gold on each side of the girl. Signed 'L' (with a dot above the top) in gold underneath the woolsack. (A fairly early example of this form of Leighton's signature.) The spine is blocked in gold. From the head downwards, the decoration is: two fillets; a crown within a panel of dots and small stems; the title: '| Parliament | in the playroom | [rule] | by | ALOE |' blocked in gold; a crown, with the word: 'Lords' blocked in gold underneath it; a mace, with roses, thistles and trefoils joined to its pole; a feathered hat, with the word: 'Commons' blocked in gold underneath; two fillets; a rectangular gold lettering-piece, with a single gold fillet blocked on its borders, has the words: '| Nelson & Sons |' blocked in relief inside; two gold fillets blocked at the tail.

Dry, *JL* no. 388.

366 Leighton, John

Edwards, Matilda Barbara Betham. *Holidays among the mountains: or, Scenes and Stories of Wales. With Illustrations by F. J. Skill.* London: Griffith and Farran (Successors to Newbery & Harris,) Corner of St. Paul's Churchyard, 1861. London: Savill and Edwards, Printers, Chandos Street, Covent Garden. vi, 218 p., 4 plates. With thirty-two pages of publisher's titles bound at the end.
125 × 175 × 20 mm. 12807.bb.20.

The plates are hand coloured.

Gilt edges. Beige endpapers and pastedowns. Binder's Ticket on lower pastedown: '| Bound by | Burn, | 37 & 38 | Kirby St. |' Purple bead-grain cloth. Both covers blocked identically in blind on the borders and on the corners. Two fillets are blocked on the borders. On the upper corners, stems, leaves and buds are blocked. On the lower corners, flowers, stems and leaves are blocked. The upper cover central vignette is blocked in gold. At the top – the Prince of Wales' feathers and crown are blocked, with the motto: 'Ich dien', blocked in relief inside pennant shaped gold lettering pieces. Beneath this, the title words: '| Holidays among the mountains |' are blocked in relief within a gold lettering-piece. The sub-title: '| or, | Scenes & Stories of Wales | by | M. Betham Edwards |' is blocked in gold. The words: '| Illustrated | by F.J. Skill |' are blocked in gold around a shield. The shield is blocked in gold, quarterly, 2nd and 4th, gules, lions passant, argent; 1st and 3rd, argent, lions passant, gules. Signed 'JL' in gold as separate letters at the base of the shield. The spine is blocked in gold. The title words: '| Holidays | among | the | mountains |' is blocked at the head. An antelope's head is blocked in gold underneath the title.

Dry, *JL* no. 390.

367 Leighton, John

Elwes, Alfred. *Ralph Seabrooke: or, the adventures of a young artist in Piedmont and Tuscany. With Illustrations by Robert Dudley.* London: Griffith and Farran, (Successors to Newbery & Harris,) Corner of St. Paul's Churchyard, 1861. London: Savill and Edwards, Printers, Chandos Street, Covent Garden. xv, 366 p., 6 plates. With thirty two pages of publisher's advertisements bound at the end.
110 × 176 × 37 mm. 12807.bb.31.

Yellow endpapers and pastedowns. Purple dotted-line horizontal-grain cloth. Blocked identically in blind on both covers. A single fillet is blocked on the borders. Inside this, a repeating oval ribbon pattern is blocked, with a clover leaf shape on the corners. In the inner rectangle are leaves on the corners, all in relief. There are three thin fillets, which cross each other to form a smaller rectangle. This innermost rectangle also has leaves blocked in blind on the corners. The spine is fully blocked in gold. From the head downwards, the decoration is: an artist's palette, in gold; a book cover, blocked as a gold lettering-piece; the title: '| Ralph | Seabrooke |' blocked in relief within the book cover; the words: '| by | Alfred | Elwes. |' are blocked in gold; a tree which supports two shields; the word '| Illustrated |' is blocked on the tail in gold, within a rectangle formed by a single gold fillet; unsigned (the signature probably obscured by a label).

Dry, *JL* no. 391. Pantazzi, *JL* p. 272. Shows the same spine, with the monogram 'JL' blocked in gold just above the word 'Illustrated'.

368 Leighton, John

Fraser, Robert William. *Head and hand or thought and action in relation to success and happiness*. London: Houlston and Wright 65 Paternoster Row, 1861. Edinburgh: Printed by Grant Brothers, 14 St James' Square. 272 p., 1 plate.

117 × 172 × 20 mm. 10603.aa.11.

The plate is signed 'J. M. Corner'.

Text sewn on two tapes. Gilt edges. Light grey endpapers and pastedowns. Binder's ticket on lower pastedown: '| Bound by | Burn | 37 & 38 | Kirby St. |' Mauve bead-grain cloth. Both covers blocked identically in blind on the borders on the corners. Two fillets are blocked on the borders, the outer thick, the inner thin. A sea shell is blocked in blind on each corner. The upper cover central vignette is blocked in gold. It shows a scene directly related to the text on page 43, which describes a sailor cutting off the hands of one of the survivors of a wrecked ship, who is clinging to the boat's rudder. The sailor in the rear of the boat holds an upraised sabre. He has already cut off the right hand of the man in the water, and is about to cut off the left hand. On the rudder, the words: '| See page | 43 |' are blocked in relief. The title: '| Head & hand |' is blocked in relief on the stern of the boat. The words: '| By the | Rev. R. W. Fraser | M. A. |' are blocked in gold beneath the boat. Signed 'JL' in gold as a separate letters at the base of the vignette. The spine is blocked in gold and in relief. A single gold fillet is blocked on the perimeter. From the head downwards, the decoration is: two fillets; the title: '| Head | & | hand |' blocked in relief within rectangular gold lettering-pieces, with '&' blocked within a circular gold lettering-piece – all the lettering-pieces have a single fillet on their borders; the sub-title: 'or | thought | & | action. |' blocked in gold; the word: '| Fraser |' blocked in relief within a rectangular gold lettering-piece, with a single fillet on its borders; a bust of a young boy is blocked above a shield, azure, with a hand blocked within; two gold lettering-pieces shaped as ribbons hang down from the shield, with the words: '| Success & | happiness |' blocked in relief within the ribbons; a rifle and a quill, crossed, are blocked between the ribbons; gold hatch leaves; two fillets; the words: '| London | Houlston & Wright |' are blocked in gold within a rectangle formed by a single gold fillet; two fillets blocked in gold at the tail.

Dry, *JL* no. 392.

369 Leighton, John

Fraser, Robert William. *Seaside divinity. With illustrations by Henry Noel Humphreys, J. Wolf, G. H. Andrews, T. W. Wood and J. B. Zwecker. Engraved by the Dalziel Brothers.* London: James Hogg and Sons, 1861. London: Printed by Spottiswoode and Co. New Street Square. xii, 378 p. With ten pages of publisher's titles bound at the end.

122 × 202 × 35 mm. 7004.b.9.

Light yellow endpapers and pastedowns. Binder's ticket on lower pastedown: '| Bound | by | Leighton | Son and | Hodge |'. Green coarse pebble-grain cloth. Three fillets are blocked in blind on the borders of both covers. The upper cover has a central vignette, blocked in gold and in blind. It consists of a large roundel. The roundel is formed by seven borders: 1 & 2. thin gold fillets; 3. a 'sea wave' border, with horizontal gold hatch; 4. a thin gold fillet; 5. a gold fillet with repeating dots blocked in relief within it; 6 & 7. thin gold fillets. On the outside, there are four small roundels, one each at the head and at the tail and the sides. Each is formed of two thin circular fillets, blocked in gold. In each roundel is blocked, clockwise from the head: a starfish, seaweed, a crab (whose claws hold the rules), an octopus. The centre of the roundel has the title: '| Seaside | divinity |' blocked in relief inside two rectangular gold letter-pieces, each with a single gold fillet on its borders. Appearing from behind these lettering-pieces are seaweed and other sea plants, blocked in gold. Signed 'JL' in gold as separate letters, beneath the lettering-pieces. The spine is blocked in gold. From the head downwards, the decoration is: two fillets blocked in gold; seaweed and plants inside a rope panel, all in gold; two rectangular gold lettering-pieces, each with a single gold fillet on its borders, have the words: '| Seaside | divinity |' blocked in relief inside; a scallop, blocked in gold; the words: '| By | the Rev. | R. W. Fraser M.A. |' blocked in relief inside the scallop; near the tail, the word: '| Illustrated |' blocked in gold inside a rectangle formed by a single 'rope-like' fillet; at the tail, two fillets are blocked in gold.

Ball, *App*. no. 61 p. Dry, *JL* no. 393.

370 Leighton, John

Hitopadesa. *The Book of Good Counsels: from the Sanskrit of the 'Hitopadesa.' By Edwin Arnold, M.A. . . . With illustrations by Harrison Weir.* London: Smith Elder, and Co., 65, Cornhill, 1861. London: Printed by Smith, Elder and Co., Little Green Arbour Court, Old Bailey, E.C. xii, 167 p., 4 plates.

130 × 196 × 20 mm. 14070.c.19.

The plates are signed 'H. Weir' and 'Dalziel'.

Yellow endpapers and pastedowns. Green coarse pebble-grain cloth. Both covers blocked identically in blind on the borders and on the corners. A single fillet is blocked in blind on the borders. A leaf and stem pattern is blocked in blind on the corners. A single shell shape is blocked on the centre head and on the centre tail. A central oval frame is formed by double fillets. The upper cover has a central vignette blocked in gold. It shows a male peacock, its feathers displayed in a fan-shape. The title word: '| The |' is blocked in gold above the peacock. The words: '| Book of Good |' are blocked in a semi-circle in relief, within the tips of the feathers of the peacock; the word: '| Counsels |' is blocked in relief, within a semi-circular horizontal hatch gold lettering-piece; the words: '| from the Sanskrit | of the | Hitopadesa |' are blocked in gold underneath the peacock, within curling stems. Signed 'JL' in gold as separate letters at the base of the vignette. The spine is blocked in gold and in relief. From the head downwards, the decoration is: a gold fillet; 'tear-drop' decoration blocked in gold; six rectangular gold lettering-pieces contain the words: '| The | Book | of | Good | Counsels | Arnold |', blocked in relief; these six

lettering-piece with a single gold fillet on its borders; a gold fillet is blocked at the tail.

Dry, *JL* no. 408.

381 Leighton, John

Robinson, Frederick William. *Twelve o'clock. A Christmas story.* London: Hurst and Blackett, Publishers, Successors to Henry Colborn, 13, Great Marlborough Street, 1861. London: Printed by R. Born, Gloucester Street, Regent's Park. [6], 318 p., 2 plates.
126 × 195 × 26 mm. 12632.cc.30.

The frontispiece plate is signed: 'J B Zwecker'; 'Pearson Sc.'

White endpapers and pastedowns. Purple morocco horizontal-grain cloth. Both covers blocked identically in blind and in relief. Two fillets are blocked on the borders, the outer thin, the inner thick. The inner rectangle is blocked with honeysuckle-shaped flowers and stems, with a single honeysuckle flower on each corner, and two larger ones on the centre, extending to the centre head and the centre tail – all of these are blocked in relief. The spine is blocked in gold and in relief. Two gold fillets are blocked at the head and at the tail. From the head downwards, the decoration is: a fillet; a man with his arms resting on the face of a pendulum clock; the clock face is a gold lettering-piece, with the roman numerals blocked in relief; at the centre of the clock, the words: '| Twelve | o' | clock |' blocked in relief within hatched gold – the word 'twelve' and the word 'clock' are blocked in a semi-circular fashion, with the ' o' blocked on the centre of the clock face as the spindle; the base of the clock is a gold lettering-piece with the words: '| A | Christmas | story | by the author of | Grandmother's | money. |' blocked in relief inside; signed 'JL' in relief at the base of the clock; near the tail of the spine, the words: '| London | Hurst & Blackett. |' are blocked in gold, within a small panel formed by a single fillet.

Dry, *JL* no. 412.

382 Leighton, John

S., A. *Stray cuttings from wild flowers etc. By a Clergyman's granddaughter . . .* London: Simpkin Marshall & Co. Robert Taylor, Chepstow: W.N. Johns, Newport: F.G. Dowty, Bridgewater, 1861. Printed by Edward Howell, Liverpool. xv, 214 p.
127 × 172 × 12 mm. 11650.aaa.27.

Gilt edges. Yellow endpapers and pastedowns. Binder's ticket on lower pastedown: '| Bound by | Bone & Son. | 76, Fleet St. London. |' Purple bead-grain cloth. Both covers blocked identically on the borders, the corners, and on the sides – in blind on the lower cover, and in gold on the upper. Two gold fillets are blocked on the borders. Inside this, a wide border is blocked in gold, with curling stems, flowers and leaves – all blocked in relief within it. A third inner border of repeating single flowers and stems is blocked in gold. Gold lettering-pieces are blocked on the inner corner, with leaf and stem decoration inside, blocked in relief. Inside these, a fourth border of flowers and leaves is blocked in gold between two fillets. The upper cover central vignette is blocked in gold. It shows a bouquet of flowers at the base, with stems and small flowers forming a circle. The title: '| Stray cuttings | from | wild flowers |' is blocked in gold on the centre. The spine is blocked in gold. From the head downwards, the decoration is: lily flowers in gold; the title: '| Stray | cuttings | from | wild flowers |' blocked in gold within a rectangle formed by a single fillet; more lily flowers, with their bases serving as strings for a lyre blocked below; lily leaves and roots are blocked near the tail; signed 'JL' in gold as a monogram near the tail; a 'diamonds' pattern is formed by gold fillets; two fillets in gold are blocked at the tail.

383 Leighton, John

Shakespeare, William. *The beauties of Shakspeare [sic]. With a general index. . . . A new edition.* London: William Tegg, 1861. Billing, Printer and Stereotyper, Guildford, Surrey. viii, 11–308 p., 2 plates.
107 × 173 × 26 mm. 11765.b.52.

Plate 1 is the Frontispiece. Plate 2 is the half title-page. Drawn by H. Corbould, engraved by C. Heath.

Light yellow endpapers and pastedowns. Blue morocco horizontal-grain cloth. Both covers blocked identically in blind on the borders and on the corners. Two fillets are blocked on the borders. On each corner, a group of three spade-shaped leaves is blocked in blind and in relief. The upper cover central vignette is blocked in gold and in relief. A bust of Shakespeare is blocked on the centre. Just above it, the words: 'Nat 1564 Obit. 1616' are blocked in gold. Above and below the bust, the words: '| Dodd's | Beauties | of | Shakspeare [sic] |' are blocked in relief, within four gold lettering-pieces, three of which are rectangles; all have a single gold fillet blocked on their borders. The word: 'of' is blocked in relief within a circular gold lettering-piece. To the left and the right of the bust, fuchsia leaves, buds and a single flower with long stamens are blocked in gold. Signed 'JL' in gold as separate letters at the base of the vignette. The spine is blocked in gold and in relief. The words: '| Dodd's | Beauties | of | Shakspeare [sic] |' are blocked in relief within four rectangular gold lettering-pieces – all within single gold fillets blocked on their borders, and surrounded by small curling stem decoration blocked in gold. The lettering-pieces are 'mounted' on a pole, blocked in gold.

Dry, *JL* no. 387.

384 Leighton, John

Wood, John George. *The boy's own book of natural history. Illustrated with Three Hundred and Thirty Engravings.* London: Routledge, Warne, & Routledge, Farringdon Street; and 56, Walker Street, New York, 1861. London: R. Clay, Printer, Bread Street Hill. xii, 378 p., 5 plates. With two pages of publisher's titles bound at the end.
110 × 175 × 38 mm. 7205.b.34.

Some of the plates are signed 'Dalziel'. The plate between pp. 24–25 is signed 'H. Weir'.

Text sewn on three sawn-in cords. Yellow endpapers and pastedowns. Brown morocco vertical-grain cloth. Both covers identically blocked in blind on the borders and on the corners. Two fillets are blocked on the borders, the outer thick, the inner thin. A tracery of stems and leaves is blocked on each corner. The upper cover central vignette is blocked in gold. It shows a gold lettering-piece, blocked as an open book. A snake curls around the head and left fore-edge of the book, its tongue chasing a lizard. A rat, a butterfly, and bird are also blocked around the book. The uppermost pages of the book are curled upwards; the outline of animals are blocked in relief on the pages underneath. The title: '| Boy's | own book | of |' is blocked in relief within the open book; '| Natural history |' are blocked in gold underneath the book. The spine is blocked in gold. A single gold fillet is blocked on the perimeter. From the head downwards, the decoration is: a frame formed by two gold fillets forms a trefoil; within the frame, the words: '| The | boy's own | book | of | natural | history | Wood. |' blocked in gold; bulrushes, birds, and an otter on a bank eating fish; the words: '| 300 illustrations |' are blocked in gold between two gold fillets at the tail. (Spine label likely to obscure JL signature near the tail.)

Dry, *JL* no. 415.

385 Leighton, John

Annie Elton; or, the cottage and the farm. Edinburgh: John Maclaren. London: Hamilton, Adams, & Co., 1862. Turnbull and Spears, Printers, Edinburgh. [1], 328 p., 2 plates.
110 × 175 × 30 mm. 12805.bbb.20.

The title page and frontispiece are plates. The frontispiece is signed: 'J. McWhirter' and 'R. Paterson Sc.'

Text sewn on two cords. Bolts uncut. Binder's ticket on lower pastedown: '| Bound by | Burn. London. | Postage | 4D. |' Brown endpapers and pastedowns. Red bead-grain cloth. Both covers are identically blocked in blind on the borders, on the corners and on the sides. Two fillets are blocked on the borders, the outer thin, the inner thick. Small single five-petal flower heads and their stems are blocked in blind on the corners. Groups of five flower-heads are blocked on the centre head, on the centre tail, with two groups blocked on each side. The upper cover vignette is blocked in gold. It is 'onion-shaped', formed by crossed fuchsia branches rising from the tail. There is a single fuchsia flower blocked at the head and one on each side. All have long stamens. The title: '| Annie Elton | or | the cottage | and | the farm |' is blocked in gold on the centre. Signed 'JL' in gold as a monogram at the base of the vignette. The spine is blocked in gold. From the head downwards, the decoration is: a gold fillet; a decorated gold fillet; a decorative-piece in gold; the title: '| Annie Elton | or | the cottage | and | the farm |' blocked in gold; a horizontal hatch gold 'Spanish' motif and fillets are blocked near the tail; at the tail, four gold fillets are blocked, then a decorated gold fillet and a plain gold fillet.

386 Leighton, John

Aylmer, J. E. *Distant homes; or, the Graham Family in New Zealand. With illustrations by J. Jackson.* London: Griffith and Farran, (Successors to Newbery and Harris), Corner of St. Paul's Churchyard, 1862. London: Printed by J. Wertheimer and Co., Circus Place, Finsbury. vii, 199 p., 4 plates. With thirty-two pages of publisher's titles bound at the end.
132 × 173 × 25 mm. 12804.f.12.

The plates are hand coloured.

Gilt edges. Beige endpapers and pastedowns. Purple bead-grain cloth. Both covers blocked identically in blind on the borders and on the corners. Six fillets are blocked on the borders, the outermost being the thickest. There is a stem and leaf pattern on each corner, extending onto the sides and the centre head and the centre tail. The upper cover central vignette is blocked in gold and relief. It shows the portico of a native house, with a pediment jutting out. At the apex of the pediment, a 'fairy figure' is blocked, its arms crossed. The title: '| Distant homes |' is blocked in relief on the pediment; the words: '| or the | Graham Family |' are blocked in gold in the pediment recess, which is blocked in hatch gold; the words: '| in New Zealand |' are blocked in relief within the base of the pediment. The pediment is suspended on a wooden pole, blocked in gold. To the right of the pole, a maori figure is blocked in gold, his right hand holding a spear. To the left of the pole, a plant and steps lean against it. Signed 'JL' in relief as separate letters at the base of the pole. The spine is blocked in gold. From the head downwards, the decoration is: the head of a maori; the title: '| Distant | homes | or the | Graham | Family | in | New | Zealand |' blocked in gold; a gold fillet; two gold fillets are blocked at the tail.

Dry, *JL* no. 417.

387 Leighton, John

Bowman, Anne. *How to make the best of it: A Domestic Tale for Young Ladies . . .* London: Routledge, Warne & Routledge, Farringdon Street; New York: 56, Walker Street, 1862. Cox and Wyman, Printers, Great Queen Street, London. [2], 416 p., 5 plates.
110 × 175 × 46 mm. 12806.cc.18.

The plates are engraved by Dalziel.

Original beige endpaper bound at the front. Red bead-grain cloth. Both covers blocked identically in blind on the borders and on the corners. Two fillets are blocked on the borders. Sea-shell motifs are blocked in relief on the centre head, the centre tail, with two on each side. The upper cover vignette is blocked in gold. It shows a three masted paddle steamer, with full sail on the foremast. The word: '| Osten |' is blocked in relief on the (right) paddle cover. Above the steamer, the title: '| How to make |' is blocked in relief within a semi-circular gold lettering-piece, with a single gold fillet on its borders; the word: 'the' is blocked in relief within a horizontal hatch gold lettering-piece with a gold fillet blocked on its borders. Below the

steamer, the words: '| Best of it |' are blocked in relief within a gold lettering-piece with a single gold fillet blocked on its borders; the words: '| a | domestic tale | for | young ladies. |' are blocked in gold within a bowl-shaped panel formed by two gold fillets. Signed 'JL' in gold as separate letters at the base the vignette. [The spine is missing.]

Dry, *JL* no. 418.

388 Leighton, John

Broderip, Frances Freeling. *Tiny Tadpole, and other tales. With Illustrations by her Brother, Thomas Hood.* London: Griffith and Farran, (Successors to Newbery and Harris,) Corner of St. Paul's Churchyard, 1862. London: Printed by J. Wertheimer and Co., Circus Place, Finsbury. [8], 176 p., 6 plates. With thirty-two pages of publisher's titles bound at the end.
128 × 175 × 23 mm. 12804.g.23.

The plates are hand coloured. Printed in page three of the publisher's titles: 'Super royal 16mo. price 3s. 6d. cloth; 4s 6d. coloured [plates], gilt edges.'

Yellow endpapers and pastedowns. Red bead-grain cloth. Both covers identically blocked in blind on the borders and on the corners. Two fillets are blocked on the borders. A conch shell and seaweed fronds are blocked in blind on each corner. The upper cover vignette is blocked in gold. The title words: '| Tiny Tadpole |' are blocked in gold in a semi-circle. The words: '| and | other tales |' are blocked in gold in fanciful letters within a pond life scene. This scene has butterflies, a bird, water lilies, a frog, a fish – all blocked in gold. Signed 'JL' in gold as separate letters at the base of the vignette. The spine is blocked in gold and in blind, and in relief. Small cartouches are blocked in relief at the head and at the tail, between single fillets, blocked in blind. On the middle to upper portion of the spine, a pennant-shaped gold lettering-piece is blocked around bulrushes. The title: '| Tiny | Tadpole |' is blocked in relief within the pennant. (The spine is not signed.)

Dry, *JL* no. 420.

389 Leighton, John

Davenport, Emma Anne Georgina. *Live toys; or anecdotes of four-legged and other pets. With illustrations by Harrison Weir.* London: Griffith and Farran, (Successors to Newbery & Harris), Corner of St. Paul's Churchyard, 1862. London: Printed by Wertheimer and Co., Circus Place, Finsbury. [7], 140 p., 4 plates. With thirty-two pages of publisher's titles bound at the end.
128 × 175 × 15 mm. 12804.g.7.

The plates are hand-coloured.

Text sewn on two sawn-in cords. Gilt edges. Beige endpapers and pastedowns. Purple wave horizontal-grain cloth. Both covers identically blocked in blind on the borders and on the corners. Two fillets are blocked on the borders. Plants and large flowers are blocked on the lower corners, with stems rising up each side, to sprout leaves on the upper corners. The upper cover vignette is blocked in gold. It shows on the left, a donkey's head; on the right, a horse's head. Between, a dog is crouched on its hind legs on a three-legged stool. The dog is wearing a conical hat, and holds a pipe. At the base of the stool legs, a cat, a cage, a ball of wool, and a small bird are blocked in gold. The thread from the wool unwinds to run up between and around all the three animals. The title: '| Live | toys |' is blocked in gold, in fanciful letters, between the stool legs. Signed 'JL' in gold as separate letters at the base of the vignette. The spine is blocked in gold. From the head downwards, the decoration is: birds on branches; the title: '| Live | toys |' blocked in gold; a squirrel is sitting on an oak branch, eating acorns.

Dry, *JL* no. 421.

390 Leighton, John

E., A.L.O. *pseud.* [i.e. Tucker, Charlotte M.] *The Shepherd of Bethlehem, King of Israel.* London: T. Nelson & Sons, Paternoster Row; Edinburgh and New York, 1862. iv, 9–334 p., 8 plates. With two pages of publisher's titles bound at the end.
120 × 185 × 30 mm. 4409.g.22.

The plates are signed 'F(?). Borders'.

Text sewn on three sawn-in cords. Yellow endpapers and pastedowns. Green wave vertical-grain cloth. Both covers blocked identically in blind on the borders, on the corners, and on the sides. Seven fillets are blocked in blind on the borders. Inside this, a border is blocked in blind, with a repeating pattern of flowers and small leaves blocked in relief. Single medallions are blocked on the centre head and the centre tail, with four-headed leaves inside each, blocked in relief. An inner border of a single fillet, blocked in blind, has repeating dots inside, blocked in relief. A thin fillet forms the inner rectangle. The upper cover vignette is blocked in gold. It shows a reproduction of the plate opposite page 88., entitled: 'David & the Giant'. Above and below the figure of David, the title: '| The | Shepherd | of | Bethlehem | King of Israel |' is blocked in gold. The spine is blocked in gold. A single gold fillet is blocked on the perimeter. From the head downwards, the decoration is: a thin gold fillet; a fillet, containing repeating dots blocked in blind; horizontal hatch gold leaves and stems; a panel formed by fillets contains the title: '| The | Shepherd | of | Bethlehem | King of | Israel |' blocked in gold; '| By | A.L.O.E. |' is blocked in gold underneath the panel; Salome holding the head of St John; at the tail, within a panel which has a single gold fillet on its perimeter, hatched leaf and diamond decoration is blocked within a rectangle formed by a single gold fillet; signed 'JL' in gold as separate letters at the feet of the figure of Salome.

Dry, *JL* no. 423.

391 Leighton, John

E., A.L.O. *pseud.* [i.e.Tucker, Charlotte M.] *The light in the robber's cave.* London: T. Nelson & Sons, Paternoster Row; Edinburgh and New York, 1862. 223 p., 2 plates.
115 × 170 × 22 mm. 12806.bb.43.

The half title page has the title: 'The | robber's cave | a story of Italy | '.

Yellow endpapers and pastedowns. Blue pebble-grain cloth. Both covers are blocked identically in blind on the borders and on the corners. Three fillets are blocked on the borders, one thick between two thin. Groups of three horse chestnut leaves are blocked in relief on each corner. The central frame is four sided, with an onion-shaped head and tail. The upper cover central vignette is blocked in gold. It shows a man, his back to us, playing a stringed instrument. He wears a hat and a cloak. His right foot is raised, on a rock, to support the instrument. Curling stems and leaves are blocked on each side and below him. The title words: '| The Robbers Cave |' are blocked in gold in rustic letters above the man. Below him, the words: 'A story of Italy' are blocked in relief within a rectangular gold lettering-piece, with a single fillet blocked on its border; '| By |' is blocked in gold; 'A.L.O.E.' is blocked in relief within a rectangular gold lettering-piece with a single fillet blocked on its borders. Signed 'JL' in relief as separate letters within the rock below the man's right foot. The spine is blocked in gold. A single fillet is blocked on the perimeter. From the head downwards, the decoration is: two hanging nets (loaded with plunder), which have small tassels at their base; the title: 'The | Robbers | Cave | a | Story | of | Italy |' blocked in gold within a panel formed by a single fillet; a hat, a mask, two crossed pistols, and a bag of gold – all blocked within a panel formed by two fillets, which crosses at the corners at its base to form straps; the words: '| By | A.L.O.E. |' are blocked in gold within a rectangle formed by a single fillet.

Dry, *JL* no. 424.

392 Leighton, John

G., E. *Narrative poems; and a Beam for Mental Darkness. For the benefit of the idiot and his institution. By E.G. Author of 'Adventures of a Sunbeam,' and other stories.* London: Dean & Son, 11, Ludgate Hill, E.C., [1862]. Dean and Son, Printers, 11 Ludgate Hill, London. [1], 96 p., 3 plates. With four pages of publisher's titles bound at the end.
122 × 173 × 15 mm. 11651.aaa.32.

The frontispiece plate is signed: 'Staples'; the plate opposite page 13 is signed 'Folkard'. Bound in after the main text: 'Second visit to Earlswood [Red Hill, Surrey], (The Asylum for Idiots,) May 17, adjourned to June 8, 1861.' 30, [2] p., 1 plate. Printed by: George Unwin, Gresham Steam Press, Bucklersbury, London, E.C.

Gilt edges. Yellow endpapers and pastedowns. Purple morocco horizontal-grain cloth. Both covers blocked identically in blind on the borders, on the corners and on the sides, the head and the tail. Two fillets are blocked on the borders, the outer thick, the inner thin. Curling stems emerge from branches (which start at the centre sides). The stems end in leaves, buds, flowers, and in a single flower, with daisy-like petals blocked in relief on each corner. The branches form an oval central frame. The upper cover vignette is blocked in gold. It shows crossed branches at the base, with stems rising to form a circle around the centre. There are thin leaves and flowers on the stems. On the centre: '| Narrative poems [blocked in a semi-circle] | and a | Beam | for | Mental Darkness [blocked in a semi-circle] |' are blocked in gold. Signed 'JL' in gold as a monogram at the base of the vignette. The spine is blocked in gold. Groups of ivy-like leaves are blocked above and below the title words: '| Narrative | poems |'. These are blocked in gold, with a branch-like fillet blocked in gold on each side of the letters.

Dry, *JL* no. 425.

393 Leighton, John

Hadley, Caroline. *Stories of old: or Bible Narratives suited to the capacity of young children. Illustrated by seven engravings. First Series. Old Testament.* London: Smith Elder & Co., 65, Cornhill, 1862. London: Printed by Smith, Elder and Co., Little Green Arbour Court, Old Bailey, E.C. iv, 311 p., 7 plates.
112 × 182 × 22 mm. 3127.bb.37. [First Series].

The plates are signed: 'Walter Crane del' and 'Swain Sc.'

Edges speckled with red ink. Yellow endpapers and pastedowns. Blue morocco horizontal-grain cloth. Both covers blocked identically in blind on the borders and on the corners. A circle and leaf pattern is blocked in blind and in relief on each corner, extending down each side. The upper cover has a central vignette blocked in gold. It shows a mandorla, formed by two gold fillets. It has a cross on its top, and three small leaves at its base. Inside, a dove is blocked at the head, with two angels beneath holding an open Bible, which is blocked as a gold lettering-piece. In the opening, the words: '| Search | the | Script | ures |' are blocked in relief. Between the angels, the title: '| Stories | of | old | Bible | narratives | for | young | children |' is blocked in gold, with the exception of the words: 'Stories' and 'old', which are blocked in relief within rectangular gold lettering-pieces, with single gold fillets on their borders. Signed 'JL' in relief as separate letters, within the three leaves at the base of the mandorla. The spine is blocked in gold. A single gold fillet is blocked on the perimeter. From the head downwards, the decoration is: a gold fillet; a spade-shape, with small leaf decoration inside; the words: '| Stories | of | Old Testament | narratives | for | young | children | [rule] | Hadley. |' blocked in gold. The words: 'Stories' and 'old' are blocked in relief within rectangular gold lettering-pieces, with single gold fillets on their borders; a medieval window and an arch; the arch contains firstly, a triangle within a circle, secondly, two horizontal hatch gold panels – the one on the left showing a staff and a snake, the one on the right showing a cross; leaf decoration within a spade-shape; near the tail, the words: '| Smith, Elder & Co. |' are blocked in gold, within a rectangle formed by a single gold fillet; two gold fillets blocked at the tail.

394 Leighton, John

Hadley, Caroline. *Stories of old: or Bible Narratives suited to the capacity of young children. Illustrated by seven engravings. Second*

Series. New Testament. London: Smith Elder & Co., 65, Cornhill, 1862. London: Printed by Smith, Elder and Co., Little Green Arbour Court, Old Bailey, E.C. iv, 255 p., 7 plates.
112 × 182 × 22 mm. 3127.bb.37. [Second Series].

The plates are signed 'W. Crane' and 'Swain', and are signed as for the First Series.

Text sewn on three sawn-in cords. Yellow endpapers and pastedowns. Purple wave vertical-grain cloth. The design blocked on the covers and the spine is identical to that on the First Series, for the Old Testament. On the spine, the word 'New' is substituted for 'Old'.

395 Leighton, John FIG. 51

Hibberd, Shirley. *Brambles and bay leaves: essays on things homely and beautiful. Second edition, corrected and revised.* London: Groombridge and Sons, 5, Paternoster Row, 1862. London: W.H. Collingridge, 117 to 199, Aldergate Street, London E.C. viii, 212 p.
123 × 190 × 30 mm. 12354.bb.32.

Gilt edges. Bevelled boards. Yellow endpapers and pastedowns. Binder's ticket on lower pastedown: '| S. Curtis. | Binder. |' Blue bead-grain cloth. Both covers are blocked identically in blind on the borders and on the corners. Two fillets are blocked in blind on the borders of both covers. Bay leaves are blocked in blind on the corners of both covers. The upper cover vignette is blocked in gold. It has the title word: '| Brambles | and'; '| leaves |' blocked in gold above and below the word 'Bay', whose letters are blocked in relief within three bay-leaf gold lettering-pieces. Signed 'JL' in gold as separate letters at base. The spine is blocked in gold. A single gold fillet is blocked on the perimeter. From the head downwards, the decoration is: a single gold fillet; an arch with tendrils and leaves; three bees, one large, two small; a bird in flight; reeds in water; a grasshopper at the base of the reeds; a gold fillet; a rectangle formed by a single gold fillet, with a single gold dot in each corner; a gold fillet is blocked across the tail.

Dry, *JL* no. 426.

FIG. 51

396 Leighton, John PLATE XXXVIII

Howitt, William and Howitt, Mary. *Ruined abbeys and castles of Great Britain. The Photographic Illustrations by Bedford, Sedgefield, Wilson, Fenton and others.*. London: A.W. Bennett, 5, Bishopsgate Without, 1862. London: Richard Barratt, Printer, Mark Lane. [7], 228 p., 27 photographs.
170 × 230 × 35 mm. C.44.d.8.

Bevelled boards. Gilt edges. Purple coarse pebble-grain cloth. Both covers are blocked identically in gold and in blind and in relief. The design blocked on the border is mostly the same as for BL C.44.d.7., except that the fillet in blind is not blocked, and a repeating pattern of hatched stars, circles and crosses is blocked in gold. Around the central medallion, the title: '| Abbeys & Castles of Great Britain |' is blocked in relief within a blind circular fillet. The photographs pasted within the central circles of each cover are different from BL C.44.d.7. The upper cover photograph is of Conway Castle, repeating the reproduction on p. 107. The spine is blocked in gold. A single gold fillet is blocked on the perimeter. From the head downwards, the decoration is: a single gold fillet; a shield with a crown and rose blocked within it, surmounted by castellation – all surrounded by stars blocked in gold; the title: 'Abbeys | & | Castles | of Great Britain [gothic letters] | [rule] | Howitt. |' blocked in gold; a mandorla formed by four gold fillets, with a 'weather-vane' hen atop it; a gold circle is blocked above and below the mandorla, each with a star blocked in relief inside; a shield is blocked within the mandorla, gules, with a crown and a cross; two gold candlesticks; two gold fillets; a diamond decorative pattern in gold, blocked within a rectangle formed by a single gold fillet; two gold fillets are blocked at the tail. Unsigned.

McLean, *VPBB* p. 104. Suggests that this design is by Leighton. Morris & Levin, *APB* p. 34, no .45. Design blocked on dark green morocco.

397 Leighton, John

Lee, Holme *pseud.* [i.e. Miss Harriet Parr.] *Tuflongbo's journey in search of ogres; with some account of his early life, and how his shoes got worn out. With six illustrations by H. Sanderson.* London: Smith Elder, and Co., 65, Cornhill, 1862. London:

Printed by Smith, Elder & Co., 15 Old Bailey, E.C. vii, 240 p., 6 plates.
112 × 185 × 25 mm. 12808.bb.40.

Text sewn on three sawn-in cords. Light yellow endpapers and pastedowns. Mauve dot and line horizontal-grain cloth. Both covers blocked identically in blind on the borders and on the corners. Two fillets are blocked on the borders, the outer thick, the inner thin. Circles, a single fleur-de-lis, and two leaves are blocked on each corner, with a four-petal flower blocked within each circle. The upper cover central vignette is blocked in gold. It shows Tuflongbo, wearing a backpack, and a feathered hat, with a walking stick held in his right hand. He is climbing a hill, with a church outlined in the distance to his right. Small stars are blocked around him, and a bat in flight is blocked above him. The title: '| Tuflongbo's | journey |' is blocked on his left in gold; the words: '| In search | of ogres |' are blocked on his right; below, the words: '| By | Holme Lee |' are blocked in gold. Signed 'JL' in gold as separate letters on the right hand base of the vignette. The spine is blocked in gold and relief. From the head downwards, the decoration is: a medallion; the title: '| Tuflongbo's | journey | in search | of | ogres |' blocked in relief within five rectangular gold lettering-pieces, each with a single gold fillet blocked on its borders; Tuflongbo stands near the base, with a pole beside him; at the top or the pole hang his hat and his backpack (a gold lettering-piece), which has the words: '| By | Holme | Lee |' blocked in relief within it; near the tail, the words: '| London | Smith Elder & Co |' are blocked in gold within a rectangle formed by a single gold fillet; a fillet is blocked at the tail.

Dry, *JL* no. 431.

398 Leighton, John

Mayhew, Henry. *London labour and the London poor; a cyclopaedia of the condition and earnings of those that will [italics] work, those that cannot[italics] work, and those that will not[italics] work. Those that will not work. Comprising, prostitutes. Thieves. Swindlers. Beggars. By several contributors. With an introductory essay on the agencies at present in operation in the metropolis for the suppression of vice and crime. By the Rev. William Tuckniss, B.A. With illustrations.* London: Griffin, Bohn, and Company, Stationers' Hall Court, 1862. xl, 504 p., 14 plates.
155 × 235 × 40 mm. Compiler's copy

This 'Extra Volume' is vol. 4 of the set. The BL sets of the 1861–62 edition are at shelfmarks: 08275.bb.28. – the copyright copy; and 08286.e.19. – the former Reading Room copy [i.e. purchased]. The text of Vol. 4 of these copies is the same as this copy. Neither of these two sets has original covers. The Newbery Library, Chicago has a set of three volumes in original covers at shelfmark Bon. 11246. Published: London: Griffin, Bohn, and Comp[any], Stationers' Hall Court, 1861. Printed by William Clowes and Sons, Stamford Street.

All three volumes at the Newbery Library have dark red pebble-grain cloth. Yellow endpapers and pastedowns. All volumes are blocked identically on the covers in blind and in relief, with two fillets on the borders, and 'spade-shapes' on the corners, formed by three fillets (one thick between two thin). There is no upper cover central vignette. On the spines, all three volumes have designs blocked that are identical to the design for the Extra Volume. The words: '| I[–III.] | London | Street | Folk |' are blocked in relief within the medallion on the centre of the spine. All are signed 'JL' in gold as separate letters near the tail. The Extra Volume is at Bon.11247. It has purple horizontal wave-grain cloth. The upper cover central vignette is same as for the Compiler's copy.

Text sewn on three sawn-in cords. White endpapers and pastedowns. Purple wave horizontal-grain cloth. Both covers identically blocked in blind on the borders, the corners and the sides. Two fillets are blocked on the borders, the outer thick, the inner thin. More fillets blocked inside this form onion-shapes on each corner, and almost complete circles at the head and at the tail. The upper cover has a central vignette blocked in gold. Part of the title: '| London | Labour | and the |' is blocked in gold on either side of the lantern and dome of St. Paul's Cathedral. Below this, a shield is blocked, showing the City of London coat of arms. The words: '| London | Poor |' are blocked in relief vertically and horizontally within the cross inside the shield. The motto: '| Dirige | domine | nos |' is blocked in relief within a pennant-shaped gold lettering-piece below the shield. A tracery of thorn-like stems is blocked in gold on either side of the shield. Signed 'JL' in gold as separate letters at the base of the vignette. The spine is blocked in gold. A gas lamp-post is blocked from tail to head. The gas lantern is blocked at the head, with a flame and rays inside. From the ladder bar of the lamp-post, a rectangular banner is hanging. This is formed by a single gold fillet. The title: '| London | Labour | and the | London | Poor. |' is blocked in gold inside the banner. A medallion gold lettering-piece is blocked in gold beneath the banner, with the words: '| Extra volume |' and a six-point star blocked in relief inside the medallion. At the base of the lamp-post, a group of objects is blocked on the ground: a broom, a hat, a stick, a basket, and a long-handled axe. Signed 'JL' in gold as separate letters underneath these objects. The word: '| Illustrated |' is blocked in gold within a rectangle formed by a single gold fillet.

399 Leighton, John

Owen, William. *Pictorial Sunday Readings: comprising A series of Scripture Subjects, treated with special reference to the tastes and requirements of families; and forming a comprehensive repertory of Biblical knowledge.* London: James Sangster and Co., Paternoster Row, [1862]. [London]: John Sangster, 36, Paternoster Row, E.C. 2 volumes bound in one.
153 × 210 × 75 mm. 3127.cc.20.

Vol. I. xii, 324 p., 40 plates.
Vol. II. [8], 304 p., 40 plates.

Some of the plates are signed: 'H. Weir'.

In BM C19 Binding of quarter morocco and blue morocco vertical-grain cloth. Board edges are gauffered. Marbled edges,

endpapers and pastedowns. Originally issued in parts with paper covers. Parts 1 to 10 form volume I. Parts 11 to 20 form volume II. The upper cover verso and lower cover recto have no printing. On the verso of each lower cover: 'To be completed in about eighteen Monthly Parts, price One Shilling, each containing Four Coloured Engravings, with Thirty-two pages of bold, clear Letter-press on a very superior paper, from type entirely new.' All the paper covers are pink-dyed. The covers are bound in sequence. The upper cover design is the same for all the parts. Two fillets are printed on the borders. Inside these, four quotations are printed, one for each side. On the head: 'Train up a child in the way he should go'; on the right hand side: 'The law was given to Moses, but grace and truth came by Jesus Christ'; on the tail: 'And when he is old, he will not depart from it'; on the left hand side: 'Thy word is a lamp unto my feet, and a light unto my path'. The title is printed inside the central rectangle, on the left: '| Pictorial | Sunday | Readings. By the | Rev. William Owen, | Author of "Memoir of Havelock." ' On the right hand side, and at the base, an oriental scene is printed, of desert plants and trees, with a town in the background. Camels and their escort approach the town gate. Signed 'JL' as a monogram on the right hand corner at the base. In a rectangular panel at the base is a cartouche with the imprint: 'London: | James Sangster & Co. | 36 Paternoster Row. |'; at the tail printed on the left: 'Part 1(–20)'; on the right: '[Price 1s.]'

On the upper cover of part 20 a label is pasted on, with the description: '| Pictorial Sunday Readings | two vols., cloth extra gilt. | [rule] | The Publishers have much pleasure, now that the above work | is completed, to undertake the binding in a manner suitable to its beauty and costliness. For this purpose, a set of emblematic designs | in colour and gold have been designed by John Leighton, Esq. | F.S.A. The Travellers will submit specimens of the binding in | cloth or morocco. Cloth cases can be had of any bookseller at 4s. the set. | [rule] | London: J. Sangster & Co., 36, Paternoster Row. |'

Dry, *JL* no. 434. Muira, *MP* p. 55, no. 6.

400 Leighton, John FIG. 52

Periodical Publications. – *London.* – *Art Union Monthly Journal. The Art Journal Illustrated Catalogue of the International Exhibition 1862.* London; New York: James S. Virtue, [1862]. London: Printed by James S. Virtue, City Road. xii, 324 p.

250 × 340 × 30 mm. 1505/179.

Gilt edges. Cream endpapers and pastedowns. Blue morocco horizontal-grain cloth. Both covers are blocked identically in blind on the borders and on the corners. There are four fillets blocked on the borders. Roses are blocked within medallions on the corners. Leaves surround these medallions, on the sides. The central block on the upper cover is blocked in gold and in relief. Outside the central oval, there are four small medallions blocked in gold on the head, on the tail and on the sides. The medallion at the head shows the word: 'Europe', blocked in relief, with the head of a horse. At the sides, 'Asia' and Africa',

FIG. 52

blocked in relief, are represented by an elephant and a camel. At the base 'America' is represented by a reindeer. Each of the medallions is surrounded by small decoration, blocked in gold. On the border of the central oval is a fillet, blocked in gold, with repeating dots blocked in relief inside it. This fillet joins each of the medallions to the central oval. Between the medallions, patterns of clover leaves, thistles, rose flowers and leaves are blocked in gold. There is a thick hatch gold fillet on the inner border of the central oval. Inside this, a thin double fillet is blocked in gold. At the centre of the oval, the monogram of Victoria and Albert is surmounted by a crown. Underneath it, the words: 'International Exhibition' are blocked in gold. (The capital letters 'I' and 'E' are hatched.) Underneath the monogram, the date '1862' is blocked in relief inside a gold hatched lettering-piece. Around the gold lettering-piece, a ribbon is blocked. Signed 'JL' at the base in gold as separate letters. The spine is blocked in gold and in blind. On the panel at the head, an ornament is blocked in blind in the shape of a lozenge. The title is blocked in gold on the second panel. A lozenge is blocked in blind in the third panel. In the fourth panel '1862' is blocked in gold. A lozenge shape is blocked in the fifth panel in blind. At the tail 'Price 21/-' is blocked in gold.

401 Leighton, John

Scott, *Sir* Walter, *Bart. The poetical works. With a memoir of the Author* . . . London: T. Nelson and Sons, Paternoster Row; Edinburgh and New York, 1862. xix, 612 p.
104 × 170 × 27 mm. 11611.aa.34.

Gilt edges. Yellow endpapers and pastedowns. Purple wave vertical-grain cloth. The lower cover is blocked in blind only. There are patterns of small decoration blocked on the borders, separated by a thin fillet. 'Spade-shapes' are blocked on the corners, with thin plant decoration, blocked in relief inside each. The centre-piece is an oval, with a Britannia-like figure blocked within. At the base of the centre-piece, a medallion is blocked, which has within it a cross of St Andrew. The upper cover is blocked in gold, in blind and in relief. Three fillets are blocked in gold on the borders. Inside this, there is a repeating patterned border of 'thin leaves'; within the border, there are small recessed triangular panels, with three dots, blocked in relief, in each panel. Inside this, there are two more fillets blocked in gold, the outer of which has repeating dots within it, blocked in relief. A tracery of curling stems is blocked in gold on each inner corner. On the centre, a raised circle is blocked. Above it, the figure of a girl is blocked, from the waist upwards. Her outstretched arms hold a sun, its rays, and a quarter moon. Below the girl, the words: '| Reparabit | cornua Phoebe |' are blocked in relief. Below the circle, a hand is blocked in relief within a gold lettering-piece. The central circle is formed by thistles and crossed leaves, blocked in gold, all on a raised surface. On the very centre, a harp, and a tartan cloak draped across it, are blocked in gold. The spine is blocked in gold and in relief. A single fillet is blocked in gold on the perimeter. From the head downwards, the decoration is: two fillets in gold; two small shields, blocked as gold lettering-pieces; the shield on the left, azure, a man is bearing a cross; the shield on the right, argent, a lion rampant, gules – both figures blocked in relief; the centre of the spine has a vertical hatch gold mandorla; the words: '| the | Poetical | Works of | Sir | Walter | Scott | Bart |' are blocked in relief within the mandorla; 'WS' is blocked in gold as a monogram; a shield-shaped gold lettering-piece; the coat of arms of Sir Walter Scott (?), quarterly, 1st and 4th, argent, two stars and crescent, azure, 2nd and 3rd, argent, bend, gules with three diamonds; the motto: 'Watch Weel' blocked in relief within a ribbon-shaped gold lettering-piece; small stem decoration is blocked in gold; signed 'JL' in gold as separate letters near the tail; a single gold fillet in gold; a cartouche formed by a single fillet; two fillets are blocked in gold at the tail.

Dry, JL no. 435.

402 Leighton, John

Scott, *Sir* Walter, *Bart. The poetical works . . . Containing The Lay of the Last Minstrel, Marmion, Lady of the Lake, Don Roderick, Rokeby, Ballads, Lyrics, and Songs. With Notes.* London: Darton and Hodge, Holborn Hill, 1862. Billing, Printer and Stereotyper, Guildford, Surrey. vi, 621 p.
125 × 188 × 37 mm. Compiler's copy.

Gilt edges. Red endpapers and pastedowns. Red honeycomb-grain cloth. Both covers identically blocked in blind on the borders and on the corners. Two fillets are blocked on the borders. A thistle flower and two leaves are blocked on each corner. On the upper cover, the extended central vignette is blocked in gold, and in gold and in blind on the lower cover. It shows a spear and a billhook, blocked from tail to the head, together with a pattern of thistle stems, leaves and flowers, which form an oval shape. At the centre head, a coat of arms is blocked within a shield. It shows the arms of Scott (?). Quarterly, 1st and 4th, or; two stars and crescent, within a square, azure; 2nd and 3rd, or; on a bend azure, three mascles and a 'circle' shape; overall, an escutcheon, argent, charged with a hand, sinister. Crest, figure of Phoebe, holding sun and quarter moon, with motto: '| Reparabit Cornua Phoebe |' in gold above. At base of shield the motto: 'Watch Weel' is blocked in gold. Signed 'JL' in gold as separate letters at the base of the vignette. On the centre, a harp, a sword, a hunting horn and a tweed cloak are blocked as a group. This group is also blocked in gold on the lower cover. The spine is blocked in gold. From the head downwards, the decoration is: clover leaves and stems form an ogee arch; ivy-like leaves, stems and berries form a frame, inside which the words: '| Scott's | Poetical | Works |' are blocked in gold in gothic letters; more ivy-like leaves, stems and berries blocked in gold; thistle leaves and flowers are blocked in gold near the tail; signed 'JL' in gold as a monogram, within the roots at the plant at the tail.

403 Leighton, John

The Churchman's family magazine containing contributions by the clergy and distinguished literary men. With upwards of seventy illustrations by C. W. Cope, R.A.; J. E. Millais, A.R.A.; J. D. Watson; J. C. Horsley, A.R.A.; George Thomas; H. C. Selons; L. Huard; H. H. Armstead; F. R. Pickersgill, R.A.; T. Sulman; P. W. Justyne; H. S. Marks, and others. London: James Hogg and Sons, [1863–1866]. Harrild, Printer, London.
XX.052.4.

The University of Durham Library copy.

Vol. I. 1863. 636 p. Vol. II. 1864. 568 p. Vol. III. 1865. 576 p. Vol. IV. 1866. 572 p.

Each volume has red edges. Red endpapers and pastedowns. Blue honeycomb-grain cloth. All volumes have the same design blocked on both covers. All the lower covers are blocked in blind. The upper covers are blocked in gold. On each upper cover, there is a border pattern of 'leaves and spade' shapes. Then three fillets are blocked in gold on the borders. The design blocked within the borders shows an identical circle at the head and the tail. Each circle is made up of petals, with leaves and hatched crosses blocked between each petal. The two circles have two fillets blocked in gold on their borders, with repeating dots in blind. These fillets form a figure of eight, linking the top and bottom circle, and forming a circle on the centre. The central circle contains a trefoil, with two fillets on its borders. The title: 'The Churchman's Family Magazine' is

blocked in gold in gothic lettering. The capitals 'C', 'F' and 'M' are blocked in relief within rectangular gold lettering-pieces. At the base of the trefoil, a gold lettering-piece is blocked, with the words: 'Illustrated by Eminent Artists' blocked in relief inside. The spine is blocked in gold and relief. A single fillet is blocked in gold on the perimeter. From the head downwards, the decoration is: a rectangle formed by single fillets, with small decoration blocked inside; an arch at the head, with passion flowers and tendrils blocked left and right; the title: '| The | Churchman's | Family | Magazine | Volume I[–IV] |' blocked in gold in gothic lettering; the capital letters 'C', 'F', and 'M' are blocked in relief within rectangular gold lettering-pieces; a mandorla, with three fillets on its perimeter: one of gold only, one of gold. with dots blocked in relief, one of hatched gold, with small leaf decoration within blocked in relief; a gold lettering-piece is blocked on the centre of the mandorla, with the words: '[a cross] | Illustrated | by | Eminent | Artists |' blocked in relief; passion flowers and leaves in gold; signed 'JL' in gold as separate letters between two passion flower buds; a cartouche and two leaves, blocked in gold within a rectangular hatched gold lettering-piece, with a single fillet blocked on its border.

The British Museum de Beaumont Collection, has a copy of Volume I, Jan.–June 1863, with the same design.

de Beaumont, *RdeB1* no. 202. Goldman, *VIB* no. 202.

404 Leighton, John PLATE XXXIX

The Churchman's Family Magazine. Containing contributions by the clergy and distinguished literary men. [The title page for Volume I continues:] With upwards of seventy illustrations, by C. W. Cope, R.A.; J. E. Millais, A.R.A.; J. D. Watson; J. C. Horsley, A.R.A.; George Thomas; H. C. Selons; L. Huard; H. H. Armstead; F. R. Pickersgill, R.A.; T. Sulman; P. W. Justyne; H. S. Marks, and others. London: James Hogg and Sons, [1863–1873].

P.P.357.b.

The BL copy has fourteen bound volumes. Bound by the BM in the C19 [1/4 leather, marbled endpapers and pastedowns, edges of boards gauffered]. The paper covers have been bound in sequence for most volumes. Each part has several plates.

The volumes are:

Volume I. 636 p. 137 × 232 × 51 mm. Parts 1–6; Jan–June 1863. Orange paper covers. Printer: Harrild Printer London.

Volume II. 568 p. 137 × 230 × 50 mm. Parts 7–12; July–Dec 1863. Orange paper covers. Printer: as Vol. I.

Volume III. 576 p. 137 × 230 × 50 mm. Parts 13–18; Jan–June 1864. Orange paper covers. Parts 17 & 18 have the picture removed, and a list of contents inserted. (Leighton's signature is still at the bottom of the cover.) Printer: as Vol. I.

Volume IV. 570 p. 138 × 230 × 48 mm. Parts 19–24; July–Dec 1864. Orange paper covers. Upper cover format as for parts 17–18. Printer: as Vol. I.

Volume V. 572 p. 140 × 230 × 42 mm. Parts 25–30; Jan–June 1865. Orange paper covers. Upper cover format as for parts 17 &18. Printer: as Vol. I.

Volume VI. 572 p. 140 × 230 × 44 mm. Parts 31–36; July–Dec 1865. Ditto. Printer: as Vol. I.

Volume VII. 572, [30] p. 140 × 230 × 45 mm. Parts 37–42; Jan–June 1866. Ditto.

Volume VIII. 571 p. 139 × 230 × 40 mm. Parts 43–48; July–Dec 1866. Ditto.

Volume XVI. 572 p. 138 × 230 × 34 mm. Vol II, parts 1–6 (91–96); July–Dec 1870. Brown paper covers. Design reverts to the format of Parts 1–16. Published by W. Mackintosh. Printer: London: C.W. Bradley, Printer, 3, Russell-Court, Brydes-Street, Strand, W.C.

Volume XVII. 576 p. 137 × 230 × 37 mm. Parts 97–102; Jan–June 1871. Ditto.

Volume XVIII. 476 p. 136 × 228 × 29 mm. Parts 103–108; July–Dec 1871. Ditto.

Volume XVIII [i.e. XIX]. 576 p. 136 × 228 × 32 mm. Parts 109–114; Jan–June 1872. No paper covers bound in. Publisher: Office – 14, York Street, Covent Garden. Printer: London: C. W. Bradley, Printer, 3, Russell-Court, Brydes-Street, Strand, W.C.

Volume V [i.e. XX]. 576 p. 137 × 230 × 35 mm. Parts 115–120; July–Dec 1872. No paper covers bound in. Publisher: Office: – 24, Paternoster Row, London E.C.

Volume XX [i.e. XXI]. 336 p. 136 × 228 × 25 mm. Parts 121–124; Jan–April 1873. Blue paper covers for parts 121 and 124 bound in; the same design printed as for parts 1–16, without Leighton's signature. Publisher: W. Macintosh, 24, Paternoster Row.

Originally issued in monthly parts with paper covers. The majority of these are bound in sequence. The upper cover for each part has a design by Leighton. Printed at top left: 'No. 1[–124]'; at the top right: 'Price 1s.'. Four fillets on borders, with a repeating dots border between the middle two fillets. The design shows an arch, with ivy branches growing up its pillars, with leaves and flowers printed at the top left and right. Printed within the arch: '| The | Churchman's | Family Magazine |'. Beneath these words is a rural scene, with the following decoration: a church, foreground, to the left; a vicarage to the right, and horses grazing in a field in front of the vicarage; hills in the background; pond, bottom left; a boundary wall at the bottom. Printed on the wall: 'Illustrated | January [February, etc] 1863 |'. Underneath this: '| London: James Hogg & Sons. |' [for parts 1–48] is printed within a cartouche. Signed 'J. Leighton F.S.A.' at the centre tail.

This design, with only the substitution of the list of contents for parts 17–48 instead of the illustration, appears to have been used throughout the series. The verso of the upper cover and both recto and verso of the lower covers have advertisements.

King, *WHR* p. 324.

405 Leighton, John FIG. 53

Golden words. The rich and precious jewel of God's Holy Word. Prayer. The Lord's Supper. Christ Mystical. The Sabbath. Public Worship. The Art of Hearing. Walking with God. Faith. Repentance. And passages on miscellaneous subjects. Being selections from the writings of Dean Addison, Bishop Babington. Dr. Barrow, Dr. Bates. Thomas Bacon, John Bradford, Bishop Coverdale, Ralph Cudworth, Edward Dering, Dr. Donne, Anthony Farindon, Sir Matthew Hale, Bishop Hall, Richard Hooker, Bishop Hooper, Bishop Hopkins, Roger Hutchinson, Bishop Jewell, Archbishop Leighton, Dr. Lightfoot, Bishop Patrick, Bishop Pearson, Archbishop Sandys, Henry Smith, John Smith, Dr. South, Bishop Jeremy Taylor, William Tyndale, Henry Vaughan, John Wycliff, Bishop Wilkins, and George Wither . . . Oxford and London: John Henry and James Parker. Birmingham: Henry Wright, New Street, 1863. [Birmingham]: Printed by Josiah Allen, jun., 9 & 10 Livery Street. xlix, 356 p.

128 × 197 × 40 mm. 4408.ee.20.

Bolts uncut. Bevelled boards. Grey endpapers and pastedowns. Brown pebble-grain cloth. Both covers blocked identically in blind. The upper cover has additional decoration in gold. A single fillet is blocked in blind on the borders. On each corner, a fleur-de-lis is blocked in blind. The inner rectangle has a circle blocked in blind on each corner, each circle with five stars blocked in gold within it. On the inner border, there is a pediment, formed by fillets, blocked on the centre sides, on the centre and centre tail. The inner rectangle has two fillets blocked in blind on its borders, one of which has repeating stars within it blocked in relief. The other fillet is blocked in blind on the inner borders. On the upper cover, there are additional decorative features blocked in gold: 1. fleurs-de-lis on the outer corners of the inner rectangle; 2. small decoration in gold within the 'pediments'; 3. a monument to Bishop Hooper blocked in gold on the centre; 4. within the base of the monument, the words: '| Bishop Hooper | Protestant Matyr MDLV |' are blocked in relief; 5. above and below the monument, the title words: '| Golden | Words. |' are blocked in gold within rectangles, each formed by a single fillet blocked in blind. Signed 'JL' in gold as separate letters below the monument. The spine is blocked in gold and in blind. From the head downwards, the decoration is: fleurs-de-lis blocked in blind; stars blocked in relief within a circle bordered by a fillet blocked in blind; a pediment and triangular small decoration beneath it, blocked in gold; [these three pieces of decoration are repeated, blocked near the tail of the spine]; the title: '| Golden | Words |' blocked in gold within three overlapping triangles, which have stars blocked within; a small leaf; the words: '| J. H. & J. Parker |' are blocked in gold at the tail, within a rectangle formed by two fillets blocked in blind.

FIG. 53

406 Leighton, John

A Welcome: original contributions in poetry and prose. London: Emily Faithfull, Printer and Publisher in Ordinary to Her Majesty, Princes Street, Hanover Square, and 83A Farringdon Street, 1863. [London]: Emily Faithfull, Printer in Ordinary to Her Majesty, Victoria Press, 83A Farringdon Street, E.C. vi, 291 p.

140 × 205 × 30 mm. 12273.c.8.

The monogram of the Victoria Press is printed on the title page. In the publisher's titles at the end of BL11649.g.23. this work is stated to be: 'On Rose-tinted Paper, in Green Cloth, 10s 6d. On Rose-tinted Paper, in White Calf, £1 1s.'

Gilt edges. Bevelled boards. Pink endpapers and pastedowns. Binder's ticket on lower pastedown: '| Bound by | Westley's & Co. | London. |' Green pebble-grain cloth. Both covers blocked identically in gold and in blind. Two fillets are blocked in blind on the borders. Inside this, a wide horizontal hatch fillet is blocked in gold. This is followed by a single thin fillet blocked in gold. At the centre is blocked a single crown, in gold. The spine is blocked in gold and in blind. Four fillets are blocked in blind at the head and at the tail. Beneath the head, the Prince of Wales' feathers are blocked in gold. The motto: '| Ich dien |' is blocked in relief within a scroll-shaped gold lettering piece. Beneath this, the title words: '| A Welcome | [rule] | March | 1863. |' are blocked in gold inside a panel formed by a single gold fillet. Underneath the title, a shield is

blocked in gold: argent, three lions, azure; hearts, gules. Beneath the shield, the motto: '| Folkets Kiaeligheds. min stryke. |' is blocked in relief within a semi-circular gold lettering piece. Signed 'JL' in gold as separate letters beneath the motto. The word: '| Faithfull |' is blocked in gold near the tail.

Dry, *JL* no. 462

407 Leighton, John

Adams, Henry Gardiner. *Our feathered families: a popular and poetical description of the birds of song and their congeners which are found in Britain. With practical hints for the breeding, rearing, and general management of song birds in confinement. With upwards of Fifty Illustrations by Wm. Harvey, Luke Clennel, and W. S. Coleman.* London: James Hogg and Sons, [1863]. London: Printed by Spottiswoode and Co. New-Street Square. 301 p., 1 plate. With two pages of publisher's titles bound at the end.
115 × 175 × 25 mm. 7284.a.9.

Hogg's 'Illustrated books for young readers', no. 6. Two other books in the same series are at this shelfmark. No. 7 is 'Birds of prey'. Green honeycomb-grain. 'Bound by Burn 37 & 38 Kirby St.'. No. 10 is 'Game and water birds', which has the printed list for the series. Red honeycomb-grain cloth. Both volumes also printed by Spottiswoode. These two volumes have the same blocking for the series on the lower half of their spines as for no. 6.

The plate is signed: 'Keyl' [i.e. F. W. Keyl] and 'E. Evans'.

Text sewn on two sawn-in cords. Beige endpapers and pastedowns. Binder's ticket on lower pastedown: '| Bound by | Burn | 37 & 38 | Kirby St. |' Green honeycomb-grain cloth. Both covers blocked identically on the borders and on the corners, in blind on the lower, and in gold on the upper. Two fillets are blocked on the borders, the inner shaped as joined branches. A single bird feather is blocked on each corner. The upper cover is blocked in gold. It shows a bird perched on a thistle plant, picking seeds out of the thistle heads. The words: '| Our Feathered Families (blocked in a semi-circle) | the | Birds | of Song |' are blocked in gold in rustic lettering above the centre. Some of the letters end in tendrils. The words: '| By H. G. Adams. |' are blocked below the centre in gold in rustic lettering. The upper half of the spine is missing. The lower half of the spine has a design for the series. The decoration downwards is: the words: '| Illustrated | books |' blocked in relief within ribbon-shaped gold lettering-pieces; the words: '| For young readers |' are blocked in relief within a circular gold lettering-piece; a circular fillet, shaped as a rope has the words: '| Books | with a | meaning |' blocked in gold within the circle; the price '3/6' is blocked in relief with a medallion gold lettering-piece, which has two fillets on its border; small decoration is blocked on either side of this medallion; two fillets are blocked at the tail in gold.

Dry, *JL* nos. 436 & 437.

408 Leighton, John

FIG. 54

Aleph *pseud.* [i.e. William Harvey, *of Islington.*] *London scenes and London people: anecdotes, reminiscences, and sketches of places, personages, events customs and curiosities of London city, past and present.* London: W. H. Collingridge, City Press, Aldersgate Street, 1863. London: W.H. Collingridge, City Press, Aldersgate Street, E.C. xi, 365 p., 17 plates With an eighteen page list of subscribers bound at the end.
135 × 203 × 35 mm. 10349.d.14.

With carte-de-visite photographs of George and Eliza Cruikshank inserted at the front. Written on the verso of the front endpaper: '| This book | is presented to | "The British Museum" | in memory of | George Cruikshank, Artist, by his Widow | Eliza Cruikshank | December 23rd 1887 | her 80th Birthday |' [See also BL copy C.109.b.4., a WH Rogers design on Goldsmith, The Vicar of Wakefield. Presentation copy from Mrs E Cruikshank.]

In the publisher's advertisements bound at the end of BL 10348.cc.8., The Old City . . ., this work is advertised as: 'Antique cloth, price 7s. 6d., illustrated by numerous superior Wood Engravings, . . .'

Bevelled boards. Red dyed edges. Dark red endpapers and pastedowns. Dark red pebble-grain cloth. Both covers identically blocked in blind with a single blind fillet blocked on the borders, and patterns blocked on the borders and on the sides, into which are set octagons blocked in relief. The upper cover has a vignette, blocked in gold, set in a square central panel, featuring a watchman holding a wooden staff and a lamp, and a soldier, in Elizabethan breastplate armour, hosiery,

FIG. 54

thigh-length boots, with his hands on the butt of his sword, which has its point in the ground. These two figures support the shield of the Corporation of London, with motto 'Domine dirige nos', blocked underneath in relief inside a gold lettering-piece shaped as a pennant. The title: '| London Scenes | and | London People |' is blocked in gold above and below the centre-piece. The spine is fully blocked in gold. From the head downwards, the decoration is: the title: '| London | Scenes | and | London | People |' blocked within a hanging sign, which is formed by two gold fillets, one of which has repeating dots blocked in relief within it; a flag of the City of London hanging from a pole; beneath the flag, the pole is criss-crossed by a pennant-shaped gold lettering-piece, in which the words: '| London | City | past | & | present |' are blocked in relief; signed 'JL' in relief, as separate letters at the base of the pole; the word 'Collingridge' is blocked in gold within a rectangle formed by a single gold fillet; a gold fillet is blocked at the tail. [The 'JL' signature is very faded.]

Dry, *JL* no. 438.

409 Leighton, John

Ballantyne, Robert Michael. *The wild man of the West. A Tale of the Rocky Mountains. With illustrations by Zwecker.* London: Routledge, Warne & Routledge, Farringdon Street; New York: 56, Walker Street, 1863. Cox and Wyman, Printers, Great Queen Street, London. viii, 408 p., 8 plates.
110 × 174 × 40 mm. 12808.bb.26.

The plates are signed: 'J B Zwecker' and Dalziel'.

Text sewn on two sawn-in cords. Beige endpapers and pastedowns. Rust-red honeycomb-grain cloth. Both covers blocked identically in blind on the borders. Three fillets are blocked on the borders. On the inner corners, triangles, formed by two fillets blocked in blind, have leaf decoration blocked within in relief. There is an inner border pattern of stems and leaves. The upper cover central vignette is blocked in gold. It shows a man holding a whip in his right, upraised, hand. He is astride a bison. The title: '| The | wild man | of the | West. |' is blocked in gold in rustic lettering on either side of the man, and below the bison. A fillet is blocked in gold, and the word: '| Illustrated |' is blocked in gold below it. Signed 'JL' in relief within a small leaf-shaped gold lettering-piece at the base of the vignette. The spine is blocked in gold. From the head downwards, the decoration is: an arched panel, blocked in gold, is formed by a single fillet; a wolf's head is blocked inside this, together with the words: '| The | wild man | of the | West | [rule] | Ballantyne |' – all in gold; a group of objects: two crossed muskets, a game bird, a crocodile; plants are blocked near the tail; the word: '| Illustrated |' is blocked in gold within a rectangle formed by a single branch-like fillet at the tail.

Dry, *JL* no. 439.

410 Leighton, John

Bennett, Charles Henry. *London people: sketched from life.* London: Smith, Elder, and Co., 65, Cornhill, 1863. London: Printed by Smith, Elder and Co., Little Green Arbour Court, Old Bailey, E.C. 143 p.
165 × 215 × 25 mm. 12355.cc.4.

Gilt edges. Bevelled boards. Original yellow endpaper bound at the front. Two fillets are blocked on each cover, on the lower cover in blind, and on the upper cover in gold. The upper cover has a central vignette, blocked in gold. It features a fox, holding a mask in its left hand, and a stick in its right hand. The fox is wearing slippers. Pairs of masks are blocked on either side of the fox. Above and below the fox are the title and author words: '| London people | by | Charles Bennett. |' blocked in gold Signed 'JL' in relief as separate letters, within a small leaf blocked in gold at the base of the vignette. The spine is blocked in gold and in relief. Three fillets are blocked in gold at the head and at the tail. A lamp-post is blocked in gold up the spine. At the head, the lamp, with a crown on top, is blocked in gold. From the ladder bar, a gold lettering-piece, shaped as a pennant, is hung, with the words: '| London | people. |' blocked in relief inside. Near the base of the lamp-post, the words: '| Sketched | from | life |' are blocked in relief within a pennant-shaped gold lettering-piece, which is wrapped around the post. The imprint: '| London: | Smith | Elder & Co. |' is blocked in gold at the tail, within a rectangle formed by two fillets.

Dry, *JL* no. 440 Oldfield, *BC* no. 73.

411 Leighton, John

Bethell, Augusta, afterwards, Parker, Hon. Augusta. *Maud Latimer: A Tale for Young People. With four illustrations.* London: Smith, Elder and Co., 65, Cornhill, 1863. London: Printed by Smith, Elder and Co., 15 ½, Old Bailey, E.C. [4], 202 p., 4 plates. With two pages of publisher's titles bound at the end.
117 × 185 × 22 mm. 12808.aaa.21.

The plates are signed: 'Swain Sc.'

Light yellow endpapers and pastedowns. Green dot and ribbon diagonal-grain cloth. Both covers blocked identically in blind on the borders and on the corners. Two fillets are blocked on the borders, the outer thick, the inner thin. On each corner, curling leaves and stems are blocked forming circles, with small leaves blocked in relief inside. The upper cover central vignette is blocked in gold. Two small butterflies are blocked at the top in gold. The title: '| Maud Latimer |' is blocked in gold in a semicircle, with tendrils attached to the capitals 'M' and 'R'. Two girls, mounted on ponies, are shaking hands. The title: '| A tale | for | young people |' is blocked in gold. Signed 'JL' in gold as separate letters at the base of the vignette. The spine is blocked in gold. A single fillet is blocked in gold on the perimeter. The contents of the design are shaped in the design of a bookcase. From the head downwards, the decoration is: a diamond-pattern glass front to the book case; a split pediment with a vase in the gap; the title: '| Maud | Latimer |' blocked in gold

within a 'panel' formed by the base of the pediment and of a bookshelf; a gold lettering-piece shows books upright on the shelf, with all the spine decoration for the books blocked in relief; the words: 'A tale' are blocked in relief within the cover, blocked as a gold lettering-piece, of a book laid on top of the shelf of books; the words: '| For the | young |' are blocked in relief on the spines of the books on the shelf; a hand holds a book-shaped gold lettering-piece between more upright books on a shelf below; the words: '| By | the Hon | Augusta | Bethell |' in relief within the front cover of the book held upright; an urn with two handles stands upon a pile of books; the words: '| London | Smith Elder | & Co. |' are blocked in gold at the tail. (Stylistically a JL spine design – the label probably obscures the signature.)

412 Leighton, John

Beverley, May. *Romantic passages in English history. With Illustrations by Robert Barnes.* London: James Hogg and Sons, [1863]. Harrild, Printer, London. 316 p., 6 plates. With four pages of publisher's titles bound at the end.
115 × 175 × 30 mm. 9504.b.7.

Hogg's 'Illustrated books for young readers'. no. 8.

Beige endpapers and pastedowns. Binder's ticket on lower pastedown: '| Bound | by | Burn | 37 & 38 | Kirby St. |' Green honeycomb-grain cloth. Both covers blocked identically on the borders and on the corners, in blind on the lower and in gold on the upper. Two fillets are blocked on the borders, the inner of which is branch-shaped, crossing on the corners. Two oak leaves and three clusters of acorns are blocked on each corner. The upper cover vignette is blocked in gold. It shows a royal coat of arms; the lion and unicorn support the central medallion gold lettering-piece, with the words: '| Romantic | passages | in | English | history |' blocked inside in relief. The words: 'By May Beverley' are blocked in relief within a rectangular gold lettering-piece, with a single fillet blocked in gold on its borders. Signed 'JL' in gold as separate letters at the base of the vignette. The spine is blocked in gold and in relief. From the head downwards, the decoration is: two fillets blocked in gold; the words: '| Romantic | passages | in | English | History | By | May | Beverley |' blocked in relief within seven rectangular gold lettering-pieces, each with a single gold fillet on its borders; rose and thistle plants are blocked between these seven lettering-pieces, with two clover leaves at their base; signed 'JL' in gold as separate letters between the clover leaves; [the lower half of the spine has a design for the series] the words: '| Illustrated | books |' are blocked in relief within a ribbon-shaped gold lettering-piece; the words: '| For young readers' are blocked in relief within a circular gold lettering-piece; a circular fillet, shaped as a rope has the words: '| Books | with a | meaning |' blocked in gold within the circle; the price '3/6' is blocked in relief with a medallion gold lettering-piece, which has two fillets on its border; small decoration is blocked in gold on either side of this medallion; two fillets are blocked at the tail in gold.

Dry, *JL* no. 441.

413 Leighton, John

Broderip, Frances Freeling. *My Grandmother's budget of stories and songs. With illustrations by her brother, Thomas Hood.* London: Griffith and Farran, Successors to Newbery and Harris, Corner of St. Paul's Churchyard, 1863. London: Printed by Wertheimer and Co., Circus Place, Finsbury Circus. [3], 200 p., 6 plates. With thirty-two pages of publisher's titles bound at the end.
127 × 176 × 20 mm. 12808.bb.29.

On page three of the publisher's titles at the end, the details for this work are: 'Price 3s. 6d. cloth; 4s. 6d. coloured, gilt edges.' The plates are hand-coloured and signed with Hood's monogram 'TH'; also signed 'C.A Ferrier Sc.'

Text sewn on three sawn-in cords. Gilt edges. Light yellow endpapers and pastedowns. Binder's ticket on lower pastedown: '| Bound by | Bone & Son, | 76, Fleet Street, | London. |' Purple morocco horizontal-grain cloth. Both covers identically blocked in blind on the borders and on the corners. Two fillets are blocked on the borders. A curling leaf and stem pattern is blocked on the corners, with some of the stems and leaves blocked in relief. On the upper cover, the central vignette is blocked in gold. It shows a dining room armchair, with curved arms and legs, a high back, and two birds on top of the back. A walking stick, blocked in gold, is propped against the chair. On the seat of the chair, a book with two clasps and spectacles is blocked in gold. A bag of money hangs from a cord looped over the left arm of the chair. A larger book, with five spine panels, is propped against the right hand leg of the chair. A footstool is blocked underneath the middle of the chair. A ball of wool, with two knitting needles in it, is blocked by the left hand side of the chair. A length of the wool is curled around the chair leg and the footstool. Signed 'JL' in gold as a monogram at the base of the vignette. The title: '| Grandmother's | Budget |' is blocked in gold to the left of the chair; to the right of the chair, the words: '| of Stories | & Songs |' are blocked in gold. The spine is blocked in gold and in relief. Three fillets are blocked at the head and at the tail, the middle fillet having straps blocked in relief as 'figures of eight'. The title: '| My | Grand- | Mother's | Budget | of | Stories | & | Songs. |' is blocked in gold; underneath this, a group of small leaves and flowers is blocked in gold.

Dry, *JL* no. 443.

414 Leighton, John

Burrow, John Holme. *Adventures of Alfan; or, the magic amulet. With Eight Illustrations by J. D. Watson.* London: Smith, Elder & Co., 65 Cornhill, 1863. Edinburgh: Printed by Ballantyne and Company, Paul's Work. viii, 393 p., 8 plates.
128 × 198 × 35 mm. 12808.bbb.15.

The plates are signed 'JDW' and 'Dalziel'.

Text sewn on three sawn-in cords. Some of the bolts are uncut. Grey endpapers and pastedowns. Red pebble-grain cloth. Both covers identically blocked in blind on the borders

and on the corners. Three fillets are blocked on the borders. Sprigs of ivy stems, leaves and berries are blocked on each corner. The upper cover vignette is blocked in gold and in relief. It shows Alfan in oriental dress, with a turban and a feather in it. He is mounted on his horse, which is richly caparisoned. At the head of the vignette, a quarter moon is blocked, and the title words: '| The | adventures | of Alfan |' are blocked in relief within four gold lettering-pieces – three are rectangular, with the word: 'of' blocked within a diamond-shaped gold lettering-piece. Below Alfan and the horse, the words: '| or | the magic | amulet. |' are blocked in relief within a bowl-shaped vertical hatch gold lettering-piece. On either side of Alfan, a pattern of thin curling stems and small vertical hatch gold leaves is blocked, which join the upper and lower portions of the vignette. The spine is blocked in gold and in relief. From the head downwards, the decoration is: oriental shapes, some blocked in horizontal hatch gold; a rectangular panel is formed by a single fillet; within the panel, the title: '| The | adventures | of | Alfan. |' blocked in gold; the word: 'or' is blocked in relief within a hatched gold five-point star; the word: 'the' is blocked in gold; the words: 'magic amulet' are blocked in relief within a quarter moon, which is blocked in gold; more oriental shapes, some blocked in horizontal hatch gold; the words: '| By | John Holme | Burrow | M A |' are blocked in relief within a gold lettering-piece with arrow-head shapes at top and bottom. [Tail of spine missing.]

Dry, *JL* no. 445.

415 Leighton, John PLATE XL

Davenport, Emma Anne Georgina. *Fickle Flora and her seaside friends. Illustrated by John Absolon.* London: Griffith & Farran, Successors to Newbery and Harris Corner of St. Paul's Churchyard, 1863. Edinburgh: Printed by R. & R. Clark. iv, 164 p., 4 plates. With thirty two pages of publisher's advertisements bound at the end.

127 × 175 × 20 mm. 12808.b.30.

In the publisher's titles at the end, this work is advertised as: 'Super royal 16mo. price 3s. 6d. cloth; 4s 6d. coloured, gilt edges.' The plates are hand-coloured.

Gilt edges. Light yellow endpapers and pastedowns. Binder's ticket on lower pastedown: '| Bound by | Bone and Son, | [rule] | 76 Fleet Street, | London. |'. Red dot and line vertical-grain cloth. Both covers are blocked in blind identically, on the borders and on the corners. A single fillet is blocked in blind on the borders. Inside this, single fillets form rectangles on the sides, the head and on the tail, with four-leaf decoration blocked on each corner in relief. The inner corners have curling stem decoration blocked in relief. The upper cover has a central vignette blocked in gold, featuring a straw hatted teenage girl (Flora?), a basket on her right arm, her right hand holding a fishing net, her left hand holding a shell. The title: '| Fickle | Flora | and her | sea-side | friends |' is blocked in gold, in fanciful rustic letters, with tendrils. Signed 'JL' in gold as separate letters within seaweed at the base of vignette. The spine is blocked in gold and blind and in relief. Two fillets are blocked in blind at the head and at the tail, with repeating triangles blocked in relief. From the head downwards, the decoration is: a starfish; the title: '| Fickle | Flora | & Her | Sea-side | Friends |' blocked in gold in rustic letters; a group of sea plants and seaweed is blocked in gold underneath the title.

King, *JL* p. 238.

416 Leighton, John

E., A.L.O. *pseud.* [i.e.Tucker, Charlotte M.] *The Crown of Success; or, four heads to furnish. A Tale.* London: T. Nelson & Sons, Paternoster Row; Edinburgh and New York, 1863. 246 p., 4 plates.

105 × 170 × 24 mm. 12806.bb.44.

The plates are signed 'K.H.' [i.e.Keeley Halswelle?]

Yellow endpapers and pastedowns. Blue morocco horizontal-grain cloth. Both covers identically blocked in blind on the borders and on the corners. Three fillets are blocked on the borders. Horse chestnut leaves and fruit are blocked on the corners, in relief. The upper cover has a central vignette blocked in gold. It shows a gaol doorway, with a barred door. The figure of a small man stands by the bars. He wears robes and a crown in the shape of a capital 'A'. In his left hand, he carries a key; his right hand is outstretched through the bars of the door. The word: 'The' is blocked in gold above the door arch. Within the arch (which is a gold lettering-piece), the words: ' "The Crown of Success" reading and writing' are blocked in relief. Between the bars of the door, the words: 'or four heads to furnish' are blocked in gold. Within the base (which is a hatched gold lettering-piece), the words: 'By A.L.O.E.' are blocked in relief. Signed JL' in relief as single letters to the left and the right of the door base. The spine is blocked in gold. Two fillets are blocked on the perimeter. From the head downwards, the decoration is: a crown in gold; the word: 'MERIT', blocked in relief within the crown; then the title words: '| The | Crown | of | Success | or | four | heads | to | furnish. |'; from the tail upwards, the 'ladder of learning' is blocked in gold; a boy is climbing its rungs, holding a piece of paper (with scroll ends), which is a gold lettering-piece; the words: 'or four heads to furnish' are blocked in relief within the paper; the words: 'by A.L.O.E.' are blocked in gold beneath this; a paint pot and brush are at the bottom of the ladder; signed 'JL' in relief on the pot; at the tail, the words: 'T. Nelson & Sons' are blocked in gold, within a rectangle formed by a single gold fillet.

The Renier Collection copy has the same design blocked on green bead-grain cloth.

Dry, *JL* no. 447.

417 Leighton, John FIG. 55

Edwards, Matilda Barbara Betham. *Scenes and stories of the Rhine. With illustrations by F. W. Keyl.* London: Griffith and Farran, Successors to Newbery and Harris, Corner of St Paul's Churchyard, 1863. London: Savill and Edwards, Printers,

FIG. 55

Chandos Street, Covent Garden. viii, 214 p., 4 plates. With 32 pages of publisher's titles bound at the end.
130 × 177 × 22 mm. 12808.bb.38.

The plates are hand coloured. Printed in the publisher's titles, page 3: 'Super royal 16mo. price 3s 6d. cloth; 4s. 6d. coloured, gilt edges.'

Gilt edges. Original light yellow upper endpaper bound at the front. Red dot-and-line horizontal-grain cloth. Both covers are blocked identically on the borders and corners in blind. A fillet is blocked on the borders and leaf and scroll stem decoration in relief on the corners. The upper cover has a central vignette blocked in gold. It shows, from the top: a crown, the title words: '| Scenes & stories |', a shield, or, with an eagle, murrey, blocked inside in relief. In the centre is blocked a paddle steamer with a jib at the front and a flag at the rear. The title word 'of' is blocked in relief on the paddle wheel housing. The steamer is surrounded to the left and to the right by vine leaves, branches, and it is set against a background of Rhineland scenery, with a castle on a hilltop. The words: '| The Rhine | By | M. Betham | Edwards. |' are blocked in gold below the steamer. At the base, a single vine leaf, blocked in gold, contains the signature 'JL', blocked in relief as separate letters.

Dry, *JL* no. 448.

418 Leighton, John

Fyfe, J. Hamilton. *British enterprise beyond the seas; or, The Planting of Our Colonies.* London: T. Nelson & Sons, Paternoster Row; Edinburgh and New York, 1863. 263 p., 4 plates.
117 × 180 × 28 mm. 10026.cc.14.

Gilt edges. Yellow endpapers and pastedowns. Blue pebble-grain cloth. The lower cover is blocked in blind, and in relief. On the borders are: 1. Two fillets are blocked in the borders, one thick, one thin; 2. a decorated border, showing a repeating pattern of curling stems and leaves; 3. two fillets blocked in blind. The inner rectangle has leaf and stem patterns blocked in relief on each corner. The upper cover is blocked in gold. Three thin fillets are blocked on the borders. On each corner, a medallion is blocked. Each is surrounded by fillets and a decorated border. Within each medallion, the following are blocked: left-hand top – 'Europe' and a horse; right-hand top – 'Asia' and an elephant; left-hand bottom – 'Africa' and a camel; right-hand bottom – 'America' and a stag. On the sides, head and tail, fillets join the medallions. A trident is blocked near the head. Below this, the title: '| British enterprise | beyond | the seas |' is blocked above the centre; below the centre, the title: '| or the | planting of | our colonies |' is blocked. A royal coat of arms is blocked on the centre. Around the centre, thin stems and leaves are blocked in gold. Three 'wave lines' are blocked in relief across the cover from head to tail as a background. Signed 'JL' in gold as a monogram in a loop where the stems join at the base. The spine is blocked in gold and in relief. A gold fillet is blocked around the perimeter. A fillet is blocked at the head and at the tail. The letters 'V R' are blocked in hatch gold at the head, on either side of an arch. Below the arch, a lion is blocked standing on a crown. Beneath this, a gold lettering-piece is blocked, shaped as a shield. The words: '| British | enterprise | beyond the | seas |' are blocked in relief within the shield. Underneath this, a medallion gold lettering-piece is blocked, and the words: '| By | J H | Fyfe |' are blocked in relief within it. A rose bush is blocked from the base upwards to meet the medallion. Seven rectangular gold lettering pieces are blocked across the rose bush. In each rectangle are blocked the names of colonies in relief: '| Australias | Indies | Canadas | Cape of Good Hope | New Zealand | New Foundland | [seventh obscured by the label] |'. A rectangle formed by three gold fillets is blocked at the tail.

419 Leighton, John

Goodrich, Samuel Griswold. *The story of Peter Parley's own life. From the personal narrative of the late Samuel Goodrich, ('Peter Parley.') Edited by his friend and admirer, Frank Freeman. With illustrations.* London: Sampson Low, Son & Co., 47 Ludgate Hill, 1863. London: Strangeways and Walden, Printers, 28 Castle St. Leicester Sq. xvi, 304 p., 6 plates. With sixteen pages of publisher's titles bound at the end.
120 × 175 × 25 mm. 10881.aa.12.

Text sewn on two sawn-in cords. Cream endpapers and pastedowns. Purple wave vertical-grain cloth. Both covers blocked identically on the borders, with a repeating decorative leaf pattern blocked in relief between two fillets blocked in blind. On the lower cover, a single large fleur-de-lis is blocked on the centre. On the upper cover, there is a central roundel blocked in gold. The title words '| Peter Parleys | own life. |' are blocked in rustic lettering in gold at the head and tail of the roundel. The perimeter of the roundel resembles a rope. Inside the roundel, a sailor stands on a quay, waving at a rowing boat on the sea, which has four occupants, two rowing. Signed 'JL' in gold as separate letters at the base of the vignette. On the spine, the head has the title: '| Peter | Parley's | Own | Life |' blocked in rustic lettering. Underneath this is a medallion with a coat of arms of the United States, and the motto: 'E. pluribus unum' blocked underneath in relief within a curving gold lettering-piece. Below this, are blocked the words: '| Delight | Benedict | School |', with, beneath, a picture of a schoolboy, satchel over shoulder, standing on tiptoe on a box – all in gold. The boy's right arm is outstretched to pull a bell. Signed 'JL' in relief as separate letters on the box. The imprint: '| London | Low. Son & Co |' is blocked in relief within a rectangular gold lettering-piece, with a single gold fillet blocked on its borders. Double gold fillets are blocked above and below the rectangle.

Dry, *JL* no. 449.

420 Leighton, John

Grant, Alexander Henley. *Half-hours with our sacred poets. Edited with biographical sketches, By Alexander H. Grant, M.A. With illustrations by H. S. Marks.* London: James Hogg and Sons, [1863]. Harrild, Printer, London. 374 p., 6 plates. With ten pages of publisher's titles bound at the end.
116 × 173 × 34 mm. 11602.bb.10.

The plates are signed 'HSM' and 'W. Thomas Sc.'

[No original endpapers or pastedowns.] Binder's ticket on lower pastedown: '| Bound by | Burn | 37 & 38 | Kirby St. |' Red honeycomb-grain cloth. Both covers identically blocked on the borders, in blind on the lower, in gold on the upper. On the upper cover, a gold fillet is blocked on the borders, with a border of repeating five-point stars, blocked in hatch gold. Larger five-point stars are blocked on each corner in gold. The upper cover has a central vignette blocked in gold. It shows a lyre, which is formed by two winged angels rising from the base. The title: '| Half hours |' is blocked in gold in a semi-circle just above the angels' heads; the words: '| With | our | sacred | poets. |' are blocked in gold between and over the strings of the lyre. The words: '| By. | A. H. | Grant | M.A. |' are blocked in relief within the gold plinth at the base of the lyre. The spine is blocked in gold. From the head downwards, the decoration is: two fillets, blocked in gold; a star; a panel formed by a curling fillet; the title: '| Half hours | with | our | sacred | poets. |' blocked in gold within the panel; an hour-glass; the words: '| by A. H. Grant M.A. |' are blocked in relief within a rectangular gold lettering-piece, with a single gold fillet blocked on its borders; hatch gold leaves; signed 'JL' in relief as a monogram, within a small 'tear-drop' gold lettering-piece; the word: '| Illustrated |' is blocked in gold near the tail; two gold fillets blocked in gold at the tail.

Dry, *JL* no. 450.

421 Leighton, John

PLATE XLI

Grant, Henry. *Mariquita.* [Shield with monogram of Emily Faithfull & Co, and the motto: 'Non nobis solum'.] London: Emily Faithfull, Printer and Publisher in Ordinary to Her Majesty, Victoria Press, Princes Street, Hanover Square, and 83A, Farringdon Street, 1863. London: Emily Faithfull, Printer and Publisher in Ordinary to Her Majesty, Victoria Press, 83A Farringdon Street, E.C. xii, 302 p., 1 plate. With two pages of publisher's titles bound at the end.
143 × 228 × 27 mm. 11649.g.23.

The plate is a photograph of a drawing [of Mariquita?] pasted onto the verso of the half-title page, and signed on the recto: 'John Beattie, Clifton.'

The text is sewn on two sawn-in cords. Some of the bolts are uncut. Light yellow endpapers and pastedowns. Binder's ticket on lower pastedown: '| Bound by | Westley's | & Co. | London. |' Green morocco horizontal-grain cloth. Both covers blocked identically, in blind on the lower, in gold and in blind on the upper. Four fillets are blocked on the borders: a single wide fillet in blind, then a hatch fillet, blocked between two thin fillets – all three in gold on the upper cover. Bulrushes rise from a pond at the base up the sides to arch at the centre head. Lilies and leaves are blocked in the pond at the base. The word: '| Mariquita |' is blocked on the centre in gold, in horizontal hatch gothic letters. Signed 'JL' in gold as separate letters at the base. The spine is blocked in gold and in blind. Five fillets are blocked at the head and at the tail, one in blind; then vertical hatch blocked between two thin fillets – all three in gold; one fillet in blind. The word: '| Mariquita |' is blocked in gold, in gothic letters near the head.

Dry, *JL* no. 451.

422 Leighton, John

Grant, James. *Dick Rodney; or, the adventures of an Eton boy. Illustrated by Keeley Halswelle.* London: Routledge, Warne and Routledge, Farringdon Street. New York: 56, Walker Street, 1863. London: Savill and Edwards, Printers, Chandos Street, Covent Garden. vii, 436 p., 8 plates. With four pages of publisher's titles bound at the end.
108 × 172 × 38 mm. 12806.bb.34.

The plates are signed: 'K. Halswelle' and 'Dalziel'.

[No original endpapers or pastedowns.] Blue rib vertical-grain cloth. Both covers blocked identically in blind on the borders and on the corners. Two fillets are blocked in blind on the borders. 'Leaf and petal' decoration is blocked in relief within a single circle blocked on each corner. More leaf decoration is

blocked in relief on the sides, the head and the tail. The central frame is formed as an oval by joined semi-circular fillets, blocked in blind. The upper cover central vignette is blocked in gold. It shows a sailor climbing a ship's rigging. A rope and pulley winds down from above him, to his left, then across and below him. The words: '| Dick | Rodney |' and 'By | James | Grant |' are blocked in gold on either side of the sailor. Signed 'JL' in gold as a monogram at the base of the vignette. The spine is blocked in gold and in relief. A single fillet is blocked in gold on the perimeter, forming a semi-circular arch at the head. From the head downwards, the decoration is: a weather vane; a gold lettering-piece, with cord and tassels on its borders, has the title: '| Dick | Rodney | or the | adventures | of an | Eton | boy. |' blocked in relief within it; the word '| Grant |' is blocked in relief within a rectangular gold lettering-piece; then the head and shoulders of a sailing officer; a boy, seated on a chair, holding a model boat in his left hand; a fillet in gold; the word '| Illustrated |' is blocked in gold within a rectangle formed by a single gold fillet; a fillet is blocked in gold at the tail.

Dry, *JL* no. 452.

423 Leighton, John PLATE XLII

Hood, Thomas. *The loves of Tom Tucker and Little Bo-Peep. A rhyming rigmarole. Written and illustrated by Thomas Hood.* London: Griffith and Farran, Successors to Newbery and Harris, Corner of St. Paul's Churchyard, 1863. London: Printed by J. Wertheimer and Co. Circus Place, Finsbury Circus. 33 p.

191 × 250 × 9 mm. 12806.h.40.

The illustrations are hand coloured.

Text sewn on three sawn-in cords. White paper over boards, with a red quarter cloth spine with morocco horizontal-grain. The lower cover has a list of Griffith and Farran titles. The upper cover has five fillets printed on the borders: two are in black, one thick fillet in blue, and then two more in black. Sheeps' heads are printed on each corner within a pointed circle, which has black and green fillets. The remainder of the cover has a yellow dye. There are two medallions on the centre. Each is in blue, and is formed by a circular 'branch', with convolvulus flowers, leaves and tendrils on the upper portion. The head of 'Tom.' [Tucker] is on the left; the head of 'Bo!' [Peep] is on the right. Each is printed within the medallions. The medallions are joined by a shepherd's crook and a stick with a bowed ribbon. The title: '| The | loves of | Tom Tucker |' is printed in 'branch-like' letters above the medallions. The words: '| & | Little Bo-Peep. |' are printed below the two medallions. The word '| By |' is printed between 'Thomas' and 'Hood'; it is printed in black on a loaf of bread, which has a bread knife suspended half-way through it. The imprint is printed below this in black type, apart from the words: 'Griffith & Farran', which are printed in blue. Signed '| Luke Limner, Del. |' in black underneath the imprint.

424 Leighton, John

Lee, Holme *pseud.* [i.e. Miss Harriet Parr.] *The true, pathetic history of Poor Match. With four illustrations.* London: Smith Elder, and Co., 65, Cornhill, 1863. London: Printed by Smith, Elder and Co., Little Green Arbour Court, Old Bailey, E.C. viii, 219 p., 4 plates. With four pages of publisher's titles bound at the end.

115 × 185 × 20 mm. 12808.aaa.30.

Three of the four plates are signed: 'W. Crane del', and two are signed 'Ed Evans'. The publisher's titles at the end states: 'With four illustrations by Walter Crane'.

Text sewn on three sawn-in cords. Most of the bolts are uncut. Yellow endpapers and pastedowns. Mauve dot and line diagonal-grain cloth. Both covers blocked identically in blind on the borders and on the corners. Two fillets are blocked on the borders. Straps and curling stem decoration are blocked on each corner and on the sides. The central frame is formed as an 'elongated quatrefoil' shape. The upper cover has a central vignette blocked in gold. It shows Match (a terrier dog), holding a leather shoe in his mouth. The shoe has a long lace which is not threaded in the lace holes. Instead, it curls out above and below Match. All this is blocked within a half-circle formed by a single gold fillet. The title: '| The | History | of |' is blocked in gold above the half circle; the words: '| Poor Match |' are blocked at the base of the half-circle – all in gold. A swallow and a small star are blocked at the base of the vignette. Signed 'JL' in gold as separate letters to the left and to the right at the base of the half-circle. The spine is blocked in gold. A single gold fillet is blocked on the perimeter, which forms a circular arch at the head. From the head downwards, the decoration is: the monogram 'PM', blocked in gold within the entrance of a kennel; the words: '| The | true, | pathetic | history | of | Poor | Match | by | Holme | Lee. |' blocked in gold; a figure of a bearded man, with robes and a shoulder ruff; two fillets in gold; the words: '| London | Smith, Elder & Co |' are blocked in gold within a rectangle formed by a single fillet; two gold fillets are blocked in gold at the tail.

Dry, *JL* no. 454.

425 Leighton, John PLATE XLIII

London III. International Exhibition of 1862. *International Exhibition, 1862. Reports by the Juries on the subjects in the thirty-six classes into which the Exhibition was divided.* London: Printed for the Society of Arts by William Clowes & Sons, Stamford Street and Charing Cross, 1863. [London]: William Clowes & Sons, Stamford Street and Charing Cross. [The pagination is printed separately for each class.] With fourteen pages of advertisements bound at the end.

190 × 272 × 90 mm. 7957.e.33.

In the report for Class XXVIII, Section D, Bookbinding, p. 11, is printed:

> 'The designs for cloth, by Luke Limner, in the case of J. Leighton [the Bookbinder], exhibit a rare dergee of merit,

> evincing, as they do, a laudable desire to develop the power of origination, which, though it may seem at times grotesque and peculiar, is, for this very reason, worthy of commendation, because it dares to be uncommon. The resort to Grecian, Roman, and Egyptian ornaments is most successful, and while the treatment of colours might be more harmonious, it must be admitted that any attempt to free us from the tyrannical chain of precedent should meet with sympathy if it be not permitted to nourish itself upon encouragement.'

The original cloth upper cover is bound at the front. Original cover size: 178 × 264 mm. Blue morocco horizontal-grain cloth. There are two fillets blocked in blind on the borders. Inside these are blocked, in blind and in relief, shields of the various exhibiting countries. Clockwise from the top, they are: Belgium, France, Prussia, Holland, America, Austria, Spain, Denmark, Turkey, Pope [i.e. the Vatican], Portugal, Italy, Russia, Sweden. In all of the shields, the symbol representing the country is blocked in relief. The name of the country is blocked in blind, within blind lettering-pieces, shaped as pennants. There are two shields at the centre of the base, which are inscribed in relief with the words: '| India, | Australia, | Cape |', and '| Canadas, | Ceylon, | Natal |'. The central rectangle has a mandorla blocked inside. Above and below it are blocked in gold the words: 'International Exhibition' in gothic letters. The perimeter of the mandorla has a wide fillet, blocked between two thin fillets – all in gold. The words: 'Reports of the International Juries by Authority of H.M. Commissioners' are blocked inside the wide gold perimeter fillets in relief. Inside the mandorla, the British royal coat of arms is blocked in gold. The initials 'IL' [sic] are blocked in gold as separate fanciful letters immediately underneath the coat of arms. The words: '| London | 1862 |' are blocked underneath the coat of arms in relief, within a shield, argent, horizontal hatch.

Dry, *JL* no. 429.

426 Leighton, John FIG. 56

Murray, Andrew. *The book of the Royal Horticultural Society. 1862–1863. With Illustrations and Photographs by John Leighton F.S.A., Thomas Scott, and C. Thurston Thompson.* London: Bradbury & Evans, 11, Bouverie Street, 1863. London: Bradbury and Evans, Printers Extraordinary to the Queen, Whitefriars. xii, 225 p., 1 fold-out plate, 13 photographs.
235 × 305 × 40 mm. C.43.d.1.

Bevelled boards. Gilt edges. Pink endpapers and pastedowns. Green dotted line vertical-grain cloth. Both covers are blocked in gold and black, with an identical design. Four fillets are blocked on the borders: 1. a gold fillet; 2. a hatch gold fillet; 3. a gold fillet, with repeating dots blocked in relief within it; 4. a black fillet. Inside this, a Chinese fret pattern is blocked in gold and in black. On the centre head and on the centre tail, a cartouche is blocked in gold. Inside this, an inner border is formed by a black fillet, and a gold fillet with small decoration blocked on each corner. The central medallion is a monogram of the Royal Horticultural Society, blocked in gold on a purple paper onlay; the medallion is surmounted by a crown blocked in gold. Below the medallion, a thistle, a rose and a shamrock are blocked in gold. The medallion is surrounded by three fillets and by a pattern of flowers and hatch leaves blocked in gold, and more leaves blocked in black. The spine is blocked in gold and in black. A single black fillet is blocked at the head and at the tail. From the head downwards, the decoration is: a gold crown; the monogram of Victoria and Albert, with the motto: '| Treu und Fest | Dieu & mon droit |' blocked above and below the monogram in gold; the title: '| The | book | of the | Royal | Horticultural | Society. |' blocked in relief within six rectangular gold lettering-pieces, with single fillets blocked in gold on the borders of each; hatch gold leaf and black leaf decoration surrounds the title; the medallion of the Royal Horticultural Society is blocked in gold, with the words: '| RHS | INST | MAR VII, | 1804 |' blocked in relief inside; below this, an arabesque is blocked in gold and in black; the words: '| London | Bradbury & Evans |' are blocked in relief inside a rectangular gold lettering-piece, with a single gold fillet blocked on its borders. Unsigned.

FIG. 56

Another copy of this work is also in the British Library (but not shelfmarked at 27.3.2000). It has a deluxe leather binding. Size: 270 × 340 × 50 mm. Gutta percha binding, now given way. Bevelled boards. Gilt edges. Pink moiré horizontal ribbed endpapers and pastedowns. Green morocco leather. Both covers

blocked identically in gold and in black, with the same design as for C.43.d.1. The central medallion is signed 'JL' in gold as separate letters at its base. The spine is blocked in gold and in black and in relief. It has the same blockwork as above; additionally, the date: '| 1863 |' is blocked in gold underneath 'Bradbury and Evans'.

Ball, *VPB* p. 82 ref. 13. Dry *JL* no. 457. King, *JL* p. 249.

427 Leighton, John

Scott, *Sir* Walter *Bart. The Lady of the Lake.* London: A.W. Bennett, 5, Bishopsgate Without, 1863. London: Richard Barrett, Printer, 13, Mark Lane, London. [7], 215 pp.
160 × 200 × 40 mm. 1347.f.19.

The text is accompanied by fourteen photographs, the frontispiece by George Washington Wilson, the other thirteen by T. Ogle.

Bevelled boards. (The text block and case received conservation treatment in 1993.) Purple honeycomb-grain cloth. Both covers blocked identically in gold and in relief. The outer border has a semi-circular arch design, blocked in gold; inside each semi-circle is a leaf blocked in blind. There is a recessed central mandorla blocked on each cover. In it stands the Lady, an oar in her left hand, clasping the prow of the boat (in the shape of a swan) immediately behind her. There are medallions, formed by two gold fillets, blocked on each side of the mandorla; to the left, a horse; to the right, a stag. Running vertically below and above the medallions are two lines of verse, blocked in relief. On the left, the lines read: 'But stumbling in the rugged dell. The gallant horse exhausted fell.' On the right: 'Then dashing down a darksome den. Soon lost to hound & hunters ken.' The medallions are within a lattice work of branches interspersed with vine leaves and grapes. Above the mandorla is blocked a swan, with its wings unfolded. Beneath the mandorla, a cross is blocked. The title words: 'The Lady' are blocked above the mandorla in relief, within a hatch gold lettering-piece. The words: 'of the lake' are blocked in relief below the mandorla. Behind this, a medallion is blocked in gold, with a beaded border, and three crossed arrows blocked inside it. Signed 'JL' in gold as separate letters at the base of the mandorla. The spine is missing.

The same copy is in the Newbery Library, Chicago; shelfmark: WING. ZP.845.B43. This copy is bound in red honeycomb-grain cloth, and has the spine. The spine is blocked in gold. A single gold fillet is blocked on the perimeter. From the head downwards, the decoration is: two gold fillets; a single gold blocked on the inner perimeter, which forms an arch near the head; circles, stars and two leaves are blocked in gold on either side of the arch; the title: '| The Lady | of the Lake |' blocked in gold in gothic lettering, with the two capital 'L's blocked in relief within rectangular gold lettering-pieces; the words: '| Illustrated | by | Photography |' are blocked in gold in gothic letters; from near the tail to below the title, a sword, planted with the ground at the tail, is blocked in gold; ribbon-shaped gold lettering-pieces wind downwards around the sword; the words: '| It forth at length | sufficed to scratch | whose sinury strength | few were the arms |' are blocked in relief within the ribbon; bulrushes grow from the ground at the tail up around the sword; signed 'JL' in gold as separate letters to the left and to the right of the ground around the sword tip; a gold fillet; the publisher: '| Bennett |' is blocked in gold within a rectangle formed by two gold fillet; a gold fillet at the tail.

Dry, *JL* no. 459

428 Leighton, John PLATE XLIV

Wise, John R. *The New Forest: its History and its Scenery. With 63 Illustrations, Drawn by Walter Crane, Engraved by W.J. Linton, and Two Maps.* London: Smith, Elder and Co., 65, Cornhill, 1863. Richard Clay, London. x, 336 p. With four pages of publisher's titles bound at the end.
175 × 245 × 42 mm. RdeB.M.7.

The British Museum de Beaumont copy.

Gilt edges. Bevelled boards. Yellow endpapers and pastedowns. Green pebble-grain cloth. Both covers blocked identically in gold, in blind and in relief. A repeating flower and stem pattern is blocked in gold on the borders; inside this, two gold fillets are blocked on the borders, with repeating dots blocked in gold between them. Triangular panels are blocked on each inner corner. Each has a horizontal hatch gold medallion blocked inside. The medallions are surrounded by fern-like leaves, blocked in gold. Within each medallion, a woodpecker, a kingfisher, an owl, and a bird of prey are blocked in gold. Two mandorlas are blocked on the centre. The outer mandorla has a zig-zag border, blocked in gold. On the border of the mandorla, branch-shaped gold fillets form panels at the head, the tail and on the sides. Within each panel, a stag's head, a fox, a horse's head, a squirrel and a stoat are blocked in gold. Further recessed panels are blocked between these four: they have single gold fillets blocked on their borders and leaves and stems are blocked in relief within each. The inner mandorla shows ivy and flowers, leaves and berries, blocked in gold. An arrow, pointing downwards, is blocked from top to bottom of the inner mandorla. The word: '| the |' is blocked in relief within a rectangular gold lettering-piece, around the tail feathers of the arrow; the words: '| New Forest |' are blocked in gold in gothic letters, with the capitals 'N' and 'F' blocked within gold lettering-pieces, which have single gold fillets on their borders; the words: '| its | History | and Scenery |' are blocked in relief in gothic letters, within ribbon-shaped gold lettering-pieces. Signed 'JL' in gold as separate letters underneath the tip of the arrow. The spine is blocked in gold and relief. A single gold fillet is blocked on the perimeter. From the head downwards, the decoration is: groups of flowers and leaves above and below a shield, gules, rose and crown; a mandorla blocked as a gold lettering-piece; the title: '| The | New | Forest | [rule] | Its History | & | Scenery |' blocked in relief in gothic letters within the mandorla; the words: '| Iohn R. Wise |' are blocked in relief within a rectangular gold lettering-piece; near the tail, a heron is blocked; it is in water, surrounded by bulrushes; fern-like leaves are blocked

underneath this; a gold fillet; the word: '| London |' is blocked in gold, in gothic letters, within a rectangle formed by a single fillet; the words: '| Smith Elder & Co |' are blocked in relief within a gold lettering-piece; a gold fillet is blocked at the tail. Dry, *JL* no. 463. de Beaumont, *RdeB1* no.404. Goldman, *VIB* no. 404. Oldfield, *BC* no. 60.

429 Leighton, John FIG. 57

Wordsworth, William, *Poet Laureate. Wordsworth's poems for the young. With fifty illustrations by John MacWhirter and John Pettie, and a vignette by J. E. Millais. Engraved by Dalziel Brothers.* London: Alexander Strahan & Co., 1863. London: Dalziel Brothers, Engravers and Printers, Camden Press. x, 92 p. With ten pages of publisher's titles bound at the end.
150 × 195 × 15 mm. 11642.aaa.52.

On page 5 of the publisher's titles at the end: 'Now Ready, Wordsworth's Poems for Children [sic] . . . In small Quarto, Elegantly Printed and Bound, 6s.'

Bevelled boards. Gilt edges. Brown endpapers and pastedowns. Binder's ticket on lower pastedown: '| Bound by | Burn | 37 & 38 | Kirby St. |' Red honeycomb-grain cloth. The lower cover is blocked in blind. The upper cover is blocked in gold and black. A single gold fillet is blocked on the borders. Inside this, another gold fillet is blocked on the borders, and is curved on the corners. Repeating dots are blocked in relief within this second fillet. A small decoration is blocked in gold on each corner. An wide inner border of overlapping black fillets cross to form repeating 'three window' arches. Flowers and leaves, some hatched, are blocked in gold within the windows. The central rectangle is formed by three gold fillets, the middle of which has repeating dots blocked in relief within it. At the centre, a thin fillet is blocked in black. Above the centre, six 5-point stars are blocked in gold. The words: '| Wordsworth's | Poems | for | the Young. |' are blocked in gold. A small plant and roots are blocked at the base of the central rectangle. Signed 'JL' in gold as separate letters by the roots. The spine is blocked in gold. A single gold fillet is blocked at the head and at the tail. Single gold fillets make three rectangular panels. The small panels at the head and at the tail have identical triangles and plant decoration blocked in gold inside them. The longer rectangle occupying the centre of the spine has the words: '| Wordsworth's Poems for the Young. |' blocked in gold inside it, along the spine.

The British Museum de Beaumont copy is at RdeB.M.9.

Dry, *JL* no .464. de Beaumont, *RdeB1* no. 422. Cites a copy in orange honeycomb-grain cloth. Goldman, *VIB* no. 422. Oldfield, *BC* no. 59. Pantazzi, *JL* p. 266.

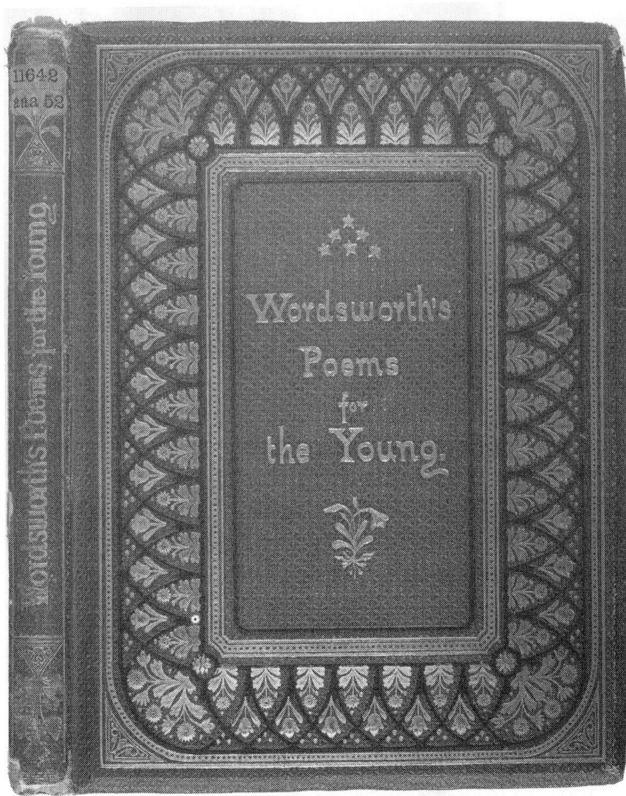

FIG. 57

430 Leighton, John

Old English ballads. A collection of favourite ballads of the olden time. With fifty illustrations by Birket Foster, Joseph Nash, Frederick Tayler, George Thomas, John Absolon, and John Franklin. London: Ward and Lock, 158, Fleet Street, 1864. London: R. Clay, Son, and Taylor, Printers. xi, 272 p. With four pages of publisher's advertisements bound at the end.
170 × 232 × 40 mm. 1347.h.11.

Bevelled boards. Gilt edges. Yellow endpapers and pastedowns. Binder's ticket on lower pastedown: '| Bound by | Leighton | Son and | Hodge. |'. Red pebble-grain cloth. Both covers are fully blocked in gold and in blind with the same design. The outer border of each cover is blocked in gold, with a repeating alternating flower pattern, attached to a fillet. Inside this are: 1. a border of repeating dots, blocked in gold; 2. a fillet in gold; 3. a repeating pattern of circles and dots, blocked in relief within a wide blind fillet. The central rectangle has a fillet border in gold, with small four-cornered stars blocked in relief within the fillet. To the corners of the central rectangle are circles, showing flower tracery in relief. The mandorla displays the title letters, which are surrounded by small circles, blocked in relief. The capital letters 'O', 'E', 'B' are blocked in relief, with the other letters '[O]ld', '[E]nglish', '[B]allads' being blocked in gold in rustic fanciful letters. Branches and tracery emerge from the ends of the letters. The spine is fully blocked in gold. Five panels and three rectangles are delineated by gold fillets. There are four circles in gold, blocked within the spine panels. Circular ivy stems, hatched leaves and berries are blocked in gold within the four circles. The title: '| Old | English | ballads |' is blocked in gold, in rustic letters, with the capital letters of each word blocked in relief, within gold lettering-pieces. Signed 'JL' in gold as separate letters near the tail. The words: '| London | Ward & Lock |' are blocked in gold within a rectangular panel blocked at the tail.

—— Another copy. London: Ward and Lock, 158, Fleet Street, 1864. London: R.Clay, Son, and Taylor, Printers. xi, 272 p. With four pages of publisher's titles bound at the end.
172 × 235 × 38 mm. RdeB.J.13.

The British Museum de Beaumont copy.

Text sewn on three tapes. Gilt edges. Bevelled boards. Yellow endpapers and pastedowns. Bookseller's stamp on upper endpaper recto, right hand corner: '| W. Croker | Mall | Waterford |'. Written on the upper endpaper recto: '| To Adelia Gates | with the kindest wishes | of Harry & Minnie Sargent | Waterford. 2nd October 1867. |' Plum sand-grain cloth. Both covers blocked identically in gold, in blind and relief. On the borders are: 1. a pattern of repeating small plants is blocked in gold; 2. two fillets are blocked, with a pattern of repeating dots blocked between these fillets – all in gold; 3. a border, blocked in blind, which shows a repeating pattern of circles and four dots, blocked in relief; 4. a gold fillet, with repeating four-point stars blocked in relief within the fillet. Circles are blocked on each inner corner, with a single fillet on its border, which has plant decoration blocked in relief inside it. (This corner decoration is repeated on BL 12808.bb.35. Household tales and popular stories . . . Brothers Grimm. 1862.) The central mandorla is formed by a single fillet, blocked in gold. It is slightly recessed. A background pattern of circles with five dots is blocked in relief within the mandorla. The title: '| Old | English | Ballads |' is blocked in gold in exaggerated gothic letters, with tendrils attached to the letter ends. The capitals 'O', 'E', and 'B' are blocked in relief within rectangular gold lettering-pieces. The spine is blocked in gold. It is divided into five main panels by gold fillets which form rectangles and squares. From the head downwards, the decoration is: two gold fillets; inside panel 1: a circle is formed by two fillets, and has also vertical hatch ivy leaf decoration on its borders; inside panel 2: the title: '| Old | English | Ballads |' blocked in gold, in gothic letters – the capitals being blocked within rectangular gold lettering-pieces; inside panel 3: the decoration is as for panel 1 – and between it and panel 4, a rectangle is formed by a single gold fillet, with small decoration in gold and a small circle inside it; inside panel 4: the decoration as for panel 1, and the rectangle as above; inside panel 5: the decoration as for panel 1, and the rectangle as above – within the small central circle, the initials 'J. L.' are blocked in gold as separate letters (unusual to have full stops after each initial); The words: '| London | Ward. Lock & Tyler. |' are blocked in gold within a rectangle formed by a single gold fillet; a gold fillet is blocked at the tail.

Ball, *VPB* p. 166. de Beaumont, *RdeB1* no. 237. Goldman, *VIB* no. 237. McLean, *Cundall* p. 86. Morris & Levin, *APB* p. 64, no. 128. A design by Warren is illustrated.

431 Leighton, John PLATE XLV

Barham, Richard Harris. *The Ingoldsby Legends or mirth and marvels, by Thomas Ingoldsby, Esquire. With sixty illustrations by George Cruikshank, John Leech and John Tenniel.* London: Richard Bentley, Publisher in Ordinary to Her Majesty, 1864. R. Clay, Son, and Taylor, Printers, London. xii, 428 p.
190 × 240 × 45 mm. 11660.f.1.

Bevelled boards. Gilt edges. Plain dark green endpapers. Binder's ticket on lower pastedown: '| Bound by | Burn | 37 & 38 | Kirby St. |' Maroon pebble-grain cloth. Both covers are blocked identically in gold and in blind. At the four corners, twin intertwined dragons are blocked in gold. The outer border in gold is of a repeating pattern of acorns at the end of leaves, interspersed with a triple leaf motif, which is enclosed in arches. The inner border features a medallion on each corner, with the head and shoulders of a fanciful character blocked within each. There is also a medallion and fanciful character within blocked on the centre of each side. Two shields with pseudo-devices within are blocked in gold and in relief on each side. Fillets and 'cord-shaped' fillets and emblems are blocked in gold between the medallions and the shields on the inner border. The inner corners have decoration blocked in blind. The central mandorla has several borders, blocked in gold. Within it at the head, a lion is blocked, holding a shield, saltire ermine. The tail of the lion loops on either side of the shield to enclose the initials 'T' and 'I'. The title: '| The | Ingoldsby | Legends |' is blocked in relief within a shield-shaped gold lettering-piece. The initials, 'JL', are blocked in relief as separate letters at the base of the title. The spine is blocked in gold and in blind. A single gold fillet is blocked on the perimeter, with three fillets blocked in blind inside this. Pairs of oak leaves and acorns are blocked in gold at the head. The inner panel runs from tail to head, formed by two gold fillets, which are semi-circular at the head. At the head of the inner panel, a rat and a frog are on either side of a medallion with a figure resembling Mephistopheles within – all in gold. The title: '| The | Ingoldsby | Legends | Illustrated |' is blocked in gold. The decoration below this shows a magpie with a ring in its mouth, astride a hat. The hat is above a sword, a spear and a bishop's staff, all crossing behind a shield. A cross and rosary, and a cat of nine tails are blocked to the left and to the right beneath the shield. The shield shows an owl displayed, wings inverted, sable. Above the owl, a bat soaring, or. The lower half of the sword impales a head, and a half moon. Signed 'JL', in gold as separate letters, beneath the half moon. The words: '| Richard Bentley |' are blocked in relief within a rectangular gold lettering-piece, with two gold fillets blocked on its borders. Beneath this, a rectangle is formed by a single fillet blocked in blind. Acorn and scallop decoration is blocked in gold at the tail.

—— Another copy. London: Richard Bentley, Publisher in Ordinary to Her Majesty, 1864. R. Clay, Son, and Taylor, Printers, London. xxi, 428 p.
175 × 238 × 42 mm. 1347.k.6.

The same text as at BL 11660.f.1. and at BL C.129.d.3.

(Dunn & Wilson, rebound 1990s.) Original brown upper endpaper bound at the front. Original upper and lower covers used as doublures, with the outer borders lost. The doublure size is 122 × 190 mm. Green pebble-grain cloth. Both covers are

blocked identically in gold and in blind. At the four corners, twin intertwined dragons are blocked in gold. The outer border in gold is of a repeating pattern of acorns at the end of leaves, interspersed with a triple leaf motif, which is enclosed in arches. The inner border features a medallion on each corner, with the head and shoulders of a fanciful character blocked within each. There is also a medallion and fanciful character within blocked on the centre of each side. Two shields with pseudo-devices within are blocked in gold and in relief on each side. Fillets and 'cord-shaped' fillets and emblems are blocked in gold between the medallions and the shields on the inner border. The inner corners have decoration blocked in blind. The central mandorla has several borders, blocked in gold. Within it at the head, a lion is blocked, holding a shield, saltire ermine. The tail of the lion loops on either side of the shield to enclose the initials 'T' and 'I'. The title: '| The | Ingoldsby | Legends |' is blocked in relief within a shield-shaped gold lettering-piece. The initials, 'JL', are blocked in relief as separate letters at the base of the title.

PLATE XLV

—— Another copy. London: Richard Bentley, Publisher in Ordinary to Her Majesty, 1864. R. Clay, Son, and Taylor, Printers, London. xii, 428 p.
178 × 242 × 45 mm. C.129.d.3.

Bevelled boards. Gilt edges. Plain dark green endpapers. Brown dot and line horizontal-grain cloth. On the lower pastedown are two tickets. The binder's ticket is: '| Bound by | Burn | 37 & 38 | Kirby St. |' The bookseller's ticket is: '| W. & E. Pickering, | new and second-hand | Booksellers, Stationers, etc | 3 Bridge Street, | Bath. |' Both covers are blocked identically in gold and in blind. At the four corners, twin intertwined dragons are blocked in gold. The outer border in gold is of a repeating pattern of acorns at the end of leaves, interspersed with a triple leaf motif, which is enclosed in arches. The inner border features a medallion on each corner, with the head and shoulders of a fanciful character blocked within each. There is also a medallion and fanciful character within blocked on the centre of each side. Two shields with pseudo-devices within are blocked in gold and in relief on each side. Fillets and 'cord-shaped' fillets and emblems are blocked in gold between the medallions and the shields on the inner border. The inner corners have decoration blocked in blind. The central mandorla has several borders, blocked in gold. Within it at the head, a lion is blocked, holding a shield, saltire ermine. The tail of the lion loops on either side of the shield to enclose the initials 'T' and 'I'. The title: '| The | Ingoldsby | Legends |' is blocked in relief within a shield-shaped gold lettering-piece. The initials, 'JL', are blocked in relief as separate letters at the base of the title. The spine is blocked in gold and in blind. A single gold fillet is blocked on the perimeter, with three fillets blocked in blind inside this. Pairs of oak leaves and acorns are blocked in gold at the head. The inner panel runs from tail to head, formed by two gold fillets, which are semi-circular at the head. At the head of the inner panel, a rat and a frog are on either side of a medallion with a figure resembling Mephistopheles within – all in gold. The title: '| The | Ingoldsby | Legends | Illustrated |' is blocked in gold. The decoration below this shows a magpie with a ring in its mouth, astride a hat. The hat is above a sword, a spear and a bishop's staff, all crossing behind a shield. A cross and rosary, and a cat of nine tails are blocked to the left and to the right beneath the shield. The shield shows an owl displayed, wings inverted, sable. Above the owl, a bat soaring, or. The lower half of the sword impales a head, and a half moon. Signed 'JL', in gold as separate letters, beneath the half moon. The words: '| Richard Bentley |' are blocked in relief within a rectangular gold lettering-piece, with two gold fillets blocked on its borders. Beneath this, a rectangle is formed by a single fillet blocked in blind. Acorn and scallop decoration is blocked in gold at the tail.

Ball, *VPB* p. 108. Discusses print runs and binders for this work. de Beaumont, *RDeB1* no. 19. Goldman, *VIB* no. 19. King, *JL* pp. 240–241.

432 Leighton, John

Bogatzky, Carl Heinrich von. *Golden treasury for the children of God. New edition.* London: William Tegg, 1864. xvi, 368 p.
120 × 176 × 30 mm. 4409.dd.9.

Bevelled boards. Red edges. Brown endpapers and pastedowns. Binder's ticket on lower pastedown: '| Bound by | Westleys | & Co. | London. |'. Purple pebble-grain cloth. Both covers are blocked identically in blind, with two fillets blocked on borders. Groups of three fillets are blocked in blind forming an inner rectangle, which also divide each cover into three panels. Fleurs-de-lis are blocked in gold in the panels at the head and at the tail. The central medallion is blocked in blind and in relief, featuring a star and a quatrefoil, which are interlinked. The spine is blocked in gold. A single gold fillet is blocked on the perimeter. From the head downwards, the decoration is: a pattern of quatrefoils blocked within squares in gold and in relief; three gothic arches; a cross blocked in gold in the middle of the three arches; the words: '| Bogatzky's | Golden | Treasury. |' blocked in gold; a cross patonce; a gold fillet; three gothic arches and leaf and stem decoration blocked in gold; a pattern of quatrefoils, as above; signed 'JL' in gold as separate letters near the tail.

433 Leighton, John

PLATE XLVI

Defoe, Daniel. *The life and adventures of Robinson Crusoe of York, Mariner. Complete edition containing the first and second parts, carefully compared with the original edition of 1719. Illustrated in oil-colours by Kronheim.* London: Published by Knight & Son, 12 Clerkenwell Close, [1864]. London: Knight, Printer, Bartholomew Close. iv, 249 p., 12 plates
155 × 226 × 35 mm. 12613.gg.8.

Bevelled boards. Gilt edges. White endpapers and pastedowns. Green hexagon-grain cloth. Both covers are blocked identically in blind on the borders, on the corners, and on the sides. Two fillets are blocked on the borders, the outer thick, the inner thin.

A scallop is blocked in blind on each corner, surrounded in a circle by seaweed stems and leaves blocked in blind, which extend up each side. A single seaweed leaf is blocked in blind on the centre head and on the centre tail. The upper cover vignette is blocked in gold. It shows the rear of a warship and its dinghy, with a sailor seated in it. The title: '| The | life and | adventures | | of Robinson | Crusoe. |' is blocked in gold above and below the ship. Signed 'JL' in gold as separate letters at base of vignette. The spine is blocked in gold. A single gold fillet is blocked on the perimeter, which curves at the head. At the head, a medallion of Crusoe is blocked, with the word 'Illustration of' blocked around the medallion. The words: '| Robinson | Crusoe |' are blocked in gold beneath the medallion. A mast is blocked in gold from the tail of the spine to beneath the title. It supports a pennant-shaped gold lettering-piece at the top with the words '| of York | Mariner |' blocked in relief within it. Below, a group of objects is blocked in gold: a sword, rifle, spade, axe, arrow, parasol – all crossing behind a copy of the Holy Bible whose title is blocked in relief on its upper cover. At the tail, two gold fillets are blocked, then the words: '| London | Knight & Son |' are blocked in relief within a rectangular gold lettering-piece. A gold fillet is blocked underneath this.

Dry, *JL* no. 470. King, *JL* p. 240.

434 Leighton, John PLATE XLVII

Defoe, Daniel. *Life and adventures of Robinson Crusoe. Including a memoir of the author, and an essay on his writings. A new edition, illustrated by Phiz.* London: Routledge, Warne & Routledge, Broadway, Ludgate Hill; New York: 129, Grand Street, 1864. Cox & Wyman, Printers, Great Queen Street, London. 15, 589 p., 5 plates.
110 × 170 × 46 mm. 1607/618.

Bevelled boards. Gilt edges. A ticket is pasted on the front pastedown: '| Bookseller and stationer, | J. Gilbert, | 18, Gracechurch Street, London, E.C. | Engraver & Printer. |' Blue pebble-grain cloth. Both covers have the same 'background' design blocked on the borders, on the corners and on the sides. The lower cover is blocked in blind and in relief only. The upper cover has three fillets blocked in gold on the borders, the middle being hatched. A pattern of flowers with long stamens and curling stems is blocked in gold on the corners and on the head and on the tail. All of this pattern is blocked in relief as well. The central frame has two fillets blocked in gold on its borders. The central vignette is blocked in gold, depicting Crusoe, and Man Friday, each shouldering a pole, over which game has been hung. A dog underneath is looking at the dead game, its front right paw raised up. The title: '| Robinson | Crusoe |' is blocked in gold in rustic lettering above and below the central figures. Signed 'JL' in gold underneath the dog. The spine is blocked in gold and in relief. A branch-like gold fillet is blocked on the perimeter. From the head downwards, the decoration is: a parrot perched on a palm leaf umbrella, with a palm tree blocked on each side of the parrot; the words: '| Robinson | Crusoe |' blocked in relief within two pennant-shaped gold lettering-pieces; a spar, with knotted rope hanging from each side; a group of objects, crossed together: a saw, an axe, two swords, a harpoon, a bow; signed 'JL' in gold as separate letters at the base of this group; the word: '| Illustrated |' is blocked in relief within a rectangular gold lettering-piece with a single gold fillet blocked on its borders.

King, *JL* p. 240.

435 Leighton, John PLATE XLVIII

Defoe, Daniel. *The life and adventures of Robinson Crusoe. With a portrait; and one hundred illustrations by J. D. Watson, engraved by the Brothers Dalziel.* London: Routledge, Warne and Routledge, Farringdon Street; and Walker Street, New York, 1864. London: R. Clay, Son, and Taylor, Bread Street Hill. xx, 498 p. With two pages of publisher's titles bound at the end.
173 × 233 × 50 mm. 12613.dd.14.

Gilt edges. Bevelled boards. Brown pebble-grain cloth. Both covers are blocked identically in gold, in blind and in relief. There is a thin fillet blocked on the outer border in gold, with three stars blocked in gold on the outer corners. Inside this on the borders are: 1. gold dots blocked between two gold fillets; 2. 'wave' border decoration. There are on the inner corners in gold four medallions with the arms of London, Hull, York, with the fourth inscribed with the name of 'JN Fernandez'. A gold fillet surrounds each coat of arms; it also has repeating dots blocked in relief within it. This fillet, containing dots, crosses to form the central rectangle, and also the central diamond. The outer rectangles between the coats of arms have curling stems blocked in blind, with leaves blocked in relief. There are scallops blocked in gold on the sides and on the head and on the tail. Within the inner rectangle in each corner, triangles are blocked in relief, each formed by four fillets blocked in blind. Within the central diamond, two gold fillets are blocked on the borders, and gold hatch stars are blocked as background. 'Rope-like' fillets form three circles, with the figures of Crusoe and Man Friday blocked in gold within the two smaller circles above and below the centre, which shows a fully-rigged man of war, blocked in gold. Beneath this, the words: '| Robinson Crusoe. | Nat. 1632. |' are blocked in gold. Signed 'JL' in gold as separate letters beneath the medallion of Man Friday. Spine missing.

The British Museum de Beaumont copy is at RdeB.G.20.

Ball, *App.* 64g. Copy with blue pebble-grain cloth. Ball, *VPB* pp. 77–78, plate 10. de Beaumont, *RdeB1* no. 76. Dry, *JL* no. 469. Goldman, *VIB* no. 76. King, *JL* p. 240. McLean, *VBD* p. 111. Reproduces a copy in blue cloth, bound by Leighton Son & Hodge. Pantazzi, *JL* p. 268. Reproduces a copy in blue cloth, bound by Leighton Son & Hodge.

436 Leighton, John

Doyle, James E. *A chronicle of England. B.C.55–A.D.1485. Written and illustrated by James E. Doyle. The designs engraved and printed in colours by Edmund Evans.* London: Longman, Green, Longman, Roberts & Green, 1864. London: Edmund

Evans, Engraver and Printer, Raquet Court, Fleet Street. viii, 462 p.
200 × 270 × 50 mm. 9503.h.3

Original upper and lower covers used as doublures. Doublure size: 190 × 268 mm. Brown pebble-grain cloth. Both covers identically blocked in gold and in blind. A single fillet and repeating small circles are blocked in gold on the borders. Fleurs-de-lis are blocked on the borders in gold. Inside this, three gold fillets are blocked. Then an inner border of diamond-shaped leaves is blocked in gold, interspersed with diamonds and triangles formed by fillets blocked in blind. The coats of arms of England, Ireland, Scotland (and Wales ?) are blocked in gold and in relief on the corners. The borders of the central rectangle are formed by: 1. three gold fillets; 2. two fillets blocked in blind; 3. a wide gold fillet, with trefoils and leaves blocked in relief within it. Three fillets are blocked in blind on the borders of a chequer board of thistles, roses, & shamrocks blocked in gold above and below the centre. On the centre, the royal coat of arms is blocked within a trefoil, itself blocked within a medallion, which is formed by a single gold fillet, with repeating dots blocked within. Signed 'JL' in gold as separate letters underneath the coat of arms. Signed 'Timbury Sc.' in gold at bottom right hand corner of each cover.

Ball, *VPB* p. 72, ref. 8. Dry, *JL* no. 471. King, *JL* p. 241. McLean, *VPBB* p. 114. Shows a copy bound in red pebble-grain cloth.

437 Leighton, John

Howitt, William. *Ruined abbeys and castles of Great Britain and Ireland. Second series. The photographic illustrations by Thompson, Sedgefield, Ogle and Hemphill.* London: Alfred W. Bennett, 5, Bishopsgate Without, 1864. London: Richard Barratt, Printer, Mark Lane. 224 p., 26 photographs.
168 × 223 × 30 mm. C.44.d.7.

Bevelled boards. Gilt edges. Binder's ticket on lower pastedown: '| Bound by | Westleys | and Co. | London. |'. Blue pebble-grain cloth. Both covers are blocked identically in gold and blind. There are four borders: 1. dog-tooth decoration attached to a fillet; 2. a gold fillet, with repeating dots blocked in relief within it; 3. a fillet blocked in blind; 4 thin gold fillets blocked on the borders of each corner. Crowns, roses and thistles are blocked in gold on border of inner corners. Four mandorlas are blocked in gold, on the centre head, the centre tail, and the centre sides. Each mandorla has a shield blocked within it. Within each shield are: a bell; a bishop's mitre; a portcullis; a helmet. The central medallion contains the title blocked around the perimeter in gold, surrounding an onlaid photographic print. The lower cover has a different onlaid photographic print within the central medallion. The spine is blocked in gold. Two gold fillets are blocked on the perimeter. From the head downwards, the decoration is: an arch, formed by five gold fillets; a shield, with horizontal hatch and a harp within, surmounted by an obelisk – all surrounded by stars; the title: '| Abbeys & | Castles of | Great | Britain | & Ireland | [rule] | Howitt |' blocked in gold; a bishop's mitre is blocked on top of a mandorla, which is formed by three gold fillets; inside the mandorla – a bishop's mitre is blocked above a shield – parted palewise, gules, azure, with crossed keys; a pattern of stems and hatch clover leaves surrounds the shield; three goblets blocked in gold; three gold fillets; near the tail, the word: '| Bennett. |' is blocked in gold within a rectangle formed by a single fillet; at the tail, a single gold fillet. Unsigned.

McLean, *VPBB* p. 104. Suggests that the 1862 edition is by Leighton, and this design is very similar to the 1862 edition.

438 Leighton, John

PLATE XLIX

Linton, Eliza Lynn [GK: Lynn, afterwards Linton, Elizabeth.] *The Lake Country. With a Map And One Hundred Illustrations Drawn and Engraved By W. J. Linton.* London: Smith, Elder and Co., 65, Cornhill, 1864. London: Printed by Clay, Son, and Taylor, Bread Street Hill, E.C. xl, 351 p., 4 plates, 1 map.
180 × 246 × 48 mm. RdeB.I.14.

Gilt edges. Bevelled boards. Binder's ticket on lower pastedown: '| Bound | by | Leighton | Son and Hodge. |' Green pebble-green cloth. Both covers identically blocked in gold, in blind and in relief. Dragon flies are blocked on each corner. Blocked on the borders are: 1. a single gold fillet; 2 a gold fillet with repeating dots blocked in relief within; 3. a fillet blocked in blind, with repeating stars and dots blocked within it; 4. as for number 2; 5 & 6 two thin gold fillets. There are four fishes blocked in gold on the inner corners, holding scrolls in their mouths, on which is blocked in relief a lake name. The four lake names are 'Windermere; Ulles Water; Derwent Water; Rydal Water'. The central vignette, blocked in gold, shows bulrushes, leaves and ferns surrounding the title. In the centre there is a swan-shaped boat with mast. It holds a winged figure seated in the rear. The title: '| The | Lake | Country |' is blocked in relief within three horizontal hatch rectangular gold lettering-pieces, which are blocked above and below the centre. Signed 'JL' in gold as a monogram at the base of the vignette. The spine is blocked in gold and in relief. A single fillet is blocked in gold on the perimeter. The majority of the spine shows an elongated oval, formed by seven gold fillets. These are (from the outer inwards): 1. a thin gold fillet; 2. a gold fillet with repeating dots inside it, blocked in relief; 3. a thin gold fillet; 4. a thin gold fillet; 5. a fillet blocked in blind, with repeating dots and stars blocked inside it in relief; 6. a fillet blocked in blind; 7. a thin fillet in gold. Inside the oval, from the head downwards, the decoration is: a group of stars blocked in gold; the title: '| The | Lake | Country |' blocked in relief within a horizontal hatch gold triangle; the words: '| By (in gold) | E. Lynn Linton (blocked in relief, within a rectangular gold lettering-piece) |'; the words: '| Illustrated | by | W.J. Linton |' are blocked in gold; three small birds in flight, blocked in gold; a group of water plants and bulrushes, in gold; a fish in water, in gold; signed 'JL' in gold as separate letters underneath the fish; at the tail, an oval is blocked, formed by four fillets; inside the oval, there is horizontal hatch gold blocking; the word: '| London |' is blocked in relief within a rectangular gold lettering-piece,

with a single fillet blocked in relief on its perimeter; the words: '| Smith Elder & Co |' are blocked in relief; the oval has a single small decorative piece blocked in gold outside it on each corner.

—— Another copy. London: Smith Elder & Co., 65, Cornhill, 1864. London: Printed by Clay, Son, and Taylor, Bread Street Hill, E.C. xl, 351 p., 1 plate.
172 × 240 × 40 mm. 10369. p. 5.

Original yellow endpaper bound at front. Original upper cover trimmed and used as a doublure. Doublure size: 160 × 230 mm. [No original lower cover.] Purple pebble-grain cloth. The upper cover is fully blocked in gold. Dragon flies are blocked on each corner. There are two fillets blocked on the borders in gold; each has lines of beads blocked in relief. Between these two borders is a border of stars and dots blocked in blind. There are four fishes blocked in gold on the inner corners, holding scrolls in their mouths, on which is printed in relief a lake name. The four lake names are 'Windermere; Ulles Water; Derwent Water; Rydal Water'. The central vignette, blocked in gold, shows bulrushes, leaves and ferns surrounding the title. In the centre there is a swan-shaped boat with mast. It holds a winged figure seated in the rear. The words 'The Lake Country' are blocked in relief. Signed 'JL' in gold in separate letters at the base of the vignette.

de Beaumont, *RdeB1* no. 173. Goldman, *VIB* no. 173. Dry, *JL* no. 472. McLean, *VPBB* p. 110. Shows a copy bound in blue pebble-grain cloth.

439 Leighton, John

Lushington, Henrietta. *Littlehope Hall.* London: Smith, Elder & Co., Cornhill, 1864. Printed by R. & R. Clark, Edinburgh. vii, 256 p., 1 plate.
115 × 187 × 25 mm. 12804.cc.38.

The plate is signed: 'Dalziel'.

Text sewn on three sawn-in cords. Light yellow endpapers and pastedowns. Both covers identically blocked in blind. Four fillets are blocked on the borders. A circle, formed by two fillets, is blocked on each corner. A quatrefoil leaf is blocked in each circle. An 'arrow-head' leaf is blocked on each side of each circle. Two fillets are blocked in blind to form the central oval frame. The upper cover central vignette is blocked in gold. It shows a stylised view of Littlehope Hall. A weather vane (with a sailing ship on its apex) is atop a steeply sloping tiled roof, which has wooden hammer beam supports. A chimney stack is blocked to the left of the roof; an attic window is blocked on the centre, with a bird cage hanging just inside. A flagpole and pennant are blocked to the right of the roof. A pattern of ivy stems, horizontal hatch gold leaves and berries is blocked at the base, and up to the left of the roof. The title words: '| Littlehope Hall. |' are blocked in gold, underneath the attic window; the capitals 'L' and 'H' are blocked in relief within square gold lettering-pieces, with single gold fillets blocked on their borders. Signed 'JL' in gold as separate letters at the base of the vignette. The spine is blocked in gold. A single gold fillet is blocked on the perimeter. From the head downwards, the decoration is: two fillets in gold; a rope and anchor; the title: '| Littlehope Hall. |' blocked in gold – the capitals 'L' and 'H' being blocked in relief within rectangular gold lettering-pieces, with a single gold fillet blocked on their borders; the words: '| by | Henrietta | Lushington |' are blocked in gold, in 'cursive script' letters; two flags, crossed, with a pole blocked between them; at the top of the flagpole, a pennant-shaped gold lettering-piece winds downwards round the pole; the words: 'Impene | trable |' are blocked in relief within the pennant; a wreath, with the word: '| Trafal | gar. |' blocked in gold inside; curling stem decoration; signed 'JL' in gold as separate letters near the tail; at the tail, the words: '| Smith Elder & Co. |' are blocked in gold, within a rectangle formed by a single gold fillet.

Dry, *JL* no. 473.

440 Leighton, John

Walsh, J. H. *The British cookery book: uniting a good style with economy, and adapted to all persons in every clime containing many unpublished recipes in daily use, by private families. Collected by a committee of ladies, and edited by J. H. Walsh, F.R.C.S. New edition, with Engravings.* London: Routledge, Warne and Routledge, Broadway, Ludgate Hill. New York; 129, Grand Street, 1864. [London]: M'Corquodale and Co., Printers, London-Works, Newton. viii, 375 p., 5 plates.
105 × 172 × 35 mm. BL [not shelfmarked]

Text sewn on two tapes. Beige endpapers and pastedowns. Green bead-grain cloth on covers. Red morocco leather on the spine. A vertical gold fillet is blocked on the leather and cloth join on each cover. The upper cover has a central vignette blocked in gold and in relief. It shows a central medallion blocked as a gold lettering-piece. The medallion is supported by a stag's head and antlers. Bunches of fruit and vegetables hang from the antlers by string – all blocked in gold. On the left and right of the medallion, a pig's head and ram's head are blocked in gold. Atop the medallion, two chickens and a turkey in a bowl, with flowers on either side, are blocked in gold. The medallion has the title: '| The | British | Cookery | Book |' blocked in relief. Signed 'JL' in gold as separate letters at the base of the vignette. The spine is blocked in gold. Two gold fillets are blocked on the perimeter. The inner fillet forms a semi-circle at the head. From the head downwards, the decoration is: the title: '| The | British | Cookery | Book |' blocked in gold; a cooking pot suspended from a cord, being heated by two torches below; a perfume bottle, surrounded by a cord and by small plants; a bull's head; a fishing net and the catch of three fishes and a lobster; the words: '| With | [gold fillet] | Illustrations |' are blocked in gold; at the tail, '| J. H. Walsh |' is blocked in gold within a rectangle formed by a single gold fillet.

441 Leighton, John PLATE L

White, Lewis Borrett. *English sacred poetry of the olden time. Collected and Arranged By the Rev. White . . .* London: The

Religious Tract Society; 56 Paternoster Row, 65 St. Paul's Churchyard; and 164 Piccadilly, 1864. London: R. Clay, Son, and Taylor, Printers, Bread Street Hill. xvi, 190 p.
155 × 225 × 25 mm. C.109.d.8.

Bevelled boards. Gilt edges. Cream endpapers and pastedowns. Binder's ticket on lower pastedown: '| Bound by | Westleys | & Co | London. |'. Blue pebble-grain cloth. Both covers blocked identically in gold and in relief. On the borders, there is an outer border of repeating tracery and flowers. Five gold fillets are blocked on the inner borders with gold hatch blocked between numbers four and five. More fillets are blocked in blind and in relief inside this, which surround the four medallions blocked on the corners of the inner border Poets' names are blocked in relief within each medallion. They are: '| Spenser | Milton | Ken | Herbert |'. An elaborate central medallion is formed by several gold fillets. It contains the title. The words 'English' and 'of the olden time' are blocked in gold. The words 'sacred' and 'poetry' are blocked in relief, inside rectangular gold lettering pieces. Signed 'JL' in gold as separate letters at the bottom of the tracery of the medallion. The spine is blocked in gold. A single gold fillet is blocked on the perimeter. From the head downwards, the decoration is: tracery in gold; a gold medallion showing a crown within; the title is blocked within a panel formed by two gold fillets and gold hatch between them; the title: '| English | sacred | poetry | of the | olden time | Chaucer | to | Ken |' blocked in gold and in relief; the words: 'sacred' and 'poetry' are blocked in relief within rectangular gold lettering-pieces; the words 'Chaucer to Ken' are blocked in relief within a cup-shaped gold lettering-piece; tracery blocked in gold forms a medallion, and a rectangle; a gold medallion with stars blocked within it; gold tracery is blocked at the tail; the medallions blocked at the head, the middle and at the tail are surrounded by line decoration, blocked in relief.

The gold blocking on this copy is fresher and sharper than that of BL 3441.e.72. This copy is the copyright deposit copy, date stamped 2 DE[CEMBER 18]63, and was placed originally at 1347.g.23.

PLATE L

—— Another copy. London: The Religious Tract Society; 56 Paternoster Row, 65 St. Paul's Churchyard; and 164 Piccadilly, 1864. London: R. Clay, Son, and Taylor, Printers, Bread Street Hill. xvi, 190 p.
155 × 225 × 25 mm. 3441.e.72.

Bevelled boards. Gilt edges. White endpapers and pastedowns. Binder's ticket on lower pastedown: '| Bound by | Westleys | & Co | London. |' Green pebble-grain cloth. Both covers and spine blocked identically as for BL C.109.d.8.

Ball, *App.* no. 64f. Copy of purple fine morocco-grain cloth. Dry, *JL* no. 478. Pantazzi, *JL* p. 272. The illustration is of the spine only.

442 Leighton, John

Gems from the poets illustrated from original designs by A. F. Lydon. London: Charles Griffin and Company, Stationer's Hall Court, [1860?]. B. Fawcett, Engraver and Printer, East Lodge, Driffield. [3], 62 p., 29 colour plates
175 × 255 × 29 mm. Private Collection. [Tom Valentine]

Gilt edges. Bevelled boards. Dark green endpapers and pastedowns. Green sand-grain cloth. Both covers blocked identically on the borders, in blind on the lower cover and in gold on the upper cover. On the outer border, there are four gold fillets, with a hatch gold repeating pattern of nearly joined triangles. Inside this, a border of leaves and branches is blocked in gold, with the leaves within picked out in relief. On the centre of the upper cover, the vignette is blocked in gold. A roundel is blocked in gold on the centre as a diaper gold lettering-piece. The title: '| Gems | from the | poets |' is blocked in relief inside three separate rectangular gold lettering pieces, each with a single fillet blocked in relief on the borders of each. Rose branches, stems, leaves and flowers form four circles on the outside of the roundel. Within the circle at the head, two birds are nesting. Eggs in a nest are blocked in the circle to the left. The newly hatched young are displayed in a nest on the right. A pair of birds are perched on a branch at the bottom. Signed 'JL' in gold as separate letters underneath the birds on the branch, at the base of the vignette.

The spine is blocked in gold and in relief. A single gold fillet is blocked on the perimeter. From the head downwards, the decoration is: two arabesques – 1. leaf and stem decoration blocked in relief within horizontal gold hatch; 2. a diamond shape with horizontal gold hatch; the title: '| Gems | from the | Poets |' blocked in relief within three gold lettering-pieces, which themselves have four diaper gold lettering-pieces blocked above and below it, each with a single five-point gold star blocked within; a diamond gold horizontal hatch gold lettering-piece with leaf decoration in relief within; a circle gold horizontal hatch gold lettering-piece with a repeating leaf and stem pattern blocked in relief within; an arabesque, with horizontal gold hatch and leaves blocked in relief within; an arabesque, the same as at the head; signed 'JL' in gold as separate letters; the imprint: '| C. Griffin | and Compy |' blocked in relief within a rectangular gold lettering-piece, with a single gold fillet blocked on its borders; two gold fillets blocked at the tail. [The BL copy is at 1347.k.12., without original covers]

This design surrounding the central circle is the same as for 'Sunshine in the country', B.L. 1347.f.9.

Ball, *VPB* p. 164 cites the 1860 Groombridge edition, with a design by Albert Warren. McLean, *VBD* p. 204 reproduces the title page of the 1860 edition. 'Printed in gold and colours by Benjamin Fawcett'. McLean, *VPBB* p. 92. Shows the Groombridge 1860 edition.

443 Leighton, John

PLATE LI

Home thoughts and home scenes. In original poems by Jean Ingelow The Hon. Mrs. Norton Dora Greenwell Amelia B. Edwards Mrs. Tom Talyor Jennett Humphreys and the Author of 'John Halifax Gentleman.' and pictures by A. B. Houghton, engraved by the Brothers Dalziel. London: Routledge, Warne, and Routledge. Broadway, Ludgate Hill, 1865. [London]: Dalziel Brothers,

Engravers and Printers, Camden Press. [5 p.] 35 plates, xxxv pages of poems printed on verso only. With two pages of publisher's titles bound at the end.
205 × 260 × 40 mm. RdeB.H.21.

The British Museum de Beaumont copy.

The plates are signed with Houghton's monogram and 'Dalziel'.

Gilt edges. Bevelled boards. Light yellow endpapers and pastedowns. Binder's ticket on lower pastedown: '| Bound by | Bone & Son, | [rule] | 76, Fleet Street, London. |' Red sand-grain cloth. Both covers blocked identically in gold and in relief. There are several border decorations: 1. an outer border of gold hatch leaves and curling stems, blocked in gold; 2. a strapwork border, blocked in gold, with dots blocked in relief inside the straps; 3. two thin fillets, blocked in gold; 4. two fillets, blocked in gold, with a repeating 'three leaf' pattern and gold hatch blocked between them; 5. a thin fillet blocked in gold; 6. a border blocked in relief; the words: 'Dalziel's Gift Book' are blocked in relief on each side; the word '1865' is blocked at the centre head in relief; the words: 'For 1865' are blocked in relief on the centre tail in relief – all these words form part of this border; 7. a fillet is blocked in gold, which forms the border of the inner central rectangle. The inner rectangle formed by these borders has rectangles at the head and at the tail formed by double gold fillets. Within the rectangle at the head, the words: 'Original poems' are blocked; within the rectangle at the tail, the words: 'and pictures' are blocked – both in gold and in relief. There is horizontal hatch gold around the words. A mandorla is blocked on the centre, with vertical gold hatch leaves and stems around it. The mandorla has multiple fillets on its borders, the outermost of which has small decoration blocked between two fillets. Within the mandorla, the title; '| Home | Thoughts | and | Home | Scenes |' is blocked in relief within four rectangular hatch gold lettering-pieces. The capital letters of the title are blocked in relief within their own gold lettering-pieces, and they are surrounded by small decoration also blocked in relief. Signed 'JL' in gold as separate letters at the base of the mandorla. The spine is blocked in gold and in relief. From the head downwards, the decoration is: a semi-circle, with vertical hatch gold leaves and stems; crossing straps in gold, and dots blocked within them in relief; a single gold fillet runs down the length of the spine from the straps – each fillet has dots blocked in relief inside it; the title: '| Home | Thoughts | and | Home | Scenes. |' blocked in gold within a panel formed by a single gold fillet; the words: '| original | poems & | pictures |' are blocked in relief within three rectangular gold lettering-pieces, which themselves are blocked in the middle of a horizontal gold hatch decorated mandorla; vertical hatch leaf and riotous stem decoration is blocked in gold above and below the mandorla; signed 'JL' in gold as separate letters near the base of this decoration; crossing straps in gold and dots blocked within them in relief; a semi-circle, with vertical hatch gold leaves and stems at the tail.

The 1868 edition is also in the British Museum Robin de Beaumont Collection. Shelfmark: RdeB.H.22.The title, pagination, size, printer and binder are all the same. The imprint is: | George Routledge and Sons, | The Broadway, Ludgate. | New York: 416 Broome Street, | 1868 | The design on the covers is the same as for 1865, with two exceptions: 1. the lower cover is blocked in blind only; 2. The '1865' and 'For 1865' are not blocked on the upper cover – small decoration has replaced the date.

de Beaumont, *RdeB1* no. 127. Dry, *JL* no. 487. Goldman, *VIB* no. 127.

444 Leighton, John PLATE LII

The voices of the year or the poet's kalendar containing the choicest pastorals in our language . . . Illustrated. London: Charles Griffin and Company, Stationer's Hall Court, 1865. London: Levey & Co., Printers, Great New Street, Fetter Lane, E.C. [7], 544 p., 4 plates.
165 × 248 × 42 mm. 11651.h.9.

Bevelled boards. Gilt edges. Dark green endpapers and pastedowns. Purple sand-grain cloth. Blocked in gold and black on both covers, with an identical design. There is a single fillet blocked in gold on the borders. Inside this, there is a border of repeating half circles attached to a fillet, both blocked in black. Inside the half circles, small flowers and branch patterns interspersed with dots are blocked in gold. The border of the inner rectangle is of a fillet blocked in gold, with repeating dots blocked in blind. On the corners of the inner rectangle trees are blocked, representing the four seasons. Each tree is within a 'pear-drop' shape, formed of two thin fillets, blocked in gold. All the strapwork around these tear-drops and around the centre circles is formed by three fillets, one thick between two thin ones, the thick having repeating dots blocked in relief within it. The strapwork is zoomorphic, ending in the heads of birds, whose beaks are gripping the strapwork. The infill within the inner rectangle is a diamond pattern, with each diamond being formed by dotted gold lines. In each diamond, a hatch four pointed leaf is blocked in gold, with a cross, blocked in relief, across each leaf. The cross ends with four small dots, blocked in gold. The central circle is formed by a single fillet blocked in gold, with repeating dots blocked in relief within it. Inside, semi-circles are blocked in black, with repeating flower patterns inside, blocked in gold. The inner central circle is formed by a single fillet in gold, with repeating dots blocked in relief within it. The central medallion is a gold lettering-piece, with hatch on the inner portion. The words: '| The poets kalendar | Illustrated |' and '| The | Voices | of the | Year |' are blocked in relief within the medallion. Signed 'JL' in gold as separate letters in a small shield at the base of the medallion. The spine is blocked in gold and in relief. A single gold fillet is blocked on the perimeter. From the head downwards, the decoration is: a pattern of curling stems and stars blocked in gold; a single gold fillet, round arched at the head, with repeating dots blocked in relief within it; the words: '| The | Voices | of | The Year |' blocked in relief within four rectangular gold lettering-pieces, each with a single fillet blocked on its borders; the words: '| or | the Poets | Kalendar |' blocked in gold within a rectangular

gold lettering-piece with a a single gold fillet blocked on its borders; an arabesque gold lettering-piece has a lyre blocked in relief within it; a diamond pattern of hatch gold leaves surrounds the lettering down the spine; signed 'JL' in relief as separate letters beneath the lyre; the imprint: '| C. Griffin & Co. |' is blocked in relief with a rectangular gold lettering-piece with a a single gold fillet on its borders; three gold fillets are blocked at the tail.

Dry, *JL* no. 496. King, *JL* p. 242. McLean, *VPBB* p. 124. Copy bound in blue cloth.

445 Leighton, John

Aleph *pseud.* [i.e. William Harvey, *of Islington.*] *The Old City, and its highways and byways. Sketches of curious customs, characters, incidents, scenes, and events, illustrative of London life in olden times.* London: W .H. Collingridge, City Press, Aldersgate Street, E.C., 1865. London: W. H. Collingridge, Printer, Aldersgate Street, E.C. viii, 387 p. Original cover size: 125 × 195 mm. With a twelve page list of subscribers, and a four page advertisement for 'London scenes and London people', bound at the end

135 × 205 × 37 mm. 10348.cc.8.

Red dyed edges. Rebound in 1981, with the original upper cover bound at the front. Dark brown pebble-grain cloth. The upper cover is blocked in blind and in relief identically on the borders, as for 'London scenes and London people' [BL 10349.d.14.].The upper cover has a vignette, blocked in gold, set in a square central panel, featuring two gryphons, holding the Corporation of London coat of arms, with the motto 'Domine dirige nos' underneath. Signed 'JL' in gold as separate letters underneath the motto. The title: '| Ye | Old | City |' is blocked in gold, with the capital letters 'O' and 'L' blocked in blind inside square hatch gold lettering-pieces. Above the title letters is an old man's head, crowned, with his beard teeming with fish. There is a shield blocked on each side of the man's head.

Dry, *JL* no. 480.

446 Leighton, John

Barham, Richard Harris. *The Ingoldsby Legends or mirth and marvels, by Thomas Ingoldsby, Esquire. With illustrations by George Cruikshank, John Leech and John Tenniel.* London: Richard Bentley, Publisher in Ordinary to Her Majesty, 1865. R. Clay, Son, and Taylor, Printers, London. xiv, 512 p.

170 × 235 × 42 mm. 11651.f.2.

(BM, rebound C19.) Original dark green endpaper bound at the front. Original upper and lower covers used as doublures. The doublure size is 160 × 230 mm. Purple sand-grain cloth. Both covers are identically blocked in gold. At the four corners, twin intertwined dragons are blocked in gold. The outer border in gold is of a repeating pattern of acorns at the end of leaves, interspersed with a triple leaf motif, which is enclosed in arches. The inner border features a medallion on each corner, with the head and shoulders of a fanciful character blocked within each. There is also a medallion and fanciful character within blocked on the centre of each side. Two shields with pseudo-devices are blocked in gold and in relief on each side. Fillets and 'cord-shaped' fillets and emblems are blocked in gold between the medallions and the shields on the inner border. The inner corners have decoration blocked in blind. The central mandorla has several borders, blocked in gold. Within it at the head, a lion is blocked, holding a shield, saltire ermine. The tail of the lion loops on either side of the shield to enclose the initials 'T' and 'I'. The title: '| The | Ingoldsby | Legends |' is blocked in relief within a shield-shaped gold lettering-piece. The initials, 'JL', are blocked in relief as separate letters at the base of the title.

Ball, *App.* 65i. Cites copy bound in brown sand-grain cloth. King, *JL* pp. 240–241.

447 Leighton, John

Bethell, afterwards Parker, Hon. Augusta . *Echoes of an old bell and other tales of fairy love. Illustrated by F. W. Keyl.* London: Griffith & Farran, (Successors to Newbery & Harris), Corner of St. Paul's Churchyard, 1865. Printed by R. & R. Clark, Edinburgh. [4], 199 p., 4 plates. With thirty-two pages of publisher's titles bound at the end.

127 × 175 × 24 mm. 12805.ccc.16.

Text sewn on three sawn-in cords. Red ink speckled edges. White endpapers and pastedowns. Binder's ticket on lower pastedown: 'Bound by | Bone & Son. | 76, Fleet Street, | London. |' Both covers identically blocked in blind on the border and on the corners. Three fillets are blocked on the borders Intertwining stem and leaf decoration is blocked in blind on each corner. The upper cover central vignette is blocked in gold. It shows a church bell, a headstock, bell wheel, and clapper. The bell has the figure of a male winged angel on it, blocked in relief. The title: 'Echoes | of an | old bell |' is blocked in gold above, to the left and to the right of the bell. A bird is blocked in gold above the word 'Echoes'. Groups of leaves, of stems and | or berries are blocked to the left and the right of the bell. They are attached to twin branches, which rise from the base of the vignette. Signed 'JL' in gold as separate letters at the base of the vignette. The spine is blocked in gold. Five fillets are blocked in blind at the head. A fillet, shaped as a bell-rope, forms two panels. In the first panel are: a bird; the title words: 'Echoes | of an | old | bell |' blocked in gold. In the second panel are: the words: '| by | the Hon. | Augusta | Bethell |' blocked in gold. [The base of the spine is missing.]

Dry, *JL* no. 481.

448 Leighton, John

Black, Adam and Charles, *Publishers. Black's guide to the counties of Hereford and Monmouth. With illustrations. Second edition.* Edinburgh: Adam and Charles Black, 1865. Printed by R. & R.

Clark, Edinburgh. xi, 155 p., 2 plates, 2 maps, one fold-out. With forty-eight pages of advertisements bound at the end.
110 × 172 × 20 mm. 10368.bb.26.

Text sewn on two tapes. Edges speckled with red ink. Yellow endpapers and pastedowns. '| Clue index | to the | principal places in Hereford and Monmouth Shires. |' printed on the upper pastedown. Index to 'Black's Travelling Maps' printed on the upper endpaper. A list of Black's guide books is printed on the lower endpaper and pastedown. Both covers have two fillets blocked in blind on the borders, the outer thick, the inner thin. The upper cover central vignette is blocked in gold. On the centre the title: '| Black's | guide | to | Hereford | and | Monmouth | shires. |' is blocked in gold. To the left and the right of the title, the coats of arms of each county are blocked. The coats of arms are joined by apple tree branches, with groups of apples and leaves. At the base of the vignette, the branches are tied by a ribbon. Signed 'JL' in gold as separate letters above the ribbon. The spine is not blocked.

The eighth edition of 1883 is at BL 10347.bb.22. 174 p., 2 plates, 2 maps, 1 fold-out. With one hundred and eight pages of advertisements bound at the end. Printed by R. & R. Clark, Edinburgh. 112 × 170 × 23 mm. Yellow endpapers and pastedowns, with indexes and lists printed on them. Green sand-grain cloth. The same design is blocked on the covers as for the second edition. On the spine, the words: 'Hereford & Monmouth' are blocked in gold along its length.

Dry, *JL* no. 482.

449 Leighton, John

Broderip, Frances Freeling. *Crosspatch, the cricket and the counterpane, A Patchwork of Story and Song. Illustrated by her brother, Thomas Hood.* London: Griffith and Farran, (Successors to Newbery & Harris), Corner of St. Paul's Churchyard, 1865. Printed by Wertheimer and Co., Finsbury Circus, London. [4], 188 p., 6 plates. With thirty-two pages of publisher's titles bound a the end.
127 × 175 × 25 mm. 12804.cc.28.

The plates are hand coloured and are signed 'TH' and 'C.A. Ferrier Sc.'. On page three of the publisher's titles bound at the end: 'Super royal 16mo. price 3s.6d. cloth, 4s.6d. coloured, gilt edges.'

Gilt edges. Light yellow endpapers and pastedowns. Binder's ticket on lower pastedown: '| Bound by | Bone & Son, | [rule] | 76, Fleet Street, | London. |' Red sand-grain cloth. Both covers identically blocked in blind on the borders and on the corners. Five fillets are blocked on the borders, the innermost of which has leaf decoration attached to it, with a circle and leaf blocked on each corner. The lower cover central vignette is blocked in blind, showing a square divided into four, with a leaf, blocked in relief, within each quarter. Four more leaves are blocked in relief on each side of the square. The upper cover central vignette is blocked in gold. It shows a lady, wearing a conical hat, standing on a three-legged stool. She is holding a patchwork in her hands, it being divided into squares. The squares have various decorative patterns, all blocked in relief. The title words: '| Cross | patch |' are blocked in relief within the squares. Above these words: '| Story | & | song' are each blocked in relief within one square. Signed 'JL' in gold as a monogram at the base of the vignette. The spine is blocked in gold and in blind. From the head downwards, the decoration is: a fillet, a Greek roll, a fillet – all in blind; the words: '| Crosspatch | the | cricket | and the | counterpane | Broderip. |' blocked in gold; a figure of the cricket, blocked in gold; at the tail: a fillet; a Greek roll, a fillet – all blocked in blind.

Dry, *JL* no. 484. King, *JL* p. 238.

450 Leighton, John

Broderip, Frances Freeling. *Merry songs for little voices. Set to music by Thomas Murby . . . With forty illustrations.* London: Griffith and Farran (Successors to Newbery and Harris,) The Corner of Saint Paul's Churchyard, 1865. London: W. Clowes and Sons, Type-Music and General Printers, Stamford Street, and Charing Cross. viii, 75 p. With four pages of publisher's titles bound at the end.
173 × 217 × 11 mm. 11650.f.21.

Many of the illustrations are signed with the monogram 'TH' [i.e. Thomas Hood.]

Yellow endpapers and pastedowns. Red coarse pebble-grain cloth. Both covers blocked identically in blind on the borders, on the sides, and on the head and the tail. Two fillets are blocked on the borders, the outer thick, the inner thin. The same curling stem patterns are blocked in blind on each corner. On the centre head and centre tail, the curling stem pattern ends in straps. The upper cover central vignette is blocked in gold. A five point hatched star is blocked at the head. Below it, the words: '| Merry songs |' are blocked in gold. Below this, a stylised lyre is blocked in gold. Its sides are in the form of a single winged angel, male on the left, and female on the right. The male angel holds a tuning fork in his right hand, and an open book (blocked as a gold lettering-piece) in his left. The book has the words: '| By | Mrs | Broderip |' blocked in relief on its covers. The female angel on the right holds a small posy of flowers in her left hand; she also holds an open book (blocked as a gold lettering-piece) in her right hand. The words: '| Music by | T | Murby |' are blocked in relief on its covers. The strings of the lyre run downwards from the angel's wings to the tie-bar at the base. The title word: 'for' is blocked in gold between the strings. The word '| Illustrated |' is blocked in relief with the tie-bar, which is a rectangular gold lettering-piece with diagonal hatch. The words: '| By | Thomas Hood |' are blocked in relief within the base of the lyre (a gold lettering-piece). The words: '| Little voices |' are blocked in relief within a rectangular gold lettering-piece, which has diagonal hatch, and a gold fillet blocked on its borders. Signed 'JL' in relief as separate letters, within a small circular gold lettering-piece at the base of the vignette. The spine is blocked in gold and in blind. From the head downwards, the decoration is: two fillets blocked in blind;

a head blocked between two wings; the title: '| Merry | songs | for | little | voices |' blocked in gold; a lyre. [Lower portion of the spine is missing.]

Dry, *JL* no. 483.

451 Leighton, John PLATE LIII

Cats, Jacob. *Moral emblems with aphorisms, adages, and proverbs, of all ages and nations. With illustrations freely rendered, from designs found in their works, by John Leighton, F.S.A. The whole translated and edited, with additions, by Richard Pigot, Member of the Leyden Society of Netherlands Literature.* Third edition. London: Longmans, Green, Reader, and Dyer, 1865. R.Clay, London. xvi, 242 p.
205 × 275 × 31 mm. 12305.m.18.

Bevelled boards. Gilt edges. White endpapers and pastedowns. Stamped on lower pastedown: '| [Bound] by Simpson & Renshaw |'. Red sand-grain cloth. Both covers blocked in gold and black, with an identical design. The borders are blocked with: 1. a single gold fillet; 2. a black fillet blocked between two thin gold fillets. Inside this, elaborate strapwork is blocked in with the same fillet work of a black fillet between two thin gold fillets. Leaves and stems are blocked in gold at the head, the tail and the sides, and on the corners. The strapwork forms a central rectangle, whose corners are blocked in black, with letters blocked in relief. The phrases are: '| Animi | pabullum |', in the top left and the bottom right hand corners. The words '| Animi | medicina |' are blocked in the top right and bottom left corners. The central mandorla is formed by three gold fillets. In the mandorla, the capitals 'M' and 'E' are blocked in gold. The words: ' [M]oral' and '[E]mblems' are blocked in relief, within rectangular gold lettering-pieces. Signed 'JL', in gold as separate letters, at the base of the mandorla. The title is surrounded by a dense pattern of curling stems and horizontal hatch leaves, with a cross near the base of the mandorla. The spine is blocked in gold and black and in relief. The strapwork is as for the covers. From the head downwards, the decoration is: on the upper half, in gold, a mandorla is blocked with horizontal gold hatch. The words: '| Moral | Emblems | By | Jacob Cats | & | Robert Fairlie. |' blocked in relief within lettering-pieces, each with a single fillet on its borders; a panel gold horizontal hatch lettering-piece, with the words: '| Illustrated | by | John Leighton | F S A |' blocked in relief within lettering-pieces, with single fillets blocked in relief on their borders; more strapwork; signed 'JL' in gold as separate letters above the imprint: '| London | Longmans & Co |', which is blocked in relief within a rectangular gold lettering-piece, with a single gold fillet blocked on its borders; a black fillet blocked between two gold fillets; two gold fillets blocked at the tail.

Ball, *VPB* pp. 54, 61, 82. King, *JL* pp. 241–242.

452 Leighton, John

Cowper, William. *The task a poem. Illustrated by Birket Foster.* London: James Nisbet and Co. Berners Street, 1865. Edinburgh: Printed by R. & R. Clark. [13], 263 p.
153 × 210 × 29 mm. RdeB.G.19.

The British Museum de Beaumont copy.

Text sewn on two tapes. Gilt edges. Bevelled boards. Yellow endpapers and pastedowns. Binder's ticket on lower pastedown: '| Bound by | Edmonds & Remnants | [rule] | London |' Blue morocco vertical-grain cloth. Both covers are blocked identically in gold. Three fillets are blocked on the borders in gold. On the spine side of each cover, nine stylised leaves and four dots are blocked from head to tail. An inner border of crossing semi-circles is blocked in gold. Small leaf and curling stem decoration is blocked inside each semi-circle. The central rectangle formed by these semi-circles is itself divided into three panels by gold fillets. In the panel at the head, a lozenge-shape is blocked in gold on the centre. The middle rectangle has small flowers blocked on its corners. The words: '| The Task | Illustrated |' are blocked in gold, with elaborate tendrils attached to the ends of some of the letters. The spine is blocked in gold. A single gold fillet is blocked on the perimeter. From the head downwards, the decoration is: two gold fillets; the words: '| The | Task | Illustrated |' blocked in gold within a rectangular panel, which is formed by a single fillet; two crossing semi-circles and small leaf decoration are blocked within a rectangle formed by a single fillet; three circles have leaf and stem decoration blocked within each; two crossing semi-circles and small leaf decoration are blocked within a rectangle formed by a single fillet; signed 'JL' in gold as a monogram at the centre of this decoration; the words: 'Nisbet & Co.' are blocked in gold within a rectangle formed by a single fillet; a fillet is blocked in gold at the tail.

de Beaumont, *RdeB1* no. 71. Goldman, *VIB* no. 71. McLean, V*BD* pp. 116–117. Oldfield, *BC* no. 51. Exhibited the New York Robert Carter edition of 1855, with a design by Leighton.

453 Leighton, John

Cundall, Joseph. *A book of favourite modern ballads. Illustrated with engravings from drawings by J. C. Horsley, A.R.A., Edward Duncan, G. H. Thomas, Edward H. Corbould, Birket Foster, C. W. Cope, R. A. Harrison Weir, W. Harvey, A. Solomon, etc.* London: Ward, Lock, & Tyler, 158 Fleet Street; and 107 Dorset Street, Salisbury Square, 1865. London: Edmund Evans, Engraver & Printer. xiv, 168 p.
165 × 230 × 35 mm. 1347.g.25.

Printed in colours by Edmund Evans. [The editor's preface is signed J.C. i.e. Joseph Cundall.]

Gilt edges. Bevelled boards. Original yellow endpaper bound at the front. Blue sand-grain cloth. On the upper cover, the outer design is fully blocked in gold. The borders have a repeating pattern of hatched leaves within a square, both attached to a gold fillet. Inside this, a fillet is blocked in blind, with small

flowers blocked in relief on each corner. The central oval is recessed, and has a Renaissance strap panel and tracery blocked on its borders. A painted onlay has been pasted within the recess. The onlay features a young girl leaning against the base of a statue, looking at a young man seated holding a harp. The lower cover has the same outer design as the upper cover, blocked in blind. The lower cover has a central vignette blocked in gold of a harp and leaves, and is signed 'JL' in gold as a monogram at the base. This vignette is used also on the covers of Ralph Waldo Emerson, Poems, 1850, [BL shelfmark: 11689.a.44.]; and on both covers of Sophia Milligen, Original poems . . ., 1856, [BL shelfmark: 11649.c.4.]. The spine is fully blocked in gold. A single gold fillet is blocked on the perimeter. From the head downwards, the decoration is: a rectangle formed by a single fillet, with gold leaf decoration, with dots blocked in relief inside; two tassels and tracery above a Renaissance oval panel, which has the title: '| A | book | of | favourite | modern | ballads. |' blocked in gold within it; more gold tracery surrounds a suspended bunch of fruit – all blocked in gold; within a Renaissance strap gold lettering-piece, the words: '| London | Ward Lock & Tyler |' are blocked in relief; a gold fillet; gold leaf decoration and dots blocked inside in relief are all within a rectangle at the tail. [Another edition of 'Favourite modern ballads', 1859 is at 1347.i.13.]

Ball, *VPB* p. 164. States that the ornamental designs of the 1859 edition are by Warren. King, *JL* p. 239. McLean, *Cundall* pp. 20–21, 34, 36, 38, 85.

454 Leighton, John

Dalton, William. *The wasps of the ocean: or little waif and the pirate of the Eastern seas. A romance of travel and adventure in China and Siam. With illustrations.* London: E. Marlborough & Co., Ave Maria Lane, [1865]. London: Henry C. Berry & Co., Gloucester Street, Regent's Park, N.W. viii, 412 p., 6 plates. With eight pages of publisher's titles bound at the front.
125 × 190 × 35 mm. 12805.h.20.

Bevelled boards. Light brown endpapers and pastedowns. Green morocco horizontal-grain cloth. The lower cover is blocked in blind, with the decoration on the borders and on the sides identical for both covers. The upper cover is blocked in gold and in blind. On the upper cover, two fillets are blocked in gold on the borders. Inside this, a border panel is blocked in blind, showing joined stems, leaves and flowers. The central rectangular panel has a trefoil blocked in gold on each corner, and a gold fillet border. The central vignette is blocked in gold, and shows the rear of a sailing ship, which has its sail and pennant flying. The rear of the ship has the features of a face and a large open mouth. Beneath the rear of the ship, a shark, blocked in gold, is swimming in the sea. The title: 'Wasps of the ocean' is blocked in gold and in relief within the mainsail. The mainsail is blocked in gold with hatch. The words: 'W. Dalton' are blocked in relief on the rear of the ship. Signed 'JL' in gold as separate letters at the base of the vignette. The spine is blocked in full gold. There is a single fillet blocked in gold around the perimeter. A large wasp is blocked in gold at the head.; underneath, the title 'Wasps of the ocean' is blocked in gold. The word: 'Dalton' is blocked underneath the title inside a rectangular gold lettering piece. Beneath this, a chinaman is blocked in gold. At the tail, the imprint is blocked in gold, inside a rectangle formed by a single fillet. Signed 'JL' in gold as separate letters, underneath the chinaman.

Dry, *JL* no. 485.

455 Leighton, John

Fraser, Robert William. *Head and hand or Thought and Action in reference to success and happiness. New edition.* London and Edinburgh: William and Robert Chambers, [1865]. Edinburgh: Printed by William Grant, 52 West Register Street. 264 p., 4 plates.
115 × 172 × 25 mm. 10604.aaa.13.

Text sewn on two tapes. The design has been blocked after casing in. Brown endpapers and pastedowns. Red pebble-grain cloth. Both covers blocked identically in blind on the borders and on the corners. Two fillets are blocked on the borders. Inside this, a third fillet is blocked in blind, with trefoils and dots blocked in relief within it. Small berries are blocked in relief on each corner. The upper cover central vignette is the same as for BL 10603.aa.11 (the 1861 edition). The incident described is on page 40 of this edition, not page 43. The author's name, blocked underneath the boat for the 1861 edition, has been replaced by sea water for this issue. The spine design is the same as for the 1861 edition, with two exceptions: the author word: 'Fraser' is omitted; the word 'W & R Chambers' is substituted for 'Houlston & Wright'.

Dry, *JL* no. 392. The 1861 edition.

456 Leighton, John PLATE LIV

Hood, Thomas, *the Elder. Jingles and jokes for the little folks. Illustrated by C. H.Bennett, W.Brunton, Paul Gray, and T. Morten.* London: Cassell, Petter and Galpin, Ludgate Hill, E.C., 1865. London: Cassell, Petter and Galpin, Belle Sauvage Works, Ludgate Hill, E.C. vii, 9–76 p. With four pages of publisher's titles bound at the end.
150 × 196 × 15 mm. 11648.cc.40.

Bevelled boards. Gilt edges. Red sand-grain cloth. Both covers blocked identically, in gold on the upper, in blind on the lower. The design features a border of joined flowers. Then a gold fillet is blocked on the borders, with repeating dots blocked in relief inside. Inside this, a thin gold fillet joins six gold medallions blocked on the corners and on the sides. The four corner medallions contain stars with faces and arms and legs. The two medallions on the sides contain a snail and a butterfly in relief within hatch gold. Sunflowers, with faces and leaves, are blocked above and below the two medallions on the sides. Above the centre, a gold lettering-piece shaped as a clock, has face-like features and roman numerals blocked in relief within.

The large central medallion is blocked in gold. In the border of the medallion, the words: '| Jingles and jokes for little folks |' are blocked in relief. The words: '| Tom Hood |' are blocked in gold. The pendulum of the clock forms the 'o' of Tom [Hood]. On the centre tail, the weights of the clock press down upon a book, and they have trapped one of the 'little folk' inside the book. Signed 'JL' in gold as separate letters underneath the book. [Spine missing.]

The National Library of Scotland copy is at shelfmark K.194.a. Text sewn on two sawn-in cords. Gilt edges. Bevelled boards. Purple sand-grain cloth. The covers are blocked as for the BL copy. The spine is blocked in gold and in relief; the title: '| Jingles & Jokes for Little Folks |' is blocked in relief along the spine within a gold hatch cartouche, with a sunflower and hatch gold leaves blocked at each end of the cartouche. Each sunflower has a 'face' blocked in relief within it. At the head and at the tail, vertical gold hatch is blocked, with triangles, and gold dots within it, all between two gold fillets.

Dry, *JL* no. 488. King, *JL* pp. 242, 244; illustration, p. 243.

457 Leighton, John

Shakespeare, William. *The dramatic works. With copious glossarial notes and biographical notice.* 2 vols. Edinburgh: Gall & Inglis, 6 George Street; London: Houlston & Wright, [1865]. Vol 1: xviii, 1020 p. 110 × 173 × 55 mm. Vol. 2: [2], 1094 p.
110 × 173 × 57 mm. 11765.aaa.29.

Gilt edges. Bevelled boards. Light yellow endpapers and pastedowns. Red bead-grain cloth. Both covers are blocked identically. The design is blocked in blind and in relief on the lower cover and in gold and in blind and in relief on the upper cover. Blocked on the borders are: 1. a repeating pattern of flower heads and triangles blocked in gold; 2. a gold fillet, with small leaf decoration blocked in relief within it; 3. a single gold fillet. Inside the inner rectangle, the corners are formed by two gold fillets, and curling stems and hatch gold leaves are blocked on each of the corners in gold. At the head and at the tail are two small circles, formed by two gold fillets, the outer of which has dots blocked in relief inside. On the centre of each circle a single flower is blocked in gold. A pattern is blocked in relief between the two. The central panel is of an arabesque. Around its perimeter fillets are blocked in gold, and decoration blocked in blind. At the centre of the panel, a lyre is blocked in gold. The two arms of the lyre have swans' necks at the top. The strings of the lyre are picked out in blind. The lyre is bisected by the word '| Shakespeare |', blocked in gold. The lyre is on a plinth, and the whole is surrounded by a circle, alternating in gold and in hatch, which in turn is encircled by interlocking curling stems and leaves. Signed 'JL' in gold as separate letters at the base of the central panel. The spines of both volumes are identical and blocked in gold. Two gold fillets are blocked on the perimeter, the outer thicker than the inner. From the head downwards, the decoration is: a gold fillet with a repeating pattern of leaf decoration blocked inside in relief; a gold fillet; three circles and arabesques, with small decoration blocked within; a medallion, blocked as a vertical gold hatch lettering-piece, surrounded by four gold fillets, which form straps at its head and its tail; the words: '| The | Dramatic | Works | of | Shakespeare | Vol. I. |' blocked inside the medallion, with the words: 'Dramatic; Shakespeare; Vol. I.' being blocked within rectangles, with single fillets blocked in relief on their borders; more hatch leaf and curling stem decoration is blocked beneath the medallion; three circles and arabesques; a gold fillet; a gold fillet with vertical hatch, triangles and dots blocked in relief inside it; the words: '| Family Edition |' are blocked in gold within a rectangle formed by a single fillet; a gold fillet; at the tail, a gold fillet with a repeating pattern of leaf decoration blocked inside in relief.

458 Leighton, John PLATE LV

Swift, Jonathan. *Gulliver's travels into several remote regions of the world. A New Edition. With explanatory notes and a Life of the Author, by John Francis Waller, LL.D. Illustrated by T. Morten.* London: Cassell, Petter, and Galpin, La Belle Sauvage Yard, Ludgate Hill, E.C., [1865]. [London]: Cassell, Petter and Galpin, La Belle Sauvage Yard, E.C. xliii, 352 p.
191 × 270 × 32 mm. 12612.i.13.

Issued in eleven parts. Each part cost 6d.

Both covers for each issue are bound in. Paper cover size: 182 × 260 mm. The paper is beige coloured, and printed in black. There is a star on each corner, then five fillets on the borders. Between the second and third fillets, a dentelle border is printed. Three medallions are at the head, each with a figure. They are: 'Laputian'; 'Yahoo, Houyhnhnm'; 'Struldbrug'. The title '| Cassell's | Illustrated | Gulliver's | Travels |' is printed at the centre. The capital 'G' is highly ornamented. A hand and a small figure within it are below the title. There is a medallion at the tail on the left and on the right. Each shows a sea monster [the Leighton 'dolphin']. The design on the upper cover for each part is signed 'Luke Limner F.S.A.' and 'H. Leighton Sc.' between the fillets at the tail. The imprint: '| London | Cassell Petter & Galpin | La Belle Sauvage Road. | E.C. |' is printed between medallions on the centre tail. Stylistically, this design is close to Leighton's for: 'Voices of the year or poet's kalendar . . .', at BL 11651.h.9.

459 Leighton, John FIG. 58

Tennyson, Alfred. *A selection from the works.* London: Edward Moxon & Co., Dover Street, 1865. London: Printed by Bradbury, and Evans, Whitefriars. vii, 256 p.
130 × 170 × 30 mm. 1607/6176.

Printed at the head of the title page: 'Moxon's miniature poets.' On verso of title page: 'The woodcuts and cover from designs by John Leighton, F.S.A.' Many of the ornamental head-pieces are signed 'JL' as separate letters; the lettering-piece is signed 'L', with a full stop above it.

Bevelled boards. Grey endpapers and pastedowns. Red pebble-grain cloth. Both covers blocked identically. The upper cover is blocked in gold; the lower cover in blind and relief.

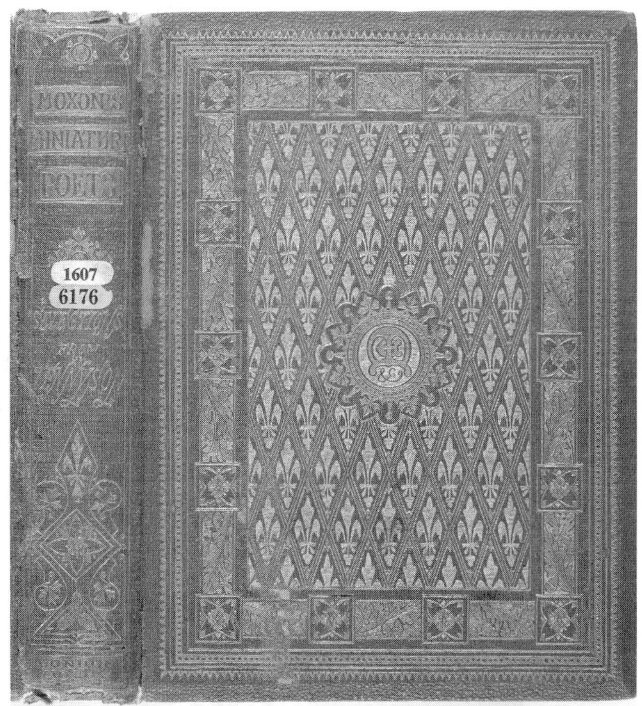

FIG. 58

Three decorative borders are blocked in gold: 1. 'dog-tooth'; 2. a gold fillet; 3. a gold fillet with repeating dots blocked in relief inside. The inner border features alternately: squares containing flowers and quatrefoils, and rectangles which contain acorns and oak leaves. A gold fillet is blocked on the perimter of the the central panel. The panel is of hatch fleurs-de-lis, blocked within diamonds. At the centre, the gold monogram of Moxon is blocked. The spine is blocked in gold and in relief, two gold fillets are blocked on the perimeter, the inner of which forms a semi-circle at the head. From the head downwards, the decoration is: the words: '| Moxon's | Miniature | Poets |' blocked in relief within three rectangular gold lettering-pieces, each with single border fillets blocked in gold; a decorative device blocked in gold; the words: '| Selections | from | Tennyson |' blocked in gold in letters with exaggerated serifs; decoration blocked within fillets, showing hatched fleurs-de-lis, and three acorns and leaves and a quatrefoil flower – all blocked within a panel formed by a single gold fillet; at the tail, the words: '| London | Moxon |' are blocked in relief within a rectangular gold lettering-piece, with a single gold fillet blocked on its borders.

Dry, *JL* no. 491. King, *JL* p. 249. McLean, *VPBB* p. 122. Shows a copy bound in brown cloth. Pantazzi, *JL* p. 265. Copy bound in red morocco cloth.

460 **Leighton, John** FIG. 59

Thompson, D'Arcy Wentworth. *Fun and Earnest; or, rhymes with reason. Illustrated by Charles H. Bennett.* London: Griffith & Farran, (Successors to Newbery and Harris,) Corner of St. Paul's Churchyard, 1865. London: R. Clay, Son, and Taylor,

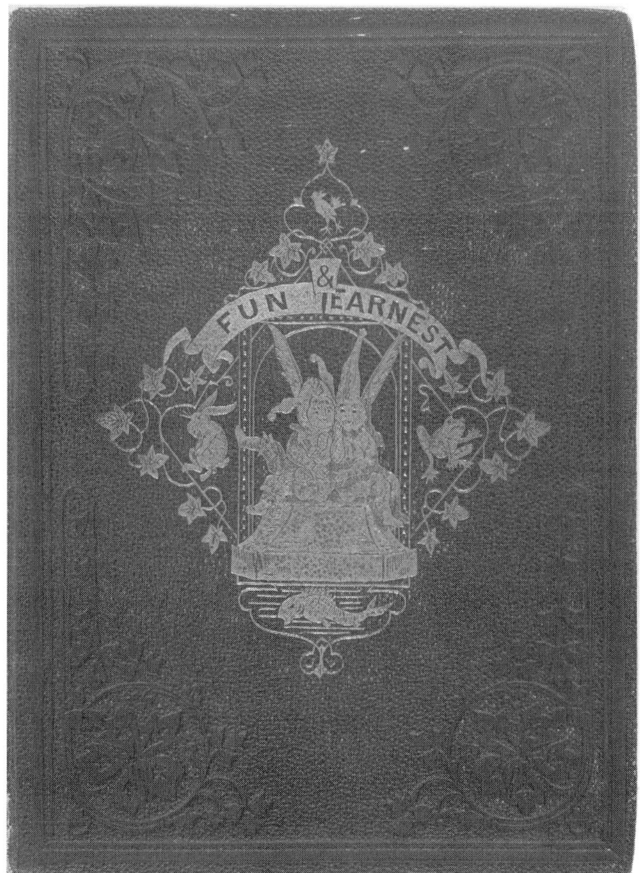

FIG. 59

Printers, Bread Street Hill. [3], 80 p., 8 plates. With thirty-two pages of publisher's titles bound at the end.
136 × 185 × 15 mm. 11649.aa.10.

Beige endpapers and pastedowns. Mauve pebble-grain cloth. Both covers are blocked identically in blind on the borders and on the corners. Two fillets are blocked on the borders, with plant and leaf patterns blocked on the corners and sides. The upper cover has a central vignette blocked in gold. Ivy leaves and stems are blocked around the perimeter. A rabbit is blocked on the left, a frog on the right and a fish at the base. In the middle, sitting on a plinth, are two 'party-like' figures in costume. Signed 'JL' in gold as separate letters at the base of the vignette. The spine is blocked in gold. The title: '| Fun | & | Earnest |' is blocked in gold. There are two circles, blocked above and below the title, with star shaped lettering pieces inside. Inside each star, a face is blocked in relief, one smiling, the other frowning. [This decoration is similar to the stars on Hood, Jingles and jokes . . .]

Dry, *JL* no. 494. King, *JL* p. 249.

461 **Leighton, John**

A round of days described in original poems by some of our most celebrated poets, and in pictures by eminent artists, engraved by the Brothers Dalziel. London: George Routledge and Sons,

Broadway, Ludgate Hill, 1866. [London]: Dalziel Brothers, Engravers and Printers, Camden Press. [6], 93 p. With two pages of publisher's titles bound at the end.
200 × 262 × 35 mm. RdeB.K.16.

The British Museum de Beaumont copy.

The text is printed only on the rectos.

Gilt edges. Bevelled boards. Binder's ticket on lower pastedown, left hand corner, tail: '| Bound | by | Leighton | Son and | Hodge |'. Bookseller's ticket on lower pastedown, left hand corner, head: '| J. Brothers, | Bookseller | & Stationer | High St. | Maidstone |'. Written on upper endpaper: '| Bryan Lewis | from his affectionate friend R. Cooper | 1 Sept 1866 |'. Green sand-grain cloth. Both covers identically blocked in gold and in relief. A thin gold fillet is blocked on the outer borders. Inside, there is a paper onlay on the inner borders. It is painted in blue and in red, and blocked with a pattern of four pointed ovals and diamonds. On the middle of each side, there are larger ovals; on each corner, there is a 'spade-shape'. All these have single gold fillets on their borders, and leaf and flower patterns blocked in gold inside. Between them, double fillets in red relief outline each pattern in blue, and groups of three clover leaves and stems are blocked in red relief. The centre of the cover has a thin mandorla, which is formed by a paper onlay painted blue and red, and blocked in gold. Groups of leaves and buds are blocked in gold on the blue at the head, the tail and the sides, within straps blocked in gold. The words: '| A | round | of |' are blocked in gold above the central medallion; the word: '| Days |' is blocked in red relief within the central hatched gold medallion; the word: '| Illustrated |' is blocked in gold in a semi-circle within the blue outer rim of the central medallion. Beneath the medallion, the words: '| Dalziel's | Fine Art | Gift | Book |' are blocked in red relief, within a horizontal hatch gold lettering-piece. Signed 'JL' in gold as separate letters at the base of the gold lettering-piece. The spine is blocked in gold. A single gold fillet is blocked on the perimeter. From the head downwards, the decoration is: a medallion, with a horizontal hatch gold fleur-de-lis blocked within it; an 'arrow head' shape, with small leaf and stem decoration blocked within; the words: '| A | round | of | days | Illustrated |' blocked in gold within a panel formed by a single gold fillet; more leaf and stem decoration is blocked within two decorative panels; a medallion – the same as blocked at the head; a gold fillet; the word: '| Routledge |' is blocked in gold, within a rectangle formed by a single fillet; at the tail, a gold fillet.

Dry, *JL* no. 507. de Beaumont, *RdeB1* no. 346. Goldman, *VIB* no. 346. Morris & Levin, *APB* p. 104, no. 231. Oldfield, *BC* no. 61. Pantazzi, *JL* p. 269.

462 Leighton, John

Swiss pictures drawn with pen and pencil. The illustrations by Mr. E. Whymper, F.R.G.S. . . . London: The Religious Tract Society, 56 Paternoster Row, 65 St. Paul's Churchyard; & 164 Piccadilly, [1866]. London: Printed by William Clowes and Sons, Stamford Street, and Charing Cross. 214[2], p, 1 plate.
200 × 285 × 20 mm. 1783.a.11.

The frontispiece plate is signed: 'E. Whymper, London; By Hodson's chromographic process.'

Text sewn on three sawn-in cords (in pieces). Gilt edges. Yellow endpapers and pastedowns. Binder's ticket on lower pastedown: '| Bound by | Westley's | & Co. | London. |'. Green sand-grain cloth. Five fillets are blocked on the borders of both covers, in blind on the lower and in gold on the upper. These are – two outer fillets, and a group of three inner fillets. On the centre of the lower cover, a large circle is blocked in blind, with a pattern of curling stems, of leaves and flowers blocked in relief within it. Inside this, a repeating pattern of leaves, small decoration and flowers is blocked in blind. Flower head petals are outlined on the very centre. The upper cover vignette is blocked in gold. The title: '| Swiss Pictures |' is blocked in gold in gothic letters above the centre; the sub-title: '| Drawn | by | Pen & | Pencil. |' is blocked in gold underneath the centre. The centre shows a lady on a horse, side saddle. The horse is feeding. The lady has an open book on her lap. Both the lady and the horse are surrounded by vine stems and leaves, to the left, and by palm tree stems and leaves, to the right. Below, between the sub-title words, a group of travelling objects is blocked in gold. There is a suitcase, which is on top of an umbrella and a stick. On top of the suitcase, a map, a telescope, a purse are blocked in gold. In front of the suitcase, a bottle and a 'Passeporte' are blocked in gold. Signed 'JL' in gold as a monogram beneath the bottle. Spine missing.

Dry *JL* no. 509.

463 Leighton, John

The Warringtons abroad: or twelve months in Germany, Italy, and Egypt. With numerous illustrations. London: Seeley, Jackson, and Halliday, 54 Fleet Street, 1866. London: Strangeways and Walden, Printers, Castle St. Leicester Sq. vi, 140 p., 19 plates.
170 × 212 × 25 mm. 12805.i.57.

Some of the plates are signed 'ET' and Aeterington'.

[Text originally sewn on three sawn-in cords, two of which are laced into each board. Yellow endpapers and pastedowns. Both now lost.] Red sand-grain cloth. Both covers blocked identically in blind on the borders, on the corners, on the sides, on the head and on the tail. Two fillets are blocked on the borders, the outer thick, the inner thin. Groups of three fillets (one thick between two thin) form cartouches on each side of the cover. There is circular decoration blocked in relief within each cartouche. The central portion has straps blocked on the head and on the tail, and diamond shapes above and below the central frame. The upper cover has four smaller diamond-shaped gold lettering-pieces blocked inside diamonds formed by the straps. The small diamonds have decoration blocked inside. At the head: horizontal hatch gold, with a star and a 'Turkish' moon; on the right and left hand side: a double headed eagle, with a ball and sceptre held in its claws; on the tail: an eagle and arrows; – all decoration is blocked in relief. The upper cover central vignette is blocked in gold. This shows an Egyptian entrance, with a pediment at its head, and 'reed-like' columns blocked on

each side. On the centre, the words: '| The | Warringtons |' are blocked in gold. Below this, a felucca is on the water, a pyramid, and small palm trees are blocked in gold. Signed 'JL' in gold as separate letters on the right-hand base of the vignette. The base of the centre-piece is a rectangular gold lettering-piece with a single fillet blocked on its borders. The word: '| Abroad |' is blocked in relief within this, plus a small decorative device on each side of this word. The spine is blocked in gold. The top third is missing. The title: '| [The] Warringtons | abroad |' is blocked in gold on the middle. Below this, small leaf and stem decoration is blocked in gold.

Dry, *JL* no. 512.

464 Leighton, John

Barham, Richard Harris. *The Ingoldsby Legends or mirth and marvels, by Thomas Ingoldsby, Esquire. With illustrations by George Cruikshank, John Leech and John Tenniel.* London: Richard Bentley, Publisher in Ordinary to Her Majesty, 1866. R.Clay, Sons, and Taylor, Printers, London. xiv, 514 p.
170 × 235 × 40 mm. 11651.f.3.

(BM, rebound C19.) Original dark green endpaper bound at the front. Original upper and lower covers used as doublures. The doublure size is 170 × 230 mm.

Green sand-grain cloth. Both covers are identically blocked in gold and in blind. At the four corners, twin intertwined dragons are blocked in gold. The outer border in gold is of a repeating pattern of acorns at the end of leaves, interspersed with a triple leaf motif, which is enclosed in arches. The inner border features a medallion on each corner, with the head and shoulders of a fanciful character blocked within each. There is also a medallion and fanciful character within blocked on the centre of each side. Two shields with pseudo-devices within are blocked in gold and in relief on each side. Fillets and 'cord-shaped' fillets and emblems are blocked in gold between the medallions and the shields on the inner border. The inner corners have decoration blocked in blind. The central mandorla has several borders, blocked in gold. Within it at the head, a lion is blocked, holding a shield, saltire ermine. The tail of the lion loops on either side of the shield to enclose the initials 'T' and 'I'. The title: '| The | Ingoldsby | Legends |' is blocked in relief within a shield-shaped gold lettering-piece. The initials, 'JL', are blocked in relief as separate letters at the base of the title.

King, *JL* pp. 240–241.

465 Leighton, John

Bulwer Lytton, Edward George. *Harold, the last of the Saxon kings. A New Edition.* London: George Routledge and Sons, Broadway, Ludgate Hill; New York: 129 Grand Street, 1866. [London]: Printed by Cox (Bros.) and Wyman, Great Queen Street. viii, 352 p., 1 plate. With three pages of publisher's titles bound at the front and at the end.
110 × 175 × 30 mm. 12603.cc.3.

Text sewn on three sawn-in cords. Yellow endpapers and pastedowns. Bookseller's ticket on upper pastedown: '| Bookseller & Stationer | [rule] | J. Gilbert, | 18 Gracechurch Street | London E.C. | [rule] | Engraver & Printer. |' Blue bead-grain cloth. Both covers identically blocked in blind. On the outer borders, six fillets are blocked in two groups of three. Between these, the fillet in the middle has a repeating pattern of crossed stems and dots. The fillets cross on the corners, forming squares. A single cross is blocked in relief within each corner square. Three fillets are blocked on the inner borders. The central vignette on each cover is lozenge-shaped, with small leaves and lines blocked in relief within it. The spine is blocked in gold. Two fillets are blocked in gold on the perimeter. From the head downwards, the decoration is: two fillets in gold; a 'lamp and its stand' is blocked from the tail to near the head; it has a bowl emitting light on its top; within a panel, the words: '| Harold | [rule] | Sir Bulwer Lytton. |' are blocked in gold; signed 'JL' in gold as separate letters at the base of the lamp stand; a fillet in gold; a rectangle formed by a single gold fillet; two fillets are blocked in gold at the tail.

Dry, *JL* no. 503.

466 Leighton, John

Duffy, Charles Gavan. *The Ballad Poetry of Ireland. Edited by the Hon. Charles Gavan Duffy . . . Thirty-ninth edition.* London: James Duffy, 15, Wellington Quay, and 22, Paternoster Row, 1866. London: Cox and Wyman, Printers, Great Queen Street, Lincoln's inn Fields, W.C. 232 p., 1 plate.
122 × 152 × 23 mm. 11622.aa.42.

The frontispiece plate is an engraved portrait of C. Gavan Duffy.

Original upper cover used as a doublure. Doublure size: 107 × 140 mm. Blue sand-grain cloth. Two fillets are blocked in gold on the borders. A single shamrock is blocked in gold on each corner. The central vignette is blocked in gold. It shows shamrock stems and leaves, which form into two 'heart' shaped frames, one on top of the other. In the upper frame, the title word: '| Ballad |' and an Irish harp are blocked. Tendrils are attached to the base of the letters 'B' and 'd'. In the lower frame, the words: '| Poetry | of Ireland. |' are blocked in gold. A tendril is attached to the 't' of 'Poetry'. Signed 'JL' in gold as a monogram at the base of the vignette.

Dry, *JL* no. 497.

467 Leighton, John PLATE LVI

Hodgkin, John Eliot. *Monograms, ancient & modern, their history & art-treatment, with examples collected and designed by John Eliot Hodgkin, F.S.A.* London: Longmans & Co, 1866. [79 plates].
120 × 140 × 30 mm. 7855.a.34.

The whole book is shaped in the form of a shield. Bevelled boards. Red edges. Red endpapers and pastedowns. Green

sand-grain cloth. Both covers are blocked identically in gold, black and red. The design features a helm surmounting a shield, surrounded by pennants and groups of plants blocked in gold. The shield, or, is blocked in gold on a red bead-grain cloth onlay. The shield features different monograms on upper and lower covers. On the lower cover shield, the initials 'JEH' [i.e. John Eliot Hodgkin] are blocked. Signed 'JL' in relief as a monogram at base of shield. The spine is in gold, with the title: '| Monograms |' blocked in relief, in gothic letters, along the spine within a rectangular gold lettering-piece.

The National Library of Scotland copy is at shelfmark Cn.9. The single leaves are sewn overcast onto three cords, and the endpapers and pastedowns have not been disturbed, so this may be the original structure.

Dry, *JL* no. 499. King, *JL* pp. 244–245; illustration p. 244. Morris & Levin, *APB* p. 100, no. 222. Pantazzi, *JL* p. 270.

468 Leighton, John

PLATE LVII

Jerrold, Douglas William. *Mrs Caudle's curtain lectures. Illustrated by Charles Keene.* London: Bradbury, Evans & Co., 11 Bouverie Street, 1866. London: Bradbury, Evans, and Co., Printers, Whitefriars. xx, 190 p., 1 plate. With one page of publisher's titles bound at the end.

167 × 213 × 25 mm. C.109.c.11.

The board edges are gauffered; the turn-ins are blocked in gold, with a repeating pattern of ovals and diamonds. Gilt edges. Light yellow endpapers and pastedowns. Red calf. Both covers identically blocked in gold and in blind and relief. Eight patterns blocked on the borders: 1. a fillet in gold with repeating dots in relief; 2. a thin fillet in gold; 3. a border of hatched five point stars and gold dots; 4. a thin fillet in gold; 5. a fillet blocked in blind; 6. a fillet blocked in blind with repeating dots blocked in relief; 7. a fillet blocked in blind; 8 a thin fillet, in gold. A four poster bed fills the rest of each cover. It is end-on to the viewer. The decorative features of the bed – the bed linen, the back of the bed, the columns – are outlined in relief by blocking in blind. A rail hung between the two post supports two curtains, which are hung on wooden rings. On the left curtain, the words: '| The curtain | lectures |' are blocked in gold; on the right curtain, the words: '| of | Mrs. | Caudle |' are blocked in gold. Five hatched five-point stars are blocked in gold below each group of words. Between the curtains on the back of the bed, a circular clock face is blocked in gold, with its Arabic hour numbers blocked in relief. In the middle of the foreground, between the curtains, a table is blocked with a lamp on its top, both blocked in relief. The candle flame and its rays inside the lamp are blocked in gold. On the table plinth, the word: '| Illustrated |' is blocked in gold. Underneath the table, a water pitcher and a bowl are blocked in relief. The words: '| By | C |' are blocked on gold on the pitcher; the word: '| Keene |' is blocked in gold on the bowl. Signed 'JL' in relief as separate letters on either side of the bowl. The spine is blocked in gold. A single fillet is blocked in gold on the perimeter. From the head downwards, the decoration is: hatched stars and a quarter moon, with a face; the words: '| Mrs. | Caudle's | curtain | lectures | [a set of teeth!] | Douglas | Jerrold. |' blocked in gold (the author words are blocked in relief within two rectangular gold lettering-pieces); the words: '| Caudle's | curtain | wedding | ring |' blocked in gold round a ring, which has an eagle perched within it; the words: '| Illustrated | by | Charles | Keene. |' blocked in gold; miscellaneous decorative patterns, some in hatched gold; near the tail: '| London | Bradbury, | Evans & Co. |' are blocked in gold within a rectangle formed by a single gold fillet; two fillets are blocked in gold at the tail.

Dry, *JL* no. 501. King, *JL* p. 249.

469 Leighton, John

Jerrold, Douglas William. *Mrs. Caudle's curtain lectures. Illustrated by Charles Keene.* London: Bradbury, Evans, & Co., 11 Bouverie Street, 1866. Whitefriars: Bradbury, Evans, and Co., Printers Extraordinary to the Queen. xiv, 190 p., 1 colour plate. With ten pages of publisher's titles bound at the end.

170 × 214 × 25 mm. RdeB.I.7.

The British Museum de Beaumont copy.

This copy is printed on blue paper.

Text sewn on three sawn-in cords. Gilt edges. Bevelled boards. Dark green endpapers and pastedowns. Purple sand-grain cloth. Binder's ticket on lower pastedown: '| Bound | by | Leighton | Son and | Hodge. |' This copy has the same upper cover and spine design as for the BL copy at C.109.c.11. The lower cover is blocked in blind only. It has the same border design as for the upper cover, and the lettering is blocked in blind only. There is no decoration of the bed, as is blocked on the upper cover.

Another copy is at RdeB.I.8. Text sewn on three sawn-in cords. Gilt edges. Bevelled boards. 'Red chequer board' endpapers and pastedowns. Binder's ticket on lower pastedown: '| Bound by | Edmonds & Remnants | [rule] | London |'. Red sand-grain cloth. This copy has the same upper cover and spine design as for BL copy at C.109.c.11. The blocking is in blind only on the lower cover. The decoration of the bed is blocked on the lower cover.

de Beaumont, *RdeB1* nos. 145–46. Dry, *JL* no. 501. Goldman, *VIB* nos. 145–146. King, *JL* p. 249.

470 Leighton, John

Pennell, Harry Cholmondeley. *Fishing gossip or stray leaves from the note-books of several anglers.* Edinburgh: Adam & Charles Black, 1866. xi, 329 p., 1 plate. With two pages of publisher's titles bound at the end.

127 × 198 × 30 mm. 7906.bb.9.

Text sewn on two tapes. Green endpapers and pastedowns. The book plates of Arthur Potts and George Watson are pasted on the upper pastedown and endpaper respectively. Brown criss-cross grain cloth. Both covers blocked identically in blind only. Two fillets blocked on the borders, the outer thick, the inner

thin. An inner rectangle is formed by two fillets, with an 'arrow-head' blocked on each corner. The spine is blocked in gold. From the head downwards, the decoration is: three fillets in gold; the title: '| Fishing | Gossip |' blocked in gold; a group of objects associated with fishing – a Neptune's tripod, an eel, a fishing net, and a fish inside it, a slatted mat, and a fishing line; near the base of this group, a gold hatched rectangular lettering-piece is blocked, with a single fillet on its borders; the word 'Pennell' is blocked in relief within it. Signed 'JL' in gold as a monogram underneath the rectangular lettering-piece. [This is one of the smallest Leighton monograms, being one millimetre square.]

Dry, *JL* no. 505. Gaskell, *NIB* p. 242, fig. 91.

471 Leighton, John

Pepper, John Henry. *The playbook of metals: including personal narratives of visits to coal, lead, copper, and tin mines; with a Large Number of Interesting Experiments relating to alchemy and the chemistry of the fifty metallic elements. With Three Hundred Illustrations. A new edition.* London: George Routledge and Sons, Broadway, Ludgate Hill. New York: 129 Grand Street, 1866. London: Savill and Edwards, Printers, Chandos Street, Covent Garden. viii, 504 p., 1 plate.
122 × 187 × 38 mm. 1608/3771.

The plate is signed 'E. Evans Sc.'

Gilt edges. White endpapers and pastedowns. [The upper endpaper is missing.] Dark red sand-grain cloth. Both covers identically blocked in blind on the borders, the corners, and the sides. Two fillets are blocked on the borders. Curling stem and leaf decoration, ending in two circles, is blocked in blind on each corner. Three more fillets are blocked on the inner borders. The upper cover central vignette is blocked in gold. It shows a central medallion, with the words: '| The | playbook | of | metals |' blocked in relief within four gold lettering-pieces, three rectangular, and one circular, each with a single fillet blocked in relief on its borders. Vertical hatch gold fills the remainder of the space at the centre. Two fillets are blocked on the border of the medallion. Signs denoting the elements surround the medallion. Above it, the head of a man is blocked, with long hair and a beard; his left and right hands have smoking bottles resting on his palms; his little fingers hold up handles on the end of cords, and beads on the cords. Two beakers are blocked at the base. Signed 'JL' in gold as separate letters at the base. The spine is blocked in gold. A single gold fillet is blocked on the perimeter. From the head downwards, the decoration is: two fillets; an arch, with a beam and a wheel; a chain hangs from the wheel, and runs down the spine to hold a frame to which a basket is tied; four boys hold onto the chain, above two men in the basket, one of whom has a spade over his right shoulder; above this group, the words: '| The | playbook | of metals. | Pepper |' are blocked in relief, within a ribbon-shaped gold lettering-piece which is wrapped around the hanging chain; signed 'JL' in relief as separate letters at the base of the basket; a gold fillet; near the tail, the words: '| 300 engravings |' are blocked within a rectangle formed by a single gold fillet; a gold fillet is blocked at the tail.

Dry, *JL* no. 406. The 1861 edition.

472 Leighton, John PLATE LVIII

Pigot, Richard. *The Life of Man, symbolised by the months of the year in a series of illustrations by John Leighton, F.S.A. and pourtrayed [sic] In their Seasons and Phases, with passages selected from ancient and modern authors.* [Renaissance bolt and strap design of Leighton & Co.] London: Longmans, Green, Reader & Dyer, Paternoster Row. 1866. London: Whitefriars Bradbury, Evans & Co., Printers Extraordinary to the Queen. xii, 240 p., 48 plates.
225 × 288 × 45 mm. C.109.f.2.

Each page of text has a motto printed on each side, on the head and on the tail, between two border fillets. The half title page verso has a reproduction of Leighton's, originally printed as the wood engraving heading the List of Plates in 'Suggestions in design', published in 1852–1853. The print represents the artist (inventor), engraver (art-workman), printer (producer) and virtuoso (consumer), amid ivy foliage. Beneath the Caxton quotation is printed a shield with a lion rampant, with the words: 'Light on s' [i.e. Leighton's] printed in the pennant underneath the shield. All the titled plates – 'infant', 'schoolboy', etc, are signed 'JL'. Many of the illustrations are signed 'L' with a full stop above, or a plain 'L'. On p. viii: 'My best thanks are due . . . to my Brother Mr. H. Leighton for the ingenious way many of them [the plates] are executed.' On p. vii: 'The smaller designs and devices in the volume are engraved by Leighton, Williamson, Green, Dalziel, Cooper, Woods, Pearson, Jewitt and Servain.' The frontispiece plate, and the plates for April and December are signed 'H. Leighton Sc.'.

Bevelled boards. Gilt edges on head and tail. On the fore-edge, the gilt is overlaid alternately with red ink to index each month. Binder's ticket on lower pastedown: '| Bound by | Edmonds & Remnants, | London |'. Orange sand-grain cloth. Both covers are blocked identically in gold and black. On the borders are blocked: 1. 'dog-tooth' pattern in gold; 2. a black fillet, with repeating stars blocked in relief within it – all between two gold fillets. These black and gold fillets form numerous panels on the inner borders and on the corners. There are patterns of plant and hatch leaves blocked in gold in the panels. Medallions, formed by two gold fillets, are blocked on the centre head, centre tail, and on the sides. Each medallion has horizontal gold hatch and the head of a figure blocked in relief within; these are: 1. an infant; 2. a schoolboy; 3. a father; 4. an old man. A shield on each corner is formed by two gold fillets, with small hatch leaf and stem decoration blocked between these fillets. Horizontal gold hatch is blocked within each shield, plus trees representing the four seasons. The central mandorla is an onlay of red sand-grain cloth. Around its edge are nine borders. These are: 1. a single gold fillet; 2. a thick gold fillet; 3.–5. borders of gold diamonds, flowers and dots, blocked in gold and in black between two thin gold fillets; 6. a fillet

blocked in black, with flower heads blocked in relief within 7. & 8. two thin gold fillets; 9. repeating gold dots. The mandorla features Eve offering Adam the apple, blocked in gold. A gold lettering-piece shaped as a pennant around their feet states: 'As | one | of | us | to | know | good | & | evil |', blocked in relief; 'Genesis III. Ch. XXII.V.' is blocked in gold. The title words are blocked in a shield. The words: '| The Life | of |' are blocked in relief within the shield, or; the word '| Man |' is blocked in gold with the edges of each letter blocked in relief, sable. A cross is blocked in relief below this. Above this shield, Eve's outstretched left arm, offering the apple to Adam, supports armour of shoulders and a helm. The helm contains a skull. Above this is blocked a serpent, crowned, which is curled around an apple tree. There are eleven circles around the apple tree, blocked in gold and the zodiac signs in the circles are blocked in relief. Signed 'JL' in gold as a monogram at the base of pennant. The 'J' and the 'L' are joined dipthong fashion. The spine is fully blocked in gold and black. A single gold fillet is blocked on the perimeter. From the head downwards, the decoration is: dog-tooth decoration in gold; a black fillet within a rectangle formed by a single gold fillet; strapwork – consisting of a black fillet blocked between two gold fillets; small stem and hatch flower decoration is blocked within the strapwork; a rectangular panel formed by a single fillet; the title: '| The | Life of | Man | symbolised | by the | months | of the | year |' blocked in gold within the panel; a single flower head is blocked in gold on each corner of the panel; strap and small gold decoration; a mandorla is formed by the strapwork; within the mandorla are blocked: 1. a five point star, 2. an hour-glass with wings, 3. a shield, or, is formed by two thin gold fillets; the word: '| Illustrated | by | Iohn [sic] | Leighton | FSA |' are blocked in relief in gothic letters within the shield; strapwork and small gold decoration; the words: '| London: | Longmans & Co. |' are blocked in gold in gothic letters within a rectangle formed by a single fillet; a black fillet is blocked within a rectangle formed by a single gold fillet; gold dog-tooth decoration is blocked across the spine at the tail. This is the copyright deposit copy, dated 4 JA[NUARY 18] 66.

PLATE LVIII

—— Another copy. BL C.109.f.4.

Text sewn on three tapes. Bevelled Boards. Gilt edges. Brown endpapers and pastedowns. Binder's ticket on lower pastedown: '| Bound by | Edmonds & Remnants, | London |'. Green sand-grain cloth. Both covers and the spine are blocked identically in gold and black, as for BL C.109.f.2. This copy was donated; dated 31.12.[19]59.

Ball, *App.* 66f. Design on green sand-grain cloth. Ball, *VPB* pp. 54–55, 61-ref. 17. King, *JL* p. 242. McLean, *VPBB* p. 90. Morris & Levin, *APB* p. 36, no. 50. Design on green sand-grain cloth. Pantazzi, *JL* pp. 266, 269. The illustration on p. 269 shows a copy bound in green sand-grain cloth.

473 Leighton, John

Raleigh, Alexander. *The Story of Jonah The Prophet.* [Engraved Map of the Mediterranean, entitled:] *Sketch-map of Mediterranean Sea.* Edinburgh: Adam and Charles Black, 1866. Printed by R&R Clark, Edinburgh. [7], 322 p., 1 plate. With four pages of publisher's titles bound at the end.

134 × 204 × 28 mm. 3166.bb.57.

The frontispiece engraving of Jonah's tomb is signed 'Dalziel' from a sketch by J. L. Porter.

Text sewn on two tapes. Black endpapers and pastedowns. Red pebble-grain cloth. Both covers blocked identically in blind on the borders. Four fillets are blocked in blind on the borders, the three inner ones having rounded corners. The upper cover central vignette is blocked in gold. It shows a medallion, formed by a single gold fillet, with Jonah, the whale and waves inside. The title: '| Story | of | Jonah |' is blocked in horizontal hatch gold above the figure of Jonah. Signed 'JL' in gold as separate letters at the base of the vignette. The spine is blocked in gold. From the head downwards, the decoration is: a gold fillet at the head; the words: '| The | Story | of | Jonah | Raleigh |' blocked in gold within a panel formed by a single 'rope-like' fillet. Near the tail, a dolphin is blocked, with ribbon-shaped gold lettering-piece around it; the words: '| A&C | Black |' are blocked in relief within the ribbon; three gold fillets are blocked at the tail, the middle of which is 'rope-like'.

474 Leighton, John

Smith, Richard Henry. *Twigs for nests or Notes on Nursery Nurture. With illustrations in graphotype.* London: James Nisbet and Co. Berners Street, 1866. Printed by R. & R. Clark, Edinburgh. xi, 144 p. With four pages of publisher's titles bound at the end.

140 × 197 × 15 mm. 12355.bb.38.

Gilt edges. Bevelled boards. Grey endpapers and pastedowns. Green sand-grain cloth. Both covers are blocked identically on the borders and on the corners – in blind on the lower and in gold on the upper. Three fillets are blocked on the borders. Small leaf and flower plant decoration is blocked on each corner. A fourth fillet is blocked inside, which has semi-circular corners. The upper cover central vignette is blocked in gold. The title: '| Twigs | for | nests. |' is blocked in gold, in rustic lettering, with 'twig-like' tendrils attached to several of the letters. Signed 'JL' in gold as a monogram at the base of the vignette. The spine is blocked in gold. From the head downwards, the decoration is: two gold fillets; a 'dotted' fillet; a gold fillet; two more gold fillets; the title: '| Twigs | for | nests |' blocked in gold; a decorated fillet; near the tail of the spine: four fillets; the words: '| London | Nisbet & Co. |' are blocked in gold; two fillets; a fillet of repeating dots; two fillets at the tail – all in gold.

Dry, *JL* no. 511.

475 Leighton, John

Tonkin, Sarah Eliza. *Rostherne mere, and other poems.* Manchester: Palmer & Howe, 1 and 3 Bond Street; London, Simpkin, Marshall, & Co., 1866. Manchester: Printed by Palmer & Howe. viii, 224 p.
132 × 170 × 20 mm. 11647.aaa.6.

Bevelled boards. Gilt edges. Grey endpapers and pastedowns. Blue pebble-grain cloth. Both covers identically blocked, in gold and relief on the upper and in blind and relief on the lower. On the upper cover, a 'dog-tooth' border is blocked in gold. Inside this, a single gold fillet is blocked on the borders. On each outer corner, triangular gold lettering-pieces are blocked each with three dots blocked inside in relief. Three inner borders (rounded at the corners) consist of: 1. a single gold fillet; 2. a single gold fillet with repeating dots blocked inside it in relief; 3. a hatch gold fillet. On each inner corner, a round gold lettering-piece is blocked, with flower heads and stems blocked inside in relief. The centre-piece is blocked in gold. It shows decoration, with fillets on the outside delineating a vase-shape. The spine is blocked in gold. A single gold fillet is blocked on the perimeter. Further single gold fillets form panels down the spine. From the head downwards, the contents of the panels are: 1. stem, leaf and bud decoration blocked in gold; 2. the words: '| Rostherne | Mere | and | other | poems. |' are blocked in gold; 3. plant stem leaf, and bud decoration, with one open flower – all in gold; 4. the words: '| S. E. Tonkin. |' are blocked in gold, within a circle formed by two fillets; 5. plant, leaf, and stem decoration blocked in gold; signed 'JL' in gold as a monogram at the base of the plant; 6. the words: '| Palmer & Howe |' are blocked in gold at the tail.

Dry, *JL* no. 510.

476 Leighton, John

Bible. *The Holy Bible containing the Old and New Testaments. With illustrations by Gustave Doré.* 2 vols. London: Cassell, Petter and Galpin, [1867]. Unpaginated.
X+.220.52.

The University of Durham Library copy.

Blue sand-grain cloth. Both covers identically blocked in blind on the borders, on the corners and on the sides. The upper cover of each volume has a large oval-shaped centre-piece blocked in gold. Within it, there are four roundels and four shields. The very centre has the title words. Signed 'IL' [sic] in gold as separate letters underneath the shield entitled 'Golgotha', at the base of the design. The spines are fully blocked in gold, with an elaborate design – the same for both volumes.

477 Leighton, John

Eliot, George. *Novels. Vol. I[–VI]. With illustrations.* Wlliam Blackwood and Sons, Edinburgh and London, [1867–1870]. Printed by William Blackwood and Sons, Edinburgh.
12603.f.15.

Vol. I. Adam Bede. vi, 486 p. Issued in 7 parts, each part in green paper wrappers. Bound as one volume. 128 × 188 × 35 mm.
Vol. II. Mill on the Floss. vi, 486 p. Issued as parts 8–16, each part in green paper wrappers. Bound as one volume. 127 × 188 × 38 mm.
Vol. III. Silas Marner. 158 p. Issued as parts 17–18, each part in green paper wrappers. Bound as one volume. 126 × 188 × 16 mm.
Vol. IV. Scenes of Clerical Life. 330 p. Issued as parts 19–23, each part in green paper wrappers. Bound as one volume. 128 × 188 × 26 mm.
Vol. V. Felix Holt. 430 p. Issued as parts 24–30, each part in green paper wrappers. Bound as one volume. 127 × 188 × 31 mm.
Vol VI. Romola. v, 504 p. Dark brown endpapers and pastedowns. Red sand-grain cloth. Both covers blocked identically in blind on the borders. The upper cover has a gold central medallion. The title and imprint are blocked in gold on the spine. Unsigned. Date stamped in blue: '31 AU[GUST 18]78'.

Originally issued in parts, each with green paper wrappers. The lower cover of each part is blank on the recto, and the verso has a list of Blackwood's titles, frequently entitled 'Blackwood's Standard Novels' series. The upper cover verso is blank. Each upper cover recto is printed in black with a design of John Leighton. [It is typical of Leighton's work in the 1860s, for example 'Voices of the year'.] On the borders, are printed: 1. a fillet; 2. repeating dots; 3. a dog-tooth pattern. Each curves on the corners. A medallion is shown on each corner, formed by dots and fillets. Within each medallion, there are pictures of: 1. a carpenter's shop; 2. a mill and its water wheel; 3. a loom; 4. a graveyard and tombs. Adjacent to each are: top left – the part number 'No 1[-30]'; top right – 'Sixpence'; bottom left – 'Ilustrations'; bottom right – 'By J. D. Cooper'. At the top between the medallions, the words: '| The novels | & | Tales |' are printed 'in relief' within three black lettering-pieces. The words: '| of | George Eliot |' are printed below this, with the capitals 'G' and 'E' printed within black lettering-pieces. Underneath this, each individual book title is printed within a picture frame, which has tendrils at its top left and right corners. Between the medallions at the base, the words: '| W. Blackwood & Sons. |' are printed in relief within a black lettering-piece. The words: '| Edinburgh | & London |' are printed within two rectangles, each formed by double fillets. Each upper cover is signed within the lower border: 'John Leighton' and 'HL SD' [i.e. Henry Leighton 'sculpted'.]

Gray, *Eliot Review* no. 29, pp. 52–56; no. 30, p. 61.

478 Leighton, John PLATE LIX

Hall, Anna Maria. *The Prince of the fair family. A fairy tale. By Mrs S. C. Hall.* London: Chapman and Hall, 193, Piccadilly, 1867. London: Virtue and Co, Printers, City Road. [8], 160 p.
165 × 225 × 28 mm. 12806.f.49.

Printed at end of list of illustrations: 'The cover from a design by John Leighton, F.S.A.'

Text sewn on three sawn-in cords. Gilt edges. Bevelled boards. Green sand-grain cloth. Yellow endpapers and pastedowns. Binder's ticket on lower pastedown: '| Bound by | Virtue & Co | City Road | London |'. Both covers blocked identically in gold and in relief. The outer border is a thin fillet, interspersed with a five dot 'dice' pattern. A butterfly is blocked on each corner. The inner border consists of flower heads stamped on raised circles (i.e. the areas around the circles have been recessed by pressure). These are surrounded by semi-circular fillets, and small decoration. The central vignette is blocked in gold. At its head, the title: '| The | Prince | of the Fair Family [in a semi-circle] |' is blocked in gold. The central roundel has a single gold fillet blocked on its borders. Within, small stars are blocked in gold around the inner perimeter. A King and Queen fairy are seated underneath the canopy of a toadstool (blocked in gold), the King asleep, a wooden spoon held in his right hand. The Queen holds a staff in her left hand, and looks upwards to the winged putto seated on top of the canopy. At the base of the canopy, the subtitle: '| A Fairy Tale |' is blocked in relief. Underneath the King and the Queen, a sea creature (the JL sea creature) has a gold ribbon wrapped around it. The words: '| By Mrs. S. C. Hall |' are blocked in relief within the ribbon. Signed 'JL' in relief within seaweed blocked in gold underneath the sea creature. The spine is blocked in gold. A single gold fillet is blocked on the perimeter. From the head downwards, the decoration is: a dragon-fly; the title: '| The | Prince | of | The Fair Family. | a Fairy Tale | by | Mrs S. C. Hall [in relief within a rectangular gold lettering-piece] |' blocked in gold; from near the tail to below the title, a fairy is clinging onto a dandelion-like plant, and blowing upwards, scattering ripened seed heads to the wind; a beetle and a locust are blocked at the base of the plant; a gold fillet; an imprint: '| London: | Chapman | and Hall |' is blocked in gold within a rectangle formed by a single gold fillet; at the tail, a gold fillet is blocked, with dots blocked in relief within it.

Dry, *JL* no. 516. King, *JL* p. 242.

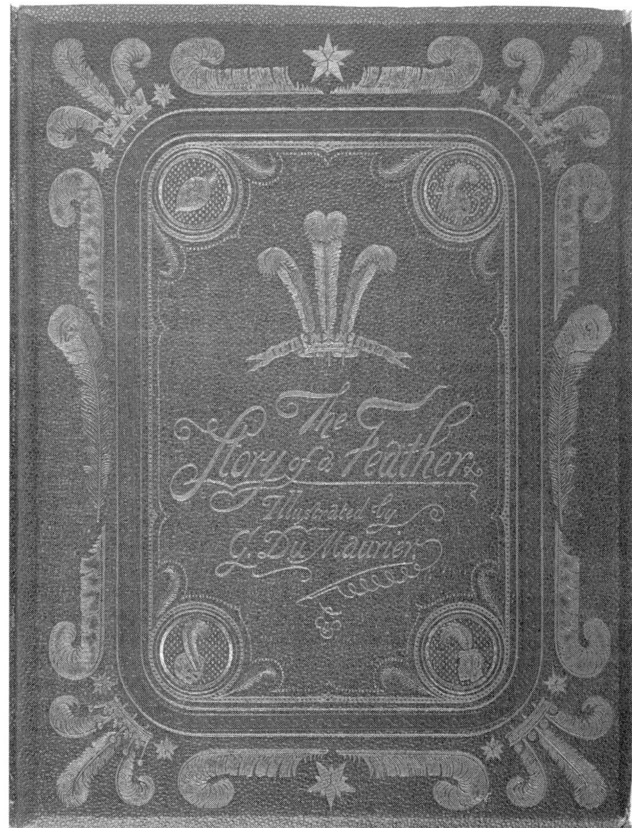

FIG. 60

479 Leighton, John FIG. 60

Jerrold, Douglas William. *The story of a Feather. Illustrated by G. du Maurier*. London: Bradbury, Evans & Co., 11 Bouverie Street, 1867. London: Bradbury, Evans, and Co., Printers Extraordinary to the Queen, Whitefriars. xv, 259 p. With four pages of publisher's titles bound at the end.

170 × 215 × 30 mm. 12619.g.26.

Bevelled boards. Gilt edges. Dark green endpapers and pastedowns. Purple pebble-grain cloth. The lower cover is blocked in blind with two fillets on the borders. A third fillet, inside, has strapwork blocked on the corners. A fourth fillet is blocked inside this, with a leaf pattern blocked in relief within it. The centre-piece is blocked in gold. It consists of three feathers of the Prince of Wales, and a crown. The motto: '| Ich dien. |' is blocked in relief at the base, in a pennant-shaped gold lettering-piece. The upper cover is fully blocked in gold. On the outer four corners are blocked the Prince of Wales' three feathers and crown. The crowns are different at the head and at the tail. On the border at the head and the tail, two feathers are blocked in gold, separated by a five point star. Down each side, three feathers are blocked. The middle of the three feathers has an eye at the top. Inside the outer border are two thin fillets blocked in gold. Between these, a fillet is blocked in blind, with a leaf pattern blocked in relief within it. Inside this, forming the central rectangle, a fillet is blocked in gold with repeating dots blocked in relief within it. On the corners inside the central rectangle, medallions are blocked, each with three different outer circles. These are: a fillet in gold, with repeating dots blocked in relief inside; a thin gold fillet; hatch gold. Each medallion contains a decorative element. In the upper two, an egg and a skull and a feather are blocked. In the lower two medallions, a skull and a feather are blocked, and, a monkey wearing a hat with a chin-strap and a feather. The background of each of the medallions is small dots, blocked in gold. Each inner corner medallion has two feathers blocked in gold alongside it. A 'fillet' of gold dots separates the corner medallions from the centre panel. The centre panel is decorated with the feathers, crown and motto of the Prince of Wales. Beneath this, the words: '| The | Story of a Feather | Illustrated by G. Du Maurier. |' are blocked in an elaborate 'scroll-like' manner, as though written with a quill pen, with much letter-end flourishes. Signed 'JL' in gold as a monogram at the base of the words 'Du Maurier'.

The spine is fully blocked in gold. From the head downwards, the decoration is: the Prince of Wales' feathers and crown; an ostrich-like bird's head, wearing spectacles, is gripping two objects in its beak: firstly, it holds a pennant-shaped gold lettering-piece, bearing the words: '| Ich dien |' blocked in relief, and also, it holds the string for a banner, which forms a decorated frame for the title; the banner has two crossed arrows behind it, their tips at the base and their heads at the top; the title and author: '| The | Story | of | a | Feather | By | Douglas | Jerrold. |' blocked within the banner in gold; inside an inverted egg-shaped lettering-piece is blocked a crouched bird-like figure; the words: '| Illustrated | edition |' and the imprint are all blocked in gold; signed 'JL' in gold as separate letters; the imprint: '| London | Bradbury | Evans & Co. |' is blocked in gold at the tail.

Dry, *JL* no. 517.

480 Leighton, John PLATE LX

Payn, James. *The Lakes in Sunshine: being photographic and other Pictures of the Lake District of Westmorland and North Lancashire. With descriptive letterpress.* [Vol. I.] Windermere: J. Garnett, 1867. Windermere: Printed by J. Garnett. x, 105 p., 16 plates of photographs, 1 fold-out map.

220 × 287 × 25 mm. 10358.h.21.

The coloured fold-out map is signed: London: Simpkin, Marshall & Co., Windermere. J. Garnett. Engraved by J. Bartholemew, Edinh.[sic] Leighton drew the title page engraving for vol I, of two symbolical wood-engravings, with the Arms of Windermere & Furness Abbey. Also, he drew the monogram and imprint on the title page verso.

Bevelled boards. Gilt edges. Beige endpapers and pastedowns. Blue sand-grain cloth. Both covers are blocked identically in gold and in black. There is a wide border blocked in gold, consisting of a repeating pattern of bulrushes, leaves, small flowers and stars. On the corners, a fern is blocked between two antlers. At the centre of each side of the border, foxgloves are blocked. At the centre of the head and of the tail of the border, holly leaves and berries are blocked. On the inner border are: 1. a black fillet; 2. a gold fillet with repeating 'tear-drops' blocked in relief within it; 3. a 'wave' border, blocked in black. Inside this is a thin fillet, with small leaves and flowers blocked on the corners in gold. The central vignette shows a lake scene, with mountains, clouds, birds, fish. There is a small sailing boat on the water. A man is blocked in the boat, standing with a pole in the left hand and guiding a sail rope with his right. A lady with a small parasol is seated in the rear of the boat. The title: '| The | Lakes | in Sunshine |' is blocked in rustic letters, above and below the boat. The spine is blocked in gold. From the head downwards, the decoration is: a sun and its rays; the title: '| The | Lakes | in | Sunshine |' blocked in gold; the word: '| Illustrated |' is blocked in relief inside a hatch gold lettering-piece; a small crouched swan is blocked in a frame; the word '| Payn |' is blocked in gold underneath the swan, with a single fan-circle blocked below this in gold [denoting Vol. 1]; a group of bulrushes and its leaves are blocked in gold near the base; signed 'JL' in gold as separate letters at the base of the bulrushes, with a gold fillet blocked underneath; the word '| Garnett |' is blocked in relief inside a rectangular gold lettering-piece, with a single gold fillet blocked on its borders; three gold fillets are blocked at the tail.

——: *being photographic and other Pictures of the Lake District of Cumberland. With descriptive letterpress.* [Vol. II.] London: Simpkin, Marshall, & Co; Windermere: J. Garnett, 1870. Windermere: Printed by J. Garnett. viii, 94 p., 10 plates of photographs.

225 × 287 × 25 mm. 10358.h.21.

Bevelled boards. Gilt edges. Yellow endpapers and pastedowns. Blue sand-grain cloth. The design blocked on the covers and on the spine is the same as the first volume published in 1867. The spine has two 'fan-circles' blocked in gold, denoting Vol. II.

Dry, *JL* nos. 530 & 544.

481 Leighton, John

Periodical Publications – *London. Peter Parley's Annual. A Christmas and New Year's present for Young People. Edited by William Martin.* London: Darton and Co., 42, Paternoster Row, 1867. [London]: William Stevens, Printer, 37, Bell Yard, Temple Bar. 320 p., 8 plates. With thirty pages of advertisements bound at the end.

137 × 197 × 32 mm. P.P.6750. [1867]

The plates are in colour and are signed 'Leighton Bros.'

Text sewn on three sawn-in cords. Gilt edges. Bevelled boards. Rust-red endpapers and pastedowns. Written on the verso of the upper endpaper: '| Julia E. Parry | Heathside | Wimbledon Common | 1869. |' Red sand-grain cloth. Both covers blocked identically in blind on the lower and in gold on the upper. A dog tooth border is blocked in gold, then two more fillets on borders, and, between these, a border of dots, small trefoils and stems – with zig-zag fillets and hatch vertical lines between the trefoils. Single spinning toys are blocked on each corner. At the centre of the head, a kite is blocked with tassels. Within it, a boy, a girl, a moon and a sun are blocked in relief. At the centre of the tail, the decoration blocked is: cricket stumps and bails, bat, ball, and a racquet. Kite streamers are blocked behind these. Moths are blocked on each inner corner. The centre of the design is surrounded by two borders blocked in gold. On the borders of the centre are: 1. a gold fillet with repeating dots and stars blocked in relief within it; 2. a zig-zag and hatch pattern blocked in gold and in relief. On the centre itself, a man, holding a book, is seated on a horse. The book has the words: '| Only | once | a | year |' blocked in relief within. A dog, standing on its hind legs, is blocked below the horse's head. A milestone is blocked underneath the horse's belly. The words: '| To | Eton | X |' are blocked in relief within it. Above the centre, the words: '| Peter Parley's |' are blocked in relief within a gold circular lettering-piece with scroll ends; below the centre, the word '| Annual |' is blocked in relief, within a gold

lettering-piece with scroll ends. The spine is blocked in gold. A border of repeating gold dots is blocked on the perimeter. From the head downwards, the decoration is: a neo-classical vase, with birds perched on it; the title: '| Peter | Parley's | Annual |' blocked in relief within three gold lettering-pieces; '| 1867. |' is blocked within a hatch horizontal gold lettering-piece; all the words are blocked within a frame formed by a cord-shaped single gold fillet; a squirrel; a girl playing croquet, also within a frame formed by a cord-shaped single fillet; a crowned and winged female figure holds up a cartouche with scroll ends, in gold; '| Illustrated |' is blocked in relief within this cartouche; signed 'JL' in gold as separate letters below this; near the tail: '| London | Darton & Co.' | are blocked in relief within a rectangular gold lettering-piece, with a single cord-shaped fillet blocked on its perimeter. Two gold fillets are blocked at the tail.

Dry, *JL* no. 521.

482 Leighton, John

Thackeray, Anne Isabella, afterwards Ritchie, Anne Isabella, *Lady. The village on the cliff. With six illustrations by Frederick Walker*. Second edition. London: Smith Elder & Co., 65, Cornhill, 1867. London: Printed by Smith, Elder and Co., Old Bailey, E.C. [6], 318 p., 6 plates. With four pages of publisher's titles bound at the end.

146 × 230 × 31 mm. 1560/202.

The plates are signed 'F. W.' and 'Swain Sc.'

Text sewn on three sawn-in cords. Yellow endpapers and pastedowns. Sale ticket on upper pastedown: '| Lewes Sale | 1923 | [rule] | Ex Libris | George Eliot |' Green sand-grain cloth. Both covers identically blocked in blind on the borders. Two fillets are blocked in blind on the borders. Inside this, a wide Greek roll is blocked around the borders, interspersed with flowers blocked in blind, the Greek roll being highlighted in relief. A single fillet in blind forms the inner rectangle. The upper cover central vignette is blocked in gold. It shows a painter's easel, with a painting standing on it; the painting shows the portrait of a lady, who is wearing a Dutch cap. The painter's wrist-stick and palette are propped against the easel. The words: '| The | Village |' are blocked in gold on the left hand side of the easel; '| on | the Cliff. |' are blocked in gold on the right hand side of the easel. Signed 'JL' in relief within the base of each of the easel legs. The spine is blocked in gold and relief. From the head downwards, the decoration is: the top of a church tower; this shows two bells, with the bell-wheels in quarter profile; the title: '| The | Village | on | the | Cliff. |' blocked in gold; a Neptune's trident and its pole are blocked in gold below the title, down to the tail; a group of objects are supported by it, held together by a rope; there are two flags, a painter's wrist-stick and palette; a sea creature is blocked below these objects [the Leighton dolphin]; The words: '| London | Smith | Elder | & | Co. |' are blocked in relief within five pennant-shaped gold lettering-pieces, which curl around the pole of the trident; signed 'L' – with a full stop above the letter – in gold at the tail. [This is the first combination of the double and single monograms of JL seen.]

Dry, *JL* no. 522.

483 Leighton, John

Wheeler, C. A. *Sportascrapiana. Cricket and shooting. Pedestrian, equestrian, rifle, and pistol doings. Lion hunting and deer stalking, by Celebrated Sportsmen: with hitherto unpublished anecdotes of the nineteenth century, from George IV. to the Sweep. Edited by CAW*. London: Simpkin, Marshall, & Co., Stationer's Hall Court, E.C., 1867. London: Printed by W. H. Collingridge, Aldersgate Street. xvi, 328 p.

127 × 185 × 32 mm. 7905.bb.37.

On the title page, the device of the author is printed – a crow within a shield, its beak uplifted to a scroll with the author's letters , 'CAW', printed within it.

Bevelled boards. White endpapers and pastedowns. Green sand-grain cloth. On both covers, two fillets are blocked in blind on the borders. The upper cover central vignette is blocked in gold. On the centre, a shield is blocked. Quarterly: or, crossed pistols, gules; on a pale azure, a cricket bat, two stumps, bail, and ball. Crossed rifles blocked behind the shield. Crest – a stag's head and antlers. Supporters – dexter, a dog; sinister, a crow. A pennant-shaped gold lettering-piece is wrapped around the front of the shield. It continues around a dog and the crow. The words: '| Scrapiana | By C. A. W. |' are blocked in relief within this lettering-piece. A ribbon-shaped gold lettering-piece is blocked below the shield. The words: '| Vive | Le | Sport |' are blocked in relief within this lettering-piece. Signed 'JL' in gold as separate letters at the base of the vignette. The spine is blocked in gold. Two gold fillets are blocked at the head and at the tail. Two gold fillets are blocked on the perimeter. From the head downwards, the decoration is: a cat's head; a cricket bat is blocked down the spine in gold; the word: '| Sportascrapiana |' blocked in relief (one letter per line) within the bat; a cricket ball in gold is blocked beneath this; a dog is blocked in gold.

The 1868 edition is at BL 7906.aa.38. xvi, 301 p. No original covers. An advertisement on the verso of page 301 reads: '| Sportascrapiana | [rule] | The original edition [i.e. 1867], | Larger type, on superior thick toned paper and handsomely | bound, can be had at | 7s. 6d. |'.

484 Leighton, John

Gems of nature and art. Embellished with twenty-four illustrations from eminent artists, printed in colours. London: Groombridge and Sons, Paternoster Row, 1868. B. Fawcett, Engraver and Printer, Driffield. vi, 72 p., 24 plates. A number of the plates are signed: 'A F Lydon'; two are signed 'J W Wood'.

185 × 255 × 30 mm. 7206.k.32.

Bevelled boards. Gilt edges. Brown sand-grain cloth. Both covers are blocked identically in gold, in black and in relief. Single fillets form squares on each corner, and a butterfly is blocked

within each corner square. Five rectangular panels are also formed by fillets – one on each side, one at the head, one at the tail, and one at the centre. These five panels and the squares on each corner are separated by five fillets, blocked in gold horizontally and vertically. Four of the fillets are thin; the thick fillet in the middle has repeating dots and 'flower heads' blocked in relief inside. Quatrefoils are blocked where the broad fillets intersect. Within the rectangle at the head, a classical head and helmet is blocked in gold, within a medallion formed by two fillets. The inner of these two fillets has repeating dots blocked inside it. Inside the rectangle at the base, a crouching female figure is blocked within a medallion. Two medallions are blocked on each side – all formed by the same fillets. All four have plants, representing the four seasons, blocked inside in gold. All the four medallions have 'arrow head' decoration on each side, blocked in black. The central rectangle has a thin single fillet on its borders. Eight medallions – each formed by two gold fillets – are blocked around the perimeter, three down each side, one at the head and one at the tail. Inside this, a 'stadium-shape' is formed by a single fillet blocked in gold, with an inner border consisting of stars and dots, blocked in black. On the centre is a white paper onlay, with borders and decoration blocked in hatched gold and in relief. The title words: '| Gems | of |' are blocked in relief, within a trefoil-shaped gold lettering-piece, with a single fillet on its borders; the word: '| Nature |' is blocked in relief with a rectangular gold lettering-piece with a single fillet blocked on its borders; the words: '| & | art. |' are blocked in relief within a trefoil-shaped gold lettering-piece with a single fillet blocked on its borders. The spine is blocked in gold. A single gold fillet is blocked on its perimeter. It is divided into four panels by single fillets and three broad single gold fillets with circles and dots blocked in relief within – the same as on the upper cover. From the head downwards, the decoration is: two fillets; panel 1 – a face and rays within a medallion, formed by four fillets; a broad gold fillet; panel 2 – the words: '| Gems | of | nature | and | art. |' blocked in gold; a broad gold fillet; panel 3 – a winged putto holds a sword and a helmet, and stands on a hatched gold medallion, which shows an owl blocked inside; two twisted snakes; signed 'L' in gold underneath these snakes; a broad gold fillet; the words: '| London | Groombridge |' are blocked in relief within two rectangular gold lettering-pieces, which are blocked within a medallion formed by two fillets; two gold fillets are blocked at the tail.

Ball, *App.* no. 60j. Cites the 1860 edition with the same design blocked. Ball, *VPB* p. 54, 61. Dry, *JL* no. 526. McLean, *Fawcett* p. 147, no. 58. McLean, *VBD* Plate XIV, reproduces the Title Page and Frontispiece of this work.

485 Leighton, John — PLATE LXI

Scotland: her songs and scenery. As sung by her bards, and seen in the camera. London: A. W. Bennett, 5 Bishopsgate Without, 1868. [London]: Unwin Brothers, Printers, Bucklersbury, E.C. viii, 192 p., 14 plates of photographs.
152 × 200 × 32 mm. 11651.e.11.

Ten photographs are by S. Thompson; four are by P. Ewing. The photographs printed by Russell Sedgefield.

Bevelled boards. Gilt edges White endpapers and pastedowns. Green sand-grain cloth. Both covers are blocked in gold and in blind, with an identical design. The border is blocked in gold, with a repeating pattern of roses and thistles, and with crowns in gold on the corners. The inner border is blocked in blind with a cartouche pattern. On the borders of the inner rectangle, a fillet is blocked in gold, with thistles blocked on the corners. At the head of the inner rectangle, a crowned lion is blocked in gold, sejant, double queued; it holds a cross in left front paw, and a sword in right front paw. The flag of St. Andrew is held by the lion's right rear paw, the flag of the lion of England through the left rear paw. The lion is atop a pennant-shaped gold lettering-piece, containing the word: '| Scotland |', blocked in relief. The words '| Her Songs and Scenery |' are in gold in gothic letters; below this, a shield is blocked, argent, with a lion rampant, gules; the shield is surrounded by leaves and flowers. Above this shield, the rays of a sun lance the letters of the words: '| Photographically illustrated |', blocked in gold in a semi-circle. Signed 'JL' in gold as separate letters at the base of the shield. The spine is blocked in gold. A single gold fillet is blocked on the perimeter. From the head downwards, the decoration is: a crown, blocked in gold; double five-point stars in gold; the title: '| Scotland | her | Songs | & | Scenery |' blocked in gold; a mandorla, filled with stars, plus a figure of a man with a wooden cross – all blocked in gold; a harp, surrounded by delicate plants; signed 'JL' in gold as separate letters; the imprint: '| London | Bennett |' is blocked in gold, within a panel formed by a single gold fillet; strapwork and fillets in gold; a gold fillet is blocked at the tail.

The same outer border of thistles and roses is reproduced on two other volumes: B.L. 11651.e.26. Scott. *Marmion.* A. W. Bennett, 1866; B.L. 11651.e.25. Scott. *Lay of the Last Minstrel* . . . Provost & Co., 1872 (With six photographs by Russell Sedgefield)

Dry, *JL* no. 531.

486 Leighton, John — PLATE LXII

Bunsen, Christian Carl Josias von, *Baron. Lyra Germanica: The Christian Life. Translated from the German by Catherine Winkworth and illustrated by John Leighton F.S.A., E. Armitage A.R.A. & F. Madox Brown.* London: Longmans Green Reader & Dyer, 1868. London: Printed by R. Clay, Son, and Taylor. xvi, 254 p. With two pages of publisher's titles bound at the end.
168 × 235 × 35 mm. 3434.f.19.

Below the title, a medallion is printed, showing a medieval boat on the sea, with three winged angels at the prow and the stern. There is a single central sail, and a dolphin in the foreground. On the perimeter of the medallion: 'Let the heaven & earth praise him. The seas & every thing that moveth therein.'

The title page verso contains a medallion '| In memoriam Emma [Leighton] | Born Sunday. Xmas.Day.1825 | Died.August.20.AD.1867. | To a dear sister who during pain

and suffering found solace in these hymns. This travail concluded. The day of her decease is dedicated.' [At the Leighton family tomb in St. Mary's Church, Harrow, the shield for Emma Leighton is on the West end of the tomb. The inscription on the shield is: 'Emma Born Sun. +mas day 1825. Died Aug 20 1867.'] Underneath the medallion, the initials 'EL' are printed on either side of a heart. The illustrations engraved by Bolton Butterworth and Heath Cooper, Dalziel, Green, Leighton, Pearson, Swain, Williamson and Whymper.

Text sewn on two tapes. Bevelled boards. Gilt edges. Red endpapers and pastedowns. Binder's ticket on lower pastedown: '| Bound by | Edmonds & Remnants. | [rule] | London |'. Green pebble-grain cloth, with red pebble-grain cloth onlay, which forms the mandorla. Both covers identically blocked in gold and blind and relief. On the borders, the fillets are blocked in gold, the outermost with 'dog-tooth' pattern. Inside this, intersecting pairs of three fillets are blocked in gold on the borders. Between the pairs, a repeating pattern is blocked of stars in gold and five dots in relief. Animals and heads are blocked on the four corners. Strapwork weaves around these heads and animals. In the mandorla, a crowned angel is blocked at prayer, with an open book in front. The angel's wings rise to form the outer edge of a lyre, with the points of the angel's crown rising to become the strings of the lyre. The title: '| Lyra | Germanica | The | Christian | Life |' is blocked in gold above and below the lyre. The border of the mandorla contains the quotes, blocked in gold: 'Sing unto the Lord. Bless his name. Show forth his salvation from day to day. Give thanks unto the Lord for he is good. For his mercy endureth forever.' A small trefoil formed by a gold fillet, plus hatch gold within is blocked above and below the mandorla. The trefoil at the head has the word: '| IHS |' in relief within the trefoil; at the tail, the trefoil has: '| INRI | L |' in relief. This copy lacks the spine.

Ball, *App.* 64k. Cites 1864 edition, with green morocco-grain cloth, bound by Edmonds & Remnants. Ball, *VPB* p. 82. de Beaumont, *RdeB1* no. 403. Dry, *JL* no. 528. Goldman, *VIB* no. 403. King, *JL* p. 242. McLean, *VPBB* p. 131, reproduces the spine and cover. Morris & Levin, *APB* p. 35, no. 49. Oldfield, *BC* no. 58. Pantazzi, *JL* p. 269.

487 Leighton, John

Corbet, Robert St. John. *Who will be Queen of the Tournament? And other stories*. London: Cassell, Petter, and Galpin, and 596 Broadway, New York, [1868]. London: Cassell, Petter, and Galpin, Belle Sauvage Works, Ludgate Hill, E.C. 224 p., 7 plates. With eight pages of publisher's titles bound at the end.
130 × 175 × 30 mm. 12622.aa.23.

Some of the plates are signed: 'FWL'.

Text sewn on two sawn-in cords. Brown endpapers and pastedowns. Purple sand-grain cloth. On both covers, the borders, the corners, the sides and the head and the tail are blocked identically in blind on the lower cover, and in black on the upper. Two fillets are blocked on the borders, the outer has 'dog-tooth' decoration; the inner fillet is thin. On each side of the cover, a knight's lance 'supports' the central inverted heart-shaped frame, which is formed by a single black fillet. Just below the tip of each lance, a pennant is fastened, and a single lion is blocked within each pennant. Two shields are blocked at the head and at the tail. At the head, left: argent, two hearts; or, one heart. At the head, right: argent, lion rampant. At the tail, left: argent, flower and sword; right: argent, a harp – all in black. The upper cover central vignette is blocked in gold and in relief. It shows a knight in full armour on his charger, which has two shields attached to its trappings. The knight holds his lance upright in his right hand. A pennant is attached to the top of the lance – all blocked in gold. Small stem and leaf decoration is blocked in gold on each side of the knight. Underneath the horse, the words: '| The Queen of the |' are blocked in gold; the word: 'Tournament' is blocked in relief within a rectangular gold lettering-piece. Signed 'JL' in relief as separate letters within a small leaf-shaped gold lettering-piece blocked at the base of the vignette. The spine is blocked in gold and in black. From the head downwards, the decoration is: the tip of a knight's lance; a crown; a shield, vert; the title: '| Queen | of the | Tournament |' blocked in relief within the shield; a wreath is blocked in front of the shaft of the lance; near the base, two pennant-shaped gold lettering-pieces are blocked in gold; within the pennant on the left, the words: '| London | and | New York |' are blocked in relief; within the pennant on the right, the words: '| Cassell | Petter & Galpin |' are blocked in relief. Line work, blocked in black, surrounds all the decoration blocked in gold, from head to the tail; a fillet is blocked in black at the tail.

Dry, *JL* no. 523.

488 Leighton, John PLATE LXIII

Hatton, Joseph. *Pippins and Cheese*. London: Bradbury, Evans, & Co., 11, Bouverie St., 1868. London]: Bradbury, Evans, and Co., Printers, Whitefriars. viii, 332 p.
118 × 177 × 31 mm. 12352.bb.33.

The title page has an engraved vignette by Leighton. This is oval-shaped, bordered by pippin apples, and shows a manservant, wearing an apron, holding bowls of pippins and cheese in front of a table. Printed within a pennant on either side of the oval: '| There's | Pippins | & | Cheese | To | Come |'. Signed 'L', as a monogram at the base of these words, with the full-stop above the top of the 'L'.

Text sewn on three sawn-in cords. Bevelled boards. Grey endpapers and pastedowns. Orange ungrained cloth. The lower cover is blocked in blind only. Three fillets are blocked on the borders, the middle fillet having repeating dots within it, blocked in relief. The centre-piece is lozenge-shaped. Each tip of the diamond has a three-pointed leaf blocked on it. The upper cover is blocked in gold and in black. A single fillet and small squares are blocked on the border in black. Two groups of three fillets are blocked in black on each side, and on the head and on the tail, which divide the cover into rectangles. These fillets intersect to form squares on the corners. An apple tree is blocked in black within the central rectangle, with the perimeter of its leaves blocked on the outer rectangles. At the head of

the central rectangle, a line, blocked in black, hangs from the fillets. Six apples, blocked in gold, are attached to the line. Each letter of the word: 'Pippins' is blocked in relief within each apple. Above the apples, a knife and a ball of string are blocked in gold, with the end of the string curling away. Underneath the apples, a third of a block of cheese is blocked as a gold lettering-piece. The title words: '| & | cheese. |' are blocked in relief within the cheese. Three apples are blocked in black at the base of the apple tree. Signed 'L' (with a full stop above the top of the 'L') in black underneath these three apples. [There is a 'modernistic' look to this design, inspired by the fillets and the small squares.] The spine is blocked in gold and in relief. From the head downwards, the decoration is: a fillet in black; a butterfly in black; three fillets in black; a hand and an implement (an apple corer?); the words: '| Pippins | & | Cheese by | Joseph Hatton. |' blocked in gold and in relief: the ampersand is wrapped around the handle of a cheese cutter; the words 'cheese by' are blocked in relief within a half circle cheese block; an apple is blocked underneath the word: 'Hatton'; a small apple tree and grass are blocked in black; three black fillets; '| London. | Bradbury Evans | and Co. |' are blocked in gold within a rectangle formed by a single gold fillet; a fillet is blocked in black at the tail.

Dry, *JL* no. 527.

489 Leighton, John

Hey, Wilhelm. *One hundred picture fables, drawn by Otto Speckter, engraved and printed in colours by the Brothers Dalziel. With rhymes translated from the German of F. Hey by H. W. Dulcken, PH.D.* London: George Routledge and Sons, The Broadway, Ludgate; New York: 416 Broome Street, 1868. London: Dalziel Brothers, Engravers & Printers, Camden Press. [4]101 p., 52 plates. With six pages of publisher's titles bound at the end.
140 × 190 × 20 mm. 12304.bbb.32.

Light yellow endpapers and pastedowns. Blue sand-grain cloth. The borders and corners of both covers are blocked identically in blind. There are five fillets blocked in blind on the borders, and stylised leaf and flower decoration on the corners. The upper cover has a square centre-piece, blocked in gold. It shows a cat, with a bird perched on its head, and a mouse below it. The word: '| Picture |' is blocked in relief, within a gold hatched lettering-piece. The lower serif of the capital 'P' supports the cat on a ledge. The words: '| Fables | By | Otto | Speckter. |' are blocked in gold below this. Through the design runs a fuchsia plant, with delicate leaves, stems and four flowers. The stamens of the flowers are elongated. Signed 'JL' in gold as separate letters at the left hand base of the central square. The head of the 'J' is interwoven in small strapwork. The spine is blocked in gold. The title: '| 100 | Picture | Fables | by | Otto | Speckter |' is blocked in gold in a 'picture frame' panel, which is formed by a single gold fillet with repeating dots blocked in relief within it. Below is a parrot on a perch, with a chain on its leg. The chain end-ring is around the stand supporting the perch. A monkey is tugging the end of the chain in an attempt to pull the parrot off its perch.

Dry, *JL* no. 539.

490 Leighton, John PLATE LXIV

Hood, Tom. *Jingles and jokes for The Little Folks. Illustrated by C. H. Bennett. W. Brunton, Paul Gray, and T. Morten.* London: Cassell, Petter, and Galpin, Ludgate Hill, E.C.; and 596, Broadway, New York, [1868]. London: Cassell, Petter, and Galpin, Belle Sauvage Works, Ludgate Hill, E.C. 76 p. With four pages of publisher's titles bound at the end.
147 × 204 × 10 mm. 12807.f.53.

The plates are signed 'Linton' or 'Linton Sc'.

White endpapers and pastedowns. Pink paper over boards. The lower cover has a list of Cassell's titles. The upper cover has mostly the same design as blocked on the upper cloth cover of BL 11648.cc.40. A grey fillet is printed on the borders. Inside, there is a border of joined leaves and stems in yellow, surrounded by red and black ribs. A star is printed on each corner, each within a black medallion, with red fillet borders. Inside each star, a grotesque face is shown. On the centre left side, a butterfly is shown. On the centre right side, a snail is shown. There are panels, with horizontal red ribs, printed between the corners and the central circle. On the centre of the head, a clock face is shown. The weights of the clock press down on a book, within an oval, on the centre tail – trapping the little folks inside the book. The imprint: '| Cassell, Petter & Galpin | London & New York |' is printed underneath the book. The central circle has two groups of red fillets on its borders, with a thick black border printed between these. The title: '| Jingles & Jokes for little folks |' is printed in pink within the circular black border. On the centre, the words: '| Tom Hood |' are printed. The 'o' of 'Tom' is the clock pendulum. Below the central circle, two clock weights press down upon the upper cover of a closed book, which has one of the 'little Folk' trapped in the pages. The word: 'Hood' is printed inside a scroll-piece. On the spine, the words: 'Price One Shilling' are printed in black from the tail up to the head. [Unsigned, but a Leighton design.]

King, *JL* pp. 242, 244.

491 Leighton, John

Kingston, William Henry Giles. *The boy's own book of boats. Including vessels of every rig and size to be found floating on the waters in all parts of the world: together with complete instructions how to make sailing models. With numerous illustrations, drawn by Edward Weedon, engraved by W. J. Linton. New Edition. Revised throughout.* London: Sampson, Low, Son and Marston, Milton House, Ludgate Hill, 1868. London: R. Clay, Son, and Taylor, Printers, Bread Street Hill. xi, 336 p. With twenty-eight pages of publisher's titles bound at the end.
117 × 172 × 30 mm. 8806.b.34.

White endpapers and pastedowns. Red sand-grain cloth. Both covers identically blocked in blind. Four fillets are blocked on the borders. A medallion is blocked on the centre, showing four spade-shapes and flowers inside. The spine has the same design as the 1861 edition, at BL 8806.b.33.

The Gall & Inglis edition of 1871 is at BL 8806.b.35.

492 Leighton, John

Periodical Publications – *London. Peter Parley's Annual. A Christmas and New Year's present for Young People. With eight full page illustrations in oil colours, and numerous wood engravings by eminent artists.* London: Darton and Co., 42, Paternoster Row, 1868. London: Printed by Wertheimer, Lea and Co., Circus Place, Finsbury. 312 p., 8 plates. With thirty-two pages of advertisements bound at the end.

135 × 187 × 35 mm. P.P.6750. [1868.]

The plates are in colour and signed 'W. Dickes'.

Gilt edges. Bevelled boards. Rust-red endpapers and pastedowns. Red sand-grain cloth. Both covers identically blocked, in blind on the lower, and in gold on the upper. The design is the same as for 1867, with only the date on the spine being altered.

Dry, *JL* no. 529.

493 Leighton, John

Periodical Publications – *London. The Epicure's Year Book and Table Companion* . . . London: Bradbury, Evans, & Co., 11 Bouverie Street, 1868. London: Bradbury, Evans, and Co., Printers, Whitefriars. xxiv, 234 p. With five pages of advertisements bound at the end.

115 × 168 × 28 mm. P.P.2488.w.[1868–1869]

A coat of arms of the Epicures by Leighton is engraved on the title page, and signed with his monogram.

Bevelled boards. Dark green endpapers and pastedowns. All pages have double red fillets printed on the borders, with a small diamond of straps in each corner. Green ungrained cloth. Bevelled boards. Binder's ticket on lower pastedown: '| Bound by | Edmonds & Remnants. | London'. The borders and corners of both covers are blocked identically in blind and in relief. A single fillet is blocked in blind on the borders, with 'tooth' decoration blocked in relief within the fillet. The fillet is curved at the corners. On the lower cover, a medallion is blocked on each corner. Each medallion is formed by a single fillet, with dots blocked within it in relief. On the centre base within each medallion, a single word is blocked in relief. Clockwise, the words are: 'Pepper; Salt; Vinegar; Mustard'. On the upper cover, an additional fillet is blocked in gold on the perimeter of each medallion. On the centre of each medallion, the head of an allegorical figure is blocked in gold. Each represents the physical state induced by the substance: i.e. pepper – sneezing; salt – the taste on the tongue; vinegar – sour looks; mustard – a hot tongue. The upper cover has a central vignette blocked in gold. A medallion is blocked on the centre of the vignette; it has a single thin fillet blocked in gold on its perimeter, and a thicker one blocked in gold inside this. Within the thick fillet, the words: 'Fish. Flesh. Fowl. Fire & Fuel' are blocked in relief. A cooking pot and a fire are blocked on the centre. Above , a bull's head supports the cooking pot; the bull's head has a cord through the ring on its nose. A fish and a fowl 'support' the medallion. The words: '| The | Epicure's | Year Book |' are blocked in gold above and on each side of the bull's head. Below the fish and the fowl, a single fillet forms three scroll-shapes. Within each scroll-shape, the words: '| Les animaux | se repaissent |'; '| L'homme d'esprit | seul sait manger |'; '| L'homme mange |' – are all blocked in gold. The year numbers: '18' and '68.' are blocked in gold on each side of a crossed set of cutlery – a knife, a fork and a spoon, which are blocked in gold. Signed 'L' in gold above the cutlery group. The spine is blocked in gold. From the head downwards, the decoration is: a small lamp and its rays – in gold; a curved panel, formed by a single fillet; the title words: '| The | Epicure's | Year | Book |' blocked in gold; the year '1868' is blocked in relief, within a rectangular gold lettering-piece, with a single gold fillet blocked on its borders; at the tail, the words: '| Bradbury, | Evans, | & Co. |' are blocked in gold within a rectangle formed by a single gold fillet.

Dry, *JL* no. 524.

—— *The Epicure's Year Book for 1869.* [Engraving showing: 'A Representative Kitchen.'] *Second year.* London: Bradbury, Evans, & Co., 11, Bouverie Street, E.C., 1869. London: Bradbury, Evans, and Co., Printers, Whitefriars. xxiv, 184, [32] p.

115 × 165 × 24 mm.

Text sewn on three sawn-in cords. Bevelled boards. Dark green endpapers and pastedowns. Red ungrained cloth. All the blocking is identical with the 1868 copy, with the exception of '1869' on the upper cover and on the spine, instead of '1868'. Signed 'L' above '1869'.

Dry, *JL* no. 534.

494 Leighton, John

Davenport, Emma Anne Georgina. *Constance and Nellie; or, the lost will. With a frontispiece by T. S. Wale.* [Monogram of Griffith & Farran.] London: Griffith and Farran, (Successors to Newbery and Harris,) Corner of St. Paul's Churchyard, 1869. Murray and Gibb, Edinburgh, Printers to Her Majesty's Stationery Office. vii, 232 p., 1 plate. With thirty-six pages of publisher's titles bound at the end.

105 × 170 × 22 mm. 12804.e.24.

The frontispiece plate is signed 'Pearson Sc.'

Text sewn on three sawn-in cords. Gilt edges. Brown endpapers and pastedowns. Red sand-grain cloth. Both covers blocked identically on the borders, in blind on the lower and in black on the upper. On the upper cover, a black fillet is blocked on the borders, then a 'dog-tooth' border is blocked in black. A single black fillet forms a rectangle at the head and at the tail. Within the rectangle at the head, three five-point stars are

blocked in gold, the middle being in horizontal hatch; within the lower rectangle, five five-point stars are blocked in gold, two being in hatch. On the inner corners, groups of three leaves are blocked in black. The upper cover vignette is blocked in gold. On the centre, an open chest is blocked, with books and letters inside it. Letters are also racked on the inside of the chest's lid. Behind the lid, a book rests on its fore-edges. A document rests against the front of the chest, with an inkwell and quill beside it. A bunch of keys and a flower are blocked below the chest. The title: '| Constance & Nellie |' is blocked in gold in a semi-circle above the chest. The capitals 'C' and 'N' are blocked in relief within rectangular gold lettering-pieces with single gold fillets on their borders; the words: '| or | the Lost Will |' are blocked in gold in gothic letters below the chest. Signed 'L' in relief on the bottom right hand corner of the chest. The spine is blocked in gold. From the head downwards, the decoration is: a gold fillet; a row of decorated triangles, blocked in gold; a gothic arch and two columns forma panel mid-spine; a hand, with a pointing index finger, is blocked in the arch; the title: '| Constance | & | Nellie, | or | the | lost | will. |' blocked in gold within the panel; a bunch of six keys is blocked underneath the title, hanging from a decorated cord, which joins the bases of the arch columns; passion flower leaves and berries are blocked at the head of the arch and below the bunch of keys; a spider hangs from a thread at the base of the leaves; the words: '| London | Griffith & Farran |' are blocked in gold; triangles are blocked in gold; a gold fillet is blocked at the tail.

Dry, *JL* no. 533.

495 Leighton, John

Hutton, Barbara. *Heroes of the Crusades. With illustrations by P. Priolo.* London: Griffith and Farran, Successors to Newbery and Harris, Corner of St. Paul's Churchyard, 1869. Murray and Gibb, Edinburgh, Printers to Her Majesty's Stationery Office. xv, 351 p., 6 plates. With thirty-two pages of publisher's titles bound at the end.

120 × 184 × 30 mm. 9055.aaa.36.

Some of the plates are signed 'PP' and 'Jenkins Sc.'.

Gilt edges. Brown endpapers and pastedowns. Brown ungrained cloth. Both covers have an identical design blocked on the borders, the corners, the sides, the head and the tail, in blind on the lower cover, and in black on the upper cover. Three fillets are blocked on the borders, the middle fillet having repeating semi-circular dots blocked in relief along it. 'Onion-shaped' tracery is blocked on each corner. On the upper cover, a medallion, each formed by two fillets, is blocked on each corner in gold. Within each medallion, a cross, a quarter moon, and two horizontal hatch five-point stars are blocked in gold. Between the corners, a pattern of thin stems is blocked in black, forming a frame around the centre. The upper cover vignette is blocked in gold. It shows a crusader, in full armour, on his caparisoned charger. He holds an axe in his left hand. In his right, he holds a pole with a banner-shaped gold lettering-piece at its head. The title: '| Heroes | of the | Crusades |' is blocked in relief within the banner. The Crusader also holds a shield, or, lion rampant, gules. Underneath the horse's hooves a sword, a stick and a banner are blocked in gold. The spine is blocked in gold and in black. Curling fillets, blocked in black, form three panels on the spine. From the head downwards, the decoration is: two fillets in black; within the first panel: a cross, a quarter moon, and two five-point stars are blocked in gold; within the second panel, the title: '| Heroes | of | the | Crusades |' blocked in gold; within the third panel, an axe, an anchor and rope, a sword are blocked in gold as a crossed group; [the signature 'JL' is likely to be signed underneath this group – a label obscures this.]; the words: '| Griffith & Farran |' are blocked in gold within two rectangles formed by single fillets in black, the inner of which has another black fillet above and below the words.

Dry, *JL* no. 536

496 Leighton, John

Leighton, John. *To The Royal Academy of Arts Upon the Condition and Future of its Library.* [London]: Royal Institution of Great Britain, 1869. [London]: Bradbury, Evans & Co., Printers Extraordinary to the Queen. 4 p.

195 × 240 × 2 mm. 11900.ee.33.

100 copies only printed. Signed at end: 'Royal Institution of Great Britain, Jan. 1869'

Plain brown thin covers of board. On front cover is pasted a bookplate of John Leighton, signed '| Iohn | Leigh | ton | LIMNER |'. It shows a picture of St. Luke drawing. Written on the cover is: '| For | the Library | of the British Museum |'. On the verso of the front cover is Leighton's bookplate [almost certainly a later one], with his coat of arms, and motto: '| Libros y amigos | pocos y buenos |'.

497 Leighton, John

PLATE LXV

Lemon, Mark. *Tinykin's transformations. A Child's Story. Illustrated by Charles Green.* London: Bradbury, Evans, & Co., 11, Bouverie Street, 1869. London: Bradbury, Evans, and Co., Printers, Whitefriars. x, 183 p., 4 plates.

142 × 195 × 25 mm. 12807.ee.21.

Engravings signed by Swain.

Gilt edges. Grey endpapers and pastedowns. Orange sand-grain cloth. The lower cover is blocked in blind. Three fillets are blocked on the borders. The fourth, innermost fillet is semi-circular on each corner, with small flower plants blocked in blind. The central vignette, also in blind, features circles and strapwork. The upper cover is blocked in gold and black. The title: '| Tiny's Transformations |' is blocked in black; it is surrounded by curling stems and straps blocked in black. Two cartouches with zigzags are blocked in black above and below the title. The stars at corners are blocked in gold. A single gold fillet is blocked on the upper and on the lower borders, with repeating dots blocked in relief within it. At the head, a winged fairy is seated in a quarter moon, blowing a horn and beating a

drum. At the tail, a group of fairy grotesques is blocked in gold, dancing above water of pond and bulrushes. The pond contains two fishes. The words: '| By | Mark Lemon. |' are blocked in black above the fairies. Signed 'L' at bottom right hand corner of upper cover. The spine is blocked in gold. From the head downwards, the decoration is: a stag's head and antlers; a ribbon-shaped gold lettering-piece, with the title: '| Tiny | Kin's | Trans | for | ma | tions |' blocked in relief within the ribbon; a fish; above and below the title – a rectangle is formed by two gold fillets with leaf-like decoration blocked in gold; an animal blocked in gold; the imprint: '| Bradbury | Evans & Co. |' is blocked in gold; two gold fillets are blocked at the tail, one thin, one thick.

The British Museum de Beaumont copy is shelved at RdeB.C.28.

de Beaumont, *RdeB1* no. 164. Dry, *JL* no. 537. Goldman, *VIB* no. 164. King, *JL* p. 245.

498 Leighton, John

Oxenham, Frances Mary. *Not yet: A Tale of the Present Day*. London: Burns, Oates, & Co., 17, 18 Portman St, and 63 Paternoster Row, 1869. London: Levey and Co, . Printers, Great New Street, Fetter Lane, E.C. [4], 403 p. With eight pages of publisher's titles bound at the end.

106 × 121 × 30 mm. 4410.h.27.

Bevelled boards. Brown endpapers and pastedowns. Blue ungrained cloth. The lower cover is blocked in blind only. On the outer border are blocked three fillets, with small decorated circles on the corners. Inside this, three more fillets are blocked to form an inner rectangle, which has flowers blocked on the corners. The upper cover has the same design for the borders as the lower cover, with the outer fillets blocked in black, and the inner fillets blocked in gold. The flowers on the corners of the inner rectangle are the same as the lower cover and blocked in gold. Near the head of the inner rectangle, a vignette is blocked in gold. This shows a tracery of flowers and leaves, with the title words: '| Not yet |' blocked in relief within a ribbon-shaped gold lettering-piece. At the base of the rectangle the words: '| A tale by | F.M. Oxenham |' are blocked in gold. The spine is blocked in gold. It has a single gold fillet blocked on the perimeter. From the head downwards, the decoration is: a gold fillet; flowers and fleurs-de-lis; the title: '| Not | Yet |' blocked in gold, within a frame; three lily flowers and leaves; signed 'JL' in gold as a monogram near the tail; at the tail, a repeating dot pattern in gold is blocked between two gold fillets.

Dry, *JL* no. 538.

499 Leighton, John

FIG. 61

Scott, *Sir* Walter *Bart. The Lady of the Lake*. Edinburgh: Adam & Charles Black, 1869. [1], 339 pp.

115 × 177 × 32 mm. 11645.bb.8.

Text accompanied by eleven photographs by George Washington Wilson, Aberdeen.

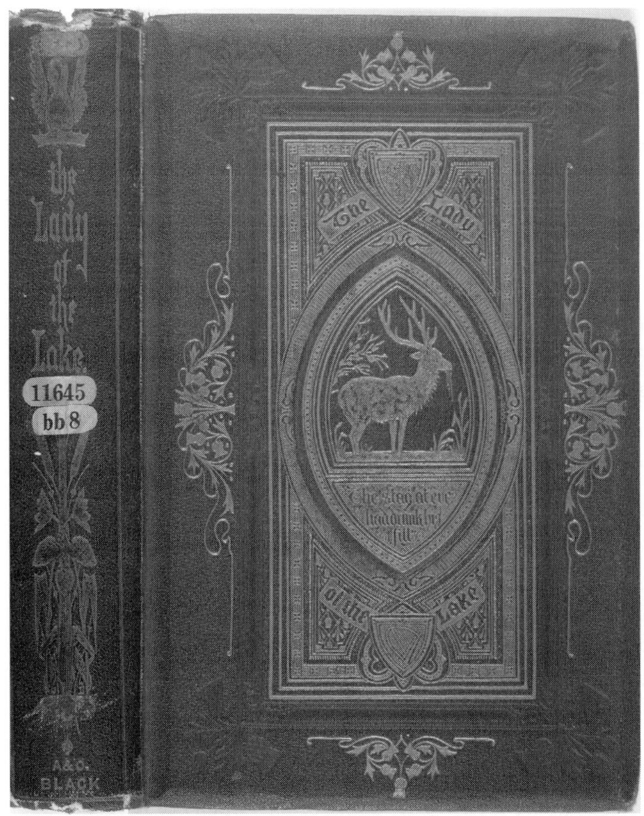

FIG. 61

Bevelled boards. Gilt edges. Blue sand-grain cloth covers. Both covers blocked identically in gold and in blind. The mandorla is recessed on both covers. It features a stag drinking water, with the quotation: 'The stag at eve had drunk his fill', blocked in relief. On the lower cover, the central mandorla only is blocked in gold. On the upper cover, the mandorla is surrounded by a rectangle, which features two shields. On the inner border, thistle plants are blocked in gold, which are also in blind on the corners of the outer border. The title: '| The Lady | of the Lake |' is blocked in relief above and below the mandorla. The spine is blocked in gold. A single gold fillet is blocked on the perimeter. From the head downwards, the decoration is: a swan atop a crown – in gold; the title: '| The | Lady | of | the | Lake. |' blocked in gold in gothic letters; a sword is blocked in gold from near the tail up to below the title; bulrushes, flowers and leaves are blocked in gold around the sword; signed 'JL' in gold as separate letters at the hilt of the sword; the words: '| A&C | Black |' are blocked in gold at the tail.

Dry, *JL* no. 460. Cites the A&C Black 1863 edition.

500 Leighton, John

Archer, Thomas. *Alexandra: A Gift Book to the Alexandra Orphanage for Infants, Hornsey Rise. Edited by Thomas Archer. Contributed, Drawn, Engraved, Printed, Bound, and Published Gratuitously For the Benefit of the Institution. All Rights reserved by the Authors*. London: James Clarke & Co., 13, Fleet Street. James Nisbet & Co., 21, Berners Street, Oxford Street, [1870.].

London: C.P. Alvey, Printer, Atlas Works, Museum Street, W.C. viii, 167 p., 10 plates. With four pages bound at the end, printed on purple dyed paper, advertising the Alexandra Orphanage for Infants, Hornsey Rise, and the Orphan Working School, Haverstock Hill.

168 × 215 × 27 mm. 12331.g.15.

Bound at the front are: 1. a photograph of the Principal Entrance of the Alexandra Orphanage with the children and adults posing in a group on the steps; 2. the half title page has a coloured lithograph, signed 'Leighton Brothers.'

Gilt edges. Bevelled boards. Light yellow endpapers and pastedowns. Binder's ticket on the lower pastedown: '| Bound | by | Leighton | Son and | Hodge. |' Blue sand-grain cloth. The lower cover is blocked in blind only. Two fillets are blocked on the borders. Inside this, double fillets are blocked on each side, and on the head and the tail to form rectangles, with squares blocked on each corner. A diamond pattern is blocked within each square. An oval central panel is formed by two fillets. The upper cover is blocked in gold and in black. A single fillet is blocked on the borders, intersecting at each corner. Groups of four stars are blocked in gold at the points of intersection at the head; groups of three stars are blocked at the points of intersection at the tail. An inner black fillet forms curling leaves in black at the head, and also at the tail, which also has a diamond-shaped frame formed by this fillet. On the centre head, a coronet of the Prince of Wales and three feathers are blocked in gold. Two oil lamps hang from the leaves at the head in gold, as does a basket, suspended on a cord, which has a baby asleep inside it. To the right of the basket – a fairy is blocked in gold, with a wand and an oil container in her left hand, and her right hand held over the baby. Small stars and a moon are blocked beside this. The title; '| The | Alexandra. |' is blocked in gold. Below this, a small bird's nest is blocked in gold. On the centre base, a shield is blocked – or, dotted, with the monogram 'AO' [the capital 'A' within the capital 'O'], blocked in vertical and horizontal gold hatch, within the shield. Above and below the shield, the words 'Hornsey' and 'Rise' are blocked in gold. Signed 'L' in gold below the birds' nest. The spine is blocked in gold and in black. From the head downwards, the decoration is: two fillets in black; the Prince of Wales' feathers in gold; '| The | Alexandra |' blocked in gold; two fillets in black at the tail.

Dry, *JL* no. 541.

501 Leighton, John FIG. 62

Capern, Edward. *Wayside warbles. Second edition, with numerous additions*. London: Simpkin, Marshall & Co. Birmingham; E.C. Osborne, 1870. E. C. Osborne, Printer, Birmingham. xix, 384 p. With eight pages listing other titles by the author bound at the end.

123 × 185 × 30 mm. 11651.bbb.7.

Bevelled boards. Gilt edges. Grey endpapers and pastedowns. Green dot and line diagonal-grain cloth. The lower cover is blocked in blind only. There are three fillets blocked in blind on

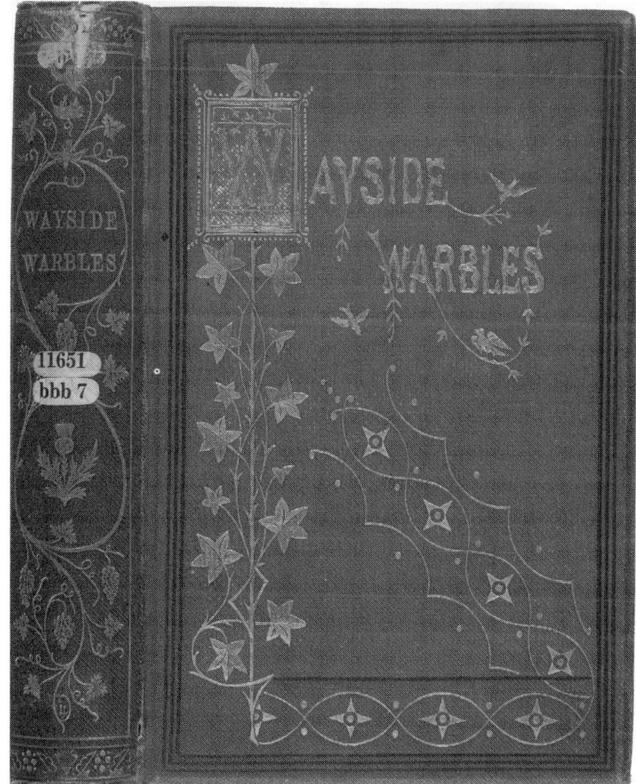

FIG. 62

the borders. On the centre, a circle of ribbons is blocked. The upper cover is blocked in gold and in black. Three fillets are blocked on the borders in black; there is a tracery of stars and intersecting lines, blocked diagonally in gold on the right of the cover. On the spine side of the cover, ivy leaves blocked in gold run up a branch which ends in a red paper onlay. The onlay has two gold fillets and dots blocked in gold on its borders. Within, the capital letter 'W', of the word 'Wayside' is blocked in gold. The title: '| [W]ayside | Warbles |' is blocked in gold in rustic letters across the top third of the cover. The spine is blocked in gold. At the head and at the tail, between single gold fillets, a berry and leaf pattern is blocked in gold. A single gold fillet is blocked on the perimeter of the rest of the spine. A looping branch, blocked in gold, is blocked down the spine, with bunches of grapes, leaves, and tendrils attached. Near the head, two adult birds, a nest and two chicks are blocked in gold. The branch forms two circles. The title: '| Wayside | Warbles |' is blocked in gold in the upper circle. A thistle flower, and leaves are blocked in gold within the lower circle. The monogram 'JL' is blocked in gold at the tail.

Dry, *JL* no. 543.

502 Leighton, John FIG. 63

Limner, Luke *pseud.* [i.e. John Leighton.] *Madre Natura versus The Moloch of Fashion. A Social Essay, with twenty five illustrations*. London: Bradbury, Evans, & Co., 11 Bouverie St., 1870. London: Bradbury, Evans, and Co., Printers, Whitefriars. [vi],

FIG. 63

101 p. The paper covers measure 115 × 172 mm. With ten pages of publisher's titles bound at rear.
120 × 180 × 19 mm. 7743.aaa.64.

Rebound by Dunn & Wilson in 1986. Issued in paper covers. The upper cover is printed in red and black on yellow paper. The red fillet on the borders intersects at the corners, with four black dots at their crossing. On the centre, a lady, fully dressed, is holding a fan in her left hand. This is a copy of the engraving on page 9. '| Price two shillings. | Book postage one penny. |' printed on the upper cover on the head and on the tail. The rest of the cover has the title and the imprint, printed in red and in black. The lower cover shows a lady at her toilette, in front of a mirror on a stand. The title page displays in italics: '| The MANTUA-MAKERS' ARMS. | [rule] |' These are described on the title page verso, in the form of an inverted triangle:

> '| On a shield sable , a Corset proper; crest, upon a wreath of roses, | an Hour-glass or, typical of golden hours wasted. Supporters, | Harpies: the dexter 'Fashion' crowned with a chig | -non or, corsetted and crinoletted proper, her train | being decorated with bows, and the wings with | scissors; the sinister, 'Vanity', crowned | with a coronet of pearls and straw | -berry leaves, bears the wings of a papillon, eyed proper, the | queue à la Paon. Motto, | 'FASHION UNTO DEATH |'.

The arms shows the claw of each of the Harpies pulling tight the laces of a corset. The same arms appear, with the same description, in the fourth edition of 1874, at 7743.aaa.65. They are also blocked in black and gilt on the upper cover of the fourth edition of 1874.

King, *JL* p. 245.

503 Leighton, John

Meteyard, Eliza. *The hallowed spots of Ancient London. Historical, biographical, and antiquarian sketches, illustrative of places and events as they appeared and occurred in the olden time. New edition.* London: Charles Griffin and Company, 10, Stationers Hall Court, 1870. London: Printed by R. Clay, Son, and Taylor, Bread Street Hill. xii, 291, xiip.
165 × 215 × 28 mm. 1570/1482.

The engravings are by C. W. Sheeres.

Gilt edges. White endpapers and pastedowns. The upper endpaper has the bookplate of Thomas Cabban. Red sand-grain cloth. Both covers are blocked identically on the borders, in blind on the lower, in gold on the upper. A single fillet is blocked on the borders. Double thin fillets are blocked at the head, the tail and on the sides, intersecting to form squares on the corners. At these intersections, four small circles are blocked in gold. (These are similar to Rossetti's 'Goblin Market'.) An inner rectangle is blocked on the upper cover, formed by four fillets blocked in black. There are two fleurs-de-lis blocked at the head and the tail, at the end of these fillets. The centre-piece is a blue paper onlay. It is shaped as a shield, and has portions of the arms of the Corporation of London. A single fillet is blocked in gold around its perimeter. A sword is blocked on the upper left hand corner. The title: '| The | Hallowed Spots | of | Ancient London |' is blocked in gold, on the onlay. The words: '| Domine | Dirige Nos |' are blocked in relief underneath the shield within two ribbon-shaped gold lettering-pieces. The spine is blocked in gold. A single fillet is blocked in gold on the perimeter. From the head downwards, the decoration is: a gold fillet; a vertical hatch gold fillet; oval panels formed by three fillets; a sword blade is blocked upwards from mid-spine to near the head; the sword has a crown on its tip; the title: '| The | Hallowed | Spots | of | Ancient | London. |' blocked in relief within six rectangular gold-lettering-pieces; these six gold lettering-pieces wind around the sword blade; flowers, leaves and stems and a 'castellated' crown are all blocked in gold within an oval panel; signed 'JL' in gold as a monogram, within a small panel; stars surround panels on the lower half of the spine; a vertical hatch gold fillet; the words: '| C Griffin & Co. |' are blocked in gold within a rectangle formed by two gold fillets; a vertical hatch gold fillet; two fillets are blocked in gold at the tail.

Dry, *JL* no. 433. The 1862 edition.

504 Leighton, John

Mortimer, F. L. *Near home; or, the countries of Europe described. With anecdotes and Numerous Illustrations . . . Thirty-third Thousand.* London: Hatchard and Co. 187 Piccadilly, 1870. London: Printed by G. Barclay, Castle St. Leicester Sq. xvi, 402 p., 1 fold-out map. With eighteen pages of publisher's titles bound at the end.
110 × 177 × 32 mm. 10106.b.8.

Light yellow endpapers and pastedowns. Red rib vertical-grain cloth. Both covers blocked identically in blind and in relief on the borders and on the corners. A single fillet is blocked in blind on the borders. On each corner, straps are blocked in relief. The upper cover central vignette is blocked in gold. It shows a boy seated on a curling branch. He is reading from a sheet of paper, with his right arm resting upon a folio book. He is surrounded by curling stems, with small leaves and berries attached. The words: '| Near | Home |' are blocked in gold above and below the boy. Signed 'JL' in gold as a monogram at the base of the vignette. The spine is blocked in gold. A single gold fillet is blocked on the perimeter. A tree (and its roots) is blocked from the tail up the spine, with two main branches rising up each side of the spine to form two arches near the head. The arches are interspersed with small leaves and berries in gold. The words: '| Near | Home; | or, | Europe | described. |' are blocked in gold near the head. Below this, more branches of the tree provide support for a scroll and a pile of four books blocked in gold, the upper three of which are titled: '| Travels | Voyages | Gazetteer |' blocked in relief within the tail of each book. On top of the books, a putto supports a globe with two feathers on top. More berries and leaves and curling branches are blocked in gold near the base of the tree. A gold fillet is blocked near the tail. A plant pattern is blocked at the tail.

505 Leighton, John PLATE LXVI

Pouchet, Felix Archimede. *The universe: or, the infinitely great and the infinitely little. Translated from the French. Illustrated by 343 engravings on wood and four coloured plates. From drawings by A. Faguet, Mesnel, Emile Bayard, and J. Stewart.* London: Blackie & Son, Paternoster Row; Glasgow and Edinburgh, 1870. Glasgow: W. G. Blackie and Co., Printers, Villafield. xx, 791 p., 4 plates. With eight pages of publisher's titles bound at the end.
175 × 260 × 60 mm. 7001.g.12.

The monogram of Blackie, XXB&SXX, is printed on the title page with the motto: XXLucem Libris. DisseminamusXX.

Bevelled boards. Yellow endpapers and pastedowns. Brown sand-grain cloth. Both covers are blocked identically in gold, which has been blocked with different use of black and gold on each cover. On the lower cover, a single thin fillet is blocked in black on the border, and four small circles are blocked in black on the corners. Inside, there are two more fillets on the borders in black, one thick, the other thin. These both curve at the corners. There is a medallion formed by three fillets blocked on the centre head and tail inside the borders. Both medallions are blocked in black. In the medallion at the head are blocked: 'Air, water, fire'. In the medallion at the tail is blocked '| vegetable | animal | mineral |'. Motifs represent each word. Adjoining each medallion are small line decorations which join two 'looped square' patterns. The central medallion is formed by three fillets blocked in gold. The words 'The' and 'universe' are at the top and the bottom of the outer circles. In the inner circle, an armillary sphere is blocked in gold, showing latitude and longitude, together with the degrees blocked in relief. Some of the signs of the zodiac are inside, each name being blocked in relief. At the base of the armillary sphere, 'L' is signed in gold, with a full stop above the 'L'. On the upper cover, the small medallions at the head and the tail are formed by four fillets, three in black, the fourth in gold. The same elements as for the lower cover are blocked within each medallion, in gold. Around the central medallion are alternate hatch leaf patterns and 'ball and spike' decoration, both blocked in gold. Black ink is blocked between the stars of the outer circle. Around the armillary sphere is black ink, ribbed, and stars in outline, showing the brown cloth. Also signed 'L' at the base of the globe, with the full stop above the 'L'. The spine is blocked in gold and in black. A black fillet is blocked at the head. From the head downwards, the decoration is: within a panel at the head is the figure of an astronomer, seated on a stool, with a telescope, compasses and a globe, all blocked in gold; the title: '| The | Universe | or | the infinitely great | and the | infinitely | little. |' blocked in gold, surrounded by a medallion, formed by three fillets, blocked in gold and in black; within a panel below the title, a man is seated on a stool, looking into a microscope, and, behind him are a book and a plant in a pot; the word: '| Pouchet |' is blocked in gold, with a flower head blocked on each side and below this word; triangles blocked in black; a black fillet; the words: '| Blackie & Son |' are blocked in gold between two gold fillets; a black fillet is blocked at the tail.

Dry, *JL* no. 545. King, *JL* p. 245. Pantazzi, *JL* p. 272 Shows a different spine from this, the 1870 edition.

506 Leighton, John

Taylor, James. *The Family History of England. Civil, military, social, commercial, & religious. From the earliest period to the passing of the Reform Bill, 1867.* [6 vols.] London: William Mackenzie, 22 Paternoster Row, E.C.; 47 Howard St Glasgow; 59 South Bridge Edinburgh, [1870–1873]. Glasgow: Printed by William Mackenzie, 43 & 45 Howard Street, Glasgow.
9504.h.1.

Vol. I. vi, 402, lxiv, p. , 9 plates, 1 map. 183 × 271 × 38 mm.
Vol. II. vii, 336p, 11 plates (2 fold-out), 1 map. 183 × 270 × 35 mm.
Vol. III. viii, 360, xl, p. , 12 plates. 182 × 269 × 37 mm.
Vol. IV. vii, 336, lx, p. , 10 plates (1 fold-out), 1 map. 183 × 270 × 35 mm.
Vol. V. viii, 400 p., 7 plates, 1 map. 182 × 270 × 35 mm.
Vol. VI. viii, 344, lvi, p. , 6 plates, 2 maps. 182 × 270 × 434 mm.

BM C19 binding. Gauffered edges. Nonpareil marble on edges, on pastedowns, and on endpapers. This copy originally issued in paper parts. The Prospectus to Part 1 states: 'The work will be completed in Thirty Parts, imperial 8vo, price Two Shillings each, or six volumes, beautifully bound in cloth, bevel boards and cut edges, price Twelve Shillings each. Each part will contain Eighty pages letterpress and Two beautiful Engravings, Maps, Portraits or Plans of Battles.' The upper and lower covers for Parts 1 and 30 are bound at the end of Vol. VI. The upper cover design is by Leighton on pink paper, printed in black and in red. The same design, printed in colours on a plate, is tipped into the front of each of the six bound volumes. The description below is for the design printed in several colours on the plate at the front of each volume.

Yellow fillet printed on the borders. Coats of arms on the left and right hand corners: arms: gules, three lions passant-guardant, argent; or, lion rampant, gules. The arch above the title has within it the words: '| Illustrated with maps portraits views and other engravings |'. Within the arch, the title: '| The | Family | History of England | Civil, military, social | commercial & religious | from the earliest period | to the passing of the Reform Bill, 1867. | Vol. I.[–VI.] |' is printed in blue, in red and in brown. Lions are printed at the left and right base of the arch. The lion on the left holds a flag showing a blue cross, and a fleur-de-lis; the lion on the right holds a flag of St. Andrew. A red medallion is printed underneath the title, with a red triangle within; the words: '| King | Lords | Commons |' are printed in white outline, inside the triangle. The words: '| Magna | Carta | Bill | of Rights | Reform Bill. |' are printed on each side of the medallion in blue and in yellow. The medallion is crossed by a mace and a sword, each printed in blue and yellow. The initials 'W' and 'M' are printed in medieval letters, within smaller medallions on either side of the central one. The imprint: '| London [blue] | William Mackenzie [white letters within red] | 22 Paternoster Row, E.C [brown] | 47, Howard St. Glasgow, 59 South Bridge, Edinburgh. [brown] |' is printed on the centre of the tail. On the left and right at the tail, plinths are printed in blue. Ivy leaves are printed in green above each. On the left plinth, an Irish harp is in red, within a shield in green; on the right plinth, the arms are: gules, quartered, four lions passant, argent. Signed at the base of the left plinth: '| Luke Limner F.S.A. Del. |'; at the base of the right plinth: '| H. Leighton Sc. |' – both printed in blue.

Dry, *JL* no. 546. King, *JL* p. 247. Muira, *MP* p. 93, plate B.

507 Leighton, John

Wheatley, Henry Benjamin. *Round about Piccadilly and Pall Mall; or, a ramble from the Haymarket to Hyde Park. Consisting of a retrospect of the various changes that have occurred in the court end of London* . . . London: Smith Elder & Co., 15 Waterloo Place, 1870. London: Printed by Smith, Elder and Co., Old Bailey, E.C. xii, 405 p., 4 plates.
135 × 212 × 58 mm. 2366.b.11.

Conserved and rebound in 1989. Original upper cover used as a doublure. Doublure size: 127 × 208 mm.

Brown sand-grain cloth. The upper cover is blocked in gold and black. The outer border is blocked in gold with a 'dog-tooth' pattern. An inner border consists of a broad black fillet, with leaves blocked in relief within it – all blocked between two thin black fillets. The cover divides into three: at the head, there is fan tracery in black in a rectangle; in the centre, there is a square with an outer border, blocked in black. Inside the square are blocked in gold a sedan chair, a porter, two water pumps, and a street lamp with an ornate stand. The title: '| Round about | Piccadilly | Pall Mall. |' is blocked in gold At the tail, is a street map of Piccadilly and environs blocked in gold, with the roads and the names in relief. Signed 'L' in relief at bottom left hand corner of map.

Dry, *JL* no. 547.

508 Leighton, John

Pouchet, Felix Archimede. *The universe: or, the infinitely great and the infinitely little. New edition. Embodying the author's latest improvements. Illustrated by 343 engravings on wood and Four Coloured Plates. From drawings by A. Faguet, Mesnel, Emile Bayard, and J. Stewart.* London: Blackie & Son, Paternoster Row, 1871. Glasgow: W. G. Blackie and Co., Printers, Villafield. xx, 818 p., 4 plates. With eight pages of publisher's titles bound at the end.
175 × 260 × 75 mm. 7001.g.13.

The monogram of Blackie, XXB&SXX, is printed on the title page with the motto: XXLucem Libris. DisseminamusXX.

Bevelled boards. Yellow endpapers and pastedowns. Green sand-grain cloth. This edition has an identical design for the covers and the spine as the 1870 edition at BL 7001.g.12.

King, *JL* p. 245. Pantazzi, *JL* p. 272 Shows a different spine from this, the 1871 edition.

509 Leighton, John

The literary bouquet: Gathered from Favourite Authors. Illustrated with numerous drawings on wood by eminent artists. . . . Edinburgh: William P. Nimmo, 1872. Muir and Patterson, Printers, Edinburgh. 160 p.
168 × 215 × 22 mm. 12330.g.29.

Text sewn on two tapes. Gilt edges. Bevelled boards. Beige endpapers and pastedowns. Green sand-grain cloth. Both covers blocked identically, in blind and in relief on the lower and in gold and black and in relief on the upper. The upper cover has four fillets blocked on the borders: 1. fillet in gold; 2. fillet in black, with a single leaf on each corner; 3. fillet in gold, curved at each corner; 4. a repeating pattern of two thin fillets with alternating black and gold dots. On each inner corner, a medallion is blocked in gold, with a background blocked in black. Symmetrical leaf and plant decoration blocked in black and in gold on each side joins the medallions. Curling stem and leaf

decoration is blocked on the centre head and on the centre tail in gold and in black. Fillets are blocked around this decoration in black. On the centre of the cover, a medallion is blocked. From the outside inwards are: 1. a single circular fillet in black; 2. a single circular fillet in gold; 3. a border blocked in black, with stars blocked in gold, together with the words: 'Literary Bouquet' blocked in gold within the border; 4. a circular fillet blocked in gold, with a Greek roll blocked in relief inside it; 5. a circular fillet blocked in gold. On the centre within the medallion, the bust of a classical figure, plus a helmet are blocked in gold against a background blocked in black. The spine is blocked in gold and in black. From the head downwards, the decoration is: a fillet in black; a fillet in gold; a girl's head, blocked in gold, within a medallion formed by a single fillet; the title: '| The | Literary | Bouquet |' blocked in gold; symmetrical leaf and stem decoration is blocked in gold and in black; a girl's head, blocked in gold, within a medallion formed by a single fillet; the word: '| Nimmo |' is blocked in gold, within a half circle formed by a single fillet; a fillet in black at the base. [The spine label is likely to obscure the signature of Leighton.]

Dry, *JL* no. 553. Cites copy in Bodleian Library, at 270 e.113.

510 Leighton, John

Black, Adam, *Publisher* and Black, Charles, *Publisher. Black's picturesque guide to the English Lakes including the geology of the district. By John Phillips. Outline mountain views by Mr. Flintoft. Illustrations by Birket Foster. Seventeenth edition.* Edinburgh: Adam and Charles Black, 1872. xxx, 239 p., 1 fold-out map; 4 maps; 6 plates. With seventy-two pages of advertisements bound at the end.

110 × 172 × 27 mm. 10360.bb.42.

The fold-out map of the Lake District bound at the front was drawn and engraved by W. Hughes, 6 Brook Street, Holborn, London.

Edges speckled with red ink. Light yellow endpapers and pastedowns. On the front endpaper and pastedown is printed an Index Map. On the lower endpaper is printed 'Comparative view of Lakes'. On the lower pastedown is printed 'Comparative heights of mountains'. Dark green sand-grain cloth. The upper cover design of this edition is the same as for the 1858 and 1861 editions at BL. 10358.d.14. and 10358.c.8. The spine has three fillets blocked in gold at the head and the tail. The title: '| Black's | Guide | to the | Lakes |' is blocked near the head in gold. The rest of the spine decoration is as for 1858 and 1861.

511 Leighton, John

Black, Adam, *Publisher* and Black, Charles, *Publisher. Black's picturesque tourist of Ireland. Illustrated with a map of Ireland, and several plans and views. Twelfth edition.* Edinburgh: Adam & Charles Black, 1872. 423 p., ten maps and plans, some fold-out.

105 × 160 × 35 mm. 10390.aa.1.

The fore-edge has place names printed down its length.

Yellow endpapers and pastedowns . The front endpaper and pastedown shows a map of Ireland. The rear endpaper and pastedown has an advertisement listing Black's guide books. Green sand-grain cloth. Both covers have two fillets blocked in blind on the borders. The upper cover has a central vignette blocked in gold. It shows an Irish harp, on a rocky plinth. The title words: 'Black's guide to' are blocked in gold above the harp. The word: 'Ireland' is blocked in gold across the strings of the harp. The spine is blocked in gold. It shows the title words, blocked in gold, inside a panel formed by two fillets, which connect above and below to clover leaf decoration. Signed 'JL' in gold as separate letters at the base of the design. Fillets are blocked in blind at the head and at the tail.

The sixteenth edition of 1881 is at BL 10390.bbb.29. 423 p. Ten maps and plans, some fold-out. With 108 pages of advertisements bound at the rear. Place names and page numbers are stamped on the centre of the fore-edge. The endpapers and pastedowns are the same as the twelfth edition. Green sand-grain cloth. The design blocked on the covers and the spine is the same as the twelfth edition. The nineteenth edition of 1885 is at BL 10390.bbb.12. The twentieth edition of 1887 is at BL 10390.bbb.21. The twenty-first edition of 1891 is at BL 10390.aaaa.24. These last three have much the same design as the twelfth edition. However, the initials 'JL' are absent from the spine.

512 Leighton, John

Brough, Robert Barnabas. *Character Sketches, Development Drawings, and Original Pictures of Wit and Humour. Done in permanent lines for posterity by Charles H. Bennett & Robert B. Brough. Illustrated with ninety-four engravings, and many head-pieces and finials.* London: Ward, Lock, and Tyler, Warwick House, Paternoster Row, [1872]. London: Bradbury, Evans, and Co., Printers, Whitefriars. x, 390 p., 19 plates. With two pages of publisher's titles bound at the end.

170 × 250 × 40 mm. 12330.i.11.

Gilt edges. Bevelled boards. Yellow endpapers and pastedowns. Blue sand-grain cloth. Both covers blocked identically, in blind only on the lower, and in gold and black on the upper. Three fillets are blocked on the borders – one in black and two in gold, and these are curved at the fore-edge. A single star is blocked in gold on each fore-edge corner. A medallion is blocked on the fore-edge at the head and at the tail. Each has a single fillet blocked on its border, and each has a green paper onlay blocked in gold. At the head, the decoration on the medallion is: a butterfly, and a mirror, with the word: 'Vanitas', blocked in gold. At the tail, the decoration is: a snake and a mirror, with the word: 'Veritas', blocked in gold. Rectangles formed by black fillets divide the upper cover into three panels. Each panel has fillets on its borders blocked in gold and in black. The upper and lower of the three panels have red paper onlays, which are blocked in black, with the words: '| Character. Sketches |' and 'Development drawings' blocked in relief to show the red onlay.

On the spine side of the upper cover, a green paper onlay is pasted, which has three fillets blocked on its borders, one in black, two in gold. One of the gold fillets has repeating dots blocked in relief inside it. The decoration on the green paper onlay shows an urn blocked in gold, with ram's head handles. The urn contains flowers blocked in gold and the leaves are blocked in relief, showing the green onlay. The flower heads have 'facial' features outlined by blocking in black. Signed 'JL' in relief as separate letters at the base of the urn. Six stars are blocked to the right of this green onlay, at the head and at the tail, two in gold, and four in black. On the fore-edge side of the upper cover, the central rectangle is formed by a single fillet blocked in black. The decoration within shows a book, with candle and ivy leaves blocked on each side – all in gold. The candle has just been snuffed out by a candle snuffer, blocked in black. Underneath the book, crossed quills are blocked in gold. On each page of the open book, two silhouettes are blocked. To the left is a bearded man blocked in gold, against a background blocked in black. To the right is another man in gold against a background in black. [Are these silhouettes of Bennett and Brough?] Above and below the book, the words: '| By | Charles H. Bennett. | & | Robert Brough. |' are blocked in gold. The spine is blocked in gold and in black. From the head downwards, the decoration is: a fillet in black; the title: '| Character | sketches | and | development | drawings. |' blocked in gold; a black lettering-piece, with straps and animal heads in gold inside it; this lettering-piece has a fillet blocked in gold above it and a fillet in black below it; three stars – two in gold, one in black; an oval formed by a single gold fillet; within the oval – face masks are blocked in black and in gold, together with a lighted candle and leaves blocked in gold; three stars – two in black, one in gold; a black lettering-piece, with joined heads and decoration blocked in gold inside; this lettering-piece has fillets blocked in black above and below it; the words: '| By | Charles H. | Bennett. | and | Robert | Brough. |' are blocked in gold; two fillets in gold; one fillet in black; the word: '| London. |' is blocked in gold at the tail.

Dry, *JL* no. 552.

513 Leighton, John

Shakespeare, William. *The library Shakespeare. Illustrated by Sir John Gilbert, George Cruikshank, and R. Dudley*. [3 vols.] London: William Mackenzie, [1873–1875]. Printed by William Mackenzie, 43 & 45 Howard Street, Glasgow.

J/11764.m.1.

Vol. I. Comedies. London: William Mackenzie, 22 Paternoster Row; South Bridge, Edinburgh; Howard Street, Glasgow, [1873]. [3], 396 p., 27 plates. 252 × 315 × 55 mm. The upper and lower paper covers of parts 1–10 are bound at the end.

Vol. II. Tragedies. London: William Mackenzie, 69, Ludgate Hill, E.C.; South Bridge, Edinburgh; Howard Street, Glasgow, [1873–75]. [2], 406 p., 16 plates. 252 × 312 × 43 mm. The upper and lower paper covers of parts 11–20 are bound at the end.

Vol. III. Historical; plays, &c. London: William Mackenzie, 22 Paternoster Row; South Bridge, Edinburgh; Howard Street, Glasgow, [1875]. [2], 476 p., 20 plates. 250 × 312 × 68 mm. The upper and lower paper covers of parts 21–32 are bound at the end. Bound at the end of Vol. III. are: Notes critical and explanatory, by Samuel Neil. The notes for each volume are paginated separately: Vol. I xvi, 62p, 4 plates. Vol. II. 50 p. Vol. III. 32 p. The upper and lower paper covers for the notes are entitled 'Division 12'; 'price 6s.6d.'

Originally issued in thirty-two parts, in paper covers. The 'Address' is printed on the verso of the lower cover of Part 1. It announces that the work is to be published in eight divisions, in cloth at 10/6 each. '. . . Also in Thirty Parts at Two Shillings each.' This set is bound into three volumes, with the paper covers for each part bound at the end of each volume.

In the three volumes, the plates that are coloured are pasted onto backing sheets, signed by each artist and produced by William Mackenzie. The black and white engravings used as the frontispieces of each play are signed by each artist and engraved by Dalziel.

The paper covers for all the parts are printed the same. The upper cover design has bead and fillet borders. At the centre head, there is a portrait bust of Shakespeare, within a Renaissance bolt frame. On the corners, a shield is printed within renaissance panels. The words: '| Mackenzie's | Illustrated | Family | Library |' are printed within a ribbon winding around the bolt, which extends on each side of the bust of Shakespeare. On the centre, two female figures [Lady Macbeth and Ophelia, perhaps] hold up a notice on stage boards, announcing the title: 'The | Library | Shakspeare[sic] | Illustrated | by | nearly | 800 superb engravings | from original designs | by | Sir John Gilbert. | George Cruikshank. | and R. Dudley. |'; the word: '| Shakespeare |' is printed in red. To the left and the right below the stage boards, a winged putto is shown. Two swords support a shield, centre. Within ribbons, the words: '| Sweet swan of Avon | Upon the banks of Thames | That did so please Eliza. | And our James. |' are printed. The imprint below this is: '| William Mackenzie |' – printed in white within a brown rectangle with a white border – '| 22 Paternoster Row | London | 47. Howard St. | Glasgow | South Bridge | Edinburgh |'. Signed at the left hand base: 'John Leighton. F.S.A.' Signed at the right hand base: 'HL Sc' as a monogram [i.e. Henry Leighton].

Dry, *JL* no. 555.

514 Leighton, John

Barham, Richard Harris. *The Ingoldsby Legends or mirth and marvels, by Thomas Ingoldsby, Esquire. With sixty illustrations by George Cruikshank, John Leech and John Tenniel.* London: Richard Bentley and Son, Publisher in Ordinary to Her Majesty, 1874. R. Clay, Son, and Taylor, Printers, London. xii, 514 p.

170 × 235 × 50 mm. C. 70.d.10.

The verso of the front endpaper has the title written out in Eliza Cruikshank's hand.

On the recto of the frontispiece is written the dedication: '| This book | is presented to | the "British Museum" | in Memory of | George Cruikshank. Artist | by his Widow | Eliza Cruikshank | December 23rd 1887. | her 80th birthday. |' Above the dedication, two cartes de visite are pasted. They are of Eliza and George Cruikshank, and each is signed in their own hand. The title page is signed '| Geo Cruikshank 1874 | and his wife, Eliza Cruikshank |'. The first page of the preface to the original edition is signed: '| Geo Cruikshank 1874 |'.

Text sewn on three tapes. Bevelled boards. Gilt edges. Plain dark green endpapers. Purple sand-grain cloth. Both covers are blocked identically in gold and in blind. At the four corners, twin intertwined dragons are blocked in gold. The outer border in gold is of a repeating pattern of acorns at the end of leaves, interspersed with a triple leaf motif, which is enclosed in arches. The inner border features a medallion on each corner, with the head and shoulders of a fanciful character blocked within each. There is also a medallion and fanciful character within blocked on the centre of each side. Two shields with pseudo-devices within are blocked in gold and in relief on each side. Fillets and 'cord-shaped' fillets and emblems are blocked in gold between the medallions and the shields on the inner border. The inner corners have decoration blocked in blind. The central mandorla has several borders, blocked in gold. Within it at the head, a lion is blocked, holding a shield, saltire ermine. The tail of the lion loops on either side of the shield to enclose the initials 'T' and 'I'. The title: '| The | Ingoldsby | Legends |' is blocked in relief within a shield-shaped gold lettering-piece. The initials, 'JL', are blocked in relief as separate letters at the base of the title. The spine is blocked in gold and in blind. A single gold fillet is blocked on the perimeter, with three fillets blocked in blind inside this. Pairs of oak leaves and acorns are blocked in gold at the head. The inner panel runs from tail to head, formed by two gold fillets, which are semi-circular at the head. At the head of the inner panel, a rat and a frog are on either side of a medallion with a figure resembling Mephistopheles within – all in gold. The title: '| The | Ingoldsby | Legends | Illustrated |' is blocked in gold. The decoration below this shows a magpie with a ring in its mouth, astride a hat. The hat is above a sword, a spear and a bishop's staff, all crossing behind a shield. A cross and rosary, and a cat of nine tails are blocked to the left and to the right beneath the shield. The shield shows an owl displayed, wings inverted, sable. Above the owl, a bat soaring, or. The lower half of the sword impales a head, and a half moon. Signed 'JL', in gold as separate letters, beneath the half moon. The words: '| Richard Bentley |' are blocked in relief within a rectangular gold lettering-piece, with two gold fillets blocked on its borders. Beneath this, a rectangle is formed by a single fillet blocked in blind. Acorn and scallop decoration is blocked in gold at the tail. This copy formerly shelved at 11611.h.12.

King, *JL* pp. 240–241.

515 Leighton, John

PLATE LXVII

Limner, Luke *pseud.* [i.e. John Leighton.] *Madre Natura versus The Moloch of Fashion. A Social Essay, with thirty illustrations. Fourth edition.* [Coat of Arms of the Mantua Makers.] London: Chatto & Windus, Piccadilly, 1874. London: R. Clay, Son, and Taylor, Printers. 119 p. With forty eight pages of publisher's titles bound at the end.

115 × 175 × 17 mm. 7743.aaa.65.

Red edges. Brown endpapers and pastedowns. Binder's ticket on lower pastedown: '| Bound | by | Leighton | Son and | Hodge. |'. Grey ungrained cloth covers. Both covers are blocked identically in black on the borders to resemble the lace work of a corset. The corners have the ends of the laces, knotted. The Mantua makers coat of arms is blocked in gold and black on the centre of the upper cover. On the verso of the title page, the following description is printed describing the coat of arms:

> '| THE MANTUA MAKERS ARMS | On a shield sable, a corset proper; crest, upon a wreath of roses | , an Hour-glass or, typical of golden hours wasted. Supporters, | Harpies: the dexter 'Fashion' crowned with a chig- | non or, corsetted and crinoletted proper, her train | being decorated with bows, and the wings with | scissors; the sinister, 'Vanity', crowned | with a coronet of pearls and straw- | berry leaves, bears the wings of | a papillon, eyed proper, the | queue à la Paon. Motto, | 'FASHION UNTO | DEATH!' [A la mode, a la mort]. |'

The claws of the Harpies are pulling the corset laces tightly. The lower cover has a vignette blocked in black at the centre, a reproduction of the illustration on page 9. This shows a lady at her toilette, in front of a mirror. The BL copy lacks the spine. The spine of the copy in the John Johnson Collection is blocked in gold and black, and shows a wire frame, in the shape of a female model, with skirt hoops and corset prominent. Robin de Beaumont informed the compiler at 1.95 that the dedication is to John Marshall, who was Rossetti's physician; a doctor to the Department of Science and Art. [The Bodleian Library copies are Johnson f.2724 and 150.g.11(10). Issued originally in paper wrappers in 1870.]

King, *JL* p. 245; illustration p. 246.

516 Leighton, John

King, Edward. *The Southern States of North America: a record of journeys in Louisiana, Texas, the Indian Territory, Missouri, Arkansas, Mississippi, Alabama, Georgia, Florida, South Carolina, North Carolina, Kentucky, Tennessee, Virginia, West Virginia and Maryland. Profusely illustrated from original sketches by J. Wells Champney.* London: Blackie & Son, Paternoster Buildings, E.C.; Glasgow and Edinburgh, 1875. Glasgow: W.G. Blackie & Co, Printers, Villafield. 906 p., 4 plates, 1 map. With two pages of publisher's titles bound at the end, and four pages bound at the front.

180 × 255 × 65 mm. 10410.w.1

Gilt edges. Bevelled boards. Yellow endpapers and pastedowns. Brown fine rib diagonal-grain cloth. The lower cover is blocked in black only. Two fillets are blocked in black on the borders. The cover is divided into three by two horizontal fillets, blocked in black. Panels are formed inside these divisions by single fillets blocked in black. Within the first and third panels, flowers and leaves are blocked. Within the central panel, single flowers are blocked on the perimeter. The centre-piece is a medallion formed by four circular fillets. Leaf decoration is blocked in black within the medallion. The upper cover is blocked in gold and in black. The same fillets on the borders and the same panels are blocked in black. Within the first panel at the head, a medallion is formed by three fillets – one blocked in black and two blocked in gold. Within, the word: 'rice' is blocked in gold. In the third panel at the base, two medallions are blocked, formed by the same three fillets. Inside these fillets, the words: 'Tobacco' and 'Cotton' are blocked in gold. The upper cover centre-piece shows four medallions joined by chain links blocked in gold. The medallions show: an eagle (with its wings blocked outside the medallion); a lady's head; a crocodile; a black man's head. The spine is blocked in gold and in black. A single fillet is blocked on the perimeter in gold. From the head downwards, the decoration is: the US flag; a 'house' formed by 'timber-like' gold fillets, with black borders; '| The |', blocked in gold; '| Southern | States |' blocked in relief within rectangular gold lettering-pieces; '| of |' blocked in gold; '| North | America |' blocked within a vertical hatch gold lettering-piece; '| copiously | illustrated |' blocked in gold; a helmet on a pole above a wooden crate – all in gold; two double five-pointed stars, one blocked in black, the other in horizontal hatch gold; the letters 'N' and 'S' are blocked in relief within each star; a horizontal hatch black lettering-piece, with a decorated gold fillet blocked on its borders; a staff with wings and two snakes – in gold; two sacks are blocked in gold, with the words: 'rice' and 'corn' blocked in relief within each sack; two barrels are blocked in gold, with the words: 'tobacco' and 'sugar' blocked in relief within each barrel; two bales of cotton are blocked in gold, with the word: 'cotton' blocked in relief within the upper, and the letters 'JL' in relief as separate letters within the lower bale; at the tail, the words: '| Blackie & Son. |' are blocked in gold within a rectangle formed by two fillets, one of gold and one of black.

517 Leighton, John

Knatchbull-Hugessen, E. H. *Whispers from fairyland*. London: Longmans, Green, and Co., 1875. London: Printed by Spottiswoode and Co., New-Street Square and Parliament Street. xi, 345 p., 8 plates. With two pages of publisher's titles bound at the end.
125 × 187 × 35 mm. 12803.g.7.

The plates are signed 'WJW' and 'Pearson Sc'.

Light yellow endpapers and pastedowns. Red fine rib diagonal-grain cloth. On both covers, the borders and corners are blocked identically, in blind on the lower and in black on the upper. On the upper cover, three fillets are blocked on the borders, the middle fillet having small repeating half circles blocked along it. On each corner, a leaf and stem pattern is blocked in black. The upper cover central vignette is blocked in gold. It reproduces the illustration bound opposite page 173, entitled: 'Mollie and the Devil-Fish'. Mollie is rowing a boat on stormy waters, with the Devil-Fish arising out of the waves on her left. The title: '| Whispers | from | Fairy-Land. |' is blocked in gold above and below the vignette. On the stern-end of the rowing boat, the monograms 'HK' and HC' are blocked, reversed, in relief. The spine is blocked in gold and black. A single gold fillet is blocked on the perimeter. From the head downwards, the decoration is: a clenched fist in gold; a dancing figure, blocked in gold, surrounded by leaf and stem decoration blocked in black; the word: '| Whispers |' blocked in relief within a rectangular gold lettering-piece; a pair of lips and teeth – blocked in gold; the words: '| from | Fairy-Land | [rule] | E. H. Knatchbull – | Hugessen. |' blocked in gold; a figure of a man with a pipe, who is looking at a Tom Thumb-like figure standing on a table; a Don Quixote-like figure is seated on a boar; signed 'L' in gold near the left hand base; a fillet in gold; the publisher 'Longmans & Co.' is blocked in gold between dotted lines and a rectangle formed by a single fillet – all in gold.

Dry, *JL* no. 557.

518 Leighton, John

Michell, Nicholas. *Ruins of many lands. A descriptive poem. With Illustrations on steel. Sixth edition*. London: William Tegg and Co., Pancras Lane, Cheapside, 1875. viii, 9–440p, 7 plates. With thirty four pages of publisher's titles bound at the end.
125 × 190 × 35 mm. 11647.c.1.

Grey endpapers and pastedowns. Brown sand-grain cloth. Both covers have identical blind blocking on the borders and on the corners. Two fillets are blocked on the borders. Thin curling leaves and stems are blocked in blind on each corner. The upper cover central vignette is blocked in gold and is the same as for the second edition of 1850. Leighton's initials are omitted from the bottom of the design. The spine is blocked in gold. From the head downwards, the decoration is: two gold fillets; a row of stylised leaves in gold; a gold fillet; the words: '| Ruins | of | many lands | [rule] | Michell. |' blocked in gold; a gold fillet; a small decorative device, incorporating a heart shape; the word: '| Illustrated. |' blocked in gold; a gold fillet; the words: '| Tegg, London |' in gold; a gold fillet; stylised leaves in gold; two gold fillets are blocked at the tail.

King, *JL* p. 240. Pantazzi, *JL* p. 263.

519 Leighton, John

Raleigh, Alexander. *The Story of Jonah The Prophet*. [Engraved map of the Mediterranean entitled: 'Sketch-map of Mediterranean Sea'.] Edinburgh: Adam and Charles Black, 1875. Printed by R. & R. Clark, Edinburgh. [9], 322 p. With four pages of publisher's titles bound at the end.
120 × 186 × 30 mm. 3166.de.65.

The frontispiece plate is the same as the 1866 edition.

Black endpapers and pastedowns. Binder's ticket on lower pastedown: '| Bound by | Burn | & Co |'. Red thin rib diagonal-grain cloth. The same fillets are blocked on the borders of both covers, in blind on the lower, in black on the upper. Two fillets are blocked on the outer border. The three fillets blocked inside form an arch at the head. On the upper cover, reed plants are blocked in black on the inner corners and on the centre tail. The upper cover vignette is blocked in gold. It shows a medallion, formed by a single gold fillet, with Jonah, the whale and waves inside. The title: '| Story | of | Jonah |' is blocked in horizontal hatch gold above the figure of Jonah. Signed 'JL' in gold as separate letters at the base of the vignette. The spine is blocked in gold and in black. From the head downwards, the decoration is: three fillets, the middle in gold, between two in black; the words: '| The | Story | of | Jonah | Raleigh |' blocked in gold within a panel formed by a single 'rope-like' gold fillet; a reed plant is blocked in black, between two black fillets; near the base, a dolphin is blocked in gold , with ribbon-shaped gold lettering-piece around it; the words: '| A&C | Black |' are blocked in relief within the ribbon; three fillets are blocked at the tail, the middle in gold between two in black.

520 Leighton, John

Black, Adam, *Publisher* and Black, Charles, *Publisher*. *Black's Tourist guide to Derbyshire Its towns, watering places, dales, and mansions. Twelfth edition With a Map of the County, Plans of Chatsworth and Haddon Hall, and several Illustrations.* Edinburgh: Adam and Charles Black, 1876. vii, 285 p., 6 plates, 1 fold-out map. With twelve pages of advertisements bound at the end.

115 × 172 × 25 mm. 1607/4086.

A sketch map showing position of Derbyshire is printed on the front endpaper. A List of Black's Guide books is printed on the rear endpaper and pastedown.

Yellow endpapers and pastedowns. Green sand-grain cloth. Two fillets are blocked in blind on the borders of both covers. The upper cover central vignette is blocked in gold. It shows a shield, or, a stag within a wooden paddock. The word: '| Derby |' is blocked in relief at the base of the shield. Signed 'JL' in relief underneath this. Above and below the shield, the words: '| Black's | Guide | to | Derbyshire |' are blocked in gold in rustic letters, with tendrils and small leaves attached to the letters. '| Black's Guide to Derbyshire |' is blocked in gold along the spine.

521 Leighton, John

Pouchet, Felix Archimede. *The universe: or, the infinitely great and the infinitely little. Third edition. The translation revised. Illustrated by 270 engravings on wood, from drawings by A. Faguet, Mesnel, and Emile Bayard.* London: Blackie & Son, Paternoster Buildings, E.C.; Glasgow and Edinburgh, 1876. Glasgow: W.G. Blackie and Co., Printers, Villafield. xvi, 564 p., 1 plate. With a one page press notice bound at the front and four pages of publisher's advertisements bound at the rear.

150 × 220 × 45 mm. 7001.eee.4.

British Museum rebind C19. The black and white plates are printed on separate sheets, but paginated with the main sequence. The original upper cover is used as a doublure. Doublure size: 140 × 212 mm. Brown fine rib diagonal-grain cloth. The cover is blocked in black and in gold and relief. A single black fillet is blocked on the borders. Inside this, a black fillet is blocked, with ovals blocked in relief within it. The cover is divided into three by the black fillet and the ovals in relief, and also by the use of a black fillet which forms rectangular panels. In the upper and lower panels are half medallions, with tracery in gold and in black. The central panel has the same armillary sphere, blocked in gold and in black, as the 1870 and 1871 editions, The sphere is surrounded by stars and dots, blocked in black. At the base of the sphere, 'L' is signed in gold, with a full stop above the 'L'. The outer circle has the subtitle 'The infinitely great and the infinitely little' blocked in gold, with black blocking between the letters. Around the whole medallion is a square and four triangular points, blocked in gold and in black. There are leaves and circles blocked within the triangles, and leaves on the corners of the square.

King, *JL* p. 245. Pantazzi, *JL* p. 272.

522 Leighton, John

Black, Adam, *Publisher* and Black, Charles, *Publisher*. *Black's guide to Devonshire. With Maps and Illustrations.* Edinburgh: Adam and Charles Black, 1877. vii, 96–291 p., 5 plates, 3 fold-out maps. With one hundred and twelve pages of advertisements bound at the end.

113 × 172 × 22 mm. 10368.cc.29.

Edges speckled with red ink. This copy belonged to Henry Spencer Ashbee. Book label of Ashbee pasted on the upper pastedown. Yellow endpapers and pastedowns. An 'Index Map . . . to Dorset, Devon & Cornwall' is printed on the upper endpaper and pastedown. A 'List of Black's Guide-Books' is printed in purple on the lower endpaper and pastedown. Green sand-grain cloth. Two fillets are blocked in blind on the borders of both covers, the outer fillet is thick, the inner is thin. The upper cover central vignette is blocked in gold. The words: '| Black's | guide [in rustic letters] | to |' are blocked in gold. A shield is blocked as a gold lettering-piece, which shows the walls of Exeter. The word: '| Exeter |' is blocked in relief within the shield, underneath the walls. Signed 'JL' in relief as separate letters underneath the word 'Exeter'. The word: '| Devonshire |' is blocked in gold in rustic letters underneath the shield. Small stems and leaves are blocked in gold and attached to the rustic letters. The spine has the single word: '| Devonshire |' blocked in gold along its length.

Dry, *JL* no. 558.

523 Leighton, John

Macfarlane, Charles and Thomson, Thomas. *The comprehensive history of England; civil and military, religions, intellectual and social. From the earliest period to the suppression of the Sepoy revolt. The whole revised and edited by the Rev. Thomas Thomson. Continued to signing of the Treaty of San Stefano. Illustrated by eleven hundred engravings.* 4 vols. London: Blackie & Son: Paternoster Buildings; Glasgow and Edinburgh, [1877–1878]. Glasgow: W.G. Blackie & Co., Printers, Villafield.

9503.g.1.

Vol. I. Earliest period to Henry VIII. xiii, 848 p., 6 plates. 173 × 255 × 55 mm.
Vol. II. Edward VI. to James II. viii, 800 p., 6 plates. 173 × 255 × 52 mm.
Vol. III. William III, to George III, A.D. 1792. viii, 872 p., 6 plates. 173 × 255 × 55 mm.
Vol. IV. George III., A.D. 1792, to Victoria, A.D. 1878. viii, 982 p., 6 plates. 173 × 255 × 61 mm.

BM Binding. Red pebble-grain cloth; quarter red leather; six spine panels, with title blocked in gold within panel two. Marbled endpapers and pastedowns, and edges, consisting of: Old Dutch, variant; small wave, variant; bouquet marble, variant. Originally issued in parts with paper covers, at 3s. per part. The upper and lower covers for parts 1 and 24 are bound at the end of Vol. IV. Each upper cover has the same design by John Leighton. Cream paper, printed in green and in brown. Medallions are printed on each corner, of the Kings of England, with smaller medallions showing a book or a scroll inscribed with the achievements of a particular monarch. They are: William the Conqueror: 'Doomsday Book'; King John: 'Magna Cart.'; Oliver Cromwell: 'Oliver Protector'; Henry VIII: 'Holy Bible'. At the centre head, a crown is printed above the words: '| Illustrated by | above eleven hundred engravings | on steel and wood. |' The centre of the cover is occupied by a large medallion, which is punctuated by a triangle. Around the perimeter of the medallion, the words: '| Far as the breeze can bear the billows foam. Survey our Empire and behold our home. |' are printed in gothic letters. The title: '| The comprehensive [within a scroll] | history | of | England. [blocked between two green rules.] | From the earliest period | to the present time. | Civil, military, religious, intellectual, & | social. |' is printed in brown and green letters around within, and below the triangle. The large medallion contains three smaller medallions, the outer two of which are bordered with two fillets and beads between them. Within each of the three are: on the left – Queen Elizabeth; on the right – Queen Mary (?); in the middle, the motto: '| Patria juncta in uno |' with three crowns around the perimeter, and a crown, a thistle, a shamrock and a rose intermingling. Signed 'JL' in green as separate letters underneath the crown. At the base of the main medallion: '| Blackie | & | Son. |' is printed within a shield, which is surrounded by clusters of oak leaves and acorns. On the centre tail: '| London | Glasgow. & Edinburgh. |' is printed in green letters within two brown rectangles, each with single fillets on their borders.

524 Leighton, John

Burns, Robert. *The National Burns. Edited by Rev. George Gilfillan, including the airs of all the songs and an original life of Burns by the editor.* 2vols. London; Glasgow; Edinburgh: William Mackenzie, 1879–1880.
200 × 260 mm. 11611.h.10.

Vol. I. cxxviii, 232 p., 24 plates. 40 mm thick.
Vol. II. 353, 7 p. 37 mm thick.

The head-piece engraving of Vol I., page 1 is signed 'H. L. Sc'. The printed title pages of both volumes are designed by John Leighton and engraved by H. Leighton.

Originally issued in fifteen parts with paper covers. Bound at the end of volume 2 are the front and rear paper covers of parts 1 and 15. On the verso of the rear cover of part 1 is a Prospectus for the work. Each part cost two shillings each, with each part containing forty-eight pages of letterpress and two plates. The paper covers are blue. The inks used for the upper covers recto are blue and red for part 1 and blue and yellow for part 15. The design is of monumental baroque, containing a portrait of Burns at the top in a broken pediment. The title is printed identically to the title page. Underneath the title are a bard, holding a harp, and a young lady in a cloak, seated, holding a scroll, showing music. Signed 'John Leighton F.S.A.' and 'H. Leighton Sc.' at the tail of each upper cover.

—— Another copy. London; Glasgow; Edinburgh: William Mackenzie, [ca.1880?]. cxxxviii, 1–232; 1–352 p., 30 plates.

NG.1166.a.5.

The National Library of Scotland copy.

The title page for this copy is the paper cover. Two volumes are bound into this copy. These are the same as the British Library copy at 11611.h.10. [i.e. the design is signed by John Leighton.] Signed at the tail: 'John Leighton F.S.A.'; 'H. Leighton Sc.' However, they are printed in monochrome only. Marbled endpapers and pastedowns. Blue half morocco. A bust of Burns is blocked in gold on the centre of the upper cover.

Dry, *JL* no. 562. King, *JL* p. 247.

525 Leighton, John

Hozier, Henry Montague. *The Russo-Turkish War: including an account of the rise and decline of the Ottoman power, and the History of the Eastern Question. Edited by Captain H. M. Hozier, F.C.S., F.G.S.* London: William Mackenzie, 69 Ludgate Hill, E.C.; Edinburgh, Glasgow, Dublin, [1879]. Printed by William Mackenzie, London, Edinburgh, and Glasgow. iii, 954 p., 24 plates, 8 maps.
210 × 275 × 73 mm. 9135.ff.19.

The Prospectus for the work is printed on the lower cover of Part 1. 'The work . . . will be published in Fifteen Parts, price Two Shillings each, each containing Sixty-Four Pages Letterpress and two Plates; or in Thirty Parts at One Shilling each; or in Five Divisions, handsomely bound in cloth, bevel boards and gilt edges, price Eight Shillings and Sixpence each.' The upper and

lower covers for parts 1 and 30 are bound at the end of the Library copy. The lower cover of part 30 has publisher's titles.

The paper has been dyed pink. The upper covers are printed in red and in black. Each upper cover has the same design. There is a red fillet printed on the borders. The top left and right hand corners have medallions. The medallion on the left shows possibly the Arkhangel Cathedral in Moscow; the medallion on the right shows Santa Sophia in Constantinople. Between the medallions, a Russian eagle is printed in black on the centre. The eagle holds a ball and a sceptre in its claws. The word '| The |' is printed in red within the eagle's tail feathers. The words: '| Russo-Turkish |' are printed in red, with black edges, within a pennant. The word: '| War |' is printed in black against the background of the dome of a mosque. Below this a moon and star are printed in white within a black circle, and underneath this, the words: '| Including an account of the | rise and decline | of the Ottoman power, | and the | History of the Eastern Question. | Edited by | Capt. H. M. Hozier, F.I.S., F.G.S. | [rule] | With numerous illustrations. |' are printed within a panel. On each side of the panel, a soldier of the Russian and Turkish armed forces is printed. Each holds weapons. There are two open books at the left and right hand base, each with text. Signed 'John Leighton F.S.A' below the Russian soldier. Signed 'H. L [possibly Henry Leighton] Sc.' on the right underneath the Turkish soldier. At the centre of the base, the words: '| William Mackenzie |' are printed in red within a black rectangular lettering-piece. The words: '| London Glasgow & Edinburgh |' are printed in black within red rectangular lettering-pieces.

The National Library of Scotland copy is at shelfmark A.82.a. It is bound in two volumes. It has the same title pages as the BL copy, and the same pagination. The binding of the NLS copy is modern buckram.

Dry, *JL* no. 560. King, *JL* p. 247.

526 Leighton, John

Moore, Thomas, *The Poet. The National Moore. Centenary edition including the airs of the Irish Melodies National airs &c and a memoir by J. F. Waller LL.D. M.R.I.A.* 4 vols. London & 6. D'Olier St. Dublin: William Mackenzie, [1879].

BCL.C689, 780–782

- Div. I. 200 × 253 × 23 mm. xvi, 168 p., 4 plates. Shelfmark: Mus.K.m.421.
- Div. I. 200 × 252 × 21 mm. xvi, 168 p., 4 plates. Shelfmark: BCL.C781.
- Div. II. 200 × 252 × 25 mm. p. 169–344, 4 plates. Shelfmark: BCL.C689.
- Div. III. 200 × 253 × 25 mm.. p. 345–528, 4 plates. Shelfmark: BCL.C782.
- Div. IV. 200 × 252 × 23 mm. p. 529–700, 4 plates. Shelfmark: BCL.C780.

The National Library of Scotland copy.

The title page for each Division is the paper cover for the publication. These paper covers have the same design as for the British Library copy at shelfmark 11611.h.9. They are signed at the tail with: 'John Leighton F.S.A.' and 'D. W. Williamson Sc.'. However, the printing is not distinctly in green and brown as for the BL copy. The NLS copy is issued in four divisions in cloth was priced at 10 shillings and sixpence for each division. All the divisions issued in cloth have the same cover design.

Gilt edges. Bevelled boards. Yellow endpapers and pastedowns. Green pebble-grain cloth. The lower covers are blocked in blind only. The design on the borders, corners, head tail and sides is the same as is blocked on the upper covers in gold and in black. The centre of each lower cover has a block which shows a Maltese cross, with spade-shaped single leaves around it. The upper covers are blocked in gold and in black. A fillet is blocked in black on the borders. Within it, a 'wave' pattern is blocked in gold. On the corners, six stars are blocked, three in hatch gold, three in black. On each inner corner, a circle is blocked in black. Clover leaves are outlined in relief within each circle. Each circle also contains a five pointed star, blocked in gold. At the points of the star, are the letters of the word 'MOORE', each blocked in relief. On the centre of each star, a leaf shape is blocked in hatch gold, the centre stems showing in relief. Shamrock leaves and stems are blocked in black at the head, the tail and the sides. A large medallion is blocked on the centre, formed by double fillets blocked in gold. Inside this, a 'wave pattern' border is blocked in gold. Adjacent to this, the words: 'The hearts and the voices of Erin prolong. Through the answering future thy name & thy song.' are blocked in gold. The centrepiece is an onlay of red diaper-grain cloth. On the perimeter of the onlay are: 1. a hatch fillet; 2. a gold fillet; 3. a gold fillet, with repeating dots in relief within it. A lady, dressed in classical robes, is seated in the middle. Her right hand holds a harp on her right knee. Her left hand hold a musical instrument. The lady has long flowing hair with leaves in it. To the left of the lady, a 'dolphin' is blocked. [This dolphin is a device created by Leighton. There is a drawing of it in the John Johnson Collection, Bodleian Library. See also BL 10002.f.5., where dolphins are used to adorn the trident.]

The spines are blocked in gold and in black. A single fillet in black is blocked at the head and at the tail. At the head, a fruit bowl and its stand are blocked in gold. The bowl is surrounded by grapes, vine leaves and tendrils, blocked in black. Beneath this, the title: '| The | National | Moore | [rule] | Centenary | edition |' is in gold. Underneath this, gold lettering-piece, shaped as an inverted clover leaf, is blocked. Inside it: '| Div. I.[–IV.] |' is blocked in relief. The clover leaf has a black fillet border, and three more smaller clover leaves are blocked in black around the larger one. Beneath this, a spear, with a pineapple on its tip, is blocked in gold. A pitcher is blocked half way down the spear. The spear and pitcher are surrounded by vine leaves, blocked in black. Near the tail, the imprint: '| William Mackenzie | London and | Dublin |' is blocked in gold. Fillets in black are blocked above and below the imprint.

The overall design and central onlay are not signed. The design is attributed to Leighton on stylistic grounds.

527 Leighton, John

Proctor, Adelaide Anne. *Legends and lyrics. With an introduction by Charles Dickens. Illustrated by W. T. C. Dobson, A.R.A., Samuel Palmer, J. Tenniel, George H. Thomas, Lorenz Frohlich, W. H. Millais, G. Du Maurier, W. P. Burton, J. D. Watson, Charles Keene, J. M. Carrick, M. E. Edwards, T. Morten. Seventh edition.* London: George Bell and Sons, York Street, Covent Garden, 1879. London: Chiswick Press: C.Whittingham, Tooks Court, Chancery Lane. [21], 330 p., 21 plates.
163 × 220 × 45 mm. 11657.g.14.

Printed at the base of the list of Illustrations: 'The engravings are by Mr Horace Harral.'

Gilt edges. Bevelled boards. Yellow endpapers and pastedowns. Brown sand-grain cloth. The same design is blocked on both covers. On the lower cover, the blocking is in blind only. On the upper cover, the blockwork is in gold and in black. On the borders are blocked 1. a repeating pattern of single flower heads and stems in gold; 2. a fillet blocked in gold, and, within it, small dots, circles and diamonds are blocked in relief; 3. a single gold fillet. The strapwork, blocked in black, forms many small panels, in which the dotted stem and leaf decoration is blocked in gold. There are small flower head patterns, and small fillets around the edge of each small panel. Above the central mandorla, the title words: '| Legends & lyrics |' are blocked in gold, within a rectangle formed by a single fillet. Below the mandorla, the words: '| By | A. A. Proctor |' are blocked in gold, within a rectangle formed by four gold fillets. The mandorla has four borders, the innermost of which is hatched. At the centre, a lyre is blocked in relief, within a hatched gold lettering-piece. Signed 'JL' in relief as separate letters, at the base of the lyre. The spine is blocked in gold and in black. As on the borders of the covers, the same repeating flowers and stems are blocked in gold at the head and at the tail. There is a single fillet blocked on the perimeter, with the same decoration in relief as for the upper cover. The spine is divided into panels by strapwork, blocked in black, around the panel borders. From the head, the blocking within the panels consists of: 1. small decoration in gold; 2. the words: '| Legends | & | Lyrics | by | A. A. Proctor |' are blocked in gold inside a panel formed by two gold fillets; 3. a hatched gold lettering-piece, shaped as a mandorla, with flowers in horizontal hatch blocked in relief inside; 4. the imprint: '| London | Bell and | Daldy. |' is blocked in relief in a hatched rectangular gold lettering-piece, with two gold fillets blocked on its borders. .

Dry, *JL* no. 506. Cites the 1866 edition.

528 Leighton, John

Burns, Robert. *The National Burns.* [Specimen Book.] [London]: [William Mackenzie], [ca.1880?]. Unpaginated
APS.491.17.

The National Library of Scotland copy.

Pages sewn on three tapes. Gilt edges. Yellow endpapers and pastedowns. Full brown morocco. The same design is blocked on the borders of both covers, in blind on the lower, and in gold and in blind on the upper cover. On the upper cover, there are two fillets blocked in gold on the borders. Inside this, a wide border of small tools is blocked in gold. Two more fillets are blocked in blind inside the wide border. The word: 'Specimen' is blocked in gold in gothic letters on the centre of the upper cover.

The original cloth upper cover for the edition in cloth is used as a doublure. The original cloth spine is pasted onto the upper endpaper. The design blocked on both the upper cover and the spine is the same as for the copy at NLS shelfmark 1169.a.20. [i.e. with central medallion onlay showing design of lady with classical dress; design signed by Leighton].

The upper covers for the parts are bound at the front, together with the Prospectus. The design for the upper paper cover is the same as the BL copy at 11611.h.10. [i.e. blue paper, with two tone printing in blue and yellow]. The cover is signed: 'John Leighton F.S.A.'; 'H. Leighton Sc.' The work is described in the Prospectus as being available in fifteen parts at two shillings each; or in thirty parts at one shilling each. [Later the work would be available in four Divisions at Ten shillings and sixpence each, but this is not stated in the Prospectus.]

There is specimen text of the 'Life of Burns'. This is followed by specimen text of Burns' works. At the end are two sheets headed: 'Duplicate list of Subscribers | for The National Burns |'. There are columns for the Names and Addresses for Subscribers. Addresses have been entered of Subscribers at addresses in Haleswroth, Framlingham in Suffolk, and in Norwich, and also for King's Lynn, Ipswich and Bedford. At the end, an engraved portrait of Burns is bound in. In the Prospectus, this is described: '. . . on its [the work's] completion every subscriber will receive a copy of a magnificent life-size portrait of Burns [the one in the Specimen Book] on returning the tickets which appear on the covers of the last eight parts, for packing and delivery of which the nominal charge of sixpence will be made.'

This book has the appearance of being a salesman's book. To allow potential Subscribers to purchase either the cloth volumes or the parts issued in paper covers, specimens of the completed designs and the text had to be available for viewing.

529 Leighton, John

Burns, Robert. *The National Burns. Edited by George Gilfillan, including all the airs of the songs and an original life of Burns by the Editor.* 4 vols. London; Glasgow; Edinburgh: William Mackenzie, [ca.1880?]. Two volumes bound in four Divisions.
NG.1169.a.20.

Div. I. 200 × 252 × 30 mm. xxxii, 152 p., 8 plates.	Vol. I.
Div. II. 200 × 252 × 30 mm. p. xxxiii–lxiv, 153–232, 8 plates. pp. 1–64 of Vol. II.	Vol. I.
Div. III. 197 × 252 × 25 mm. p. lxv–xcvi, 64–208, 8 plates.	Vol. II.
Div. IV. 200 × 353 × 25 mm. p. xcvii–cxxxvi, 209–356, [8], 6 plates, 1 map.	Vol. II.

The National Library of Scotland copy.

The Life of Burns is paginated i–cxxxvi, and it is bound at the front of all four volumes. The Prospectus for the work is bound at the front of Div. I. 'The work will be published in Four Divisions, handsomely bound in cloth, bevel boards and gilt edges, price Ten Shillings and Sixpence each; or in Fifteen Parts, at Two Shillings each, each part containing forty-eight pages letterpress . . . and Two Plates.' The title pages of each volume of this copy are the paper covers. These are the same as the British Library copy at 11611.h.10. However, they are printed in monochrome only. Each title page is signed: 'John Leighton F.S.A.'; 'H. Leighton Sc.'

All volumes sewn on three sawn-in cords. Gilt edges. Yellow endpapers and pastedowns. Green pebble-grain cloth. The same design has been blocked on all the covers and the spines. The lower covers are blocked in blind only. There are two fillets blocked on the borders. An inner rectangle is formed by two more fillets, with two leaves, a four-headed flower and a single strap blocked at each corner. On the centre, a lozenge is blocked in blind, which is formed out of interlocking 'paper clip' shapes. The lozenge has a small diamond at its centre, with four water-drops within it. The upper covers are blocked in gold, black and relief. A fillet is blocked in black on the borders. Within the fillet, a 'wave pattern' border is blocked in gold. The corners, the head, the tail, and the sides have symmetrical leaf, stem, and flower decoration, all blocked in black. The stems have several flowers hanging from them, like lilies of the valley. Sunflowers are blocked in black on the centre head and on the centre tail. On each inner corner, a single five-pointed star gold lettering-piece is blocked in gold, surrounded by smaller stars. Within each star, the letters 'BURNS' are blocked in relief. Above the medallion, a ribbon is blocked in gold. On each side, a small medallion is blocked, which has a surround of flames blocked in black and balls in gold. In the small medallion to the left, a square gold lettering-piece has the letters '| NAT | 1759 |' blocked in relief. In the small medallion on the right, the square gold lettering-piece has the letters '| OBIT | 1796 |' blocked in relief.

The central medallion is an onlay of red rib-diagonal grain cloth. The perimeter of the medallion is blocked with: 1&2. single gold fillets; 3. repeating gold balls; 4&5. single gold fillets 5. a black fillet. On the centre, a lady is seated. She is wearing a classical dress. A harp is blocked on the ground to her right; and pan pipes on the ground to her left. Below this a plinth is blocked in gold. Signed 'JL' in relief as separate letters to the left and right of the plinth. The spines are blocked in gold and in black. A black fillet is blocked at the head and at the tail, and within it, a 'wave' pattern is blocked in gold. At the head a sunflower, leaves, and also three pointed flowers on a single stem are blocked in gold. Below this, the words: '| The | National | Burns | [rule] | Rev | George | Gillfillan | Div I[–IV] |' are blocked in gold. The Letters 'Div I' are blocked within a thistle, which is blocked in black. Underneath this, more sunflowers and leaves are blocked in gold. At the tail, the imprint: '| William | Mackenzie |' is blocked in gold. Below this, small stem decoration is blocked in black.

Dry, *JL* no. 562. Pantazzi, *JL* p. 271. Illustrates a bound copy of the same work, in dark green morocco-grain cloth.

530 Leighton, John

Leighton, John. *Suggestions in design being a comprehensive series of original sketches in various styles of ornament. Arranged for application in the decorative and constructive arts. With descriptive and historical letterpress, by James K. Colling*. London: Blackie & Son, 49 & 50 Old Bailey, London, Glasgow, Edinburgh, [1880]. xii, 176p, 101 plates.
250 × 320 × 40 mm. 1812.a.35.

The publication was originally issued in parts. Paper cover size: 240 × 310 mm. The upper and lower covers for the first and last parts are bound at the end. Each issue had green paper covers. The front cover of part 1 is the same as for the title page. On the lower covers are publisher's advertisements. On the upper cover is a star, containing 'Medals awarded to John Leighton F.S.A.'. The medals, clockwise are:

Fine Arts Award 1851
First Class Paris 1855
Prize medal London 1862
Service Medal London 1862
First Class Paris 1867
Fine Arts Philadelphia 1876

The lithograph frontispiece is a re-working of that of the 1852 edition. Each plate has 'John Leighton F.S.A' printed on the bottom right hand corner. For the 1880 edition, Leighton's monogram is no longer invariably the crossed 'JL'. There are many examples also of a capital 'L' with a full stop above it. (See plates 49, 51, 55, 57, 59.) The plates are lithographs from stone – black on a 'light khaki' background. In plate 52, blazonry, figure 5 shows a ship and a whale. A proof copy of this figure is in the John Johnson Collection in the Bodleian Library. In the various artistic styles of the plates, Leighton's taste for the extravagant and the humorous finds full rein. For example, see plate 63, fig. 6, described as 'Rebus I(eye) L, with olive branch'. This is a parody of Leightons's monogram.

531 Leighton, John

Moore, Thomas, *The Poet. The National Moore. Centenary Edition including the airs of the Irish Melodies national airs &c and a memoir by J. F. Waller*. London & 6 D'Olier St. Dublin.: William Mackenzie, [1880]. xvi, 700 p., 16 plates.
205 × 261 × 70 mm. 11611.h.9.

BM binding. Edges and endpapers and pastedowns marbled with antique spot pattern. Brown pebble-grain cloth.

This work, according to the Prospectus, was issued in Four Divisions in cloth (bevelled boards, gilt edges, price 10 | 6d for each Division); or in 15 parts, 2/- each, (with paper covers), each part containing forty-eight pages of letterpress and one steel engraving. The British Library copy has the paper covers for parts 1 and 15 bound at the end. The upper cover of each

part has a design by John Leighton. The paper is white, printed in green and brown. There is a green fillet on the borders. 'Arrow-shapes' are on each corner. In each arrow is a clover-leaf which contains the words 'Thomas Moore'. The word: '| Thomas |' is printed within the clover leaf; the word: '| Moore |' is printed within a star inside the clover-leaf. On the central area, a robed lady harpist holds a laurel branch above a medallion depicting Thomas Moore. The words '| The | National |' are printed in brown; the word '| Moore |' is printed in green – with the capital 'M' in brown and in green; the words '| Centenary Edition | including the |' are printed in brown; the words: '| Airs of the Irish Melodies |' are printed in green, with brown edging, with the capitals 'I' and 'M' printed in brown only; the words: '| National Airs &c |' are printed in green within a brown rectangle; the word: '| J. F. Waller |' is printed in green within a brown rectangle. Signed at the base: '| John Leighton F.S.A.; D. W. Williamson Sc. |'. The prospectus for the work is printed on the lower cover of Part 1.

Muira, *MP* p. 85, no. 25.

532 Leighton, John

Morris, Francis Orpen. *A series of picturesque views of seats of the noblemen and gentlemen of Great Britain and Ireland. With descriptive and historical letterpress. Edited by the Rev. F. O. Morris, B.A . . .. Vol. I[–VI].* London: William Mackenzie, 69 Ludgate Hill. Edinburgh and Dublin, [ca.1880]. B. Fawcett, Engraver and Printer, Driffield.

YA.1987.b.173.

Vol. I. vi, 91 p., 40 plates. 215 × 285 × 42 mm.
Vol. II. vi, 80 p., 40 plates. 215 × 285 × 40 mm.
Vol. III. iv, 80 p., 40 plates. 215 × 285 × 42 mm.
Vol. IV. iv, 82 p., 40plates. 215 × 285 × 38 mm.
Vol. V. iv, 80 p., 40 plates. 215 × 285 × 40 mm.
Vol. VI. iv, 88 p., 40 plates. 215 × 285 × 37 mm.

All volumes have: gilt edges; bevelled boards; gloster marbled endpapers and pastedowns; red morocco leather. All volumes are identically blocked in gold, in blind and in relief. Three fillets are blocked on the outer border – two in gold, the third in blind. The inner border has dog-tooth and Greek roll decoration blocked between two fillets, with squares on the inner corners, and small medallion gold lettering-pieces blocked within the squares. Also blocked on each inner corner is a hatched gold 'diamond and leaf' shape, with a single dot. These are joined by a single fillet blocked in blind between. The central vignette blocked on each cover is a large royal coat of arms. 'The words: '| Dieu | et mon droit |' are blocked in gold between the lion and the unicorn. The title words: '| County seats | of the | Noblemen | & | Gentlemen | of | Great Britain | & | Ireland |' are blocked in relief within five joined rectangular gold lettering-pieces which have scroll ends. The joins of the rectangular gold lettering-pieces contain the words 'of the' and the '&' and the word 'of'. Signed 'JL' in relief as separate letters above the words: 'County seats'. The spines are identically blocked in gold. They are divided into six panels by bands and by fillets in gold on each side of each band. In the panels from the head are: 1. A crown in gold; 2. '| County | seats |', blocked in gold in fanciful letters; 3. 'Vol | I.[–VI.] |' in gold; panels 4–6: a crown in gold; at the tail a Greek roll is blocked in gold between fillets.

The National Library of Scotland copy has the same blocking on brown sand-grain cloth.

Dry, *JL* no. 504. Cites the 1866 edition. McLean, *Fawcett* pp. 17–22; p. 138, no. 53c. Muira, *MP* p. 88, no.28.

533 Leighton, John

Black, Adam, *Publisher* and Black, Charles, *Publisher. Black's picturesque guide to the English Lakes including the geology of the district by John Phillips . . . Outline mountain views by Mr. Flintoft. Illustrations by Birket Foster. Twentieth edition.* Edinburgh: Adam and Charles Black, 1882. xxiv, 293 p., 5 outline views, , 6 maps, 1 fold-out map. With one hundred and nine pages of advertisements bound at the end.
110 × 170 × 30 mm. 10352.e.34.

The fold-out map bound near the front is printed in black and was drawn and engraved by W. Hughes, 6 Brook Street, Holborn, London.

Yellow endpapers and pastedowns. On the front endpaper and pastedown is printed an Index Map. On the lower endpaper is printed 'Comparative view of Lakes'. On the lower pastedown is printed 'Comparative heights of mountains'. Dark green sand-grain cloth. The upper cover design of this edition is the same as for the 1858 and 1861, and 1872 editions at BL. 10358.d.14.; 10358.c.8.; 10360.bb42. The spine has three fillets blocked in gold at the head and the tail. The title: '| Black's | Guide | to the | Lakes |' is blocked near the head in gold. The rest of the spine decoration is as for 1858 and 1861, and 1872.

534 Leighton, John

Ewald, Alexander Charles. *The Right Hon. Benjamin Disraeli, Earl of Beaconsfield, K.G., and his times.* 5 vols. London: William Mackenzie, 69 Ludgate Hill, E.C.; Edinburgh, & Dublin, 1882. Printed by William Mackenzie, 43 & 45 Howard Street, Glasgow. Two volumes bound in five Divisions.

BCL.B5572–5576

Div. I. 187 × 273 × 27 mm. 240 p., 6 plates.	Vol. I.
Div. II. 187 × 273 × 27 mm. p. 241–480, 6 plates.	
Div. III. 187 × 273 × 27 mm. p. 481–600, 6 plates. pp. 1–120	Vol. II.
Div. IV. 187 × 273 × 30 mm. pp. 121–360, 6 plates.	
Div. V. 185 × 271 × 24 mm. pp. 361–599, 6 plates.	

The National Library of Scotland copy.

At colophon of Vols. I & II: 'Printed by William Mackenzie, 43 & 45 Howard Street, Glasgow.'

All the Divisions have the same cover design. Gilt edges. Bevelled boards. Yellow endpapers and pastedowns. Blue pebble-grain cloth. The lower covers are blocked in blind only.

Two fillets are blocked on the borders, the outer thick, the inner thin. Inside these, a third fillet is blocked, semi-circular on each corner, together with a circle blocked in blind. A Renaissance oval shape is blocked on the centre, consisting of small leaf and stem decoration; strapwork protrudes from the oval at the head, the tail and the sides. On the upper covers, the blocking is in gold and in black. On the outer border, two fillets are blocked in gold. Single five-pointed stars are blocked in gold on each corner between the fillets. Inside this, a single fillet is blocked in black. This 'feathers' at each corner, to surround a medallion blocked in gold. Inside each medallion, shown in relief, are: top left hand – 'Vivian Grey' blocked inside an open book; top right hand – a crown and 'VR' blocked below it; bottom left hand – a cross, a moon and 'Cyprus' blocked below; bottom right hand – a pyramid and the word 'SUEZ'. On the centre is an oval. An Earl's coronet is blocked in gold and in black above the oval. On its outer perimeter, a pattern of spear points and a single ball is blocked in gold. Inside this successively are: a black border; a 'crown and ball' pattern, repeated. Between the points of the crowns, groups of three leaves are blocked in gold. On the very centre, the Beaconsfield coat of arms is blocked. Arms – per saltire argent, two lions rampant in fesse and a castle and an eagle in pale; crest – upon the battlements of a tower proper a castellated crown. Supporters: dexter, an eagle proper; sinister, a lion proper, both gorged with a collar (argent) pendent therefrom by a chain a castle, argent. The motto: '| Forti | nihil | difficile |' is blocked in relief at the base of the coat of arms, within a gold lettering-piece shaped as a pennant. At the base of the oval, a block of St. George on a horse spearing a dragon, is blocked in gold. Signed 'L', plus the 'full stop', in black on all volumes underneath the motto.

All spines are blocked in gold and in black with the same design. There is a single fillet blocked at the head and at the tail. From the head, the decoration is: a crown blocked, with the letters 'V' and 'R' to the left and right of it, all in gold. Below the crown the words: 'Kaiser. I. Hind.' are blocked in gold. The title: '| The Right Hon: | The | Earl of | Beaconsfield | K.G. | and his | times |' blocked in gold. A garter roundel is blocked in gold. Its border contains the motto: 'Honi.soit.qui.mal.y. pense.', blocked in relief. On its centre, the words: 'Div I[–V]' are blocked in gold. Below this, a mace is blocked, then two scrolls across the mace, all in gold. Within each scroll, the words: '| Treaty | of Berlin | Household | Suffrage |' are blocked in relief. A banner hangs from a cord attached to the mace. The banner has tassels on each of its corners. It has a crown and 'VR' blocked on its centre in relief. Underneath the mace is a gold lettering-piece shaped as a shield, which shows: an open book, a mace, two birds, a bell and a tree – all blocked in relief. Around the mace and the shield, leaves and stems are blocked in black. Signed 'JL' in black as separate letters at the base of the shield. At the tail, the words: '| William | Mackenzie |' are blocked in gold, within a black rectangle, formed by a single black fillet.

Dry, *JL* no. 566.

535 Leighton, John PLATE LXVIII

Ross, Frederick. *The ruined abbeys of Britain. Illustrated with coloured plates and wood engravings from drawings by A. F. Lydon.* 2 vols. London: William Mackenzie, 69, Ludgate Hill. Edinburgh: Dublin, [1882]. B.Fawcett, Engraver and Printer, Driffield.

1788.b.9.

Vol. I. viii, 148 p., 6 coloured plates. 272 × 370 × 27 mm.
Vol. II. 149–288 p., 6 coloured plates. 272 × 370 × 27 mm.

Gilt edges. Bevelled boards. Dark green endpapers and pastedowns. Dark green morocco straight-grain cloth. The covers and spines of both volumes are blocked identically in gold, in black and in blind. The lower covers are blocked in blind only. Three fillets are blocked on the borders. Two more fillets form an inner rectangle. Inside this, two more fillets are blocked, with circular corners. A small plant is blocked on each corner. On the centre, a small rectangle is blocked, with decoration in blind on its corners. Inside it, the decoration is blocked in relief. On the upper cover, a fillet is blocked in black on the borders. Further fillets in black divide the cover into panels. On the left hand side, the panel is a thin rectangle, stretching from head to tail. It has filigree decoration inside the fillets, and four leaves blocked in black on each corner. In the middle of this panel, there is a mandorla, an onlay of red rib diagonal-grain cloth, blocked in gold and in black. The perimeter of the mandorla has three fillets, one blocked in black and two in gold, with small decoration in gold at its head and its tail. There is an inner border of small dots in gold, which highlights the red cloth, and, inside this, another fillet is blocked in gold. The centre of the mandorla shows two saints, male and female, at prayer within two decorated gothic arches. The saints' clothing is picked out in relief. A cross, two candles, candlesticks and a font are blocked in gold between the saints. Signed 'L' in relief at the base of the font. A winged angel, holding a shield, is blocked at the base of the mandorla. The shield shows an abbey. The angel's wings 'support' the upper portion of the mandorla. All the detail of the angel and the shield is picked out in relief.

On the centre and the right of the upper cover, the black fillets form five panels. From the head, panels one, three, and five have single leaves blocked in black on each corner. Panels two and four are black rectangular lettering-pieces, with gothic lettering blocked in gold. Panel two has the words: '| The Ruined Abbeys |'; panel four has the words: '| of Britain |'. A dragon is blocked in gold to the right of the word 'Britain'. The spines of both volumes are identical apart from the volume numbers. Fillets are blocked in gold and in black at the head and the tail. At the head, an abbot's coat of arms is blocked in gold and in relief with the motto: '| Built | in | faith |' blocked in relief at its base. Underneath, the words: '| The | Ruined | Abbeys | of | Britain | by Frederick | Ross. | Vol. I. [II.] |' are blocked in gold. Beneath this, an abbot's crook is blocked in gold. The words: '| William | Mackenzie |' are blocked in gold, with a fillet blocked in black at the tail.

The National Library of Scotland copy is at shelfmark

A.23.a. The two volumes are the same as the BL copy, with the same cover design.

Dry, *JL* no. 568. Gaskell, *NIB* p. 243, fig. 103(a). McLean, *Fawcett* pp. 17–22, details Lydon's work for Fawcett. McLean, *VBD* p. 204. Lydon was '. . . the mainstay of Fawcett's art department for about thirty years, until he left for London in about 1883.'

536 Leighton, John

Taylor, James. *The age we live in: a history of the nineteenth century, from the peace of 1815 to the present time.* 7 vols. London: William Mackenzie, 69 Ludgate Hill, E.C., Edinburgh and Dublin, [1882–1884]. Glasgow: Printed by William Mackenzie, 43 and 45 Howard Street, Glasgow.
Four volumes in seven Divisions.

C.30.b.

Div. I. 188 × 273 × 23 mm. 240 p., 6 plates. Div. II. 188 × 271 × 23 mm. pp. 241–480, 6 plates.	Vol. I.
Div. III. 188 × 271 × 27 mm. 1–240 p., 6 plates. Div. IV. 187 × 271 × 25 mm. pp. 241–471, 6 plates. p. 1–8 of Vol. III.	Vol. II.
Div. V. 187 × 271 × 25 mm. pp. 9–248, 6 plates. Div. VI. 185 × 270 × 24 mm. pp. 249–368, 6 plates, 4 maps. pp. 1–120 of Vol. IV.	Vol. III.
Div. VII. 186 × 270 × 25 mm. pp. 121–360, 6 plates, 1 map.	Vol. IV.

The National Library of Scotland copy.

This copy is stamped 'Advocates Library Edinburgh'.

The Prospectus bound at the front of Div. I states that the work: '. . .will be completed in Seven Divisions, handsomely bound in cloth, bevel boards and gilt edges, price Eight Shillings and Six-Pence each; . . .' There are forty-two engravings – six per Division. A copy with paper covers is at BL shelfmark 9079.l.3.

Gilt edges. Bevelled boards. Yellow endpapers and pastedowns. All the seven volumes have the same design on both covers and on the spines. Brown pebble-grain cloth. The lower covers are blocked in blind only. There is a single fillet blocked on the borders. Inside this, a double fillet is blocked, with straps and small leaves on each corner. The upper covers are blocked in gold, in black, in red and in relief. On the borders are: 1. a fillet in black, with a 'tooth | cog' repeating pattern; 2. two fillets blocked in gold, with a 'vein' pattern between; 3. a fillet is blocked in black. There are eight medallions blocked on each cover, which detail achievements of the nineteenth century. A medallion is blocked on each inner corner, two on each side. Each is gold hatch, with lettering blocked in relief within. Each has a surround, blocked in black, resembling a 'cog wheel'. The lettering and decoration in each medallion is:

- left hand top: 'Land transit', showing a winged wheel.
- left hand side: 'Free trade', showing a winged staff and two snakes coiled around it.
- left hand side: 'Abolition slavery', showing two hands and arms, with handcuffs and chains on the wrists.
- left hand bottom: 'Electric light', showing two bulbs and electric current.
- right hand top: 'Steam navigation', showing a winged wheel, with cogs.
- right hand side: 'Prepaid postage', showing envelopes and stamps.
- right hand side: 'International exhibitions N S', showing two clasped hands.
- right hand bottom: 'Steam printing', showing a printing roller and wings.

Between each medallion, eight-pointed stars are blocked in gold, with cables, fleurs-de-lis and tridents blocked in black. At the centre of the head, a sun and two stars are blocked in gold. The word '| Photo | graphy |' is blocked in black on either side of this sun. At the centre of the tail, the words 'Telegraph & Telephone' are blocked in gold. On either side of these words, telegraph posts are blocked in gold with the telegraph wires blocked in black. The central oval has borders of black dots; then gold dots and semi-circles; then small ball decoration; then a gold fillet. Within the oval, there are three panels. The upper and lower of these are blocked in hatch gold lettering-pieces. In the upper panel the words: '| The | Age |' are blocked in black. In the middle panel, the words: '| we live in |' are blocked in black. In the lower panel, the words: 'A history of the XIX century' are blocked in black. Above the oval, a crown is blocked in gold. Below the oval, the letters: 'VR' are blocked in gold as a monogram with a rose and thistle stems blocked in black, and are intertwined. Signed 'L' (with the 'full stop' above) in relief at the base of the oval.

The spines are blocked with the same design in gold and in black. Gold and black single fillets are blocked at the head and at the tail. At the head, a crown is blocked in gold. Beneath this, the title: '| The | age | we | live | in | A | History | of the | XIX | century | [rule] | Div. I.[–VII.] |' is blocked in gold. Underneath this, an inverted Napoleonic staff is blocked, with its stem blocked in black. At its base, an eagle and an emblem are blocked in gold to form a circle, with a capital 'N' blocked in relief inside. A sword, a pennant, blocked in gold and a cluster of leaves (blocked in black) criss-cross the staff. The word: 'Waterloo' is blocked in relief within the pennant. At the tail, a trident is blocked in black. Underneath this are: a 'wave' border; a fillet in black; the imprint: '| William | Mackenzie |', in gold. Signed 'JL' in relief as separate letters within the 'wave' border.

Dry, *JL* no. 570.

537 Leighton, John

PLATE LXX

Ewald, Alexander Charles. *The Right Hon. Benjamin Disraeli, Earl of Beaconsfield, K.G., and his times.* 2 vols. London: William Mackenzie, 69 Ludgate Hill, E.C., Edinburgh and Dublin, 1883. Printed by William Mackenzie, 43 & 45 Howard Street, Glasgow.

10815.g.9.

Vol. I: 600 p., 12 plates. 185 × 272 × 50 mm.
Vol. II: 598 p., 18 plates. 185 × 272 × 48 mm.

Both volumes bound by the BM. Red pebble grain cloth. Quarter leather. Old Dutch marbled edges, endpapers and pastedowns. Originally issued, according to the Prospectus, in Five Divisions, bound in cloth, bevelled boards, gilt edges, price 8/6d each; or in fifteen parts (with paper covers), price 2/- each, containing 80 pages of letterpress and two plate illustrations. The British Library copy is made up from the latter. The sheets were originally stab-stitched, before the BM binding.

The paper covers for Parts 1 and 15 are bound at the end of Vol II. The covers are light blue-dyed paper. The upper covers are printed in dark blue with the fillets in black. Fillets are on borders in black. On the spine side of the upper cover, a single black fillet creates a rectangular frame, stretching from head to tail. Inside, achievements of Disraeli's career are shown. From the head these are: 'Kaiser I Hind. 1876.', within a heart-shaped panel; a mace with a flag and royal coat of arms, and '1868'; a medallion showing a pyramid, with 'Cyprus Suez Canal' inscribed within it; a scroll, inscribed: '| June | 1878 | Treaty of | Berlin |'; a shield, showing the Glasgow University coat of arms, with '| Lord | Rector | Univ. Glasgow | 1873 |'; the words: 'K G 1878' are printed below the Glasgow University shield. A Garter star is printed below this. Signed at the base of the rectangle: '| John Leighton F.S.A. |' Also signed 'JL' as separate letters near the head, beneath the small cross. The right hand side of the upper cover is split by black fillets into three frames. At the head, in a semi-circle are the words and motifs: '| 1826 "Vivian Grey", | Nat. 1804 Obit 1881, | [a crown, denoting Earldom], 1876; '| "Endymion" 1880.' Underneath the semi-circle are the title words: '| The Right Hon: | Benjamin Disraeli. |' In the middle frame, the words continue: '| Earl of Beaconsfield. K.G. | and his times |'. In the bottom frame the title continues: '| By | Alexander C. Ewald, F.S.A . . . | Illustrated with numerous | portraits engraved on steel. |' Above the imprint at the tail is a coat of arms. Arms – per saltire argent, two lions rampant in fesse and a castle and an eagle in pale; crest – upon the battlements of a tower proper a castellated crown. Supporters: dexter, an eagle proper; sinister, a lion proper, both gorged with a collar (argent) pendent therefrom by a chain a castle, argent. At the base, the motto: '| Forti nihil difficile |' is printed within a scroll-shaped pennant. The verso of the lower cover of Part 1 has the 'Prospectus'; that of Part 15 has three publisher's titles.

Muira, *MP* pp. 96–97.

538 Leighton, John

Milner, Thomas. *The gallery of geography, a Pictorial and Descriptive Tour of the World*. London: William Mackenzie, 69 Ludgate Hill, Edinburgh and Dublin, [1884]. Printed by William Mackenzie, 43 & 45 Howard Street, Glasgow. 1198 p., 36 maps, 25 plates.

175 × 262 × 93 mm. 10002.f.5.

BM rebind of C19. Parts were issued in paper covers. The upper and lower covers of parts 1 and 15 are bound at the end. The Prospectus printed on the lower cover verso of Part 1 states: 'It will be completed in Six Divisions, cloth antique, bevel boards and cut edges, price Six Shillings and Sixpence each; or in Fifteen Parts, price Two Shillings each, containing Eighty pages of letterpress and Four Maps or Steel engravings in each Part.'

The paper upper covers for parts 1 and 15 have the same design printed. The paper is blue-dyed and printed in blue and red. A scallop and two stars are on each upper corner. 'Part 1' and 'Price 2s.' are printed on the top left and right corners. An arch is formed at the head by a border of a blue fillet with red stars printed within it. On the outside of this is a 'wave' border, in blue. The word '| Milner's |' is printed in blue at the head. From the base to the head runs a mast, in blue. A trident is on top of the mast. It has two dolphins on either side of the central spike. [These dolphins are very much a Leighton device. See NLS BCL.C781. – The National Moore – for another example of its use.] Beneath the trident, a pennant curls downwards around the mast. The words: '| Gallery of | geography |' are printed within the pennant in blue. To the right and left of the pennant is the subtitle: '| A | Pictorial | & | Descriptive | Tour | of the | World. |', printed in red. Beneath the pennant, a medallion is printed, which contains a classical head and three fishes. The motto around the perimeter reads: '| Far as the breeze can bear the billows foam | Survey our Empire & behold our home |'. Underneath this, a coronet of three sails and two ship ends is printed. The imprint is below this: '| London [in blue] | William Mackenzie | 69 Ludgate Hill [in red] | Edinburgh [a]nd Dublin [in blue] |'. Signed: '| John Leighton F.S.A. |' at the base of the design. Signed '| Williamson Sc. |' underneath the word 'Edinburgh'. The lower cover verso of part 15 has publisher's titles.

539 Leighton, John

Taylor, James. *The age we live in: a history of the nineteenth century, from the peace of 1815 to the present time*. 4 vols. London: William Mackenzie, 69 Ludgate Hill, E.C., Edinburgh and Dublin, 1884. William Mackenzie, 43 & 45 Howard Street, Glasgow.

190 × 274 × mm. J/9079.l.3.

Issued in 7 divisions, bound in cloth, at a cost of 8/6 each. The alternative format of issue was in 24 parts, containing two steel engravings per part, at a cost of 2/- each. The British Library copy has the front and rear covers of parts 1 and 21 bound at the rear of vol. 4, and parts 22–24 in their original paper wrappers, each part being stab-stitched. On the verso of the lower cover of part 1 is printed a Prospectus for the work. Each part cost two shillings, each issued with eighty pages and two steel engravings. The paper is blue and it is printed in blue and in red. On the borders are: 1. a red 'dog-tooth' border; 2. a border, printed in blue, of 'baroque' decorations, printed between blue double fillets. There are nine medallions, four on the corners, two on the sides and three near the head. They are printed in blue and in red. Each corner medallion is formed by a single fillet. Each

medallion on the side is formed by a single blue fillet and repeating beads. The two medallions near the head are formed by: 1. a red fillet; 2. a blue fillet and shading; 3. a red fillet printed between two blue fillets. The medallion on the centre head is formed by a red fillet printed between two blue fillets. Printed in each medallion, clockwise from the centre head: 1. '| Photography |' plus a sun and its rays; 2. '| Steam | navigation |' plus a winged waterwheel; 3. '| Penny | postage | , plus stamped envelopes'; 4. '| International | exhibition |' plus two hands in a handshake, with the compass points '| N | E | S | W' around the hands; 5. '| Steam | printing' plus a winged printing ink roller; 6. '| Electric | light |' plus two cables generating electricity; 7. '| Abolition | of slavery |' plus hands, from which manacles are falling away; 8. '| Free | Trade |' plus a winged staff; 9. '| Land | transit |' plus a winged wheel. On either side of the medallion at the centre head, the words: '| Telegraph | Telephone |' are printed between the wires of two telegraph poles. Below this, the words: '| Wellington | Waterloo |' are printed on either side of a vignette of Wellington and his horse, Copenhagen. The central medallion displays the crowned head of Queen Victoria, with the words '| India, Canada, South-Africa, Australia |' printed round the outside of the medallion. The title: '| The age | we live in |' is printed around the central medallion. The central medallion has red 'dog-tooth' decoration around its border in red, with red 'rays' emanating from the dog-tooth. The effect is to make the medallion like the centre of the sun. Within a rectangular cartouche, the sub-title: '| A history of the 19th century | from the peace of 1815 to the present day |' is printed. The words: '| By James, Taylor, A.M., D.D., F.S.A., | . . . |' are underneath the sub-title. The imprint: |' William Mackenzie |' is printed in red within a black semi-circle; '| 69, Ludgate Hill | Edinburgh London Dublin |' are printed in blue beneath. The design is signed 'John Leighton F.S.A.' underneath the publisher's name.

Dry, *JL* no. 570. King, *JL* p. 247; front cover illustration of this BLJ issue.

540 Leighton, John

Simon, G. Eugene. *China: its social, political, and religious life . From the French of G. Eug. Simon.* London: Sampson Low, Marston, Searle, & Rivington, St. Dunstan's House, Fetter Lane, Fleet Street, E.C., 1887. London: Printed by William Clowes and Sons, Limited, Stamford Street and Charing Cross. [3], 342 p.
132 × 196 × 36 mm. 10058.cc.17.

[Rebound 1980.] Original upper cover bound at the front; size: 125 × 187 mm. Yellow rib diagonal-grain cloth. The design is blocked in gold and in black. It shows a Chinese lantern, with ten bells suspended from its roof. The word: '| China |' is blocked in gold in 'Chinese style' lettering, within the centre of the lantern. The words: '| its social political |' are blocked in black on either side of the base of the lantern; the words: '| and religious life |' are blocked in black below the lantern. Signed 'JL' in black as separate letters at the base of the lantern.

Dry, *JL* no. 572.

541 Leighton, John

Black, Adam, *Publisher* and Black, Charles, *Publisher. Black's picturesque guide to the English Lakes including the geology of the district by John Phillips . . . Outline mountain views by Mr. Flintoft. Illustrations by Birket Foster. Twenty-first edition.* Edinburgh: Adam and Charles Black, 1888. xxv, 293 p., 15 plates, 1 fold-out map. With one hundred and twenty-eight pages of advertisements bound at the end.
110 × 170 × 328 mm. 10347.aa.38.

The fold-out map bound near the front is printed in black and yellow and was 'Published by A&C Black London'.

Edges speckled with red ink. Light yellow endpapers and pastedowns. On the upper endpaper and pastedown is printed an Index Map. On the lower endpaper is printed 'Comparative view of Lakes'. On the lower pastedown is printed 'Comparative heights of mountains'. Dark brown sand-grain cloth. The upper cover design of this edition is the same as for the 1858 and 1861, 1872 and 1882 editions at BL. 10358.d.14.; 10358.c.8.; 10360.bb42; 10352.3.34. The spine has three fillets blocked in gold at the head and the tail. The title: '| Black's | Guide | to the | Lakes |' is blocked near the head in gold. The rest of the spine decoration is as for 1858 and 1861, and 1872.

542 Leighton, John

Leighton, John. *The unification of London: the need and the remedy.* [Third edition.] London: Elliot Stock, 62 Paternoster Row, City, 1895. viii, 64p, 2 maps.
140 × 213 × 12 mm. 10350.de.38.

On the title page, the Leighton shield is printed beneath the title: argent, a lion rampant, gules, motto: '| Light | on | s |'.

Original paper covers bound in. The upper cover features the Corporation of London coat of arms and the mace in red and black, supported by two gryphons, who stand on the motto: '| Domine dirige nos |'. Beneath the coat of arms is an open book, with the half title and author printed inside it. Signed 'L' 1897 '| Third edition |'. The whole upper cover is framed with staves, surrounded by green. A bee and a beehive are printed on the top corners. 'Price one shilling.' is printed at the head. The following text is quoted round the sides: '| The Rt. Hon. G. J. Goschen, M.P. says: 'Local government is a chaos | of authorities, of rates and of areas'. |' At the tail is quoted: ' "| Our remedies | oft within ourselves do lie. |" Shakspere [sic] |'. On rear cover is an advertisement for the Book Plate Annual and Armorial Year Book.

King, *JL* p. 247.

543 Leighton, John

Burns, Robert. *The National Burns including the airs of all the songs in the staff and tonic sol-fa notations; edited, With an Original Life of Burns, by the Rev, George Gilfillan.* 4 vols. London: William Mackenzie, 69 Ludgate Hill, Edinburgh and Glasgow, [ca.1896]. Two volumes bound in four Divisions.

NG.1178.b.1.

Div. I. 201 × 255 × 25 mm. cxx, 88 p., 8 plates. Div. II. 201 × 255 × 27 mm. p. 89–232, 8 plates. pp. 1–80, Colophon: 'End of Vol I'.	Vol. I.
Div. III. 200 × 255 × 25 mm. 200 p., 8 plates. Div. IV. 200 × 255 × 25 mm. pp. 201–408, [8], 6 plates)	Vol. II.

The National Library of Scotland copy.

The monogram of William Mackenzie is printed on the title page above the imprint. The Life of Burns is paginated i–cxx, and it is bound at the front of Div. I. The title page is the same for all the volumes. [These are not paper covers.] This appears to be a different edition from NLS shelfmark NG.1169.a.20., as the latter has a longer Life of Burns, of cxxxvi pages. From the Prospectus at the front of Div. I: 'The work will be published in Four Divisions, handsomely bound in cloth, bevel boards and gilt edges, price Ten Shillings and Sixpence each; or in Fifteen Parts at Two Shillings each . . .'

Gilt edges. Bevelled boards. Yellow endpapers and pastedowns. Green pebble-grain cloth. The cover design is the same for all the volumes. The lower covers are blocked in blind only. There are two fillets on the borders. An inner rectangle is formed by two more fillets, a dot, and a four-headed flower and a single strap blocked on each corner. On the centre, a lozenge is blocked, with ornamental decoration. [This lozenge is different from those on the lower covers of NG.1169.a.20.] The upper covers are blocked in gold, black and relief. A fillet is blocked in black on the borders. Within the fillet, a 'wave pattern' border is blocked in gold. The corners, the head, the tail, and the sides have symmetrical leaf, stem, and flower decoration, all blocked in black. The stems have several flowers hanging from them, like lilies of the valley. Sunflowers are blocked in black on the centre head and on the centre tail. On each inner corner, a single five-pointed star gold lettering-piece is blocked in gold, surrounded by smaller stars. Within each star, the letters 'BURNS' are blocked in relief. The central medallion is an onlay of red ungrained cloth. Around its perimeter, a repeating pattern of 'flame-points' and balls, is blocked in gold. The perimeter of the onlay has five borders: 1&2. single gold fillets; 3. repeating balls; 4&5 single gold fillets. Above the medallion, a ribbon is blocked in gold. On each side, a small medallion is blocked, which has a surround of flames blocked in black and balls in gold. In the small medallion to the left, a square gold lettering-piece has the letters '| NAT | 1759 |' blocked in relief. In the small medallion on the right, the square gold lettering-piece has the letters '| OBIT | 1796 |' blocked in relief. Within the central medallion, the head and shoulders portrait of Burns as a young man is blocked in gold. Unsigned. The spine is blocked in gold and in black. A black fillet is blocked at the head and at the tail, and within it, a 'wave' pattern is blocked in gold. At the head a sunflower, leaves, and also three pointed flowers on a single stem are blocked in gold. Below this, the words: '| The | National | Burns | [rule] | Rev | George | Gilfillan | Div I[–IV] |' are blocked in gold. The Letters 'Div I' are blocked within a thistle, which is blocked in black. Underneath this, more sunflowers and leaves are blocked in gold. At the tail, the imprint: '| William | Mackenzie |' is blocked in gold. Below this, small stem decoration is blocked in black.

544 Leighton, John

FIG. 64

Taylor, James. *The age we live in: a history of the nineteenth century, from the Peace of 1815 to the present time* [i.e. 1895.] London: William Mackenzie, 69 Ludgate Hill, E.C., Edinburgh: Dublin, [1896]. Printed by William Mackenzie, 43, 45 Howard Street, Glasgow. Four volumes bound in eight Divisions.

9079.l.23.

Div. I. [2], 240 p., 6 plates. 186 × 267 × 28 mm. Div. II. pp. 241–480, 6 plates. 186 × 267 × 27 mm.	Vol. I.
Div. III. 240 p., 6 plates. 185 × 266 × 28 mm. Div. IV. pp. 241–470, 6 plates. 185 × 269 × 27 mm.	Vol. II.

FIG. 64

Pp. 1–8 of Vol III. are bound at the end of Div. IV.
Div V. pp. 9–248, 6 plates. 185 × 269 × 26 mm.
Div. VI. pp. 249–368, 6 plates. 187 × 269 × 26 mm. } Vol. III.
Pp. 1–120 of Vol IV are bound at the end of Div. VI.
Div. VII. pp. 121–360, 6 plates. 186 × 268 × 25 mm.
Div. VIII. pp. 361–648, 6 plates. 187 × 270 × 32 mm. } Vol. IV.

All the plates are bound at the front of each Division.

The text of all volumes is sewn on three tapes. All volumes have gilt edges, bevelled boards and yellow endpapers and pastedowns. All have a gift stamp on the upper endpaper which has the words: '| A gift from the people of Shildon | to the Men and Women serving | in the Forces, with gratitude and best wishes. | Chairman, Shildon U.D.C. |' A Prospectus for the work is bound at the front of Div. I., which states: 'The work will be supplied to subscribers only, and completed in Eight Divisions, bound in cloth, bevelled boards, gilt edges, price Eight Shillings and Sixpence each, containing six steel engravings and 240 pages of letterpress; or in 24 parts, price Two Shillings each.'

Olive-green morocco vertical-grain cloth. All the volumes are blocked with the same design, except for the Div. number on each spine. The lower covers are blocked in blind only. There is a single fillet blocked on the borders. Inside this, there are two more fillets with strapwork and small decoration blocked on each corner. The upper covers are blocked in gold, black, light brown and relief. The border at the head is blocked in black, between two thin black fillets. It has five-point stars blocked in light brown. Below this, five flower heads are blocked, three in black and two in light brown. The main panel has a black fillet on three sides, not the fore-edge. On the left hand side, a royal mace is blocked in gold. There is a sword crossing the mace. The blade of the sword is blocked in black, and the handle in gold. The sun and its rays are blocked in gold near the right hand corner. A sprig of leaves and berries, blocked in black, crosses over the mace and the sword. A snake, blocked in black with its scales highlighted in relief, curls from the right of the mace downwards with its head near the centre at the base of the right hand corner. The snake's body swirls around a number of objects: at the left hand base are three books, each on top of the other. Book 1 is a black lettering-piece, with the words: '| The | past |' blocked in relief within it. Book 2 is in landscape format, a gold lettering-piece shaped as open pages. The words: '| A history of the XIX cent. |' are blocked in relief. The words immediately underneath this are: '| The present |', blocked in relief. The book at the bottom is blocked in gold and has the words; '| The future |' blocked in black along its spine. The blade of a scythe, blocked in gold, curls through the open book in the middle. The handle of the scythe, blocked in black, curves away to the right hand side of the panel, and passes underneath a winged hour-glass, blocked in gold. The wooden holder of the hour-glass is blocked in gold, black and light brown. A border at the base is blocked in black and light brown, forming 'waves'. This border is blocked between two thin black fillets. Signed 'L', with a dot above the 'L', on the left at the tail. The spines are blocked in gold and in black. The spine has two fillets blocked in gold and in black at the head and the tail. A crown is blocked in gold at the head. Beneath this, the words: '| The | age | we | live | in | A | History | of | the | XIX | century. | Div. I.[–VIII.]'. Beneath this, a figure of Britannia is blocked in gold. She holds a spear in her right hand. Attached to the head of the spear is a pennant-shaped gold lettering-piece. It has the motto: '| Canal | de Suez |' blocked in relief. Her left hand holds upright a pole, inverted. A flag is blocked as a gold lettering-piece at its top near the ground, with the word: '| Britannia |' blocked in relief within the flag. Britannia stands on a sea monster, which is blocked in gold. Underneath this, a trident is blocked in black above waves which are blocked in gold. At the tail the words: '| William Mackenzie |' are blocked in gold, between two black fillets.

Leighton, SID, 1880. plate 56 Shows similar examples of Leighton's later monogram. Dry, *JL* no. 573.

545 Leighton, John PLATE LXIX

Leighton, John. *Tubular Transit for London. First edition.* London: 1902. Imprinted at The Crown Press, Devonshire Street, Bishopsgate, within the City of London, In the First Year of the Reign of His Majesty King Edward the Seventh. 16 p.

130 × 210 × 20 mm. 8235.bb.87(4).

The frontispiece shows a portrait of John Leighton. JL proposes a hexagonal layout for the distribution of the central London transportation system: 'London as it is vs. London as it should be. Chaos vs. Kosmos.' Original paper covers. The upper cover is mostly the same design as for the Unification of London [BL shelfmark 10350.de.38.]. It features the Corporation of London coat of arms in red and black, supported by two gryphons, and the mace, with the motto 'Domine dirige nos' underneath. The border of the upper cover is framed with staves, surrounded by greenery. A bee and a beehive are printed on the top corners. Printed at the top in red is '| The system Leighton |'. The lower cover has a hexagon divided into triangles, showing North, North-East, South-East, South, South-West, North-West. The South triangle is sub-divided into sixteen smaller triangles.

King, *JL* p. 248 – portrait of Leighton. Pantazzi, *JL* p. 273. Originally published in *The Graphic*, 12.2.1870 as *London Indexed* [Plan for dividing London into hexagonal superficial miles].

546 Leighton, John and Dudley, Robert

Smith, Richard Henry. *Expositions of great pictures. Illustrated by Photographs.* London: James Nisbet and Co., 21, Berners Street, 1863. Edinburgh: Printed by Ballantyne and Company. [3], 101 p., 8 plates of photographs. With two pages of publisher's titles bound at the end.

148 × 210 × 20 mm. 7869.r.39.

Gilt edges. Bevelled boards. Light yellow endpapers and pastedowns. Green pebble-grain cloth. Binder's ticket on lower pastedown: '| Bound by | Leighton | Son and | Hodge. |' Both covers are blocked in blind on the borders with the same design. There is a repeating plant pattern on the borders, with two fillets blocked inside this, one thick, one thin. On the corners inside this, small plants are blocked in relief. On both covers, the central oval is formed by two fillets blocked in blind. On the upper cover, the central mandorla is blocked in gold and in relief. A single gold fillet is blocked on its borders. The outer border of the mandorla is of hearts, each linked by two gold fillets, with small plants blocked between each heart. The leaves of the plants are hatched. Inside this, a wide oval fillet is blocked in gold, with small leaves and dots blocked within in relief. Then there are three more thin oval fillets, all blocked in gold. On the centre, two interlinked hatched gold hearts have the words: '| Expositions | of | great | pictures |' blocked in relief within. The small line decoration around the words is also picked out in relief. A small single heart is blocked in gold above and below the centre, each with a head blocked in gold in its middle. Signed 'JL' in gold as separate letters at the base of the heart below the centre. The spine is blocked in gold. There is a single thin gold fillet around the perimeter of the spine. At the head, there is a small rectangle formed by a single fillet, blocked in gold, with spirals blocked inside. The middle of the spine has a cartouche, formed by two gold fillets, with the title: '| Expositions of great pictures |' blocked in gold inside. A small cartouche is blocked above and below this central cartouche, with leaves, stems and a flower, all blocked in gold inside each cartouche. A circle formed by two gold fillets is blocked near the base, with '| Nisbet | & Co. | London |' blocked in gold inside. Signed 'RD' in gold as separate letters within a rectangle formed by a single fillet at the tail.

Ball, *VPB* p. 72, ref. 3; p. 148. On p. 148, Ball states that the spine design is a re-use of the block of 1860 used on the spine of Smith's 'Expositions of the cartoons of Raphael', 1860. Dry, *JL* no. 461.

547 Pugin, Augustus Welby Northmore FIG. 65

Pugin, Augustus Welby Northmore. *A treatise on chancel screens and rood lofts, Their Antiquity, Use and Symbolic Signification. Illustrated with figures copied on stone from drawings by the author* . . . London: Charles Dolman, 61, New Bond Street, and 48A, Paternoster Row, 1851. [London]: Printed by Cox (Brothers) and Wyman, Great Queen Street, Lincoln's-Inn Fields. viii, 124 p., 14 plates.
207 × 265 × 20 mm. 7820.g.40.

Plates 1, 5, 7, show Pugin's monogram.

Green rib horizontal-grain cloth. Both covers are blocked identically. The lower cover is in blind only, the upper in gold and in blind. Two fillets are blocked in blind on the borders, the outer thick, the inner thin. A circle, formed by a single gold fillet, is blocked in each corner. Inside each circle, a quatrefoil, four flower heads, four large dots and small dots are blocked in gold, together with a circle and small four-leaf decoration on

FIG. 65

the middle. A gold fillet, with repeating semi-circles and three-leaf decoration, joins the corner circles and forms the central rectangle. On the centre, an elaborate cross is blocked in gold.

Atterbury and Wainwright. *Pugin*, p. 159. Illustration 301. Wainright suggests that the design for this book is by Pugin, as he had control of the artwork for the plates.

548 Ralston, William

Dulcken, Henry William. *Old friends and new friends. Tales, fables, and emblems. In prose and verse. Profusely illustrated.* London: Frederick Warne and Co., Bedford Street, Covent Garden, [1867]. [London]: Dalziel Brothers, Engravers and Printers, Camden Press. [7], 310 p. With two pages of publisher's titles bound at the end.
140 × 190 × 29 mm. RdeB.B.19.

The British Museum de Beaumont copy.

On the title page verso: '| The pictures in this book | are drawn by J. D. Watson J. B. Zwecker A. B. Houghton | T. Dalziel H. Weir A. Pasquier | J. Gilbert H. K. Browne A. W. Bayes | and Engraved by the Brothers Dalziel. |'.

Bevelled boards. Light yellow endpapers and pastedowns. Green sand-grain cloth. Both covers blocked identically in blind with three fillets on the borders. The upper cover vignette

is blocked in gold, in black and in relief. The design is square-shaped, with a bird's head, a donkey's head, a small bird, and a goat's head blocked on each side of the square, forming an outer diamond. These heads have a border of curling stems and small vertical gold hatch leaves. The square itself is formed by three fillets, one in black between two in gold. The black fillet has repeating dots inside it, blocked in relief. Inside the square, more vertical hatch gold leaves and stems surround three gold lettering-pieces, which have the title: '| Old friends | and | new friends |' blocked in relief in each lettering-piece. The upper and lower of these three lettering-pieces are semi-circular and have vertical hatch borders in gold on their tops and bases. The word: 'Illustrated' is blocked in relief within a gold scroll-shaped lettering-piece at the base of the vignette. Signed 'WR' in gold as a monogram, beneath the small bird blocked in gold near the base of the vignette. The spine is blocked in gold, in black and in relief. From the head downwards, the decoration is: three gold fillets; panels are formed by two fillets: one in gold and one in black, with repeating dots inside it blocked in relief; within three gold lettering-pieces, the title: '| Old friends | and | new friends |' blocked in relief; the words: '| Tales, fables | and | emblems |' blocked in gold within a rectangle formed by a single gold fillet; the word: '| Illustrated |' is blocked in relief within a semi-circular gold lettering-piece; leaf, stem and star decoration is blocked in gold near the base; the words: '| F. Warne & Co |' are blocked in gold; three gold fillets are blocked at the tail.

de Beaumont, *RdeB1* no. 95. Goldman, *VIB* no. 95. Jones & Brown, *WR* no. 11.

549 Ralston, William FIG. 66

Golden thoughts from golden fountains. Arranged in fifty two divisions. Illustrations by eminent artists, engraved by the Brothers Dalziel. London: Frederick Warne and Company, Bedford Street, Covent Garden, [1868]. [London]: Dalziel Brothers, Engravers and Printers, Camden Press. xvi, 290 p. With two pages of publisher's titles bound at the end.

182 × 252 × 40 mm. 11651.i.11.

Gilt edges. Bevelled boards. Gilt edges. Green sand-grain cloth. Both covers blocked identically in gold, red, black and in blind. The outer border has a 'three dot and quarter fan' repeating pattern, blocked in gold between two fillets – all in gold. The inner border has a repeating pattern in gold, consisting of: trefoils and twin stems, crossing stems and hatch leaves, with four gold dots interspersed. 'Sea shells' are blocked in blind underneath each pair of leaves. The inner border has a single gold fillet. At the head, the tail and the sides, this fillet joins border fillets to form straps. Panels at the head and at the tail are rectangular, with six semi-circles blocked within and one at each end of the panel. Stem and dot patterns are blocked in red relief, surrounding the words: '| Golden Thoughts | Golden Fountains |', which are blocked in green relief within rectangular gold lettering-pieces. On the centre, a circle and four medallions are blocked, all formed by fillets and border decoration. Within each medallion, four 'spade-shapes' and dots are blocked in red relief. Within the border of the circle, stem and quatrefoil decoration is blocked in red relief. Within the circle, on the centre, the following are blocked: 1. 'shells' in relief; 2. a rectangular gold lettering-piece with dots and a single fillet on its head and on its tail; 3. small decoration is blocked in red relief. 4. the word: '| From |' is blocked in green relief within a gold lettering-piece. Curling stem decoration is blocked in black around the title words and the central circle. Signed 'WR' in green relief as a monogram beneath the word 'Fountains'. The spine is blocked in gold, in black, in red and in relief. 'Dog tooth and dots' perimeter decoration is blocked in gold. From the head downwards, the decoration is: a thin gold fillet; straps, semi-circles, dots – all in gold; small black decoration; the words: '| Golden | Thoughts | from | Golden | Fountains | [rule] |' blocked in relief within a single gold lettering-piece panel, which has a single border fillet blocked in red; The word: '| Illustrated |' is blocked in relief within the same panel, and it is also within a rectangle formed by two fillets blocked in relief; a quatrefoil is blocked in gold above and below a medallion, with gold and red decoration within; within the medallion, dots and a cross are blocked in gold; small decoration in black and gold dots surround the quatrefoils and medallion; the words: '| F. Warne & Co. |' are blocked in relief within a rectangular gold lettering-piece, with a single thin border fillet blocked in relief; a gold fillet is blocked at the tail.

Ball, *VPB* p. 159. Jones & Brown, *WR* no. 3.

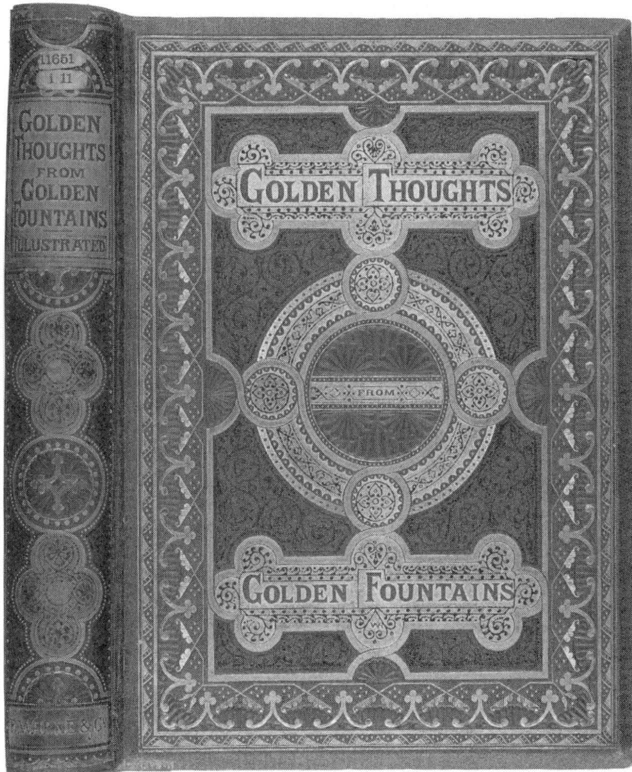

FIG. 66

550 Ralston, William

Songs for the little ones at home. Illustrated with Sixteen Coloured and Sixteen Tinted Pictures, from designs by eminent artists. London: Ward , Lock, and Tyler, Warwick House, Paternoster Row, E.C., [1868]. [London]: Printed by Jas. Wade, 18, Tavistock-street, Covent-garden, W.C. xi, 148 p.m 32 plates.
135 × 182 × 32 mm. 11602.cc.30.

The coloured plates are engraved by Leighton Brothers.

Red ink edges. Brown endpapers and pastedowns. Red sand-grain cloth. Both covers are blocked identically on the borders and on the corners. The lower cover is blocked in blind only. It has a central vignette, oval in shape, of a renaissance design, featuring strapwork. The upper cover is blocked in gold and in black. Blocked on the borders are: 1. a gold fillet; 2 & 4. repeating gold dots; 3. a black fillet between 2 & 4, with repeating dots blocked in relief within it; 5. a border is blocked of small leaves, joined by stems and small circles. There is 'flower and vase' decoration on each corner. The central vignette is blocked in gold. The borders of the vignette are formed by: 1. repeating gold dots; 2. a black fillet, with repeating dots blocked in relief within it; 3. a gold fillet. Around the vignette is elaborate curling stem and leaf decoration, all blocked in gold. The centre shows birds nesting in a tree, with the tree branch overhanging water, containing bulrushes and water lilies. The title: '| Songs | for the |' is blocked above the centre; the words: '| Little ones |' are blocked below the centre, within a rectangular frame, all in gold. Signed 'WR' in gold at the base of the vignette. The spine is blocked in gold and in black. From the head the decoration is: a fillet and small decoration in gold; two dotted gold fillets above and below a black fillet, with dots blocked in relief within it; the title: '| Songs | for the | little ones |' blocked within a gold frame formed by a gold fillet and dots; lilies on water; the words: '| Sixteen | coloured pictures |' blocked within a decorated frame, formed by a single gold fillet; decoration and two dotted fillets are blocked above and below a black fillet, with dots blocked in relief within it; '| London | Ward, Lock & Tyler |' are blocked in gold near the tail, within a rectangle formed by a single gold fillet; two fillets blocked in gold at the tail.

Ball, *VPB* p. 159. Not in his 'WR' list. Jones & Brown, *WR* no. 10.

551 Ralston, William

Aesop. *Aesop's fables. Illustrated by Ernest Griset. With text based chiefly upon Croxall, La Fontaine, and L'Estrange. Revised and rewritten by J. B. Rundell.* London: Cassell, Petter and Galpin: and 596, Broadway, New York, [1869]. Cassell, Petter and Galpin, Belle Sauvage Works, London, E.C. xii, 244 p. With eight pages of publisher's titles bound at the end.
190 × 270 × 30 mm. 12305.i.26.

Bevelled boards. Gilt edges, Cream endpapers and pastedowns. Green sand-grain cloth. The lower cover is blocked in blind, with fillets blocked on the borders and a leaf and flower pattern on the corners and the sides. The upper cover is blocked in gold and in black. A single fillet is blocked in gold on the outer border; and in black on the inner border. Three stars are blocked in gold on the upper corners. At the top left hand corner is a fox, seated, and a pelican, with its beak in a tankard placed on a stool. The words: '| Aesop's | Fables [in hatch]. |' are blocked in gold, in fanciful letters. Pond waters are blocked at the bottom of the upper cover, above which reeds are blocked. The word 'Illustrated' is blocked in relief within a hatch scroll-like gold lettering-piece. the words: '| Ernest Griset |' are blocked in relief, within a lower scroll-like gold lettering-piece. To the right above the pond waters is a dog, leaning over the pond to look at the fish in it. Signed 'WR' in gold as a monogram at the right hand side, just above the pond waters. The spine is blocked in gold and in black. A single gold fillet is blocked on the perimeter. From the head downwards, the decoration is: black and gold curling stem and flower decoration; the words: '| Aesop's | Fables |' are blocked in relief within two rectangular gold lettering-pieces, with decoration blocked in gold and black above and below these words; the words: '| Illustrated | by | Ernest | Griset | [rule] |' are blocked in gold, within a cartouche formed by a single black fillet; more stem, flower, and leaf decoration is blocked in gold and in black; a gold fillet; repeating dots blocked in gold; the words: '| London & New York | Cassell, Petter & Galpin |' are blocked in gold; repeating dots in gold; a gold fillet; at the tail, two fillets are blocked in black.

Ball, VPB p. 147. de Beaumont, *RdeB1* no. 3. The 1872 Edition. Goldman, *VIB* no. 3. Jones & Brown, *WR* no. 14.

552 Ralston, William

Byrne, Janet. *Picture teaching for young and old.* London: Cassell, Petter and Galpin, [1869]. Cassell, Petter and Galpin, Belle Sauvage Works, London, E.C. [vii] 184 p. With sixteen pages of publisher's advertisements bound at the end.
170 × 223 × 18 mm. 12807.f.72.

Cream endpapers and pastedowns. Purple sand-grain cloth. Both covers blocked in blind, with an identical design. A single fillet is blocked in blind on the borders. There is a tracery of intersecting lines, ending in 'three-point' patterns. The upper cover centre piece is blocked in gold. The words: '| [P]icture | [T]eaching |' are blocked in relief within scroll-shaped gold lettering-pieces; the capital letter 'P' is blocked in hatch gold. From its base, string holds up a slate board, which has a wooden frame – both blocked as a gold lettering-piece. The capital letter 'T', together with Arabic numbers, are blocked in relief within the slate board. A 'Lily of the valley' plant in gold intersects the two scrolls. A bird is perched on the lower scroll. Signed 'WR' in gold as a monogram underneath the board containing the capital 'T'. The spine is blocked in gold and in relief. A cartouche is blocked in gold along the spine, with a single fillet in relief on its perimeter. The words: '| [four dots] Picture Teaching [four dots] |' are blocked in relief within the cartouche. Plant decoration is blocked in gold at the head and at the tail of the cartouche.

Jones & Brown, *WR* no. 18.

553 Ralston, William

Mayhew, Henry and Mayhew, T. A. *The magic of kindness. or, the wondrous story of the good yarn. By the brothers Mayhew. With illustrations by Walter Crane.* London and New York: Cassell, Petter and Galpin, [1869]. London: Cassell, Petter and Galpin, Belle Sauvage Works, London, E.C. iv, 220 p., 8 plates. With eight pages of publisher's titles bound at the end.
125 × 170 × 27 mm. 12808.b.26.

Bevelled boards. Cream endpapers and pastedowns. Brown sand-grain cloth. The upper and lower covers are blocked with fillets in black on the borders. The upper cover has a central square, blocked in gold. The square has a border fillet. Inside the square is an angel, holding an olive branch in her right hand, and a cross in her left hand. A turbaned oriental (a sick man?) is on the ground. Oriental domes are situated in the distance, behind the two figures. The title letters are blocked in gold. Signed 'WR', in relief, on bottom left hand corner of the square. The spine is blocked in gold. A single gold fillet is blocked on the perimeter. A gold fillet and gold dots form four panels on the spine. In panel one, black fillets and gold leaf and stem decoration are blocked; in panel two, the title: '| The | Magic | of | Kindness |' is blocked in gold; in panel three, black fillets surround leaf and stem decoration blocked in gold, and also surround the words: '| By the | Brothers | Mayhew |', blocked in gold; more gold leaf and stem decoration; in panel four, the words: '| London & New York | Cassell Petter & Galpin |' are blocked in gold, within a rectangle formed by a single gold fillet.

Ball, *VPB* p. 159. Jones & Brown, *WR* no. 22.

554 Ralston, William

Quiz *pseud.* [i.e. Charles Dickens.] *Sketches of young couples, young ladies, young gentlemen. Illustrated by Phiz.* [i.e. Hablot Knight Browne.] London: Cassell, Petter and Galpin; and 596, Broadway, New York, [1869]. Cassell, Petter and Galpin, Belle Sauvage Works, London, E.C. v, 238 p., 17 plates. With two pages of publisher's titles bound at the end.
120 × 180 × 25 mm. 12331.bb.32.

Bevelled boards. Brown endpapers and pastedowns. Green fine bead-grain cloth. Blocked in blind on lower cover, with three fillets blocked on the borders. The upper cover is blocked in gold, red and black. One fillet on the upper cover borders is blocked in red, with two inside blocked in black. The word 'Sketches', has the capital 'S' in relief, and it is in the shape of an artist's palette, with a pennant in gold trailing from it. The rest of the word: '[S]ketches' is blocked in relief, on a red onlay, which is surrounded by gold blocking. The words: '| Young couples |' have two chickens walking along a line above. The 'Y' of '| Young ladies |' on the line below is formed of a pair of scissors through which an arrow's tail feathers are inserted. The head of the arrow pierces two hearts, situated immediately above the letters '[Y]oung ladies'. The words: '| Young Gentlemen |' are blocked in gold underneath this. The word: '| by |' is blocked in relief within a 'watch-face' held by a man sitting on the capital 'Q' of the word 'Quiz'. The word 'Quiz' is in fanciful letters, blocked in gold, with the centre of the 'Q' being pierced by a pen, also blocked in gold, that goes from top to bottom of the design. Signed 'WR' in gold by the side of the capital 'Q'. The words: '| Illustrated by Phiz |' are blocked in gold underneath this. The spine is blocked in gold, in black and in red. From the head downwards, the decoration is: two black fillets; an artist holding brushes sitting on a painter's palette; the word: '| Sketches |' blocked in relief within the palette; the words: '| By | Quiz | [pens in gold] | Illustrated | by | Phiz. |' blocked in gold; dots are blocked in gold across the spine; the words: '| London & New York | Cassell, Petter & Galpin |' are blocked in gold; two black fillets; a red fillet is blocked at the tail.

Ball, *VPB* p. 157. Jones & Brown, *WR* no. 15. Muir, *VIB* p. 125.

555 Rogers, William Harry

The Art Journal Illustrated Catalogue. The Industry of All Nations 1851. London: Published for the Proprietors, By George Virtue, [1851]. [London]: Bradbury and Evans, (Printers Extraordinary to the Queen), Whitefriars. xxvi, 328 p.+XVI*, VIII+, VIII**, XXII***
250 × 330 × 37 mm. De Beaumont. Private Collection.

Gilt edges. Bevelled boards. Gauffered edges and turn-ins. Light yellow endpapers and pastedowns. Green morocco. Both covers blocked identically in gold. On the borders of the covers, two fillets are blocked. Between them a repeating pattern of curling leaves and stems, with a single leaf blocked within each curled stem. The centre-piece of each cover is an elaborate frame, formed by large leaf and curling stems, blocked in gold. At the head of the frame, a group of objects is suspended from knotted ribbons: 1. an artist's palette; 2. a mallet; 3. a group of paint brushes inserted through the thumb-hole of the palette. The title: '| The | Art-Journal | Illustrated Catalogue | of the [gothic letters] | Industry | of all nations [gothic letters] |' is blocked in gold within the central frame. Underneath the title, '| 1851 |' is blocked in gold within a hatched gold lettering-piece, styled as a renaissance panel. Signed 'WHR' in gold as a monogram underneath the date. The spine is blocked in gold. Three gold fillets are blocked at the head. On the centre, the date '1851' is blocked within a highly-ornamented frame. Three fillets in gold are blocked near the tail, with three more fillets in gold at the tail.

The BL copy of the text is at shelfmark: RB.31.c.162.

Ball, *VPB* p. 155. King, *WHR* p. 319. Pantazzi, *4D* p. 91.

556 Rogers, William Harry PLATE LXXI

Alastor *pseud.* [i.e. J. Orton.] *'Excelsior;' or, the realms of poesie.* London: William Pickering, 1852. London: C. Whittingham, Chiswick. xvi, 148 p.
140 × 197 × 20 mm. 11805.c.20.

With two pages of reviews of the 1851 edition of 'Excelsior', and one page announcing 'The Enthusiast. A Poem.' by Alastor – all bound at the end.

Green endpapers and pastedowns. Blue wave diagonal-grain cloth. Both covers are blocked identically in gold, with the same design as for the 1851 edition. The blocking on the covers is identical to the 1851 edition. The size of the design is 107 × 160 mm, possibly the same block. There is a single fillet blocked in gold on the borders, with straps and stars in gold on the corners. The title: '| Excelsior |' is blocked in relief, in a pennant-shaped gold lettering-piece underneath the upper portion of a globe. From the globe, a right hand emerges, an index finger pointing to the stars and a crescent moon blocked above. The spine is fully blocked in gold, showing lilies and leaves, running from the tail to the head. '| Excelsior |' is blocked in gold diagonally across the spine near the head. Signed 'WHR' in gold as a monogram at the tail. This copy is blue date stamped '19 MR [MARCH 18]52'.

Ball, *VPB* p. 155. Cites this edition, but not the privately printed one of 1851. King, *WHR* p. 320.

557 Rogers, William Harry

Frere, A. F. *Wonder Castle a structure of seven stories. With a frontispiece by E. H. Wehnert.* London: Addey and Co. 21 Old Bond Street, 1853. London: Printed by Petter, Duff, and Co. Playhouse Yard, Blackfriars. vii, 181 p., 1 plate.
140 × 190 × 15 mm. 12806.e.43.

Gilt edges. Light yellow endpapers and pastedowns. Diaper-grain cloth. Dyed with a light and dark red marbled pattern. Two fillets are blocked in blind on the borders of both covers, the outer thick, the inner thin. The upper cover has 'Wonder Castle' blocked in gold on the centre, in fanciful letters. (The capital 'W' is stylistically much that of Rogers – with looped serifs at the base.) The capital 'C' has castellation, running rightwards to the 'a'. A hand and a wrist ruff are blocked between these two letters. The spine is blocked in gold. The title: '| Wonder Castle |' is blocked in gold along the spine, in the same fanciful letters as for the upper cover. At the head and the base, a hand and a wrist ruff, both attached to a tether, are blocked in gold. Within the tether line at the base, the monogram 'WHR' is incorporated.

King, *WHR* p. 320.

558 Rogers, William Harry

Passing thoughts in sonnet stanzas. With other poems, Original and Translated . . . London: Arthur Hall, Virtue and Co., 1854. London: Printed by J. Wertheimer and Co., Finsbury Circus. xv, 245 p. With sixteen pages of publisher's titles bound at the end.
145 × 220 × 25 mm. 11647.e.46.

Gilt edges. Yellow endpapers and pastedowns. Binder's ticket on lower pastedown: '| Bound by | Westleys | & Co. | London. |' Navy blue moiré rib horizontal-grain cloth. Both covers are identically blocked in blind on the borders and on the corners. There are two fillets blocked on the borders. On the corners, rose stems, leaves and two rose flowers are blocked in blind, with the rose heads blocked in relief. The upper cover central vignette is blocked in gold. It shows corn plants, with convolvulus growing up around them, the whole forming a circle. The roots of the corn plants are tendrils, a characteristic feature of Rogers. Signed 'WHR' in gold as a monogram at the base of the vignette. The spine is blocked in gold and in blind. Two fillets are blocked in gold at the head and at the tail. Flowers, leaves, stems are blocked at the head and underneath the title. The title words: '| Passing | thoughts |' are blocked in gold; there is a small leaf decoration blocked in gold underneath the title.

559 Rogers, William Harry

Edgar, John George. *History for boys or annals of the nations of modern Europe. With eight illustrations.* London: David Bogue, 86 Fleet Street, 1855. London: Printed by G. Barclay, Castle St. Leicester Sq. vii, 425 p., 6 plates. With three pages of publisher's titles bound at the front, and two pages bound at the end.
110 × 178 × 35 mm. 9007.b.14.

Bolts uncut. Yellow endpapers and pastedowns. Binder's ticket on lower pastedown: '| Bound by | Bone & Son | [rule] | 76, Fleet Street, | London. |' Red morocco horizontal-grain cloth. Both covers blocked identically in blind and in relief. Two fillets are blocked in blind on the borders. The rest of each cover is blocked in relief with a pattern of stems, five-petal flowers, and 'spade-shaped' leaves. Near the centre, the stems curl, to form circles. The spine is blocked in gold. A single fillet is blocked in gold on the perimeter. From the head downwards, the decoration is: a crown, blocked in gold; a shield-shaped panel, formed by a single fillet blocked in gold; the title: '| History | for | boys |' blocked in gold within this panel; a quill and a sword are blocked above, below and 'behind' the panel; two crossed flags, bearing the arms of England and of Turkey are blocked in gold; the flag-pole in the middle of the flags has an eagle blocked on its top; in the middle of the flags, where the flags cross, a ribbon-shaped gold lettering-piece is blocked, with: '| J. G. Edgar |' blocked in relief inside it; small curling stem and leaf decoration is blocked in gold between and below the flags. (The monogram 'WHR' is possibly blocked below this, but a label prevents sight of this.)

560 Rogers, William Harry

Goldsmith, Oliver. *The Vicar of Wakefield. A tale. Illustrated by George Thomas.* London: Published for Joseph Cundall by Sampson Low and Son, 47 Ludgate Hill, 1855. London: R. Clay, Printer, Bread Street Hill. viii, 219 p. With sixteen pages of publisher's advertisements bound at the end.
150 × 210 × mm. C.109.b.4.

Text sewn on two cords. Bevelled boards. Gilt edges. Yellow endpapers and pastedowns. Orange morocco vertical grain cloth. Both covers blocked with an identical design, in blind on the lower cover, in gold on the upper cover. The design shows elaborate panel, strapwork and plant stem tracery. The title:

'| The | Vicar | of | Wakefield |' is blocked in gold on the centre. This copy belonged to George Cruikshank and then to his wife Eliza. On the front pastedown is his dedication to her: '| From | Ge Cruikshank | to his dear wife | Eliza | March 7th 1855 |'. On the front endpaper signed carte de visite photographs of Cruikshank and of his wife are pasted. Beneath both is the dedication: '| This book | is presented to | the British Museum | in memory of | George Cruikshank, Artist | by his widow | Eliza Cruikshank | December 23rd 1887 | her 80th birthday |'. [Other presentation copies from Mrs Cruikshank are at: 1. BL 10349.d.14. Aleph. London scenes; 2. C.70.d.10. R. H. Barham. The Ingoldsby Legends ; 3. C.61.b.27. S. C. Hall. A Book of Memories.] The spine is blocked in gold. From the head downwards, the decoration is: a square panel, formed by a thick gold fillet blocked between two thin fillets; straps in gold; the title: '| The | Vicar | of | Wakefield. |' blocked in gold within a panel of stem tracery; straps and a square panel – both blocked in gold; the words: '| Illustrated | by | George Thomas. |' blocked in gold; a panel in gold, with a strap at its head and at the tail; a semi-circle of a strap is blocked near the tail; signed 'WHR' in gold as a monogram at the tail. (The monogram is cunningly inserted in small decorative work, also blocked in gold.) This copy was formerly shelved at 12604.h.19. The British Museum de Beaumont copy is shelved at RdeB.H.13.

Ball, *VPB* p. 155. de Beaumont, *RdeB1* no. 118. A copy in red wavy grain cloth, bound by Bone. Goldman, *VIB* no. 118. King, *WHR* p. 320. McLean, *VPB* p. 51. Says this design is signed by Rogers. The copy shown is in orange cloth, bound by Bone. Pantazzi, *4D* p. 91.

561 Rogers, William Harry

Lee, R. *Playing at settlers; or, the faggot-house. With Illustrations by John Gilbert*. London: Grant and Griffith , Successors to Newbery and Harris, corner of St Paul's Churchyard, 1855. London: T.E. Metcalf, Printer, 63, Snow Hill. [3], 94 p., 4 plates. With eight pages of publisher's titles bound at the end.

125 × 175 × 12 mm. 12806.d.23.

The plates are signed with Gilbert's monogram, and also signed 'Henry Linton Sc.'.

Red ink speckled edges. Yellow endpapers and pastedowns. Binder's ticket on lower pastedown: '| Bound by | Bone & Son, | [rule] | 76, Fleet Street, | London. |' Green wave diagonal-grain cloth. The borders and the corners are identically blocked in blind on both covers. Two fillets are blocked on the borders. Curling stems and leaves are blocked on each corner in blind. The central vignette is the same for both covers, blocked in blind on the lower cover, and in gold on the upper. On the lower cover, the title is not blocked. The vignette consists of six joined branches, with convolvulus leaves and flowers winding around the branches. On the upper cover, the title: '| Playing | at | settlers | or the | faggot | house |' is blocked in gold on the centre. Signed 'WHR' in gold as a monogram at the base of the vignette. The spine is missing.

562 Rogers, William Harry

In honorem. Songs of the brave. Poems and odes by Campbell, Wolfe, Collins, Byron, Tennyson, and Mackay. London: Sampson Low, Son & Co. 47, Ludgate Hill, 1856. [London]: R. Clay, Printer, Bread Street Hill. 46 p. With two pages of publisher's titles bound at the end.

133 × 202 × 13 mm. RdeB.K.24.

The British Museum de Beaumont copy.

The monogram of Joseph Cundall is printed on the title page verso.

Gutta percha binding. Gilt edges. Bevelled boards. Yellow endpapers and pastedowns. Binder's ticket on lower pastedown: '| Bound by | Bone & Son | [rule] | 76, Fleet Street, | London. |' Blue morocco horizontal-grain cloth. Both covers identically blocked in blind on the borders and on the corners. Three fillets are blocked on the borders. A pattern of intertwined stems and leaves is blocked in blind on each corner, together with a laurel wreath and ribbon. Stems and leaves are blocked on each side. [This is the same blocking as for RdeB.K.25.] The upper cover central vignette is blocked in gold. It shows a pattern of roses, thistle and clover stems and leaves, supported by a single branch at the base. At the head of the vignette, small five-point stars are blocked. At the top, the words: 'In Honorem' are blocked in relief, within a ribbon-shaped gold lettering-piece. The title: '| Songs of the Brave |' is blocked in gold in gothic letters in a semi-circle between the stems. Signed 'WHR' in gold as a monogram, at the base of the vignette. [A small monogram – only 2 mm across.] The spine is blocked in gold. The title: '| Songs | of | the | Brave |' is blocked in gold in gothic letters, with rose, stem and decoration blocked in gold above and below the title.

de Beaumont, *RdeB1* no. 361. Goldman, *VIB* no.361. King, *WHR* p. 320.

563 Rogers, William Harry

Songs of the brave. The Soldier's Dream, and other poems and odes. By Campbell, Wolfe, Collins, Byron, Tennyson, and Mackay. Illustrated with twenty-six engravings, from drawings by Edward Duncan, Birket Foster, George Thomas, etc. London: Sampson Low, Son & Co. 47, Ludgate Hill, 1856. [London]: R. Clay, Printer, Bread Street Hill. 46 p. With two pages of publisher's titles bound at the end.

138 × 200 × 12 mm. RdeB.K.25.

The British Museum de Beaumont copy.

The monogram of Joseph Cundall is printed on the title page.

Gilt edges. Yellow endpapers and pastedowns. Blue wave diagonal-grain cloth. Both covers blocked identically in blind. Three fillets are blocked on the borders. A pattern of intertwined stems and leaves is blocked on each corner, together with a laurel wreath and ribbon. Stems and leaves are blocked on each side. [This is the same blocking as for RdeB.K.24.] The upper cover vignette is blocked in gold. It shows stems forming a circle, with small leaves and buds off the stems. The title:

'| The Soldier's Dream [in a semi-circle] | and | Other Poems. |' is blocked in gold in gothic letters above and below the centre. On the centre, a hussar's helmet, a sword, and an anchor are all blocked in gold. Signed 'WHR' in gold as a monogram at the base of the vignette. The spine is blocked in gold. The title: '| The | Soldier's | Dream. | &c. |' is blocked in gold in gothic letters, with branch, stem, and leaf decoration blocked between, above and below the title in gold.

de Beaumont, *RdeB1* no. 362. Goldman, *VIB* no. 362.

564 Rogers, William Harry

Sabbath bells chimed by the poets . . . Illustrated by Birket Foster. London: Bell and Daldy, 186, Fleet Street, 1856. [London]: Chiswick Press: C. Whittingham, Tooks Court, Chancery Lane. 112 p.
162 × 232 × 22 mm. C.30.h.19.

The title page verso has Joseph Cundall's monogram in colour within a wreath of flowers. The engravings are on wood and printed in colours by Edmund Evans.

Gilt edges. Bevelled boards. Light brown endpapers and pastedowns. Binder's ticket on lower pastedown: 'Bound by | Bone & Son. | [rule] | 76, Fleet Street. | London. |' Brown morocco veritcal-grain cloth. Both covers identically blocked in blind and in relief on the borders, the corners, and on the sides. A single fillet is blocked on the borders in blind. On the corners, the sides, and on the head and the tail, a pattern of curling stems, leaves and buds is blocked in relief. The outer block forms a central frame of three circles, one large, two small. The upper cover has a central vignette blocked in gold. It shows a tracery of crossed stems and pointed leaves – all blocked in gold. On the perimeter of each circle, flattened 'three leaves', are blocked in relief within gold lettering-pieces. These 'three leaves' end in three berries blocked in gold. On the centre, the words: '| Sabbath | Bells. |' are blocked in gold, in fanciful letters. Signed 'WHR' in gold as a monogram at the base of the vignette. The spine is blocked in gold. From the head downwards, the decoration is: a diamond, a circle, leaves and berries; the words: '| Sabbath | Bells. |' blocked in gold within a circular panel, formed by a single fillet; more tracery of leaves and stems and buds; signed 'WHR' in gold as a monogram at the base of the decoration.

Previous shelfmarks: 1346.h.33.; C.30.k.11.

Ball, *VPB* p. 155. McLean, *VPBB* p. 66. Reproduces a copy in blue cloth. Pantazzi, *4D* p. 91 no. V.

565 Rogers, William Harry

The Children's Bible Picture-Book. Illustrated with eighty engravings. London: Bell and Daldy, 186, Fleet Street, 1858. London: Printed by G. Barclay, Castle St. Leicester Sq. xii, 322 p.
130 × 177 × 33 mm. 3127.c.10.

Several of the engravings are signed: 'E. Skill Sc.'

Text sewn on three sawn-in cords. Gilt edges. Yellow endpapers and pastedowns. Binder's ticket on lower pastedown: '| Bound by | Bone & Son. | [rule] | 76, Fleet Street, | London. |' Dark blue wave diagonal-grain cloth. Both covers identically blocked in blind on the borders, the corners and on the sides. A single fillet is blocked on the borders. A pattern of passion flowers, leaves and stems are blocked in relief on the corners, the sides and on the head and the tail. The oval-shaped central frame has two fillets and fleurs-de-lis blocked on its borders. The upper cover central vignette is blocked in gold. It shows passion plant flowers, leaves, buds, stems and tendrils blocked in gold surrounding the title on the centre: '| The | Children's | Bible | Picture Book |' blocked in gold. Signed 'WHR' in gold as a monogram at the base of the vignette. The spine is blocked in gold, blind and in relief. A single fillet is blocked in blind on the perimeter. From the head downwards, the decoration is: two passion plant leaves, blocked in relief; the title: '| The | Children's | BIBLE | Picture | Book |' blocked in gold within a panel formed by a single gold fillet; a group of five passion plant leaves with a flower at the centre is blocked in relief; a fleur-de-lis near the tail; a quatrefoil, formed by a single fillet in blind, has three passion plant leaves and one flower blocked within in relief.

566 Rogers, William Harry

Maitland, Julia Charlotte. *Historical acting charades; or, Amusements for winter evenings. New Edition.* London: Griffith and Farran, Late Grant & Griffith, Successors to Newbery & Harris, Corner of St. Paul's Churchyard, 1858. London: Savill and Edwards, Printers, Chandos Street. viii, 229 p. With twenty four pages of publisher's titles bound at the end.
110 × 175 × 20 mm. 12807.b.41.

Yellow endpapers and pastedowns. Green morocco horizontal-grain cloth. Both covers blocked identically in blind on the borders and on the corners. Two fillets are blocked on the borders. Curling stems, trefoil leaves and flowers are blocked in blind on each corner. The upper cover vignette is blocked in gold. It is diamond-shaped, and formed by intermingling holly branch, stems, leaves and berries. A sprig of mistletoe and a ribbon hang down from the top. The title: '| Historical | Acting | Charades. |' is blocked in gold in fanciful letters inside the diamond on the centre. The spine is blocked in gold. A pattern of holly branches, leaves and berries is blocked down the spine, the branches forming panels. The title: '| Historical | Acting | Charades |' is blocked in gold within the panel near the head. The oval-shaped panel at the centre has leaves blocked in gold within it. The 'spade-shaped' panel near the base has three passion plant leaves blocked in gold inside, together with the signature 'WHR' blocked in gold as a monogram.

567 Rogers, William Harry

Wordsworth, William. *Pastoral poems. Illustrated with numerous engravings* [by Birket Foster, George Thomas, Henry Warren].

London: Sampson Low, Son & Co., 47 Ludgate Hill, 1858. Printed by Edmund Evans, London. 55 p.
137 × 202 × 15 mm. 1347.f.4.

The monogram of Joseph Cundall is printed on the title page verso. The illustrations engraved by William Thomas, Edmund Evans, James Cooper, Thomas Bolton, and S. V. Slader.

Bevelled boards. Gilt edges. Yellow endpapers and pastedowns. Blue bead-grain cloth. Both covers are blocked identically in blind and in relief. On the borders, there is a pattern of plant tracery blocked in relief. There is a floral medallion blocked on each inner corner. Within the recessed central rectangle, a 'spider's web' pattern is blocked in relief. The upper cover oval central panel is blocked in gold, with floral patterns surrounding the title. The title: '| Wordsworth's | Pastoral | Poems |' is blocked in gold in gothic letters; it is surrounded by a pattern of thin stems, of flowers and hatch leaves – all blocked in gold. The spine is blocked in gold. A small cockerel weather vane is blocked at the head. The title: '| Wordsworth's | Pastoral | Poems. |' is blocked in gold in gothic letters, with stem decoration around the title. Signed 'WHR' in relief as a monogram at the tail, within a leaf-shaped gold lettering-piece, 3 mm across.

King, *WHR* p. 320. McLean, *Cundall* p. 80.

568 Rogers, William Harry

The home treasury of old story books. Illustrated with Fifty Engravings by Eminent Artists. London: Sampson Low, Son, and Co. 47 Ludgate Hill, 1859. London: Printed by G. Barclay, Castle St. Leicester Sq. viii, 288 p.
126 × 175 × 25 mm. 12804.d.21.

Gilt edges. Yellow endpapers and pastedowns. Binder's ticket on lower pastedown: '| Bound by | Bone & Son, | 76, Fleet St London. |' Blue wave-diagonal-grain cloth. Both covers are blocked identically in blind and in relief on the borders, on the corners, and on the sides. A fillet is blocked on the borders; on the corners, a pattern of curling stems and small leaves is blocked in relief. On the inner border, a fillet is blocked in relief, forming a single circular strap on the centre of each side, and on the centre head and on the centre tail. The upper cover vignette is blocked in gold. It shows a rose bush, with its roots, and small flowers blocked at the base. Its branches curl upwards and outwards. Leaves and flowers grow from the branches and butterflies are blocked near the flowers. The title: '| The | home treasury | of | old | story books. |' is blocked in gold between the branches and the stems. Signed 'WHR' in gold as a monogram near the base of the vignette. The spine is blocked in gold and blind and relief. From the head downwards, the decoration is: the title: '| The | home | treasury | of | old | Story Books |' blocked in gold – surrounded by rose leaves and branches; down the spine, rose leaves and branches are blocked, some outlined in relief by blind blocking, some in blind only; a fillet is blocked in blind at the tail.

King, *WHR* p. 326.

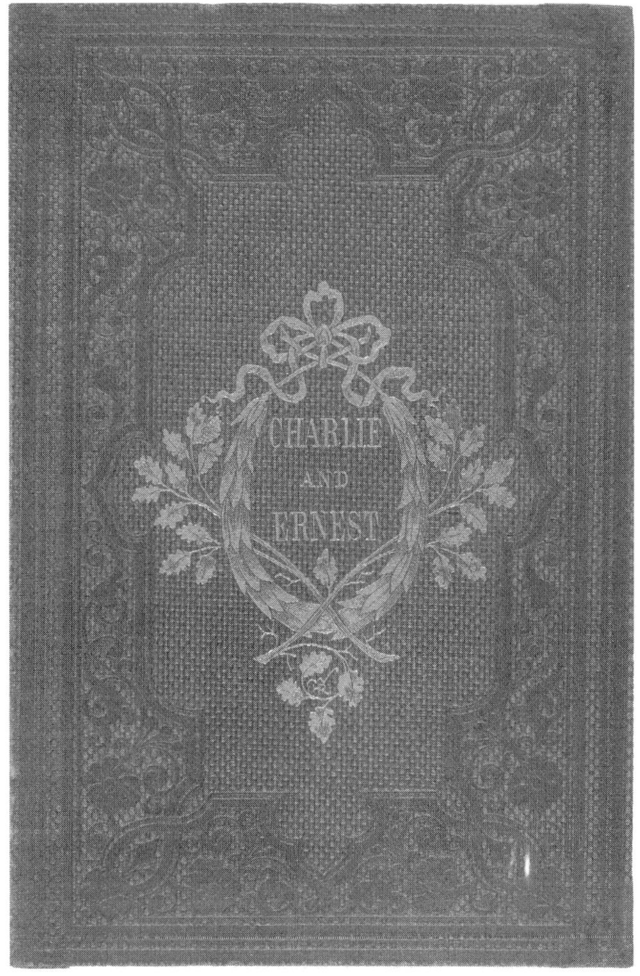

FIG. 67

569 Rogers, William Harry FIG. 67

Edwards, Matilda Barbara Betham. *Charlie and Ernest or play and work. A story of Hazelhurst school. With four illustrations . . .* Edinburgh: Edmonston and Douglas, 1859. Edinburgh: Printed by R. & R. Clark. 180 p., 4 plates.
125 × 175 × 25 mm. 12806.c.21.

Yellow endpapers and pastedowns. Binder's ticket on lower pastedown: '| Bound by | Burn | 37 & 38 Kirby St. |' Green bead-grain cloth. Both covers are blocked identically in blind. Three fillets are blocked on the borders, with patterns of tracery on the corners, the head, the tail, and the sides. The upper cover central vignette is blocked in gold. The title: '| Charlie | and | Ernest |' is blocked in gold, inside a laurel wreath hanging from ribbons at the head. Two oak branches and leaves pass through the wreath. Signed 'WHR' in gold as a monogram at the base of the vignette. [No spine.]

Ball, *VPB* p. 156.

570 Rogers, William Harry

Longfellow, Henry Wadsworth. *The Courtship of Miles Standish, and other poems. Illustrated from designs by John Absolon, Birket Foster, and Matthew S. Morgan; engraved on wood by T. Bolton.* London: W. Kent and Co. (Late D. Bogue), 86, Fleet Street, 1859. London: Savill and Edwards, Printers, Chandos Street, Covent Garden. viii, 124 p.
138 × 210 × 15 mm. RdeB.I.15.

The British Museum de Beaumont copy.

Gilt edges. Bevelled boards. Yellow endpapers and pastedowns. Binder's ticket on lower pastedown: '| Bound by | Bone & Son, | 76, Fleet St. London. |' Green morocco vertical-grain cloth. Both covers blocked identically in blind on the borders, the corners, and on the sides. Three fillets are blocked on the borders. A pattern of branches, stems and leaves is blocked in relief on each corner. On the sides, long stems with multiple leaves are blocked in relief. An oval central frame is formed by these patterns. The upper and lower cover central vignettes are blocked identically in gold and in blind. Joined stems form a diamond-shape, with leaves, flowers and dots surrounding the perimeter of the diamond – all in gold. Within the diamond, the title: '| The | Courtship | of | Miles Standish |' is blocked in gold, with the first three words being blocked in gothic letters. The 'h' of the word 'The' is joined to the vignette border decoration. Signed 'WHR' in gold as a monogram at the base of the vignette. [The 'W' is not joined to the 'HR'.] The spine is blocked in gold. The title: '| The | Courtship | of | Miles | Standish |' is blocked in gold within a panel formed by a single fillet. Flowers and decoration are blocked above and below the panel in gold.

de Beaumont, *RdeB1* no. 175. Goldman, *VIB* no. 175.

FIG. 68

571 Rogers, William Harry FIG. 68

Milton, John. *L'allegro*. London: Sampson Low, Son & Co., 47 Ludgate Hill, 1859. [London]: Printed by Richard Clay, Bread Street Hill. [2], 22 p.
135 × 202 × 15 mm. 1347.f.5.

The text is printed on the recto only. The illustrations are engraved by W. J. Linton.

Gilt edges. Bevelled boards. White endpapers and pastedowns. Blue morocco vertical-grain cloth. Both covers blocked identically in blind and relief. Four fillets are blocked on the borders, and plant and stem tracery is blocked in relief on each corner. The upper cover has a vignette blocked in gold, showing a tracery of flowers, leaves and thin branches, enclosing the words: '| Milton's | L'Allegro |', which are blocked in gold in gothic letters. The spine is blocked in gold. Above the title, a circular leaf wreath is blocked in gold. The words: '| Milton's | L'Allegro |' are blocked in gold in gothic letters. Below this, flowers and leaves are blocked within a vase – all blocked in gold. Signed 'WHR' in relief within a small leaf-shaped gold lettering-piece blocked at the tail of this decoration.

King, *WHR* p. 320; illustration p. 323.

572 Rogers, William Harry FIG. 69

Myrtle, Harriet, Mrs. *pseud.* [i.e. Lydia Falconer Miller.] *A visit to the New Forest. A tale by Harriet Myrtle. Illustrated by twenty-five engravings, from drawings by William Harvey, George Thomas, Birket Foster, and Harrison Weir.* London: Sampson Low, Son, & Co., 47 Ludgate Hill, 1859. London: Cassell, Petter and Galpin, Belle Sauvage Works, Ludgate Hill, E.C. viii, 158 p.
130 × 175 × 20 mm. 12804.e.31.

The engravings are hand coloured.

Gilt edges. Yellow endpapers and pastedowns. Binder's ticket on lower pastedown: '| Bound by | Bone & Son, | [rule] | 76 Fleet Street, | London. |' Red morocco horizontal-grain cloth. Both covers are blocked identically in blind and relief with the same design. A single fillet is blocked on the borders, and a tracery of acorns, leaves, branches is blocked in relief on the corners. There is a central vignette in gold. The words: '| A visit to | The New Forest | By Harriet Myrtle |' are blocked in relief within three rectangular gold lettering-pieces. These are interspersed with oak branches, leaves and acorns, blocked in gold. Signed 'WHR' in gold as a monogram at the base of the

FIG. 69

vignette. The serifs of the 'W' are elongated slightly. The spine is blocked in gold and in blind and in relief. At the head, oak stems, leaves are blocked in relief. The words: '| A visit to | The | New Forest | by Harriet | Myrtle. |' are blocked in gold, within a frame formed by stems and acorns blocked in gold. Upwards growing oak branches, leaves and acorns are blocked in relief from the tail to beneath the title.

Ball, *VPB* p. 156. King, *WHR* p. 326; illustration p. 323.

573 Rogers, William Harry

Wharton, Thomas. *The Hamlet an ode written in Wichwood Forest. Illustrated with fourteen etchings by Birket Foster.* London: Sampson Low, Son, and Co. 47, Ludgate Hill, 1859. [2], 12 p.
140 × 205 × 11 mm. RdeB.L.23.

The British Museum de Beaumont copy.

Gutta percha binding. Grey endpapers and pastedowns. Green sand-grain cloth. Both covers blocked identically in blind on the borders and on the corners. Four fillets are blocked on the borders. A pattern of crossed stems and two leaves is blocked on each corner. The upper cover central vignette is blocked in gold. It is diamond-shaped. The words: '| The Hamlet | an ode | By Thomas Warton [sic] | Illustrated with etchings | by | Birket Foster |' are blocked in gold in gothic letters. They are surrounded by a tracery of small leaves, of very small flower heads, and of stems, which often end in tendrils. Signed 'WHR' in gold as a monogram at the base of the vignette. The spine is not blocked.

de Beaumont, *RdeB1* no. 396. Goldman, *VIB* no. 396. King, *WHR* p. 320.

574 Rogers, William Harry

The children's picture book of birds. Illustrated with sixty-one engravings by W. Harvey. London: Sampson Low, Son, & Co. 47 Ludgate Hill, 1860. London: Printed by Spottiswoode and Co. New-Street Square.xii, 276 p.
127 × 175 × 28 mm. Renier Collection.

The Museum of Childhood copy.

Gilt edges. Yellow endpapers and pastedowns. Binder's ticket on lower pastedown: 'Bound by Bone & Son, 76, Fleet St London'. Red bead-grain cloth. Both covers identically blocked in blind on the borders and on the corners. A single fillet blocked on the borders. A lattice work of oak stems, oak leaves, and acorns is blocked on the borders. The upper cover has a diamond-shaped central vignette blocked in gold. It shows the title words: 'The children's picture book of birds.', blocked in gold. Leaves and stems grow out of the letters. Signed 'WHR' in gold as a monogram at the base of the vignette. The spine is blocked in gold and in blind. Near the head, the title: '| The | Children's | Picture Book | of | Birds |' is blocked in gold. On the rest of the spine, leaf and stem decoration is blocked in blind.

King, *WHR* p. 320.

575 Rogers, William Harry

Aikin, John and Aikin afterwards Barbauld, Anna Letitia. *Evenings at home; or the juvenile budget opened. Corrected and revised by Cecil Hartley. A new edition, illustrated with five engravings.* London: Routledge, Warne & Routledge, Farringdon Street; New York: 56, Walker Street, 1860. vii, 446 p., 6 plates.
112 × 176 × 32 mm. Renier Collection.

The Museum of Childhood copy.

Yellow endpapers and pastedowns. Blue bead-grain cloth. Both covers identically blocked in blind on the borders and on the corners. Two fillets are blocked on the borders. Leaves and three flowers – of four petals each – are blocked on each corner. The lower cover central vignette is blocked in blind. It shows an oval of joined stems and two leaves at the head, and at the tail; two pairs of leaves blocked on each side. The upper cover is blocked in gold. It shows two flower pots on stands, supported by branches at the base. The title words: 'Evenings at home' are blocked in gold within the plant stem foliage. Signed 'WHR' in gold as a monogram at the base of the vignette. The spine is blocked in gold. Plants rise from the base, with stems crossing and re-crossing up the spine. The upper stems of the plant form an oval frame for the title words: '| Evenings | at | home |', blocked near the head in gold. A plant pot is blocked underneath the title, on a table top. Signed 'WHR' in gold as a monogram near the tail.

FIG. 70

576 Rogers, William Harry FIG. 70

Bunyan, John. *Bunyan's Pilgrim's Progress. With illustrations by Charles Bennett and a preface by the Rev. Charles Kingsley.* London: Longman, Green, Longman, and Roberts, 1860. London: Printed by Spottiswoode and Co. New-Street Square. xxxv, 399 p., 45 plates.
154 × 212 × 46 mm. 4416.k.1.

Bevelled boards. Gilt edges. Brown endpapers and pastedowns. Binder's ticket on lower pastedown: '| Bound by | Westleys & Co. | London. |' Brown morocco vertical-grain cloth. Both covers are blocked in gold, in blind and in relief with an identical design. A single fillet is blocked in blind on the borders, with a pattern of repeating hearts blocked in relief within the fillet. Each cover is divided into nine panels by fillets blocked in blind. The eight outer panels all have stem and leaves and flowers blocked in relief. The central panel is blocked in gold and in relief. At its head a small butterfly is blocked in gold. A sword is blocked in gold from the base to the head of the vignette, with a Roundhead's helmet and a cross blocked on its point. The words: '| The Pilgrim's Progress | Illustrated by C. H. Bennett |' are blocked in relief within three ribbon-shaped gold lettering-pieces. Crossed leaf and stem decoration is blocked in gold between and around the lower two ribbons. Signed 'WHR' in gold as a monogram underneath 'C. H. Bennett'. Four pansy-like plants are blocked in gold at the base of the vignette. Small stars in gold surround all of the decoration. The spine is blocked in gold, in blind and in relief. From the head downwards, the decoration is: a gold fillet, with a pattern of repeating hearts, blocked in relief within it; the words: '| The | Pilgrim's Progress | Illustrated | by C. H. Bennett |' blocked in relief within a shell-shaped gold lettering-piece; interlocking broad stems are blocked in relief downwards, to near the tail; near the tail, a gold fillet is blocked, with a pattern of repeating hearts, blocked in relief within it.

Ball, *VPB* p. 156.

577 Rogers, William Harry FIG. 71

Shakespeare, William. *The most excellent historie of the Merchant of Venice.* [Illustrated by Birket Foster and others.] London: Sampson Low, Son & Co., 47 Ludgate Hill, 1860. London: Richard Clay, Bread Street Hill. vii, 95 p.
165 × 230 × 20 mm. 1347.f.6.

The monogram of Joseph Cundall is printed on the title page verso. On page vii: '| The Emblematical Devices and

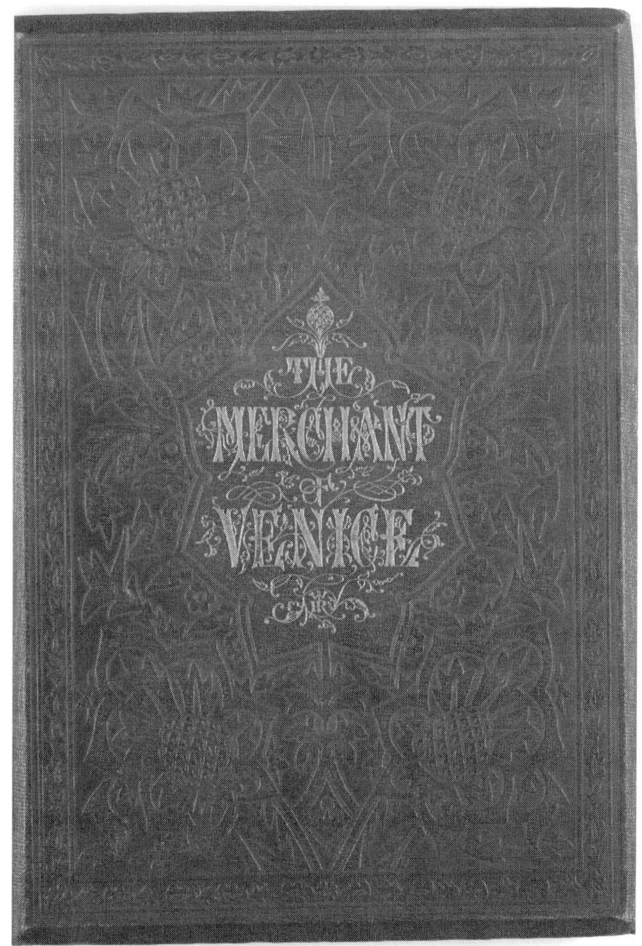

FIG. 71

Ornaments were designed by Harry Rogers | and engraved by Edmund Evans. | '

Bevelled boards. Gilt Edges. Yellow endpapers and pastedowns. Red morocco horizontal-grain cloth. Both covers blocked identically in blind and in relief. Two fillets are blocked on the borders, with a leaf border blocked in relief between the two fillets. Larger leaf patterns and flower heads are blocked in relief on the inner corners. The upper cover has a central vignette blocked in gold, with the title: '| The | Merchant | of | Venice |' blocked in fanciful letters. Signed 'WHR' in gold as a monogram at the base of the vignette. The spine is blocked in gold and blind and in relief. At the head and at the tail, plant decoration is blocked between two fillets – all in relief. Near the head, the title words: '| The | Merchant | of | Venice |' are blocked in gold, surrounded by a tracery of stems and of leaves.

King, *WHR* p. 320. Pantazzi, *4D*, p. 91, no. VIII.

578 Rogers, Willam Harry

Grey, Rose. *Double sight. A Poem.* London: McClary, 32, St. James's Street, 1861. [1], 169 p.
198 × 255 × 16 mm. 11647.f.32.

Beige endpapers and pastedowns. Binder's ticket on lower pastedown: '| Bound by | Burn | 37 & 38 | Kirby St. |' Mauve bead-grain cloth. Both covers identically blocked in blind and in relief on the borders and on the corners. Two fillets are blocked in blind on the outer and on the inner borders, the outer of each pair thick, the inner of each pair thin. Each inner corner has a leaf pattern blocked in relief. The upper cover central vignette is blocked in gold. A circular branch-like fillet has leaves and small stems blocked in gold around it. Groups of leaves are formed at the head and at the tail. The title: '| Double sight. | A Poem |' is blocked in gold on the centre. Signed 'WHR' in gold as a monogram at the base of the vignette. The spine is blocked in gold. The same small decoration and fillets are blocked at the head and at the tail. The title: '| Double | sight | A Poem |' is blocked in gold. Small leaf and stem decoration is blocked in gold beneath the title.

579 Rogers, William Harry PLATE LXXII

Quarles, Francis. *Quarles' emblems. Illustrated by Charles Bennett and W. Harry Rogers.* London: James Nisbet & Co., 21, Berners Street, 1861. [10], 321 p.
160 × 225 × 37 mm. 1347.f.11.

On the title page verso: 'The illustrations engraved by Joseph Swain and Edmund Evans'. For all full page illustrations, the page headers and footers, and the borders are emblematic. These are signed 'WHR' as a monogram. The illustrations within are signed 'CHB' as a monogram.

Gilt edges. Bevelled boards. Yellow endpapers and pastedowns. Red morocco horizontal-grain cloth. Both covers blocked identically in gold and in blind. On the outer borders, diagonal stripes are blocked between two gold fillets. Inside this, a recessed fillet is blocked in blind. On the inner borders, a pattern of flowers and leaves is blocked in gold, with the following blocked in medallions, formed by double gold circular fillets: a butterfly, a snake, an orb, a skull, a sparrow in a heart, a shell. The central rectangle has flowers blocked in blind around the central large medallion. The central medallion is blocked in gold, showing crossed tulip flowers and leaves, The title words: '| Quarles' Emblems |' are blocked in relief within a heart at the centre. Signed 'WHR' in relief as a monogram at the base of the heart. The spine is fully blocked in gold and in relief. A perimeter pattern is blocked, consisting of: 1. a 'herring bone' pattern in gold and in relief; 2. repeating gold dots; 3. hatch gold leaves and tulips intertwining down the spine. The title: '| Quarles' | Emblems |' is blocked in relief within two rectangular gold lettering-pieces. Signed 'WHR' and CHB' as joined monograms in relief, both within a heart-shaped gold lettering-piece, which has two gold fillets blocked on its borders.

The de Beaumont Private Collection copy (PLATE LXXII), has the same blocking as the BL copy.

Ball, *VPB* p. 156. King, *WHR* p. 321. McLean, *VPBB* p. 83. Oldfield, *BC* no. 76.

580 Rogers, William Harry PLATE LXXIII

Rogers, William Harry. *Spiritual Conceits, Extracted from the Writings of the Fathers, the Old English poets, &c. Illustrated by W. Harry Rogers.* [Cross and Crown motto.] London: Griffith and Farran, Corner of St. Paul's Churchyard, 1862. London: Chiswick Press: – Printed by Whittingham and Wilkins, Tooks Court, Chancery Lane. [16], 223 p.
155 × 210 × 35 mm. C.109.b.1.

On the title page verso: 'The engraving by Joseph Swain'.

Bevelled boards. Gilt edges. Brown endpapers and pastedowns. Binder's ticket on lower pastedown: '| Bound by | Bone & Son | 76, Fleet St. London. |' Green morocco vertical-grain cloth. Both covers are blocked identically in gold and in blind and in relief. On the borders there are two fillets, one blocked in gold, the next blocked in blind. Inside these, a border of repeating patterns is blocked in gold. The patterns are 'three hatch leaf' and 'hanging diamonds', each with four dots blocked inside in relief. There is a rectangular central panel, and, at the head and tail, rectangular gold lettering pieces are blocked. The one at the head contains the word: '| Spiritual |', blocked in relief; the one at the tail contains the word: '| Conceits |', blocked in relief. Each lettering piece has diagonal fillets, which are blocked in vertical and horizontal hatch. The hatched fillets alternate with those which are blocked in gold, with small dots blocked in relief. Four rose flowers are blocked in gold underneath and above the two rectangular gold lettering pieces. They are surrounded by small stars, blocked in relief. The central panel is a quatrefoil, and around its perimeter fleurs-de-lis are blocked in gold in a repeating pattern. At the very centre, surrounded by small stars and circles blocked in gold, an interlocking crown and a cross are blocked in gold. The decorative elements of the crown and cross are picked out in hatch and in relief. The spine decoration is all in gold and in relief. There is

a fillet blocked in gold around the perimeter. The spine is divided into five panels. Numbers 1, 2 and 5 are formed by a single gold fillet. At the head, panel 1 contains a crow, surrounded by small stars and circles, all in gold. Panel 2 has the title: '| Spiritual | Conceits |' blocked in relief within a square gold lettering piece. Panel 3 has a descending scroll-like gold lettering-piece, with the words: 'No Cross, No Crown' blocked in relief inside. In the centre of this panel the interlocking cross and crown are blocked. The monogram 'WHR' is blocked in relief at the base of the scroll-shaped gold lettering-piece. In panel 4, '| WH Rogers |' is blocked in relief inside a small gold lettering-piece. In panel 5, a cross, surrounded by small crowns and circles, is blocked in gold.

See 12304.e.18. 'Emblems of Christian life' which has a similar design.

Ball, *VPB* p. 158. Says that *Emblems of Christian Life* is a new edition of *Spiritual Conceits*, which he had not seen. de Beaumont, *RdeB1* no. 365. Copy in maroon cloth. Goldman, *VIB* no. 365. King, *WHR* p. 320.

581 Rogers, William Harry

Gwynne, Fanny Price. *The Tenby Souvenir: A table-book in prose and verse. Illustrated by twenty-five photographic views, by Mr. Charles Allen.* Tenby: R. Mason, High Street, 1863. R. Mason, Printer, High Street, Tenby. vii, 81 p., 25 photographs.
180 × 270 × 20 mm. 12355.k.1.

Gilt edges. Bevelled boards. Light yellow endpapers and pastedowns. Purple pebble grain cloth. Both covers blocked identically in blind on the lower and in gold on the upper. On the upper cover, a single gold fillet is blocked on the borders, and, inside, wide gold hatch, with a pattern of curling stems, and leaves encircling it. The lower cover central vignette shows curling stems and leaves; the stems join as two 'spade-shapes'. The upper cover central vignette is blocked in gold. Stems, leaves, flowers and tendrils form the central circle. The title: '| The | Tenby | Souvenir |' is blocked in gold on the centre. Signed 'WHR' in gold as a monogram at the base of the vignette. The spine is blocked in gold. The title: '| The Tenby Souvenir |' is blocked in gold along the spine, within a cartouche formed by gold fillets, with curling leaf decoration blocked in gold at each end.

582 Rogers, William Harry

Periodical Publications – *London. Our own fireside. A magazine of home literature for the Christian Family. Edited by the Rev. Charles Bullock, Rector of St. Nicholas, Worcester.* [London]: William Macintosh, Paternoster Row, [1863–64]. Benjamin Pardon, Printer, Paternoster Row, London. vi, 834 p.
172 × 258 × 51 mm. P.P.357.c.

Parts 1 to 15 are bound into one volume. Pagination continuous for Parts 1–15, Oct. 1863 to Dec. 1964.

Each part has the original upper and lower covers of orange dyed paper bound in sequence. Paper cover size: 165 × 250 mm. The recto of each upper cover has a list of contents for that part, printed within the design by Rogers for the cover. Printed on the left hand corner of each upper cover recto: 'Part 1 [–15]'; on the right hand corner of each upper cover: 'Price 6d'. The verso of each upper cover and both recto and verso of each lower cover have advertisements printed on them. The upper cover design consists of the title printed within an arch at the head. The corners of the arch have leaf decoration The arch is supported on each side by a thin column with a spiral pattern, with foliated capitals at the head of each column. The base of each column is joined to a horizontal cartouche at the tail. This has the printer's name on either side of a foliated oval panel on the centre of the cartouche. Within the panel, the month and the year of each part are printed. Signed 'WHR' as a monogram on the left hand side of the cartouche. Signed 'EW' as a monogram, on the right hand side of the cartouche. The upper covers all have the same design.

King, *WHR* p. 324.

583 Rogers, William Harry

Greenwood, James. *Curiosities of savage life. (Second series.) With woodcuts & designs by Harden S. Melville; engraved by H. Newson Woods. And coloured illustrations from water-colour drawings by F. W.Keyl and R.Huttala.* London: S. O. Beeton, 248 Strand, W.C., 1864. Hertford: Printed by Stephen Austin, Fore Street. xiv, 418 p. [9 plates]
138 × 222 × 37 mm. 10006.cc.42.

Gilt edges. Red pebble-grain cloth. Both covers are blocked in blind with an identical design on the borders and on the corners. Two fillets are blocked in blind on the borders. Leaves and circular stems are blocked on each corner, with a single flower head blocked in relief within the circle on each corner, formed by the stem. The central oval frame is formed by two fillets blocked in blind, the outer of which has repeating dots blocked in relief within it. The central vignette on the upper cover is blocked in gold, and shows a savage holding a spear. The title: '| Curiosities of | savage life |' is blocked in gold in semicircles above and below the centre. Palm tree and coconut decoration is blocked in gold around the centre, with a single tassel hanging to the lower left and lower right of the central vignette. A small snake is blocked at the base of the vignette. The spine is fully blocked in gold. A single gold fillet is blocked on the perimeter. From the head downwards, the decoration is: a gold lettering-piece, showing a savage in a canoe; the title: '| Curiosities | of | savage | life |' blocked in gold within a panel formed by three gold fillets, one thick between two thin; the word: '| by |' blocked in gold within a rectangular hatch gold lettering-piece; the words: '| James Greenwood |' blocked in gold within a rectangular hatch gold lettering-piece; a mandorla-shaped gold lettering-piece shows a savage holding an axe and a spear; small decoration and objects are blocked in gold around the mandorla; the words: '| Second series |' are blocked

in gold, surrounded by fillets and small decoration; signed 'WHR' in gold as a monogram near the right hand tail; the words: '| London | S. O. Beeton |' are blocked in gold at the tail.

Ball, *VPB* p. 156. Suggests that Vol. 2. *Savage habits and customs*, 1865, has a design by Rogers.

584 Rogers, William Harry

Shakespeare, William. *The works. Edited, with a scrupulous revision of the text, by Charles and Mary Cowden Clarke . . . In four volumes*. London: Bickers and Son, 1864. Edinburgh: Printed by Ballantyne and Company.

11762.cc.10.

Vol. I. [2], 730 p. With six pages of publisher's titles bound at the end. 147 × 236 × 55 mm. Binder's ticket on lower pastedown: '| Bound by | Bone & Son, | [rule] | 76, Fleet Street, | London. |'
Vol. II. [2], 730 p. 145 × 236 × 45 mm.
Vol. III. [2], 700 p. 144 × 236 × 48 mm.
Vol. IV. [2], 751 p. 145 × 236 × 41 mm.

All volumes have bevelled boards. Dark brown endpapers and pastedowns. Dark maroon pebble-grain cloth. The lower and upper covers are identically blocked in blind and in relief. Two fillets are blocked in blind on the borders. Inside this, there is a border of interlinked circles and diamonds, formed in relief by the blocking in blind, i.e. the blocking in blind 'highlights' the circles and the diamonds. (The pattern is reminiscent of the Jacobean brick walls outside Hatfield House.) Sprigs of leaves are blocked in relief on each inner corner. At the inner head and the inner tail, an 'onion' shape is formed by a single fillet. The upper cover central vignette of each volume is the same, blocked in gold. It shows a Renaissance bolt and strap design, with garlands hanging to the left and to the right from a thin cord. The central rectangle is formed by three gold fillets. The words: '| Shakespeare | [a lance, blocked horizontally] | Charles & Mary | Cowden Clarke. |' are blocked in gold within the frame. Signed 'WHR' in gold as a monogram near the base of the vignette. Only one-third of the spine of Vol. III survives for this set. The spine is blocked in gold and in relief. Decorative panels are formed by single fillets, with leaves and other decoration (picked out in relief) blocked inside the panels. The word: '[a lance, blocked horizontally] | Shakespeare | [a lance blocked horizontally] |' is blocked in gold between the first and second panels. The words: '| Charles & Mary | Cowden Clarke |' are blocked in gold between the second and the third panel; the words: 'Vol. III' are blocked in gold within a circle formed by a single fillet, which has repeating dots blocked in relief inside it.

There is a pencil and ink drawing for this design drawn by Rogers in the Rogers Albums , No. 1, at the Victoria and Albert Museum.

King, *WHR* p. 322.

585 Rogers, William Harry

Howell, Catherine Augusta. *Pictures of girl life. With frontispiece by F. Eltze*. London: Griffith and Farran, (Successors to Newbery & Harris), Corner of St. Paul's Churchyard, 1865. Edinburgh: Murray and Gibb, Printers, Edinburgh. [5], 259 p., 1 plate. With thirty-six pages of publisher's titles bound at the end.

110 × 176 × 25 mm. 12805.ccc.25.

The frontispiece plate is signed: 'Swain'.

Text sewn on two sawn-in cords. Beige endpapers and pastedowns. Brown sand-grain cloth. Both covers blocked identically in blind with three fillets on the borders, one thicker between two thin. The upper central vignette is blocked in gold. It shows leaves and flowers blocked in hatch gold around a square centrepiece. This is formed by three gold fillets with straps forming arabesques on each side. The title: '| Pictures | of | girl | life |' is blocked on the centre in gold. Signed 'WHR' in gold as a monogram at the base of the vignette. The spine is blocked in gold and relief. From the head downwards, the decoration is: leaves and flowers blocked in hatch gold; the title: '| Pictures | of | girl | life |' blocked in relief within three rectangular gold lettering-pieces, with the word: 'of' blocked inside a circular gold lettering-piece; more leaves and flowers in hatch gold; signed 'WHR' in gold as a monogram within a small circle near the base of these leaves and flowers.

The Cambridge University Library copy is at shelfmark 140.1.199. Bolts uncut. Beige endpapers and pastedowns. Brown sand-grain cloth. The upper cover vignette and the spine design are the same as for the BL copy.

The 1881 edition is at BL 12808.d.35. Also published by Griffith and Farran. 192 p., 1 plate by F. Eltze. Light yellow endpapers and pastedowns. Green fine rib diagonal-grain cloth. This features an unsigned design on the upper cover of apples and leaves, with panel near the head and a parlour scene, blocked on the upper cover in gold, black and platinum (?).

586 Rogers, William Harry FIG. 72

Noel, Augusta, *Lady*. *Effie's friends; or chronicles of the woods and shore. Illustrated by W. Harry Rogers*.[By Lady Augusta Noel] London: James Nisbet & Co., 21, Berners Street, 1865. London: Printed by Edmund Evans, Raquet Court, Fleet Street. [2], 192 p.

185 × 132 × 20 mm. 12804.cc.34.

Many of the printed head and tail-pieces are signed 'WHR' and 'EE' [Edmund Evans].

Text sewn on three sawn-in cords. Bevelled boards. Grey endpapers and pastedowns. Blue sand-grain cloth. Both covers identically blocked. The lower cover is blocked in blind, the upper cover is blocked in gold. Two fillets are blocked in gold on the borders, one thick, one thin. Groups of birds are blocked on three corners and a peacock feather blocked on the fourth corner – all in gold. The central vignette is blocked in gold, showing a tracery of leaves and flowers. The title: '| Effie's | Friends |' is blocked in relief within two scroll-shaped gold

FIG. 72

FIG. 73

lettering-pieces. Signed 'WHR', in gold as a monogram at the base of the vignette. The spine is blocked in gold and in relief. Two butterflies are blocked in gold at the head. The title: '| Effie's | Friends |' is blocked in relief within a gold lettering-piece, with a single gold fillet blocked on its borders; below this, a tracery of flowers and stems and a peacock's feather are blocked in gold. Signed 'WHR', in gold as a monogram at the base of the tracery. At the tail, the words: '| London | Nisbet & Co |' are blocked in gold, within a panel formed by small border decoration. The British Museum stamp is blue [copyright], dated '16 FE[BRUARY 18]65'.

Ball, *VPB* p. 158.

587 Rogers, William Harry FIG. 73

Rimmel, Eugene. *The book of perfumes. With above 250 illustrations by Bourdelin, Thomas, etc.* London: Chapman and Hall, 193, Piccadilly. To be had also of the Author, 96, Strand, 128, Regent Street, 24 Cornhill, London, 1865. Stephen Austin, Printer, Hertford. xx, 266 p., [2] p. , 13 plates.

200 × 250 × 34 mm. 7940.g.19.

Bevelled boards. The gilt edges are gauffered. Cream endpapers and pastedowns. Blue pebble-grain cloth. Both covers are blocked in gold with an identical design. On the outer border of each cover are three fillets in gold. Inside there is a leaf and branch pattern blocked in gold as a border. There are two more rules blocked in gold inside this pattern. The author and title letters are in a half circle shape, around the centre piece. The centre piece is a rebus, whose shield shows a steaming container on the left upper quarter, and a fountain on the right upper quarter. In the lower half of the shield a glass beaker on a stand is blocked. The shield is surrounded by a gold lettering-piece shaped as a pennant containing, in relief, the motto: 'Non cuique datum est haere nasum'. The pennant is pierced on the left by a branch of roses and flowers; on the right, by a bunch of flowers. The initials 'WHR' are blocked in gold at the base of this bunch of flowers. A basket of flowers is blocked in gold above the shield and the pennant. This coat of arms is also printed on the title page, and is also signed 'WHR'. The spine is fully blocked in gold. The author and title letters are blocked in relief within ribbon-shaped gold lettering-pieces, which are surrounded by rose stems, leaves and flowers. The initials 'WHR' are blocked in gold underneath the word 'Rimmel'.

King, *WHR* p. 321.

588 Rogers, William Harry FIG. 74

Heber, Reginald, *Bishop of Calcutta. Heber's Hymns Illustrated.* London: Sampson, Low, Son and Marston, Milton House, Ludgate Hill, 1867. London: Printed by W. Clowes and Sons, Stamford Street. xii, 92 p.

165 × 220 × 25 mm. 3435.k.5.

Bevelled boards. Gilt edges. Light yellow endpapers and pastedowns. Binder's ticket on lower pastedown: '| Bound by | Bone

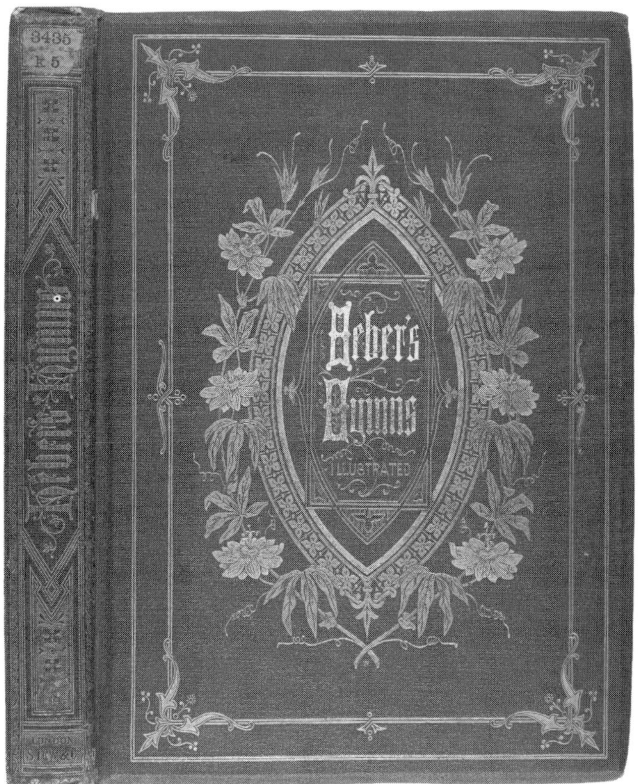

FIG. 74

& Son. | 76 Fleet St. | London E.C. |' The lower cover is blocked in blind, with fillets blocked on the borders. The central vignette is blocked in blind, showing flower tracery. Signed 'WHR' in blind as a monogram at the base of the vignette. The upper cover is blocked in gold. There are two fillets blocked on the outer border, with two more fillets and leaf tracery at the corners of the inner border. The central mandorla is formed by four leaf repeating borders blocked between two fillets. The mandorla is surrounded by passion plant leaves and flowers. Within the mandorla, inside a rectangle and an inner mandorla, the words: '| Heber's | Hymns | Illustrated |' are blocked in gold in hatched gold gothic capitals . Signed 'W' at the base of the mandorla. The spine is fully blocked in gold. Two fillets and a border are blocked around the perimeter. There are square gold lettering-pieces blocked at the head and at the tail. The words: 'London S.Low & Co.' are blocked in relief within a square gold lettering-piece at the base. The title words: '| Heber's Hymns |' are blocked in hatched gold gothic capitals along the spine, within a cartouche, which has diamond straps at each end. There is decoration blocked in relief within gold panels at head and at tail of the cartouche.

Ball, *VPB* p. 157. Pantazzi, *4D* no. XII.

589 Rogers, William Harry — PLATE LXXIV

Thornbury, Walter. *Two centuries of song; or, lyrics, madrigals, sonnets, and other occasional verses of the English poets of the last two hundred years. With critical and biographical notes . . . Illustrated by original pictures of eminent artists, drawn and engraved especially for this work. With coloured borders, designed by Henry Shaw, F.S.A. etc etc.* London: Sampson Low, Son, and Marston, Milton House, Ludgate Hill, 1867. Richard Clay, London. xii, 308 p., 20 plates.

167 × 234 × 43 mm. — RdeB.L.14.

The British Museum de Beaumont copy.

Gilt edges. Bevelled boards. Single brass clasp on the centre fore-edge. Yellow endpapers and pastedowns. Written on the upper endpaper: '| The | Lady | Henry Nevill | with every kind & good wish for 1894 | [rule] | from J. R. |' Red morocco. The turn-ins are blocked in gold with an elaborate pattern of leaves, flowers, and semi-circles. Both covers blocked identically in gold and in black. Five fillets are blocked on the borders: two pairs of fillets in gold, with one in black between these pairs. The fillet in black has a repeating pattern of flower heads and small leaves blocked in gold inside it. The cover is divided into three rectangular panels, by two sets of three fillets blocked horizontally from spine to fore-edge. The upper panel has the decoration: 1. a repeating pattern of a putto's head, its wings, an urn and a single tassel – in gold; 2. three leaves in black. The middle panel has the title: '| Two | centuries | of | song. |' blocked in gold, together with curling leaf and stem decoration blocked in gold, and a single leaf in black. The lower panel has an ornamental baroque design, blocked in gold, with two curved leaves blocked in black. The spine is blocked in gold. A single fillet is blocked on the perimeter, ending in one wide and one thin fillet blocked at the head and at the tail. The spine is divided into three rectangular panels formed by single gold fillets. Inside the panel at the head, a putto and a tassel are blocked in gold, together with three leaves blocked in black. Inside the middle panel, the title: '| Two | centuries | of | song |' is blocked in gold, together with curved leaves and stems. Inside the bottom panel, three curved leaves are blocked in black, with 'baroque' decoration in gold. Signed 'WHR' in gold as a monogram within the centre of this decoration. At the tail, a fillet is blocked in black, with leaf and stem decoration blocked in gold – all within a rectangle formed by a single gold fillet.

Ball, *VPB* p. 157.de Beaumont, *RdeB1* no. 383. Goldman, *VIB* no. 383. King, *WHR* p. 320. Pantazzi, *4D* p. 91.

590 Rogers, William Harry — FIG. 75

Tupper, Martin Farquhar. *Proverbial philosophy. (The first and second series.) Illustrated. A new edition.* London: Edward Moxon & Co., Dover Street, 1867. London: Bradbury, Evans & Co., Printers, Whitefriars. xi, 367 p.

190 × 230 × mm. — 11651.f.11.

Bevelled boards. Gilt edges. Green coarse pebble-grain cloth. On the lower cover, the borders are blocked in blind, with a 'plant pattern'. The central rectangle contains a gold lettering-piece, shaped as a pennant. The title and author letters are in relief, and, in a medallion, the Moxon monogram is blocked in gold. On the upper cover, the same 'plant design' borders are blocked in gold. The central rectangle is blocked in gold, with a

FIG. 75

diagonal chequer board pattern. Each diamond is blocked in hatch. The same pennant-shaped gold lettering-piece in the rectangle is also blocked on the upper cover, with the letters in relief and the Moxon monogram blocked in gold. The spine is fully blocked in gold, with a similar design as the upper cover. Signed 'WHR', with small initials, at the tail in gold.

Ball, *VPB* p. 158. Says this copy signed 'HR'. de Beaumont, *RdeB1* no. 387. The 1854 edition, published by Hatchard, possibly with a design by Rogers. Goldman, *VIB* no.387. King, *WHR* p. 321; col. pl. 11.

591 Rogers, William Harry — PLATE LXXV

Christian lyrics: chiefly selected from modern authors. With upwards of one hundred engravings. London: Sampson, Low, Son and Marston, Milton House, Ludgate Hill, 1868. London: Printed by W. Clowes and Sons, Stamford Street. xiv, 180 p. With four pages of publisher's titles bound at the end.

170 × 220 × 20 mm. 1570/37.

Bevelled boards. Gilt edges. Yellow endpapers and pastedowns. Binder's ticket on lower pastedown: '| Bound by | W. Bone & Son. | 76, Fleet St. | London E.C. |' The lower cover is blocked in blind, with seven fillets on the borders, one thick in the middle of six thin. A cross flory is blocked on the centre. The cross has a quatrefoil centre. The upper cover is fully blocked in gold and relief. A fillet is blocked on the border, and another fillet blocked in gold has a repeating pattern of four squares blocked in relief within it. A chequer board pattern is blocked on the corners in relief and in gold. Between these, there are four panels of thin flower tracery at the head, tail, and the two sides. The central rectangle has a gold fillet border; inside is a repeat of the chequer board pattern at the top and the bottom of the rectangle. A putto's head and wings hover above the title: '| Christian | Lyrics. |', which is blocked in gold in gothic letters. Signed 'WHR' in gold as a monogram underneath the title. The spine is fully blocked in gold and relief. At the head and at the tail, a single gold fillet and a 'dog tooth' fillet are blocked in gold. A single fillet is blocked on the perimeter. A repeating 'four squares' pattern is blocked in relief within this fillet. Just inside this, another single thin gold fillet is blocked on the perimeter. A pattern of curling stems and leaves is blocked in gold at the inner head and at the inner tail. On the centre of the spine, a single gold fillet with 'dog tooth' decoration forms a cartouche. The words: '| Christian Lyrics |' are blocked in gold in gothic letters within the cartouche.

Another copy of this work is at BL C.128.f.5. (formerly shelved at 11602.f.5.) Green sand sand-grain cloth. The same design as for BL 1570/37 is blocked on the covers and on the spine.

Ball, *VPB* p. 157. King, *WHR* p. 320; illustration p. 323. Pantazzi, *4D* no. XIV.

592 Rogers, William Harry — PLATE LXXVI

Clarke, Charles Cowden and Clarke, Mary Cowden. *'Many happy returns of the day!' A birth-day book. New edition, with numerous additional engravings* . . . London: C. Lockwood & Co., 7, Stationers' Hall Court, Ludgate Hill, [1869]. London: Harrison & Sons, Printers in Ordinary to Her Majesty, St. Martin's Lane. viii, 355 p. With four pages of publisher's titles bound at the end.

120 × 182 × 30 mm. 12808.g.23.

Gilt edges. Brown endpapers and pastedowns. Binder's ticket on lower pastedown: '| Bound by | W. Bone and Son. | 76 Fleet St. | London E.C. |' The lower cover is blocked in blind with four fillets on the borders. The upper cover is blocked in gold and black. Two fillets on the borders are blocked in black. On the upper cover, there is a tracery of plant leaves and branches in black to the right; in gold to the left. The title: '| [M]any happy | [R]eturns of the day |' is blocked in relief on green onlays (probably paper) within elongated rectangular gold lettering-pieces. The capital letters 'M' and 'R' are blocked in gold within red onlays (probably paper), which have a single gold fillet on their borders. Signed 'WHR' in black as a monogram near to the base of the design on the upper cover. The spine is blocked in gold and in black. From the head downwards, the decoration is: a single black fillet across the spine; the words: '| Many | Happy | Returns | of the | Day: |' blocked in gold in gothic letters, which are surrounded by leaf and stem decoration blocked in black; the words: '| Charles & Mary | Cowden Clarke |' blocked in relief within a rectangular gold lettering-piece, which has a single gold fillet blocked on its borders; more plant and leaf decoration blocked in gold and in black; signed 'WHR' in black as a monogram on the left hand side of the spine near the tail; a gold fillet; the words:

'| Lockwood & Co |' are blocked in gold in gothic letters; a gold fillet; a black fillet.

Ball, *VPB* p. 157. King, *WHR* p. 327; illustration p. 322.

593 Rogers, William Harry FIG. 76

Great Britain and Ireland – *Army. The great battles of the British army. A new edition, including the Indian Mutiny and the Abyssinian War. With coloured illustrations.* London: George Routledge and Sons, The Broadway, Ludgate; New York, 416 Broome Street, [1869]. London: R. Clay, Sons and Taylor, Printers, Bread Street Hill. vii, 565 p., 6 plates. [By Leighton, Brothers.] With two pages of publisher's advertisements bound at the end.

140 × 200 × mm. 9505.bbb.23.

Yellow endpapers and pastedowns. Binder's ticket on lower pastedown: '| Bound by | W. Bone and Son | 76 Fleet St. London E.C. |' Blue sand-grain cloth. The lower cover is blocked in blind. It has the same outline of the design blocked to the upper cover in gold and black. The upper cover has black fillets on the borders, with a border inside these of gold, with a leaf and stem pattern on head, fore-edge and tail. The right half of the cover has a tracery in black of plants and leaves, in geometrical patterns. The left side of the upper cover has three red onlays (probably paper), running vertically. They have been blocked in gold with the red paper showing in relief, from the top: a rose flower and leaves; thistle flowers and a leaf; clover leaves. In between the red paper onlays are two small rectangular blocks in gold, the upper featuring a flag and a palm leaf; the lower rectangle features a sword, a cuirassier's helmet and oak leaves. Signed 'WHR' in black as a monogram at the left hand tail of the upper cover. The spine is fully blocked in gold. The title is in gold and is blocked onto a red onlay (probably paper). On the left hand side of the spine, from head to tail runs a flagpole, which holds the title panel as a flag. A prominent stem, blocked in black and in gold, curls from the tail to the head, with leaves and tendrils attached to it, blocked in gold A lion rampant is blocked in gold at the tail. Signed 'WHR' in gold near the tail. At the tail: the word: '| Routledge |' is blocked in gold, between two gold fillets.

FIG. 76

King, *WHR* p. 324.

594 Rogers, William Harry

Nash, Joseph. *The Mansions of England in The Olden Time. Re-edited by J. Corbet Anderson. With the original one hundred and four illustrations, carefully reduced and executed in lithography, by Samuel Stanesby.* 4 vols. London: Henry Sotheran & Co., 136, Strand, 1869–1872. London: Printed by Wertheimer, Lea and Co., Finsbury Circus.

J/7815.e.24.

Vol. I 1869. [2], p. 1–15, plates 1–26.
Vol. II. 1870. p. 16–32, plates 27–52.
Voll. III. 1871. p. 33–55, plates 53–78.
Vol. IV. 1872. p. 57–74, plates 79–104.
All volumes measure 280 × 375 × 17 mm.

All volumes have bevelled boards. Vol I. has gilt head and tail; Vols II.–IV are gilt at the head only. All volumes have yellow endpapers and pastedowns. Red pebble-grain cloth. All covers have the same blocking on the borders, corners and on the sides, in blind on the lower cover and in gold and black on the upper. Three fillets are blocked in black on the upper covers. Decorative patterns are blocked on the corners and the middles of the sides, all in black. An inner rectangle is formed by three more fillets, blocked in black. Medallions are blocked in gold on the centres of each side, with decoration picked out in relief. The decoration within each, clockwise from the head, is: a rose, a fleur-de-lis, a helmet, a portcullis. On the corners of the inner rectangle, a crown is blocked in gold, with the capital letters 'E', 'R', 'I' each underneath a crown, and a shamrock blocked underneath the crown bottom right. The title: '| The | mansions | of England | in the | olden time | Ioseph Nash. |' is blocked in gold. The letters have small circles in them, which gives them a bisected effect. Signed 'WHR' in gold as a monogram at the base of the title lettering. The spines have decorated gold fillets blocked at the head and at the tail. The words: '| Nash's Mansions of England |' are blocked in gold along the spine, with a gold fillet at each end of the words. '| Vol. I. [–IV.] |' is blocked in gold at the tail.

Another copy of the First Series is at BL N.Tab.2014/8. [2], 16p, 26 plates. 463 × 585 × 42 mm. The Hanhart brothers are named as lithographers of the plates. Yellow endpapers and pastedowns. Green sand-grain cloth, plus quarter morocco on the spine. Two gold fillets are blocked vertically on each cover on the join of the cloth and the leather. The title and author are

blocked in gold on the upper cover in the same letters as for J/7815.e.24., with a rule between the title and the author. A single flower is blocked in gold on the centre tail of the upper cover, denoting vol. I. There are notches on the covers on the fore-edge centre, for a possible ribbon tie. The spine is not blocked.

King, *WHR* p. 324.

595 Rogers, William Harry

Ewing, Julia Horatia. *The Brownies and other tales. With illustrations by George Cruikshank.* London: Bell and Daldy, York Street, Covent Garden, 1870. London: Printed by William Clowes and Sons, Stamford Street, and Charing Cross. [2], 229 p., 4 plates. With eighteen pages of publisher's titles bound at the end.

142 × 187 × 30 mm. 12808.m.25.

The plates are signed 'G. CK' and 'H. Harral Sc.'.

Brown ungrained cloth. The lower cover is blocked with a single black fillet on its borders. The upper cover is blocked in gold and in black and relief. A single fillet is blocked on the borders. Curling stem and small leaves are blocked in black down the left hand side and across the head. An owl, a violin player, two puppies, and a bird are blocked in gold amongst the stems. Near the centre, the title words: '| The Brownies, | and other tales. |' are blocked in relief within two rectangular gold lettering-pieces, with single fillets on their borders. Signed 'WHR' in black as a monogram, just above the bird blocked on the left hand side. The spine is blocked in gold and in black. From the head downwards, the decoration is: curling stems, blocked in black; an owl is blocked in gold within these stems; the title words: '| The | Brownies | & | other tales |' blocked in gold; a violin player, blocked in gold; the name: '| J. H. Ewing |' blocked in gold; curling stems, blocked in black; a dragonfly is blocked in gold; the words: '| Bell & Daldy |' are blocked in gold at the base.

596 Rogers, William Harry PLATE LXXVII

Lydon, Alexander Frank. *Fairy Mary's dream. With illustrations by the author.* London: Groombridge and Sons, 5, Paternoster Row, 1870. B. Fawcett, Printer, Driffield. 31 p., 8 plates.

186 × 257 × 13 mm. 11651.i.19.

Bevelled boards. Gilt edges. Brown endpapers and pastedowns. Red sand-grain cloth. The lower cover is blocked in blind, with four fillets on the borders. The upper cover is blocked in gold and black. There are four fillets on the borders, all blocked in black. The title words: '| Fairy | Mary's | Dream |' are blocked in gold, and also the decoration around the letters. Each capital letter is decorated and in double size. The decoration consists of plant stems and 'fuchsia shaped' flowers. Signed 'WHR' in gold as a monogram at the base of the decoration. The spine is blocked in gold. Decorative devices are blocked in gold at the head and at the tail. The words: '| Fairy Mary's Dream |' are blocked along the spine in gold.

Ball, *VPB* p. 158. King, *WHR* p. 321; illustration p. 322. McLean, R., *Fawcett* pp. 19–22.

597 Rogers, William Harry PLATE LXXVIII

Rogers, William Harry. *Emblems of Christian life, Illustrated by W. Harry Rogers, from the writings of the Fathers, the old English poets, etc.* [device of cross (printed in red) and crown, with the motto: 'No cross no crown' printed within groups of trefoils at scroll-ends.] London: Griffith and Farran, Corner of St. Paul's Churchyard, [1870]. London: Chiswick Press: Printed by Whittingham and Wilkins, Tooks Court, Chancery Lane. [16], 224 p.

155 × 205 × 32 mm. 12304.e.18.

On the title page verso: '| The engraving by Joseph Swain |' in gothic letters, printed within a scroll attached to an engraving tool. Also printed is the monogram 'JS'. On page one of the text, the title: '| Spiritual Conceits |' is printed. All pages have a single red fillet on the borders, with a cross and crown device printed in red on each corner.

Bevelled boards. Gilt edges. Brown endpapers and pastedowns. Purple sand-grain cloth. Both covers identically blocked, in blind and relief on the lower cover and in gold and in blind and in relief on the upper. On the upper cover, a single gold fillet is blocked on the borders. Inside this, a border is blocked consisting of a pattern of dots, and of hatch 'three trefoils' shapes. Between these, there is a pattern of 'hanging diamonds'. Near the head, a rectangular panel is blocked in gold, with a single border fillet blocked in relief. Within the panel, the words: '| Emblems: of |' are blocked in relief in gothic letters. Near the tail, a similar rectangular panel is blocked in gold, with the words: '| Christian: Life |' blocked within in relief in gothic letters. The centre is occupied by an intertwined cross patonce and crown, blocked in gold and in hatch. Both are surrounded by a border of repeating fleurs-de-lis, in hatch, together with small circles and stars. A single rose is blocked on each inner corner. Further background decoration is provided by a repeating four point star pattern, blocked in relief. The spine is blocked in gold and in relief. A single gold fillet is blocked on the perimeter. From the head downwards, the decoration is: a panel formed by a single fillet; inside the panel, a small cross patonce is blocked in gold, surrounded by small stars and circles – all blocked in gold; the title: '| Emblems of | Christian | Life. |' blocked in relief in gothic letters within a gold lettering-piece; inside a long rectangle formed by a single gold fillet, a intertwined crown and cross are blocked in gold; the motto: '| no | cross | no crown |' blocked in relief within a scroll-shaped gold lettering-piece blocked above and below the crown and the cross; signed 'WHR' in relief at the base of the motto; the name: '| W.H. Rogers |' is blocked in relief in gothic letters within a rectangular gold lettering-piece; at the tail, inside a panel formed by a single gold fillet, a cross patonce is blocked, surrounded by small circles and stars – all in gold. [This is one of the most unified designs by Rogers.]

Ball, *VPB* p. 158. King, *WHR* p. 321. Oldfield, *BC* no. 77. Pantazzi, *4D* p. 90, no. 1.

598 Rogers, William Harry

The great sieges of history. A new edition, including The siege of Paris. With coloured illustrations. London: George Routledge and Sons The Broadway, Ludgate; New York, 416 Broome Street, [1871]. London: Wyman and Sons, Law and General Printers. Great Queen Street, W.C. xii, 742 p., 8 plates. With two pages of publisher's titles bound at the end.
125 × 192 × 57 mm. 9005.cc.13.

The Preface is signed 'W. R.'

Text sewn on two sawn-in cords. Beige endpapers and pastedowns. Brown pebble-grain cloth. The lower cover is blocked in blind only. The upper cover is blocked in gold, in black and in relief. On the lower cover, the decoration is blocked in blind. On the upper cover the same decoration is blocked in black. The upper cover has two fillets blocked in black on the borders. Across the head, the tail, and down the fore-edge, a border pattern of two leaves and a berry, repeated, are blocked in gold, with a single fillet in black on the inside of this. Curling leaf and stem decoration work is blocked in black on the upper cover from the fore-edge towards the spine. Towards the spine side of the upper cover, there are three pairs of panels; the left of each pair is formed by a single fillet blocked in black. The right of each pair is a blue paper onlay, blocked in gold, with plant decoration blocked inside in relief. Between the pairs of panels, rectangular panels are blocked in gold. The upper rectangular panel shows a rifle, a palm leaf and a flag blocked in gold inside; the lower has a sword, a helmet and oak leaves blocked in gold inside. Signed 'WHR' in black as a monogram in the bottom left hand corner of the upper cover. The spine is blocked in gold and in black. A single fillet is blocked up each side of the spine in black, ending at the head in leaves forming an arch. From the head downwards, the decoration is: fleur-de-lis, a rose and portcullis -all in gold; the words: 'Great | sieges | of | history |' blocked in gold on a black paper onlay, with has a single fillet in gold on its borders. From the right hand side of the tail upwards, curling stem decoration in black and in gold is blocked; a castle front in gold near the tail; signed 'WHR' in gold as a monogram near the right hand tail; two fillets in gold; the word: 'Routledge' is blocked in gold; a fillet in gold at the tail. This is the copyright copy, and date stamped '10 NO[VEMBER 18] 71'.

The Cambridge University Library copy is at shelfmark 71.7.677. Blue sand-grain cloth, with red paper onlays on the upper cover. The design blocked on this copy is the same as for the BL copy. The size of the copy is 125 × 191 × 51. The red paper onlays on the upper cover are not cut to the right size for each rectangle, so the blue sand-grain cloth of this copy shows through in relief.

King, *WHR* p. 324; col. pl. 12.

599 Rogers, William Harry

Brown, J. *Tales and Traditions of the Arabs, with A Sketch of Mahomet's Career, and his Extraordinary Night Journey To the Seven Heavens on the Back of the Wonderful Beast, Al Borak.* London: Elliot Stock, 62, Paternoster Row, [1873]. [London]: J. Ogden and Co., Printers, 172, St. John Street, E.C. vii, 120 p.
105 × 170 × 20 mm. 12431.aaa.23.

Text originally sewn on two sawn-in cords. Bevelled boards. Brown endpapers and pastedowns. Maroon sand-grain cloth. Apart from the title, both covers are blocked identically, in blind only on the lower, and in black on the upper. On the upper cover, a single fillet is blocked in black on the borders. The rest of the cover displays a pattern of long curling stems and leaves, blocked in black. Four groups of six five-pointed stars are blocked near the head and near the tail. On the centre, the title: '| Tales and | traditions of | the Arabs |' is blocked in relief within three rectangular gold lettering-pieces. Each lettering-piece has a fillet and repeating dots blocked in relief above and below it. Each lettering-piece also has a single fillet blocked in black on its borders. Signed 'WHR' in black as a monogram at the right hand corner of the upper cover. Spine missing.

600 Rogers, William Harry

Grant, James, *of the 62nd Regiment. British heroes in foreign wars of the Cavaliers of Fortune. A new edition with coloured illustrations.* London: George Routledge and Sons The Broadway, Ludgate; New York, 416 Broome Street, [1873]. London: Savill, Edwards, and Co., Printers, Chandos Street, Covent Garden. vii, 404 p., 8 plates. With four pages of publisher's advertisements bound at the end.
122 × 190 × 40 mm. 10804.b.20.

The plates are signed 'Leighton Bros.'.

In the publisher's titles at the rear: 'Routledge's Five – Shilling Juvenile Books. In fcap. 8vo. and post 8vo, Illustrated by Gilbert, Harvey, Foster, and Zwecker, gilt.' Other books listed in this series are: Great Sieges of History; Great Battles of the British Army; Great Battles of the British Navy.

Yellow endpapers and pastedowns. Blue sand-grain cloth. The lower and upper covers are blocked identically as for 'The great sieges of history' – BL 9005.cc.13. The spine is fully blocked in gold and black and relief. A single black fillet is blocked on the perimeter. From the head downwards, the decoration is: stems and quatrefoils in black; crossed spears and bayonets, in gold; a red paper onlay with a gold lettering-piece, and the words: '| British | Heroes | in | Foreign | Wars |' blocked in relief within; decoration in black and a laurel wreath; a rifle and a naval sword in gold; Neptune's trident is blocked in gold across the spine, near the tail; signed 'WHR' in gold as a monogram beneath the trident; a fillet in gold; 'Routledge' in gold; two fillets are blocked in black at the tail.

The Cambridge University Library copy is at shelfmark: 73.7.633. It has the same cover and spine design as this copy.

Ball, *VPB* p. 158. King, *WHR* p. 324.; col. pl. 12.

601 Rogers, William Harry

Low, Charles Rathbone. *The great battles of the British Navy.* London: George Routledge and Sons, The Broadway,

as at the head; signed 'IS' in gold as a monogram at the base of the shield; a rectangle, formed by a single gold fillet, has: '| Routledge & Co. |' blocked in gold within; a rectangle is blocked at the tail.

de Beaumont, *RdeB1* no. 181. Goldman, *VIB* no. 181. Oldfield, *BC* no. 83.

613 Sliegh, John PLATE LXXX

Pollock, Robert. *The course of time a poem. Illustrated edition.* Edinburgh and London: William Blackwood and Sons, 1857. Printed by R. & R. Clark, Edinburgh. xxiv, 7–359 p.
163 × 226 × 32 mm. 1347.h.13.

Gilt edges. Bevelled boards. Yellow endpapers and pastedowns. Binder's ticket on lower pastedown: '| Bound by | Edmonds and Remnants. | [rule] | London. |' Orange morocco horizontal-grain cloth. Both covers are blocked identically in gold and in relief. The borders have a dentelle pattern, with two border fillets blocked inside. On the corners, each formed by two gold fillets, plant patterns are blocked. Around the central rectangle, arabesques are blocked, with the stems and leaves in relief. The central rectangle has a fillet border, blocked in gold. Inside it, there is a flower and stem pattern on the border, and further small arabesques on the corners, both in gold. The title: '| The | Course | of | Time. |' is blocked in gold and in relief in rustic letters. The spine is blocked in gold. A single gold fillet is blocked on the perimeter. Three panels are formed down the spine by single and double gold fillets. From the head downwards, the decoration is: in panel one – stem and leaf decoration in gold, together with a triangular gold lettering-piece, with three leaves and stems blocked in relief inside it; in panel two – the title: '| The | Course | of | Time |' blocked in gold in rustic letters; in panel three – the same triangle and decoration as for panel one, together with a near-diamond shape, formed by four gold fillets, and also a quatrefoil gold lettering-piece, with small leaf decoration blocked inside it in relief; leaf and stem decoration is blocked near the tail; signed 'IS' in gold as a monogram at the tail.

Ball, *VPB* p. 163. de Beaumont, *RdeB1* nos. 267 & 268. Goldman, *VIB* nos. 267 & 268. McLean, *VPBB* p. 69. An orange cloth copy is illustrated. Pantazzi, *4D* p. 98, item V.

614 Sliegh, John

Dulcken, Henry William. *Our favourite fairy tales and famous histories: told for the hundredth time. Illustrated with three hundred pictures, engraved by the Brothers Dalziel, from original designs by eminent artists.* London: Ward and Lock, 158, Fleet Street, 1858. [5], 415 p. Some of the illustrations are hand coloured.
133 × 180 × 40 mm. RdeB.B.18.

The British Museum de Beaumont copy.

Gilt edges. White endpapers and pastedowns. Paper lace card inlaid into the upper pastedown, with a putto and garland as coloured onlays on the lace. Signed '| Emily Hippisley. | 1867. |' in ink within the central oval of the card. Blue wave vertical-grain cloth. Both covers are blocked in blind with the same design on the borders and the corners. Two fillets are blocked on the borders. Small leaves are blocked in relief on the corners. On the lower cover, the central vignette is blocked in blind. It shows an oval at the centre, with long thin stems and leaves surrounding it. On the upper cover, the central vignette is blocked in gold. It shows a diamond-shaped gold lettering-piece, with ivy leaves and stems blocked inside in relief. In the centre, a circle is blocked, with the title: '| Our favourite | fairy tales | illustrated |' blocked in gold in fanciful letters. The spine is blocked in gold and in relief. It is divided into panels by fillets blocked in gold and in relief. In the panel at the head, small ivy leaves & stems are blocked in gold. Underneath, the title: '| Our favourite | fairy tales |' is blocked in relief within a gold lettering-piece. The central panel shows more leaves and stems, with a 'four petal' motif picked out in relief at the centre. The word: 'Illustrated' is blocked below this in relief within a gold lettering-piece. The panel at the base shows the same ivy leaf pattern as is blocked at the head. Signed 'IS' in gold as a monogram within the decoration of the panel at the base. The British Library copy is at 12431.c.27. The upper cover of this copy is tipped into the front of the rebound volume. The upper cover is the same design as the de Beaumont copy. It is less worn, but has been cropped.

de Beaumont, *RdeB2* no. 106. P&D Accession no. 1996–11–4–12.

615 Sliegh, John PLATE LXXXI

Odes and sonnets illustrated. The pictures in this book are by Birket Foster, the ornamental designs by John Sliegh. Engraved and printed by the Brothers Dalziel. London: George Routledge & Co. Farringdon Street, 1859. Dalziel Brothers, Engravers and Printers, London, Camden Press, 1858. 107 p.
155 × 225 × 17 mm. 1347.g.11.

Bevelled boards. Gilt edges. Light yellow endpapers and pastedowns. Blue morocco vertical-grain cloth. Both covers are blocked with an identical design in gold, in blind, and in relief. The border is blocked with two fillets in gold. Inside, this, a repeating pattern of diamonds, trefoils, quatrefoils and small dots, is blocked. Inside this, a fillet is blocked in gold, with small 'crossed oval' shapes blocked in relief within it. Each of the inner corners has a circle blocked in gold, with flower and leaf patterns blocked in relief inside. At the head, tail and sides, panel gold lettering-pieces are blocked, with decoration of flowers and leaves blocked in relief. At the centre is a mandorla. Around its perimeter a fillet is blocked, with crossed oval shapes blocked inside in relief. The outer part of the mandorla is blocked in blind, with decorated circles blocked in relief. The central mandorla has the title: '| Odes | and | Sonnets | Illustrated |' blocked in relief inside four gold rectangular lettering-pieces. Small single flowers are blocked in gold around these lettering-pieces. Signed 'IS' in gold as a monogram at the base of the innermost mandorla. The spine has decorated panels at the head and at the tail, blocked in gold. The title: '| Odes

and Sonnets | ' is blocked in relief along the spine, inside a cartouche, with fillets and decoration around its perimeter.

Ball, *VPB* p. 91, p. 162.

616 Staples

Shakespeare, William. *The works. Illustrated.* 7 vols. London: John Tallis & Company, London & New York, [1850–51].
All volumes are the same size:
192 × 286 × 25 mm. RB.23.b.2666.

Vol. I 16, 1–230 p., 12 plates. Plate 2 is the title page.
Vol. II. p. 231–495, 12 plates.
Vol. III. 1–300 p., 12 plates. Plate 2 is the title page.
Vol. IV. p. 301–576, 12 plates.
Vol. V. 1–254 p., 12 plates. Plate 2 is the title page.
Vol. VI. Sonnets. xxxii, p. 255–488, 12 plates.
Vol. VII. Doubtful plays. 1–262 p., 12 plates. Plate 2 is the title page.

The text of all volumes is sewn on four sawn-in cords. Gilt edges. Yellow endpapers and pastedowns. Red morocco horizontal-grain cloth. All the lower covers identically blocked in blind. Two fillets are blocked on the borders, with leaf and flower decoration on the corners and on the sides. The upper covers are blocked identically in gold only. Two fillets blocked on the borders in gold. There is an inner border of interlocking leaves and stems. An angel blowing a trumpet is blocked on each top corner. The words: ' | Tallis's Illustrated Shakspere [sic]. | ' are blocked in gold around a memorial statue of Shakespeare. The words: ' | Macready Testimonial | ' are blocked below this. Near the tail, on the left and right, two classically dressed ladies hold a laurel wreath over a bust of Shakespeare, blocked at the centre, within an oval frame. Below this, the imprint: ' | J.Tallis & Co. London & New York. | ' is blocked within a cartouche. Signed ' | Staples Sc. | ' in gold to the left of the bust of Shakespeare. The spines identically blocked in gold. From the head, the decoration is: two fillets; the tomb of Shakespeare, with the bust of Shakespeare within; the words: ' | The | complete | works | of Shakspere [sic] | [two fillets] | Illustrated | '; a bust of Shakespeare within a wreath; the words: ' | Dedicated | to | W. Macready Esq. | '; two fillets; a statue of Shakespeare; the words: ' | Macready Testimonial' | [two fillets] | 'Div. I [–VII] | Price 8/6' | [fillet] | 'J. Tallis & Co. | London & New York | ' blocked at the tail.

Another set is at 011768.dd.1. Six volumes./Divisions. (Wants vol. VII.) The size of all vols. is 192 × 286 × 23 mm. Pagination for each volume is the same as above. Yellow endpapers and pastedowns. Blue morocco horizontal-grain cloth. The same design as RB.23.b.2666. above is blocked on the covers and the spines of each volume.

617 Staples, Thomas PLATE LXXXII

Acheta Domestica *pseud.* [i.e. L. M. Budgen.] *Episodes of insect life.* 3 vols. London: Reeve, Benham, and Reeve, 1849–51.
C.109.c.4.

First series. xviii, 320 p., 1 plate. Reeve, Benham, and Reeve, King William Street, Strand, 1849. Printer: Reeve, Benham, and Reeve, Lithographers, Printers and Publishers, King William Street, Strand. 137 × 207 × 22 mm.

Second series. xvi, 326 p., 1 plate. Reeve, Benham, and Reeve, King William Street, Strand. Printer: Printed by Reeve, Benham, and Reeve, Heathcote Court, Strand. 138 × 207 × 22 mm.

Third series. xvii, 434 p., 1 plate. Reeve and Benham, Henrietta Street, Covent Garden. Printer: Printed by Reeve and Nichols, Heathcote Court, Strand. With eighteen pages of publisher's titles bound at the end. 138 × 207 × 32 mm

All volumes have gilt edges, and yellow endpapers and pastedowns. On the upper pastedown of each volume is a bookplate, with the printing: ' | J. Edwin Couchman, | Hurstpierpoint. | ' The upper endpaper of each volume has the dedication: ' | Presented | to the | Revd Edward Fox | by some of his | affectionate pupils. | [rule] | Royal Armagh School. | Decr 11th 1852. | ' The half title page of each volume is blind stamped: ' | Down House | Hurstpierpoint | '. Volume 3 has a binder's ticket on the lower pastedown: ' | Bound by | Westleys & Co. | Friar Street, | London. | ' Blue rib vertical-grain cloth. Both covers and spine of each volumes are identically blocked in gold. Two gold fillets are blocked on the borders of the covers. The main block shows a 'teacher' insect, seated on a mound at the centre. His left 'hand' holds an open book on his left thigh, his right 'hand' is upraised, making a point. The 'teacher' is dressed in knee breeches and stockings, with a waistcoat, a neckcloth, and a long-tailed coat. Two other books are on the ground in front of him. Around and above the 'teacher', various other insects are gathered listening – on foliage to the left, and on branches on the right. Above the 'teacher' insect, near the centre head, a spider's web, with a spider in the middle, straddles the foliage to left and right. Signed ' | Staples Sc. | ' in gold at the base of the ground, near the two books. A quotation is blocked at the base: ' | He filled their listening ears with wondrous things | '. The spines are blocked in gold and relief. From the head downwards, the decoration is: two gold fillets; the words: ' | First [Second; Third] Series. | '; a plant is blocked up the spine, with a butterfly blocked near the head, and two large leaves underneath; the title: ' | Episodes | of | Insect | Life | ' blocked in relief in fanciful letters within the two leaves; a caterpillar is blocked on a stem near the tail. Volume 3 has: ' | Reeve & Co. | ' blocked in gold near the tail; two gold fillets blocked at the tail.

This copy was purchased on the 18.12.1947. The copyright copy, date stamped: '6 DE[CEMBER 18] 50' is at BL shelfmark 1258.f.10–12. It is in a BM quarter leather binding.

Ball, *VPB* p. 98, ref. 50. McLean, *VPBB* p. 42. Morris & Levin, *APB* p. 32 no. 40. States the cover designer as Thomas Staples. Oldfield, *BC* no. 50.

618 Sulman, Thomas PLATE LXXXIII

Kalidasa. Sakuntala. English. *Sakoontala; or, the lost ring; an Indian drama, translated into English prose and verse, from the*

Sanskrit of Kalidasa by Monier Williams, M.A., Professor of Sanskrit at the East India College, Haileybury, formerly Boden Scholar in the University of Oxford. Hertford: Printed and published by Stephen Austin, Bookseller to the East India College, 1855. Printed by Stephen Austin, Hertford. xxxvii, 128 p., 14 plates. With twenty-five pages of notes and one page of publisher's advertisement bound at the rear.
175 × 230 × 35 mm. C.30.h.8.

The note at the end of the 'List of Illustrations' reads: 'The Pictorial Borders to the Illustrations, as well as that round each page, and the other ornaments and decorations, are taken from MSS. in the British Museum and in the Library of the East India House. They have been designed by Mr T. Sulman Jun., and engraved by Mr George Measom.'

Gilt edges. Light yellow endpapers and pastedowns: each has the same oriental decorated border, and extended central lozenge. Light-green morocco diagonal-grain cloth. Both covers are blocked in gold and relief with the same design, with the exception of the central roundels. On the outermost border is a repeating pattern of semi-circles linked with alternating flower crowns. Inside this, a single fillet is blocked in gold. Signed in relief at the base, within the single gold fillet: 'T. Sulman Invt'; and, on the right: 'Knights and Keeling Sc.' Inside this, there is a border of circles and oriental-style cartouches blocked alternately in gold, with the decoration inside each being blocked in relief. Inside this, there is a border of double fillets, interlocking at intervals into hexagons. On the corners of the inner rectangle, there are oriental patterns blocked in relief within gold lettering-pieces. The curling border of the central panel is of knotted single straps, with balls in the knots. Inside the central panel, intertwined flowers and stems are blocked in gold. Above the central roundel, the word: '| Sakoontala |' is blocked in relief inside a gold lettering-piece, with scroll-like ends. Below the central roundel, the words: '| or the | lost ring |' are blocked in relief in the same way as for 'Sakoontala'. The borders of the central roundel have repeating semi-circular patterns blocked in gold. On the lower cover, these are linked to elaborate oriental decoration, which has at its very centre two interlocking squares, with decoration inside blocked in relief.

On the upper cover, the central roundel shows a man on a terrace holding out a ring in his right hand, offering it to a woman clasping her hands to her chest. There is a fountain, and other plants, behind a terrace wall.

The spine is fully blocked in gold. It has two thin gold fillets blocked on the perimeter. The decoration from the head is: a seated Buddha-like figure with four arms, blocked inside an oriental-style frame, which is formed by two gold fillets; two four-armed crowned figures, who sprout from flower heads; the title: '| Sakoontala |' is blocked in gold and in relief inside a gold lettering-piece, shaped as a cartouche, running up the spine; leaves and flowers are blocked in gold around the cartouche; an oriental figure '| Kan wa |' is blocked in the oriental panel formed by two gold fillets near the tail; the imprint: '| Hertford. | Stephen Austin |' is blocked in gold within a frame formed by a single gold fillet at the tail. This is the copyright copy, date stamped '7 NO[VEMBER 18] 56'.

Another copy of this work is at BL C.68.i.15. Date stamped 13.2.1932. 170 × 223 × 42 mm. This has a deluxe binding by Joseph Zaehnsdorf, 1814–1886. Donated by E. Zaehnsdorf to the BM in January 1932. E. Zaehnsdorf suggests that this volume was exhibited at the International Exhibition of 1862. Gilt edges, gauffered. Silk endpapers. Vellum pastedowns. Brown morocco turn-ins decorated with red and green onlays to form cartouches which are blocked in gold, with circles blocked in gold between them. The upper pastedown is elaborately tooled with small gold decoration and squares and diamonds. On the upper pastedown: '| Bound by Zaehnsdorf |' is blocked in gold near the tail. Both covers are blocked identically. Gold fillets and elaborate small gold decoration is blocked on the borders around the recessed central panel, which has oriental shaped corners. Within the central panel, a white leather onlay is blocked with a repeating pattern of quatrefoils and diamonds, delineated by a single gold fillet. Diamonds of blue, red and green onlays have small decoration blocked in gold within them. The spine is blocked in gold. Elaborate small gold decoration throughout. There are recessed oriental panels above and below the centre, with white leather onlays within the panels, together with blue and brown diamond-shaped onlays, with small decoration blocked in gold on them. On the centre of the spine a green leather onlay contains the title: '| Sakoontala |' blocked in gold in fanciful letters. A red leather onlay surrounds the green, with two gold fillets on its borders, and small decoration blocked in gold between the fillets.

Ball, *VPB* p. 92. McLean, *VBD* pp. 172–173. McLean, *VPBB* p. 57. Shows a copy in dark green leather, with the same blockwork as this copy.

619 Sutcliffe, J.

Williamson, J., Mrs. *Hymns for The Household of Faith, and Lays of the better Land . . .* London: Wertheim, Mackintosh, and Hunt, 24 Paternoster Row, and 23, Holles Street, Cavendish Square, 1861. London: Wertheim, Mackintosh, and Hunt, 24 Paternoster Row, and 23, Holles Street, Cavendish Square. xxvii, 419 p.
125 × 190 × 30 mm. 11602.d.18.

Brown endpapers and pastedowns. Green pebble-grain cloth. Both covers are blocked identically, in blind on the lower, in gold on the upper. Three fillets are blocked on the borders. The rest of the cover is blocked with a design of combined flowers, leaves, cornstalks. Winding around the design is a pennant which supports the plants. The title words: '| Hymns | for the | Household of | Faith |' are blocked in gold in gothic letters within the pennant. Signed 'J. Sutcliffe, Leeds' in gold at the base of the design. The name is 'woven' into the tendrils. The spine has two gold fillets blocked at the head and at the tail. The title: '| Hymns | for the | Household | of | Faith |' is blocked in gold in gothic letters, together with two small blocks of plants and roots.

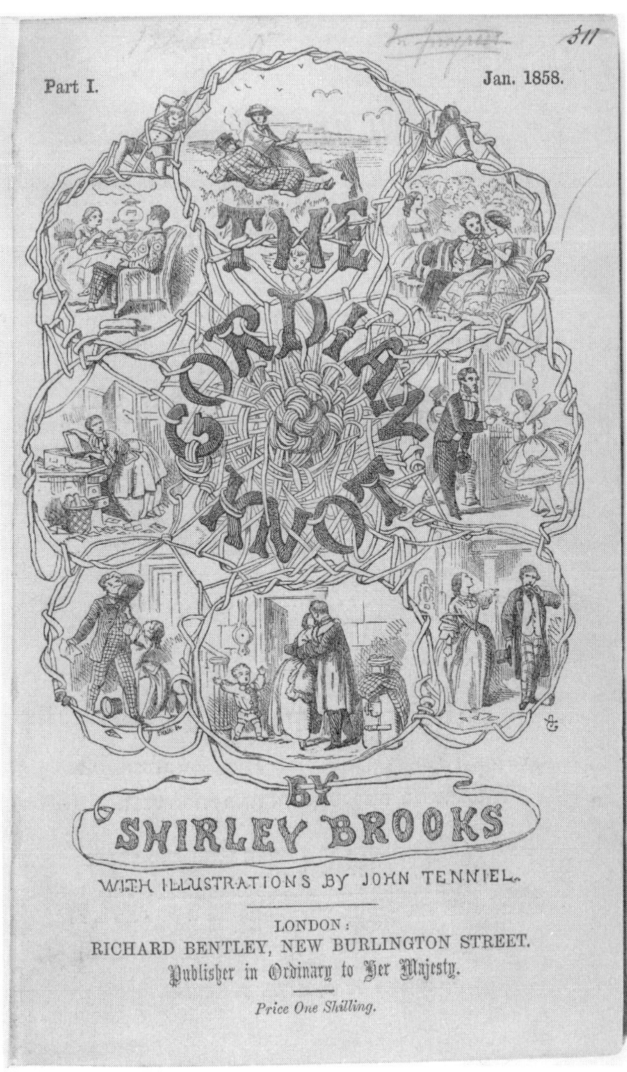

FIG. 77

620 Tenniel, John FIG. 77

Brooks, Shirley. *The Gordian Knot. A Story of Good and of Evil. With illustrations by John Tenniel.* London: Richard Bentley, New Burlington Street, 1860. London: Savill and Edwards, Printers, Chandos Street. viii, 376 p., 22 plates.
139 × 230 × 34 mm. 12622.f.9.

Text issued in parts with paper covers, between January 1858 – Part I; and December 1859 – Parts X. XI. XII. All parts priced at One Shilling, except the last three, issued together, price Three Shillings. The paper covers are bound in sequence. The verso of each part's upper cover and the recto and verso of each lower cover contain publisher's titles and advertisements. The upper cover of each part shows an engraving, signed with Tenniel's monogram, bottom right; and 'Swain Sc.', bottom left. The engraving shows a series of string knots on the centre, with the title: '| The | Gordian Knot |' all tied up by the string. The words: '| Gordian Knot |' are printed in a circle around the centre, attached to the strings. The strings loosen outwards to form eight panels, each of which contains a scene from the contents.

621 Tymms, William Robert

Tennyson, Alfred. *The May Queen.* London: Published March 1st. 1861, by Day & Son, Lithographers to the Queen. 6 Gate St. Lincoln's Inn Fields, 1861. 22 p.
205 × 272 × 15 mm. 1347.i.18.

Text printed on rectos of pages only. On page 2: 'Illuminated by Mrs. W. H. Hartley. Chromolithographed by W. R. Tymms.'

Gilt edges. Original yellow endpapers bound in. Green morocco horizontal-grain cloth. Both covers blocked identically in blind and relief on the lower, and in gold and relief on the upper. The upper cover has two fillets blocked in blind on the borders. Inside this, a border of hatch is blocked in blind and in relief. Another gold border fillet provides a frame for a pattern of dotted leaf, stem and flower decoration, which is denser on the corners and on the centre head and the centre tail. The whole forms an oval, and, from the centre tail, stems rise up to form a triangular-shaped cluster of dotted leaves, stems and flowers on the centre. Signed: '| W. R. Tymms Inv. et Del. |' in gold on the centre tail. The spine is blocked in gold. A single gold fillet blocked on each side of the spine forms a cartouche, ending in a dotted leaf head and tail. The words: '| The May Queen |' are blocked in gold in gothic letters within the cartouche.

The Day & Son catalogue bound at the rear describes this work as: 'Twenty-two pages, 4to. elegantly bound, price 21s.'

622 Tymms, William Robert

Hitopadesa. *Indian Fables, from the Sanskrit of the Hitopadesa. Translated and illustrated in colours from original designs by Florence Iacomb. Chromo-lithographed by W. R. Tymms.* London: Day & Son. Lithographers to the Queen, 6, Gate St. Lincolns Inn Fields, [1862]. [29 p.] Each leaf is printed on the recto only. With four pages of publisher's titles bound at the end.
195 × 251 × 15 mm. 12304.h.1.

On page two of the publisher's titles: 'The Work will consist of 24 pages, with appropriate borders of Flowers and Plants &c., and 12 subjects illustrating the Fables, all executed in the best style of Chromo-lithography. Size, 4to. (to be handsomely bound), price 2l. 2s.'

Gutta percha binding. Gilt edges. Yellow endpapers and pastedowns. Green morocco horizontal-grain cloth. Both covers blocked identically in blind and relief on the lower, and in gold, in blind and in relief on the upper. On the borders, the following are blocked: 1. a repeating stem, leaf and dot pattern; 2. a chevron pattern in relief, within a gold fillet; 3. a wide border in gold, with plants, leaves and flowers blocked inside in relief. This border also contains medallions – two at the head, and at the tail, and three on each side. Each medallion is formed by two fillets; clockwise from the head they show: a horse; a bird, a boar, a turtle, a dodo-like bird, an elephant, a wolf, a cat, a deer, a snake. On the borders of the inner rectangle, two gold fillets are blocked, with a repeating pattern of 'semi-circles and dots' blocked in gold between the fillets. On the corners of the inner rectangle, a pattern of leaves is blocked in relief. There is a large

central diamond. It has four borders: 1. a gold fillet; 2. gold hatch leaves; 3. chevrons blocked in relief within a gold fillet. 4. a recessed fillet, blocked in blind. The diamond on the centre is a gold lettering-piece. It has a border of semi-circles and dots, blocked in relief. The title: '| Indian | Fables | From the Sanscrit | of the | Hitopadesa |' is blocked in relief, with stems and small leaves attached to several of the letters. Signed at the centre tail: 'W. R. Tymms Inv.' in gold. The spine is blocked in gold. A cartouche is blocked along the spine. It is formed by two fillets, with repeating dots blocked between them. The title: '| Indian Fables |' is blocked in gold along the spine with small stem and leaf decoration attached to each letter.

623 Unsigned UK

The pensive wanderer, a poem, in four cantos; with Nero and the fire of Rome, an ode; and other poems. By Cambria's Bard. London: Published by the Author, 55, Upper Berkeley Street, Portman Square, [1830]. Cirencester: Printed by Bailey and Jones. xv, 140 p.

108 × 175 × 14 mm. 11642.a.49.

Yellow endpapers and pastedowns. Green dot and rib diagonal-grain cloth. Ribbon embossed with a repeating pattern of stems, leaves and flowers. Both covers are blocked identically in blind. There are two fillets blocked on the borders, which are intertwined, forming straps on the sides, and on each corner. On the inner corners, leaf and stem decoration is blocked in relief. On the upper cover, the title: '| The | pensive | wanderer |' is blocked in gold on the centre. The spine is not blocked.

624 Unsigned UK

The Juvenile Forget Me Not. A Christmas and New Year Gift, or birthday present. Edited by Mrs S. C. Hall. London: Frederick Westley and A. H. Davis, Stationers' Hall Court, 1832. London: J. Westley and Co. Ivy Lane. 221 p., 5 plates. With three pages of publisher's titles bound at the end.

Renier Collection.

The Museum of Childhood copy.

White endpapers and pastedowns. Green dyed leather. Both covers identically embossed with border decoration and a neo-classical design. A medallion is blocked just below the centre, showing four horses and their driver holding the reins – riding out of the sun. Signed 'De La Rue & Co. London' within a cartouche near the base. The spine is blocked in blind. The title and the imprint are blocked in gold within panels.

625 Unsigned UK

Budden, Maria Elizabeth. *Chit chat; or short tales in short words. Third edition enlarged. With sixteen engravings.* London: John Harris, St. Paul's Churchyard, 1834. London: Printed by Samuel Bentley, Dorset street, Fleet Street. 242 p. With six pages of publisher's titles bound at the end.

110 × 140 × 25 mm. Renier Collection.

The Museum of Childhood copy.

White endpapers and pastedowns. Red rib horizontal-grain. Ribbon embossed with a hexagon pattern. The upper cover has 'Chit-Chat' blocked on the centre in gold within a cartouche.

626 Unsigned UK

Trench, Frederick Fitzwilliam. *Short notes on the Holy Scriptures, with references: intended for daily use in families. Chiefly selections from various authors.* Dublin: Richard Moore Tims, 85, Grafton Street. James Nisbet, and Simpkin and Marshall, London; Waugh and Innes, Edinburgh, 1834. [1], 362 p.

140 × 225 × 27 mm. 3128.f.42.

Rebound 1998. No original endpapers or pastedowns. Brown pebble-grain cloth. Ribbon embossed with a pattern of 'four tool handles', stars and circles. The tool handles form 'squares', with the five-point stars in the middle, and the small circles at the end of each handle. No blocking on the covers. No original spine. [For another example of this ribbon embossing, see BL 942.a.3. Sam Belson. Simpkin and Marshall . . . 1836.]

627 Unsigned UK

Fragments from the history of John Bull. These things are an allegory. Edinburgh: William Blackwood & Sons; and T. Cadell, Strand, London, 1835. Edinburgh: Printed by Ballantyne & Co. Paul's Work. 242 p. With two pages of publisher's titles bound at the end.

110 × 176 × 20 mm. 12316.ee.23.

The bookplate of John Jocelyn is pasted onto the verso of the front endpaper. The endpapers are printed in brown, with a vertical white line pattern, which have diamonds between the lines to form a diagonal pattern. Green rib vertical-grain cloth. Ribbon embossed with hexagons across both covers and spine. There is no blocking on the covers. On the spine the title: 'John Bull' is blocked in gold near the head. A decorative device is blocked in gold above and below the title. The same rib vertical-grain and hexagons is on a copy of Scott's 'Poetical works' – BL shelfmark 11609.de.16–26.

628 Unsigned UK

The world: a poem. In Six Books. London: Thomas Hurst, St. Paul's Churchyard. 1835. [London]: Thoms, Printer, Warwick Square. 275 p.

142 × 233 × 21 mm. 991.i.24.

Original yellow endpaper bound at the front. Maroon rib vertical-grain cloth. Ribbon embossed on both covers with a pattern of beaded stems, leaves, groups of small flowers and larger

single flowers. No blocking on the covers. Spine missing. Rubbing available.

629 Unsigned UK

Sam Belson, or a visit to the beach. A Tale for Young Persons, in which the most striking and interesting phenomena peculiar to the sea-side, are familiarly explained . . . London: Simpkin, Marshall, and Co., Stationers'-Hall Court, 1836. [London]: J. Haddon and Co. Doctors' Commons. vii, 188 p.

93 × 145 × 15 mm. 942.a.3.

Text sewn on three sawn-in cords. Original yellow endpapers bound at the front. Green pebble-grain cloth. Ribbon embossed with a pattern of 'four tool handles', stars and circles. The spine is blocked in gold near the head. The title: '| Sam | Belson |' is blocked in gold, between two small flower and leaf blocks, which are also in gold. [For another example of this embossed pattern, see BL 3128.f.42. F.F. Trench. Short notes on the Holy Scriptures . . . Simpkin and Marshall, 1834.]

630 Unsigned UK

England. House of Commons. *Lists of Members. An atlas of the Divisions of the House of Commons, in the second session of the fourth Parliament of William IV, 1836; exhibiting at one view, the votes of each Member on every question. To which is prefixed, a key to the Divisions, containing the subject and substance of each, with the majority and minority. Arranged from the Authorized Lists. To be continued Annually.* London: Published by Simpkin, Marshall, and Co., Stationer's-Hall Court, 1836. [London]: Printed by Mills and Son, Gough-Square, Fleet-Street. Unpaginated. [iv, [6], B4–H4]

241 × 321 × 10 mm. 8133.k.12.

Brown rib diagonal-grain cloth. Ribbon embossed with a repeating pattern of stems, leaves and flowers, on both covers and spine. Blocked in gold on the centre of the upper cover: '| Atlas | of the | Divisions 1836. |'. No blocking on the spine. Rubbing available.

631 Unsigned UK

Stranger. *A six days' tour through the Isle of Man; or, a passing view of its present natural, social, and political aspect. By a Stranger. 1836.* Douglas: Published and sold by William Dillon, Bookseller. Sold also by Marples and Co., and Lacey, Liverpool; Thompsons, Manchester; Simpkin Marshall, and Co., London; and Cummins, Dublin, [1836]. Liverpool: D. Marples, Printers, Liverpool. v, 183 p., 1 plate.

110 × 181 × 15 mm. 10360.bbb.36.

White endpapers and pastedowns. Maroon pebble-grain cloth. Also embossed with a repeating pattern, across both covers and spine, of 'tool-handles'. These are set opposite each other, to form squares. Between adjoining squares is a small five pointed star. Rubbing available.

632 Unsigned UK

Garnet, afterwards, Godwin, Catherine Grace. *Alicia Gray; or, to be useful is to be happy.* London: John W. Parker, West Strand, 1837. London: John. W. Parker, St. Martin's Lane. 126 p., 2 plates, the frontispiece and the title page. With eight pages of publisher's titles bound at the end.

98 × 155 × 12 mm. 942.a.26.

Text sewn on two tapes. Yellow endpapers and pastedowns. Red rib horizontal-grain cloth. Ribbon embossed with a pattern of 'crazy lines', with the ends of lines forming into straps, and also into 'S' shapes. Diamond shapes are embossed, with trefoil leaves (so small as to resemble dots) on each point of the diamond. The spine is missing.

633 Unsigned UK

Roberts, W. H. *The Scottish ale-brewer: a practical treatise on the art of brewing ales according to the system practised in Scotland. In which are detailed, a simplified process of sparging (illustrated by an engraving of a newly invented self-acting sparging machine), and the method of conducting slow fermentation; containing also four tables of original gravities and altenuations, both real and apparent, with the quantity of proof spirit per cent. in the ales of the various Edinburgh brewers, ascertained by means of partial evaporation.* Edinburgh: Oliver and Boyd; Simpkin, Marshall, and Co. London, 1837. [Edinburgh]: Edinburgh Printing Company. 160, [7] p. With sixteen pages of publisher's advertisements and four pages of advertisements bound at the end.

140 × 225 × 25 mm. 1037.l.34.

Green pebble-grain cloth. Ribbon embossed with a pattern of four-pointed stars and single dots at each corner of each star. No blocking on the covers. No original spine. Rubbing available.

634 Unsigned UK

Whowell, T. *A classification of the essentials of the Christian faith or a key to the Old and New Testament: with the fulfilment in succession, of the Prophecies of Our Blessed Saviour. In one volume . . . With the past and present state of the Jews, and the appearance of their restoration.* London: Printed for the Author By Thomas Curson Hansard, Paternoster Row, 1837. [London]: Thomas Curson Hansard, Paternoster Row. xxx, 732 p. 1 fold-out coloured map.

143 × 224 × 62 mm. 3128.g.1.

The map is entitled: '| A Comprehensive Family Map of the Holy Land, | with Chart of Generations. |' The chart is entitled: '| Genealogical Chart of Scripture History, | showing the lineal descent of most of the principal characters mentioned in sacred writ, from the creation of Adam to the birth of Our Saviour. |'

[No original endpapers or pastedowns.] Blue diaper-grain cloth. Both covers blocked identically in blind, with a curling leaf and stem pattern on each corner. Groups of two semi-

circular fillets join to form a central frame with leaves blocked on the inside where the fillets meet. The spine is blocked in gold only. The title words: '| The | essentials | of the | Christian | faith. |' are blocked in gold within a square panel formed by a single thick gold fillet.

635 Unsigned UK

Story, Robert. *The outlaw; a drama in five acts.* London: Simpkin, Marshall, and Co., 1839. Printed by J. Tasher, Bookseller, etc, Skipton. 176 p.
110 × 182 × 15 mm. 841.b.22.

Original green endpaper bound at the front. Blue rib diagonal-grain cloth. Ribbon embossed with a 'zig-zag' pattern, resembling stems and leaves. The embossing is across both covers and spine. A printed paper label pasted along the spine. Rubbing available. [Rebound in 1980s, paper laminated.]

636 Unsigned UK

Jesse, Edward. *A summer's day at Hampton Court, being a guide to the Palace and gardens; with an Illustrative Catalogue of the Pictures according to the new arrangement, including those in the apartments recently opened to the public.* London: John Murray, Albemarle Street, 1840. London: Printed by William Clowes and Sons, Stamford Street. viii, 142 p. With one page of publisher's titles bound at the end.
110 × 175 × 15 mm. 010349.w.24.

Text sewn on three sawn-in cords. White endpapers and pastedowns. Rib diagonal-grain cloth. Ribbon embossed with a repeating pattern of diamonds. No blocking on covers. Rubbing available.

637 Unsigned UK

Egan, Pierce. *Fistiana; or, the oracle of the ring. Comprising a defence of British boxing; a brief history of pugilism, from the earliest ages to the present period; practical instructions for training; together with chronological tables of prize battles, from 1780 to 1840 inclusive, alphabetically arranged with the issue of each event. Scientific hints on sparring, &c. &c. &c.* London: Published by Wm. Clement Jun. At the Office of Bell's Life in London, 170, Strand, and to be had of all booksellers and newspaper agents throughout the kingdom, 1841. [London]: Whiting, Beaufort House, Strand. viii, 311 p., 5 plates.
104 × 167 × 20 mm. 7923.d.1.

Gilt edges. Yellow endpapers and pastedowns. Green rib horizontal-grain cloth. Both covers blocked identically in blind, with a 'French' pattern of curling stems and leaves, which form an oval. On the lower cover, the gold central vignette shows a basket full of wine bottles. On the ground in front of the basket, boxing gloves, a watch and a wine bottle are blocked in gold. This vignette is a copy of the engraving printed on page viii, at the end of the Address. On the upper cover, the central gold vignette shows two boxers ready to fight. This is similar to the illustration of two boxers opposite page 306, entitled: 'First positions setting to.'.

638 Unsigned UK

PLATE LXXXIV

Tattersall, George. *Sporting architecture.* London: Published Sept. 29th 1841 by R. Ackermann, Eclipse Sporting Gallery, 191 Regent Street, [1841]. London: Printed by Walter Spiers, 17 North Audley Street. vi, 97 p., 20 plates.
220 × 288 × 22 mm. 786.l.32.

Binder's ticket on lower pastedown: '| Bound by | Runting, | 7, Goldsmith-row, | Fleet Street. |' Blue rib vertical-grain cloth. Both covers have the same design blocked in blind on the borders. There are four fillets blocked on the borders: nos. 1 & 4 are thin, nos. 2 & 3 are thick. On the upper cover, the central vignette is blocked in gold. It shows a classical portico, with a pediment. The pediment has a classical goddess atop it, a bow held at the ready. On the left and the right of the pediment, a stag is blocked. The pediment is supported at its edges by four fluted columns. There are steps blocked at the base, signifying an entrance. Within the portico, at the centre, the words: '| Sporting | architecture | by | G. Tatters. | 1841. |' are blocked in gold. Unsigned. Spine missing.

Packer, *BVL* p. 130.

639 Unsigned UK

Ramsay, John. *Eglington Park Meeting and other poems* . . . Sixth edition. Edinburgh: Stirling, Kenney & Co.; J. Duncan, London; David Robertson, Glasgow; H. Crawford and Son, Kilmarnock, 1843. Kilmarnock: Printed by H. Crawford and Son. 256 p.
107 × 175 × 24 mm. 11643.aa.50.

On the title page: 'Price Three Shillings and Sixpence.'

Original yellow endpaper bound in at the front. Brown rib vertical-grain cloth. No blocking on either cover. The spine has the words: '| Ramsay. | Poems |' blocked in gold near the head. Above and below this, a small decorative device is blocked in gold.

640 Unsigned UK

The Good Shunammite ii Kings, Chap iv, v. vvvi. [All letters in gothic style, printed in colours.] [London]: [Longman Brown Green and Longmans], [1847]. xxi p.
117 × 170 × 15 mm. C30.b.2.

All the pages are chromolithographed. The colophon reads: '| This book | was completed | for Longman | Brown Green | and Longmans the last day | of October at the Studio of | Lewis Gruner in the year | of our Lord MDCCCXLVIII. |'

Gilt edges. Marbled endpapers and pastedowns (the same as BL C.72.a.7.). Black 'papier mache' covers, with an identical design. The edges and turn-ins of the covers are blocked in gold

with the same patterns as for C.72.a.7.; possibly the same binding company. Executed in the 'monastic style' (Cundall, cited in McLean, VBD, p. 210). Each cover is divided by rules into nine panels. The four corner panels have circles and ovals. The panels at the head and at the tail contain vines and grapes. The panels on each side have vines, grapes and one medallion. The medallion on the left has the head of a lady; the one on the right has the head of a bearded man. The largest panel is the central rectangle, with vine leaves and grapes surrounding the central circle. This has a border of joined trefoil leaves and stems. Within, the title: '| The | Good | Shunammite | 2 Kings .iv.8. |' is blocked in relief within a ribbon. The spine is of black leather. The title: '| The Good Shunammite |' is blocked in relief within a cartouche along its centre. Vine leaf and strap decoration is blocked in relief above and below the cartouche.

Ball, *VPB* p. 144. McLean, *VBD* pp. 92, 210. '. . .probably printed at the establishment of Owen Jones . . .'

641 Unsigned UK

Templeton, Andrew. *Poems on the hopes and fears, the joys and the sorrows, of man.* Stirling: Printed in the Observer Office, 1847. 156 p.

114 × 194 × 10 mm. 11644.eeee.7.

Text sewn on two sawn-in cords. Yellow endpapers and pastedowns. Green rib diagonal-grain cloth. Ribbon embossed with a repeating 'grapevine' pattern, showing clusters of grapes. The words: '| Poems | by | A. Templeton. |' are blocked in gold on the upper cover. Rubbing available.

642 Unsigned UK

Brooks, Henry F. *The Victories of the Sutlej, A Prize Poem, to which the Vice-Chancellor' first prize was awarded at Trinity College, Dublin, in Hilary Term, 1847. Together with The Sailor's Christmas Eve, and Other Pieces.* [The arms of Trinity College are printed below the title.] Dublin: Arthur B. Keene, 6, College-Green. Longman &Co., London. Beilby, Birmingham. Deardon, Nottingham. Metcalf, East Retford, 1848. Dublin: Printed at the University Press, By M. H. Gill. vx, 90 p.

108 × 175 × 10 mm. 11645.d.27.

Text sewn on three sawn-in cords. Gilt edges. Yellow endpapers and pastedowns. Binder's ticket on lower pastedown: '| Cavenagh | Bookbinder, | 26, Wicklow St | Dublin. |' Dark red rib diagonal-grain cloth, with light red horizontal stripes. Both covers identically blocked in gold on the borders and on the corners. Two fillets are blocked in gold on the borders, and a single leaf outline blocked in gold on each corner. The lower cover central vignette shows a lozenge as a gold lettering-piece with a 'strap and stem' decoration blocked in relief within it. The upper cover central vignette is blocked in gold. A frame is formed by six curved broad leaves, blocked in pairs at the head, the tail and the sides. On the centre, the title: '| The | Victories | of | The Sutlej |' is blocked in gold. The spine is blocked in gold and in relief. At the tail, the head of a flagpole supports a pennant-shaped gold lettering-piece, which is blocked in horizontal gold hatch, and runs along the spine to the head. The title: '| The Victories of The Sutlej &c |' is blocked in relief within the pennant.

643 Unsigned UK

Gatty, Alfred. *The bell: its origin, history, and uses.* London: George Bell, 186, Fleet Street, 1848. Printed by J. C. Platt, Sheffield. [1], ix, 117 p.

115 × 193 × 12 mm. 7895.b.20.

Yellow endpapers and pastedowns. Binder's ticket on lower pastedown: '| Bound by | Westleys & | Clark. | London. |' Red moiré rib vertical-grain cloth. Both covers are blocked identically in blind on the borders and on the corners. Groups of three bells, their clappers showing, are blocked on each corner and on the centre head and on the centre tail. Pairs of bells, their clappers showing, are blocked on each side at the centre. All the bells are joined by bell ropes. A single fillet, blocked in blind, forms the central rectangle. On the centre of the of the upper cover, the title: '| The bell. |' is blocked in gold. The spine is blocked in gold and in blind. Groups of four fillets in blind divide the spine into five panels. The title: '| The | bell. |' is blocked in gold within the second panel.

644 Unsigned UK

Liturgies. *The Book of Common Prayer, and administration of The Sacraments and other rites and ceremonies of the Church, according to the use of the United Church of England and Ireland* . . . London: Printed by G. E. Eyre and W. Spottiswoode, Printers to the Queen's Most Excellent Majesty, and sold at their warehouse, 189 Fleet Street, 1848. Unpaginated [A12–Y12, Z6]

95 × 150 × 63 mm. C.72.a.7(1).

Text sewn on three tapes. Marbled endpapers and pastedowns. Gilt edges, with a gauffered pattern of diamonds and flower heads. Red and yellow head and tail bands. The sewing forms a hollow back. Black 'papier mache' covers and spine. Both covers have the same design. The edges and the turn-ins of the covers are blocked in gold, with a small repeating pattern showing beads, small leaves and dots. (This is the same as for C.30.b.2. The Good Shunammite.) Raised borders on each cover. The design shows a central figure of a robed Jesus, right hand upraised, surrounded by arches and plants, flowers. The spine is attached to the text block by leather. A profusion of plants and leaves grow within an arch, whose point is at the head. Near the head, the words: '| Church | Service |' are in relief within a lettering-piece running across the spine.

Ball, *VPB* p. 144.

645 Unsigned UK

Reinhold, Caroline. *The evening bell, or, the hour of relating entertaining anecdotes for dear young people. Translated from the German, by The Rev. Cosby Stopford Mangan . . .* Dublin: Printed at the University Press. James McGlashan, 21 D'Olier-Street. Wm. S. Orr & Co., 147 Strand, London, 1848. Dublin: Printed at the University Press, By M. H. Gill. xii, 243 p., 4 plates.

130 × 199 × 21 mm. 12805.h.39.

The plates are tinted lithographs. Each is inscribed: 'Designed and drawn on stone by Samuel Watson.' Parallel text, German and English.

Yellow endpapers and pastedowns. Binder's ticket on lower pastedown: '| Cavenagh | Bookbinder, | 26, Wicklow St. | Dublin. |' Brown rib vertical-grain cloth. Both covers blocked identically in blind on the borders and on the corners. Two fillets are blocked on the borders, the outer thick, the inner thin. Curling stem and leaf decoration is blocked on each corner. The upper cover central vignette is blocked in gold. It shows a rectangular panel, formed by a thick fillet. Ribbons and jewels are shown tied to the arch at the top of the panel. A shell is blocked at the base of the panel. Below the arch, a country scene is blocked, showing a lady dancing to a tune, which is being played on a wind instrument by a figure seated against a tree on the left. Another lady looks on. Unsigned. The spine is blocked in gold. A single fillet is blocked in gold on the perimeter. From the head downwards, the decoration is: a gold ornament-piece; the words: '| The | evening | bell | [rule] | German | and | English |' blocked in gold; 'branch and leaf' ornament is blocked in gold from the tail to beneath the title; this has a bird perched on top of the branches; at the tail, the imprint: '| Dublin | 1848 |' is blocked in gold.

Another copy of this work is at BL 12805.b.35. Size: 128 × 198 × 22 mm. '| With Illustrations by [Samuel] Watson |' printed in gothic letters on the title page. This copy has on the Dedication page to the Duchess of Kent as in BL 12805.h.39. This copy has the same cloth, endpapers and pastedowns, but no binder's ticket. It has the same blocking, but in blind only on both covers; the spine has the same blocking, but only the title is blocked in gold; no gold fillet on the perimeter.

646 Unsigned UK

Spring flowers and summer blossoms. The Snow Drop May Flowers The Wall Flower Almond Blossom Cowslips Primroses Daisies. London: Thomas Dean and Son. Threadneedle Street, [1849]. [London]: Dean and Son Printers, Threadneedle Street. 114 p., 11 plates.

125 × 180 × 11 mm. 12805.h.26.

Gilt edges. Yellow endpapers and pastedowns. Blue rib diagonal-grain cloth. The covers are also dyed alternately with light blue horizontal stripes: 1. straight; 2. zig-zag. The borders, the corners and the sides, the head and the tail are blocked identically, in blind on the lower cover, and in gold on the upper. The blocking has been done after casing-in. Two fillets are blocked on the borders, the outer thick, the inner thin. An 'acanthus leaf' pattern is blocked on the head, the tail, the corners, and on the sides, with small 'tassel-like 'hanging decoration blocked inside. The whole forms a central frame. (The same frame is blocked on the covers of BL 12805.h.40.) On the lower cover, the central vignette is blocked in gold. It shows an urn with two handles. On the upper cover, the title: '| Spring flowers | and | summer blossoms | for the young & good |' is blocked on the centre. On the spine, the title: '| Spring flowers & summer blossoms |' is blocked along the spine in gold.

Another work of this series is also shelved at 12805.h.26. The same title page, frontispiece, and both hand-coloured. 71 p., 6 plates. White endpapers and pastedowns. Blue morocco vertical-grain cloth. This volume has the same border blocking as above, without the tassels. No lower cover central vignette. The title is blocked in gold on the centre of the upper cover. No spine blocking.

Another work of this series is also shelved at 12805.h.26. The same title page, frontispiece, and both hand-coloured. 71 p., 6 plates. White endpapers and pastedowns. Green rib vertical-grain cloth. This volume has the same border blocking as above. No lower cover central vignette. The title is blocked in gold on the centre of the upper cover. No spine blocking.

647 Unsigned UK

Which is best; being stories about the five divisions of the world, and stories of the five senses. London: Thomas Dean and Son, Threadneedle-Street, [1849]. [London]: Dean and Son, Printers, Threadneedle-Street. 51 p., 8 plates. With two pages of publisher's titles bound at the end.

122 × 180 × 11 mm. 12805.h.40.

Gilt edges. Yellow endpapers and pastedowns. Pink rib diagonal-grain cloth. The covers are also dyed alternately with two blue horizontal stripes: 1. straight; 2. zig-zag. Both covers blocked identically on the borders. They are blocked after casing-in. The lower cover is blocked in blind, with the centre-piece blocked in gold. The centre-piece is quatrefoil-shaped, with small protruding leaf decoration blocked on the centre of each side. The upper cover is blocked in gold only. The fillets are blocked on the borders, the outer thick, the inner thin. 'Metal Strips', ending in leaves, are blocked on each corner. A pattern of 'acanthus leaves' is blocked on the head, the tail, and on the sides, with small ornaments on the centre head and on the centre tail. 'Hanging tassels' are blocked inside. (This is the same decoration as on BL 12805.h.26.) The whole forms a central frame. Within it on the upper cover, the title: '| Which is best? | Being stories about the | five senses and | divisions of the globe. |' is blocked in gold. The spine is blocked in gold. The title: '| Which is best |' is blocked in gold along the spine, with small ornament devices blocked at each end in gold.

648 Unsigned UK

Copley, Esther. *The comprehensive knitting-book. With nineteen illustrations.* London: William Tegg and Co., Cheapside, 1849.

London: Bradbury and Evans, Printers, Whitefriars. xii, 208 p.
220 × 145 × 15 mm. 871.h.68.

Red rib vertical-grain cloth. Both covers are blocked in blind with the same design on the borders and on the corners. Two fillets are blocked in blind on the borders. There is strapwork on each corner, together with a spray of leaves and berries which extend along the sides. On the upper cover, a central vignette is blocked in gold. It shows an extended knitting pattern arranged in a semi-circle, with knitting needles through the pattern. Above and within the semi-circle, the words: '| Esther Copley's | Comprehensive knitting book |' are blocked in gold. (No original spine.)

649 Unsigned UK

H., C. S. *Skyrack. A fairy tale.* London: C. Gilpin, 5, Bishopsgate Street Without, 1849. [London]: Printed for Charles Gilpin, 5, Bishopsgate Street Without. iv, 28 p., 4 plates.
120 × 183 × 7 mm. 12805.h.27.

The dedication is signed: 'C. S. H.'

Gilt edges. Light yellow endpapers and pastedowns. Green ripple horizontal-grain cloth. The covers are also dyed alternately with two black stripes: 1. straight; 2. a diagonal-line stripe. Both covers blocked identically, in blind on the lower, and in gold and blind on the upper. A single fillet is blocked on the borders, with an 'acanthus leaf' pattern blocked on the corners and on the sides, with ornamental pieces joining the leaf pattern blocked on the centre head, on the centre tail, and on the centre sides. The same central vignette is blocked on both covers. It shows a mature deciduous tree, with a group of three people blocked at its base. The spine is blocked in gold. The title word: 'Skyrack' is blocked in gold along the spine, with two ornamental pieces blocked in gold above and below the word. Unsigned.

Another copy of this work is at BL 12805.h.6. [1851]. 28 p. No plates. Bound in yellow paper wrappers. The upper cover reprints the title-page. The lower cover prints publisher's titles. With twenty-four pages of publisher's titles bound at the end.

650 Unsigned UK

Bartlett, William Henry. *The Nile boat; or, glimpses of the Land of Egypt. Second Edition.* London: Arthur Hall, Virtue, and Co., 25 Paternoster Row, 1850. Bungay: John Childs and Son. viii, 218 p., 33 plates. With fourteen pages of publisher's titles bound at the end.
174 × 258 × 34 mm. 10095.f.7.

Binder's ticket on lower pastedown: '| Bound by | Westleys & Co. | Friar Street, | London. |' Purple morocco vertical-grain-cloth. Both covers have the same design blocked in gold. There are five fillets blocked on the borders, the fourth of which is hatched in relief. The inner rectangle has three panels at the head and three at the tail. Fillets between the panels form straps. Each panel has decorative lines within. The central panel has decoration on the corners, with a fillet on each side. The central vignette shows a felucca. The spine is blocked in gold. A single gold fillet is blocked at the head and at the tail. There are four panels, one above, and three below the title letters. Each panel has two fillets on the outside, which cross to form straps on the corners, and on the middle of the sides, and then form an oval in the middle. The title words on the second panel: '| The | Nile | boat. |' are blocked in fanciful capitals, with the line emphasis within each letter being picked out in relief. The University of Durham copy has the same design on green morocco horizontal-grain cloth. It too has a Westley binder's ticket. Shelfmark: PK.1143.BAR.

651 Unsigned UK

Queen Philippa's Golden Booke. London: Printed for Arthur Hall, Virtue & Co. at 25 Paternoster Row, 1851. London: Printed by Richard Clay, Bread Street Hill. 231 p. With four pages of publisher's titles bound at the end.
122 × 191 × 23 mm. 11646.d.49.

The half title page is a chromolithograph. It is signed: 'W. Dickes, 5½ Old Fish St, Doctors' Commons.'

Text sewn on two tapes. Gilt edges. Bevelled Boards. Yellow endpapers and pastedowns. Blue net vertical-grain cloth. Both covers are blocked identically in gold. There is an elaborate tracery of thin stems, leaves and berries blocked in gold on the whole of each cover. Near the head, a crown and an inverted fleur-de-lis are blocked in gold. The title: '| Queen | Philippa's | Golden | Booke |' is blocked in gold on the centre, with stems and tendrils attached to the letters. The spine is blocked in gold. A crown is blocked in gold near the head. Underneath this, looping stems, plus leaves and berries, are blocked in gold. Unsigned.

652 Unsigned UK

Alastor *pseud.* [i.e. J. Orton.] *'Excelsior;' or, the realms of poesy.* London: Printed for the Author, 1851. London: George Woodfall and Son, Angel Court, Skinner Street. xii, 103 p.
127 × 175 × 12 mm. 11826.bbb.16.

Written on the front endpaper: '| Samuel Rogers Esq. | With | the sincere admiration of | the Author. | Leemont. July 1851. |'

Gilt edges. Yellow endpapers and pastedowns. Blue ripple vertical-grain cloth. Both covers are blocked identically in gold and relief. There is one fillet blocked in gold on the borders, with straps and stars on the corners. The title: '| Excelsior |' is blocked in relief in a pennant-shaped gold lettering-piece underneath the upper portion of a globe. From the globe, a right hand emerges, an index finger pointing to the stars and a crescent moon blocked above. The spine is not blocked. This copy purchased on the '9 DE[CEMBER 18]63'. Unsigned. The design on the covers is identical to the covers of the

William Pickering edition of 1852, which has Rogers' monogram 'WHR' blocked on the spine.

Ball, *VPB* p. 155. Cites the 1852 edition.

653 Unsigned UK

Great Exhibition of the Works of Industry of All Nations, 1851. *Official descriptive and illustrated catalogue. In three volumes. [and] Supplement.* London: Spicer Brothers, Wholesale Stationers; W. Clowes & Sons, Printers; Contractors to the Royal Commission, 29, New bridge Street Blackfriars, and at the Exhibition Building, 1851.

M:X.13–16.

The Durham Cathedral Library copy.

All four volumes are in original covers.

Gilt edges. Yellow endpapers and pastedowns. Binder's ticket on the lower pastedowns for volumes I–III: 'Bound by Edmonds and Remnant London'. The Supplementary volume has a binder's ticket on the lower pastedown: 'Bound by Westley's'. Blue morocco horizontal-grain cloth. The two borders are blocked in blind, the outer of which consists of repeating stylised leaves, blocked in relief. The inner border is of rectangles with cross bars, with a floral motif in the middle, all blocked in relief. [The rectangles are reminiscent of the gallery support cross-sections of the Great Exhibition Hyde Park building.] Within this, the central design is blocked in blind on the lower covers, in gold and in relief on the upper covers. The design shows Britannia, enthroned, holding out crowns of laurel above the heads of Europe and Asia. The figures of America and Africa look on. The words: '| OFFICIAL EXHIBITION ILLUSTRATED CATALOGUE |' are blocked in relief within the gold-blocked border at the base of the plinth. The spine lettering is profuse, and identical for all the volumes. The spines of all four volumes have identical blocking from the head to the middle. Near the head, the title words are blocked in gold: '| OFFICIAL | DESCRIPTIVE | AND ILLUSTRATED | CATALOGUE | OF THE | GREAT | EXHIBITION | 1851. |' Underneath the title, a royal coat of arms is blocked in gold. At the tail of each volume, the names: '| SPICER BROTHERS | CLOWES [&] SONS. |' are blocked in gold. The volume contents words are blocked beneath the royal coat of arms. They are:

'VOL. I. | [rule] | INDEX AND | INTRODUCTORY. | [rule] | SECTION I. | RAW MATERIALS, | CLASSES 1 TO 4. | [rule] | SECTION II. | MACHINERY, CLASSES 5 TO 10. | [rule] |'

'VOL. II. | [rule] | SECTION III. | MANUFACTURES | CLASSES 11 TO 29. | [rule] | SECTION IV. | FINE ARTS, | CLASS 30 | [rule] | COLONIES. | [rule] |'

'VOL. III. | [rule] | FOREIGN STATES. |'

'VOL. IV. | SUPPLEMENTAL. | [rule | ADDITIONAL | ILLUSTRATIONS | AND | DESCRIPTIONS | [rule] | 1ST. & 2ND. REPORTS | OF THE ROYAL | COMMISSION. | [rule] |'

The same design for the covers is used on the 'Reports by the Juries . . .', 2 vols, 1852. The Durham Cathedral Library copy of the Jury Reports is at shelfmark M.X.11–12. The British Library copy is at shelfmark 7955.e.12., and this has the original cloth upper covers used as doublures.

654 Unsigned UK

Hunt, Robert. *Hunt's hand-book to the Official Catalogues: an explanatory guide to the natural productions and manufactures of the Great Exhibition of the Industry of All Nations, 1851. Edited by Robert Hunt.* 2 vols. London: Spicer Brothers, and W. Clowes & Sons, contractors to the Royal Commission, 29, New Bridge Street Blackfriars, and at Hyde Park, [1851]. London: Printed by W. Clowes and Sons, Stamford Street and Charing Cross.

7956.b.25.

Vol. I. iv, 476 p., 1 fold-out plan. With one page of advertisements bound at the end. 108 × 170 × 25 mm. Another copy of Vol. I. is also at this shelfmark.

Vol. II. viii, 477–949 p. 108 × 170 × 25 mm.

Text sewn on three sawn-in cords for both volumes. Yellow endpapers and pastedowns for both volumes. Vol. I. has a binder's ticket on the lower pastedown: '| Bound by | Westley's & Co. | Friar Street, | London. |' Both volumes have blue morocco vertical-grain cloth. Both volumes are blocked with the same design. Both covers blocked identically in blind on the borders, corners and the sides. Two fillets are blocked on the borders, the outer thick, the inner thin. There is also an inner rectangle formed by a repeating pattern of small leaves, lines and spirals on each corner. Inside this, there are another two fillets blocked in blind. On the centre of each upper cover, the facade of the Crystal Palace is blocked vertically in gold. The spine is divided into five panels by groups of two horizontal fillets blocked in blind, with dots also in blind blocked between the fillets. The second panel has the words: '| Hunt's handbook | to the | Great Exhibition | 1851. | [rule] | Vol. I. [II.] |'. Fillets are blocked in blind at the head and at the tail.

655 Unsigned UK

MacLaurin, W. C. Augustine. *Fasti Christiani; or, rhymes on the kalendar. In six books.* London: C. Dolman, 61, New Bond Street, and 22, Pater Noster Row, 1851. [London]: Printed by T. Booker, at the Metropolitan Catholic Printing Office, 9, Rupert Street, Leicester Square. [7], 249 p.

137 × 221 × 19 mm. C.109.d.12.

On the title page, the author is stated to be: '| (Late Dean of Moray and Ross,) | Now a member of the Catholic Church. |'

Gilt edges. Yellow endpapers and pastedowns. Binder's ticket on lower pastedown: '| Bound by | E. Smith. | 5, Ivy Lane. | Paternoster Row. |' Blue morocco vertical-grain cloth. Both

covers identically blocked: in blind on lower, in gold and in blind on the upper. The borders on both covers are blocked in blind, showing ovals and small dots blocked in relief within a fillet blocked in blind. A fillet is blocked on the inner border, with single straps and small decoration blocked on each corner. The upper cover has a central vignette blocked in gold. It shows a harp, interlaced with small buds, flowers and stems. The spine is blocked in gold. From the head downwards, the decoration is: a panel formed by a single gold fillet, with stem and ornament decoration blocked inside; the title: '| Rhymes | on the | Kalendar |' blocked in gold; a fleur-de-lis is blocked above an angel; the angel holds a shield, gules, with a cross centred; a cross, with rays, is blocked within an arch, with a fleur-de-lis below; a pattern of small stems and buds is blocked at the tail. A single fillet is blocked on the spine perimeter from below the title to the tail.

656 Unsigned UK

FIG. 78

The Irish Tourist's illustrated handbook for visitors to Ireland in 1852. With numerous maps. Second edition. London: Office of the National Illustrated Library, 227, Strand. M'Glashan, Sackville Street, Dublin, 1852. London: Bradbury and Evans, Printers, Whitefriars. [1], xvi, 167 p., 6 fold-out maps. With sixteen pages of timetables bound at the front, and eighteen pages of advertisements bound at the end.
130 × 200 × 25 mm. 10390.b.13.

Yellow endpapers and pastedowns. Green wave diagonal-grain cloth. The lower cover has two fillets blocked in silver on the borders. It has a map blocked on it, in silver. It shows the route from London to Holyhead, then to Dublin Bay, with routes south to Wexford Harbour and to Cork Harbour. Town names on the map are blocked in relief, with names immediately adjacent to the map being blocked in silver. There are latitude and longitude lines on the map. The upper cover has a single silver fillet blocked on the borders. A background design features circular coils of stems and shamrocks. The central panel is shaped like a beaker, with curved rims. A lighthouse, a paddle steamship, an Irish harp and a steam engine are blocked in silver around the centre. An open book is blocked on the centre as a silver lettering-piece, and the words: '| The tourist's | handbook |' are blocked in relief within the book. The words: '| for | Ireland |' are blocked in silver below the book. The spine is not blocked.

FIG. 78

657 Unsigned UK

Useful knowledge for Children, with stories and pictures. London: Darton & Co., Holborn Hill, [1852]. 88 + 88 p., 1 plate.
106 × 168 × 14 mm. 12806.c.20.

Light blue endpapers and pastedowns. Binder's ticket on lower pastedown: '| Leighton | Son & | Hodge, | Shoe Lane | London. |' Blue ripple vertical-grain cloth. Both covers identically blocked, in blind on the lower, in silver on the upper. Two fillets are blocked on the borders. Elaborate strapwork and lattice work is blocked on each corner, and also on the centre sides. Curling stems form a 'figure of eight' shape, from the centre head to the centre tail. From this a tracery of thin stems, leaves and flowers fills the spaces inside and around the figure of eight. The spine is blocked (possibly in silver, now faded.) The words: '| Useful knowledge for children |' are blocked in blind along the spine, within an extended cartouche, with small decoration blocked at each end, at the head and the tail. [This design has all the appearance of a Leighton design.] Unsigned.

658 Unsigned UK

Catlow, Maria E. *Popular scripture zoology, containing a familiar history of the animals mentioned in the Bible.* London: Reeve and Co., Henrietta Street, Covent Garden, 1852. [London]: Printed by John Edward Taylor, Little Queen Street, Lincoln's Inn Fields. xvi, 360 p., 16 plates, With eight pages of publisher's titles bound at the end.
130 × 170 × 32 mm. 3126.cc.10.

Yellow endpapers and pastedowns. Binder's ticket on lower pastedown: '| Bound by | Westleys & Co. | Friar Street, |

London. |' Purple morocco vertical-grain cloth. Both covers blocked identically on the borders and on the corners. Two fillets are blocked on the borders, the outer thick, the inner thin. The corners have leaf and stem decoration blocked in blind. The central vignette is a pelican on both covers, blocked in blind on the lower and in gold on the upper. The spine is blocked in gold. Two plant stems are blocked the length of the spine, forming circular panels at the head and at the tail. The panel at the head contains the title: '| Popular | scripture | zoology. |' blocked in gold. The panel at the tail has the author: 'Catlow' blocked in gold. Unsigned.

659 Unsigned UK

Great Exhibition of the Works of Industry of All Nations. *Reports by the Juries on the subjects in the thirty classes into which the Exhibition was divided. In two volumes.* London: Spicer Brothers, Wholesale Stationers; W. Clowes & Sons, Printers; Contractors to the Royal Commission, Tudor Street, New bridge Street, Blackfriars, 1852. London: William Clowes and Sons, Stamford Street and Charing Cross, Printers to the Royal Commission.

7955.e.12.

Vol. I. 177 × 264 × 73 mm. ccv, 818, 16 p. The sixteen pages bound at the end are advertisements for the *Official Descriptive and Illustrated Catalogue of the Great Exhibition* ...

Vol. II. 180 × 265 × 70 mm. viii, 819–1828 p, 3 plates. With two pages of advertisements bound at the end.

Gilt edges. Original upper covers used as doublures. Blue morocco vertical-grain cloth. The upper covers of both volumes identically blocked in gold and in blind. The two borders are blocked in blind. the outer of which consists of repeating stylised leaves, blocked in relief. The inner border is of rectangles with cross bars, with a floral motif in the middle, all blocked in relief. [The :ectangles are reminiscent of the gallery support cross-sections of the Great Exhibition Hyde Park building.] The central rectangle is a single block. It shows Britannia, enthroned, holding out laurel wreaths to place on the heads of Europe and Asia, who are bowing their heads to receive them. The figures of Africa, left and of America, right, look on. The words: 'OFFICIAL EXHIBITION ILLUSTRATED CATALOGUE' are blocked in relief within the border, blocked in gold, at the base.

The Durham Cathedral Library copy is at shelfmark M.X.11–12. This has the original covers and spines. Each volume has the same binder's ticket on the lower pastedown: 'Bound by Edmonds & Remnant London'. The spines have identical blocking, with only the volume number changed. At the head: 'REPORTS | BY | THE JURIES. | [pallet] | VOL. I. [II.] |'. [Royal coat of arms.] 'EXHIBITION. | 1851. |' At the base, the words: 'SPICER BROTHERS. | CLOWES [&] SONS. |' are blocked in gold.

660 Unsigned UK

Longfellow, Henry Wadsworth. *Voices of the night; the seaside and the fireside; and other poems. Illustrated with sixty-four engravings on wood from designs by Jane E. Benham, Birket Foster, etc.* London: David Bogue, 86, Fleet Street, 1852. [London]: Henry Vizetelly, Printer & Engraver, Gough Square, Fleet Street. xii, 228 p.
138 × 210 × 30 mm. 11686.e.36.

Gilt edges. Bevelled boards. Yellow endpapers and pastedowns. Binder's ticket on rear pastedown: '| Leighton | Son & | Hodge, | Shoe Lane | London. |'. Blue ripple vertical-grain cloth. Both covers are blocked identically in gold. On the borders, there are bunches of lilies blocked within cartouches, which are formed by single fillets. These are within panels formed by two thin gold fillets. Quatrefoils and decoration are blocked in gold on each corner. There is a recessed central rectangular panel. On its corners, leaf and stem decoration is blocked in relief. The title: '| Longfellow's | Voices | of the | Night |' is blocked in gold, in rustic letters. The spine is blocked in gold. A single thin gold fillet is blocked on the perimeter. At the head and at the tail, a quatrefoil is blocked, with four fleurs-de-lis blocked inside. Four more fleurs-de-lis are blocked in gold on the outside of the quatrefoil, each being within a square formed by a single gold fillet. The words: '| Longfellow's Voices of the Night &c |' are blocked in gold in rustic letters along the spine, within a cartouche formed by a single fillet. Small leaf decoration is blocked in gold at each end of the cartouche. Unsigned.

Ball, *VPB* p. 163. Cites the 1858 edition of Routledge as having a design by Warren. Oldfield, *BC* no. 89.

661 Unsigned UK

Fern, Fanny *pseud.* [i.e. Sarah Payson Willis.] *Fern leaves from Fanny's portfolio. Illustrated by Birket Foster.* London: Ingram, Cooke, and Co., 1853. London: Printed by Levey, Robson, and Franklyn, Great New Street and Fetter Lane. 326 p., 8 plates. With two pages of publisher's titles bound at the end.
130 × 195 × 25 mm. 12354.f.19.

The plates are signed 'E. Evans Sc'.

Text sewn on two sawn-in cords. Yellow endpapers and pastedowns. Binder's ticket on lower pastedown: '| Leighton | Son & | Hodge, | Shoe Lane | London. |' Green morocco vertical-grain cloth. Both covers blocked identically in blind on the borders, on the sides, the head and the tail. A pattern of leaves is blocked on the corners and on the sides, which forms a central frame. The upper cover central vignette is blocked in gold. It shows a group of fern leaves and stems, which form a frame near the top of the vignette. The title: '| Fern leaves | from | Fanny's | Portfolio. |' is blocked in gold within this frame. Unsigned. The spine is blocked fully in gold. A single gold fillet is blocked on the perimeter. From the tail to the head, fern leaves and other small multi-flowered plants rise upwards, with their leaves hanging downwards. Near the head the title:

'| Fern | leaves | from | Fanny's portfolio. |' is blocked in gold. Unsigned. [Possibly the work of John Leighton.]

Dry, *JL* no. 372. (1860) The BL copy does not appear to have a signed design.

662 Unsigned UK

Moore, Thomas. *Lallah Rookh, an Oriental Romance. Illustrated with engravings from drawings by eminent artists.* London: Longman, Brown, Green, and Longmans, 1853. London: Spottiswoodes and Shaw, New-street Square. viii, 392 p. With twenty-four pages of publisher's titles bound at the end.
152 × 220 × 40 mm. 11656. p. 3.

Brown endpapers and pastedowns. Publisher's titles printed on upper and lower pastedowns. Bookseller's ticket embossed on the upper endpaper: '| Riddell | Bookseller | and | Stationer | Bath |'. Binder's ticket on lower pastedown: '| Bound by | Westleys & Co. | Friar Street | London. |' Navy blue rib vertical-grain cloth. The cloth is also dyed with light-blue horizontal stripes. Both covers are blocked identically in blind. Three fillets are blocked on the borders. Inside these, a wide border, with a repeating pattern of 'rings, diamond-drops, and clasps', is blocked in relief. A diamond-shaped vignette is blocked in relief on the centre of each cover. Within it, there is a medallion and a square. The spine is divided into five panels. Panels one, three, four and five, are square , formed by single 'rope-like' fillets blocked in relief. On the centres of each these panels, dragon's heads and bodies form a double 'S', blocked in relief. Panel two has the words: '| Moore's | Lallah | Rookh | [rule] | Illustrated |' blocked in gold. The imprint: '| London. | Longman & Co. |' is blocked in gold at the tail.

663 Unsigned UK

Palliser, John. *Solitary rambles and adventures of a hunter in the Prairies. With illustrations.* London: John Murray, Albemarle Street, 1853. London: Bradbury and Evans, Printers, Whitefriars. xv, 326 p., 8 plates. With two pages of publisher's titles bound at the end.
130 × 197 × 28 mm. 10411.c.18.

Russet-red endpapers and pastedowns. Binder's ticket on lower pastedown: '| Bound by | Remnant & Edmonds | [rule] | London |'. Brown rib horizontal-grain cloth. White dye 'wave' patterns run vertically on each cover and the spine. Two fillets are blocked in blind on the borders of both covers. The upper cover central vignette is blocked in gold. It shows a charging bison. The spine is blocked in gold. A single fillet is blocked on the perimeter, which forms a 'heart-shape' twice down each side. The words: '| Solitary | rambles | of a | hunter. | [rule] | Palliser | [rule] |' are blocked in gold. A beaver is blocked on its river dam, with small river and forest decoration arising on either side. At the tail, the words: '| London | John Murray |' are blocked in gold within a rectangle formed by a single gold fillet.

FIG. 79

664 Unsigned UK FIG. 79

Entertaining biography from Chambers' Repository. London: W. and R. Chambers 47 Paternoster Row and High Street, Edinburgh, 1855. Edinburgh: Printed by W. and R. Chambers. Unpaginated.
107 × 183 × 47 mm. 10600.bb.27.

The bookplate of Henry Spencer Ashbee is on the upper pastedown. On the upper endpaper, the bookplate of: '| Stassin et Xavier | Libraires | 22, Rue de la Banque, 22 | [rule] | . . .' is pasted. Olive green trefoil leaf trellis-grain cloth. Both covers have the same design blocked in blind on the borders and on the corners. There are two fillets blocked on the borders. On each corner, a leaf decoration design is blocked. On the upper cover, the monogram of W. & R. Chambers is blocked in gold inside a decorated medallion. The spine is blocked in gold. A single gold fillet is blocked on the perimeter. Down the length of the spine, an elaborate pattern of stems, leaves, and flowers is blocked in gold. The title: '| Entertaining | biography |' is blocked in gold near the head. '| Ashbee | Collection |' red leather label is pasted near the tail. [Rebound and paper laminated 1995. No original endpapers or pastedowns.]

Ball, *VPB* p. 140.

665 Unsigned UK

Henderson, Thalia Susannah. *Olga; or, Russia in the tenth century. An Historical Poem.* London: Hamilton Adams & Co. 33, Paternoster Row; James Nisbet & Co. Berners Street, 1855. London: R.Clay, Printer, Bread Street Hill. viii, 326 p.
110 × 177 × 25 mm. 11648.e.12.

Uncut bolts. Yellow endpapers and pastedowns. Binder's ticket on lower pastedown: '| Bound by | Westleys & Co. | London. |'. Vertical rib-grain cloth, dyed with red and black horizontal stripes. The borders of both covers are blocked in blind with the same design. Two fillets are blocked in blind on the borders, the outer thin, the inner thick. A third inner border of an 'edging pattern' is blocked in blind. The upper cover has a central vignette blocked in gold. It shows a wreath of ivy branches, leaves and flowers, with the title word: '| Olga |' blocked in Cyrillic characters in the middle. The same vignette is blocked in blind on the lower cover. The spine has decoration blocked in gold. A single fillet is blocked in gold at the head and at the tail. '| Olga |' is blocked in gold at the head, with ivy branch, stem and leaf decoration blocked in gold underneath.

666 Unsigned UK

Parley, Peter. *Faggots for the fireside, or tales of fact and fancy. With twelve tinted illustrations.* London: Grant and Griffith, Successors to Newbery and Harris, Corner of St Paul's Churchyard, 1855. 320 p., 12 plates. With eight pages of publisher's titles bound at the end.
125 × 185 × 25 mm. 12806.e.30.

Bolts uncut. Text sewn on three sawn-in cords. Yellow endpapers and pastedowns. Red fine rib vertical-grain cloth. Both covers blocked identically in blind with the same design. A single fillet is blocked on the borders. A leaf and flower pattern is blocked in blind on the corners. On the centre, more leaf and flower patterns are blocked. These surround a vase blocked within. The spine is fully blocked in gold. A single gold fillet is blocked on the perimeter. From the head downwards, the decoration is: a single gold fillet; the words: '| Faggots | for the | fireside, | or | fact & fancy | by | Peter Parley. |' blocked in gold in fanciful letters; stars are blocked in gold above and below the title; above a burning fire, a group is blocked: an owl, an Indian and a tomahawk, a man playing a violin, a mother and her baby; the fire has figures of an animal and a young lady burning in it; the words: '| Grant | & Griffith |' are blocked in gold between two gold fillets.

The USA edition of the work is at BL 12804.f.31. New York: D. Appleton & Co., 1855. v, 320 p., 12 plates. With four pages of publisher's titles bound at the end. 125 × 185 × 30 mm. Yellow endpapers and pastedowns. Green dot-grain cloth. The lower cover central vignette is blocked in gold, featuring an two handled urn, with flowers. The upper cover centre-piece is blocked in gold, showing two columns of decoration. There are two red and two white, paper onlays, blocked in gold. The spine is blocked in gold, with blue and white paper onlays.

667 Unsigned UK

Bible. Job. English. *The Book of Job illustrated with fifty engravings from drawings by John Gilbert, and with explanatory notes & poetical parallels.* London: James Nisbet and Co. Berners Street, 1857. Printed by R. & R. Clark, Edinburgh. xxx, 7–188 p. With one page of publisher's titles bound at the end.
163 × 233 × 27 mm. C.109.d.6.

The illustrations are engraved by Dalziel Brothers, J. W. Whymper, W. L. Thomas.

Gilt edges. Bevelled boards. Mauve endpapers and pastedowns. Binder's ticket on lower pastedown. '| Leighton | Son & | Hodge, | Shoe Lane | London. |' Red morocco horizontal grain cloth. Both covers blocked identically in gold, in blind and in relief. The whole design is elaborate Moorish. The outer border has a fillet blocked in gold, with small diamonds and dotted squares, repeating, blocked in relief within it. Around the large central oval, a pattern of stems, horizontal hatch leaves and flowers is blocked in gold on the corners and on the sides. Inside the oval, a flower and stem pattern is blocked in relief around the centre. On the centre, a circle is blocked, with an elaborate strap pattern within it. There is an elaborate border to this circle. Around the circle, another elaborate strap pattern of stems and leaves, surrounded by horizontal hatch, is blocked in gold. The spine is blocked in gold. A 'wavy' fillet is blocked on the perimeter, with repeating dots blocked in relief within it. An elaborate cartouche of arabesques forms an oval. Within the oval, the title: '| The | Book | of | Job. |' is blocked in gold. Hatched leaves and flowers are blocked in gold as patterns on the head and on the tail. A single fillet is blocked at the head and at the tail.

668 Unsigned UK

Burgess, Nathan G. *The ambrotype manual: a practical treatise on the art of taking positive photographs on glass, commonly known as ambrotypes. Containing all the various recipes for making collodions; preparation and use of the nitrate bath; developing solutions; varnishes, etc., etc., as practised by the most successful operators in the United States. To which is added the practice of the negative process and positive photographs on paper. Third edition.* New York: J. M. Fairchild & Co., 109 Nassau-Street, 1857. New York: R. C. Valentine, Stereotyper and Electrotypist, 17, Dutch-st, cor. Fulton, N.Y. 184 p. With four pages of publisher's titles bound at the end.
118 × 190 × 16 mm. 1399.c.13.

Text sewn on two sawn-in cords. Yellow endpapers and pastedowns. Purple trefoil leaf trellis-grain cloth. The same design is blocked in blind on both covers. There are three fillets, one thick, two thin, blocked on the borders. There is leaf and branch decoration on the inner corners and on the sides, which forms a quatrefoil central frame. A leaf and flower vignette is blocked on the centre. The spine is divided into four panels, with three fillets in blind separating each panel. The words: '| The | ambrotype | manual. | [rule] | Burgess |' are blocked in gold in fanciful letters diagonally within panel two.

Ball, *VPB* p. 140. Gives example of trefoil leaf trellis grain.

669 Unsigned UK

Lukis, William C. *An account of Church bells; with some notices of Wiltshire bells and bell-founders. Containing a copious list of founders, a comparative scale of tenor bells, and inscriptions from nearly five hundred parishes in various parts of the kingdom* . . . London: J. H. Parker, London and Oxford, 1857. London: Printed by J. B. Nichols and Sons, 25 Parliament Street. ix, 148 p., 13 plates.
142 × 230 × 16 mm. 1400.i.33.

The plates are drawn by Lukis.

No original endpapers or pastedowns. Blue morocco horizontal-grain cloth. Both covers have four fillets blocked in blind on the borders. The upper cover has a centre-piece showing a bell, blocked as a gold lettering-piece. On the bell the words: '| Church bells |' are blocked on the shoulder; '| by |' is blocked on the waist; the name: '| W. C. Lukis. MA, FSA. |' are blocked on the sound-bow: All the letters are blocked in relief. Original spine missing.

670 Unsigned UK

FIG. 80

Steggall, John. *First lines for chemists and druggists preparing for examination before the Board of the Pharmaceutical Society.*

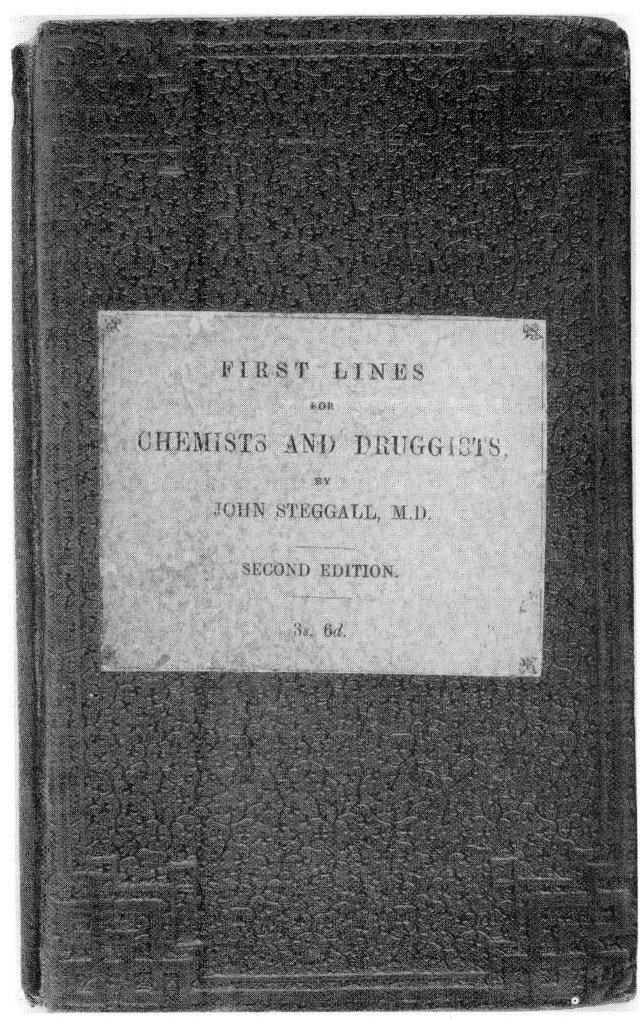

FIG. 80

Second edition. London: John Churchill, New Burlington Street, 1857. London: J. E. Adlard, Printer, Bartholomew Close. viii, 178 p. With six pages of publisher's titles bound at the end.
96 × 153 × 12 mm. 777.a.45.

Text sewn on three sawn-in cords. Yellow endpapers and pastedowns. Red trefoil leaf trellis-grain. Both covers blocked identically in blind on the borders and on the corners. There are two fillets blocked on the borders, one thick, one thin. The thick fillet forms strapwork on each corner, the thin fillet has only one strap. On the upper cover, a printed paper label is pasted on the centre. A thin fillet is printed on its borders, with small decoration on each corner. Printed on the centre of the label: '| First lines | for | chemists and druggists, | by | John Steggall, M.D. | [rule] | Second edition. | [rule] | 3s.6d. |'. The spine is not blocked.

Ball, *VPB* p. 140.

671 Unsigned UK

Waring, J. B. *Art treasures of the United Kingdom. Consisting of examples selected from the Manchester Art Treasures Exhibition, 1857. With Descriptive Essays by Owen Jones, M. Digby Wyatt, A. W. Franks, J. C. Robinson, George Scharf, Jun. & J. B. Waring. The entire work will be produced under the direction of J. B. Waring, the chromo-lithography by F. Bedford. One hundred plates, to be issued in thirty-two parts, fortnightly, at 10s. 6d. per part. 2 vols.* London: Day & Son, Lithographers to the Queen, 6, Gate Street, Lincoln's-Inn Fields, [1857]. Printed by Cox & Wyman, 74–75, Great Queen Street, Lincoln's-Inn Fields, London.
1801.a.25.

Vol. I. [31 p.], 43 p., 32 p., 33 p. 312 × 397 × 38 mm.
Vol. II. 80 p., 27 p. 312 × 395 × 35 mm.

For the two volumes there are 100 plates. The title page proper is a chromo-lithograph, with the title printed within the central oval. The dedication page states: 'The drawings on wood by R. Dudley.'

In this copy, the paper wrappers for the parts are bound in: the wrapper for part I is bound at the front of Vol. I.; those for parts II–XXXII are bound at the end of vol. II.

672 Unsigned UK

Wilkinson, *Sir* John Gardiner. *The Egyptians in the time of the Pharaohs. Being a companion to the Crystal Palace Egyptian collections. To which is added an introduction to the study of the Egyptian hieroglyphs. By Samuel Birch.* London: Published for the Crystal Palace Company by Bradbury and Evans, 11 Bouverie Street, 1857. London: Bradbury and Evans, Printers, Whitefriars. xvi, 282 p., 2 plates. With one page of publisher's titles bound at the end.
128 × 195 × 24 mm. 7704.aa.29.

Light yellow endpapers and pastedowns. Bookseller's ticket on upper pastedown: '| Randle, | music seller | Bookseller | &

Stationer, | Market Place, | Devizes. |' Book plate of Oscar Boulton on the upper pastedown. Blue morocco horizontal-grain cloth. Both covers blocked identically in blind on the borders and on the corners. There are three fillets blocked on the borders, with fans and small decoration blocked on each corner. The upper cover has a central vignette blocked in gold. It shows an Egyptian lady playing a stringed instrument. The spine is blocked in gold and in blind. A single fillet is blocked in blind at the head and at the tail. The title: '| The | Egyptians. | Sir J. G. Wilkinson; | Egyptian hieroglyphs | by | S. Birch. |' are all blocked in gold. Four small decorated fillets separate the title lettering. '| Price 7/6 |' is blocked in gold at the tail.

673 Unsigned UK

FIG. 81

Brewster, *Sir* David. *The kaleidoscope its history, theory and construction with its application to the fine and useful arts. Second edition, greatly enlarged. With fifty-six wood engravings and one plate.* London: John Murray, Albemarle Street, 1858. Edinburgh: T. Constable, Printer to Her Majesty. vii, 189 p., 1 plate. With thirty-four pages of publisher's titles bound at the end.

128 × 196 × 25 mm. 8715.c.33.

Original brown endpaper bound at the front. Binder's ticket on lower pastedown: '| Bound by | Edmonds and Remnants. | [rule] | London |'. Brown morocco horizontal-grain cloth. Both covers have two fillets blocked in blind on the borders. On the upper cover, the central vignette shows a kaleidoscope, blocked in gold. The spine is missing. Unsigned.

FIG. 81

674 Unsigned UK

PLATE LXXXV

Stanesby, Samuel. *Light for the Path of Life. From the Holy Scriptures. Designed by Samuel Stanesby.* London: Griffith & Farran, Corner of St. Paul's Churchyard, [1858]. [London]: Printed in Colors [sic] by Ashbee and Dangerfield. [4], 28 p. All pages have borders chromolithographed in gold and in colours.

140 × 187 × 20 mm. 3127.k.22.

On the title page verso: '| Illuminated by Samuel Stanesby |'.

Original gutta percha binding. Gilt edges. Bevelled boards. Brown endpapers and pastedowns. Green morocco horizontal-grain cloth. Both covers blocked identically. A single fillet is blocked in blind on the borders. Inside this, a border is blocked in relief of repeating joined circular stems, each with a three pointed leaf inside. The inner rectangle has patterns of larger leaves, with a large single flower blocked on each inner corner in relief. The central rectangle is blocked in gold. It has a border of gold dots, with spade shapes blocked at the centre head and the centre tail, and a circle on each side. The title: '| Light | for the | path of | life. |' is blocked in gold in fanciful letters, with rays blocked above and below. The spine is blocked in gold. A single gold fillet is blocked on the perimeter. At the head, rays are blocked in gold. At the tail, an oriental lamp and its rays are blocked in gold. Along the spine, the title: '| Light for the path of life |' is blocked in gold in fanciful letters. Unsigned.

675 Unsigned UK

Willmott, Robert Eldridge Aris. *Summer time in the country. Illustrated edition.* London: George Routledge & Co. Farringdon Street. New York: 18 Beekman Street, 1858. London: Printed by Richard Clay, Bread Street Hill. vii, 216 p.

150 × 206 × 27 mm. 1346.g.34.

The heading to the 'List of illustrations' reads: 'From drawings by Birket Foster, Harrison Weir, and John M. Carrick. Engraved by the Brothers Dalziel.'

Bevelled boards. Gilt edges. Yellow endpapers and pastedowns. Binder's ticket on lower pastedown: '| Leighton | Son & | Hodge, | Shoe Lane | London. |' Green morocco horizontal-grain cloth. The same design is blocked on both covers. The lower cover is blocked in blind. The two fillets on the borders are 'spiked' to resemble rose branches. Patterns of roses and rose leaves are blocked in relief on the corners. The centre piece contains the author and title lettering, blocked in blind. The upper cover is fully blocked in gold, with the addition of a leaf pattern blocked in blind around the centre piece. The words: '| Summer Time | In The Country | by | The Revd. R. A. Willmott |' are blocked in gold in elaborate gothic letters, with the capital letters being blocked in relief within rectangular gold lettering-pieces. The spine is blocked in gold. A single gold fillet, resembling 'rose-branch', is blocked on the perimeter. From the head downwards, the decoration is: roses blocked in gold; a fillet; the title: '| Summer | Time | In The | Country |'; a pattern of hatched leaves and thin stems in gold; roses are blocked near the tail; a gold fillet, resembling a 'rose-branch' is blocked at the tail.

de Beaumont, *RdeB1* no. 401. Copy with green sand-grain cloth. Goldman, *VIB* no. 401. McLean, *VBD* p. 222. Reproduces the 1864 edition. McLean, *VPBB* pp. 2–3. Reproduces the frontispiece & title page of the 1858 edition.

676 Unsigned UK

Grattan, Thomas Colley. *Civilised America. Second edition. In two volumes.* London: Bradbury and Evans, 11, Bouverie Street, 1859. London: Bradbury and Evans, Printers, Whitefriars.
140 × 218 × 72 mm. 1509/4405.

Two volumes bound as one.

Vol. I. xxiv, v–xix, 444p, 1 plate.
Vol. II. vii, 517 p., 2 maps (1 fold-out)

The fold out map is printed in black and red. It is entitled: 'Civilised America; graduated shades shewing the progress of civilisation.' Signed at the bottom: 'Del. & litho by James Wyld, Charing Cross East London.'

Gilt edges. Yellow endpapers and pastedowns. Green binder's ticket on lower pastedown: '| Bound by | Smith & Collings, | 5, Ivy Lane, | Paternoster Row. |' Mauve pebble-grain cloth. The lower cover is blocked in blind only. Three fillets are blocked on the borders: the first is plain; the next two have a herring-bone pattern blocked in relief between them, with dots blocked in relief on each corner. The central oval is formed by three fillets. The upper cover is blocked in gold and in black. From the border inwards, the decoration is: a fillet in gold on the borders; a border in gold of beads and dots; a herring-bone border, blocked in black, with single leaves blocked in gold on the corners, the centre head, the centre tail and the centre sides; a single fillet forms an inner rectangle, with a leaf and flower device blocked in gold on each inner corner. The central oval is formed by three fillets, blocked in black. The centrepiece, blocked in gold, shows a shield, shaped like the geographical outline of the USA, with stars and vertical stripes. The spine is blocked in gold. From the head downwards, the decoration is: two gold fillets; two corner-pieces in gold; a decorative arch, in which the words: '| Grattan's | America. |' blocked in gold in gothic letters.; an interlinking strap design, with the same USA shield as on the upper cover; two corner-pieces near the tail; two gold fillets are blocked at the tail.

677 Unsigned UK

PLATE LXXXVI

Lister, afterwards, Lewis, *Lady* Maria Theresa. *The semi-detached house. Edited by Lady Theresa Lewis.* London: Richard Bentley, New Burlington Street, 1859. London: Printed by A.Schulze, 13, Poland Street. [2], 327 p.
126 × 205 × 27 mm. 12632.f.4.

Light yellow endpapers and pastedowns. Binder's ticket on lower pastedown: '| Bound by | Westleys | & Co. | London. |' Dark green bead-grain cloth, with horizontal light green stripes. On both covers, four fillets are blocked in blind, two thick and two thin. The spine is blocked in gold. Two fillets are blocked in blind at the head and at the tail. The title: '| The | semi-detached | house |' is blocked in gold within a panel formed by two fillets, with small decoration blocked above and below. The words: '| By | Lady Theresa | Lewis |' are blocked in gold on the middle. '| London Bentley. |' is blocked in gold at the tail.

678 Unsigned UK

Michell, Nicolas. *Pleasure, A Poem. In seven books.* London: William Tegg & Co., 85, Queen Street, Cheapside, 1859. London: Petter and Galpin, Belle Sauvage Printing Works, Ludgate Hill, E.C. 243 p. With two pages of publisher's titles bound at the end.
128 × 195 × 21 mm. 11650.d.18.

Light yellow endpapers and pastedowns. Green bead-grain cloth. Both covers are blocked identically in blind on the borders, the corners and the sides. There are two fillets blocked on the borders. Inside this is a frame showing leaf and stem decoration, with spirals on the corners, and on the centres of the sides. The upper cover has a central vignette blocked in gold. It shows a putto, a basket of flowers on his head, standing on a pole. A bird is perched on each side of the putto on the pole. The pole is garlanded with ribbons and flower posies. A bunch of fruit hangs at the base. The spine is blocked in gold. There is a single gold fillet blocked around the perimeter. A laurel wreath is blocked at the head, with the words: '| Pleasure | [rule] | Michell |' blocked in gold underneath. In the middle of the spine, a small decorative device is blocked in gold, which shows a triangle of three shamrocks.

679 Unsigned UK

Cobbold, Robert Henry. *Pictures of the Chinese, drawn by themselves.* London: John Murray, Albemarle Street, 1860. London: Woodfall and Kinder, Printers, Angel Court, Skinner Street. vi, 220 p., 34 plates.
127 × 197 × 25 mm. 10057.b.24.

White endpapers and pastedowns. Dark green-dyed cloth with vertical light green stripes. Wave vertical-grain cloth. Two fillets are blocked in blind on the borders of both covers. On the lower cover, the central vignette is blocked in blind. It is oval-shaped, and shows a dragon surrounded by foliage, all blocked in relief. On the upper cover, the central vignette is blocked in gold. It shows a Chinaman, on tiptoe, with a wooden drum, a stick and a tablet in his hands. There is a sign on a pole attached to his back. On the spine at the head and at the tail, gold fillets are blocked, and, between them, a repeating pattern of semi-circles, leaves and small dots blocked in gold. The title: '| Pictures | of the | Chinese |' is blocked near the head in gold. Underneath this, a small decoration showing leaves is blocked in gold. At the tail, the words: '| London John Murray |' are blocked in gold.

680 Unsigned UK

Montgomery, James. *The poetical works. With a memoir. Eight Engravings on Steel.* Edinburgh: Gall & Inglis, 6 George Street. London: Houlston & Wright, [1860]. xxii, 456 p., 8 plates.
105 × 170 × 32 mm. C.129.a.18.

Gilt edges. Yellow endpapers and pastedowns. Ticket on upper pastedown: '| Sold by | James MacTaggart | Bookseller Bookbinder | & Stationer | 103 High Street | Arbroath. |' Prize bookplate on upper pastedown: '| Presented | by the Magistrates | and | Town Council of Arbroath | to | Miss Anne Hill | 2nd | of her Arithmetic Class | Under Mr Fraser | In Arbroath High School | John .... Provost. | Council Chambers | Arbroath 15th July 1863. |' Written at the top of the plate: '2nd also in Competition.' Blue wave vertical-grain cloth. Both covers blocked identically, in blind and in relief on the lower, in gold and in relief on the upper. The borders are blocked in gold with: 1. a single fillet; 2. a hatch fillet; 3. two more fillets. Inside these, there is a border of repeating 'thin-branch' motifs, blocked in relief within a horizontal hatch gold fillet. The inner rectangle has two 'dog-tooth' fillets blocked in gold on its borders. Groups of passion flower leaves are blocked in relief on the centre head, and on the centre tail, and on the centre sides, surrounded by horizontal hatch gold. Four pointed stars and dots are blocked on the inner corners in gold. On the centre, five ovals are blocked, the smallest being at the centre. All the ovals have fillets blocked on their borders. The oval on the centre has small four-point stars and dots within, and the words: '| James Montgomery |' in gold between fillets. On the lower cover, another block has been stamped in gold over the original. From the head downwards, the decoration on this block is: the word: '| Arbroath |', blocked within a ribbon; a portcullis and chains; a medallion surrounded by curling leaves; inside the medallion, the words: '| Prize | The | Magistrates | and | Town Council. |' are blocked in gold. The spine is blocked in gold. A 'tooth and dot' repeating pattern is blocked in gold on the perimeter, with a single fillet inside this on the perimeter. There is a diamond pattern blocked vertically from head to tail. Groups of passion flower leaves are blocked in relief within horizontal hatch gold lettering-pieces, on the head and on the tail. Near the head, the words: '| James Montgomery's | Poetical | Works |' are blocked in relief within three rectangular gold lettering-pieces, with single fillets on their borders. Below the title, six medallions are blocked down the spine, with five stars and four leaves blocked in relief alternately in each medallion. The words: '| Gall & Inglis |' are blocked in gold within a rectangle formed by a single gold fillet near the base. Unsigned.

Dry, *JL* no. 374.

681 Unsigned UK

Bible. Matthew. Selections. English. *The Sermon on the Mount.* [London]: [Day & Son], [1861]. Unpaginated. [26 leaves.]
445 × 575 × 35 mm. Tab.1216.a.

Each leaf is printed on the recto only.

On leaf two is printed: 'Illuminated by W & G Audsley Architects Liverpool. [Monograms of WA & GA 1861 printed in gold against a blue background, all within a quatrefoil with a red ball-bead border, and a gold border.] Illustrated by Charles Rolt. Chromolithographed by W R Tymms. Day & Son.'

In the Day & Son catalogue bound at the end of BL 12304.h.1, this work is described as: 'Copies of the above work are to be supplied to Subscribers only. Proofs, extra thick paper, full morocco, gilt (210 copies printed), 12l. 12s. . . .'

Gilt edges. Yellow endpapers and pastedowns. Binder's ticket on lower pastedown: '| Bound | by | Leighton | Son and Hodge. |' Brown morocco. Both covers blocked identically in gold and blind and relief. A number of fillets and patterns blocked inwards on the borders: 1. a wide single fillet blocked in blind; 2. two thin gold fillets; 3. a wide pattern of repeating semi-circles with 'three leaves and single ball' atop each semi-circle; 4. a thin gold fillet; 5. a wide gold fillet, with repeating dots blocked in side it in relief. This last fillet forms a large single circular strap at the centre head, the centre tail, and the centre sides. Within each of the straps, a flower head is blocked. The inner corners have a pattern of curling stems, leaves and one large flower head, all blocked in gold and in relief. The centre is formed by an elongated quatrefoil. It has multiple decoration blocked on its borders, and a 'diamond and dot' pattern blocked in relief within it. The centre of the quatrefoil is occupied by a cross flory blocked in gold. The patterns showing on each arm of the cross are blocked in relief. On the centre of the cross, and of the cover, a quatrefoil is blocked. The inscription: 'IHS' is blocked in gold within the quatrefoil. Unsigned. The spine is blocked in gold. Small decoration is blocked at the head and at the tail. The title: '| The Sermon on the Mount |' is blocked in gold in gothic letters along the spine. Unsigned.

682 Unsigned UK

Broderip, Frances Freeling. *Chrysal; or, A story with an end. Illustrated by Thomas Hood. . . .* [Monogram of Saunders, Otley, and Co., with the motto: 'Sans Changer'.] London: Saunders, Otley, and Co., 66, Brook Street, Hanover Square, W., 1861. London: F. Schoberl, Printer, 37, Dean Street, Soho, W. viii, 119 p.
162 × 212 × 17 mm. 12807.f.11.

Gilt edges. Bevelled boards. Brown endpapers and pastedowns. Binder's ticket on lower pastedown: '| Bound by | Burn. | 37 & 38 | Kirby St. |' Maroon morocco horizontal-grain cloth. Both covers are blocked identically. The design is blocked in blind and relief on the lower cover, and in gold and relief on the upper. On the upper cover, a single fillet is blocked in gold on the borders, and inside it, a horizontal hatch 'joined leaf and three dot' pattern is blocked in gold. A stylised single leaf is blocked on each corner, with the inner borders blocked with four fillets. Three of these are blocked in gold only, and the fourth has a repeating pattern of small hatched cartouches in gold and dots blocked in relief within it. The centre is occupied by a 'diamond and four pointed star' pattern blocked in relief.

The centre has a large oriental twelve point pattern, blocked in gold, with a decoration of stems, leaves and horizontal hatch blocked in relief. On the centre, a gold lettering-piece is blocked, with the title words: '| Chrysal | or | A Story | with | An End. |' blocked in relief inside. The spine is blocked in gold and in relief. From the head downwards, the decoration is: hatch gold and decoration; a vertical hatch gold fillet; the title: '| Chrysal | or | a story | with | an end. |' blocked in gold; tapering perpendicular decoration, with leaves blocked inside in relief; oriental-style decoration is blocked in gold near the base; a panel is formed by a single gold fillet; two gold fillets blocked at the tail.

683 Unsigned UK

Gatty, Margaret. *Parables from nature. By Mrs. Alfred Gatty . . . With illustrations by C. W. Cope, R.A., H. Calderon, W. Holman Hunt. W. Millais. Otto Speckter, G. Thomas, and E. Warren.* London: Bell and Daldy, 186, Fleet Street, 1861. London: Chiswick Press: Printed by Whittingham and Wilkins, Tooks Court, Chancery Lane. viii, 196 p., 14 plates. With four pages of publisher's titles bound at the end.
140 × 205 × 27 mm. 12807.e.17.

Bevelled boards. Gilt edges. Cream endpapers and pastedowns. Purple morocco horizontal-grain cloth. The same design is blocked on both covers. The lower cover is blocked in blind, the upper cover is blocked in gold. The upper cover has a fillet blocked in gold on the border. Inside the border is strapwork, highlighted in relief, which forms 'onion' shapes on the corners. There is a tracery of leaves and flowers blocked in relief around the strapwork, against a horizontal hatch gold background. In the central oval, the title words: '| Parables | from | nature | Mrs. A. Gatty |' are blocked in relief within four rectangular gold lettering-pieces, each with a single gold fillet on its borders. A tracery of small plant decoration is blocked in gold, surrounding these lettering-pieces. The spine is fully blocked in gold and relief. A single gold fillet is blocked on the perimeter. From the head downwards, the decoration is: two gold fillets; flower decoration blocked in relief within gold horizontal hatch; The words: '| Parables | from | nature | Mrs A Gatty |' blocked in gold, within a panel with fillets forming an ogee arch at the head; four gold fillets; more flower and stem decoration blocked in relief within gold horizontal hatch; an extended oval, with semi-circles is blocked on the middle of the lower half of the spine, with small leaf and flower decoration blocked in gold within it; six gold fillets are blocked at the tail. Unsigned.

Ball, *VPB* p. 156. Cites the 1864 edition.

684 Unsigned UK

Keble, J. *Keble's Morning Hymn. Illuminated by B. B-B. Chromo-Lithographed by W. R. Tymms.* London: Day and Sons Lithographers to the Queen. 6 Gate St Lincolns Inn Fields, [1861]. Unpaginated. [12 pages]
215 × 172 × 13 mm. C.30.b.40.

The Day and Son catalogue at the end of BL 12304.h.1. states of this work: 'Size small 4to., handsomely bound, with gilt edges, price 15s.'

Text printed only on the recto of each page. Text sewn on three sawn-in cords. Gilt edges. Bevelled boards. Yellow endpapers and pastedowns. Brown morocco horizontal-grain cloth. Both covers blocked identically in blind and in relief only on the lower, and in gold, in blind and in relief on the upper. Two fillets are blocked in blind on the borders, with a zig-zag border blocked between them. Two more gold fillets are blocked inside this on the borders, with repeating dots blocked in gold between these. On each inner corner, a circle is blocked. Two semi circles and an eight-point star are blocked inside. The elongated central oval (blocked horizontally) has a thin fillet in blind on its borders; then two more fillets blocked in gold, with five-point stars blocked between these. Inside, a circular gold fillet and trefoils are blocked, together with a cross and trefoils at its ends. The spine is blocked in gold. Small decoration is blocked at the head and at the tail. The title: '| Keble's Morning Hymn |' is blocked in gold along the spine from the base to the head, in gothic letters. Unsigned.

685 Unsigned UK

Red, white and blue: sketches of military life. 'By the author of Flemish interiors'. In three volumes. Vol. I. [–III.] London: Hurst and Blackett, Publishers, Successors to Henry Colborn, 13, Great Marlborough Street, 1862. Billing, Printer, 103, Hatton Garden, London, and Guildford, Surrey.
8834.f.1.

Vol. I. xv, 356 p., 2 plates. 128 × 202 × 32 mm.
Vol. II. viii, 296 p. 128 × 202 × 28 mm.
Vol. III. vi, 351 p. 128 × 202 × 32 mm. With six pages of publisher's titles bound at the end.

All three volumes have brown endpapers and pastedowns. Vol. 1 has a binder's ticket on the lower pastedown: '| Bound | by | Leighton | Son and | Hodge |'. Across both covers and the spine of each volume are three different dyed cloths. Red on the head, white in the middle, and blue at the tail. All three cloths used to cover the boards for the three volumes are of pebble-grain. All volumes are blocked with the same design on the covers and on the spines. There are two fillets blocked on the borders in blind. Inside this, a repeating border of 'cross-ribbon' and dots is blocked in relief. Inside this, a repeating pattern of 'three leaves and two flower heads' is blocked in relief. This pattern is also blocked on the lower two thirds of each spine. The heads of the spine of vols 1 and 3 are missing. The head for vol 2 shows a gold lettering-piece, shaped as a flag. The words: '| Red | White | Blue | by the author of | Flemish interiors |' are blocked in relief within four curved gold lettering pieces that flutter from the flag. Underneath the flag, '| Vol. II |' is blocked in gold. '| Hurst and Blackett |' is blocked in gold at the tail of all three volumes. There are two gold fillets at the head and at the tail of vol 2.

686 Unsigned UK

Ede, Charles. *Warm hearts in cold regions. A Tale of Arctic Life.* London: T. Nelson and Sons, Paternoster Row; Edinburgh; and New York, 1862. 192 p., 7 plates.
106 × 170 × 23 mm. 12804.bb.20.

Yellow endpapers and pastedowns. Brown coarse pebble-grain cloth. Both covers blocked identically in blind and relief on the borders and on the corners. Six fillets are blocked on the borders: 1. a thick fillet; 2. & 3. thin fillets; 4. a fillet blocked in blind, with repeating dots blocked within in relief; 5. a very thin fillet; 6. a fillet in blind. Straps are blocked in relief on each corner. The upper cover vignette is blocked in gold. It shows three men constructing an igloo. Two of the men are handling ice blocks near the top of the igloo. The third man is crawling in through the entrance 'tunnel'. Unsigned. The spine is blocked in gold. From the head downwards, the decoration is: a rectangular panel formed by a single fillet; decoration blocked in relief; a hatched gold rectangular panel, with the title: '| Warm | hearts | cold | regions |' blocked in relief within five rectangular gold lettering-pieces, each with single fillets blocked in relief on their borders; below this, a jagged 'ice landscape' is outlined in gold; within this, a polar bear perches on three small ice peaks – all blocked in gold; a vertical hatch gold rectangular gold lettering-piece, has the words: '| By | Charles Ede. R.N. |' blocked in relief within it; more jagged ice outlined in gold, with decoration blocked in relief; at the tail, a rectangle is formed by a single gold fillet.

687 Unsigned UK

Stanesby, Samuel. *Aphorisms of the Wise & Good. Illuminated by Samuel Stanesby.* London: Griffith and Farran, Corner of St. Paul's Churchyard, 1862. [London]: Printed in colors [sic] by Thomas Bessent. [iv], 28 p. All pages have borders chromolithographed in gold and in colours.
105 × 143 × 15 mm. 8408.a.36.

Page [ii] has an oval portrait photograph of John Milton with a chromolithograph surround, and the caption: 'John Milton Born, 1608 Died, 1674.' printed in colours within a ribbon underneath the portrait.

Page [iii], the title page, has the quotation on the oval border: 'In the lips of him that hath understanding wisdom is found. The tongue of the just is as choice silver.'

Page [iv], the title page verso, has the words: 'Illuminated by Saml. Stanesby. Printed in Colors [sic] by Thomas Bessent.' printed within ribbons, which surround a gold shield containing the monogram 'SS' printed in red and green.

Original gutta percha binding. Gilt edges. Bevelled boards. Yellow endpapers and pastedowns. Binder's ticket on lower pastedown: '| Hanbury & Co. | Binders, | 80, Coleman St. | E.C. |' Green morocco vertical-grain cloth. Both covers identically blocked in gold, in blind and in relief. Two borders are blocked on the covers in gold: 1. a repeating pattern of joined leaves and small circles; 2. a thin fillet. Curling stems are blocked in relief on the corners. Three overlapping ovals are blocked on the centre. The borders of the two outer ovals are purple paper onlays with fillets on edges, and blocked with curling stems and hatch gold berries. Inside this, four blue paper onlays are blocked in gold with small diamonds and decoration. The centre head and centre tail of the oval in the middle has small leaf decoration blocked in relief within a gold and hatched gold lettering-piece. On the centre, the title: '| Aphorisms of | the wise & good |' is blocked in gold. The spine is blocked in gold. Two fillets are blocked on the sides. From the tail upwards, the decoration is: a fillet and small panels; two 'spade-shapes'; from the middle to the head, the title: '| Aphorisms of the Wise & Good |' is blocked along the spine in gold. Each capital letter is in gold within a horizontal hatch gold panel with fillets blocked on either side. Small decoration and a fillet blocked at the head.

McLean, *VBD* p. 134 & p. 137.

688 Unsigned UK

Farmer, Edward. *Ned Farmer's scrap book; being a selection of poems, songs, scraps, etc. etc. Enlarged and revised . . . Third edition.* London: W. MacIntosh, 24, Paternoster Row. Derby: Bemrose & Sons, Irongate and Market-Place, 1863. [Derby]: Printed and published for the Author, by Bemrose & Sons, Irongate and Market-Place, Derby. xv, 144 p.
125 × 197 × 13 mm. 11649.aaa.12.

Text sewn on two tapes. Gilt edges. Yellow endpapers and pastedowns. Binder's ticket on upper pastedown: '| Bound by | Bemrose & Sons, | Derby. |' Brown wave vertical-grain cloth. Both covers are blocked identically in blind on the borders and on the corners. Two fillets are blocked on the borders, one thick, one thin. An inner rectangle is formed by another fillet, with straps blocked in blind on the corners and on the sides. Inside this, each corner has a spade-shaped design, with leaves and flower buds blocked in relief inside. On each side, four 'maple-shaped' leaves are blocked in blind, with two more each on the head and the centre tail. On the centre of the upper cover, the title words: '| Ned Farmer's | scrap book. |' are blocked in gold. No blocking on the spine. Unsigned.

689 Unsigned UK

Stanesby, Samuel. *The Floral Gift. An Illuminated Souvenir.* London: Griffith & Farran, Corner of St. Paul's Churchyard, [1863]. [London]: Printed in Colours by Thomas Bessent. [2], 28, [2] p. The borders of the pages are chromolithographed.
138 × 190 × 20 mm. 1347.f.20.

Printed on the title page verso: '| Illuminated by Saml. Stanesby. |'

Gilt edges. Bevelled boards. Binder's ticket on lower pastedown: | Bound by | Bone & Son, | 76, Fleet Street, | London. |' Green dot and line grain cloth. Both covers blocked identically in gold, in blind and in relief. There is a fillet blocked in gold on the borders, with two more fillets blocked in blind inside this. An inner border pattern of flower stems and heads

is blocked in relief, within a gold fillet. There is a recessed rectangular central panel, with an 'ogee arch and oval' tracery pattern blocked inside in blind, with a small leaf blocked in relief within each oval. The title: '| The Floral Gift. |' is blocked in relief, in gothic lettering, within a rectangular gold lettering-piece. Across each cover run two raised imitation medieval clasps, blocked in gold. The patterns of branches, leaves and seeds are blocked in relief within the length of the clasps. They run across the spine. The spine is blocked in gold. The spine is divided into five panels by single fillets blocked in blind. Panels two and four are the continuation of the clasps blocked on each cover. Panels, one, three and five are formed as rectangles by two gold fillets. Within the three odd numbered panels: 1. small decoration blocked in gold; 3. the title: '| The | Floral | Gift |' is blocked in gold in gothic letters, surrounded by small leaf, stem and flower decoration blocked in gold; 5. the words: '| London | Griffith | and | Farran |' and small flowers are blocked in gold. Unsigned.

Morris & Levin, *APB* p. 101, no. 224.

690 Unsigned UK

Tillotson, John. *Ireland and its scenery. Illustrated by Thirty-Five Engravings on Steel, by various artists.* London: T. J. Allman, 463 Oxford Street, [1863]. London: Printed at the City Central Press, Oxford Arms Passage, Warwick Lane, St. Paul's. 80 p., 36 plates.
190 × 250 × 25 mm. 10390.e.11.

Gilt edges. Bevelled boards. Yellow endpapers and pastedowns. Green coloured binder's ticket on lower pastedown: '| Bound by | Smith and Collings, | 5 Ivy Lane, | Paternoster Row. |' Red honeycomb-grain cloth. Both covers blocked identically on the borders, corners and sides, in blind on the lower cover, and in gold and in relief on the upper. The borders are blocked with: 1 & 2. two gold fillets; 3. a pattern of repeating leaves blocked in gold; 4. a gold fillet and repeating gold dots; 5 & 6. two gold fillets; 7. a wide inner border of a gold fillet with a curling leaf and stem blocked within it. Arabesques are blocked on each inner corner, centre sides, on the centre head and centre tail. Within the inner rectangle, tracery of small leaves and stems is blocked in relief on the corners. The central panel of the upper cover is recessed. On its outer border, a gold lettering-piece forms an oval, with plant decoration blocked in relief within it. Three gold fillets within this form inner borders. On the centre, the title: '| Ireland | and its | Scenery. |' is blocked in gold. Unsigned. The spine is not blocked.

Packer, *BVL* p. 139.

691 Unsigned UK

Waring, J. B. *Masterpieces of industrial art & sculpture at the International Exhibition, 1862. Chromo-lithographed by and under the direction of W. R. Tymms, A. Warren, and G. Macculloch, from photographs supplied by the London & Stereoscopic Company, taken exclusively for this work by Stephen Thompson. In three volumes. – Volume I. [–III.]* London: Published by Day & Son, Lithographer to the Queen and to H.R.H. The Prince of Wales, 6, Gate Street, Lincoln's-Inn Fields, 1863. London: Cox and Wyman, Printers, Great Queen Street, Lincoln's-Inn Fields.
Each volume is 300 × 432: × 50 mm – vol I; × 45 mm – vol. II; × 58 mm – vol. III. 1800.b.12.

Vol I. has 100 plates of chromolithographs. Plate 24: 'Leather Book Cover by F. Bedford for H. Shaw's "Dresses & decorations of the Middle Ages." . . .'

Vol. II. has plates 101–200. Plate 126 is entitled 'Book-covers', by Messrs J & J. Leighton, and Messrs. Leighton & Hodge, London. Four book covers are illustrated in the plate: 1. [upper and lower covers] 'Paradise regained'; the design by JL [Luke Limner] for J & J Leighton; 2. A Bible by Leighton Son & Hodge, with emblems of sacrament, designed by Owen Jones; 3. Bible – Leighton & Hodge.

Vol. III. has plates 201–300A. It has an 'Index to Letter-press; 'Notice to the Binder' re. plate number errors; 'Notice to Subscribers'. At the end of Vol. III. are: 1. the paper wrappers for the descriptive text are bound; these are beige, printed in gold; 2. the upper and lower paper wrappers for parts 1–75. Each part was issued at 15s.

In the Day and Son catalogue at the end of BL 12304.h.1, this work is advertised as: '75 parts. 5s. per Part'.

Parallel English and French text accompanies each plate.

Gilt edges, gauffered. Marbled endpapers and pastedowns. Red morocco. The wide leather turn-ins have gold fillets and plant decoration blocked in gold. All three volumes blocked with the same designs. Both covers blocked identically in gold on the covers. Fillets are blocked on the borders, and French decoration is blocked on the corners. Royal coats of arms are blocked on the centre. The spine has raised bands, which divide it into six panels. Panels two and four have the title and the volume number; panels one, three, five and six, have elaborate plant decoration in gold and in hatch. Fillets are blocked at the head and at the tail in gold. Unsigned.

692 Unsigned UK

Barter, William George Thomas. *Adventures of a summer-eve: a poem in six books and other poems.* London: Bell and Daldy, 186, Fleet Street, 1864. London: Printed by Spottiswoode and Co. New-Street Square. [2], xvi, 353 p. With thirty-three pages of publisher's titles bound at the end.
110 × 178 × 35 mm. 11649.aaa.5.

Bolts uncut. Dark brown endpapers and pastedowns. Binder's ticket on lower pastedown: '| Bound by | Bone & son, | [rule] | 76, Fleet Street, | London. |' Green bubble-grain cloth. Both covers blocked identically on the borders, in blind on the lower, and in gold on the upper. On the borders of the upper cover, hatch gold is blocked between two fillets. On the centre, the device of Bell and Daldy is blocked in gold. [A bell, an anchor, and a sea creature, hanging from ribbons; this device is printed at the head of the publisher's titles at the end.]The

spine is blocked in gold. At the head and at the tail: vertical hatch is blocked in gold between two gold fillets. Near the head, the title: '| Adventures | of a | Summer-Eve | [rule] | W.G.T. Barter. |' is blocked in gold. The imprint: '| London | Bell & Daldy' is blocked in gold near the tail. Unsigned.

693 Unsigned UK

Chatterton, Henrietta Georgiana, Maria, *Lady. Leonore. A Tale: and other poems.* London and Cambridge: Macmillan and Co., 1864. London: Printed by R. Clay, Son and Taylor, Bread Street Hill. [8], 324 p. With four pages of publisher's titles bound at the end.

110 × 175 × 30 mm. 11649.aa.2.

Text sewn on three sawn-in cords. Dark green endpapers and pastedowns. Binder's ticket on lower pastedown: '| Bound by | Burn | 37 & 38 | Kirby St. |' Brown bead line diagonal-grain cloth. (The rib grain is vertical.) Both covers have a single fillet blocked on the borders, in blind on the lower, in gold on the upper. On the lower cover, the Macmillan medallion is blocked in gold on the centre. The spine is blocked in gold. A single gold fillet is blocked at the head and at the tail. The title: '| Leonore | and other | poems | Lady | Chatterton |' is blocked in gold near the head. The imprint: '| Macmillan & Co. |' is blocked in gold near the tail.

Gaskell, *NIB* p. 242, no. 95.

694 Unsigned UK

Fox, Charles Armstrong. *A poet's playmates; or, country pictures.* Bath: Binns & Goodwin. London: E. Marlborough & Co. London: Houlston & Wright, [1864]. Bath: Printed by Binns and Goodwin. iv, 288 p. With four pages of publisher's titles bound at the end.

116 × 175 × 30 mm. 11649.aaa.11.

White endpapers and pastedowns. Blue wave horizontal-grain cloth. Both covers are blocked identically in blind. Five fillets blocked on the borders. There is a wide inner border blocked of ovals with leaves inside, and spade shapes on each corner. An inner rectangle is formed by interlocking groups of three fillets, which overlap at the head and at the tail. The spine is blocked in gold. From the head downwards, the decoration is: fillet at head; hatch gold circles and quatrefoils; a fillet; 'dog tooth' decoration; an oval blocked in hatch gold, with scroll-work at its head and at its tail; the title: '| A poet's | playmates |' blocked in relief within gold lettering-pieces; 'dog tooth' decoration; hatch gold circles and quatrefoils; a fillet at the tail.

695 Unsigned UK

Shairp, John Campbell. *Kilmahoe. A highland pastoral. With other poems.* London and Cambridge: Macmillan and Co., 1864. Edinburgh: T. Constable, Printer to the Queen, and to the University. xii, 211 p.

110 × 178 × 20 mm. 11649.aaa.9.

The Description of this work in the publisher's titles as the end of *Leonore*, BL11649.aa.2.: 'Fcap. 8vo. 5s. | '

Binder's ticket on lower pastedown: '| Bound by | Burn | 37 & 38 | Kirby St. |' Blue beaded line diagonal-grain cloth. (The rib grain is horizontal.) Both covers have a single fillet blocked on their borders, in blind on the lower and in gold on the upper. On the centre of the lower cover, the Macmillan medallion is blocked in gold. The spine is blocked in gold. A single gold fillet is blocked at the head and at the tail. The title: 'Kilmahoe | and other | poems | [rule] | Shairp |' is blocked in gold near the head. Near the tail, the imprint: '| Macmillan |' is blocked in gold.

Gaskell, *NIB* p. 242, fig. 95.

696 Unsigned UK

Thompson, D'Arcy Wentworth. *Nursery nonsense or rhymes without reason. Illustrated by C.H.Bennett.* London: Griffith & Farran, Successors to Newbery & Harris, Corner of St. Paul's Churchyard, 1864. London: Wertheimer and Co, Printers, Circus Place, Finsbury. viii, 56 p. With thirty-two pages of publisher's titles bound at the end.

135 × 185 × 12 mm. 12806.bb.13.

The illustrations are signed with Bennett's monogram: 'CHB', and are hand coloured.

Gilt edges. Bevelled boards. Brown endpapers and pastedowns. Binder's ticket on the lower pastedown: '| Bound by | Burn | 37 & 38 | Kirby St. |' Red honeycomb-grain cloth. Both covers are blocked with the same design, in blind on the lower cover, and in gold, black and relief on the upper cover. On the upper cover, there are three fillets blocked in gold on the borders. Between the outer two of these, a repeating pattern of hatch leaves is blocked in gold. Inside the fillets, there are small gold decorative pieces blocked on the corners and on the sides. There are multiple fillets blocked in gold and in black, which form single straps at the centre of the head and the centre of the tail. Leaf and stem decoration is blocked in gold on the inner corners. The central roundel is a gold lettering-piece blocked within an oval formed by fillets blocked in gold and in black. The roundel has three fillets blocked in black on its perimeter, which cross to form medallions at the head and at the tail. Each of these medallions has a head, blocked in gold. Inside the roundel, a gold lettering-piece is blocked with a hatched centre. The title: '| Nursery nonsense | or | Rhymes | Without | Reason |' is blocked in relief with tendrils leading off from many of the letters. The spine is blocked in gold. The words: '| Nursery | nonsense |' are blocked in relief within gold pennant-shaped lettering-pieces.

697 Unsigned UK

White, Henry Kirke. *The poetical works and remains of Henry Kirke White. With a life by R. Southey, LL.D.* London: T. Nelson and Sons, Paternoster Row; Edinburgh; and New York, 1864. xlvii, 340 p., 9 plates, 2 photographs.

115 × 175 × 40 mm. 11611.aa.37.

The two photographs are: 1. An oval pasted to the half title page of 'Wilford Church and Church-yard'; 2. Frontispiece: 'The house in which Henry Kirke White was born (Exchange Alley, Nottingham)'.

Gilt edges. Bevelled boards. Brown endpapers and pastedowns. Purple pebble-grain cloth. Both covers are blocked with an identical design. The design is blocked in gold and in blind on the upper cover, and in blind only on the lower. On the upper cover, five fillets are blocked in gold and blind on the borders. The corner pieces are blocked in gold, and show lyres. The central circular vignette is blocked in gold, with the author's name blocked in relief, within a rectangular gold-lettering-piece formed by two fillets. The spine is blocked in gold and in relief. A single gold fillet is blocked on the perimeter. Near the head, the words: '| Poetical | Works | of | Henry Kirk White |' are blocked in relief within three rectangular gold lettering-pieces, each surrounded by gold hatch decoration. Arabesque decoration and a lyre are blocked in gold on the middle. The words: '| With fine illustrations |' are blocked in relief near the tail, within a rectangular gold lettering-piece surrounded by gold hatch decoration.

698 Unsigned UK

Beauties of poetry and art. Embellished with Sixteen Facsimiles of Water=Colour Drawings, and other illustrations, by George Cattermole, T. Sidney Cooper, A.R.A., Edward Duncan, John Gilbert, William Hunt, R. P Leitch, George Smith, George H. Thomas, Edward H. Wehnert, Mrs. Ward, Henry Warren, Harrison Weir, and H. B. Willis. Engraved and printed by Edmund Evans. London: Ward, Lock, & Tyler, 158, Fleet Street; and 107 Dorset Street, Salisbury Square, [1865]. [London]: Edmund Evans, Engraver and Printer, Raquet Court, Fleet Street. [4], 68 p., 16 plates.

180 × 240 × 34 mm. C.109.d.11.

Gilt edges. Bevelled boards. Purple sand-grain cloth. Both covers are blocked identically in gold, in blind and in relief. On the borders are: 1. a single thin fillet; 2. a hatch fillet; 3. a single fillet; 4. a border of joined leaves, repeated; 5 a single thin gold fillet 6. a hatch fillet; 7. a single thin gold fillet. On the inner borders, three more fillets are blocked: there are two thin fillets, with a single fillet between them, blocked in gold, which has repeating dots blocked in relief within it. On the remainder of each cover, apart from the centre, is a repeating pattern of: 1. single horizontal hatch fleur-de-lis, within diamonds blocked in relief, formed by repeating gold dots; 2. between the diamonds, fillets are blocked in blind, with repeating dots within them blocked in relief. The vignette on the centre of each cover is identical: on the upper cover, it is blocked onto a blue pebble-grain onlay. The vignette is lozenge-shaped with two fillets and vertical hatch between the fillets on the borders. There is a pattern of stems, leaves, flowers, and tendrils, with the leaves blocked in vertical hatch. The title: '| Beauties of poetry | and art. |' is blocked in gold on the centre. The spine is blocked in gold. A single fillet is blocked in gold on the perimeter. From the head downwards, the decoration is: decoration as for borders of covers, nos. 2–6; the title: '| Beauties | of | poetry | and | art. |' blocked in gold, within a panel formed by a single fillet; horizontal hatch fleur-de-lis, blocked within diamonds formed by fillets; decoration as for borders of covers, nos. 2–6; a fillet; at the tail, the words: '| London | Ward, Lock & Tyler |' are blocked in gold, within a rectangle formed by two gold fillets .

Ball, *VPB* p. 165. States the design as possibly by Warren. McLean, *VBD* p. 184 & pp. 221–222.

699 Unsigned UK

Byron, George Gordon Noel, *Baron Byron. The Prisoner of Chillon. Poem by Lord Byron, Illuminated by W. & C. Audsley, Architects.* London: Printed and Published by Day & Son, London, 1865. Unpaginated. [20 p.]

225 × 318 × 20 mm. 11651.m.8.

Each page is chromolithographed on the recto only. The imprint is printed on the last page, together with: '| Chromolithographed | by | W. R. Tymms |'

Gilt edges. Bevelled boards. Cream endpapers and pastedowns. Purple pebble-grain cloth. Both covers blocked mostly identically, in blind and in relief on the lower, and in gold, in blind and in relief on the upper. On the upper cover, the following are blocked on the borders: 1. a 'dog-tooth' border in blind, with repeating dots blocked in relief within each triangle formed by the dog-tooth; 2. a single gold fillet; 3. a border pattern of repeating arches and dog-tooth, blocked in gold; 4. a single gold fillet; 5. a single gold fillet, with repeating dots blocked in relief inside it; 6. dog-tooth decoration on the inner border. On each corner, a six-lobed flower is blocked in gold, and, within each, there is a red pebble-grain cloth onlay, each with two gold fillets on its borders, and each with a shield blocked within. Each shield has a symbolic prison motif blocked in gold within it . There is a large diamond, stretching from head to tail and to each side, with a linked chain blocked in gold on its borders. Inside this, a single fillet is blocked in gold. A blue pebble-grain cloth onlay is within the diamond. There are four wide horizontal gold lettering-pieces blocked within the diamond, each with dog-tooth borders, and each with a single fillet blocked in relief below and above the dog-tooth. The words: '| The | Prisoner | of | Chillon | Byron |' are blocked in (blue) relief within the lettering-pieces, in gothic letters. On the centre, the word: '| of |' is blocked in relief within a quatrefoil-shaped gold lettering-piece, with a single fillet blocked in relief on its borders. Between outside of the diamond and the flowers, a pattern of rectangles is blocked, with a 'two leaves and flowers' motif blocked within each rectangle. The spine is blocked in gold. (The lower half and the head are missing.) Dog-tooth decoration is blocked in gold on the perimeter. Inside this, a single gold fillet is blocked on the perimeter. The title: '| The Prisoner of Chillon |' is blocked along the spine in gothic letters. The words: '| Illuminated by | W & C Audsley |' are blocked in gold along the spine at the head.

Oldfield, *BC* no. 92.

700 Unsigned UK

Jones, Owen. *The grammar of ornament. Illustrated by examples from various styles of ornament. One hundred and twelve plates.* London: Published by Day and Son, Limited, Gate Street, Lincoln's Inn Fields, [1865]. London: Day and Son, Limited, Gate Street, Lincoln's Inn Fields. [1], 157p., 100 plates.
230 × 340 × 45 mm. 1756.a.25.

Gilt edges. The centre of the original upper cover and the original spine are used as pastedowns. Maroon pebble-grain cloth. A Chinese fret is blocked in gold to form the central rectangle. The title: '| The Grammar of Ornament |' is blocked in gold near the head, within a rectangle formed by a single gold fillet. A single gold fillet is blocked on the inner borders. Inside this, another fillet, blocked on the head and on the sides, forms straps on the upper inner corners. A dense leaf and stem pattern is blocked near the tail. Out of this pattern, three long papyrus stems rise, forming three flowers. Unsigned.

701 Unsigned UK

PLATE LXXXVII

George, Hereford Brooke. *The Oberland and its Glaciers: explored and illustrated with ice-axe and camera. With twenty-eight photographic illustrations by Ernest Edwards, B.A. and a map of the Oberland.* London: Alfred W. Bennett, 5, Bishopsgate Without, 1866. London: Unwin Brothers, The Gresham Steam Press, Bucklersbury, London, E.C. xii, 243 p., 11 plates
215 × 274 × 40 mm. Cup.410.g.225.

Frontispiece map of the Oberland has: '| Published by Alfred W. Bennett, 5, Bishopsgate Without. Day & Son (Limited) Lithogrs. |' at the base.

Gilt edges. Bevelled boards. Binder's ticket on lower pastedown: | Bound by | Westleys | & Co. | London. |' Blue sand-grain cloth. Both covers blocked identically in blind on the borders. Three fillets are blocked on the head, the tail, and the sides, intersecting at the corners. Four small circles are blocked in blind at the intersections of these fillets. An inner rectangle is formed by two fillets, blocked in blind on the lower cover and in gold on the upper. On the upper cover, inside this, the central vignette is blocked in gold. It shows, on a snowy mound, an ice-axe, a camera, its shroud, and a tripod. Above the vignette, the title: '| The Oberland | and its glaciers | [rule] |' is blocked in gold. Below the vignette, the sub-title: '| Explored | and Illustrated | with | Ice-axe and Camera. |' is blocked in gold. The spine is blocked in gold. From the head downwards, the decoration is: three gold fillets; the title: '| The | Oberland | and its | glaciers | [by] | H. B. George, M.A. | F.R.G.S. |' blocked in gold; near the tail: '| A. W. Bennett. |' blocked in gold; four gold fillets are blocked in gold at the tail.

702 Unsigned UK

Teika. *Hyak Nin Is'Shin, or stanzas by a century of poets, being Japanese lyrical odes, translated into English, with explanatory notes, the text in Japanese and Roman character, and a full index. By F. V. Dickins, M.B.* London: Smith Elder & Co., 65, Cornhill, 1866. xi, 52, [1], xviii, xvp.
140 × 222 × 20 mm. 11100.d.20.

Gilt edges. Bevelled boards. Original yellow endpaper bound at the front. Both covers are blocked identically, in blind on the lower and in gold on the upper. A single fillet is blocked on the borders. On each upper corner, two oval panels are blocked. On each lower corner, a dragon's head is blocked. Down each side, Japanese text is blocked. Branches are blocked at the head and at the tail, forming an oval central frame. The title words: '| Japanese odes | with translations |' are blocked in gold in semi-circles above and below the centre. On the centre, a Japanese mountain scene is blocked. It shows a volcano (with its cone rising above a layer of cloud), a tree, a hut and a river. The spine is blocked in gold. The words: 'Japanese odes' are blocked in gold along the spine, with small plant decoration on the end of the title.

703 Unsigned UK

Ingelow, Jean. *Poems. With illustrations by G. J. Pinwell, J. W. North, J. Wolf, E. J. Poynter, E. Dalziel, T. Dalziel, A. B. Houghton and W. Small. Engraved by the brothers Dalziel.* London: Longmans, Green, Reader, & Dyer, 1867. [London]: Dalziel Brothers, Engravers and Printers, Camden Press. xv, 318 p.
170 × 237 × 38 mm. RdeB.I.2.

The British Museum de Beaumont copy.

Text sewn on three tapes. Gilt edges. Bevelled boards. Light yellow endpapers and pastedowns. Blue sand-grain cloth. Both covers blocked identically in gold and in black. Two fillets are blocked in gold on the borders. Quatrefoils are blocked in gold on each corner, with plant decoration blocked in gold ins ide. The inner borders have three patterns blocked: the first and third are of repeating fuchsia-like flowers – blocked between two fillets, all in gold. The second border (blocked between the first and the third) shows a repeating pattern of leaves and berries, blocked in relief against a black background, between two fillets blocked in black. The inner rectangle corners show straps and a small leaf blocked in gold and in black. The central oval is formed by a number of gold fillets. Within the central oval, a recessed, elongated quatrefoil is blocked. This has a light yellow paper onlay, blocked with the words: '| Poems | by | Jean Ingelow | Illustrated. |' in gold in elaborate gothic letters. The spine is blocked in gold, and in black, and in relief. A single fillet is blocked in gold on the perimeter. From the head downwards, the decoration is: a rectangle formed by a single fillet, with a fillet blocked in black inside; a decorated rectangular gold lettering-piece; an elongated rectangular panel formed by a single gold fillet; within this panel, flower head decoration is blocked in gold, with leaves blocked in relief – both surrounded by blocking in black; a quatrefoil-shaped gold lettering-piece, with the words: '| Poems | by | Jean Ingelow |' blocked inside in relief in gothic letters; below this panel, the word: '| Illustrated |' is blocked in relief, within a rectangular gold

lettering-piece, which has a single fillet blocked on its borders; another panel formed by a single gold fillet; inside this panel, leaves are blocked in relief, surrounded by small decoration blocked in black; flower head decoration is blocked in gold; five diamonds are blocked in gold, with small crosses and dots, blocked in relief within each diamond; the words: '| Longmans & Co. |' are blocked in relief within a rectangular gold lettering-piece, with a single gold fillet blocked on its borders; a rectangle formed by a single gold fillet, with a black fillet blocked inside; a single gold fillet is blocked at the tail.

Neither the covers nor the spine is signed. R. de Beaumont has written on the upper endpaper verso: 'According [to] an ink note by Ruari [McLean] in my copy of Victorian Book Binding, the binding design is by Albert Warren from Longman's list.'

de Beaumont, *RdeB1* no. 137. Goldman, *VIB* no. 137.

704 Unsigned UK

Kingston, William Henry Giles. *Paul Gerrard, the cabin boy. With illustrations.* London: George Routledge & Sons, Broadway, Ludgate Hill; New York: 416 Broome Street, 1867. [London]: Cox & Wyman, Printers, Great Queen Street, W.C. [1], 372 p., 8 plates. With eight pages of publisher's titles bound at the end.

106 × 172 × 38 mm. 12805.g.57.

The plates are signed: 'Dalziel'.

Text sewn on three sawn-in cords. Light yellow endpapers and pastedowns. Green sand-grain cloth. Both covers blocked identically on the borders, in blind on the lower and in gold on the upper. On the upper cover, there is a 'dog-tooth' border, blocked in gold, with two fillets in gold blocked on the borders inside. The upper cover central vignette is blocked in gold. It shows a semi-circular panel, which is formed by a single thick fillet blocked in gold. The panel is supported by two round columns, blocked to the left and to the right. Within the panel, a three-masted ship, its sails furled, is on the sea. Between the two columns on the centre, the words: '| Paul Gerrard | the | cabin boy. | By W. H. G. Kingston. |' are blocked in gold, within a rectangle formed by a single thick gold fillet. Unsigned. The spine is blocked in gold. From the head downwards, the decoration is: two gold fillets; the words: '| Paul Gerrard | the | Cabin Boy. | Kingston |' blocked in relief within three gold lettering-pieces, which have gold hatch borders; the word 'the' is blocked in gold within a rectangle formed by a single gold fille; between and around the gold lettering-pieces acorns, oak leaves and a ship's mast are blocked in gold; signed either 'J', or 'TJ', or 'JT' as a monogram at the base of the oak decoration; a rowing boat and an anchor are blocked in gold near the base; the word: '| Routledge |' is blocked in relief within a rectangular gold lettering-piece, with a gold hatch border; two gold fillets are blocked at the tail.

705 Unsigned UK

Whittier, John Greenleaf. *Snow-Bound; A Winter Idyll.* London: Alfred W. Bennett, 5, Bishopsgate Without, E.C., 1867. Unwin Brothers, Printers, Bucklersbury, London. 47 p., 1 plate.

132 × 185 × 13 mm. 11686.aaa.55.

The frontispiece is a photograph portrait of Whittier. On the half title page verso: 'Five photographic illustrations taken from American scenery.' On the title page verso: 'Reprinted from the American edition. (Twenty-Fifth Thousand.)'

Gilt edges. Bevelled boards. Brown endpapers and pastedowns. Binder's ticket on lower pastedown: '| Bound by | Westleys | & Co. | London. |' Blue sand-grain cloth. Both covers identically blocked on the borders and on the corners, in blind on the lower cover, in gold on the upper cover. Three fillets blocked on the borders. Flower, leaf and small decoration is blocked on each corner. On the upper cover, a circular photographic print is pasted onto a recess on the centre. It shows a winter forest snow scene. Above and below it, the words: 'Snow bound'; 'J. G. Whittier' are blocked in gold, in semi-circular 'wintry' letters. The spine has no blocking.

706 Unsigned UK

Turnely, Joseph. *Reveries of affection. In memory of that good and beloved Prince His Royal Highness the late Prince Consort who departed this life on the fourteenth day of December 1861. 'The righteous never die'.* [South Norwood, Surrey: Published for the Author, 1868.] London: Dalziel Brothers, Engravers and Printers, Camden Press. [11], 85 p., 4 photographic prints.

203 × 262 × 20 mm. 1347.k.20.

The photographs appear to be photo-montage. Three of the four are: page 2: An angel is hovering outside an upper castle rampart; page 23: Clouds; page 33: Victoria and Albert (in shadow) surrounded by clouds.

Gilt edges. Red morocco. '| Bound by Riviere |' is blocked in gold on the upper cover turn-in. Both covers have the same design blocked in gold on the borders and on the corners. The upper cover has the words: 'In memoriam' blocked in gold on the centre. The lower cover has the royal coat of arms on the centre in gold, with the motto: 'Treu und Fest'. On the spine, the six panels are formed by single gold fillets and blocked in gold with a flower on the centre of each panel. This copy is the author's dedication copy, and was purchased 8 AP[RIL 18]92. Another copy is at BL 11658.g.178.

707 Unsigned UK

Wilcocks J. C. *The sea-fisherman: comprising the chief methods of hook and line fishing in the British and other seas, and remarks on nets, boats and boating. Profusely illustrated with woodcuts of leads, baited hooks, knots, nets, and boats etc., and detailed descriptions of the same . . . Second edition, much enlarged, and almost entirely rewritten.* London: Longmans, Green, and Co., 1868. London: Printed by Spottiswoode and Co., New-Street Square and

Parliament Street. xiii, 303p, 28 plates. With sixteen pages of advertisement and thirty-two pages of publisher's titles bound at the end.
123 × 202 × 34 mm. 7907.bbb.3.

Brown endpapers and pastedowns. Blue sand-grain cloth. Both covers blocked identically with three fillets in blind on the borders, one thick between two thin. The upper cover central vignette is blocked in gold. It shows a reproduction of the engraving on page 71, entitled: 'the courge or Sand-Eel basket'. '. . . The basket is made of fine willow or osier twigs, not more than about one-eighth of an inch thickness . . .' The spine is blocked in gold. Three fillets are blocked in gold at the head and at the tail, one thick between two thin. Near the head, the words: '| The | Sea | Fisherman | Wilcocks |' are blocked in gold.

708 Unsigned UK

PLATE LXXXVIII

The Enchanted Toasting-Fork. A fairy Tale. London: Tinsley Brothers, 18, Catherine St., Strand, 1869. London: Bradbury, Evans, and Co., Printers, Whitefriars. 52 p. With one page of publisher's titles bound at the end.
148 × 190 × 17 mm. 11648.ee.7.

Purple pansy-grain cloth. The upper cover is blocked in gold. Three fillets are blocked in blind on the borders of the lower cover, two thin and one thick. The same three fillets are blocked in gold on the borders of the upper cover. On the centre, a pennant-shaped gold lettering-piece has a toasting fork driven through the folds of the pennant. In the pennant, the words: '| A Fairy Tale |' are blocked in relief. The title: '| The Enchanted | Toasting | Fork. |' is blocked above and below the pennant. The spine is blocked in gold. At the head and at the tail, a fillet and linked semi-circles are blocked in gold. The title: '| The | Enchanted | Toasting | Fork. |' is blocked in gold, in fanciful letters. Near the tail: '| Tinsley Brothers |' is blocked in gold. Unsigned.

709 Unsigned UK

Ouida *pseud.* [i.e. Marie Louise de la Ramee.] *Tricotrin. The story of a waif and stray. In three volumes. Vol. I. [–III.]* London: Chapman and Hall, 193, Piccadilly, 1869. [London]: John Childs & Son, Printers.
12626.dd.8.

Vol. I. [6], 331 p. 130 × 196 × 25 mm.
Vol. II. [4], 319 p. 130 × 197 × 25 mm.
Vol. III. [4], 413 p. 130 × 196 × 30 mm.

Light yellow endpapers of each volume bound at the front. Green pansy-grain cloth is on the boards of all three volumes. All covers are blocked identically in blind. There are three fillets blocked on the borders, with an inner border fillet. A central oval panel is blocked on each upper cover, with small decoration blocked in relief within each. The spines are blocked in gold. Small repeating flower decoration is blocked between two fillets at the head and at the tail – all in gold. The words: '| Tricotrin | by | Ouida. | [small decorative device] | Vol. I. [–III.] |' are blocked in gold near the head.

710 Unsigned UK

Raven, John James. *The church bells of Cambridgeshire; a chronicle of the principal campanological events that have occurred within the County. To which is appended a list of the inscriptions on the bells. By J. J. Raven, B.D., of Emmanuel College, Cambridge, Head Master of Yarmouth Grammar School. . . .* Lowestoft: Samuel Tymms, 60, High Street, 1869. Printed by Samuel Tymms, 60, High Street, Lowestoft. [5], 67, 36 p., 9 plates.
145 × 230 × 14 mm. 7896.aaa.1.

On the upper pastedown, the bookplate of Gilbert R. Redgrave is pasted. Below this, a slip is pasted, with the typed words: '| Ex libris | Harry Palgrave Raven | to replace a copy | destroyed | May 1941 |' Signed on the half-title page recto: '| Ex-libris | Gilbert R. Redgrave. | Dec. 1870. |'. Printed on the half-title page verso: '| Only one hundred copies printed. |'

Yellow endpapers and pastedowns. Brown horizontal-grain cloth. Both covers identically blocked in blind on the borders and on the inner corners. Two fillets are blocked on the borders, the outer thin, the inner thick. Diagonal fillets blocked on each corner join the outer fillets to two more fillets, which form the inner rectangle. On each inner corner, a leaf pattern is blocked. On the lower cover, the central vignette is blocked in gold. It shows a reproduction of figure 15, the arms of France and of England quarterly, crowned, which are on the West Wickham 4th [bell]. The upper cover central vignette is blocked in gold. It shows a reproduction of figure 23, which is a shield on the Landbeach tenor. The bird and the initials 'WP' are conjectured as the bell founder's name: William Peacocke. The text: '| In d'uo | co'fido |' is considered to be an allusion to Psalm XI, 1.

711 Unsigned UK

Svoboda, Alesander. *The seven churches of Asia. With twenty full-page photographs, taken on the spot, historical notes and itinerary. With an introduction by the Rev. H. B. Tristram, M.A., LL.D., F.R.S.* London: Sampson Low, Son and Marston, Crown Buildings, Fleet Street, 1869. London: R. Clay, Sons, and Taylor, Printers, Bread Street Hill. viii, 77 p., 20 plates of photographs.
215 × 280 × 30 mm. 1783.a.37.

There is one page bound at the end, which lists the entire sixty-two photographs taken by A. Svoboda on his expedition.

Bevelled boards. Gilt edges. Brown endpapers and pastedowns. Binder's ticket on lower pastedown: 'Bound by Burn & Co. Kirby St. E.C.' Blue sand-grain cloth. Both covers have the same design blocked on the borders, the corners and on the sides, in blind on the lower cover, and in gold and black on the upper. There are three fillets blocked on the borders. A cross is blocked on each corner. Fillets blocked in gold and black form

small rectangular panels, which have scrollwork blocked in gold, and other small decoration blocked in black and in gold. On the upper cover, the Alpha and Omega letters are blocked in black, with small decoration around them in gold. In the central panel at the head, a cross is blocked inside an inverted triangle, both in gold. At the tail, the star of David is blocked in gold. Below the cross and triangle, seven stars are blocked in gold. The title words: ' The seven' are blocked in gold above the centre. The word: 'Churches' is blocked below the centre. At the centre, seven lit candles are blocked in gold, each with a long stem, with the candleholders ending in three legs at the base. Towards the base of each, the name of each church is blocked in relief within pennant-shaped hatched gold lettering-pieces. The names are: 'Ephesus; Smyrna; Pergamos; Thyatira; Sardis; Philadelphia; Laodices'. On the left and the right of the group of candles, symbols of the cross are blocked in gold. Each of these symbols is blocked at the head and at the tail of the spine, in gold. The title words are blocked along the spine in gold.

712 Unsigned UK

Hibberd, Shirley. *Rustic adornments for homes of taste. A new edition, revised corrected, and enlarged, with nine coloured plates and two hundred and thirty wood engravings.* London: Groombridge and Sons, 5, Paternoster Row, 1870. B. Fawcett, Engraver and Printer, Driffield. vii, 402 p., 8 plates. With two pages of the 'Rustic adornment advertising sheet' bound at the front, and ten pages of advertisements and eight pages of publisher's titles bound at the end.
167 × 215 × 60 mm. 7004.bb.24.

The Frontispiece plate is signed: 'H. Briscoe del.'

Gilt edges. Bevelled boards. Binder's ticket on lower pastedown: '| Bound by | W. Bone & Son | 76 Fleet Street London E.C. |' Brown sand-grain cloth. On the lower cover, three fillets are blocked in blind on the borders. There is a central vignette blocked in blind on the lower cover, showing curling stems and leaves. The upper cover is blocked in gold and in black. Two fillets are blocked on the borders in black. A rustic branch diagonal trellis is blocked in gold on the left hand side and on the lower half of the cover. A bird cage, blocked in gold, (with a bird inside) hangs near the top. Black leaves and stems climb from the base to the top on the left hand side. A medallion is blocked in gold near the left base; it has two fillets blocked on its perimeter, one in black and one in gold. Inside it, a scene showing jungle houses is blocked in gold. On the right hand side of the cover, the words: '| Rustic | adornments | for | homes of taste | by | Shirley Hibberd |' are blocked in gold above and between the trellis. The spine is blocked in gold and in black. From the head downwards, the decoration is: '| Rustic | adornments | for | homes of taste | [rule] | Shirley Hibberd |' blocked in gold; from the base to the title words, a wooden frame formed by branches is blocked in gold; a diamond is blocked at the head of this frame, with the words: '| Coloured Illustrations |' blocked in relief within a rectangular gold lettering-piece, with a single gold fillet blocked on its borders; below this, leaf and stem decoration blocked in black; an aquarium blocked in gold, within a half moon formed by two fillets, one in black, and one in gold; the words: '| London | Groombridge & Sons |' are blocked in gold within a rectangle formed by a single branch-like gold fillet; two fillets and leaf decoration are blocked in black at the tail.

713 Unsigned UK

Prosser, Mrs. *Original Fables. Profusely Illustrated by Ernest Griset, Harrison Weir, Noel Humphreys, and other eminent Artists.* London: The Religious Tract Society, 56, Paternoster Row; 65, St. Paul's Churchyard; and 164 Piccadilly, [1870]. London: Printed by W. Clowes and Sons, Stamford Street and Charing Cross. viii, 248 p.
138 × 190 × 23 mm. 12304.cc.35.

Gilt edges. Bevelled boards. Brown endpapers and pastedowns. Binder's ticket on lower pastedown: '| Bound by | Lewis & Sons, | Gough Square | Fleet St. | London |'. Brown dot and line diagonal-grain cloth. The lower cover is blocked in blind only. Three fillets are blocked on the borders, the outermost thick, the two inner thin. The central vignette shows four joined circles, with a leaf blocked in each. A diamond is blocked between the four circles on the centre. The upper cover is blocked in gold and black. A fillet is blocked on the borders in black. On the corners and sides, there is a 'trellis' pattern of thin stems, leaves and flowers, joined to thin supports – all blocked in black. The words: '| Original fables | by Mrs. Prosser |' are blocked in gold. The capital 'O' of 'Original' is a green paper onlay which has gold blocked on its recessed centre and fillets on its borders. A group of leaves, of birds and an ass, dressed in a coat and glasses, are blocked to the left of the 'O'. The spine is blocked in gold and in black. A single fillet is blocked in black on the perimeter of the upper and the lower panels. From the head downwards, the decoration is: a fillet in black; a curling stem and leaf, blocked in a panel in black; the title words: '| Original | Fables |' blocked in relief within two rectangular gold lettering-pieces – the capitals 'O' and 'F' being blocked within horizontal hatch gold lettering-pieces; the words: 'Mrs Prosser' blocked in gold within a rectangle formed by a single fillet blocked in black; a tracery of curling stems blocked in black surrounds a flying bird and a cockerel on a weather vane – both in gold; a fillet is blocked in black at the tail.

Packer, *BVL* p. 92.

714 Unsigned UK

Thompson, Stephen. *Venice and the Poets. With photographic illustrations. Edited and illustrated by Stephen Thompson. . . .* London: Provost & Co., 5, Bishopsgate Without, E.C., 1870. iv, 47 p., 10 photographs.
220 × 286 × 15 mm. 11651.k.15.

Bevelled boards. Gilt edges. Dark green endpapers and pastedowns. Purple pebble-grain cloth. Both covers blocked identi-

cally on the borders and the corners. Two fillets are blocked in blind on the borders, the outer thick, the inner thin. There is tracery blocked in gold on the corners, in gold on the upper cover and in blind on the lower. On the upper cover, the central vignette is blocked in gold. It shows the Doge's Palace and the tower of St Mark's, with a gondola blocked in the foreground on the water. The title: '| Venice | and the poets |' is blocked in gold. On the spine, the title: '| Venice and the poets |' is blocked in gold. Unsigned.

715 Unsigned UK

Hall, Samuel Carter. *A Book of Memories of Great Men and Women of the age, from personal acquaintance* . . . London: Virtue & Co., City Road and Ivy Lane, 1871. London: Printed by Virtue and Co., City Road. xv, 488 p.
166 × 232 × 42 mm. C.61.b.27.

On the front endpaper verso, two carte de visite portraits are pasted. They are autographed: 'Mrs George Cruikshank'; 'Geo Cruikshank'. Underneath them are the words: '| A Book of Memories. | This book | is presented to | "The British Museum" | in memory of | George Cruikshank. Artist | by his Widow | Eliza Cruikshank | December 23rd 1887 | her 80th Birthday |'.

The half title page recto has two carte de visite portraits pasted at the head. They are autographed: '| SC Hall'; 'Anna Maria | Mrs. S. C Hall' |. Underneath are the words: '| To Mr & Mrs George Cruikshank | with the affectionate regards | of their very dear friends. S. C. Hall | Anna Maria Hall |'.

Gilt edges. Bevelled boards. Yellow endpapers and pastedowns. Binder's ticket on lower pastedown: '| Bound by | Virtue & Co | City Road. | 294. |' Green pebble-grain cloth. The lower cover is blocked in black only. Four fillets are blocked on the borders. The central medallion shows laurel leaves in a circle, with a lamp on the centre. The upper cover is blocked in gold and in black. Two fillets are blocked in black on the borders, with the design between them being of black dots. Rectangles are formed at the head and at the tail by single fillets blocked in black. Half ovals, also formed by fillets, are blocked inside. Within the rectangle at the head, two stars and the words: '| A | book of memories |' are blocked in gold. In the rectangle at the tail, two stars and the words: '| of | great men & women of the age. |' are blocked in gold. The centre panel has a quatrefoil formed by two fillets blocked in black. A star is blocked in gold at the centre head of the central panel. The central medallion is the same as the lower cover, but blocked in gold, with the addition of a second circular fillet in black. The spine is blocked in black and in gold. Two fillets are blocked on the perimeter in black, with repeating dots between them. From the head downwards, the decoration is: an arch, blocked in black; the word: '| Memories. |' blocked in gold, within an arch; a fillet blocked in black; a star blocked in gold within a near-circle formed by two fillets blocked in black; a fillet runs down each side of the spine to near the tail from this near-circle; a medallion is blocked on the centre of the spine, formed by three fillets: gold, black, gold; a lamp is blocked in gold inside the medallion; a semi-circle formed by a single fillet is blocked near the base; inside the arch: '| S. C. Hall | F.S.A. |' is blocked in gold.

Formerly shelved at: 10804.ee.12. The title letters are 'modernistic' in style, having prominent 'weighted' serifs at their tips.

—— Another copy is at BL.10856.ee.5. Copyright copy. The original upper cover and spine are bound in at the front. Rebound by Chivers, 1980.

716 Unsigned UK

Hood, Thomas. *Poems. Illustrated by Birket Foster.* London: E. Moxon, Son & Co., Dover Street, 1871. viii, 109 p., 22 plates. With three pages of publisher's titles bound at the end.
220 × 285 × 30 mm. 11651.k.5.

Gilt edges. Bevelled boards. Beige endpapers and pastedowns. Binder's ticket on lower pastedown: '| Bound | by | Leighton | Son and | Hodge |'. Purple sand-grain cloth. On the lower cover, two fillets are blocked in blind on the borders. The central medallion is of a repeating 'ball and leaves' motif, together with the monogram of Moxon. The upper cover is blocked in gold. The design is of a large flywheel, to the right of the cover. The 'drive shaft' is linked to it and is blocked across the cover to the spine. Behind the wheel, a garden trellis has flowers and branches blocked on it, all in gold. Two groups of fillets, each ending in four 'circlets' are blocked in gold on each corner. The title and imprint: '| Hood's Poems | Illustrated | by Birket Foster | E. Moxon Son & Co. | 1871 |' are blocked in relief within ribbon-shaped gold lettering-pieces, which 'hang' from the trellis and from the fly wheel. At the head and at the tail, there is a wide border blocked in gold, with flower heads and other ornamental patterns blocked within squares. The spine is blocked in gold and in relief. A single gold fillet is blocked on the perimeter. The title: '| Poems. | Hood. Foster |' is blocked in relief along the spine, within a long gold lettering-piece, shaped as a 'driveshaft'. Small decoration is blocked in gold within squares at the head and at the tail, together with two small circles in gold.

McLean, *VPBB* p. 129.

717 Unsigned UK

Burnand, *Sir* Francis Cowley. *MoKeanna! A treble temptation. &c., &c., &c.* London: Bradbury, Agnew, & Co., 10, Bouverie St, 1873. [London]: Bradbury, Agnew & Co., Printers, Whitefriars. [8], 270 p., 4 plates.
115 × 165 × 22 mm. 12331.aaa.49.

Red rib diagonal-grain cloth (faint diagonals). The lower cover is blocked in blind only. Three fillets are blocked on the borders, one thick between two thin. The upper cover is blocked in black only. A single fillet is blocked on the borders. The two figures of a seal and person (wrapped in a costume of leaves) are

reproductions of those on the plate between pages 174–5, entitled: 'Beauty and Fashion a la mode insulaire'. The title: '| MoKeanna! |' is blocked in black in oriental lettering; the words: '| A | Treble | Temptation | By | F. C. Burnand. |' are blocked in black. The spine has the title: '| MoKeanna! |' blocked in gold along it.

de Beaumont, *RdeB1* no. 44. Goldman, *VIB* no. 44.

718 Unsigned UK

Dunkin, Edwin Hadlow Wise. *The Church Bells of Cornwall: their archaeology past and present condition. . . .* Printed for the Author by Bemrose & Sons, London and Derby, 1878. Bemrose and Sons, Printers, London and Derby. [7], 94 p., 3 plates.
143 × 227 × 12 mm. 10360.ff.7.

Yellow endpapers and pastedowns. Brown pebble-grain cloth. Both covers identically blocked in blind on the borders with two fillets, the inner of which resembles joined-up bell rope sallies. The upper cover centre-piece shows a bell, which is blocked as a gold lettering-piece. It has no inscriptions on it. Above and below the bell, the title: '| Church Bells | of | Cornwall |' is blocked in gold. The spine is blocked in gold. Three fillets are blocked in gold at the head and at the tail. The title: '| The Church Bells of Cornwall |' is blocked in gold along the spine.

719 Unsigned UK

D'Anvers, N. *pseud.* [i.e. Nancy R. E. Meugens, afterwards, Bell.] *Some account of the great buildings of London: historical and descriptive. With Thirteen Autotype Illustrations by F. York.* London: Marcus Ward & Co., 67 & 68 Chandos Street, W.C; and Royal Ulster Works, Belfast, 1879. [5], 56 p., 14 plates of photographs.
175 × 255 × 18 mm. 10352.i.4.

Each plate is inscribed: 'F. York, Photographer; Autotype, S.S.B. & Co.'. The fourteen autotypes, or carbon prints, were used some fourteen years after the process was improved by Swan in 1864.

Bevelled boards. White endpapers and pastedowns. Red sand-grain cloth. The lower cover is blocked in blind, with two fillets blocked on the borders. The upper cover is blocked in gold and in black. There is a black fillet blocked on the borders. Inside this, the design divides into three. At the head, a rectangular gold lettering-piece is blocked, showing the Tower of London. This is bordered with ornament blocked in black. In the middle, is a roundel gold lettering-piece, showing St. Paul's cathedral dome and the west front facade. To either side of the roundel, coats of arms are blocked: to the left the Arms of the Corporation of London; to the right, the Arms of Westminster. These are blocked in gold and in relief, and are surrounded by leaves and by branches, blocked in black. At the tail, the rectangular gold lettering-piece shows Westminster Abbey. This is also surrounded by ornament blocked in black. The words: '| Great Buildings |' are blocked above the roundel in gold, with black edges. The word: '| of |' is blocked in gold below the roundel; the word: '| London |' is blocked below the roundel in gold, with black edges. The spine is blocked in gold and in black. Fillets in black are blocked on the head and on the tail. From the head downwards, the decoration is: a rose blocked in gold and in relief; the title: '| Great | Buildings | of | London |' blocked in relief within a gold lettering-piece; the word: '| D'Anvers |' blocked in gold between two fillets in black; Nelson's column is blocked in gold and in relief on the middle of the spine; the imprint: '| Marcus | Ward & Co |' is blocked in relief within a gold lettering-piece near the tail.

Martin, *Photos* pp. 82, 83.

720 Unsigned UK

Holmes, Frederick Morrell. *Faith's Father: a story of child-life in London bye-ways.* London; Paris; New York: Cassell, Petter and Galpin & Co., [1880]. London: Cassell, Petter and Galpin, Belle Sauvage Works, London, E.C. 159 p. With four pages of publisher's titles bound at the rear.
125 × 190 × 15 mm. 12809.k.23.

Buff endpapers and pastedowns. Red ungrained cloth. Both covers blocked in gold and in black. The design is continuous across both covers and the spine. The lower cover is blocked in black only. It shows a broad leaf and stem design, with a spider hanging from a thread. The upper cover is blocked in gold, in black and in relief. On the upper portion, there is a gold lettering-piece shaped as a fan, with the title: '| Faith's | Father |' blocked in relief within. To the left of the fan, a black square is blocked, together with an insect in flight. Below this, stem, leaf and flower decoration is blocked in black. On the lower half, a man, wearing a backpack, is looking through a telescope mounted on a wooden stand. The spine is blocked in gold and in black. The title: '| Faith's | Father |' is blocked in gold, with two leaves below it blocked in black.

721 Unsigned UK

Maggs, J. *Round Europe with the crowd.* London: W. H. Allen & Co., 13, Waterloo Place, S.W., 1880. [London]: Witherby & Co., Printers, 74, Cornhill; Newman's Court, Cornhill; and 325A, High Holborn, W.C. vii, 362 p.
125 × 187 × 30 mm. 10107.ee.9.

White endpapers and pastedowns. Grey ungrained cloth. The lower cover is blocked in black. A single black fillet is blocked on the borders. The central panel is a double diamond-shape, formed by three fillets, with small decoration on its corners – all blocked in black. The upper cover is blocked in gold and in black. Four fillets are blocked in black at the head and at the tail. The rest of the blocking is in gold. On the centre, a globe is blocked, showing countries' latitude and longitude, in relief. A man sits astride the globe, dressed in seventeenth century style clothes. Decorative stems and leaves form four circles around the globe. In each circle, the following are blocked: a train; a paddle steamer, named 'Ohio'; mountains; a volcano. Satyr-like heads are blocked in gold at the head and on the tail. One star is

blocked in gold on each side of the globe. The spine is blocked in gold. From the head downwards, the decoration is: curling stem decoration; the title: '| Round Europe | with | The Crowd | [rule] | J. Maggs |' blocked in gold between fillets blocked in gold; two circles, as for the upper cover, with the paddle steamer and the volcano blocked within each circle; at the tail, the imprint: '| W. H.Allen & Co. |' is blocked in gold between two groups of two gold fillets.

722 Unsigned UK

Wood, Charles William. *The Cruise of The Reserve Squadron.* London: Richard Bentley & Son, New Burlington St. Publishers in Ordinary to Her Majesty the Queen, 1883. London: Simmons & Botten, Printers, Shoe Lane, E.C. xii, 239 p., 62 plates

127 × 195 × 35 mm. 10161.de.12.

Light yellow endpapers and pastedowns. Blue ungrained cloth. The lower cover has a small central vignette, blocked in gold. It shows a sailor, in contemporary clothes, a sword in his right hand, and a Union Jack in his left hand, a cannon and cannon balls, which are stacked in a pile. Underneath the sailor, the initials '| H.M.S. |' are blocked in gold, and the word: '| Defence |' is blocked in relief, within a gold lettering-piece shaped as the end of an anchor. The upper cover is blocked in gold, red, olive green and platinum [?]. It shows a mast, in gold, with the Union Jack at the top, and two flags below. The title words are blocked below this. The words: '| The cruise |' are blocked in gold; '| of the |' are blocked in platinum; the words: '| Reserve Squadron |' are blocked in gold in 'rope-shaped' letters. There is a platinum fillet blocked at the tail. The spine is blocked in gold. There are gold fillets at the head and at the tail. The title: '| The | Cruise | of the | Reserve | Squadron |' is blocked in gold. Underneath this, the upper rigging of a sailing ship is blocked in gold. The publisher's name '| Bentley |' is blocked in gold near the tail.

723 V., L

Jewry, afterwards Valentine, Laura. *Gems of national poetry. Compiled and edited by Mrs Valentine. With illustrations and steel portrait.* London: Frederick Warne & Co., Bedford Street, Strand, [1880]. [London]: Dalziel Brothers, Engravers and Printers, Camden Press. [4], 540 p., 9 plates.

125 × 185 × 35 mm. 11604.b.1/4.

The Lansdowne Poets [series].

Gilt edges. Bevelled boards. Brown endpapers and pastedowns. Red diagonal rib-grain cloth (the grain is faint). The lower cover is blocked in blind, with, on the borders, four fillets and a repeating leaf pattern blocked in the middle in blind. On the centre is blocked a medallion, with '35' blocked inside. The upper cover is blocked in gold and black. There is a black fillet blocked on the border. The words: '| Lansdowne poets |' are blocked in black at the head. Signed 'LV' as a monogram within a shield formed by a single fillet. The words '| National poetry |' are blocked in black, with red in relief as 'double' lettering, all inside a rectangle blocked in hatch gold. The decoration is in black, with thistles and flowers around a lyre, which is blocked in black and gold. The word: '| Illustrations |' is blocked in relief within a scroll-shaped gold lettering-piece. The spine is blocked in gold and in black. From the head downwards, the decoration is: repeating gold dots across spine; small circles and two dots blocked in relief within a gold fillet; the words: '| Lansdowne | Poets. |' blocked in black within a panel formed by two black fillets; three black fillets; the words: '| Gems | of | National | Poetry |' blocked in relief within a gold lettering-piece panel, which has vertical hatch at its head and at its tail; decoration blocked in black; a vase is blocked in gold, with a surround blocked in black; leaf and buds are blocked in relief against a background blocked in black; near the tail, the words: '| F. Warne & Co. |' blocked in relief within a rectangular gold lettering-piece, with a single fillet blocked in relief on its borders; two black fillets at the tail.

Ball, *VPB* p. 158. States that the 1866 edition of this work has a design recorded in the V&A catalogue with a cover design by Rogers.

724 W

Kingston, William Henry Giles. *Infant amusements; or, how to make a nursery happy. With practical hints to parents and nurses on the moral and physical training of children.* London: Griffith and Farran, Corner of St. Paul's Churchyard, 1867. Gilbert and Rivington, Printers, St. John's Square, London. xviii, 183 p., 1 plate. With thirty-two pages of publisher's titles bound at the end.

126 × 197 × 23 mm. 12806.ccc.27.

The frontispiece plate is signed: 'Kate Greenaway del'.

Yellow endpapers and pastedowns. Green sand-grain cloth. Both covers blocked identically in blind on the borders, on the corners, and on the sides. Two fillets are blocked in blind on the borders, the outer thick, the inner thin. On the inner border, two parallel fillets blocked in blind cross regularly to form cartouches. On each corner, the fillets cross and are surrounded by leaves. The whole forms the inner rectangle. The upper cover central vignette is blocked in gold and in relief. On the centre, two interlocking scroll-like gold lettering-pieces are blocked, each with hatch gold borders. They form semi-circular shapes which cross. The title: '| Infant | Amusements |' is blocked in relief within each gold lettering-piece. Above and below these, groups of leaves and flowers are blocked in gold. Signed 'W' in relief within a circular gold lettering-piece near the base of the vignette. The spine is blocked in gold, in blind and in relief. Three fillets are blocked in blind at the head and at the base of the spine. The title: '| Infant | amusements |' is blocked in relief within two semi-circular scroll-shaped gold lettering-pieces, with leaves and flowers blocked above and below. Near the tail: the words: '| London | Griffith & Farran |' are blocked in gold.

725 W

Loud, Clara. *A wreath from the woods. Poems. . . .* Dover: Published by Batcheller & Co., King's Arms Library; Canterbury: R. Austen, 43 & 44, Burygate Street, 1868. Chivers, Printer, Palace Street, Canterbury. viii, 128 p.
107 × 165 × 15 mm. 11647.aaa.34.

Text sewn on two thin cords. Yellow endpapers and pastedowns. Mauve pansy-grain cloth. Both covers blocked identically in blind on the borders and on the corners. Two fillets are blocked on the borders, one thick, one thin. There is leaf and stem decoration blocked on each corner. The upper cover has a central vignette blocked in gold. It shows two stems at the base, which rise to form a circle. There are stems, small leaves and flowers blocked around the circle. Inside the circle, the title: '| A Wreath | from the | Woods |' is blocked in gold. Signed 'W' in gold at the base of the vignette. At the head of the spine, the word: '| Poems |' is blocked in gold between two gold fillets. A small decorative device is blocked beneath. Another decorative device is blocked in gold at the tail, with two gold fillets underneath.

726 W

Sauvage, Elie. *The Little Gipsy. Illustrated by Lorenz Frölich. Translated by Anna Blackwell.* London: Griffith and Farran, Successors to Newbery and Harris, Corner of St. Paul's Churchyard, 1869. Gilbert and Rivington, Printers, St. John's Square, London. vii, 150 p. With two pages of publisher's titles bound at the end.
162 × 221 × 21 mm. 12805.i.54.

On page one of the publisher's catalogue: 'Small 4vo., price 5s. cloth; 6s cloth elegant, gilt edges.'

Gilt edges. Bevelled boards. Grey endpapers and pastedowns. Binder's ticket on lower pastedown: '| Bound by | W. Bone & Son. | 76. Fleet St. | London E.C. |' Red ungrained cloth. Both covers blocked identically in black on the borders. Five fillets are blocked on the borders. An interlinked pattern of stems and of leaves is blocked in black on the sides, the head and the tail. On the sides, the stems form a 'figure of eight'. On the head and on the tail, the stems form a trefoil. The upper cover central vignette is blocked in gold. It shows a central oval formed by two 'rope-shaped' fillets, with a pattern of ivy leaves and berries blocked between them. At the head and at the base, the words: '| The Little Gipsy | Illustrated by | Lorenz Frölich |' are blocked in relief within three rectangular gold lettering-pieces; the top and bottom lettering-pieces have a single gold fillet blocked on their borders. On the centre, the figure of the Little Gipsy is blocked. She is wearing a ragged full length dress and holds a bowl in her left hand. On the title page, the same engraving is signed: 'L. Frolich'. The upper cover vignette is signed 'W' in gold at the base of the Gipsy's feet. The spine is blocked in gold and in relief. A single gold fillet is blocked on the perimeter. At the head, the decoration is: two gold fillets; small decoration in gold; a line of dots in gold. Along the spine, from tail to head, the words: '| Illustrated | The Little Gipsy | By Frölich |' are blocked in relief within three gold lettering-pieces with their borders picked out by single fillets blocked in relief. The words are surrounded by ivy and berry decoration, blocked in gold. At the tail are: two gold fillets; the words: '| Griffith | and | Farran |' are blocked in relief within a square gold lettering-piece; two gold fillets.

727 W., A.

Grant, James. *Jack Manly: His Adventures by Sea and Land. With illustrations.* London: Routledge, Warne and Routledge, Farringdon Street. New York: 56, Walker Street, 1861. London: Savill, and Edwards, Printers, Chandos Street, Covent Garden. vii, 436 p. 8 plates. With four pages of publisher's titles bound at the end.
110 × 172 × 42 mm. 12806.cc.37.

The plates are signed 'Keeley Halswelle' and 'Dalziel'.

Yellow endpapers and pastedowns. Green morocco vertical-grain cloth. Both covers blocked identically in blind on the borders and on the corners. Two fillets are blocked on the borders. Roundels are blocked in blind on each corner, with a rose blocked in relief within each. The upper cover central vignette is blocked in gold. It shows a young man seated on a wooden barrel. An anchor is blocked to his right and a telescope and a clam are blocked below him. Curling stems and small leaves surround the centre, forming a 'diamond-shape'. The spine is blocked in gold and in relief. Double gold fillets are blocked down each side and a single gold fillet is blocked at the head and at the tail. From the head downwards, the decoration is: a wooden stave; from the stave hangs a gold lettering-piece, shaped to resemble a canvas sail; the words: '| Jack Manly's | adventures | by | Sea & Land | [rule] | Grant. |' blocked in relief within the sail; an anchor, a sword and a rifle – all three surrounded by sea plant decoration in gold; the word: '| Illustrated |' is blocked in relief within a rectangular gold lettering-piece, which has repeating dots blocked in relief above and below on its border; more sea plant decoration; signed 'AW' in gold as a monogram at the tail.

728 W., A.

Du Chaillu, Paul Belloni. *Stories of the Gorilla Country. Narrated for young people. With numerous illustrations.* London: Sampson Low, Son, & Marston, Milton House, Ludgate Hill, 1868. London: Printed by William Clowes and Sons, Stamford Street and Charing Cross. xii, 294 p., 7 plates. With twenty-four pages of publisher's titles bound at the end.
116 × 175 × 30 mm. 10096.aaa.36.

Light yellow endpapers and pastedowns. Binder's ticket on lower pastedown: '| Bound by | Bone & Son. | 76 Fleet St. | London E.C. |' Purple sand-grain cloth. The lower cover is blocked in blind only. Four fillets are blocked on the borders, the inner three of which are thin. The centre-piece is diamond-shaped, and is formed of leaves and straps. The upper cover is blocked in gold and in relief. The same four fillets are blocked in

gold on the borders as for the lower cover. On the centre of the upper cover, a gorilla is blocked, walking on the ground. Above the gorilla, a gold lettering-piece is blocked, shaped as a banner. The title: '| Stories | of | the | Gorilla Country |' is blocked in relief within the banner. Below the gorilla, the words: '| By | Paul du Chaillu. |' are blocked in gold. The spine is blocked in gold and in relief. A single fillet is blocked in gold on the perimeter. Inside this, there is another single fillet, 'branch-shaped', blocked in gold on the perimeter. From the head downwards, the decoration is: palm leaves; the title: '| Stories | of the | Gorilla | Country |' blocked in relief within a panel-shaped gold lettering-piece; snakes surround the words: '| P. Du Chaillu |', which are blocked in relief within a rectangular gold lettering-piece, with a single fillet blocked on its borders; the words: '| Numerous | illustrations |' blocked in relief within another gold lettering-piece, with a single fillet on its borders; a flamingo, with its beak dipped in water; bulrushes; the words: 'London | Sampson Low & Co |' are blocked in relief within a gold lettering-piece, with a single fillet blocked on its borders in gold; signed 'AW' in gold as separate letters at the tail.

The Cambridge University Library copy is at CUL.140.4.235. Bound in blue sand-grain cloth.

['AW' may be the initials of Albert Warren.]

729 Warren, Albert

Campe, Joachim Henrich. *Robinson the Younger; or, The New Crusoe. Translated from the German of J. H. Campe. With illustrations.* London: G. Routledge & Co. Farringdon Street; New York: 18, Beekman Street, 1855. [London]: Printed by Cox (Bros.) and Wyman, Great Queen Street. vii, 240 p., 2 plates With eight pages of publisher's titles bound at the end.

108 × 177 × 23 mm. 12806.d.13.

The half title page and Frontispiece plates are signed 'Dalziel Sc.'

Original upper cover bound at the front; size 110 × 167 mm. Red ripple horizontal-grain cloth. A single fillet is blocked in blind on the borders. On each corner, a single strap is blocked, with stems and leaves curling around the fillets. The upper cover central vignette is blocked in gold. It shows stems, leaves and berries joined to form an oval. A parrot is blocked at the top of the oval; an axe, bow and arrows are blocked at the bottom. On the centre, the words: '| Robinson | the | Younger | or the | New Crusoe |' are blocked in gold, in fanciful lettering. Signed 'W' (or 'AW', as a monogram) at the base. Possibly a design by Albert Warren.

The Renier Collection copy of this work, of 1855, has the same design on blue ripple horizontal-grain cloth covers. The 1866 edition also has 240 p., the same vignette and spine design, on green wave horizontal-grain cloth.

730 Warren, Albert

Bloomfield, Robert. *The farmer's boy. Illustrated with Thirty Engravings, from Drawings by Birket Foster, Harrison Weir, and G. E. Hicks.* London: Sampson Low, Son & Co. 47, Ludgate Hill, 1857. London: Printed by Richard Clay, Bread Street Hill. iv, 68 p.

134 × 203 × 20 mm. 1346.g.33.

Gilt edges. Bevelled boards. Light yellow endpapers and pastedowns. Green morocco horizontal-grain cloth. Both covers are blocked identically in blind and in relief on the borders and on the corners. Fillets are blocked in blind on the borders, and patterns of branches and leaves in relief on the corners. The upper cover has a central design, blocked in gold. It shows branches, leaves and flowers, which surround the words: '| The | Farmer's | Boy | By | Bloomfield |', blocked in gold in fanciful letters. Signed with a monogram underneath the word 'Bloomfield'. The spine is blocked in gold The title: '| The | Farmer's | Boy |' is blocked in gold. A branch, stem and leaf pattern is blocked in gold above and below the title. Formerly shelved at C.30.g.

Ball, *VPB* p. 163. States that the V&A catalogue attributes this design to Warren.

731 Warren, Albert

Longfellow, Henry Wadsworth. *The voices of the night, ballads, and other poems. With illustrations by John Gilbert, engraved by the Brothers Dalziel.* London: George Routledge & Co. Farringdon Street, 1857. London: Printed by Richard Clay, Bread Street Hill. vi, 118 p.

150 × 208 × 15 mm. 1347.g.2.

Gilt edges. Bevelled boards. Yellow endpapers and pastedowns. Binder's ticket on lower pastedown: '| Bound by | Bone & Son, | 76, Fleet Street, | London. |' Blue morocco vertical-grain cloth. Both covers are blocked with the same design, in blind on the lower and in gold on the upper. Two gold fillets are blocked on the borders, the inner of which intertwines with a plant pattern blocked on the corners. The words: '| Voices of the Night | [rule] | Ballads | and Other Poems | [rule] | H. W. Longfellow | [rule] | Illustrated by | John Gilbert |' are blocked in fanciful lettering. Signed 'AW', as a monogram, at the base of the central design. The spine is blocked in gold. The title: '| Voices of the Night. Ballads &c |' is blocked along the spine, with leaf and stem decoration blocked in gold at the head and at the tail.

732 Warren, Albert PLATE LXXXIX

Beattie, James. *The Minstrel. With thirty-three designs by Birket Foster, engraved by the Brothers Dalziel.* London: George Routledge & Co., Farringdon Street; New York: 18 Beekman-Street, 1858. London: Printed by Richard Clay, Bread Street Hill. vii, 91 p.

150 × 207 × 15 mm. C.129.c.7.

Gilt edges. Bevelled boards. Yellow endpapers and pastedowns. Bookplate on upper pastedown. Binder's ticket on lower pastedown: '| Bound by | Bone & Son, | [rule] | 76, Fleet Street, |

London. | ' Blue morocco horizontal-grain cloth. Both covers are blocked with the same design in gold, in relief and in black. Between two fillets blocked in gold on the borders, there is a wide border showing a repeating pattern of stylised leaves and flowers, blocked in gold and in relief. The inner rectangle has a pattern of large flowers blocked in black. The central vignette is blocked in gold as a lettering-piece. The words: ' | Beattie's | Minstrel | ' are blocked in relief inside it. The letters are in large gothic type, surrounded by a tracery of thin stems, which are blocked in relief. The words: ' | Illustrated | by Birket Foster | ' are also blocked in relief, in sans serif capitals. Signed 'AW' as a monogram in relief at the base of the vignette. The spine is blocked in gold. The words: ' | Beattie's Minstrel | ' are blocked in gold along the spine within a cartouche formed by a single fillet, with gold leaf and flower decoration blocked at each end at the head and at the tail. Formerly shelved at 11611.bb.14. Donated and dated 30.6.1955.

—— Another copy. London: George Routledge & Co. Farringdon Street. New York: 18 Beekman Street, 1858. London: Printed by Richard Clay, Bread Street Hill. vii, 91 p.
150 × 205 × 17 mm. 11659.b.20.

Gilt edges. Bevelled boards. Yellow pastedowns. Red ungrained cloth. Both covers are blocked identically in gold, in relief and in black. There is a single fillet blocked in gold on the borders. Inside this, there is another border showing a repeating pattern of stylised leaves and flowers, blocked in gold and in relief. The inner rectangle has a pattern of large flowers blocked in black. The central vignette is blocked in gold. The words: ' | Beattie's | Minstrel | ' are blocked in relief. The letters are in gothic, surrounded by a tracery of thin stems, blocked in relief. The words ' | Illustrated by | Birket Foster | ' are also blocked in relief, in sans serif capitals. Signed 'AW' as a monogram in relief at the base of the vignette. The spine is blocked in gold. The words: ' | Beattie's Minstrel | ' are blocked in gold, within a cartouche formed by a single gold fillet. With gold leaf and flower decoration blocked at each end at head and at the tail. Donated copy, no date of accession.

Ball, *VPB* p. 51; p. 61, ref. 4; p. 163. McLean, *VPBB* p. 76. Copy in blue cloth. Oldfield, *BC* no. 87.

733 Warren, Albert

Burns, Robert. *Poems and songs. Illustrated with numerous engravings.* London: Bell and Daldy, 186, Fleet Street; Edinburgh: J. Menzies, 1858. London: Printed by Richard Clay, Bread Street Hill. xvi, 272 p.
165 × 225 × 35 mm. 1347.h.6.

Monogram of Joseph Cundall is printed on the verso of the title page.

Original yellow endpaper bound at the front. The original lower cover used as a doublure. Doublure size is 152 × 218 mm. Brown pebble-grain cloth. The design is a 'Renaissance panel'. There is a horizontal hatch fillet blocked in gold on the borders. Medallions and scrollwork are blocked on the corners in gold and in relief. Cartouches are blocked on the sides, the head and the tail in gold and in relief. Plant stem and leaf decoration is blocked in relief between all the above. The central rectangle has two fillets blocked in hatch gold, with a pattern of repeating diamonds between the fillets. The central oval has a border of scrollwork, The words: ' | Poems | and | songs | by | Robt. Burns | ' are blocked in relief within the central oval.

Ball, *VPB* pp. 163, 166. States this design was signed on the spine.

734 Warren, Albert FIG. 82

Mackay, Charles. *The home affections pourtrayed by the poets. Selected and edited by Charles Mackay. Illustrated with one hundred engravings, drawn by eminent artists, and engraved by the Brothers Dalziel.* London: George Routledge & Co., Farringdon Street. New York: 18, Beekman-Street, 1858. London: Printed by Richard Clay, Bread Street Hill. xv, 391 p.
170 × 230 × 35 mm. 1347.h.12.

Gilt edges. Bevelled boards. Original yellow endpaper bound in at the front. Red morocco vertical-grain cloth. Both covers have

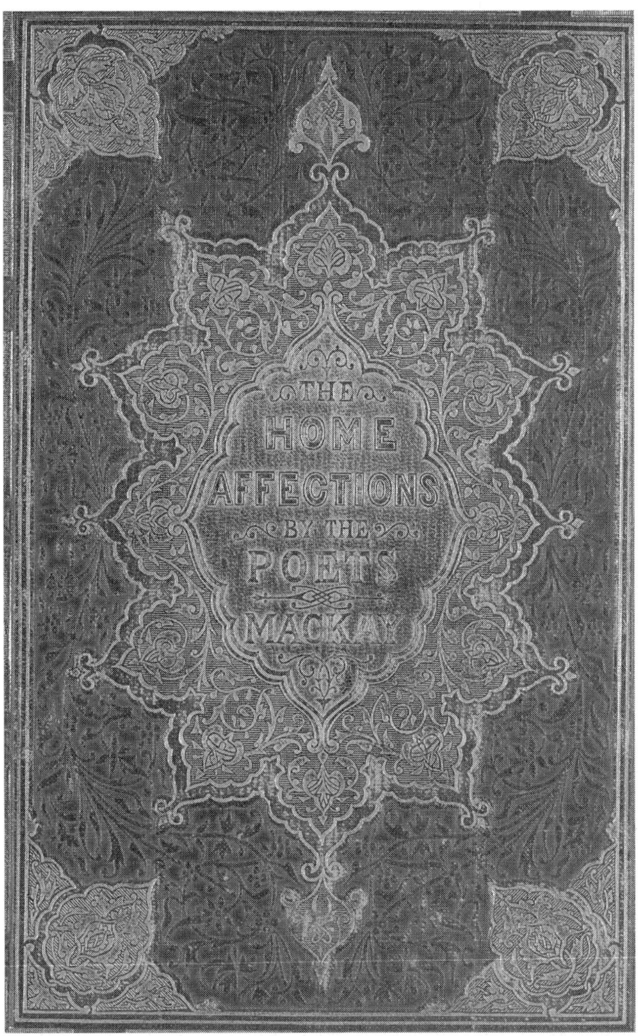

FIG. 82

an identical design blocked in gold, in blind and in relief. The borders are blocked in gold, with a 'Christmas tree' repeating pattern. Three fillets are blocked in gold on the borders. On the outer rectangle, raised cartouches are blocked in gold and in relief, with small zig-zag patterns blocked in relief between. Between the outer and inner rectangles, two fillets are blocked in gold. On the corners of the inner rectangle, plant patterns are blocked, within horizontal hatch arabesques. The central decoration is Moorish in design, with a twelve-pointed design and horizontal hatch blocking. The tracery of plants and leaves has the patterns picked out in relief. The words: '| The | Home | Affections | by the | Poets | Mackay |' are blocked in gold and in relief on the central panel. The spine is blocked in gold. There is a tracery of leaves and stems blocked in gold down the spine. The words: '| The | Home | Affections | by the | Poets | Mackay |' are blocked in relief, within a gold lettering-piece. Signed 'AW' in relief as a monogram, with the 'A' being inside the 'W'. It is above the word '| Illustrated |' blocked in relief within a horizontal hatch gold lettering-piece. The publisher: '| Routledge |' is blocked in relief within a vertical hatch gold lettering-piece blocked near the tail.

Ball, *VPB* p. 163. '. . .reissued in 1866 with the same design'. de Beaumont, *RdeB1* no. 193. Goldman, *VIB* no. 193. Morris & Levin, *APB* p. 108, no. 244.

735 Warren, Albert FIG. 83

Milton, John. *Comus. A mask. With thirty illustrations by Pickersgill, Birket Foster, Harrison Weir, &c. Engraved by the Brothers Dalziel.* London: George Routledge & Co. Farringdon Street. New York: 18 Beekman Street, 1858. London: Printed by Richard Clay, Bread Street Hill. viii, 91 p.
150 × 210 × 20 mm. 1347.g.3.

Gilt edges. Bevelled boards. Original light yellow endpaper bound in at the front. Blue morocco vertical-grain cloth. Both covers are blocked identically in gold and in black. There are two fillets blocked in gold on the borders, in gold. Between them, a wide horizontal hatch border is blocked in gold, with a pattern of repeating stems, leaves and flowers blocked in relief. Within the inner rectangle, flowers and leaves are blocked in black around the centre. The central vignette is blocked as a gold lettering-piece, within an arabesque. On the inner border of the vignette, a fillet is blocked in relief. The words: 'Milton's Comus. Illustrated', are blocked in relief in fanciful letters. Signed 'AW', with the 'A' inside the base of the 'W', in relief as a monogram at the base of the vignette. The spine is blocked in gold. '| Milton's Comus |' is blocked in gold along the spine, within a cartouche formed by a gold fillet, with leaf decoration blocked in gold at the head and at the tail. There are other copies of this design on Longfellow 'The courtship of Miles Standish and other poems', Routledge, 1859, BL shelfmark 1347.f.2.; and on Wordsworth 'The deserted cottage', Routledge, 1859, BL shelfmark 1347.g.5.

Ball, *VPB* p. 163. Pantazzi, *4D* p. 95. Cites a copy in 'bright green [cloth]'.

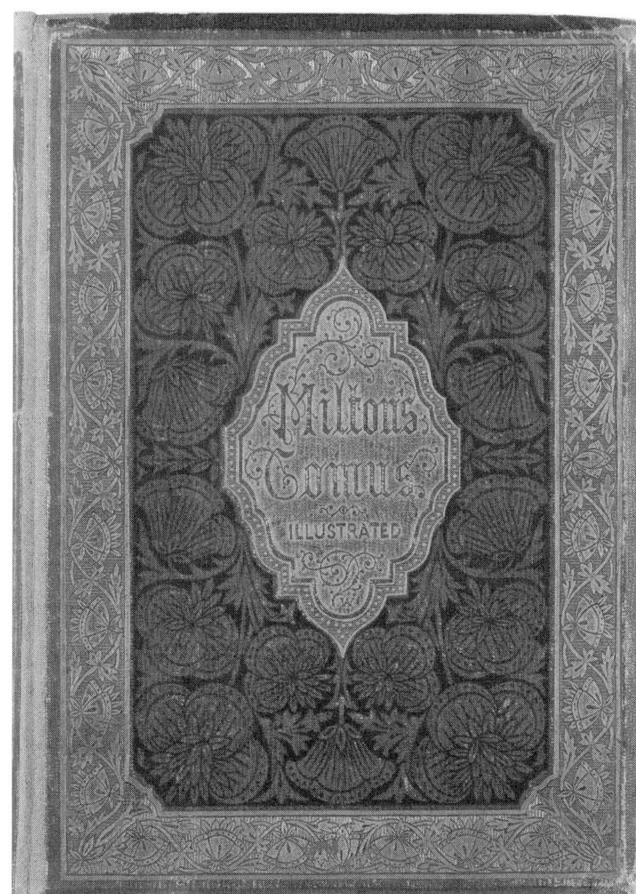

FIG. 83

736 Warren, Albert

Goldsmith, Oliver. *The deserted village. Illustrated by the Etching Club.* London: Sampson Low, Son & Co., 47 Ludgate Hill, 1859. London: Printed by R. Clay, Bread Street Hill. 46 p.
135 × 205 × 10 mm. RB.23.a.5278.

Gilt edges. Yellow endpapers and pastedowns. Green morocco vertical-grain cloth. Both covers are blocked in blind with the same design. Fillets are blocked on the borders. Leaf and stem patterns are blocked on the inner border and on the sides. Strapwork is blocked on the corners. On the upper cover, the central vignette is blocked in gold and in relief. The vignette is onion-shaped. On the outside of it, a tracery of leaves and stems is blocked in gold. The border of the vignette is a rule, blocked in relief. The title words: 'The deserted village' are blocked, surrounded by a tracery of thin stems and leaves, all in relief. The gold blocking surrounds the lettering and the tracery. Signed 'AW' in relief as separate letters at the base of the vignette. The spine is blocked in gold, with small designs above and below the title. The 1855 edition is at BL shelfmark 11640.ee.51. It has a cover design by John Leighton.

McLean, *VPBB* p. 78. Shows the 1855 edition, with a different design by John Leighton.

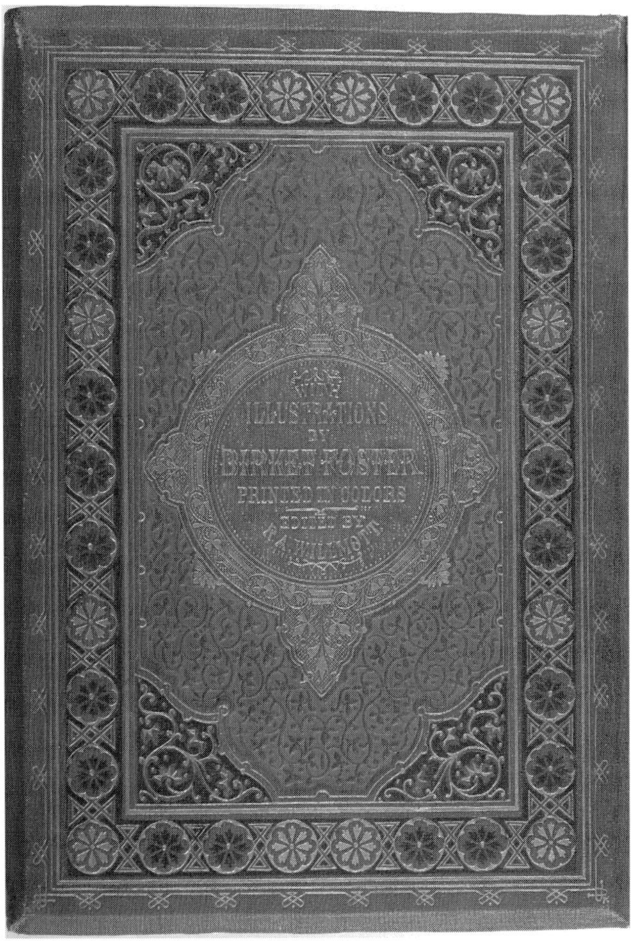

FIG. 84

737 Warren, Albert

FIG. 84

Goldsmith, Oliver. *The poems of Oliver Goldsmith. Edited by Robert Aris Willmott. With illustrations by Birket Foster and H.N. Humphreys. Printed in colors* [sic] *from wood blocks.* London: George Routledge and Co., Farringdon Street; New York: 18, Beekman-Street, 1859. London: Edmund Evans, Engraver and Printer. xvi, 160 p.

165 × 230 × 30 mm. C.109.d.7.

Gilt edges. Bevelled boards. Yellow endpapers and pastedowns. Red morocco vertical-grain cloth. Both covers are blocked identically in gold and in black. The three fillets on the borders are blocked in gold, with a repeating 'figure of eight' pattern blocked on the outside. The inner border is of shell-shaped medallions, blocked in gold and in black. There are two fillets blocked on the inner border. The central rectangle has leaf and stem tracery blocked in gold and in black on the corners. Around the sides of the inner rectangle, recessed and blocked in relief, is a repeating pattern of three-pointed leaves and stems. The central roundel is surrounded by a filigree with leaves and stems blocked in gold. On the lower cover, the words: '| With | illustrations | by | Birket Foster. | Printed in colors. Edited by R. A. Willmott. |' are blocked in gold inside the roundel. On the upper cover, the words: '| The | poems | of | Oliver | Goldsmith |' are blocked in gold in elaborate lettering. It is likely that Warren's monogram , 'AW', is blocked in gold at the base of the roundel, within the tracery at the base of the roundel on each cover. The spine is blocked in gold and in black. There is 'Moorish' ornament blocked at the head and at the tail, blocked in gold and relief. The words: '| The | Poems | of | Oliver | Goldsmith | [rule] | Illustrated |' are blocked in gold, with seven gold fillets blocked underneath. On the middle, there is a mandorla blocked in gold and in relief. This copy formerly shelved at 1347.g.9.

Ball, *VPB* p. 164. States that Warren's '. . .monogram [is] in central roundel of covers'. McLean, *VPBB* p. 82. Shows the Routledge edition of 1860 in red pebble-grain cloth, with the same design. Pantazzi, *4D* p. 96. Says the design is unsigned.

738 Warren, Albert

Thomson, James. *The Seasons Illustrated by Birket Foster, F.R. Pickersgill, J. Wolf, G. Thomas, and Noel Humphreys.* London: James Nisbet & Co. Berners Street, 1859. Printed by R. & R. Clark, Edinburgh. [7], 228 p.

153 × 210 × 28 mm. RdeB.L.12.

The British Museum de Beaumont copy.

Text sewn on three tapes. Gilt edges. Bevelled boards. Cream endpapers and pastedowns. Binder's ticket on lower pastedown: '| Leighton | Son & | Hodge, | Shoe Lane | London. |' Blue morocco horizontal-grain cloth. Both covers blocked identically in gold, in blind and in relief. A wide gold border is blocked and within the border, a repeating pattern of four leaves and berries is blocked in relief. On each corner, a four-petal flower is blocked within a square. On the inner corners and on the sides, groups of stems and of leaves are blocked, each representing a season, with small leaves blocked in relief around them. The central frame is formed by ivy leaves and berries, which surround the central hexagon. This is blocked as a gold lettering-piece, bordered by a single fillet. The title: '| Thomson's | Seasons |' is blocked in relief within the lettering-piece. Small leaves and stem decoration is blocked in relief around the title. Signed 'AW' in relief as a monogram at the base of the hexagon. The spine is blocked in gold. A single gold fillet is blocked on the perimeter. From the head downwards, the decoration is: leaves and dots blocked between two fillets; a gold fillet; ivy leaves and berries; leaves and a quatrefoil with gold dots inside it; a hexagon gold lettering-piece with the title: '| Thomson's Seasons |' blocked in relief inside; leaves and a quatrefoil with dots inside it; ivy leaves and berries; a gold fillet; leaves and dots are blocked in gold between two fillets. Unsigned.

de Beaumont, *RdeB1* no. 381. Goldman, *VIB* no. 381.

739 Warren, Albert

Goldsmith, Oliver. *The poems. Edited by Robert Aris Willmott. A new edition with illustrations by Birket Foster and H. N. Humphreys. Printed in colours by Edmund Evans.* London:

Routledge, Warne and Routledge, Farringdon Street; and 56, Walker Street, New York, 1860. London: Edmund Evans, Engraver and Printer, Raquet Court, Fleet Street. xxii, 162 p.
165 × 235 × 30 mm. 1347.g.16.

Gilt edges. Bevelled boards. Original yellow endpaper bound at the front. Blue morocco vertical-grain cloth. The design on the covers is the same as that for the 1859 edition. [BL copy at C.109.d.7.] The blocking on this edition is in gold and blind only (i.e. where the blockwork was in black for the 1859 edition, it is in blind for this edition). The spine is fully blocked in gold and in blind. A mandorla in gold and in relief is blocked in the middle. Moorish designs are blocked at the head and at the tail, in gold and in relief. The same monograms are on the central roundels of both covers as for the 1859 edition.

740 Warren, Albert PLATE XC

Miller, Thomas. *Common wayside flowers. Illustrated by Birket Foster.* London: Routledge, Warne and Routledge, Farringdon Street; and 56, Walker Street, New York, 1860. London: Edmund Evans, Engraver and Printer, Raquet Court, Fleet Street, London. [7], 185 p.
178 × 227 × 30 mm. C.44.d.6.

Gilt edges Bevelled boards. Brown morocco horizontal-grain cloth. Both covers identically blocked in gold. The paper onlays are also identical for both covers. Three fillets are blocked on the borders, the two inner being shaped as branches, with ivy leaves being blocked between them. The veins of the leaves are outlined in relief. The fillets intersect at the corners to form small squares. A single fillet is blocked on the borders of each of the four inner corner panels. A printed paper onlay showing 'wayside flowers' is laid onto each inner corner. Each onlay has been varnished. The centre panel is diamond-shaped, with 'branch-like' fillets and ivy leaves on its borders. The title: '| Common | Wayside | Flowers |' and the name: '| Birket Foster |' are blocked in rustic-style letters. Between the two, the words: '| Illustrations by |' are blocked in gold. Signed 'AW' in gold as separate letters on the centre tail of each cover. The spine is blocked in gold. A single branch-shaped fillet is blocked on the perimeter. From the head downwards, the decoration is: at the head, ivy leaves are blocked in a panel, formed by a single 'branch-like' fillet; a gold lettering-piece, with ivy leaves blocked in relief inside it, and a branch-shaped single fillet on its borders – is blocked above and below the title words; the title words: '| Common | wayside | flowers |' blocked in relief on a blue paper onlay, within a gold lettering piece; in the middle of the spine, within another gold lettering-piece, the words: '| with | illustrations | by | Birket Foster |' are blocked in relief on a red paper onlay; foxgloves are blocked in gold; the words: '| Routledge & Co |' are blocked in relief on a blue paper onlay, inside a gold lettering-piece; at the tail, ivy leaves are blocked within a rectangle formed by a single branch-like gold fillet.

Ball, *VPB* p. 164. McLean, *VPBB* p. 53. 'Perhaps the most sensational of all the cut-out paper and gold blocking bindings.' Morris & Levin, *APB* p. 66, no. 133. Pantazzi, *4D* p. 94.

741 Warren, Albert

Moore, Thomas. *Lallah Rookh: an oriental romance. With illustrations, engraved by Edmund Evans, from original drawings by G H Thomas, F R Pickersgill, R.A., Birket Foster, E. H. Corbould, etc, etc.* London: Routledge, Warne, & Routledge, Farringdon St; New York: 56, Walker Street, 1860. London: Printed by Edmund Evans, Raquet Court. [6], 303 p., 1 plate.
170 × 230 × 40 mm. C.109.d.9.

Text sewn on three tapes. Gilt edges. Bevelled boards. Cream endpapers and pastedowns. Binder's ticket on lower pastedown: '| Bound | by | Leighton | Son and | Hodge |'. Blue morocco vertical-grain cloth. Both covers are blocked identically in gold and in blind. The recessed strapwork is blocked in blind as wide fillets, with small decoration blocked in relief inside them. The strapwork forms arabesques. They intermingle with the decorative panels which are blocked on gold. At the centre, the oriental-shaped gold lettering-piece contains the words: '| Lallah Rookh | by | Thomas Moore |', blocked in relief. Similar elaborate arabesques and decorative patterns are blocked on the spine. The words: '| Lallah Rookh | [rule] | Moore | [rule] | Illustrated |' are blocked in relief inside a gold lettering-piece. (The book label at the tail covers a possible Warren monogram.)

Ball, *VPB* p. 164. Morris & Levin, *APB* p. 54, no. 101. Nos. 102 & 103 show variants. Oldfield, *BC* no. 81. Cites 1868 Routledge edition. Pantazzi, *4D* p. 94. Illustrates upper cover and spine.

742 Warren, Albert

Bowman, Anne. *Among the Tartar tents; or, the lost fathers. A Tale . . .* London: Bell and Daldy, 186, Fleet Street, 1861. London: Strangeways and Walden, Printers, Castle St. Leicester Sq. xii, 324 p., 2 plates.
125 × 190 × 32 mm. 10056.aa.11.

Light brown endpapers and pastedowns. Binder's ticket on lower pastedown: '| Bound by | Bone & Son, | 76, Fleet St. London. |' Green morocco horizontal-grain cloth. Both covers are blocked identically in blind and in relief. Two fillets are blocked on the borders. A leaf and curling stem pattern is blocked on each corner, and on the sides, with the centres of the leaves being blocked in relief. Two fillets form an oval frame at the centre. The spine is blocked in gold and in relief. A single fillet is blocked on the perimeter in gold. From the head downwards, the decoration is: a 'dotted' gold fillet; two gold fillets; small plant decoration is blocked in gold. a gold lettering-piece panel, which contains four rectangular lettering-pieces, which are picked out by being formed by double fillets blocked in relief on their borders; the title: '| Among | the | Tartar | tents |' blocked in relief within the four gold lettering-pieces; a small circular gold lettering-piece has the word: '| by |' blocked in relief within; a decorative panel gold lettering-piece formed by a single fillet, and the words: '| Anne Bowman |' blocked inside; small decoration, of stems and leaves forming patterns, is blocked in gold above and below the Author, and down the spine to near the tail; small gold decorative-piece, near the tail,

with 'bud' decoration blocked inside in relief; signed 'AW' in gold as separate letters; two gold fillets; gold dots are blocked at the tail.

743 Warren, Albert FIG. 85

Campbell, Thomas. *The pleasures of hope. Illustrated by Birket Foster, George Thomas, and Harrison Weir. Third edition.* London: Sampson Low, Son, & Co., 47, Ludgate Hill, 1861. [London]: R. Clay, Printer, Bread Street Hill. [3], 59 p.
135 × 200 × 12 mm. 11661.bb.2.

The illustrations engraved by Edmund Evans, Horace Harral, William Measom, W. T. Green, James Cooper, Thomas Bolton, and J. Greenaway. Joseph Cundall's monogram is printed on the title page verso.

Gilt edges. Light yellow endpapers and pastedowns. Written on the upper endpaper: '| Berthold Holland Smith. | Prize for Greek | A. James's Lodge, Croydon. | July 25th 1861. | Philip Smith. |' Purple morocco vertical-grain cloth. Both covers are blocked identically in blind and in relief on the borders, corners and the sides. There is a fillet on the outer border. Trefoils are blocked on the corners in relief. There is a pattern of ivy leaves, of stems blocked in relief on the sides, corners, head and tail. The patterns form a central oval, which is blank on the lower cover. The upper cover has a central vignette blocked in gold. The perimeter is of thin stems and leaves. The centre is onion-shaped, with hatch gold blocking and a border blocked in relief. At the centre is a gold lettering-piece in which are blocked in relief the words: '| The | pleasures | of hope |'. The words are surrounded by tendrils, also blocked in relief. Signed 'AW' in relief as separate letters at the base of the gold lettering-piece. The spine has the title words blocked in gold, with fillets blocked in vertical gold hatch above and below. There is small plant decoration blocked in gold above and below these fillets.

McLean, *Cundall* pp. 36, 80.

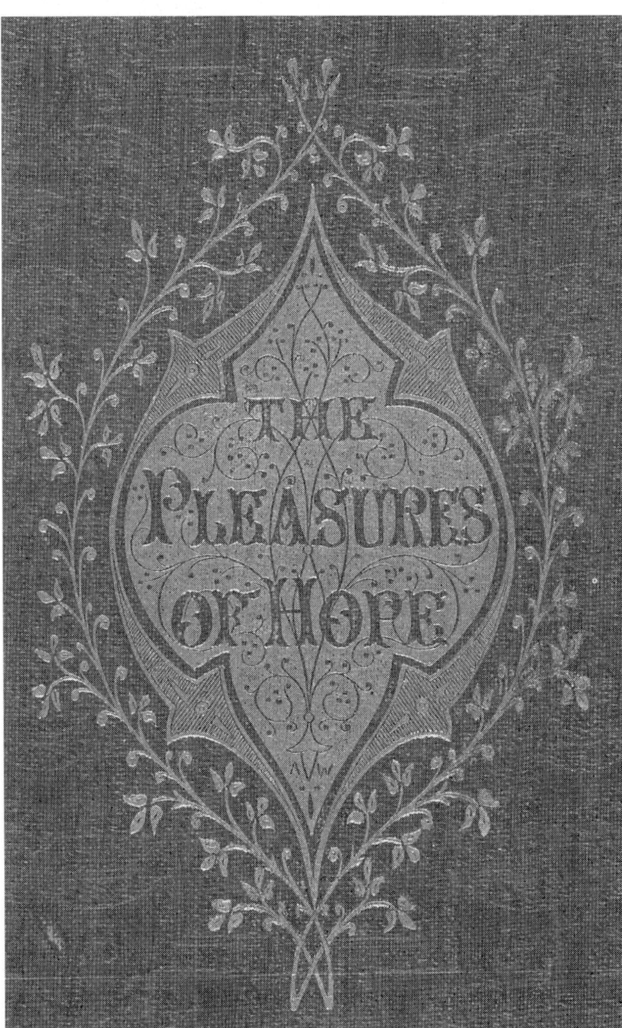

FIG. 85

744 Warren, Albert FIG. 86

Tennyson, Alfred. *The May Queen. Illustrated by E.V.B.* London: Sampson Low, Son & Co. 47, Ludgate Hill, 1861. R. Clay, Printer, Bread Street Hill, London. 39 p.
155 × 215 × 12 mm. RdeB.L.7.

The British Museum de Beaumont copy.

Text sewn on three sawn-in cords. Gilt edges. Bevelled boards. Yellow endpapers and pastedowns. Binder's ticket on lower pastedown: '| Bound by Bone & Son, | 76, Fleet St London. |' Blue morocco vertical-grain cloth. Both covers blocked in blind

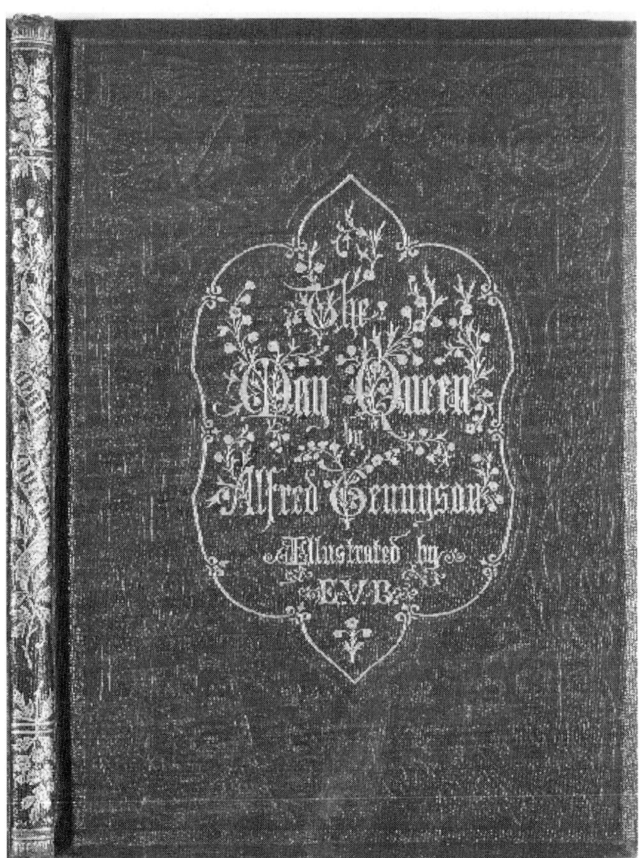

FIG. 86

and in relief identically on the corners and on the sides. The blocking shows two branches on the borders, with an elaborate pattern of curling stems, flowers and leaves blocked in relief around the branches. The whole forms the central frame. On the upper cover around the borders of the central frame, two joined fillets are blocked – one in blind the other in gold. On the centre, the words: '| The | May Queen | by | Alfred | Tennyson | Illustrated by | E.V.B. |' are blocked in gold in gothic letters. Flowers, stems, and leaves are blocked in gold between, through, and on the ends of the letters. The spine is blocked in gold and in relief. From the head downwards, the decoration is: a filigree pattern blocked in gold; two gold fillets; a ribbon-shaped gold lettering-piece runs down the spine, with the title: '| The | May | Queen. |' blocked in relief within the ribbon; two gold fillets; a branch and blossom, blocked in gold; signed 'AW' in gold as separate letters; two gold fillets; a filigree pattern is blocked in gold at the tail.

de Beaumont, *RdeB1* no. 373. Goldman, *VIB* no. 373.

745 Warren, Albert

Wilson, Mark. *The first reading book. With one hundred and twenty illustrations.* [Engraving of forest scene.] London: Sampson Low, Son, and Co. 47, Ludgate Hill, [1862]. [London]: R. Clay, Son, and Taylor, Printers, Bread Street Hill. 128 p.
123 × 180 × 15 mm. 12805.dd.41.

The frontispiece illustration on page 2 is signed 'H. Weir'.

White pastedowns. The spine is of red bead grain cloth. Red dyed paper over boards. The lower cover has a list of publisher's titles. The work is advertised as: '| Price 1s. | The child's first reader. | With 120 Pictures |'. The upper cover has on the borders: 1. a blue fillet; 2. horizontal hatch between pairs of fillets. Groups of three small leaves are printed on each corner, with more stems and leaves on the inner corners. Blue fillets form an 'hour-glass' shaped central frame. The title: '| Wilson's | First | Reader |' is printed inside three rectangles formed by single fillets. Signed 'AW' in blue letters at the centre tail.

746 Warren, Albert FIG. 87

Buchanan, Robert. *Ballad Stories of the Affections. From the Scandinavian. With illustrations by G. J. Pinwell W. Small A. B. Houghton E. Dalziel T. Dalziel J. Lawson & J. D. Watson. Engraved by the Brothers Dalziel.* London: George Routledge & Sons, Broadway, Ludgate Hill, [1866]. [London]: Dalziel Brothers, Engravers and Printers, Camden Press. [1], xiv, 174 p. With four pages of publisher's titles bound at the end.
170 × 235 × 25 mm. RdeB.G.6.

The British Museum de Beaumont copy.

Gilt edges. Bevelled boards. Light yellow endpapers and pastedowns. Binder's ticket on lower pastedown: '| Bound by | W. Bone & Son. | 76, Fleet St. | London E.C. |'. Green sand-grain cloth. Both covers blocked identically in gold and in relief. Three fillets are blocked in gold on the borders. Between these

FIG. 87

fillets, a repeating pattern of half-circles and dotted stems is blocked in gold. The central vignette is blocked in gold and in relief. It shows an oval formed by border fillets, with three-leafed groups blocked at the head and at the base. The words: '| Ballad Stories | of the | Affections | Robert Buchanan | Illustrated |' are blocked in relief within five rectangular gold lettering-pieces, with the title being blocked in gothic letters. Behind and between these, a diamond pattern is blocked in gold, with single leaves blocked in relief inside each diamond. Signed 'W' in relief within a diamond near the base of the vignette. The spine is blocked in gold. From the head downwards, the decoration is: two gold fillets; a panel, formed by two zig-zag gold fillets and hatched gold triangles; four gold fillets; a panel formed by two gold fillets, with small decoration at its head and tail; within this panel are blocked: 1. a pattern of diamonds with small leaves blocked in gold inside each diamond, 2. the title: '| Ballad | Stories | of the | Affections |' blocked in gold in gothic letters; the words: '| Robert | Buchanan |' blocked in gold within a rectangle formed by two gold fillets; signed 'W' in gold within a circle formed by two gold fillets; the word: '| Illustrated |' is blocked in gold within a rectangle formed by a single gold fillet, which has 'scroll' ends; at the tail, two gold fillets; '| Routledge |' is blocked in relief within a rectangular gold lettering-piece; two gold fillets.

de Beaumont, *RdeB1* no. 34. Goldman, *VIB* no. 34.

747 Warren, Albert

Watts, Isaac. *Divine and moral Songs for children. Illustrated.* London: Sampson Low, Son, and Marston, 1866. Richard Clay London. 116 p.
152 × 208 × 17 mm. 3437.i.15.

Gilt edges. Bevelled boards. Light yellow endpapers and pastedowns. Binder's ticket on the lower pastedown: '| Bound by | Bone & Son, | [rule] | 76, Fleet Street, | London. |' The lower cover is blocked in blind and in relief. Three fillets are blocked in blind on the borders. The centre-piece shows linked and overlapping semi-circles, formed by fillets blocked in blind, with dots blocked in relief within the inner semi-circles. On the centre, a twelve-petal single flower is blocked in blind. The upper cover is blocked in gold and in relief. Three gold fillets are blocked on the outer borders. Two fillets are blocked on the inner border, with curling stems near each corner. On each inner corner, an oval is blocked with horizontal gold hatch, and a fleur-de-lis blocked in gold within each oval. Small single ovals are blocked on the centre sides. The centre-piece shows a mandorla, with curling stems and flowers blocked on its borders. It also has a border repeating pattern of four leaves. The words: '| Watts' | Divine & moral | songs |' are blocked in relief within three gold lettering-pieces which are joined and have scroll-like ends. Each lettering-piece has a single horizontal fillet blocked above and below the letters. A bird is blocked above the title. Signed 'AW' in gold as separate letters at the base of the centre-piece. The spine is blocked in gold and in relief. From the head downwards, the decoration is: two gold fillets; a panel formed by a single gold fillet with a zig-zag pattern, and also two gold fillets blocked above and below; tassel decoration; the central portion of the spine is blocked as a gold lettering-piece, and has on its perimeter – 1. a rope-like gold fillet; 2. a single gold fillet; 3. dots blocked in relief ; within these fillets, the words: '| Watts' Divine & Moral Songs. |' blocked in relief within the rectangular gold lettering-piece; tassel decoration; three gold fillets; a panel formed by a single gold fillet; the words: '| London | S. Low & Co. |' are blocked in relief within a rectangular gold lettering-piece, all within a panel; four gold fillets are blocked at the tail.

Ball, *VPB* p. 166. Goldman, *Cat. 1* no. 184. Pantazzi, *4D* p. 94 no. IX.

748 Warren, Albert

Broderip, Frances Freeling. *Wild roses; or, Simple Stories of Country Life. With illustrations by H. Anelay.* London: Griffith and Farran, Successors to Newbery and Harris, Corner of St. Paul's Churchyard, 1867. London: Gilbert and Rivington, Printers, St. John's Square. v, 235 p., 4 plates.
123 × 192 × 28 mm. 12806.ee.16.

The plates are signed with the monogram 'HA' and 'Pearson Sc.' On page 4 of the publisher's titles at the end: 'Post 8vo., price 3s. 6d. cloth elegant; 4s. gilt edges.'

Bevelled boards. Yellow endpapers and pastedowns. Red sand-grain cloth. Both covers have the same two fillets blocked in blind on the borders . The upper cover central vignette is blocked in gold and in relief. It shows a posy of wild roses, with four gold lettering-pieces (which have hatched fillets on their borders) blocked in front of the posy. The words: '| Wild roses |' are blocked in relief within a rectangular gold lettering-piece; the word: '| or |' is blocked in relief within a circular gold lettering-piece; the words: '| simple stories of country life |' are blocked in relief within a curving gold lettering-piece; the word: '| Broderip. |' is blocked in relief within a ribbon-shaped gold lettering-piece. Signed 'AW' in gold as separate letters at the base of the vignette. The spine is blocked in gold. It has the same design as the upper cover vignette: a posy of wild roses is blocked in gold, with six rectangular gold lettering-pieces, each with a hatched gold fillet blocked on its borders; the words: '| Wild roses | or | simple stories | of | country life | Broderip. |' are blocked in relief in each of the six gold lettering-pieces.

749 Warren, Albert

Broderip, Frances Freeling. *Tales of the toys, told by themselves. With illustrations by Tom Hood.* [Monogram of Griffith and Farran.] London: Griffith and Farran, (Successors to Newbery and Harris) Corner of St. Paul's Churchyard, 1869. [London]: Wertheimer, Lea and Co., Printers, Finsbury Circus. [2], 220 p., 5 plates.
129 × 175 × 26 mm. 12807.ee.35.

The plates are hand coloured. They are signed with the monogram 'TH' and 'Ferrier Sc.'. On page four of the publisher's titles at the end: Super Royal 16mo., price 3s. 6d.cloth elegant, 4s. 6d. coloured gilt edges.

Gilt edges. [No original endpapers or pastedowns.] Binder's ticket on lower pastedown: '| Bound by | W. Bone & Son. | 76, Fleet St. | London E.C. |'. Blue sand-grain cloth. Both covers blocked identically in blind on the borders, on the corners and on the sides. A single fillet is blocked in blind on the borders. Extended leaf decoration is blocked in relief on each corner. A curved inner thin fillet, blocked in blind, forms a central frame. The upper cover central vignette is blocked in gold. There are three ribbon-shaped gold lettering-pieces blocked near the centre. The words: '| Tales of the toys | told by themselves | by Frances Freeling Broderip |' are blocked in relief within the ribbons. A coiled rope and a thin fillet twines around and behind the ribbons, forming a fleur-de-lis shape at the head and at the base of the vignette. The very centre shows a Chinese figure, a copy of the one reproduced in the plate opposite page 38. Signed 'AW' in gold as separate letters underneath the figure. The spine is blocked in gold, in blind and in relief. From the head downwards, the decoration is: three gold fillets, one thick between two thin; a kite and tail streamers; in front of the kite, four rectangular gold lettering-pieces are blocked; the words: 'Tales | of the toys | told by themselves | by | Frances Freeling Broderip. |' blocked in relief within the lettering-pieces; three pendulous stars, blocked in relief within a panel; small stem and bud decoration; two fillets blocked in blind; two thin gold fillets; the words: 'London | Griffith & Farran |' are blocked in relief within a rectangular gold lettering-piece at the tail.

Ball, *VPB* p. 166.

Routledge, Warne and Routledge, Farringdon Street; and 56, Walker Street, New York, 1860. London: Edmund Evans, Engraver and Printer, Raquet Court, Fleet Street. xxii, 162 p.
165 × 235 × 30 mm. 1347.g.16.

Gilt edges. Bevelled boards. Original yellow endpaper bound at the front. Blue morocco vertical-grain cloth. The design on the covers is the same as that for the 1859 edition. [BL copy at C.109.d.7.] The blocking on this edition is in gold and blind only (i.e. where the blockwork was in black for the 1859 edition, it is in blind for this edition). The spine is fully blocked in gold and in blind. A mandorla in gold and in relief is blocked in the middle. Moorish designs are blocked at the head and at the tail, in gold and in relief. The same monograms are on the central roundels of both covers as for the 1859 edition.

740 Warren, Albert

PLATE XC

Miller, Thomas. *Common wayside flowers. Illustrated by Birket Foster.* London: Routledge, Warne and Routledge, Farringdon Street; and 56, Walker Street, New York, 1860. London: Edmund Evans, Engraver and Printer, Raquet Court, Fleet Street, London. [7], 185 p.
178 × 227 × 30 mm. C.44.d.6.

Gilt edges Bevelled boards. Brown morocco horizontal-grain cloth. Both covers identically blocked in gold. The paper onlays are also identical for both covers. Three fillets are blocked on the borders, the two inner being shaped as branches, with ivy leaves being blocked between them. The veins of the leaves are outlined in relief. The fillets intersect at the corners to form small squares. A single fillet is blocked on the borders of each of the four inner corner panels. A printed paper onlay showing 'wayside flowers' is laid onto each inner corner. Each onlay has been varnished. The centre panel is diamond-shaped, with 'branch-like' fillets and ivy leaves on its borders. The title: '| Common | Wayside | Flowers |' and the name: '| Birket Foster |' are blocked in rustic-style letters. Between the two, the words: '| Illustrations by |' are blocked in gold. Signed 'AW' in gold as separate letters on the centre tail of each cover. The spine is blocked in gold. A single branch-shaped fillet is blocked on the perimeter. From the head downwards, the decoration is: at the head, ivy leaves are blocked in a panel, formed by a single 'branch-like' fillet; a gold lettering-piece, with ivy leaves blocked in relief inside it, and a branch-shaped single fillet on its borders – is blocked above and below the title words; the title words: '| Common | wayside | flowers |' blocked in relief on a blue paper onlay, within a gold lettering piece; in the middle of the spine, within another gold lettering-piece, the words: '| with | illustrations | by | Birket Foster |' are blocked in relief on a red paper onlay; foxgloves are blocked in gold; the words: '| Routledge & Co |' are blocked in relief on a blue paper onlay, inside a gold lettering-piece; at the tail, ivy leaves are blocked within a rectangle formed by a single branch-like gold fillet.

Ball, *VPB* p. 164. McLean, *VPBB* p. 53. 'Perhaps the most sensational of all the cut-out paper and gold blocking bindings.' Morris & Levin, *APB* p. 66, no. 133. Pantazzi, *4D* p. 94.

741 Warren, Albert

Moore, Thomas. *Lallah Rookh: an oriental romance. With illustrations, engraved by Edmund Evans, from original drawings by G H Thomas, F R Pickersgill, R.A., Birket Foster, E. H. Corbould, etc, etc.* London: Routledge, Warne, & Routledge, Farringdon St; New York: 56, Walker Street, 1860. London: Printed by Edmund Evans, Raquet Court. [6], 303 p., 1 plate.
170 × 230 × 40 mm. C.109.d.9.

Text sewn on three tapes. Gilt edges. Bevelled boards. Cream endpapers and pastedowns. Binder's ticket on lower pastedown: '| Bound | by | Leighton | Son and | Hodge |'. Blue morocco vertical-grain cloth. Both covers are blocked identically in gold and in blind. The recessed strapwork is blocked in blind as wide fillets, with small decoration blocked in relief inside them. The strapwork forms arabesques. They intermingle with the decorative panels which are blocked on gold. At the centre, the oriental-shaped gold lettering-piece contains the words: '| Lallah Rookh | by | Thomas Moore |', blocked in relief. Similar elaborate arabesques and decorative patterns are blocked on the spine. The words: '| Lallah Rookh | [rule] | Moore | [rule] | Illustrated |' are blocked in relief inside a gold lettering-piece. (The book label at the tail covers a possible Warren monogram.)

Ball, *VPB* p. 164. Morris & Levin, *APB* p. 54, no. 101. Nos. 102 & 103 show variants. Oldfield, *BC* no. 81. Cites 1868 Routledge edition. Pantazzi, *4D* p. 94. Illustrates upper cover and spine.

742 Warren, Albert

Bowman, Anne. *Among the Tartar tents; or, the lost fathers. A Tale . . .* London: Bell and Daldy, 186, Fleet Street, 1861. London: Strangeways and Walden, Printers, Castle St. Leicester Sq. xii, 324 p., 2 plates.
125 × 190 × 32 mm. 10056.aa.11.

Light brown endpapers and pastedowns. Binder's ticket on lower pastedown: '| Bound by | Bone & Son, | 76, Fleet St. London. |' Green morocco horizontal-grain cloth. Both covers are blocked identically in blind and in relief. Two fillets are blocked on the borders. A leaf and curling stem pattern is blocked on each corner, and on the sides, with the centres of the leaves being blocked in relief. Two fillets form an oval frame at the centre. The spine is blocked in gold and in relief. A single fillet is blocked on the perimeter in gold. From the head downwards, the decoration is: a 'dotted' gold fillet; two gold fillets; small plant decoration is blocked in gold. a gold lettering-piece panel, which contains four rectangular lettering-pieces, which are picked out by being formed by double fillets blocked in relief on their borders; the title: '| Among | the | Tartar | tents |' blocked in relief within the four gold lettering-pieces; a small circular gold lettering-piece has the word: '| by |' blocked in relief within; a decorative panel gold lettering-piece formed by a single fillet, and the words: '| Anne Bowman |' blocked inside; small decoration, of stems and leaves forming patterns, is blocked in gold above and below the Author, and down the spine to near the tail; small gold decorative-piece, near the tail,

with 'bud' decoration blocked inside in relief; signed 'AW' in gold as separate letters; two gold fillets; gold dots are blocked at the tail.

743 Warren, Albert FIG. 85

Campbell, Thomas. *The pleasures of hope. Illustrated by Birket Foster, George Thomas, and Harrison Weir. Third edition.* London: Sampson Low, Son, & Co., 47, Ludgate Hill, 1861. [London]: R. Clay, Printer, Bread Street Hill. [3], 59 p.
135 × 200 × 12 mm. 11661.bb.2.

The illustrations engraved by Edmund Evans, Horace Harral, William Measom, W. T. Green, James Cooper, Thomas Bolton, and J. Greenaway. Joseph Cundall's monogram is printed on the title page verso.

Gilt edges. Light yellow endpapers and pastedowns. Written on the upper endpaper: '| Berthold Holland Smith. | Prize for Greek | A. James's Lodge, Croydon. | July 25th 1861. | Philip Smith. |' Purple morocco vertical-grain cloth. Both covers are blocked identically in blind and in relief on the borders, corners and the sides. There is a fillet on the outer border. Trefoils are blocked on the corners in relief. There is a pattern of ivy leaves, of stems blocked in relief on the sides, corners, head and tail. The patterns form a central oval, which is blank on the lower cover. The upper cover has a central vignette blocked in gold. The perimeter is of thin stems and leaves. The centre is onion-shaped, with hatch gold blocking and a border blocked in relief. At the centre is a gold lettering-piece in which are blocked in relief the words: '| The | pleasures | of hope |'. The words are surrounded by tendrils, also blocked in relief. Signed 'AW' in relief as separate letters at the base of the gold lettering-piece. The spine has the title words blocked in gold, with fillets blocked in vertical gold hatch above and below. There is small plant decoration blocked in gold above and below these fillets.

McLean, *Cundall* pp. 36, 80.

FIG. 85

744 Warren, Albert FIG. 86

Tennyson, Alfred. *The May Queen. Illustrated by E.V.B.* London: Sampson Low, Son & Co. 47, Ludgate Hill, 1861. R. Clay, Printer, Bread Street Hill, London. 39 p.
155 × 215 × 12 mm. RdeB.L.7.

The British Museum de Beaumont copy.

Text sewn on three sawn-in cords. Gilt edges. Bevelled boards. Yellow endpapers and pastedowns. Binder's ticket on lower pastedown: '| Bound by Bone & Son, | 76, Fleet St London. |' Blue morocco vertical-grain cloth. Both covers blocked in blind

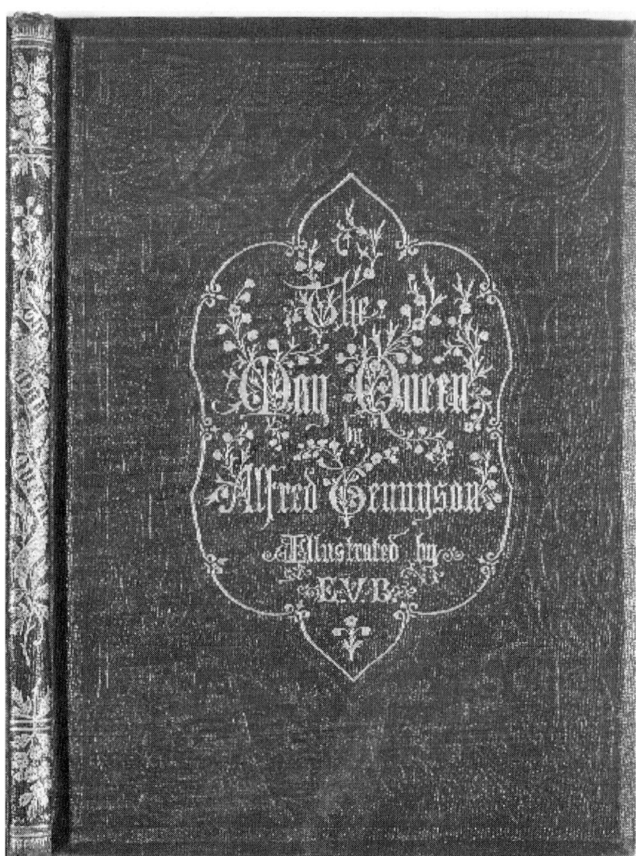

FIG. 86

747 Warren, Albert

Watts, Isaac. *Divine and moral Songs for children. Illustrated.* London: Sampson Low, Son, and Marston, 1866. Richard Clay London. 116 p.
152 × 208 × 17 mm. 3437.i.15.

Gilt edges. Bevelled boards. Light yellow endpapers and pastedowns. Binder's ticket on the lower pastedown: '| Bound by | Bone & Son, | [rule] | 76, Fleet Street, | London. |' The lower cover is blocked in blind and in relief. Three fillets are blocked in blind on the borders. The centre-piece shows linked and overlapping semi-circles, formed by fillets blocked in blind, with dots blocked in relief within the inner semi-circles. On the centre, a twelve-petal single flower is blocked in blind. The upper cover is blocked in gold and in relief. Three gold fillets are blocked on the outer borders. Two fillets are blocked on the inner border, with curling stems near each corner. On each inner corner, an oval is blocked with horizontal gold hatch, and a fleur-de-lis blocked in gold within each oval. Small single ovals are blocked on the centre sides. The centre-piece shows a mandorla, with curling stems and flowers blocked on its borders. It also has a border repeating pattern of four leaves. The words: '| Watts' | Divine & moral | songs |' are blocked in relief within three gold lettering-pieces which are joined and have scroll-like ends. Each lettering-piece has a single horizontal fillet blocked above and below the letters. A bird is blocked above the title. Signed 'AW' in gold as separate letters at the base of the centre-piece. The spine is blocked in gold and in relief. From the head downwards, the decoration is: two gold fillets; a panel formed by a single gold fillet with a zig-zag pattern, and also two gold fillets blocked above and below; tassel decoration; the central portion of the spine is blocked as a gold lettering-piece, and has on its perimeter – 1. a rope-like gold fillet; 2. a single gold fillet; 3. dots blocked in relief ; within these fillets, the words: '| Watts' Divine & Moral Songs. |' blocked in relief within the rectangular gold lettering-piece; tassel decoration; three gold fillets; a panel formed by a single gold fillet; the words: '| London | S. Low & Co. |' are blocked in relief within a rectangular gold lettering-piece, all within a panel; four gold fillets are blocked at the tail.

Ball, *VPB* p. 166. Goldman, *Cat. 1* no. 184. Pantazzi, *4D* p. 94 no. IX.

748 Warren, Albert

Broderip, Frances Freeling. *Wild roses; or, Simple Stories of Country Life. With illustrations by H. Anelay.* London: Griffith and Farran, Successors to Newbery and Harris, Corner of St. Paul's Churchyard, 1867. London: Gilbert and Rivington, Printers, St. John's Square. v, 235 p., 4 plates.
123 × 192 × 28 mm. 12806.ee.16.

The plates are signed with the monogram 'HA' and 'Pearson Sc.' On page 4 of the publisher's titles at the end: 'Post 8vo., price 3s. 6d. cloth elegant; 4s. gilt edges.'

Bevelled boards. Yellow endpapers and pastedowns. Red sand-grain cloth. Both covers have the same two fillets blocked in blind on the borders . The upper cover central vignette is blocked in gold and in relief. It shows a posy of wild roses, with four gold lettering-pieces (which have hatched fillets on their borders) blocked in front of the posy. The words: '| Wild roses |' are blocked in relief within a rectangular gold lettering-piece; the word: '| or |' is blocked in relief within a circular gold lettering-piece; the words: '| simple stories of country life |' are blocked in relief within a curving gold lettering-piece; the word: '| Broderip. |' is blocked in relief within a ribbon-shaped gold lettering-piece. Signed 'AW' in gold as separate letters at the base of the vignette. The spine is blocked in gold. It has the same design as the upper cover vignette: a posy of wild roses is blocked in gold, with six rectangular gold lettering-pieces, each with a hatched gold fillet blocked on its borders; the words: '| Wild roses | or | simple stories | of | country life | Broderip. |' are blocked in relief in each of the six gold lettering-pieces.

749 Warren, Albert

Broderip, Frances Freeling. *Tales of the toys, told by themselves. With illustrations by Tom Hood.* [Monogram of Griffith and Farran.] London: Griffith and Farran, (Successors to Newbery and Harris) Corner of St. Paul's Churchyard, 1869. [London]: Wertheimer, Lea and Co., Printers, Finsbury Circus. [2], 220 p., 5 plates.
129 × 175 × 26 mm. 12807.ee.35.

The plates are hand coloured. They are signed with the monogram 'TH' and 'Ferrier Sc.'. On page four of the publisher's titles at the end: Super Royal 16mo., price 3s. 6d.cloth elegant, 4s. 6d. coloured gilt edges.

Gilt edges. [No original endpapers or pastedowns.] Binder's ticket on lower pastedown: '| Bound by | W. Bone & Son. | 76, Fleet St. | London E.C. |'. Blue sand-grain cloth. Both covers blocked identically in blind on the borders, on the corners and on the sides. A single fillet is blocked in blind on the borders. Extended leaf decoration is blocked in relief on each corner. A curved inner thin fillet, blocked in blind, forms a central frame. The upper cover central vignette is blocked in gold. There are three ribbon-shaped gold lettering-pieces blocked near the centre. The words: '| Tales of the toys | told by themselves | by Frances Freeling Broderip |' are blocked in relief within the ribbons. A coiled rope and a thin fillet twines around and behind the ribbons, forming a fleur-de-lis shape at the head and at the base of the vignette. The very centre shows a Chinese figure, a copy of the one reproduced in the plate opposite page 38. Signed 'AW' in gold as separate letters underneath the figure. The spine is blocked in gold, in blind and in relief. From the head downwards, the decoration is: three gold fillets, one thick between two thin; a kite and tail streamers; in front of the kite, four rectangular gold lettering-pieces are blocked; the words: 'Tales | of the toys | told by themselves | by | Frances Freeling Broderip. |' blocked in relief within the lettering-pieces; three pendulous stars, blocked in relief within a panel; small stem and bud decoration; two fillets blocked in blind; two thin gold fillets; the words: 'London | Griffith & Farran |' are blocked in relief within a rectangular gold lettering-piece at the tail.

Ball, *VPB* p. 166.

and in relief identically on the corners and on the sides. The blocking shows two branches on the borders, with an elaborate pattern of curling stems, flowers and leaves blocked in relief around the branches. The whole forms the central frame. On the upper cover around the borders of the central frame, two joined fillets are blocked – one in blind the other in gold. On the centre, the words: '| The | May Queen | by | Alfred | Tennyson | Illustrated by | E.V.B. |' are blocked in gold in gothic letters. Flowers, stems, and leaves are blocked in gold between, through, and on the ends of the letters. The spine is blocked in gold and in relief. From the head downwards, the decoration is: a filigree pattern blocked in gold; two gold fillets; a ribbon-shaped gold lettering-piece runs down the spine, with the title: '| The | May | Queen. |' blocked in relief within the ribbon; two gold fillets; a branch and blossom, blocked in gold; signed 'AW' in gold as separate letters; two gold fillets; a filigree pattern is blocked in gold at the tail.

de Beaumont, *RdeB1* no. 373. Goldman, *VIB* no. 373.

745 Warren, Albert

Wilson, Mark. *The first reading book. With one hundred and twenty illustrations.* [Engraving of forest scene.] London: Sampson Low, Son, and Co. 47, Ludgate Hill, [1862]. [London]: R. Clay, Son, and Taylor, Printers, Bread Street Hill. 128 p.
123 × 180 × 15 mm. 12805.dd.41.

The frontispiece illustration on page 2 is signed 'H. Weir'.

White pastedowns. The spine is of red bead-grain cloth. Red dyed paper over boards. The lower cover has a list of publisher's titles. The work is advertised as: '| Price 1s. | The child's first reader. | With 120 Pictures |'. The upper cover has on the borders: 1. a blue fillet; 2. horizontal hatch between pairs of fillets. Groups of three small leaves are printed on each corner, with more stems and leaves on the inner corners. Blue fillets form an 'hour-glass' shaped central frame. The title: '| Wilson's | First | Reader |' is printed inside three rectangles formed by single fillets. Signed 'AW' in blue letters at the centre tail.

746 Warren, Albert FIG. 87

Buchanan, Robert. *Ballad Stories of the Affections. From the Scandinavian. With illustrations by G. J. Pinwell W. Small A. B. Houghton E. Dalziel T. Dalziel J. Lawson & J. D. Watson. Engraved by the Brothers Dalziel.* London: George Routledge & Sons, Broadway, Ludgate Hill, [1866]. [London]: Dalziel Brothers, Engravers and Printers, Camden Press. [1], xiv, 174 p. With four pages of publisher's titles bound at the end.
170 × 235 × 25 mm. RdeB.G.6.

The British Museum de Beaumont copy.

Gilt edges. Bevelled boards. Light yellow endpapers and pastedowns. Binder's ticket on lower pastedown: '| Bound by | W. Bone & Son. | 76, Fleet St. | London E.C. |'. Green sand-grain cloth. Both covers blocked identically in gold and in relief. Three fillets are blocked in gold on the borders. Between these fillets, a repeating pattern of half-circles and dotted stems is blocked in gold. The central vignette is blocked in gold and in relief. It shows an oval formed by border fillets, with three-leafed groups blocked at the head and at the base. The words: '| Ballad Stories | of the | Affections | Robert Buchanan | Illustrated |' are blocked in relief within five rectangular gold lettering-pieces, with the title being blocked in gothic letters. Behind and between these, a diamond pattern is blocked in gold, with single leaves blocked in relief inside each diamond. Signed 'W' in relief within a diamond near the base of the vignette. The spine is blocked in gold. From the head downwards, the decoration is: two gold fillets; a panel, formed by two zig-zag gold fillets and hatched gold triangles; four gold fillets; a panel formed by two gold fillets, with small decoration at its head and tail; within this panel are blocked: 1. a pattern of diamonds with small leaves blocked in gold inside each diamond, 2. the title: '| Ballad | Stories | of the | Affections |' blocked in gold in gothic letters; the words: '| Robert | Buchanan |' blocked in gold within a rectangle formed by two gold fillets; signed 'W' in gold within a circle formed by two gold fillets; the word: '| Illustrated |' is blocked in gold within a rectangle formed by a single gold fillet, which has 'scroll' ends; at the tail, two gold fillets; '| Routledge |' is blocked in relief within a rectangular gold lettering-piece; two gold fillets.

de Beaumont, *RdeB1* no. 34. Goldman, *VIB* no. 34.

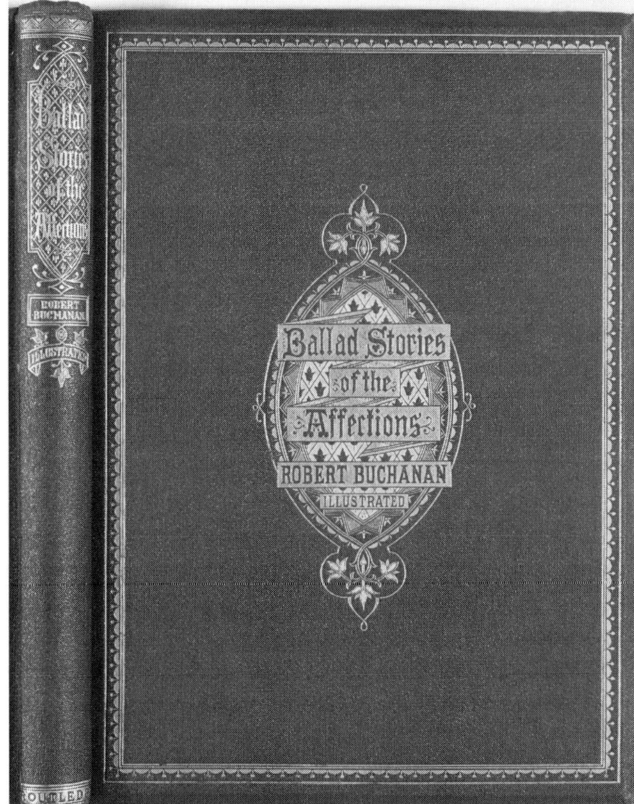

FIG. 87

COLOUR PLATES

Leighton, *SID. 1880*. Leighton, John. *Suggestions in design . . .* London: Blackie, [1880]. The USA edition, New York: D. Appleton, 1881 is reprinted as *1,100 designs and motifs from historic sources*. New York: Dover Publications Inc. [1995]. The plate numbers cited are the same for the English edition of 1880.

Martin, *Photos*. Martin, Elizabeth. *Collecting and preserving old Photographs*. London, Collins, 1988.

McLean, *Cundall*. McLean, Ruari. *Joseph Cundall. A Victorian publisher.* Pinner: Private Libraries Association, 1976.

McLean, *Fawcett*. McLean, Ruari and McLean Antonia. *Benjamin Fawcett. Engraver and Colour Printer.* Aldershot: Scolar Press, 1988.

McLean, *VBD*. McLean, Ruari. *Victorian book design and colour printing.* 2nd edition. [London] Faber & Faber [1972.]

McLean, *VPBB*. McLean, Ruari. *Victorian publishers' book-bindings in cloth and leather.* London, Gordon Fraser, 1974.

McLean, *VPBP*. McLean, Ruari. *Victorian publishers' bookbindings in paper.* London: Gordon Fraser, 1983.

Morris & Levin, *APB*. Morris, Ellen K. & Levin, Edward S. *The Art of Publishers' Bookbindings 1815–1915*. Los Angeles: William Daley Rare Books Ltd, 2000.

Muir, *VIB*. Muir, Percy. *Victorian illustrated books.* London: B. T. Batsford. [Revised impression. 1985.]

Muira, *MP*. Muira, Einen. *The art of marbled paper. Marbled patterns and how to make them.* London: Zaehnsdorf, [1988].

Oldfield, *BC. From Boards to Cloth: The Development of Publishers' Bindings in the Nineteenth Century. Guide to an Exhibition at the Thomas Fisher Rare Book Library, University of Toronto. July–September 1991*. Exhibition and Catalogue by Philip Oldfield. [Toronto: University of Toronto Library, 1991.]

Packer, *BVL*. Packer, Maurice. *Bookbinders of Victorian London.* London: British Library, 1991.

Pantazzi, *JL*. Pantazzi, Sybille. *John Leighton, 1822–1912. A versatile Victorian designer: his designs for book covers.* **In:** *The Connoisseur*, Vol. 152, April 1963. pp. 262–273.

Pantazzi, *4D*. Pantazzi, Sybille. *Four designers of English publishers' bindings of the nineties.* **In:** *Papers of the Bibliographical Society of America*. 55. 1961. pp. 88–99.

Tanselle, ***BDP***. G. Thomas Tanselle. *The bibliographical description of patterns. Studies in Bibliography*. Vol. XXIII. 1970. pp. 71–102

Other Books consulted

Houfe, Simon. *The Dictionary of 19th Century British Book Illustrators and Caricaturists.* [Revised edition] [Woodbridge: Antique Collectors Club, [1996].

Korey, Maria Elena. *Elegant Editions. Aspects of Victorian Book Design. An exhibition of books selected from the Ruari McLean Collection of Victorian Book Design and Colour Printing in the Robertson Davies Library at Massey College. Thomas Fisher Rare Book Library, University of Toronto, Massey College. 19 January–31 March 1995*. Toronto: Massey College, 1995.

Sadleir, Michael. *XIX Century Fiction. A Bibliographical Record based on his own collection. In two volumes.* Cambridge, Mass. Maurizi Martino, [1996].

Waddleton, Norman. *The Waddleton Chronology of Books with Colour Illustrations or Decorations, 15th to 20th Century*. 5th ed. 1993.

Books and Articles Referred to, with Abbreviated Titles

Atterbury and Wainwright. *Pugin.* Atterbury, Paul, and Wainwright, Clive, Editors. *Pugin. A Gothic passion.* New Haven and London: Yale University Press, [1994].

Ball, *App.* Ball, Douglas. *A catalogue of the Appleton Collection of Victorian colour printing and signed bindings.* 1979. [College of Librarianship, Aberystwyth, Wales.]

Ball, *VPB.* Ball, Douglas. *Victorian publishers' bindings.* London, Library Association, 1985.

Barber, *Rossetti.* Barber, Giles. *Rossetti, Ricketts, and Some English Publishers' Bindings of the Nineties.* **In:** *The Library.* 5th series.1970. pp. 314–330.

Buchanan-Brown, *BIGC.* Buchanan-Brown, John. *The book illustrations of George Cruikshank.* Newton Abbot: David & Charles, 1980.

Darton, *CB.* F. J. Harvey Darton. *Children's books in England. Five centuries of social life.* 3rd. ed. London, British Library, 1999.

de Beaumont, *RdeB1.* [Catalogue of] *Robin de Beaumont Collection. 1860s Illustrators, Books, Prints and Drawings. Given to the British Museum, Prints & drawings Dept., May 1992.*

de Beaumont, *RdeB2. Robin de Beaumont Collection. 1860s Illustrators. Books, Drawings & Proofs. Combined 1992 & 1996 Gifts. March 2000. [Compiled by Robin de Beaumont.]*

de Beaumont, *PB.* de Beaumont, Robin. *Nineteenth Century Publishers' Bindings 1820–1900; a brief survey from my shelves.* **In:** *The Private Library.* Fourth series. Volume 9:1. Spring 1996. 48 p.

Dry, *JL.* Dry, Graham. *John Leighton and bookbinding design in England from 1845 to 1880.* Thesis for submission to Institut für Kunstgeschichte der Universität München, 1984–85. [Copy at Cambridge University Library. The checklist at the end cites 574 titles with designs by John Leighton.]

Gaskell, *NIB.* Gaskell, Philip. *A new introduction to bibliography.* Oxford: Oxford University Press, 1972. Table 9, pp. 240–244, *The Classification of Book-cloth Grains.*

Goldman, *Cat1.* Goldman, Paul. Antiquarian Books. Catalogue no.1. [London, 1998.]

Goldman, *VIB.* Goldman, Paul. *Victorian Illustrated Books 1850–1870. The heyday of wood-engraving. The Robin de Beaumont Collection.* London, British Museum Press, 1994. Checklist of the de Beaumont Collection, nos. 1–592, pp. 126–142.

Gray, *Eliot Review.* Gray, Beryl. *E. M. W. [i.e. Edmund Morison Wimperis.] The stereotyped edition's title-page vignettes.* Also: Adams, Kathleen. *Milly Barton and Emma Gwyther.* **In:** *The George Eliot Review.* No. 29, 1998, pp. 52–56; no. 30, pp. 60–62.

Jones & Brown, *WR.* Jones, Gregory V. & Brown, Jane E. *Victorian Binding Designer WR: William Ralston, not William Harry Rogers.* **In:** *The Book Collector.* [Publication in 2002.]

King, *JL.* King, Edmund M. B. *The Book Cover Designs of John Leighton, F.S.A.* **In:** *The British Library Journal,* vol.24, no.2.Autumn 1998. pp. 234–255.

King, *WHR.* King, Edmund M. B. *The Book Cover Designs of William Harry Rogers.* **In:** *'For the Love of the Binding'. Studies in Bookbinding History Presented to Mirjam Foot.* [London]: The British Library, 2000. pp. 319–328.

Leathlean, *HNH.* Leathlean, Howard. *Henry Noel Humphreys and the Getting-Up of Books in the Mid-Nineteenth Century.* **In:** *The Book Collector.* Vol. 38. no. 2. Summer 1989. pp. 192–209.

Leathlean, *Jerrard.* Leathlean, Howard. *Paul Jerrard Publisher of 'Special Presents'.* **In:** *The Book Collector* Vol. 40. no. 2. Summer 1991. pp. 169–196.

Leighton, *SID. 1852.* Leighton, John. *Suggestions in design . . .* London: David Bogue, 1852–53. Issued originally in parts.

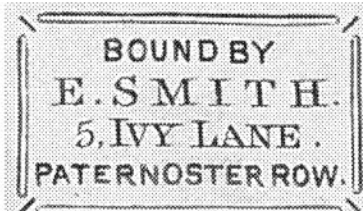

SMITH, E.
Ball 80 (additional)

VIRTUE & CO.
Ball 96A

VIRTUE & CO.
Ball 96B

WESTLEYS & CLARK
Ball 101A

WESTLEY, JOSIAH
Ball 102A

WESTLEY, JOSIAH
Ball 102A (variant)

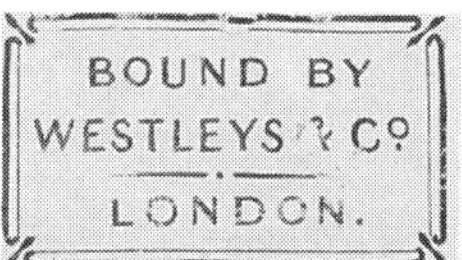

WESTLEYS & CO.
Ball 103A

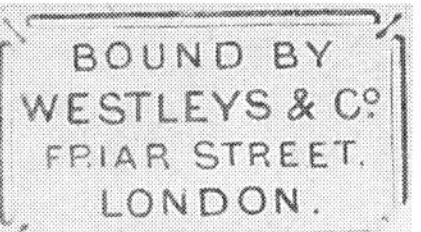

WESTLEYS & CO.
Ball 103B

WESTLEYS & CO.
Ball 103C

LEIGHTON SON & HODGE
Ball 53E

LEIGHTON SON & HODGE
Ball 53F

LEWIS & SONS
Ball 54A

MACTAGGART, JAMES
Ball (not cited)

REMNANT & EDMONDS
Ball 66E1

REMNANT EDMONDS & REMNANTS
Ball 67A (variant)

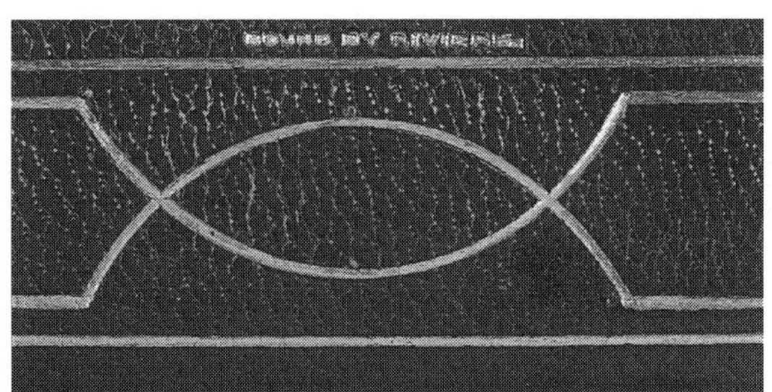

RIVIERE
Ball (not cited)

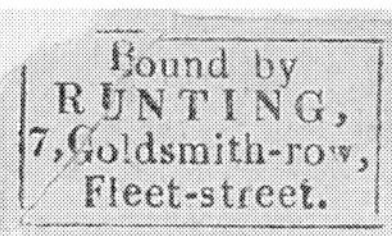

RUNTING
Ball (not cited)

SIMPSON & RENSHAW
Ball 79 (variant)

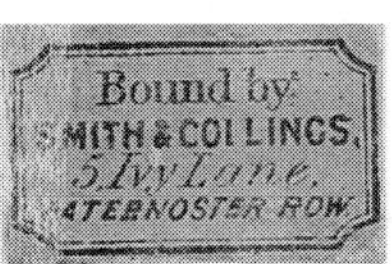

SMITH & COLLINGS
Ball 83A

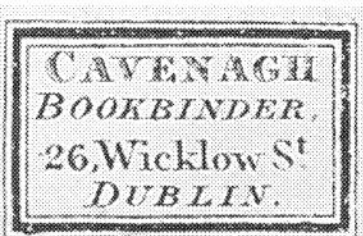

CAVENAGH
Ball 20B (variant)

CLARKE, CHARLES H.
Ball (not cited)

CURTIS, S.
Ball 23A

EDMONDS & REMNANTS
Ball 31A

GRAY, JOHN
Ball 39B

GOWANS, ADAM
Ball 37 (variant)

HANBURY & CO.
Ball 41A

HANBURY & CO.
Ball 41A (variant)

LEIGHTON SON & HODGE
Ball 53A

LEIGHTON SON & HODGE
Ball 53B

LEIGHTON SON & HODGE
Ball 53C

LEIGHTON SON & HODGE
Ball 53D

List of Bookbinders' Tickets

The bookbinders' tickets reproduced here are examples recorded whilst cataloguing binding designs for this book. Ball, in *Victorian Publisher's Bindings*, Appendix E, *Nineteenth-Century Edition Binders' Signatures*, pp. 168–192, lists and describes these (and many others) in more detail. Where the citation in Ball is identified, the number in his Appendix is given here. In the General Index of this book, the entries whose books have a particular bookbinder's ticket are grouped together by the Ball number.

The aim of the list is to record (in conjunction with the General Index entries) which books possess particular tickets. No attempt has been made to give measurements, to state the ink colour, to describe any artwork printed on the ticket, or to identify the dye colour of the paper of the ticket. Tickets are reproduced 1.5 times their actual size.

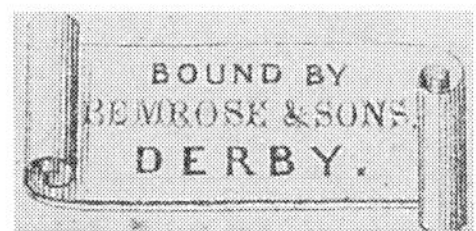

BEMROSE & SONS
Ball 14A (possibly a variant)

BONE & SON
Ball 17A

BONE & SON
Ball 17C

BONE & SON
Ball 17D

BONE & SON
Ball 17E

BURN
Ball 20A

BURN
Ball 20B

BURN
Ball 20E

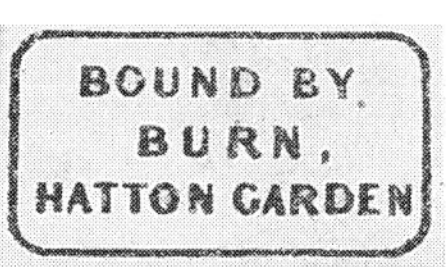

BURN
Ball 20 (not cited)

Another copy of the fifth edition is at BL X. 802/3044. Gilt edges. Rebound in 1975.

The 1982 edition was published in New Dehli by Time International Books. 171 p. 320 × 250 × 25 mm. Printed and bound by Surya Print Process, New Dehli. With an Introduction by Toby Sinclair. Brown endpapers and paste-downs. This copy has red silk cloth, ungrained. The title is blocked in gold on the upper cover and on the spine. Part of the Introduction reads: 'The book is dedicated to the great Victorian novelist – William Thackeray, who in an oblique reference in turn named one of his characters Gen. Sir Curry Rice, K.C.B. in his novel 'A shabby genteel story'. 'The plates reproduced are a poor monochrome version of the facsimiles made for the fourth edition of 1911.

750 Wyatt, Matthew Digby

Wyatt, *Sir* Matthew Digby. *The Industrial Arts of The Nineteenth Century. A series of illustrations of the choicest specimens produced by every nation at the Great Exhibition of Works of Industry, 1851. Dedicated, by Permission, to His Highness The Prince Albert.* London: Published by Day and Son, Lithographers to the Queen, 1851. viii, [64 p.], 32 plates.
335 × 493 × 20 mm. HS.74/1240.

Former National Central Library copy.

Quarter red leather spine and white endpapers and pastedowns – neither original. Light yellow paper over boards. Lithographed with an elaborate design identical on both covers – the colours being originally green, maroon and gold. On the borders are: 1. a pattern of linked cartouches, in green; 2–3. a thick and a thin fillet, in maroon; 4. spaced hatching, in maroon; 5–7. one thick maroon fillet, between two thin maroon fillets, the thick with green repeating beads within it; 8. a wide border pattern in maroon of thin curling stems and leaves; 9. on the centre sides, the head and the tail, beaded fillets form a circle, each with flower decoration within, surrounded by gold; 10. fillets as for nos 5–7; 11. spaced hatching, in maroon; 12. a maroon fillet; 13. a maroon fillet, with green overprinted within it. Within the central rectangle, an elaborate pattern of circles and straps is above and below the centre, with a diaper pattern as background. On the centre, maroon is printed, with lettering in gold. The words: '| Divis. 1st Xmas 1851. | The | Industrial Arts, | of the | Nineteenth Century, | by | M. Digby Wyatt, | Architect, | Day & Son, Lithr to the Queen. |' Signed on the lower left hand corner: '| [M] Digby Wyatt, Invt. et Del. |' The spine has lettering along the spine: '| The Industrial Arts of the Nineteenth Century Division I – Wyatt |' blocked in gold. '| 1851 | 'is blocked in gold near the tail.

McLean, *VBD* pp. 120–121.

751 Wyatt, Matthew Digby PLATE XCI

Atkinson, George Francklin. *'Curry and rice', on forty plates; or, the ingredients of social life at 'Our Station' in India.* London: Published by Day & Son, Lithographers to the Queen, Gate Street, Lincoln's Inn Fields, [1859]. London: Lithographed, Printed and Published by Day & Son, Lithographers to the Queen, 6 Gate Street, Lincoln's Inn Fields. [87 p.], 40 plates.
210 × 295 × 28 mm. 10057.v.8.

Gilt edges. Yellow endpapers and pastedowns. The upper endpaper and the title page have the bookseller's name stamped in blue ink: '| A. J. Combridge & Co. | New and old booksellers. | Bombay. |' Orange moiré fine rib vertical-grain cloth. Both covers blocked identically in blind on the borders. The borders show a repeating stem and flower pattern. On the upper cover, a rectangular block, in gold, occupies the centre. It shows a portico with a plinth, border decorations and columns – all in the Indian idiom. On the centre of this design, the veranda of an Indian colonial house is depicted, with three figures. The title: '| Curry & rice |' is blocked in relief at the head within a rectangular cartouche gold lettering-piece. Signed: '| M. Digby Wyatt Invt et Delt |' in gold at the base of the design. The spine is blocked in gold. The title: '| Curry and rice | Atkinson |' is blocked in gold along the spine, inside rectangles formed by gold fillets, also with gold borders. At the tail: 'Day and Son' is blocked in gold.

Another copy of the original issue is at BL OIOC W.4564. [87 p.], 40 plates. 210 × 290 × 35 mm. This copy is in a half morocco binding. The edges were trimmed upon rebinding, originally gilt.

The second edition is at BL 1264.e.16. [87 p.], 40 plates. 210 × 295 × 35 mm. The original upper cover is bound in at the front of this volume. It has a size of 205 × 285 mm. The upper cover has the same design blocked as for BL 10057.v.8. This is the copyright deposit copy, with the date stamp: '12 JA[NUARY 18] 59'.

The third edition is at BL OIOC W.3698. [87 p.], 40 plates. 205 × 294 × 25 mm. Red ink speckled edges. White endpapers and pastedowns. The cover design is the same as for BL 10057.v.8. The covers are worn, and the spine has been rebacked. This copy was donated to the India Office Library by Sir Theodore Tasker.

752 Wyatt, Matthew Digby

Atkinson, George Francklin. *'Curry and rice', on forty plates; or, the ingredients of social life at 'Our Station' in India. Fourth edition, with colour illustrations from the original sketches from the author.* London: W. Thacker & Co., 2, Creed Lane, E.C.; Calcutta & Simla: Thacker, Spink & Co., 1911. London: George Pulman & Sons, Ltd., The Cranford Press. [87 p.], 40 plates.
205 × 295 × 23 mm. 10058.k.24.

Gutta percha binding, now dried out. Gilt edges. The endpapers and pastedowns are decorated with 'lattice-work' pattern. Orange moiré fine rib vertical-grain cloth. Both covers blocked identically in blind on the borders. The blind blocking shows a repeating stem and flower pattern. On the upper cover, a rectangular block, in gold, occupies the centre. It shows a portico with a plinth, border decorations and columns – all in the Indian idiom. On the centre of this design, the veranda of an Indian colonial house is depicted, with three figures. The title letters 'Curry and rice' are blocked in white, within a rectangular cartouche gold lettering-piece at the head. Signed: '| M. Digby Wyatt Invt et Delt |' in gold at the base of the rectangular block. The spine is blocked in gold and in relief. The title: '| Curry and rice |' and '| Atkinson |' is blocked along the spine in gold, within rectangles formed by gold fillets and borders blocked in gold. At the tail: '| Thacker & Co. |' is blocked in gold, between two gold fillets.

The fifth edition, also published in 1911, has the sub-title: 'Fifth edition, with colour illustrations for the first time from the original sketches of the author, kindly lent by the owner, Mr Frederick Palmer, C.I.E.' This copy is at BL OIOC W.2868. The copy was donated to the India Office Library by Mrs Waller. It has been rebound.

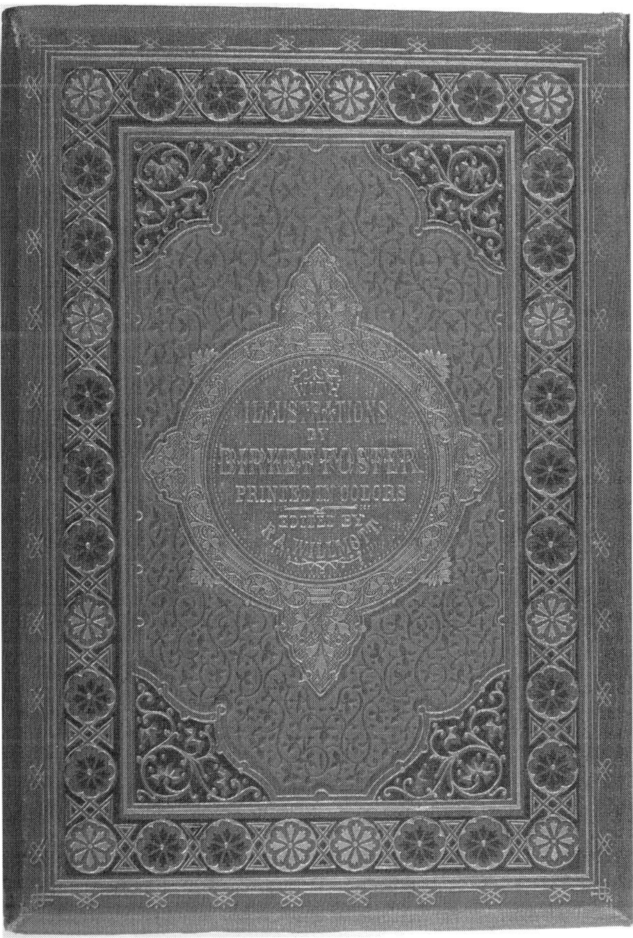

FIG. 84

737 Warren, Albert FIG. 84

Goldsmith, Oliver. *The poems of Oliver Goldsmith. Edited by Robert Aris Willmott. With illustrations by Birket Foster and H.N. Humphreys. Printed in colors* [sic] *from wood blocks.* London: George Routledge and Co., Farringdon Street; New York: 18, Beekman-Street, 1859. London: Edmund Evans, Engraver and Printer. xvi, 160 p.
165 × 230 × 30 mm. C.109.d.7.

Gilt edges. Bevelled boards. Yellow endpapers and pastedowns. Red morocco vertical-grain cloth. Both covers are blocked identically in gold and in black. The three fillets on the borders are blocked in gold, with a repeating 'figure of eight' pattern blocked on the outside. The inner border is of shell-shaped medallions, blocked in gold and in black. There are two fillets blocked on the inner border. The central rectangle has leaf and stem tracery blocked in gold and in black on the corners. Around the sides of the inner rectangle, recessed and blocked in relief, is a repeating pattern of three-pointed leaves and stems. The central roundel is surrounded by a filigree with leaves and stems blocked in gold. On the lower cover, the words: '| With | illustrations | by | Birket Foster. | Printed in colors. Edited by R. A. Willmott. |' are blocked in gold inside the roundel. On the upper cover, the words: '| The | poems | of | Oliver | Goldsmith |' are blocked in gold in elaborate lettering. It is likely that Warren's monogram , 'AW', is blocked in gold at the base of the roundel, within the tracery at the base of the roundel on each cover. The spine is blocked in gold and in black. There is 'Moorish' ornament blocked at the head and at the tail, blocked in gold and relief. The words: '| The | Poems | of | Oliver | Goldsmith | [rule] | Illustrated |' are blocked in gold, with seven gold fillets blocked underneath. On the middle, there is a mandorla blocked in gold and in relief. This copy formerly shelved at 1347.g.9.

Ball, *VPB* p. 164. States that Warren's '. . .monogram [is] in central roundel of covers'. McLean, *VPBB* p. 82. Shows the Routledge edition of 1860 in red pebble-grain cloth, with the same design. Pantazzi, *4D* p. 96. Says the design is unsigned.

738 Warren, Albert

Thomson, James. *The Seasons Illustrated by Birket Foster, F.R. Pickersgill, J. Wolf, G. Thomas, and Noel Humphreys.* London: James Nisbet & Co. Berners Street, 1859. Printed by R. & R. Clark, Edinburgh. [7], 228 p.
153 × 210 × 28 mm. RdeB.L.12.

The British Museum de Beaumont copy.

Text sewn on three tapes. Gilt edges. Bevelled boards. Cream endpapers and pastedowns. Binder's ticket on lower pastedown: '| Leighton | Son & | Hodge, | Shoe Lane | London. |' Blue morocco horizontal-grain cloth. Both covers blocked identically in gold, in blind and in relief. A wide gold border is blocked and within the border, a repeating pattern of four leaves and berries is blocked in relief. On each corner, a four-petal flower is blocked within a square. On the inner corners and on the sides, groups of stems and of leaves are blocked, each representing a season, with small leaves blocked in relief around them. The central frame is formed by ivy leaves and berries, which surround the central hexagon. This is blocked as a gold lettering-piece, bordered by a single fillet. The title: '| Thomson's | Seasons |' is blocked in relief within the lettering-piece. Small leaves and stem decoration is blocked in relief around the title. Signed 'AW' in relief as a monogram at the base of the hexagon. The spine is blocked in gold. A single gold fillet is blocked on the perimeter. From the head downwards, the decoration is: leaves and dots blocked between two fillets; a gold fillet; ivy leaves and berries; leaves and a quatrefoil with gold dots inside it; a hexagon gold lettering-piece with the title: '| Thomson's Seasons |' blocked in relief inside; leaves and a quatrefoil with dots inside it; ivy leaves and berries; a gold fillet; leaves and dots are blocked in gold between two fillets. Unsigned.

de Beaumont, *RdeB1* no. 381. Goldman, *VIB* no. 381.

739 Warren, Albert

Goldsmith, Oliver. *The poems. Edited by Robert Aris Willmott. A new edition with illustrations by Birket Foster and H. N. Humphreys. Printed in colours by Edmund Evans.* London:

an identical design blocked in gold, in blind and in relief. The borders are blocked in gold, with a 'Christmas tree' repeating pattern. Three fillets are blocked in gold on the borders. On the outer rectangle, raised cartouches are blocked in gold and in relief, with small zig-zag patterns blocked in relief between. Between the outer and inner rectangles, two fillets are blocked in gold. On the corners of the inner rectangle, plant patterns are blocked, within horizontal hatch arabesques. The central decoration is Moorish in design, with a twelve-pointed design and horizontal hatch blocking. The tracery of plants and leaves has the patterns picked out in relief. The words: '| The | Home | Affections | by the | Poets | Mackay |' are blocked in gold and in relief on the central panel. The spine is blocked in gold. There is a tracery of leaves and stems blocked in gold down the spine. The words: '| The | Home | Affections | by the | Poets | Mackay |' are blocked in relief, within a gold lettering-piece. Signed 'AW' in relief as a monogram, with the 'A' being inside the 'W'. It is above the word '| Illustrated |' blocked in relief within a horizontal hatch gold lettering-piece. The publisher: '| Routledge |' is blocked in relief within a vertical hatch gold lettering-piece blocked near the tail.

Ball, *VPB* p. 163. '. . .reissued in 1866 with the same design'. de Beaumont, *RdeB1* no. 193. Goldman, *VIB* no. 193. Morris & Levin, *APB* p. 108, no. 244.

735 Warren, Albert — FIG. 83

Milton, John. *Comus. A mask. With thirty illustrations by Pickersgill, Birket Foster, Harrison Weir, &c. Engraved by the Brothers Dalziel.* London: George Routledge & Co. Farringdon Street. New York: 18 Beekman Street, 1858. London: Printed by Richard Clay, Bread Street Hill. viii, 91 p.
150 × 210 × 20 mm. 1347.g.3.

Gilt edges. Bevelled boards. Original light yellow endpaper bound in at the front. Blue morocco vertical-grain cloth. Both covers are blocked identically in gold and in black. There are two fillets blocked in gold on the borders, in gold. Between them, a wide horizontal hatch border is blocked in gold, with a pattern of repeating stems, leaves and flowers blocked in relief. Within the inner rectangle, flowers and leaves are blocked in black around the centre. The central vignette is blocked as a gold lettering-piece, within an arabesque. On the inner border of the vignette, a fillet is blocked in relief. The words: 'Milton's Comus. Illustrated', are blocked in relief in fanciful letters. Signed 'AW', with the 'A' inside the base of the 'W', in relief as a monogram at the base of the vignette. The spine is blocked in gold. '| Milton's Comus |' is blocked in gold along the spine, within a cartouche formed by a gold fillet, with leaf decoration blocked in gold at the head and at the tail. There are other copies of this design on Longfellow 'The courtship of Miles Standish and other poems', Routledge, 1859, BL shelfmark 1347.f.2.; and on Wordsworth 'The deserted cottage', Routledge, 1859, BL shelfmark 1347.g.5.

Ball, *VPB* p. 163. Pantazzi, *4D* p. 95. Cites a copy in 'bright green [cloth]'.

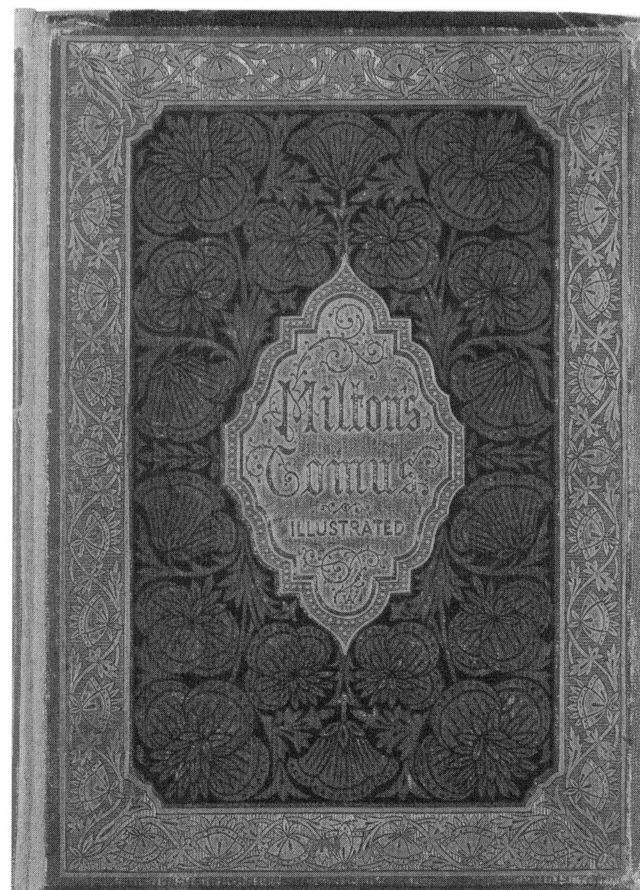

FIG. 83

736 Warren, Albert

Goldsmith, Oliver. *The deserted village. Illustrated by the Etching Club.* London: Sampson Low, Son & Co., 47 Ludgate Hill, 1859. London: Printed by R. Clay, Bread Street Hill. 46 p.
135 × 205 × 10 mm. RB.23.a.5278.

Gilt edges. Yellow endpapers and pastedowns. Green morocco vertical-grain cloth. Both covers are blocked in blind with the same design. Fillets are blocked on the borders. Leaf and stem patterns are blocked on the inner border and on the sides. Strapwork is blocked on the corners. On the upper cover, the central vignette is blocked in gold and in relief. The vignette is onion-shaped. On the outside of it, a tracery of leaves and stems is blocked in gold. The border of the vignette is a rule, blocked in relief. The title words: 'The deserted village' are blocked, surrounded by a tracery of thin stems and leaves, all in relief. The gold blocking surrounds the lettering and the tracery. Signed 'AW' in relief as separate letters at the base of the vignette. The spine is blocked in gold, with small designs above and below the title. The 1855 edition is at BL shelfmark 11640.ee.51. It has a cover design by John Leighton.

McLean, *VPBB* p. 78. Shows the 1855 edition, with a different design by John Leighton.

PLATE I **Entry No. 11**

PLATE II **Entry No. 14**

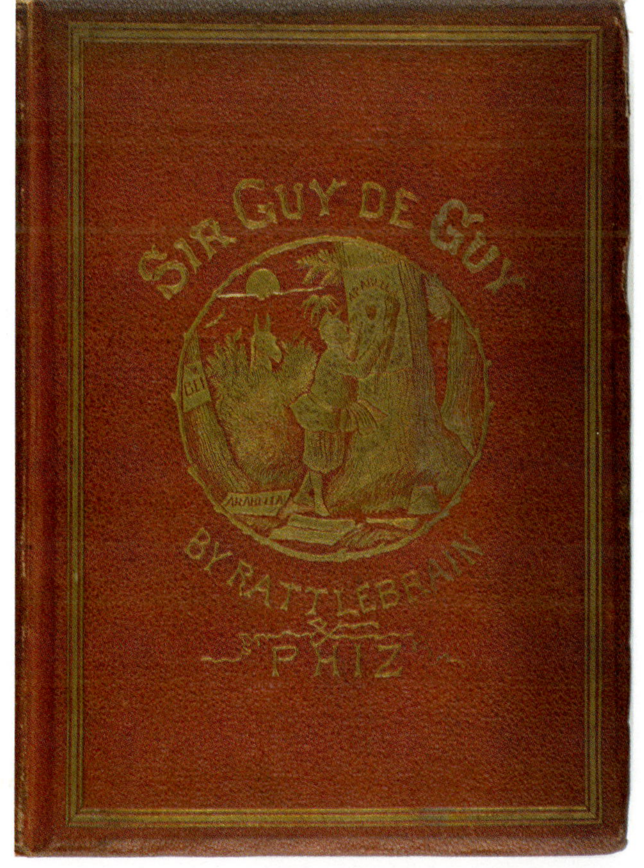

PLATE III **Entry No. 18**

PLATE IV **Entry No. 30**

PLATE V (*The British Museum*) Entry No. 32

PLATE VI Entry No. 35

PLATE VII Entry No. 56

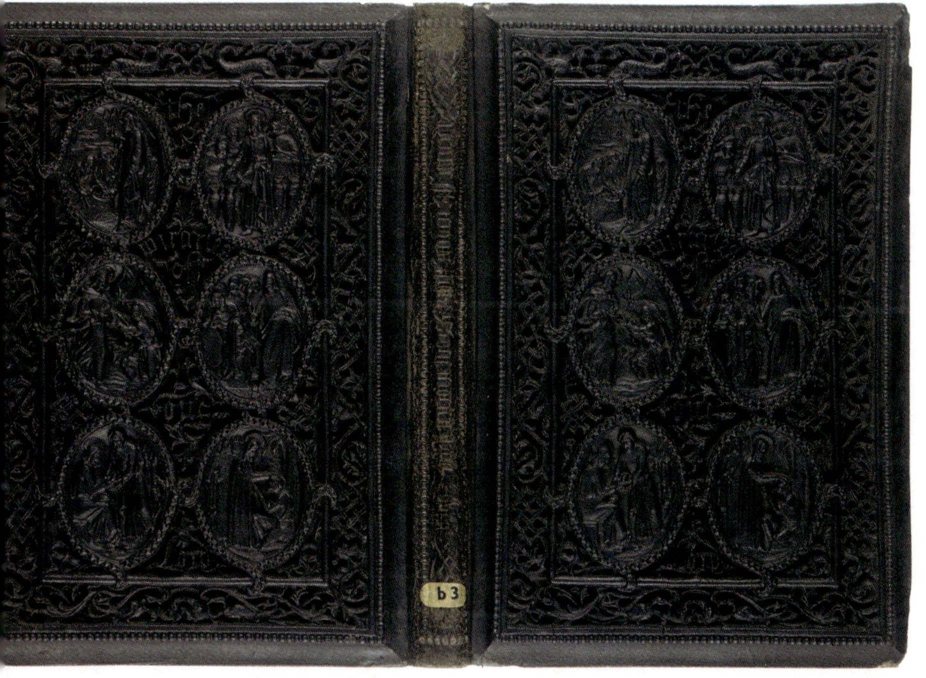

TE VIII Entry No. 57

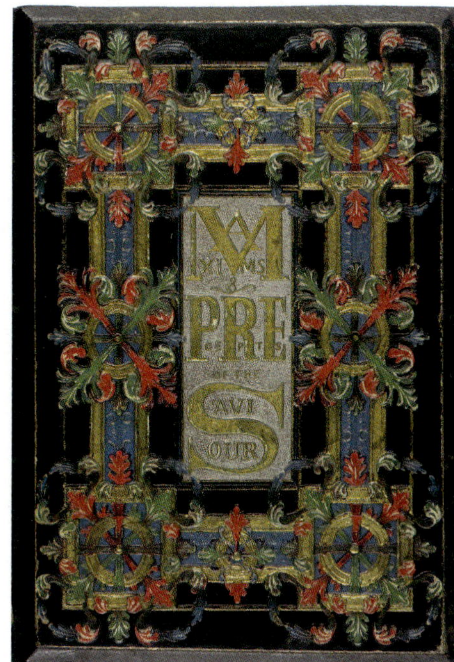

PLATE IX Entry No. 58

PLATE X Entry No. 60

PLATE XI Entry No. 61

PLATE XII

Entry No. 62

PLATE XIII

Entry No. 66

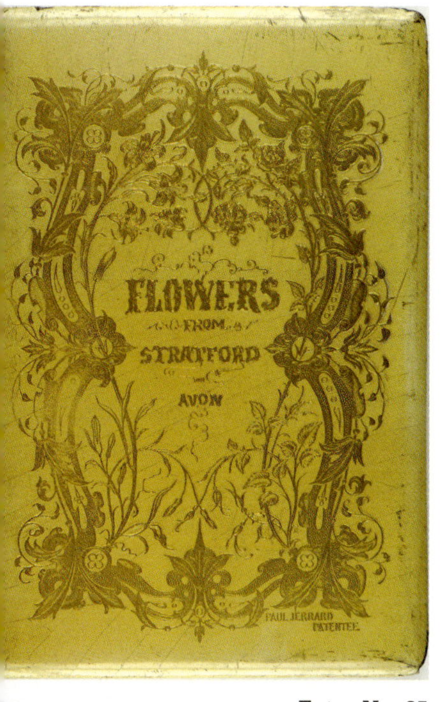

TE XIV Entry No. 65

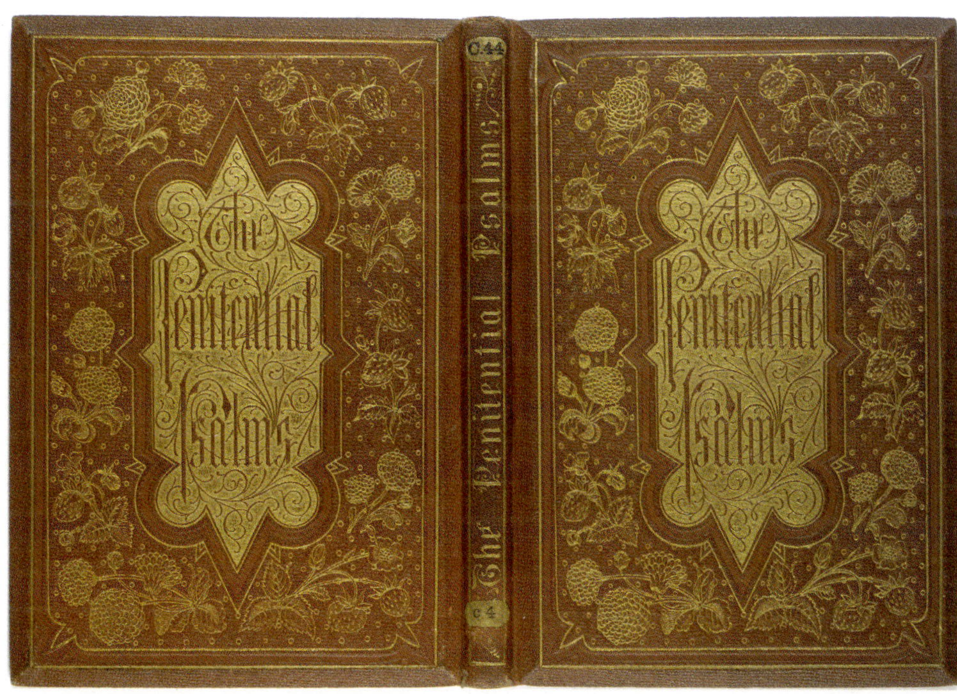

PLATE XVI Entry No. 72

TE XV (*The British Museum*) Entry No. 67

PLATE XVII Entry No. 78

PLATE XVIII Entry No. 80

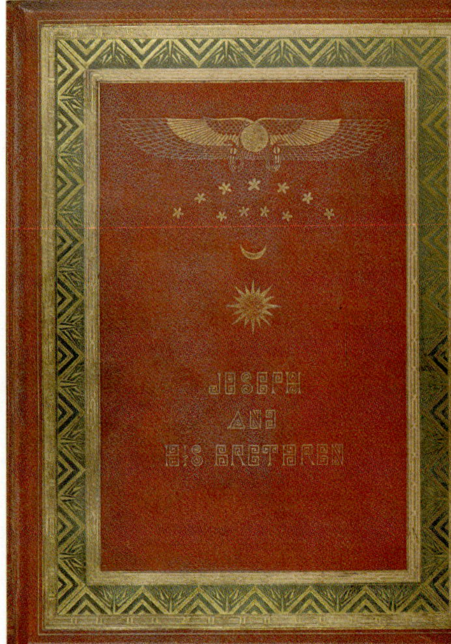

PLATE XIX Entry No

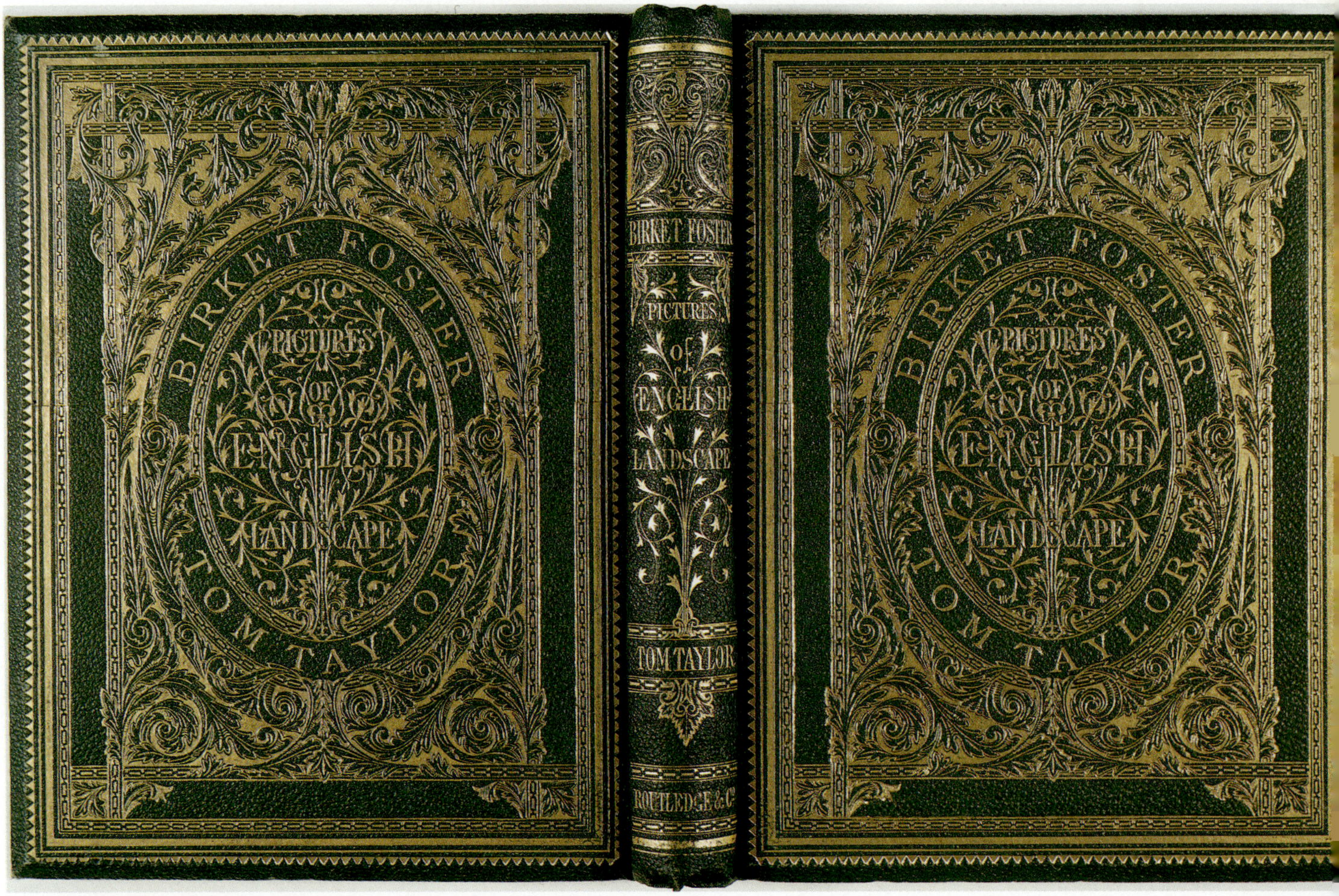

PLATE XX (*The British Museum*) Entry No

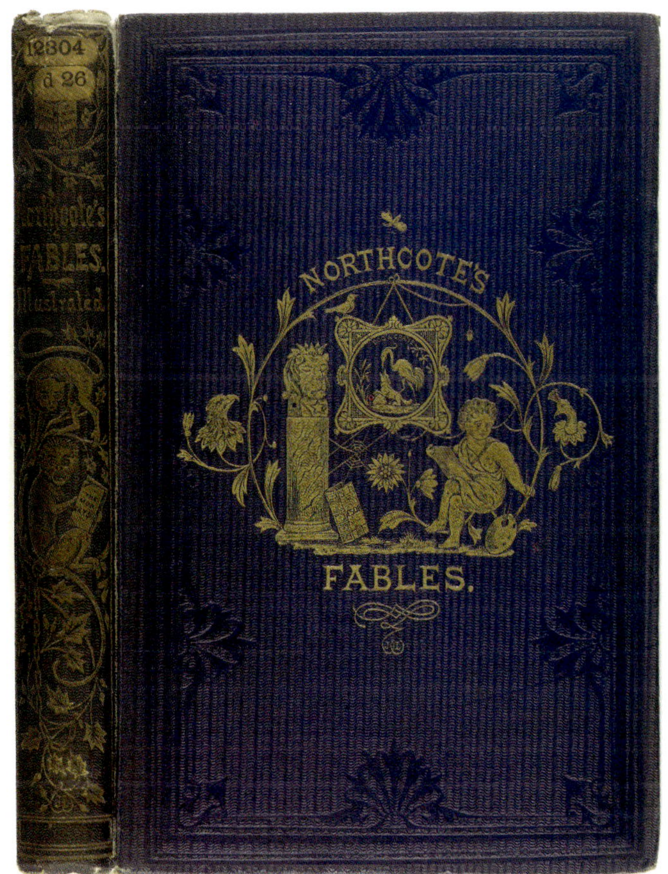

PLATE XXXII Entry No. 250

PLATE XXXIII Entry No. 258

PLATE XXXIV Entry No. 297

PLATE XXXV Entry No. 3

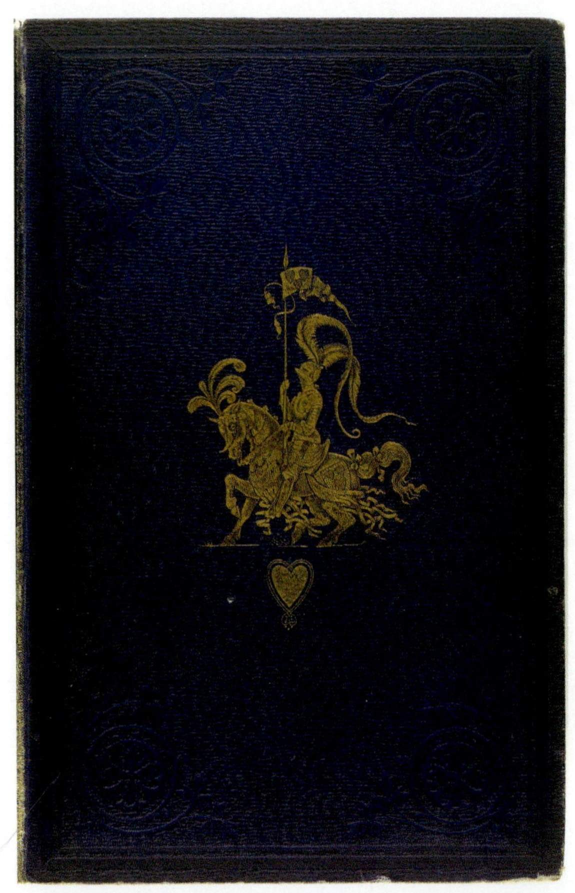

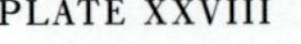

PLATE XXVIII Entry No. 228

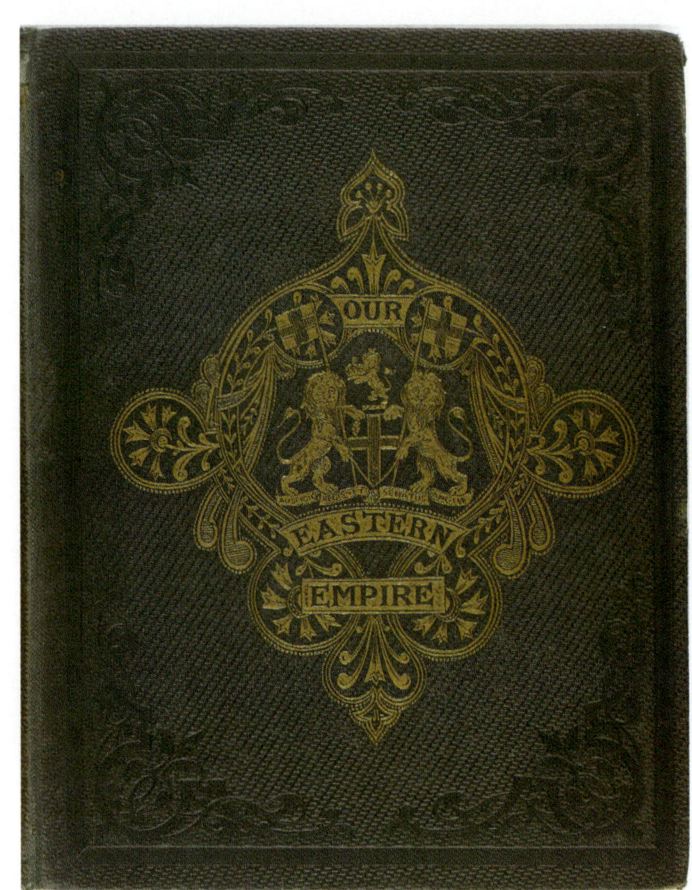

PLATE XXIX Entry No. 239

ATE XXX Entry No. 242

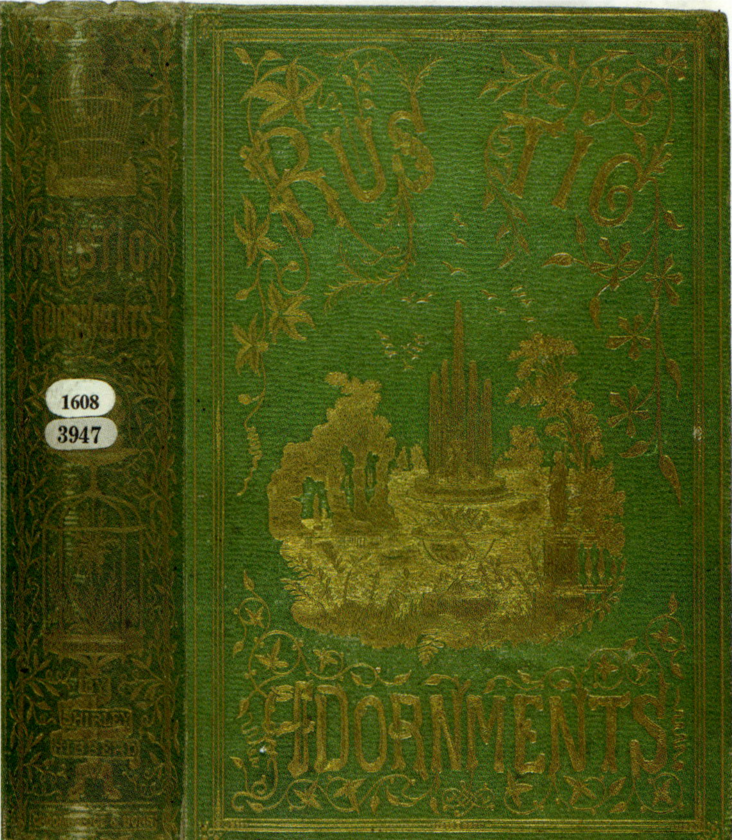

PLATE XXXI Entry No. 245

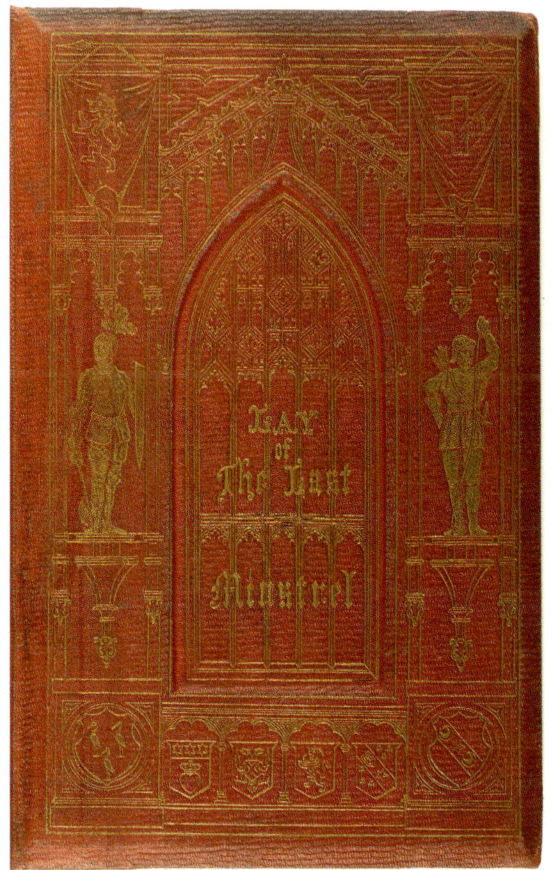

PLATE XXIV Entry No. 184

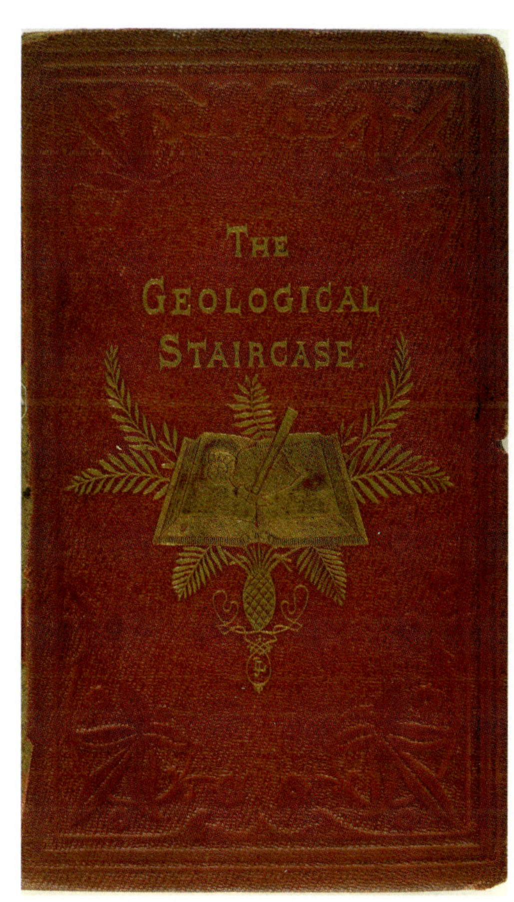

PLATE XXV Entry No. 197

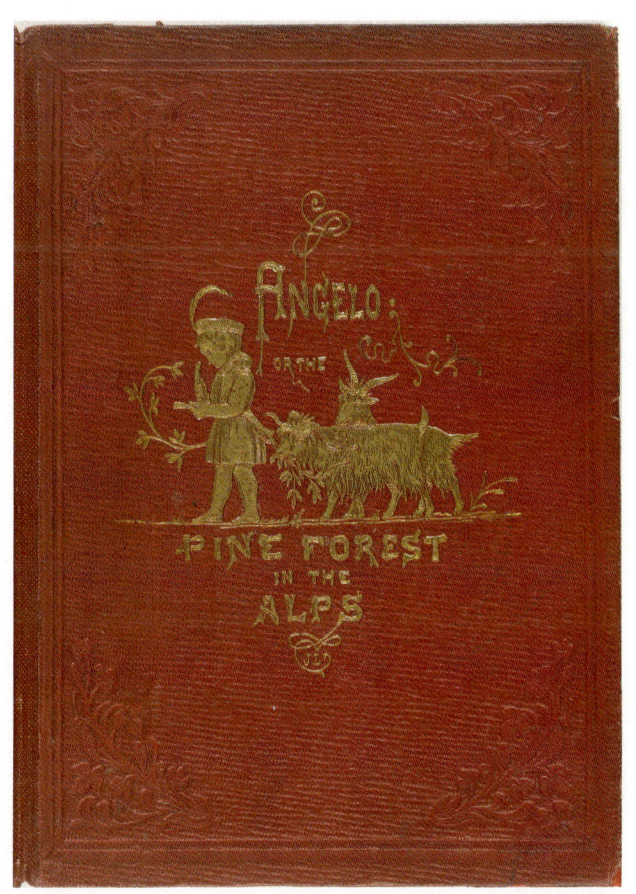

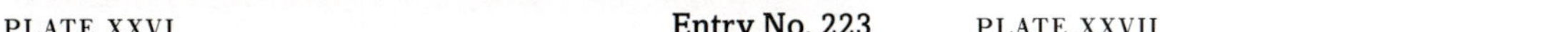

PLATE XXVI Entry No. 223

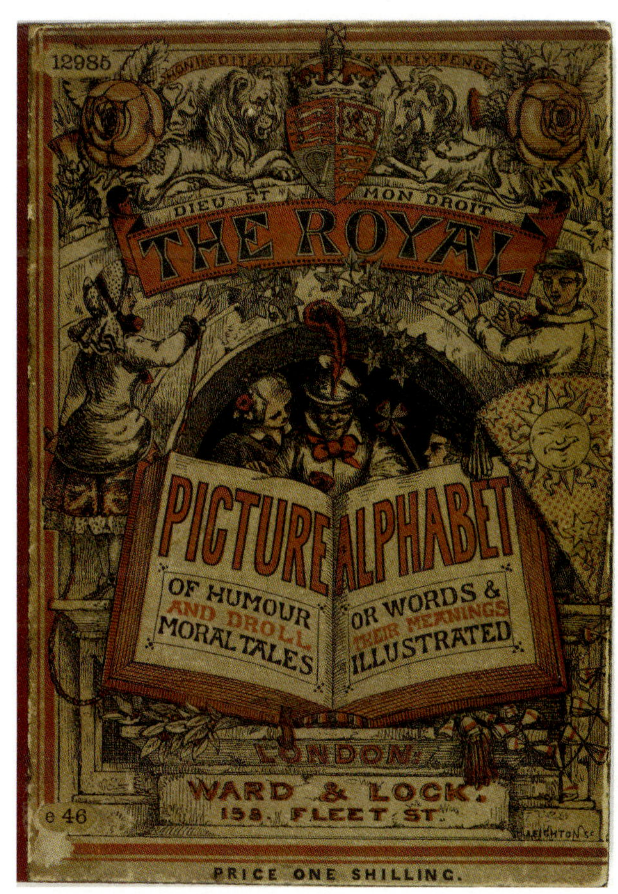

PLATE XXVII Entry No. 225

PLATE XXI

Entry No. 99

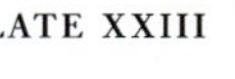
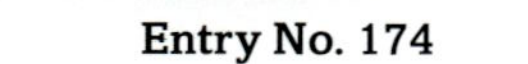

PLATE XXII

Entry No. 174

PLATE XXIII

Entry No. 114

PLATE XVIII

Entry No. 80

PLATE XIX

Entry No

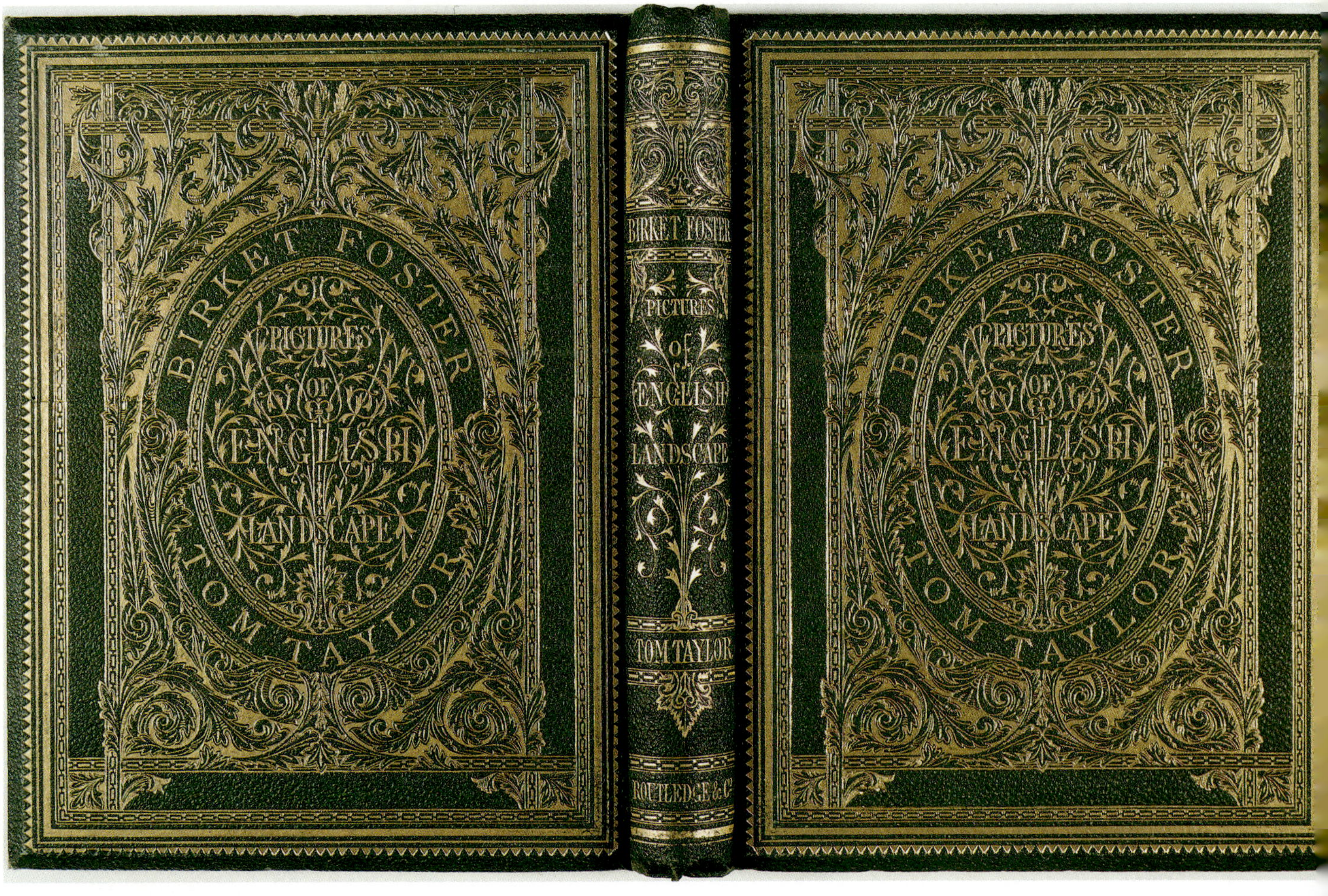

PLATE XX (*The British Museum*)

Entry No

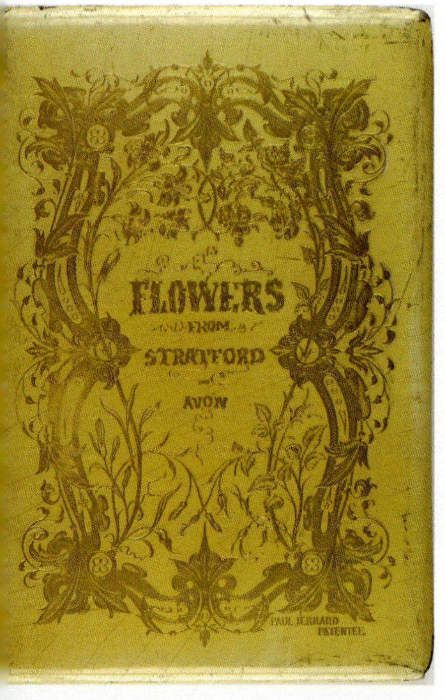

TE XIV **Entry No. 65**

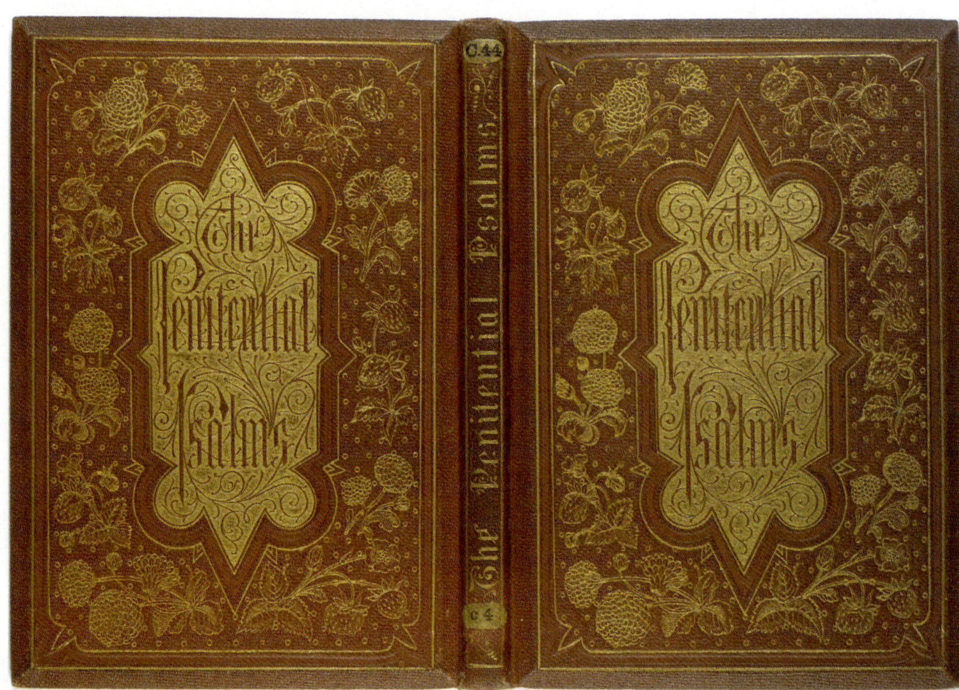

PLATE XVI **Entry No. 72**

TE XV (*The British Museum*) **Entry No. 67**

PLATE XVII **Entry No. 78**

PLATE XII

Entry No. 62

PLATE XIII

Entry No. 66

TE VIII Entry No. 57

PLATE IX Entry No. 58

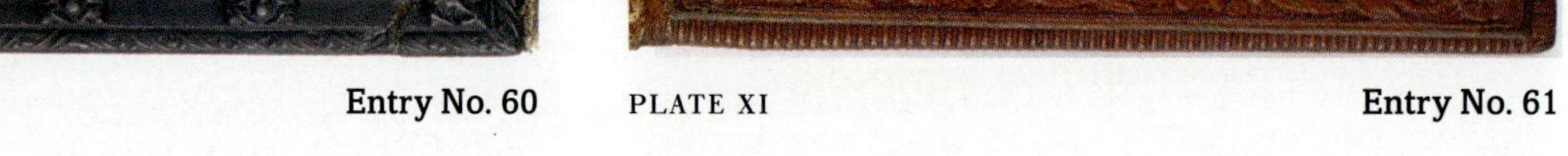

PLATE X Entry No. 60

PLATE XI Entry No. 61

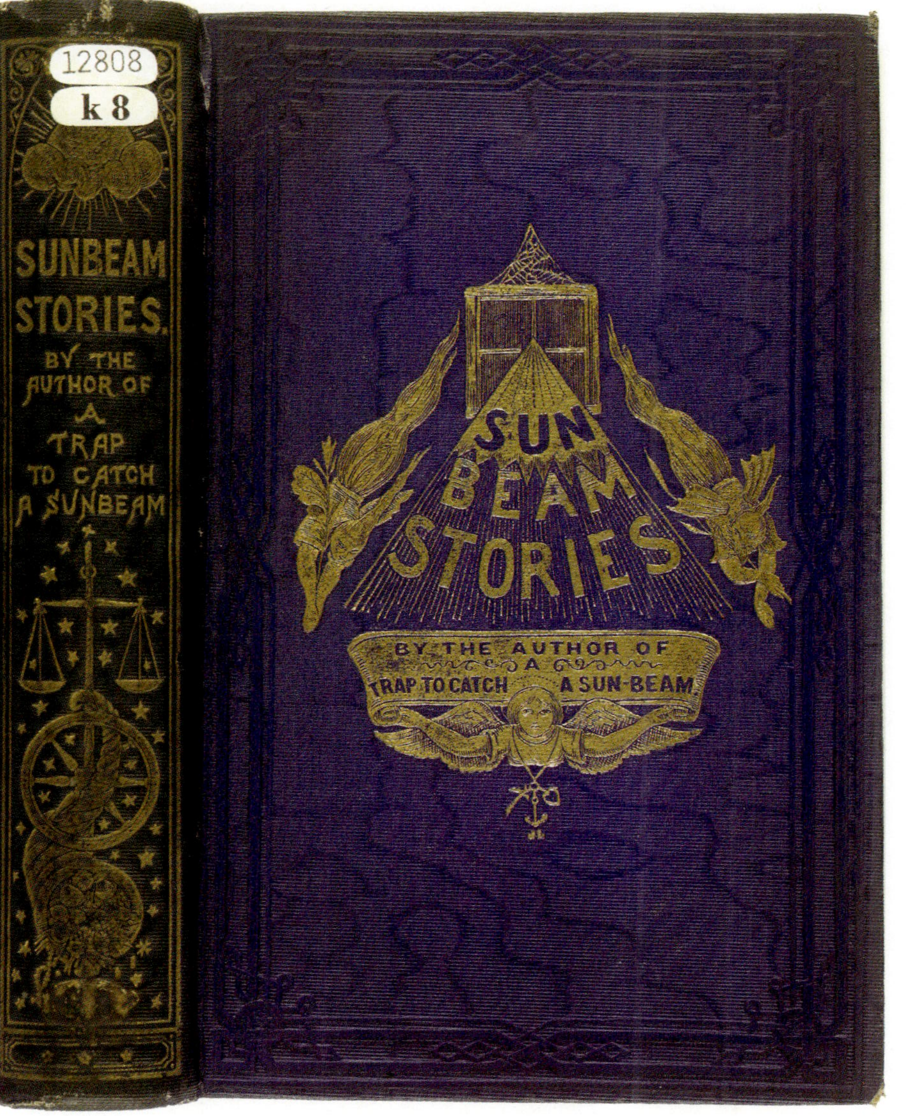

PLATE XXXVI

Entry No. 347

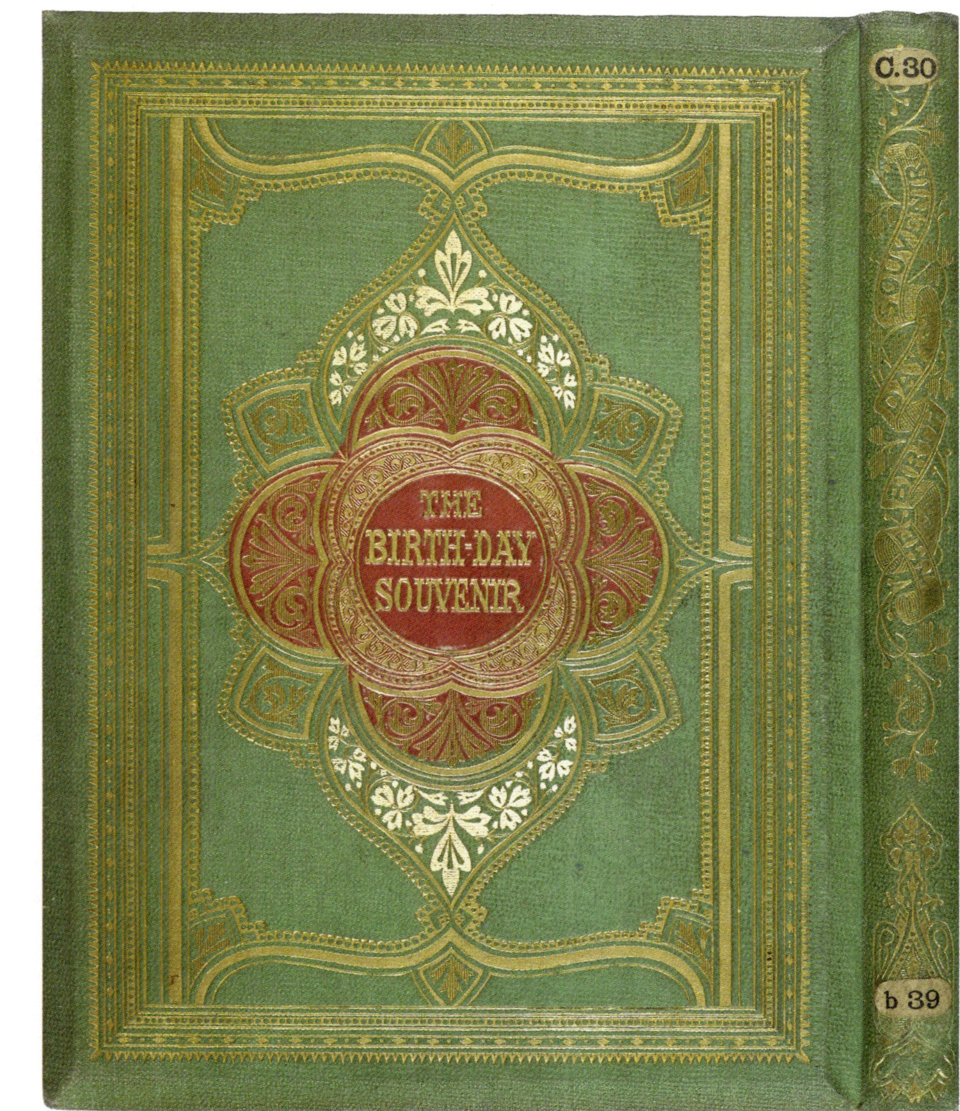

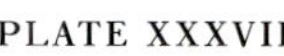

PLATE XXXVII

Entry No. 350

PLATE XXXVIII **Entry No. 396**

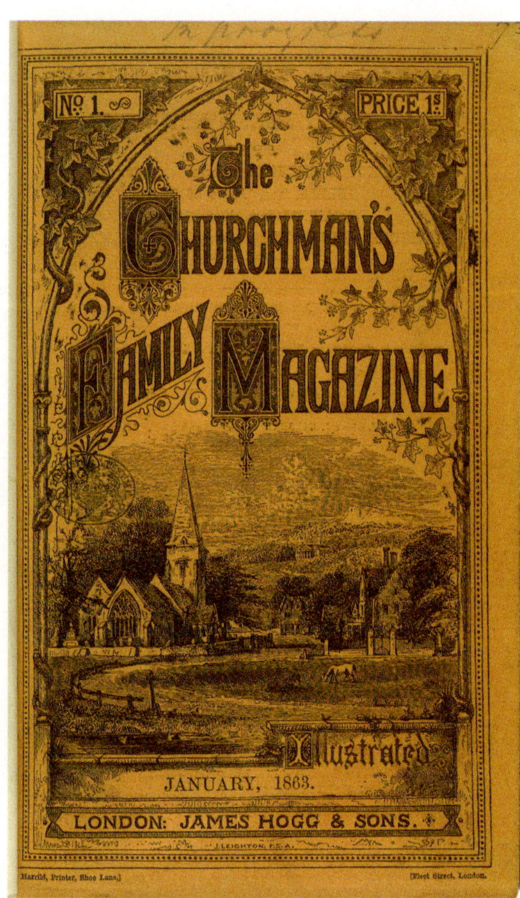

PLATE XXXIX **Entry No. 404**

PLATE XL **Entry No. 415**

PLATE XLI **Entry No. 421**

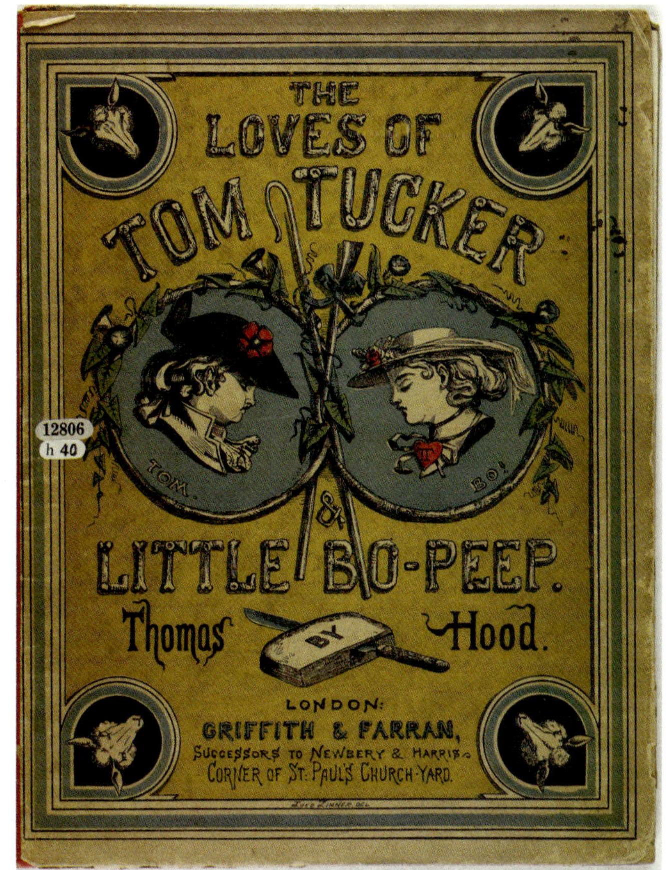

PLATE XLII Entry No. 423

PLATE XLIII Entry No. 425

PLATE XLIV (*The British Museum*) Entry No. 428

PLATE XLV

Entry No. 431

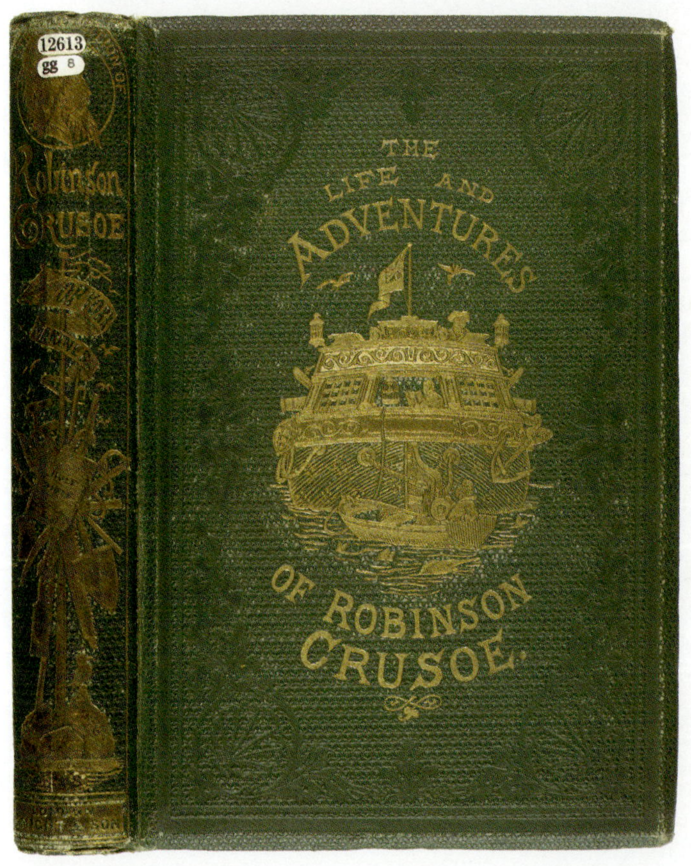

PLATE XLVI

Entry No. 433

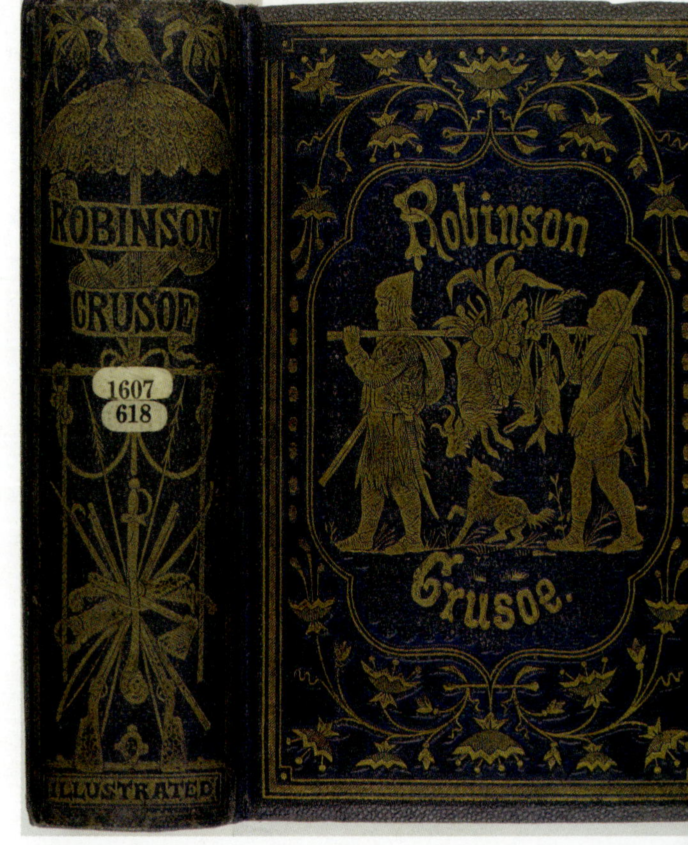

PLATE XLVII

Entry No.

PLATE XLVIII **Entry No. 435**

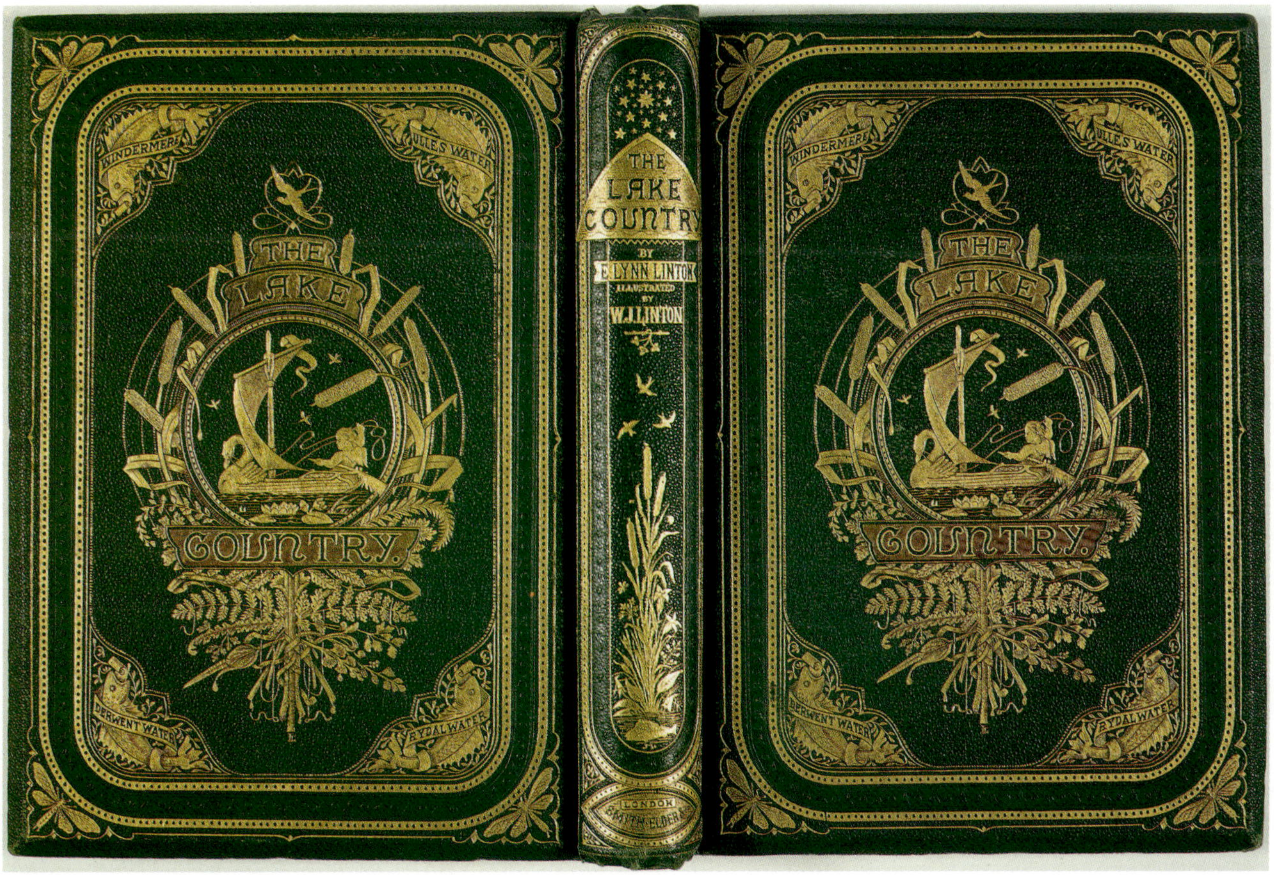

PLATE XLIX (*The British Museum*) **Entry No. 438**

PLATE L

Entry No. 441

PLATE LI (*The British Museum*)

Entry No. 443

PLATE LII

Entry No. 444

PLATE LIII

Entry No. 451

PLATE LIV

Entry No. 456

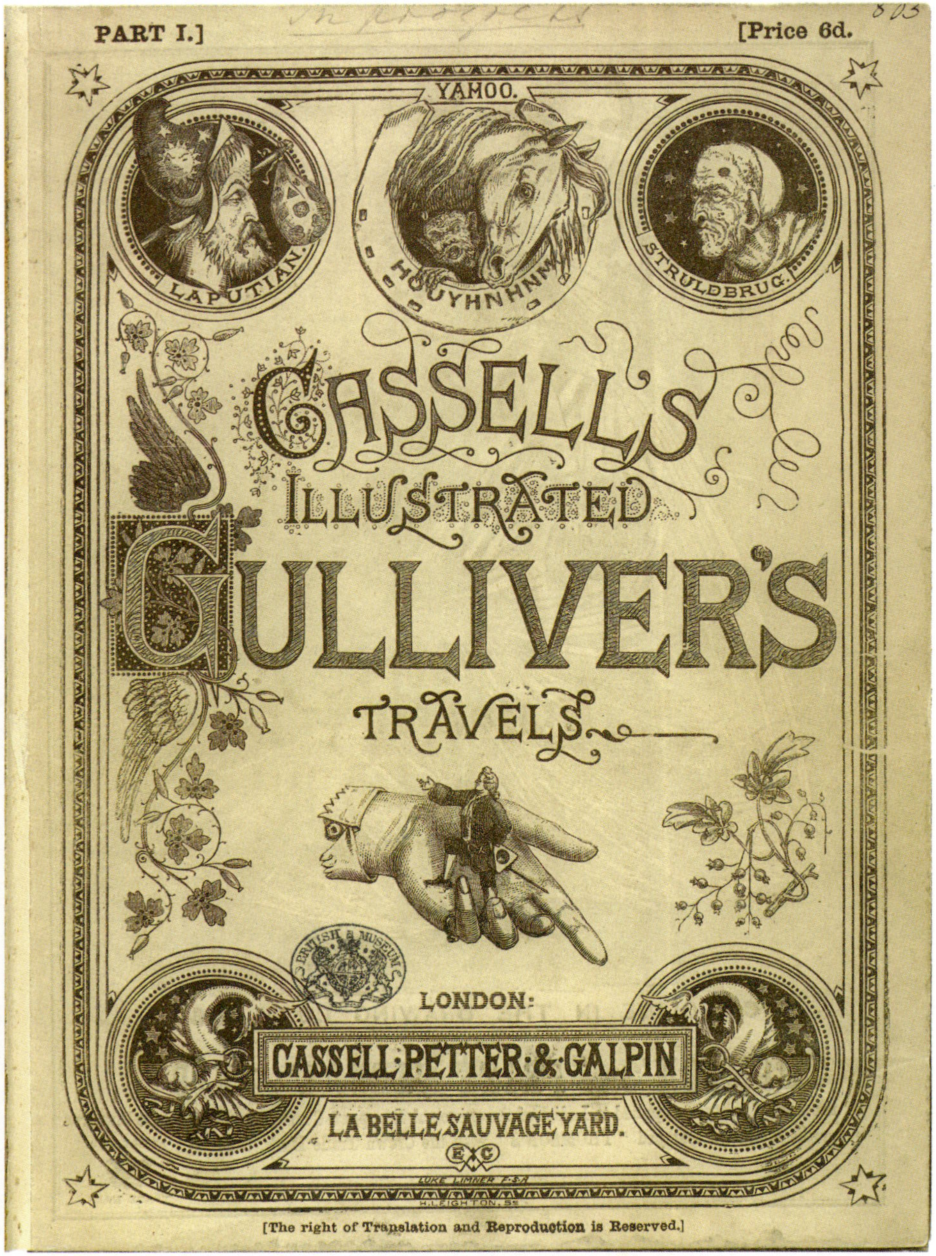

PART I.] [Price 6d.

LAPUTIAN. YAHOO. HOUYHNHNM. STRULDBRUG.

CASSELL'S ILLUSTRATED GULLIVER'S TRAVELS

LONDON:
CASSELL, PETTER & GALPIN
LA BELLE SAUVAGE YARD.
E.C.

[The right of Translation and Reproduction is Reserved.]

PLATE LV

Entry No. 458

TE LVI

Entry No. 467

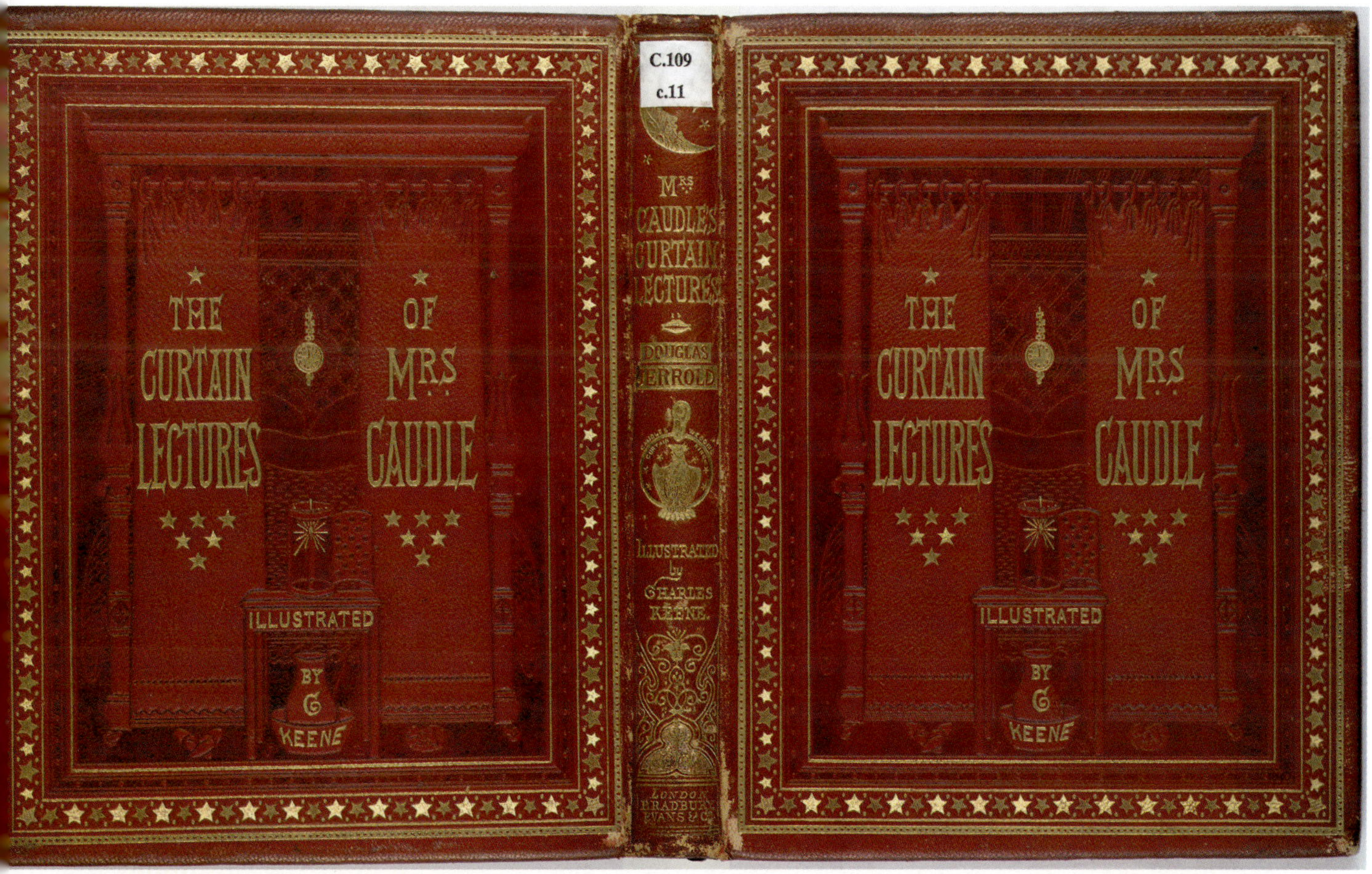

TE LVII

Entry No. 468

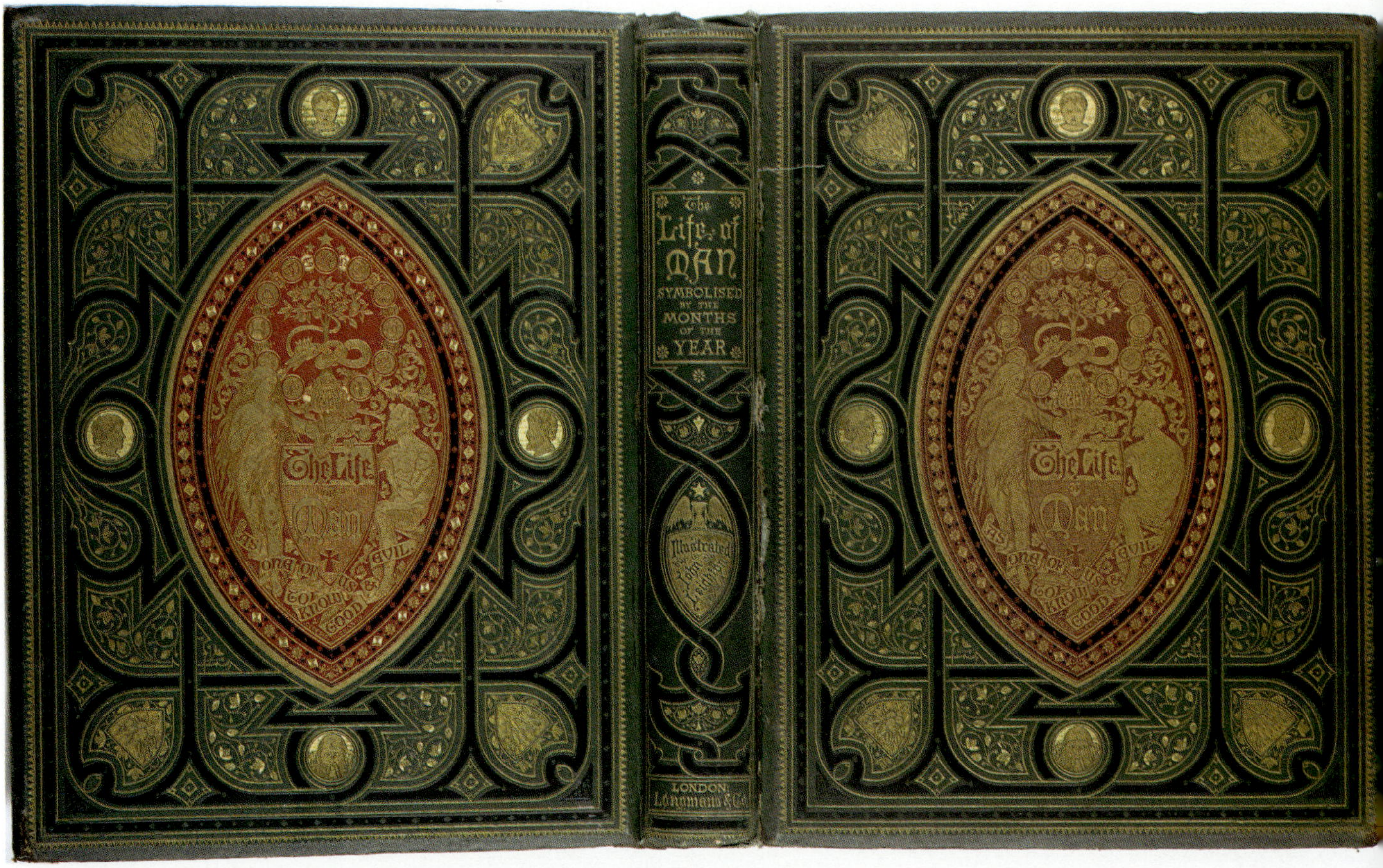

PLATE LVIII

Entry No. 47

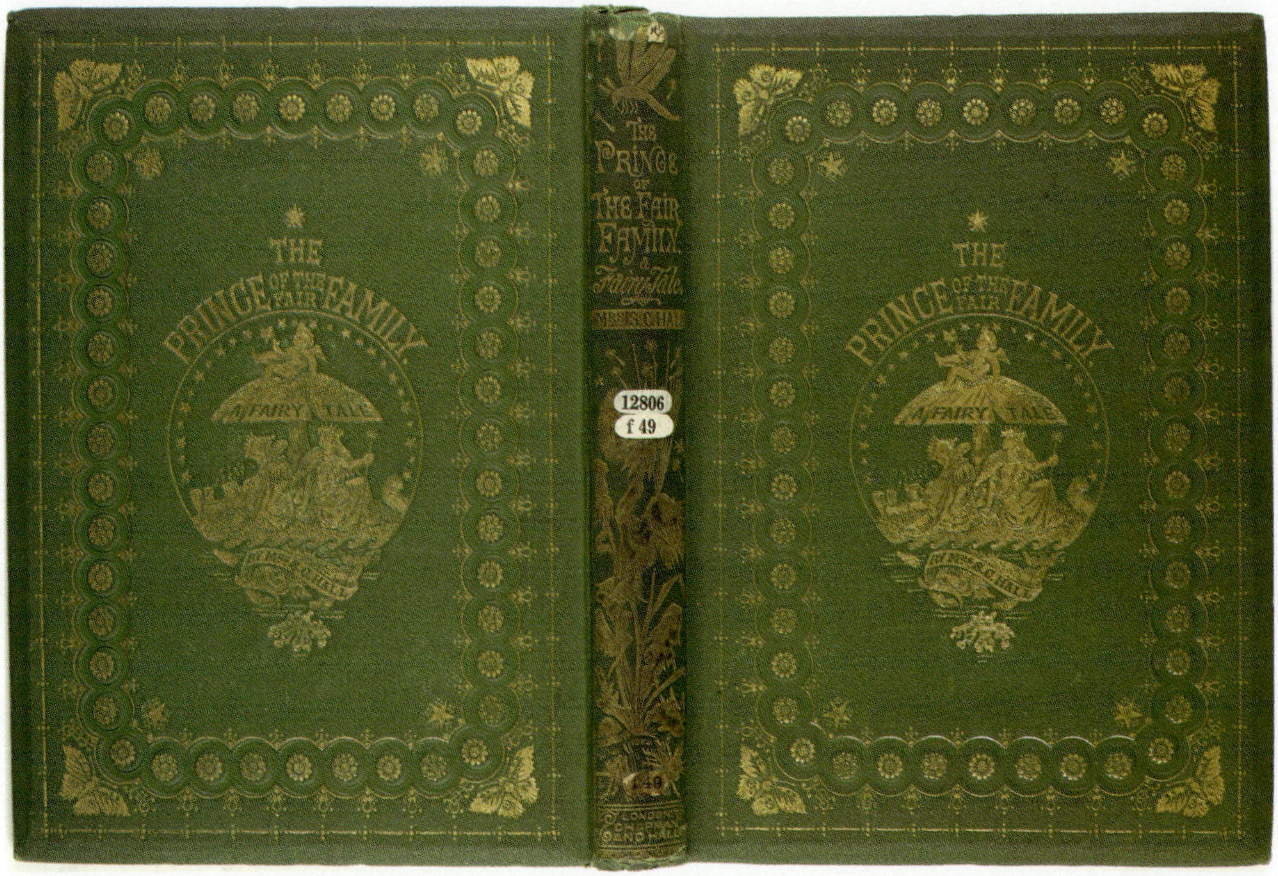

PLATE LIX

Entry No. 478

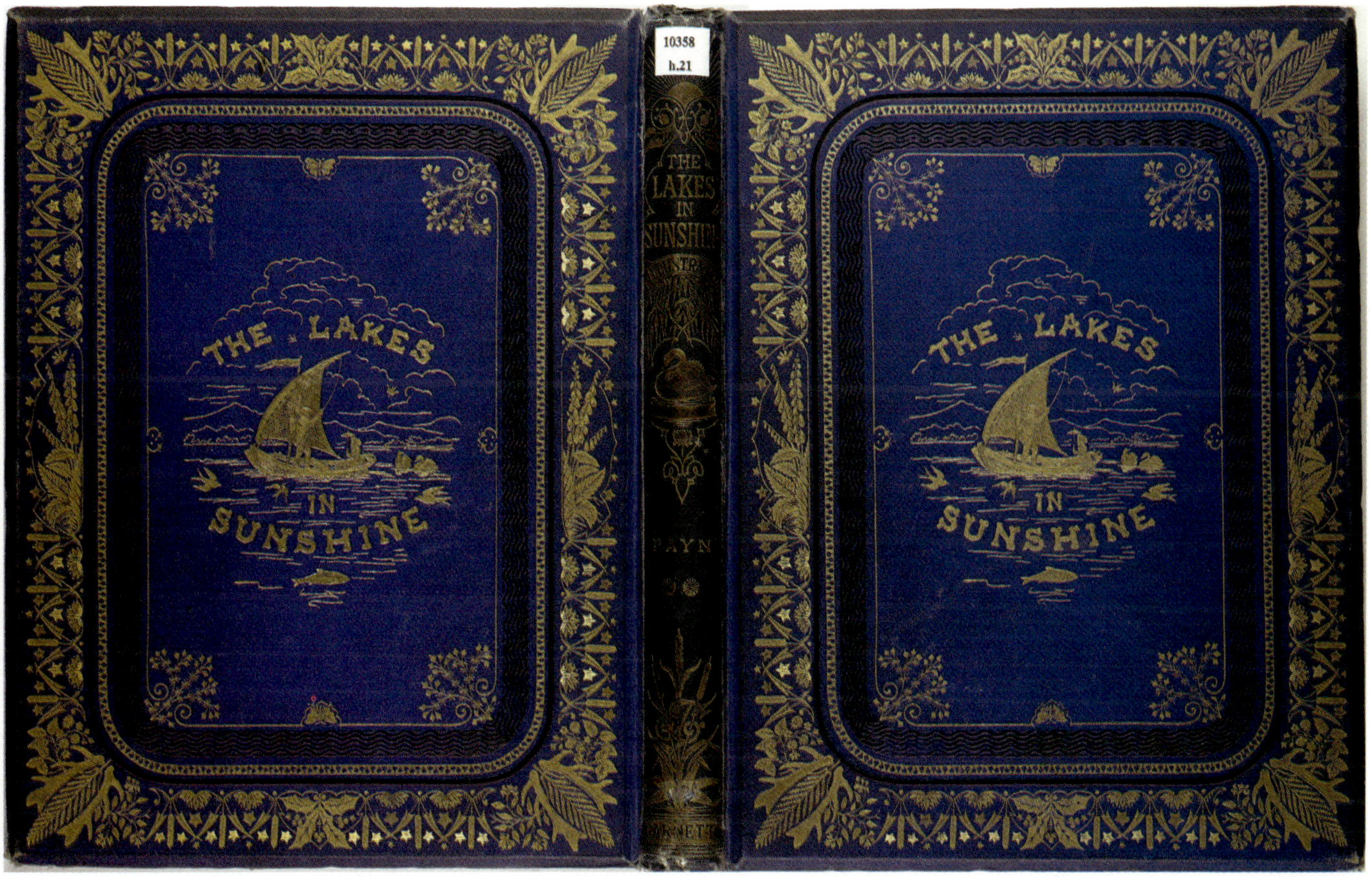

PLATE LX

Entry No. 480

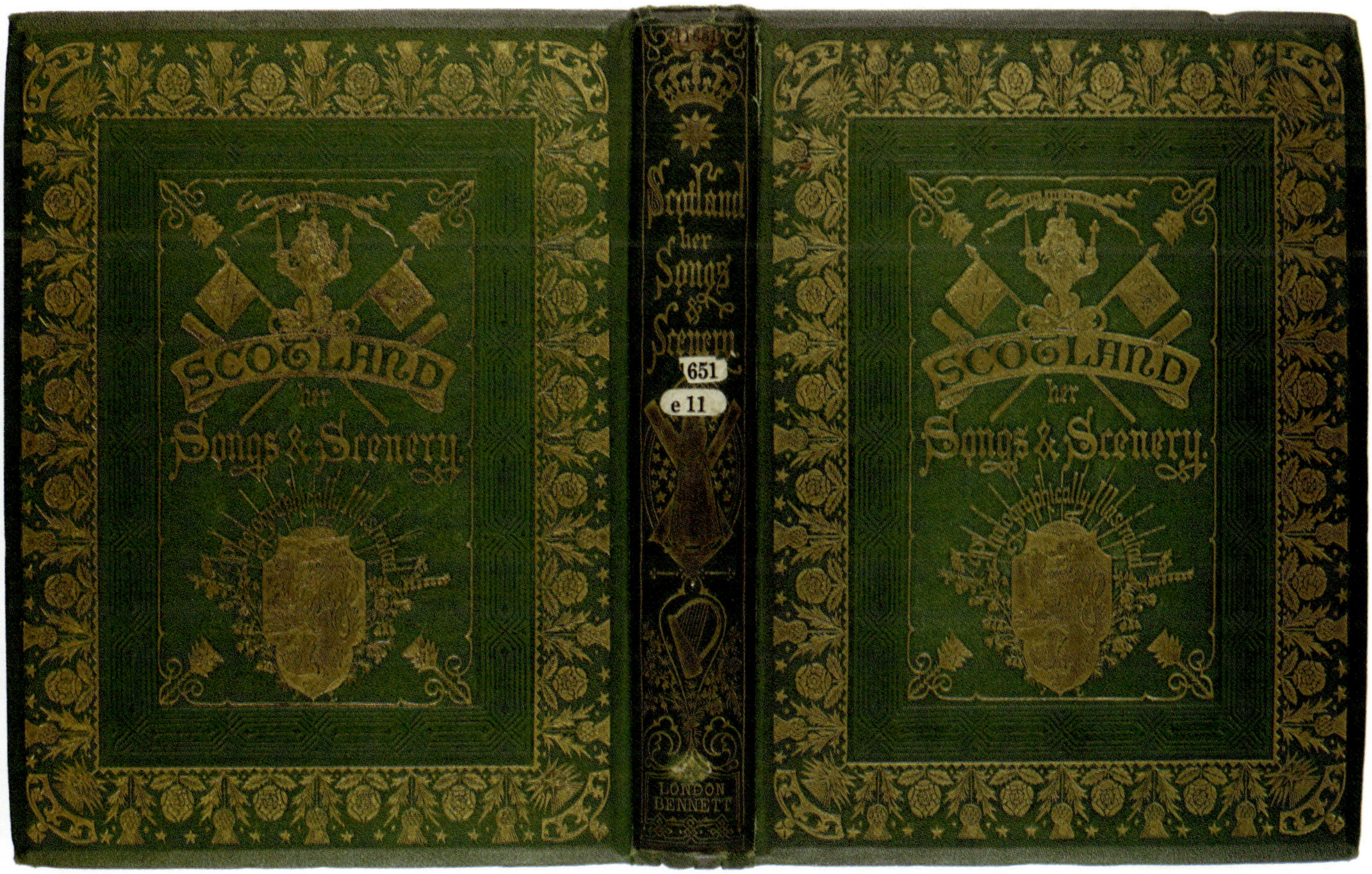

PLATE LXI

Entry No. 485

PLATE LXII Entry No. 486

PLATE LXIII Entry No. 4

PLATE LXIV Entry No.

ATE LXV Entry No. 497

PLATE LXVI Entry No. 505

PLATE LXVII Entry No. 515

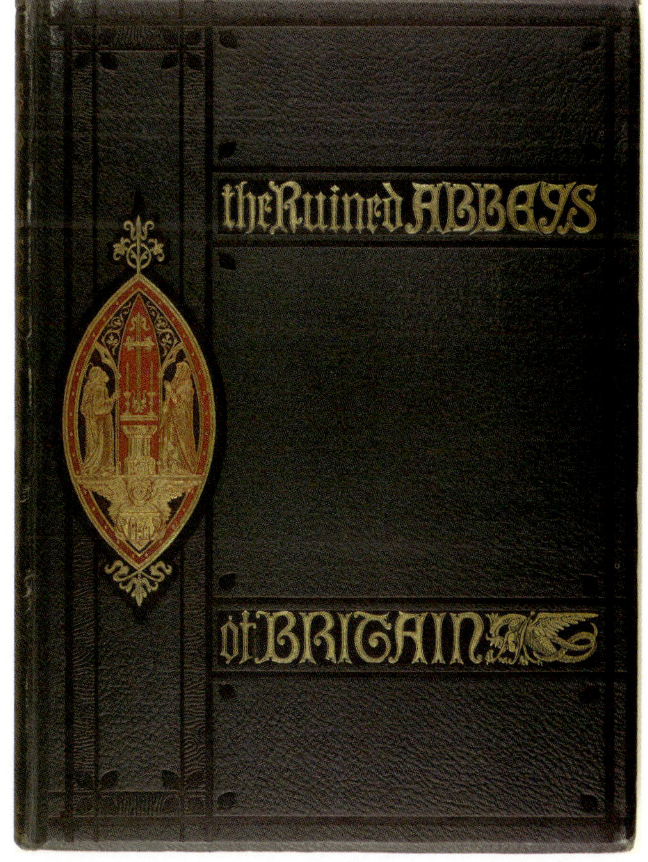

PLATE LXVIII Entry No. 535

THE SYSTEM LEIGHTON
TUBULAR TRANSIT
FOR
DOMINE DIRIGE NOS
LONDON
THE NEED & THE REMEDY.
BY JOHN LEIGHTON
F.S.A. MRI.
FIRST ADVANCE EDITION

PLATE LXX

Entry No. 537

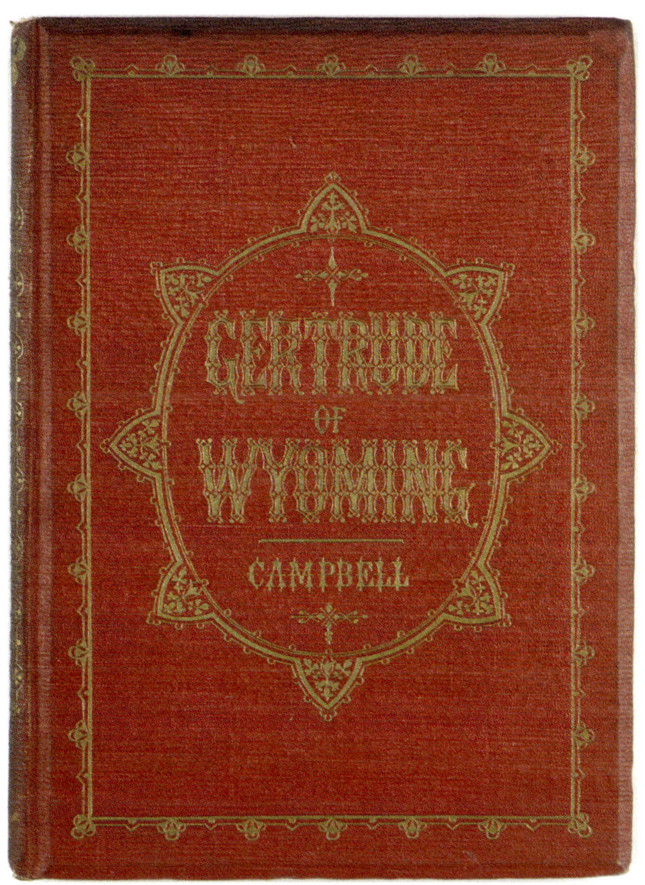

PLATE LXXIX **Entry No. 611**

PLATE LXXX **Entry No. 613**

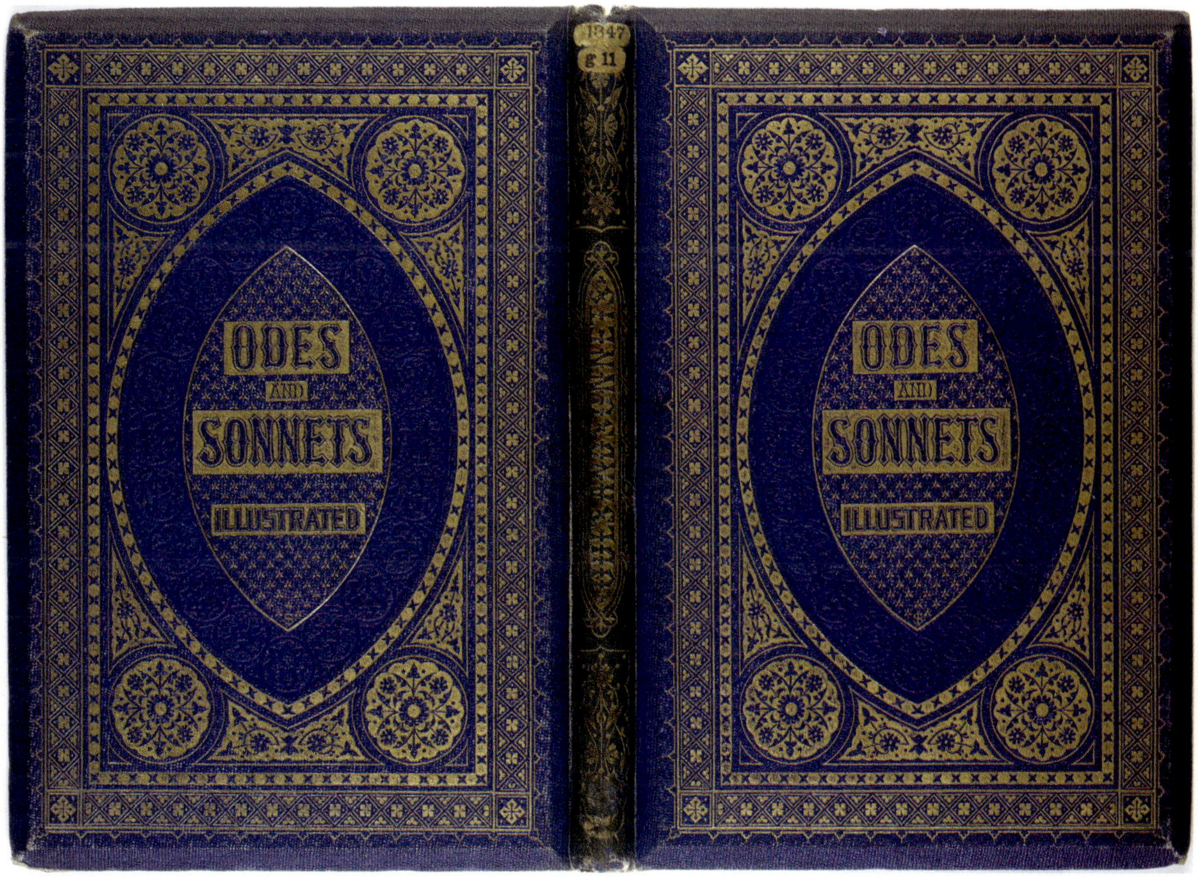

PLATE LXXXI **Entry No. 615**

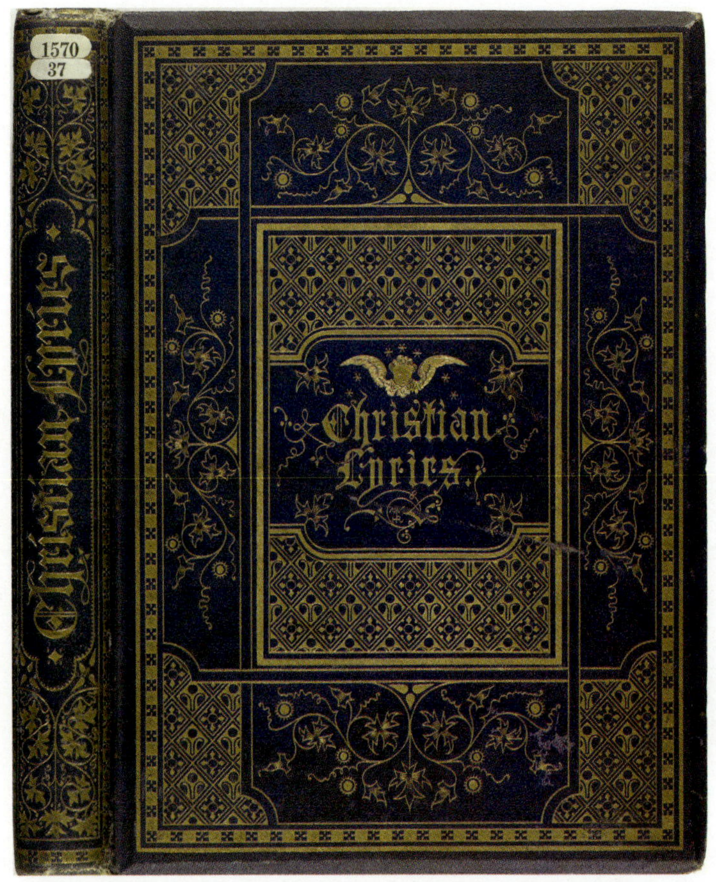

PLATE LXXV Entry No. 591

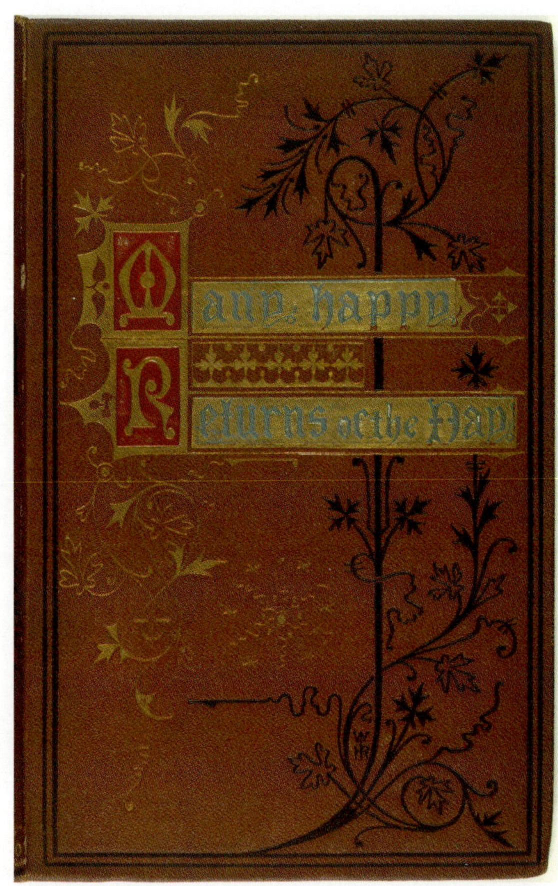

PLATE LXXVI Entry No. 592

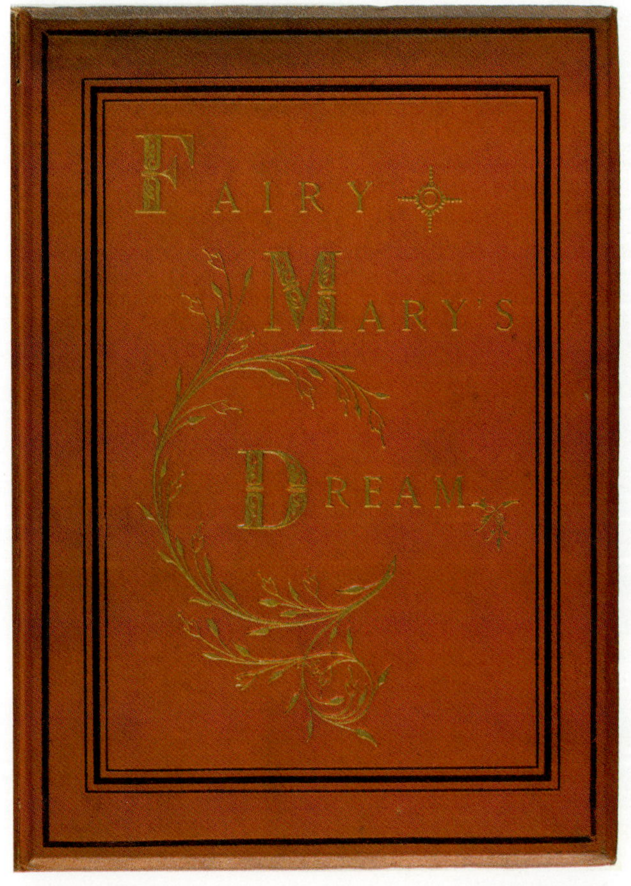

PLATE LXXVII Entry No. 596

PLATE LXXVIII Entry No. 597

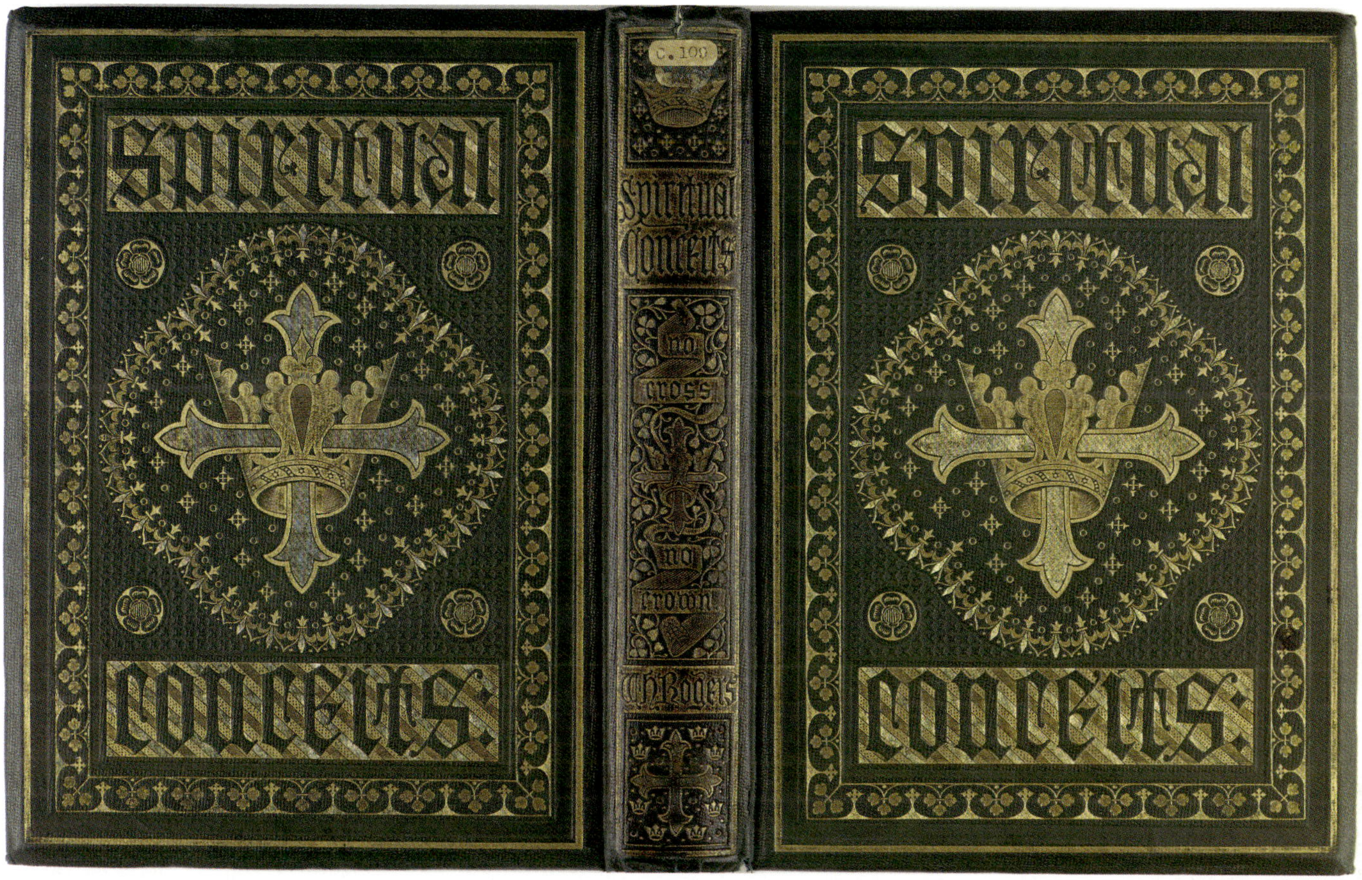

PLATE LXXIII

Entry No. 580

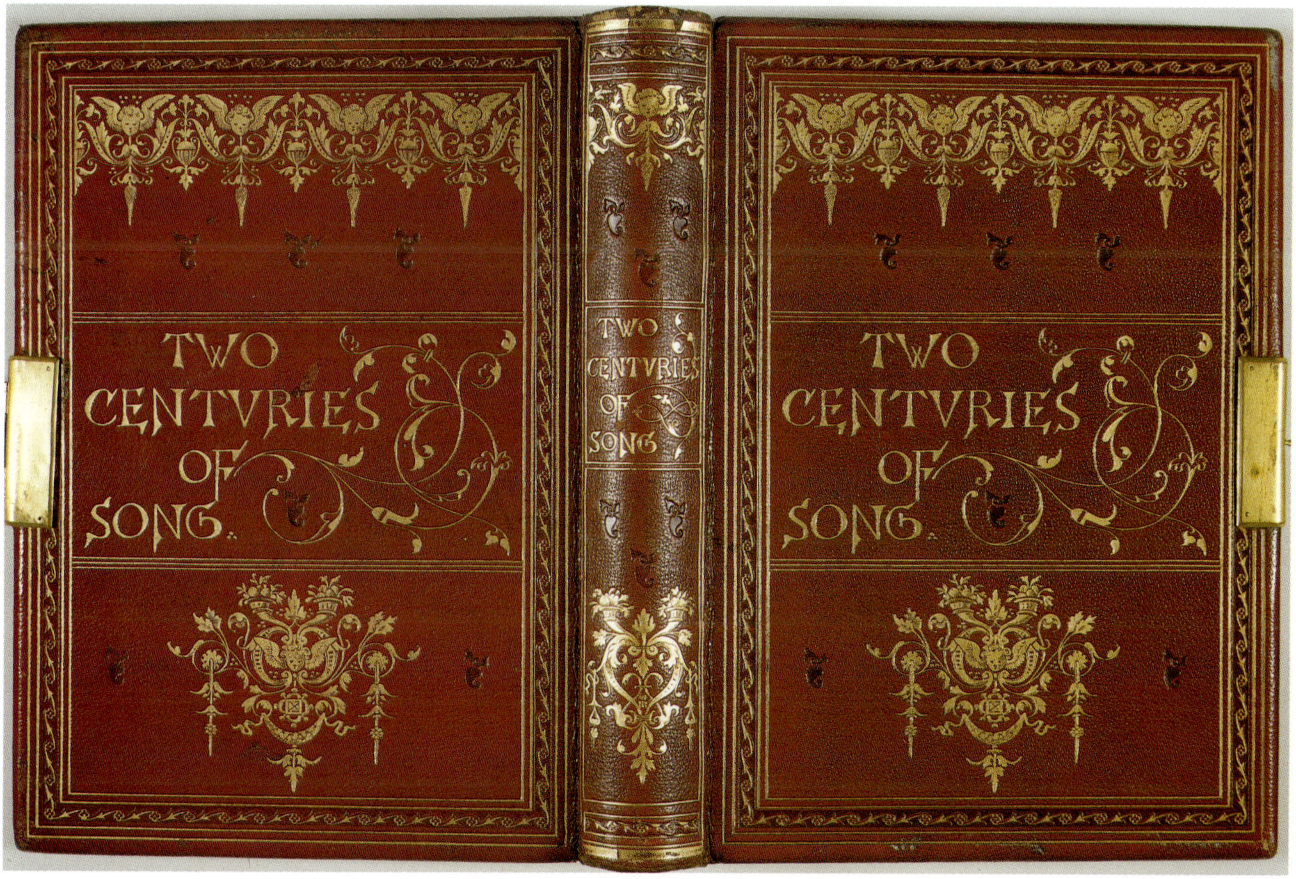

PLATE LXXIV (*The British Museum*)

Entry No. 589

PLATE LXXII (*R. de Beaumont Private Collection*) **Entry No. 579**

PLATE LXXXII

Entry No. 617

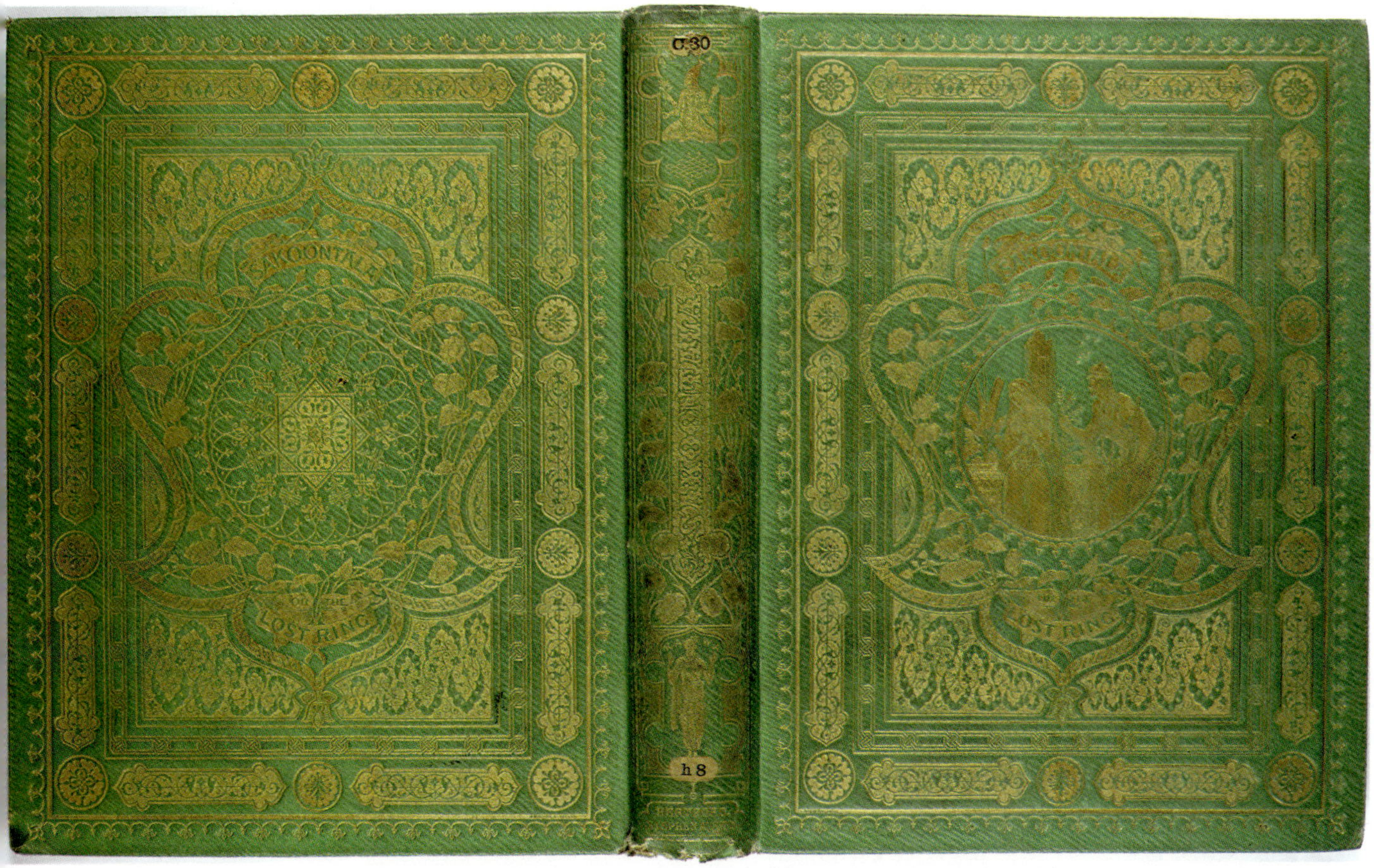

PLATE LXXXIII

Entry No. 618

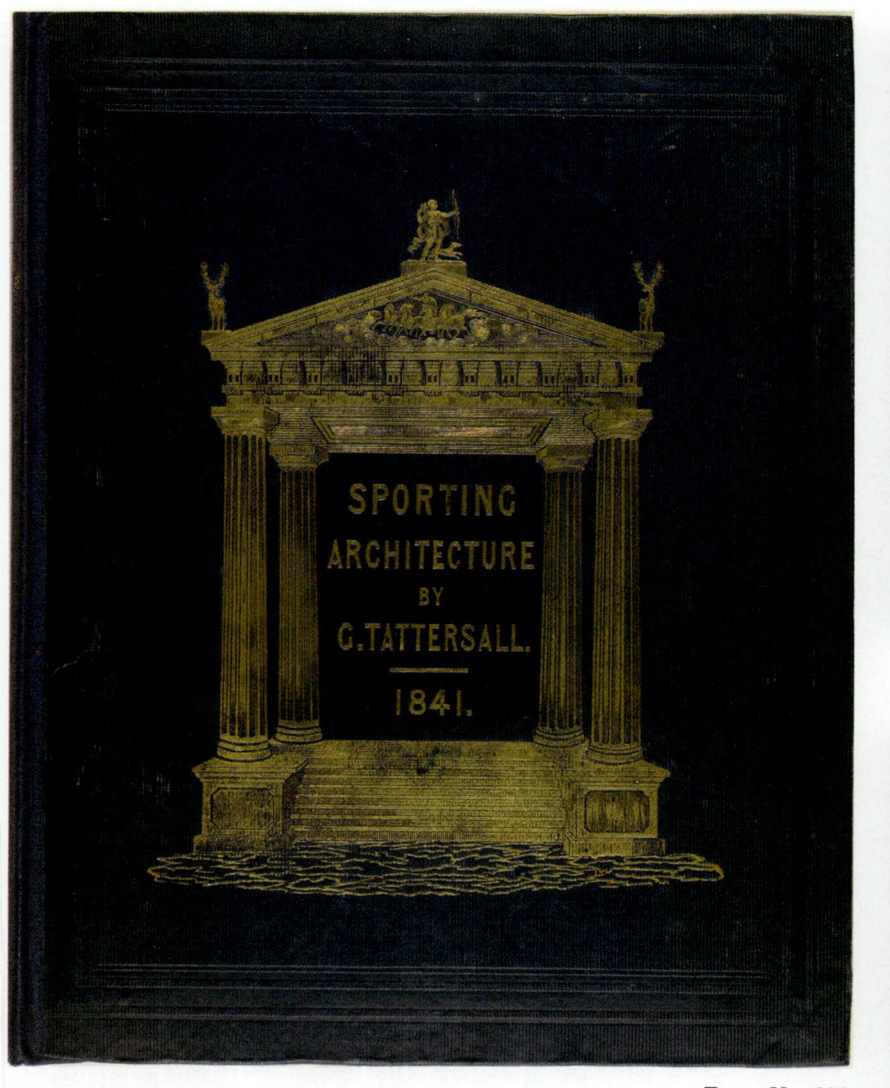

PLATE LXXXIV

Entry No. 638

PLATE LXXXV

Entry No. 674

PLATE LXXXVII

Entry No. 701

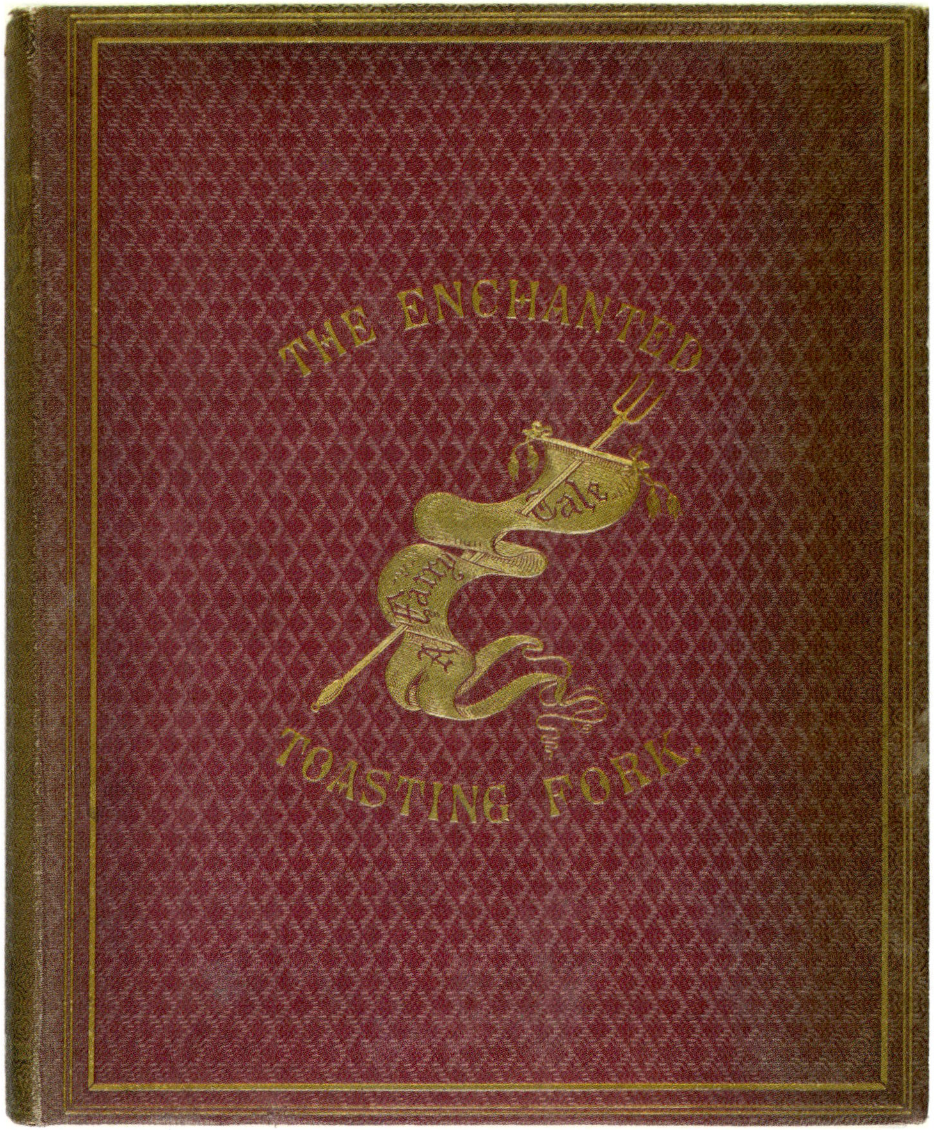

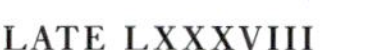

PLATE LXXXVIII

Entry No. 708

PLATE LXXXIX

Entry No. 732

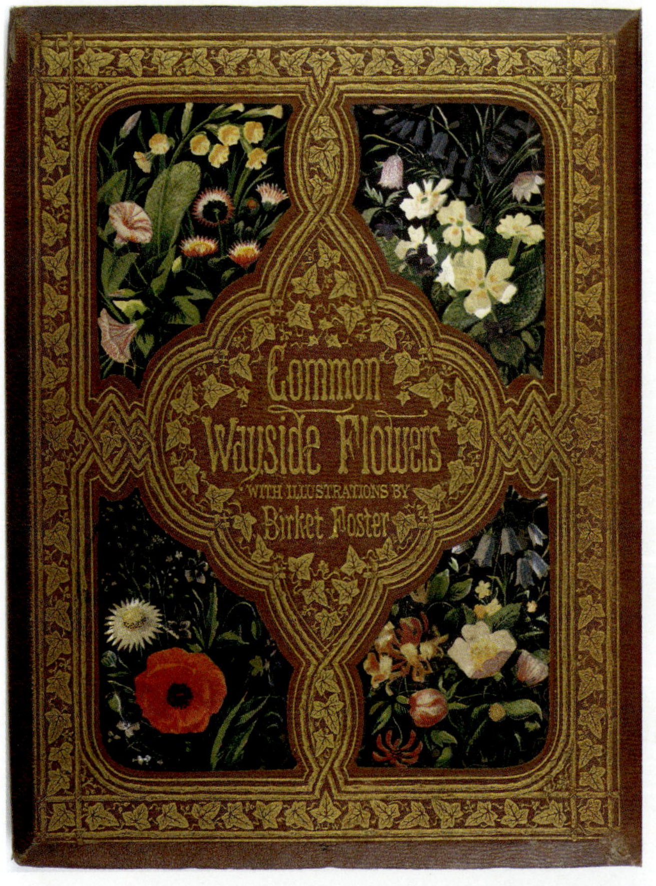

PLATE XC

Entry No. 740

PLATE XCI

Entry No. 751

INDEXES

Select Subject Index

This is not a systematic compilation. It includes some unusual grains; striped cloth; ribbon embossing; some unusual objects. Numbers cited are main entry numbers, not pages.

Title Index

Numbers cited refer to the main entry in the Bibliography, not to a page number. When at the beginning of the title, "A; The; Mrs; Mr, L', etc." have been included selectively after the last substantive word. Subtitles are generally omitted.

General Index

This index lists Authors, Bookbinders, Booksellers, Brass Block Engravers, Cover Design Artists, Editors, Illustration Engravers, Illustrators, Photographers, Printers, Publishers, Translators. See the *List of Bookbinders' Tickets* for reproductions of the tickets used by each bookbinder. Numbers cited refer to the main entry in the Bibliography, not a page number.